HOOVER'S GUIDE TO Private Companies

PROFILES OF 500 MAJOR U.S. PRIVATE ENTERPRISES

1994–1995

Hoover's Guide to Private Companies is intended to provide its readers with accurate and authoritative information about the enterprises covered in it. The Reference Press asked all profiled companies and organizations to provide information. Some did so; a number did not. The information contained herein is as accurate as we could reasonably make it. However, we do not warrant that the book is absolutely accurate or without any errors. In many cases we have relied on third-party material that we believe to be trustworthy but that we were unable to independently verify. Readers should not rely on any information contained herein in instances where such reliance might cause loss or damage. The editors and publishers specifically disclaim all warranties, including the implied warranties of merchantability and fitness for a specific purpose. This book is sold with the understanding that neither the editors nor the publisher is engaged in providing investment, financial, accounting, legal, or other professional advice.

THE REFERENCE PRESS, INC.

Copyright © 1994 by The Reference Press, Inc. All rights reserved. No part of this book may be reproduced or transmitted in any form or by any means, electronic or mechanical, including by photocopying, facsimile transmission, recording, rekeying, or using any information storage and retrieval system, without permission in writing from The Reference Press, Inc., except that brief passages may be quoted by a reviewer in a magazine, in a newspaper, on-line, or in a broadcast review.

10 9 8 7 6 5 4 3 2 1

Publisher Cataloging-In-Publication Data

Hoover's Guide to Private Companies 1994–1995. Edited by The Reference Press, Inc.

Includes indexes.
1. Business enterprises — Directories. 2. Corporations — Directories.
HF3010 338.7

ISBN 1-878753-55-X
ISSN 1073-6433

This book was produced by The Reference Press on Apple Macintosh computers using Claris Corporation's FileMaker Pro 2.1v2, Quark, Inc.'s Quark XPress 3.3, EM Software, Inc.'s Xdata 2.5, and Adobe Systems Incorporated's fonts from the Palatino and Futura families. Cover design is by Kristin M. Jackson, of Austin, Texas. Electronic prepress and printing was done by Quebecor Printing in Kingsport, Tennessee. Text paper is 60# Postmark Bright White (manufactured by Union Camp). Cover stock is Kivar #5 cloth.

Published in association with Warner Books.

Hoover's Guide to Private Companies and other Reference Press books are available from:

THE REFERENCE PRESS
6448 Highway 290 E., Suite E-104
Austin, Texas 78723
USA
Phone: 512-454-7778
Fax: 512-454-9401

WILLIAM SNYDER PUBLISHING ASSOCIATES
5, Five Mile Drive
Oxford OX2 8HT
England
Phone and fax: +44 (0)865-513186

THE STAFF

Chairman: Gary Hoover
CEO, President, and Senior Editor: Patrick J. Spain
Executive Vice-President and Editor-in-Chief: Alta Campbell
Vice-President and Senior Editor: Alan Chai
Vice-President of Sales and Marketing: Dana L. Smith
Senior Managing Editor: James R. Talbot
Director of Sales and Marketing for Electronic Products: Tom Linehan
Editor: Thomas Trotter
Desktop Publishing Manager: Holly Hans Jackson
Senior Researcher: Anita Joe
Controller: Deborah L. Dunlap
Office Manager: Tammy Fisher
Customer Service Manager: Rhonda T. Mitchell
Marketing and Publicity Coordinator: Angela J. Schoolar
Sales Assistant: Lisa Treviño

ACKNOWLEDGMENTS

Editors: Alta Campbell, Stuart Hampton, Lori McClure, Jeanne Minnich, Dixie Peterson, Patrick J. Spain, Teri C. Sperry, Deborah Stratton, James R. Talbot, Thomas Trotter

Writers: Tim Barger, Stephen N. Bole, Greg Cancelada, Dean Graber, Edward Kozek, Robert Macias, Pete Menzies, Paul Mitchell, Darla Morgan, Lisa Norman, Rebecca Patterson, Eric Rasmussen, Barbara M. Spain, Valera Stroup, Alice Wightman

Database Designers: Kristin M. Jackson, Kevin P. Taylor, Wendy Weigant

Desktop Publishers: Catherine H. Cantieri, Michelle de Ybarrondo, Holly Hans Jackson

Fact Checkers/Proofreaders: Alex Báez, Megan A. Brown, Robyn Gammill, Devon Garrett, Allan Gill, Jenny Hill, Britton E. Jackson, Rena Korb, Dan Laws, Diane Lee, Elizabeth Gagne Morgan, John Willis

Researchers: Wilson Allen, Catherine R. Butler, Carrie Faust, Tweed Chouinard, Patricia DeNike, Jill Holsinger, Anita Joe, Lori Legge, Knox Pitzer, Jr., Mike Steckel, Trip Wyckoff

Other Contributors: Ginger Dixon, Wendy Franz, Kyna Horton, Kevin P. Taylor, Heather Woolsey, Santa Yanez

THE REFERENCE PRESS MISSION STATEMENT

1. To produce business information products and services of the highest quality, accuracy, and readability.
2. To make that information available whenever, wherever, and however our customers want it through mass distribution at affordable prices.
3. To continually expand our range of products and services and our markets for those products and services.
4. To reward our employees, suppliers, and shareholders based on their contributions to the success of our enterprise.
5. To hold to the highest ethical business standards, erring on the side of generosity when in doubt.

CONTENTS

COMPANIES LISTED IN THE PRIVATE 500

Note: Company names in **boldface** indicate full-length profiles. Lightface names have capsule profiles only.

COMPANIES LISTED IN THE PRIVATE 500

Note: Company names in **boldface** indicate full-length profiles. Lightface names have capsule profiles only.

COMPANIES LISTED IN THE PRIVATE 500

Note: Company names in **boldface** indicate full-length profiles. Lightface names have capsule profiles only.

ABOUT HOOVER'S GUIDE TO PRIVATE COMPANIES

In response to requests from librarians and other business professionals for a reasonably priced, easy-to-use reference book on major privately held companies and independent commercial enterprises, The Reference Press has created *Hoover's Guide to Private Companies 1994–1995*. This first edition is the seventh in the *Hoover's* series of books profiling companies.

As we discovered in conducting the research for this book, most private companies don't readily give out information about themselves or their businesses. Unlike public companies, which are required to disclose information to shareholders, privately held entities are under no such obligation. For most privately held enterprises, secrecy is a key competitive strategy, and information is jealously guarded. The lack of legal requirements for detailed business disclosures has resulted in a scarcity of comprehensive reference material on privately held enterprises.

Since many private enterprises are major players in the U.S. economy and affect our daily lives (such as UPS, the largest package delivery service in the world), the lack of information about them is of concern not only to business professionals but to all of us. The Reference Press has attempted to overcome the obstacles and fill the information vacuum with this book — a comprehensive reference guide to the 500 largest privately held commercial enterprises (with revenues of $525 million or more)in the United States. It is more than a list of names, addresses, and sales rankings or a collection of newswire clippings. We have gone beyond the basics to bring you full-page, in-depth profiles of 125 of the most influential and interesting private businesses and quarter-page basic profiles of the 500 largest private enterprises (ranked by sales). Every profile contains the essential information that most people need to locate, communicate with, and evaluate a company. We believe no other guide to private companies provides the comprehensive information contained in *Hoover's Guide to Private Companies 1994–1995*.

The book will be updated biennially. The number of companies covered will expand with each new edition.

We recommend *Hoover's Guide to Private Companies 1994–1995* to anyone — particularly librarians, executives, salespeople, the media, job seekers, fund raisers, and students — needing a working knowledge of the major privately held companies in the United States.

SELECTION OF THE ENTERPRISES

In order to provide our readers with a more comprehensive range of information about private companies than is available elsewhere, we have attempted to include a broad spectrum of non–publicly traded enterprises in this book. For example, we feature large industrial and service companies, from agricultural giant Cargill to up-and-coming catalog house J. Crew; policyholder-owned insurers (e.g., State Farm and Pacific Mutual); agricultural and other cooperatives (e.g., Farmland Industries and Land O' Lakes); hospital/health care organizations (e.g., Blue Cross and Kaiser); the largest African American- and Hispanic-owned private companies (TLC Beatrice and Bacardi, respectively); and the largest private company owned by a woman (JM Family Enterprises).

In our effort to cover the full range of non–publicly traded commercial entities, we have included enterprises that compete in the marketplace against other private and public companies but that are usually overlooked because of their nature. For example, we've profiled companies that are public or quasi-governmental (e.g., the U.S. Postal Service, National Passenger Railroad Corporation [Amtrak], the Corporation for Public Broadcasting, and Tennessee Valley Authority).

These entities, though partially publicly funded, operate as independent commercial enterprises and derive the bulk of their revenue from customers rather than taxpayers. The same logic dictates the inclusion of utility districts (e.g., Sacramento Municipal Utility District), state university systems (e.g., University of California), and regional transportation authorities (e.g., The Port Authority of New York and New Jersey). We've added the Georgia and California state lotteries because, unlike most lottery commissions, they are not state agencies, but independently chartered businesses. United States Enrichment Corporation, on the other hand, is a government agency, but is in the midst of privatization. Other types of nontraditional companies covered in the book include joint ventures (e.g., Caltex) which, though not independent businesses, have a significant impact on the economy completely apart from that of companies that own them. We have also included 45 colleges and universities in the book. Although not usually considered commercial enterprises, these schools generate over $58 billion in annual revenues in 1993 and employ over 900,000 people.

The primary criterion for selection of the private 500 was sales. Although we have used the most current sales figure available, not all numbers are for the same year; also, some companies would not divulge exact sales figures or any figures at all; sales numbers for these companies are estimated or approximate and are marked as such. Where two companies have the same sales, the higher rank is assigned to the company with the larger number of employees.

Once we had compiled and ranked the 500 we noted that there were a number of private companies significant enough to be included even though they did not qualify by virtue of sales, such as the nation's largest law firm (Baker & McKenzie), certain charitable organizations (e.g., the Salvation Army and the United Way), and membership organizations (e.g., AARP, Teamsters, and Rotary International). We have also covered 12 investment firms (e.g., KKR and Carlyle Group), which wield influence disproportionate to their size through their investments in large private and public companies. Since sales figures are not really relevant for investment companies, we have not included any sales numbers in these profiles.

Finally we added a handful of companies that caught the imagination of the editors and that, aside from any economic impact, have been fun to research and write about. These include such companies as Irvin Feld & Kenneth Feld Productions, which operates Ringling Bros. and Barnum & Bailey Circus.

We think that you will be intrigued (as were we) and moderately surprised by the characteristics of our private 500. Although we expected to see a number of supermarkets among the top 500, the actual number of food-related businesses (110) surprised even us. At the other end of the spectrum, we found only four computer-related companies, one telecommunications business, and one maker of medical equipment.

THE 125 IN-DEPTH PROFILES

Each of the 125 in-depth profiles provides a full page of data, including an operations overview, a discussion of company strategy and history, up to 10 years of key financial data, lists of products and competitors, executives' names, headquarters address, phone and fax numbers, and a picture of the company's logo. These profiles are written in the same accessible style as the other *Hoover's Handbooks* and appear alphabetically. The company's rank in the private 500 appears in the upper right-hand corner of the profile. Those companies too small to be included in the 500 are shown as "N/R" ("not ranked").

THE 500 BASIC PROFILES

Each of the 500 basic profiles contains the company's name, headquarters address, and phone and fax numbers; the names of the chief executive officer (CEO) and chief financial officer (CFO), as well as four other key executives (usually including the human resources director and the legal counsel); the company's fiscal year-end; an industry description; the most recently available annual sales figure; and the number of employees. It also includes a brief overview of the company's operations and ownership, a list of key competitors, and a list of the company's main products, services, subsidiaries, or other relevant business. Since investment firms and schools do not compete against one another in the traditional sense, we have omitted the list of key competitors for these entities.

SOURCES OF INFORMATION

We left no stone unturned in the pursuit of information from which to write this book. We started with a database of company information developed by The Reference Press over the past few years (including information gleaned from weekly reading and clipping of some 50 business publications) and supplemented and expanded this database by identifying candidates for inclusion via the following sources: Duns Market Identifiers; Ward's private company database (maintained by Ziff-Davis unit Information Access); special-issue publications featuring privately held companies (including the *Forbes* 400, *Inc.* 500, *Hispanic Business* 500, *Black Enterprise* 100, various city business journals, and dozens of newspapers and trade journals); and on-line business information, primarily obtained through the Dow Jones News Service. We also attempted to obtain and/or verify information directly from the companies concerned through mail, fax, and telephone communication. All information is current through September 1994.

INDEXES

To help readers easily locate information, we have included three indexes — one by industry; one by headquarters location; and one of brands, companies, and people.

ELECTRONIC EDITION

The in-depth profiles (but not the basic profiles) in this book are available on Mead Data Central's LEXIS/NEXIS (HOOVER in the COMPNY file), America Online (Keyword Hoover's), CompuServe (Go Hoover), Apple eWorld (Keyword Hoover's), and other on-line services. We encourage you to use these services to access all *Hoover's* profiles.

PRICING

The mission of The Reference Press is to produce high-quality business reference products at affordable prices. The cost for each basic profile in *Hoover's Guide to Private Companies 1994–1995* is far below the price of similar information from other providers. The Reference Press believes that basic information about companies should be reasonably priced and widely available. We are leading the movement to make this a reality, and we appreciate the support that you, our readers and customers, are providing to this effort.

SUGGESTIONS

The best suggestions we receive come from our readers. We welcome your suggestions and comments and encourage you to share your thoughts with us about additional information you would like to see included in future editions. If you believe there is a need for other reasonably priced business reference books, let us know.

TOP 500 NON-PUBLICLY TRADED BUSINESS ENTERPRISES IN THE US

Rank	Company	Sales ($ mil.)
1	Blue Cross and Blue Shield Association	71,161
2	United States Postal Service	47,418
3	Cargill, Incorporated	47,100
4	The Prudential Insurance Company of America	45,974
5	Metropolitan Life Insurance Company	28,683
6	State Farm Mutual Automobile Insurance	24,463
7	Koch Industries, Inc.	20,000
8	United Parcel Service of America, Inc.	17,782
9	Caltex Petroleum Corporation	15,409
10	Continental Grain Company	15,000
11	Nationwide Insurance Enterprise	14,835
12	The Goldman Sachs Group, LP	13,200
13	Mars, Inc.	13,000
14	John Hancock Mutual Life Insurance Company	12,732
15	Kaiser Foundation Health Plan, Inc.	11,930
16	Teachers Insurance and Annuity Association	10,300
17	Northwestern Mutual Life Insurance Company	8,778
18	Publix Super Markets, Inc.	7,554
19	Bechtel Group, Inc.	7,337
20	Army & Air Force Exchange Service	7,263
21	Massachusetts Mutual Life Insurance Company	7,109
22	The Guardian Life Insurance Company of America	7,069
23	Principal Financial Group	6,600
24	R. H. Macy & Co., Inc.	6,300
25	Star Enterprise	6,252
26	Ingram Industries Inc.	6,163
27	Arthur Andersen & Co, Société Coopérative	6,017
28	Montgomery Ward Holding Corp.	6,002
29	KPMG Peat Marwick	6,000
30	USAA	5,990
31	Levi Strauss Associates Inc.	5,892
32	Liberty Mutual Insurance Group	5,859
33	Ernst & Young LLP	5,839
34	Advance Publications, Inc.	5,320
35	Tennessee Valley Authority	5,276
36	Coopers & Lybrand L.L.P.	5,220
37	Deloitte & Touche	5,000
38	The ARA Group, Inc.	4,891
39	Farmland Industries, Inc.	4,723
40	H. E. Butt Grocery Company	4,500
41	Amway Corporation	4,500
42	Thrifty PayLess Inc.	4,454
43	The Marmon Group, Inc.	4,319
44	Meijer, Inc.	4,250
45	Pathmark Stores, Inc.	4,207
46	Price Waterhouse LLP	3,890
47	American Standard Inc.	3,830
48	The University of Texas System	3,744
49	Alco Health Services Corporation	3,719
50	State University of New York	3,700

Rank	Company	Sales ($ mil.)
51	Wakefern Food Corporation	3,600
52	Mutual of Omaha Companies	3,577
53	S.C. Johnson & Son, Inc.	3,550
54	The Mutual Life Insurance Company of New York	3,493
55	New York Life Insurance Company	3,493
56	Harvest States Cooperatives	3,482
57	Hallmark Cards, Inc.	3,400
58	Penske Corporation	3,250
59	Pacific Mutual Life Insurance Company	3,210
60	Lefrak Organization Inc.	3,200
61	The Kemper National Insurance Companies	3,166
62	The Circle K Corporation	3,157
63	The Anschutz Corporation	3,134
64	Topco Associates, Inc.	2,927
65	Aid Association for Lutherans, Inc.	2,885
66	The New England	2,827
67	American Family Mutual Insurance Company	2,818
68	DHL Worldwide Express	2,800
69	Natural Gas Clearinghouse	2,791
70	MacAndrews & Forbes Holdings Inc.	2,748
71	Yucaipa Companies	2,742
72	Land O' Lakes, Inc.	2,733
73	The Dyson-Kissner-Moran Corporation	2,723
74	American Financial Corporation	2,721
75	Allmerica Financial	2,705
76	Associated Milk Producers, Inc.	2,692
77	Cox Enterprises, Inc.	2,675
78	Milliken & Co.	2,640
79	General American Life Insurance Company	2,636
80	Global Petroleum Corp.	2,622
81	Estée Lauder Inc.	2,614
82	JM Family Enterprises Inc.	2,600
83	FMR Corporation	2,570
84	Associated Wholesale Grocers Inc.	2,540
85	Hyatt Corporation	2,500
86	Hy-Vee Food Stores, Inc.	2,500
87	Steelcase Inc.	2,500
88	New United Motor Manufacturing, Inc.	2,500
89	Roundy's Inc.	2,490
90	The Grand Union Holdings Corporation	2,477
91	Red Apple Group	2,425
92	The University of Wisconsin System	2,424
93	Randalls Food Markets	2,400
94	Cotter & Company	2,356
95	Connecticut Mutual Life Insurance Company	2,310
96	The Hearst Corporation	2,300
97	Carlson Companies, Inc.	2,295
98	Lutheran Brotherhood	2,243
99	Domino's Pizza, Inc.	2,200
100	Lexmark International Inc.	2,200

TOP 500 NON-PUBLICLY TRADED BUSINESS ENTERPRISES IN THE US (CONTINUED)

Rank	Company	Sales ($ mil.)
101	Vanstar, Inc.	2,200
102	Spartan Stores Inc.	2,189
103	Peter Kiewit Sons', Inc.	2,179
104	The University of Michigan	2,162
105	Little Caesar Enterprises, Inc.	2,150
106	Dominick's Finer Foods Inc.	2,150
107	American Retail Group, Inc.	2,120
108	Giant Eagle Inc.	2,100
109	University of Illinois	2,069
110	The City University of New York	2,050
111	Farmers Union Central Exchange, Incorporated	2,048
112	Dow Corning Corporation	2,044
113	Trump Organization	2,037
114	Graybar Electric Company, Inc.	2,033
115	Ace Hardware Corporation	2,018
116	Certified Grocers of California, Ltd	2,007
117	Phar-Mor Inc.	2,000
118	Countrymark Cooperative, Inc.	2,000
119	Subway Sandwiches	2,000
120	Specialty Foods Corp.	1,998
121	Navy Exchange System	1,977
122	CONSOL Energy Inc.	1,927
123	The Port Authority of New York and New Jersey	1,921
124	Sisters of Charity Health Care Systems, Inc.	1,911
125	Mercy Health Services	1,900
126	The Detroit Medical Center	1,900
127	Core-Mark International, Inc.	1,900
128	Morse Operations	1,886
129	C&S Wholesale Grocers Inc.	1,867
130	Raley's Inc.	1,850
131	Huntsman Chemical Corporation	1,850
132	Cawsl Corp.	1,846
133	Mid-America Dairymen, Inc.	1,832
134	Metromedia Company	1,804
135	Wegmans Food Markets Inc.	1,800
136	Edward J. DeBartolo Corporation	1,800
137	Polo/Ralph Lauren Corporation	1,800
138	American Red Cross	1,796
139	Delta Dental Plan of California	1,792
140	The Minnesota Mutual Life Insurance Company	1,783
141	Schwan's Sales Enterprises, Inc.	1,780
142	Major League Baseball	1,774
143	Belk Stores Services, Inc.	1,774
144	Young Men's Christian Association	1,762
145	California State Lottery Commission	1,760
146	National Football League	1,753
147	Agway Inc.	1,711
148	Life Care Centers of America	1,700
149	J.R. Simplot Company	1,700
150	Menard, Inc.	1,700
151	Science Applications International Corporation	1,680
152	Enterprise Rent-A-Car Co.	1,659
153	Frank Consolidated Enterprises	1,658
154	TLC Beatrice International Holdings, Inc.	1,656
155	Catholic Healthcare West Inc.	1,633
156	Southern Wine & Spirits of America	1,620
157	SERVISTAR Corp.	1,619
158	Clark Enterprises, Inc.	1,600
159	Hendrick Automotive Group	1,600
160	Hardware Wholesalers, Inc.	1,600
161	University of Pennsylvania	1,594
162	Health Insurance Plan of Greater NY	1,583
163	Mayo Foundation	1,579
164	University of Minnesota	1,572
165	Sentry Insurance, A Mutual Company	1,568
166	Del Monte Foods Company	1,555
167	Stater Bros. Holdings Inc.	1,550
168	The Parsons Corporation	1,547
169	Gulf States Toyota, Inc.	1,534
170	Jordan Motors Inc.	1,532
171	US Foodservice Inc.	1,530
172	The Pennsylvania State University	1,504
173	Keystone Foods Corporation	1,500
174	United States Enrichment Corporation	1,500
175	Aectra Refining & Marketing Inc.	1,500
176	George E. Warren Corporation	1,500
177	The University of Maryland System	1,481
178	Kohler Co.	1,472
179	Indiana University	1,460
180	Maritz Inc.	1,442
181	New York Power Authority	1,430
182	The Ohio State University	1,409
183	National Railroad Passenger Corporation	1,403
184	Gold Kist Inc.	1,401
185	Saks Holdings, Inc.	1,400
186	Mid-Atlantic Cars Inc.	1,400
187	Grocers Supply Co. Inc.	1,400
188	The Salvation Army	1,398
189	Brown Brothers Harriman & Co.	1,390
190	Corporation for Public Broadcasting	1,390
191	Sinclair Oil Corporation	1,385
192	Salt River Project	1,360
193	Adventist Health System/West	1,350
194	Renco Group Inc.	1,350
195	The Golodetz Group	1,350
196	Transammonia, Inc.	1,350
197	Gates Corporation	1,340
198	The Johns Hopkins University Inc.	1,329
199	Walter Industries Inc.	1,329
200	New York University	1,324

TOP 500 NON-PUBLICLY TRADED BUSINESS ENTERPRISES IN THE US (CONTINUED)

Rank	Company	Sales ($ mil.)
201	Cornell University	1,315
202	Sammons Enterprises, Inc.	1,308
203	Harvard University	1,306
204	UniHealth America	1,303
205	"21" International Holdings, Inc.	1,301
206	Delaware North Companies Inc.	1,300
207	Perdue Farms Incorporated	1,300
208	McKinsey & Company, Inc.	1,300
209	Southwire Company, Inc.	1,300
210	Services Group of America Inc.	1,275
211	Stanford University	1,268
212	University of Washington	1,260
213	Avis, Inc.	1,260
214	Demoulas Super Markets Inc./Market Basket Inc.	1,260
215	Massachusetts Institute of Technology	1,251
216	Schneider National Inc.	1,250
217	Schreiber Foods Inc.	1,250
218	Packard Bell Electronics Inc.	1,250
219	Watchtower Bible & Tract Society of New York Inc.	1,250
220	Duke University	1,249
221	Schnuck Markets Inc.	1,225
222	Dunavant Enterprises Inc.	1,225
223	Ag Processing Inc	1,219
224	The Texas A&M University System	1,212
225	Schottenstein Stores Corporation	1,204
226	Club Corporation International	1,200
227	Helmsley Enterprises, Inc.	1,200
228	BeefAmerica, Inc.	1,200
229	C.H. Robinson Company	1,200
230	The UNO-VEN Company	1,200
231	Guardian Industries Corp.	1,200
232	Twin County Grocers Inc.	1,200
233	Pueblo Xtra International, Inc.	1,199
234	Holy Cross Health System	1,192
235	Louisiana State University System	1,191
236	Fort Howard Corporation	1,187
237	Continental Cablevision, Inc.	1,177
238	Ocean Spray Cranberries, Inc.	1,168
239	Family Restaurants Inc.	1,167
240	Golden State Foods Corporation	1,160
241	Jitney-Jungle Stores of America, Inc.	1,152
242	The University of Chicago	1,150
243	Contran Corporation	1,147
244	Georgia Lottery Corporation	1,128
245	The Golub Corporation	1,120
246	Dresser-Rand Company	1,116
247	Howard Hughes Medical Institute	1,106
248	American United Life Insurance Company	1,103
249	Oglethorpe Power Corporation	1,101
250	Save Mart Supermarkets	1,100

Rank	Company	Sales ($ mil.)
251	Crowley Maritime Corporation	1,100
252	E. & J. Gallo Winery	1,100
253	Advantis	1,100
254	J. M. Huber Corporation	1,100
255	Oxbow Corporation	1,100
256	Shurfine International, Inc.	1,100
257	VT Inc.	1,088
258	Hughes Markets, Inc.	1,087
259	Kash n' Karry Food Stores Inc.	1,086
260	Bell Communications Research Inc.	1,086
261	Cumberland Farms Inc.	1,085
262	Alamo Rent A Car, Inc.	1,080
263	Mercy Health System	1,076
264	Alex Lee Inc.	1,073
265	Associated Grocers, Incorporated	1,073
266	The University of Tennessee	1,071
267	Standard Insurance Co.	1,063
268	84 Lumber Co.	1,060
269	Sunkist Growers, Inc.	1,054
270	The Scoular Company Inc.	1,053
271	University of Southern California	1,052
272	Caterair International Corp.	1,050
273	Lennox International Inc.	1,050
274	Connell Co.	1,050
275	The University of Massachusetts	1,049
276	Prospect Motors Inc.	1,047
277	Washington University	1,046
278	U-Haul International, Inc.	1,041
279	Aurora Eby-Brown Co.	1,040
280	Columbia University in the City of New York	1,033
281	National Basketball Association	1,030
282	Holman Enterprises Inc.	1,028
283	JP Foodservice, Inc.	1,026
284	McCrory Corporation	1,024
285	Harvard Community Health Plan, Inc.	1,023
286	Provident Mutual Life Insurance Company	1,023
287	Budget Rent A Car Corporation	1,018
288	Astrum International Corp.	1,013
289	The Stroh Companies Inc.	1,010
290	Young & Rubicam Inc.	1,009
291	Trammell Crow Residential	1,007
292	Intermountain Health Care, Inc.	1,000
293	SSM Health Care System Inc.	1,000
294	Mashantucket Pequot Gaming Enterprise Inc.	1,000
295	Holiday Cos.	1,000
296	Lincoln Property Company	1,000
297	Ziff Communications Company	1,000
298	Andersen Corp.	1,000
299	Hunt Consolidated Inc.	1,000
300	General Medical Corporation	1,000

TOP 500 NON-PUBLICLY TRADED BUSINESS ENTERPRISES IN THE US (CONTINUED)

Rank	Company	Sales ($ mil.)
301	A-Mark Financial Corporation	1,000
302	Rich Products Corporation	990
303	The University of Missouri System	990
304	QuikTrip Corporation	985
305	The University of Iowa	984
306	International Data Group	980
307	Johnson & Higgins	970
308	Roll International	962
309	DynCorp	953
310	CooperSmith Inc.	952
311	Furr's Supermarkets, Inc.	950
312	Pension Benefit Guaranty Corporation	950
313	Allina Health System	948
314	Allegheny Health, Education and Research Foundation	938
315	Southern States Cooperative, Incorporated	937
316	Gilbane Building Company	936
317	National Life Insurance Co.	935
318	Group Health Cooperative of Puget Sound	934
319	University of California	932
320	Franciscan Health System	928
321	Montefiore Medical Center	927
322	GAF Corp	926
323	Lykes Bros. Inc.	915
324	Connell Limited Partnership	913
325	United Van Lines, Inc.	912
326	Hartz Group Inc.	911
327	Gordon Food Service Inc.	910
328	Young's Market Co.	910
329	International Controls Corp.	909
330	Uniroyal Chemical Company, Inc.	908
331	CF Industries, Inc.	906
332	The University of Alabama	904
333	Flying J Inc.	900
334	UOP	900
335	Baker & Taylor Inc.	900
336	Wilbur-Ellis Company	900
337	Glaval Corporation	900
338	Mark III Industries, Inc.	900
339	JPS Textile Group Inc.	885
340	Darigold Inc.	882
341	Tang Industries, Inc.	878
342	United Grocers Inc.	877
343	Zeigler Coal Holding Company	873
344	Amica Mutual Insurance Company	871
345	Long John Silver's Restaurants, Inc.	870
346	L.L. Bean, Inc.	870
347	Battelle Memorial Institute	869
348	Essex Group Inc.	869
349	AMSTED Industries Incorporated	868
350	Emory University Inc.	862

Rank	Company	Sales ($ mil.)
351	Simpson Investment Co.	860
352	Yale University	852
353	World Color Press, Inc.	850
354	Potamkin Manhattan Corp.	850
355	Home Interiors & Gifts, Inc.	850
356	Woodward & Lothrop, Incorporated	849
357	Goodwill Industries International, Inc.	849
358	Vanderbilt University	848
359	K-III Communications Corporation	845
360	The University of Kentucky	844
361	Earle M. Jorgensen Holding Company, Inc.	843
362	North Pacific Lumber Co.	840
363	The University of Nebraska	839
364	Duchossois Industries, Inc.	837
365	AmeriServ Food Co.	833
366	Carnival Hotels and Casinos	830
367	Sweetheart Holdings, Inc.	830
368	National Distributing Company, Inc.	830
369	Tennessee Restaurant Co.	829
370	GROWMARK Inc.	827
371	Tri Valley Growers	821
372	Moorman Manufacturing Company	820
373	University of Florida	816
374	Homeland Holding Corporation	811
375	The Union Central Life Insurance Company	810
376	Treasure Chest Advertising Company, Inc.	807
377	W. L. Gore & Associates Inc.	804
378	Island Lincoln-Mercury Inc.	804
379	University of Pittsburgh	801
380	Bath Iron Works Corporation	800
381	Foster Poultry Farms Inc.	800
382	Haworth, Inc.	800
383	Vought Aircraft Company	800
384	MTS Inc.	800
385	G. Heileman Brewing Company, Inc.	800
386	The Irvine Company	800
387	M. A. Mortenson Companies, Inc.	798
388	Ford Foundation	797
389	Federated Insurance Companies	796
390	Racetrac Petroleum, Inc.	795
391	Coca-Cola Bottling Co. of Chicago	793
392	H. B. Zachry Company	792
393	Gulfstream Aerospace Corporation	790
394	Associated Food Stores, Inc.	787
395	Dairymen, Inc.	784
396	Di Giorgio Corp.	782
397	The Ritz-Carlton Hotel Company, Inc.	781
398	Santa Monica Ford	778
399	Quality King Distributors Inc.	775
400	Minyard Food Stores Inc.	770

TOP 500 NON-PUBLICLY TRADED BUSINESS ENTERPRISES IN THE US (CONTINUED)

Rank	Company	Sales ($ mil.)
401	Visa International	770
402	University of Rochester	764
403	Basin Electric Power Cooperative	764
404	GSC Enterprises, Inc.	757
405	Georgetown University Inc.	749
406	The Andersons Management Corp.	747
407	Tauber Oil Company	747
408	Allison Engine Co.	740
409	Loyola University of Chicago	740
410	Mary Kay Cosmetics Inc.	737
411	Boston University	736
412	Wickland Corporation	732
413	Smithsonian Institution	729
414	King Kullen Grocery Company Inc.	720
415	UIS, Inc.	716
416	PMC Inc.	715
417	Wawa Inc.	715
418	Dillingham Construction Holdings Inc.	713
419	Towers Perrin	709
420	Prairie Farms Dairy Inc.	709
421	Bartlett and Company	708
422	Drummond Co., Inc.	707
423	Day & Zimmermann Incorporated	706
424	The Elder-Beerman Stores Corp.	705
425	Catalyst Energy Corporation	705
426	Quad/Graphics, Inc.	700
427	Big V Supermarkets Inc.	700
428	Booz, Allen & Hamilton Inc.	700
429	Brookshire Grocery Company	700
430	McCarthy Building Companies	700
431	Warren Equities Inc.	700
432	R. B. Pamplin Corporation	695
433	National Hockey League	694
434	Black and Veatch	693
435	Riceland Foods, Inc.	692
436	General Chemical Corp.	690
437	Parsons and Whittemore Inc.	685
438	Sealy Corporation	683
439	Brenlin Group	680
440	The George Washington University	677
441	Bell & Howell Co.	676
442	Slim-Fast Nutritional Foods International, Inc.	675
443	Chemcentral Corporation	675
444	Menasha Corporation	674
445	Pan-American Life Insurance Company	663
446	Lanoga Corporation	657
447	Sacramento Municipal Utility District	656
448	Fiesta Mart Inc.	650
449	Sun-Diamond Growers of California	649
450	Hensel Phelps Construction Co.	646

Rank	Company	Sales ($ mil.)
451	Silgan Holdings Inc.	646
452	Huber, Hunt & Nichols Inc.	645
453	United Artists Theatre Circuit, Inc.	643
454	Republic Engineered Steels, Inc.	642
455	Edward D. Jones & Co.	640
456	McKee Foods Corporation	640
457	Florist's Transworld Delivery Association Inc.	640
458	The Hub Group, Inc.	640
459	Westfield Companies	638
460	J. Crew Group Inc.	636
461	Coulter Corporation	635
462	The Sverdrup Corp.	635
463	Penn Mutual Life Insurance Co.	635
464	Washington Corporations	629
465	S&P Co.	628
466	Crown Holding Company	626
467	ABCO Markets Inc.	625
468	Leo Burnett Company, Inc.	622
469	Carpenter Co.	619
470	Follett Corporation	612
471	Esprit de Corp.	606
472	Sierra Pacific Industries	604
473	Calcot, Ltd.	600
474	Key Food Stores Cooperative, Inc.	600
475	Dairyman's Cooperative Creamery Association	595
476	Crawford Fitting Company Inc.	594
477	RGIS Inventory Specialists	590
478	Harbour Group Ltd.	590
479	Bashas' Inc.	586
480	Galileo International	584
481	Sunbelt Beverage Corporation	580
482	Bacardi Imports, Inc.	578
483	MediaNews Group Inc.	575
484	The Dick Group of Companies	575
485	K-Va-T Food Stores, Inc.	562
486	AMI Cos.	561
487	Asplundh Tree Expert Co.	560
488	Thrifty Oil Co.	560
489	Alling and Cory Company	557
490	Flint Ink Corporation	550
491	Metallurg, Inc.	550
492	Wisconsin Dairies Cooperative	548
493	RLC Industries Co. Inc.	548
494	American Crystal Sugar Company	543
495	West Publishing Co.	541
496	Princeton University	541
497	Encyclopaedia Britannica Inc.	540
498	MasterCard International Incorporated	540
499	D'Arcy Masius Benton & Bowles, Inc.	531
500	Ferrellgas, Inc.	525

THE 125 LEADING

Private Companies

ACE HARDWARE CORPORATION

RANK: 115

OVERVIEW

Ace Hardware is the 2nd largest dealer-owned hardware wholesaler in the US, after Cotter & Co. (True Value Hardware). Headquartered in Oak Brook, Illinois, Ace is a cooperative with more than 4,100 dealers who own 5,000 Ace Hardware stores in the US, Scandinavia, the Middle East, and Central and South America.

Ace acts as middleman between manufacturers and dealers, distributing products through 14 Retail Support Centers, and also makes its own brand-name paint. Its dealers own 100% of the company and receive dividends from Ace's net profits as well as from Ace Paint.

The company provides a variety of other services for its dealers, including training, insurance, and computer services. Dealers also pay 1.25% of their annual purchases for Ace's National Advertising program, featuring football commentator John Madden and the slogan "Ace is the place."

Ace continues to expand into new markets. In 1993 it signed a deal with Canadian building materials distributor Canfor-Weldwood Distribution to distribute Ace products in Canada. The company also announced plans to establish a subsidiary in Mexico to serve its dealers there.

ACE Hardware

Dealer-owned cooperative
Fiscal year ends: December 31

WHO

Chairman: Richard E. Laskowski
President and CEO: Roger E. Peterson
EVP and COO: David F. Hodnik
SVP Marketing and Advertising: William A. Loftus
VP Merchandising: Michael C. Bodzewski
VP Corporate Strategy and International Business: Paul M. Ingevaldson
VP Finance: Rita D. Kahle
VP, General Counsel, and Secretary: David W. League
VP Retail Support: David F. Myer
VP Information Systems: Donald L. Schuman
VP Human Resources: Fred J. Neer
Auditors: KPMG Peat Marwick

WHEN

Ace traces its roots to a group of Chicago-area hardware dealers — Frank Burke, Richard Hesse, E. Gunnard Lindquist, and Oscar Fisher — who joined together in 1924 to pool their hardware buying and their promotional costs. In 1928 the group incorporated as Ace Stores, Inc., and began operations as a wholesaler, with Burke as president. Burke stepped down a year later and was replaced by Hesse, who would remain president of the company for the next 44 years.

The company opened its first warehouse in 1929, and by 1933 Ace had 38 dealers. That same year the company held its first convention so that dealers could review and purchase merchandise. The company continued to grow during the next 2 decades, and by 1949 it had 133 dealers in 7 states.

In 1953 Ace began to allow dealers to buy stock in the company through the Ace Perpetuation Plan. In the 1960s Ace began to expand into the South and the West, and in 1969 it opened distribution centers in Benicia, California, and Atlanta, its first such facilities outside of Chicago.

In the early 1970s the do-it-yourself market began to surge as inflation pushed up the fees for plumbers and electricians. As the market grew, large home center chains began to gobble up market share from independent dealers like those franchised through Ace. In response Ace and its dealers became a part of a growing trend in the hardware industry — cooperatives.

In 1973 Richard Hesse sold Ace to its dealers for $6 million (less than half its book value), and in 1974 Ace began operating as a cooperative. Hesse stepped down, and Arthur Krausman became head of the company. In 1977 the dealers took full control when Ace's first Board of Dealer-Directors was elected.

Ace continued to expand in 1975 when it began exporting products, and in 1978 Ace signed up a number of dealers in the Eastern US. By 1979 it had dealers in all 50 states. Ace began an aggressive building program in 1980 to add distribution centers to serve its growing network of dealers.

In 1984 Ace began manufacturing its own paint when it opened a paint plant in Matteson, Illinois. By 1985 Ace had reached $1 billion in sales. That same year the company initiated its "Store of the Future Program," allowing dealers to borrow up to $200,000 to upgrade their stores and conduct market analyses.

In 1989 the company began to test a computer network, called ACENET, that allowed Ace dealers to check inventory, send and receive electronic mail, make special purchase requests, and keep up with prices on commodity items such as lumber. Also in 1989 Ace added a Lumber & Building Materials convention to its list of annual meetings.

Ace established an International Division in 1990 to handle its overseas stores. In 1992, 4 Ace dealers in Florida sued the company for allegedly signing up a wholesaler as a dealer. According to Ace's membership requirements, owner-dealers must be retailers.

In 1993 Ace opened a Retail Support Center in Princeton, Illinois.

WHERE

HQ: 2200 Kensington Ct., Oak Brook, IL 60521
Phone: 708-990-6600
Fax: 708-573-4894

Ace serves dealers with retail operations in all 50 states and in 44 countries.

Retail Support Centers

Baltimore, MD	Little Rock, AR
Charlotte, NC	Prescott Valley, AZ
Dallas, TX	Princeton, IL
Gainesville, GA	Sacramento, CA
Hartford, CT	Tampa, FL
La Crosse, WI	Toledo, OH
Lincoln, NE	Yakima, WA

WHAT

Dealer Services
Advertising
Fixtures and equipment
In-store displays
Insurance
Retail computer services
Store planning and development
Training

KEY COMPETITORS

84 Lumber	Menard
Ames	Montgomery Ward
Benjamin Moore	National Home Centers
Cotter & Co.	Payless Cashways
D. I. Y. Home Warehouse	Pratt and Lambert
Eagle Hardware & Garden	Price/Costco
Grossman's	Sears
Hardware Wholesalers	Servistar
Hechinger	Sherwin-Williams
Home Depot	Venture Stores
Imperial Chemical	Wal-Mart
Kmart	Wickes Lumber
Lowe's	Wolohan Lumber
McCoy	

HOW MUCH

	9-Year Growth	1984	1985	1986	1987	1988	1989	1990	1991	1992	1993
Sales ($ mil.)	9.0%	926	1,009	1,061	1,198	1,382	1,546	1,625	1,704	1,871	2,018
Net income ($ mil.)	8.3%	28	32	37	42	54	51	60	59	61	57
Income as % of sales	—	3.0%	3.2%	3.4%	3.5%	3.9%	3.3%	3.7%	3.5%	3.2%	2.8%
Dividends ($ mil.)	8.8%	28	31	37	44	50	53	58	58	63	59
Employees	6.0%	2,018	2,096	2,253	2,477	2,741	2,875	2,931	3,110	3,256	3,405

1993 Year-end:
Debt ratio: 27.7%
Return on equity: 31.6%
Long-term debt (mil.): $71.3

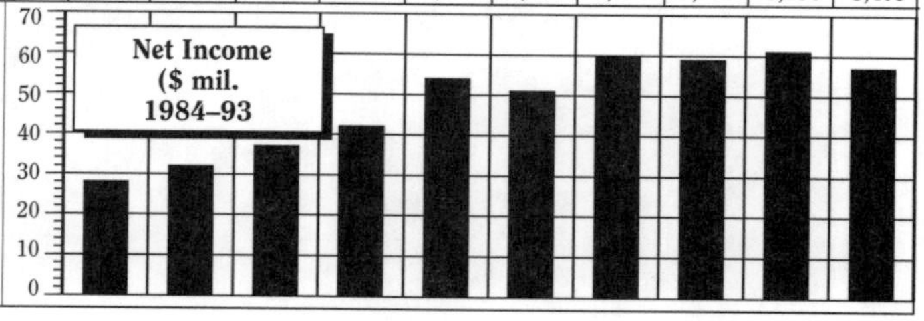

Net Income ($ mil.) 1984–93

ADVANCE PUBLICATIONS, INC.

RANK: 34

OVERVIEW

Advance Publications, owned by its founder's sons Si and Donald Newhouse, is the holding company for the US's largest privately held media group. Advance ranks among the leaders in all of its business segments: books (Random House), magazines (Condé Nast), newspapers, and cable TV.

Advance's book arm is the largest consumer publisher in the US (with over $1 billion in sales in 1992), controlling the publishers Knopf, Ballantine, and Vintage, among others. Condé Nast is one of the top 5 US magazine publishers, with 15 titles, which include *Vogue*, *The New Yorker*, and *Details*. Newhouse Newspapers publishes 26 newspapers, including the Portland *Oregonian*, Cleveland *Plain Dealer*, and New Orleans *Times-Picayune*. Its *Parade*, a magazine supplement in Sunday newspapers, leads the US in paid circulation. Newhouse Broadcasting owns the 8th largest US cable company.

Advance has formed recent ventures to increase its strength in multimedia. In 1994 Condé Nast replaced top editorial and advertising executives with relative youngsters in what Si Newhouse called "the changing of the guard."

WHEN

Solomon Neuhaus (who later became Samuel I. Newhouse) dropped out of school at 13 because of family poverty. He went to work for a lawyer who received the *Bayonne* (New Jersey) *Times* as payment for a debt. At age 16 in 1911, Newhouse was put in charge of the failing newspaper; he turned the company around. In 1922 he bought the Staten Island *Advance*, the core of Advance Publications.

Newhouse used profits from the *Advance* to buy newspapers throughout the New York area, operating out of a briefcase rather than a headquarters suite. He purchased the *Long Island Press* (1932), the Newark *Star-Ledger* (1933), the *Long Island Star-Journal* (1938), and the *Syracuse Journal* (1939). He later acquired the *Syracuse Herald-Standard* (1941), the *Jersey Journal* (1945), and the Harrisburg *Patriot* (1948). In 1955 he expanded into the South by buying the *Birmingham News* and the *Huntsville Times*.

In 1959 Newhouse entered magazine publishing when he bought Condé Nast (*Vogue, Bride's, House & Garden*) as an anniversary gift for his wife, Mitzi (joking that she had asked for a fashion magazine, so he bought her *Vogue*). In 1962 he paid $42 million for the New Orleans *Times-Picayune* and *New Orleans States-Item*, a record price broken by his 1967 purchase of the Cleveland *Plain Dealer* for $54 million. By 1967 Newhouse had also established NewChannels, which owned several cable systems (10,000 subscribers). Newhouse set yet another newspaper purchase record in 1976 by buying the Booth chain of 8 Michigan newspapers for $304 million.

Newhouse died in 1979, leaving his sons Si and Donald as trustees of the company's 10 shares of voting stock. They claimed that the estate was worth $181.9 million, taxable at $48.7 million. The IRS contested that figure. When the case — the largest ever at the time — was decided in 1990, the IRS lost.

Meanwhile the sons continued to expand Advance Publications. They entered book publishing by buying Random House, at that time the largest general-interest US book publisher, from RCA in 1980. Random House began in 1925 when Bennett Cerf bought the Modern Library from his boss. In 1927 Cerf and his partner, Donald Klopfer, began publishing luxury editions (chosen "at random") in addition to the inexpensive Modern Library books. In 1966 RCA bought Random, but bureaucratic RCA and genteel Random did not mesh.

Advance resurrected *Vanity Fair* in 1983, bought *The New Yorker* in 1985, and acquired Crown Publishing in 1989. In 1992 Si Jr. moved *Vanity Fair* editor Tina Brown to *The New Yorker*, hoping to give an edge to the eccentric weekly. In 1993 Condé Nast bought Knapp Publications (*Architectural Digest*, *Bon Appetit*).

Also in 1993 the company joined with Brøderbund Software to create children's multimedia software and bought the electronic publishing division of Bantam Doubleday Dell. That year it also offered $500 million to QVC, backing its bid for Paramount (which QVC later lost to Viacom).

The company acquired 25% of *Wired*, a leading multimedia magazine, in 1994.

HOW MUCH

	Annual Growth	1984	1985	1986	1987	1988	1989	1990	1991	1992	1993
Estimated sales ($ mil.)	12.1%	2,000	2,030	2,200	2,397	2,860	2,935	3,100	4,579	4,750	5,320
Cable TV revenues ($ mil.)	15.0%	—	—	186	203	229	295	398	440	467	496
Cable subscribers (thou.)	5.3%	850	917	1,027	1,098	1,078	1,147	1,242	1,301	—	1,350
Newspaper revenues ($ mil.)	2.9%	—	—	1,470	1,601	1,681	1,745	1,797	1,714	1,748	1,800
Newspapers	0.0%	26	26	27	26	36	26	30	32	28	26
Magazine revenues ($ mil.)	8.6%	—	—	544	678	745	842	845	941	1,042	970
Employees	0.3%	18,500	18,500	19,000	19,000	19,500	19,500	19,000	19,000	19,000	19,000

Estimated Sales ($ mil.) 1984–93

6,000
5,000
4,000
3,000
2,000
1,000
0

Private company
Fiscal year ends: December 31

WHO

Chairman and CEO: Samuel I. "Si" Newhouse, Jr., age 64
President: Donald E. Newhouse, age 63
Publisher: Richard Diamond
Chairman, President, and CEO, Random House, Inc.: Alberto Vitale
President, The Condé Nast Publications Inc.: Steven T. Florio, age 44
President, Newhouse Newspapers Metro-Suburbia, Inc.: Edwin F. Russell
Editorial Director, The Condé Nast Publications Inc.: James Truman, age 35

WHERE

HQ: 950 Fingerboard Rd., Staten Island, NY 10305
Phone: 718-981-1234
Fax: 718-981-1415

Advance Publications has newspapers and cable TV groups in the US and book and magazine operations in New York and Europe.

WHAT

The Condé Nast Publications Inc.
Allure
Architectural Digest
Bride's
Condé Nast Traveler
Details
Glamour
Gourmet
GQ
Mademoiselle
The New Yorker
Parade
Self
Vanity Fair
Vogue

Random House
Alfred A. Knopf
Ballantine Books
Beginner Books
Crown Publishers
Fawcett Books
Fodor's Travel Publications
Modern Library
Orion
Pantheon Books
Random Century (UK)
Times Books
Villard Books
Vintage Books

Newhouse Broadcasting
8th largest US cable group; 1.35 million subscribers

Newhouse Newspapers Metro-Suburbia (Selected)
Alabama
- *Birmingham News*
- *Birmingham Post-Herald*
- *The Mobile Press*
- *The Mobile Press Register*
- *The Mobile Register*

New Orleans, Louisiana
- *The Times-Picayune*

Springfield, Massachusetts
- *Union-News & Sunday Republican*

Michigan
- *The Ann Arbor News*
- *The Flint Times*
- *The Grand Rapids Press*
- *Kalamazoo Gazette*
- *Times* (Bay City)

Pascagoula, Mississippi
- *Mississippi Press*
- *Mississippi Press Register*

Jersey City, New Jersey
- *Jersey Journal*

Syracuse, New York
- *Herald-American*
- *The Post-Standard*
- *Syracuse Herald-Journal*

Cleveland, Ohio
- *Plain Dealer*

Portland, Oregon
- *The Oregonian*

Harrisburg, Pennsylvania
- *The Patriot-News*

KEY COMPETITORS

ADVO
American Express
Bertelsmann
Capital Cities/ABC
Comcast
Cox
Gannett
Hearst
Houghton Mifflin
Knight-Ridder
Liberty Media
Matra-Hachette
New York Times
News Corp.
Pearson
Publishers Group West
Reader's Digest
Reed Elsevier
Scholastic
E.W. Scripps
TCI
Thomson Corp.
Time Warner
Times Mirror
Tribune
Viacom
Washington Post

AGWAY INC.

RANK: 147

OVERVIEW

Agway is the largest farm cooperative in the Northeast and the 2nd largest in the US (after Farmland), with over 90,000 members and operations in 12 states. Agway strives to maintain a down-to-earth, friendly corporate image: its membership is limited exclusively to farmers, and each member of its 18-person board is an active dairy or crop farmer.

Agway operates in 4 business areas. Its agriculture group takes orders for feed and seed and delivers farm-related products and services. Its consumer group operates over 550 Agway stores in the suburban and rural Northeast, selling yard and garden supplies, pet food and supplies, and farm-related products. This group also operates the Country Foods unit, which markets members' commodities. (These 2 groups account for 59% of sales.) The energy arm delivers oil to over 400,000 customers (37% of sales). The financial group, which includes Telmark and Agway Insurance, offers financial services to farmers and equipment dealers (4% of sales).

Since 1992 Agway has been operating under its "Customer Driven: 1995" plan, a 2-pronged program designed to prepare it for the 21st century. It aims to secure for Agway a strong financial standing and to provide efficient, customer-driven delivery of products and services. Agway's biggest move in this direction was its 1993 decision to divest two food operations (to generate cash to strengthen core operations), which had been providing almost 50% of overall revenues.

WHEN

Agway was formed in 1964 by the merger of 3 large northeastern agricultural cooperatives: Cooperative Grange League Federation Exchange, Inc., founded in 1920; Eastern States Farmers Exchange, Inc., founded in 1918; and Pennsylvania Farm Bureau Cooperative Association, founded in 1934. The combined sales of the 3 co-ops at the time of the merger was $375 million. The idea of a merger was first discussed in 1960 when executives from GLF and Eastern States met at the annual meeting of the National Council of Farmer Cooperatives in Atlanta. A complicated merger eventually resulted, after countless meetings (and a study predicting its results conducted by Battelle Memorial Institute).

About the time of the merger, Agway indirectly acquired voting control of Curtice Burns Foods through a co-op that a group of Agway's own members owned. Curtice Burns quickly became a fast-growing food products business, which bought most of its raw materials from Agway members and which focused almost exclusively on regionally popular, niche products that larger companies ignored. Between 1971 and 1981 the subsidiary acquired at least 8 other food companies, including Nalley's Fine Foods, National Brands Beverage, and National Oats Co. In 1962 sales hovered at $13 million; 30 years later revenues were approaching $900 million.

Excited by the positive financial results of Curtice Burns, Agway purchased another food company, H. P. Hood, in 1980. Founded in 1846, Boston-based H. P. Hood was a leading maker and distributor of dairy and other food products in the Northeast.

In 1990 the plain-talking Ralph Heffner, chairman (and owner of a large farm in Pennsylvania), set his sights on reengineering Agway. He had listened to the grim forecasts from industry pundits: that more than 20,000 northeastern farms had closed down since 1990 and that 17,000 more closures were expected by 1995. Slimming down and stockpiling cash were 2 of his early goals. In 1992 more than 400 employees took early retirement, persuaded by an attractive retirement package. The energy group was trimmed considerably: 8 fuel distribution businesses were sold, and the group turned its focus from low-margin commercial accounts to higher-profit homeowner accounts. Agway's retail stores underwent renovation, getting wider aisles and brighter lighting. Perhaps most significant, Agway separated its retail arm from its agricultural services and wholesale farm supply business, forming a single-margin system by creating a virtually direct pipeline from farmer to supplier. In 1992 Agway took a $75 million hit related to restructuring costs.

In 1993 the co-op announced its intention to divest H. P. Hood, on which it had blamed a revenues slide in 1991 and 1992, and Curtice Burns. CEO Charles Saul now intends to zero in on "work simplification," eliminating layers of management to make the co-op more nimble and responsive to market changes.

HOW MUCH

	9-Year Growth	1984	1985	1986	1987	1988	1989	1990	1991	1992	1993
Sales ($ mil.)	(9.3%)	4,101	4,067	2,793	2,725	2,936	1,842	1,985	1,971	1,801	1,711
Operating income ($ mil.)	5.8%	12	14	26	11	20	11	8	(6)	(59)	20
Members	(1.4%)	103,000	102,000	102,000	102,000	99,000	95,000	95,000	95,000	91,000	91,000
Employees	(5.1%)	10,600	—	—	—	—	8,000	—	8,000	8,400	6,600

Agricultural cooperative
Fiscal year ends: June 30

WHO

Chairman: Ralph H. Heffner, age 55
VC: Charles C. Brosius, age 63
CEO, President, and General Manager: Charles F. Saul, age 60, $527,751 pay
SVP Finance and Control: Peter J. O'Neill, age 46, $283,299 pay
SVP Planning/Operations: Bruce D. Ruppert, age 41, $222,653 pay
SVP Corporate Services: David M. Hayes, age 49, $265,401 pay
Group VP, Energy Group: Stephen B. Burnett, age 46, $239,773 pay
Group VP, Agriculture Group: Joel G. Newman
Group VP, Consumer Group: John L. Norris
VP Human Resources: Robert T. Engfer, age 57
Auditors: Coopers & Lybrand

WHERE

HQ: 333 Butternut Dr., DeWitt, NY 13214-1879
Phone: 315-449-7061
Fax: 315-449-6078

Agway has more than 90,000 members in 12 northeastern states: Connecticut, Delaware, Maine, Maryland, Massachusetts, New Hampshire, New Jersey, New York, Ohio, Pennsylvania, Rhode Island, and Vermont.

WHAT

	1993 Sales		1993 Operating Margin	
	$ mil.	% of total	$ mil.	% of total
Agriculture & Consumer	1,006	59	20	36
Energy	639	37	24	44
Financial Services	70	4	11	20
Adjustments	(4)	—	—	—
Total	**1,711**	**100**	**55**	**100**

Operating Units

Agriculture Group
- Makes and delivers farm production supplies
- Operates feed, fertilizer, and seed facilities
- Provides agricultural services

Consumer Group
- Stores and franchised representatives, selling yard and garden products, pet food and supplies, and farm-related products; Country Foods stores

Energy Group
- Supplies farm and home heating fuels, power fuels, and other petroleum products

Financial Services Group
- Agway Insurance (property, health, auto, and liability insurance to farm, residential, and small business enterprises)
- Telmark Inc. (finances leases for buildings, equipment, and vehicles)

KEY COMPETITORS

ADM
Ag Processing
Ag Services of America
Allstate
American Cyanamid
Amoco
Andersons
Cargill
Caterpillar
CML Group
ConAgra
Continental Grain
Deere
Farmland Industries
General Host
Global Petroleum
Home Depot
Hormel
Kmart
Pennzoil
Prudential
Sears
State Farm
Wal-Mart
Woolworth

ALCO HEALTH SERVICES

RANK: 49

OVERVIEW

Based in Valley Forge, Pennsylvania, Alco Health Services Corporation is one of the largest pharmaceuticals distribution companies in the US (with Elib Lilly and National Intergroup's FoxMeyer unit, among others). It provides goods and services to more than 16,000 customers, including independent and chain pharmacies, hospitals, nursing homes, and clinics.

Alco provides lower-cost pharmaceuticals (90% of sales) and health, beauty, and general merchandise to small buyers who cannot drive hard bargains directly with the manufacturers. It also offers a number of services to its customers, including marketing and promotional assistance for small drugstores through its Family Pharmacy program, bulk purchasing, inventory management, and emergency delivery services through its Prime Vendor and PrimeNet merchandising programs. The company offers various discount packages for both branded and generic products.

Alco markets aggressively. It has over 200 salespeople and distributes its products from 18 facilities in the eastern US.

After the 1992 postponement of a public offering, Citicorp entities remain in control of 73% of Alco, and a group of top management members owns most of the remainder.

Private company
Fiscal year ends: September 30

WHO

Chairman, President, and CEO: John F. McNamara, age 58, $530,340 pay

Group President, Central Region: R. David Yost, age 46, $245,340 pay

Group President, Eastern Region: David M. Flowers, age 46, $234,980 pay

VP Marketing: Robert E. McHugh, age 52, $144,000 pay

VP Finance and Treasurer: Kurt J. Hilzinger, age 33, $174,000

VP, Legal Counsel, and Secretary: Teresa T. Ciccotelli, age 42

VP Human Resources and Assistant Secretary: Robert D. Gregory, age 64

Auditors: Ernst & Young

WHEN

In 1977 Tinkham Veale II decided to go into the drug wholesaling business. Veale's company, Alco Standard, already owned a variety of chemical, electrical, metallurgical, and mining companies, but by the late 1970s the company was pursuing a strategy of zeroing in on different types of distribution.

Alco's first drug wholesaler purchase was The Drug House, of Delaware and Pennsylvania; the next was Duff Brothers, of Chattanooga. In the ensuing years the company bought other wholesalers in the South, East, and Midwest. Alco's modus operandi was to buy small, well-run companies for cash and Alco stock and leave the incumbent management in charge. In this way, Alco had become the US's 3rd largest wholesale drug distributor by the early 1980s.

Alco's drug distribution drive came at a time when the US health and drug industries were undergoing considerable structural change, and the wholesaling niche grew because it was able to offer greater sales and better service to buyers than the drug manufacturers themselves could offer.

Yet Alco's growth in the 1980s came at a time of consolidation in the industry (the number of wholesalers dropped by half between 1980 and 1992).

In 1985 Alco Standard spun off its drug distribution operations as Alco Health Services Corporation, a public company, of which Alco Standard retained 60% ownership.

Alco Health continued its previous growth strategy of expanding through acquisition. The addition of Valdosta (Georgia) Drug Company and Meyers and Company (Tiffin, Ohio) boosted sales above $1 billion. Alco Health also increased its market share by offering marketing and promotional help to its independent pharmacy customers, who were beleaguered by the growth of national discounters. Alco also increased its market by targeting hospitals, nursing homes, and clinics.

This strategy paid off. Between 1983 and 1988 (including the period of its spinoff) Alco's sales grew at a compounded annual rate of 28%.

In 1988, when the US was in the midst of its LBO frenzy, an Alco management group attempted and failed to conclude an LBO. Rival McKesson then also attempted to acquire Alco Health, but this fell through because of antitrust considerations. By this time Alco Standard's interest had fallen to 49%.

Later that year management turned to Citicorp Venture Capital Corp., Ltd., for backing for another buyout attempt. This time they succeeded. A newly formed holding company, Alco Health Distribution, bought 92% of Alco Health's stock and issued debentures for the remainder.

To pay down its debt, Alco Health has curtailed its acquisitions program and cut expenses. In particular Alco Health reduced its operations from 31 facilities in 1989 to 17 in 1993. It also began to upgrade its information systems.

In late 1993 the company was named as one of 30 defendants in 14 suits filed by independent pharmacies. These suits charge Alco with discriminatory pricing policies.

WHERE

HQ: Alco Health Services Corporation, 300 Chesterfield Pkwy., Valley Forge, PA 19482
Phone: 215-296-4480
Fax: 215-647-0141

Alco owns facilities in Georgia, Indiana, Kentucky, Maryland, Missouri, Ohio, Pennsylvania, Tennessee, and Virginia and leases facilities in Kentucky, Minnesota, New Jersey, Ohio, South Dakota, Tennessee, and Texas.

WHAT

Services
Family Pharmacy (merchandising program)
Income Pax (promotional assistance)
Income RePax (bulk purchasing program)
Income RX (generic pharmaceuticals sales)
Partner Pak (promotional assistance)
PrimeNet (hospital-group purchase plan)
Prime Vendor (long-term distribution program)

	1993 Sales	
	$ mil.	% of total
Hospitals	1,554	42
Independent pharmacies, nursing homes & clinics	1,397	37
Chains	768	21
Total	**3,719**	**100**

	1993 Sales % of total
Pharmaceuticals	90
Other	10
Total	**100**

KEY COMPETITORS

Abbott Labs
American Home Products
Bausch & Lomb
Baxter
Bristol-Myers Squibb
Cardinal Distribution
Eli Lilly
Johnson & Johnson
Marion Merrell Dow
Merck
National Intergroup
Pfizer
Pharmacy Direct Network
Price/Costco
Quality King Distributors
Schering-Plough
Upjohn

HOW MUCH

	Annual Growth	1984	1985	1986	1987	1988	1989	1990	1991	1992	1993
Sales ($ mil.)	12.6%	—	—	1,226	1,831	2,059	2,297	2,564	2,827	3,330	3,719
Net income ($ mil.)	(32.7%)	—	—	16	19	20	(12)	(21)	(15)	1	1
Income as a % of sales	—	—	—	1.3%	1.0%	0.9%	—	—	—	—	—
Employees	2.3%	—	2,000	2,420	2,700	2,900	2,400	2,323	2,560	2,269	2,403

Net Income ($ mil.) 1986–93

20
10
0
-10
-20
-30

AARP

RANK: N/R

OVERVIEW

The American Association of Retired Persons (AARP) is the US's largest organization dedicated to advocacy for older citizens. It provides its over 33 million members with insurance; discounts on pharmaceuticals, car rentals, and hotel rates; other travel services; an investment program; and subscriptions to *Modern Maturity* and the *AARP Bulletin*.

The association is also one of the US's most powerful lobbies, dedicated to maintaining and expanding programs targeted to people over 50. It steadfastly opposes cuts in Social Security and Medicare entitlements, which in 1993 accounted for 38% of all federal tax receipts. This position has stirred criticism that it is working for the benefit of its constituency at the expense of the young. As a countermeasure, AARP recently began stressing intergenerational concerns. To this end it has lobbied for family leave laws and emphasized the wide variety of volunteer programs from which younger citizens benefit.

Based Washington, DC, AARP views itself as a representative of its members' interests. But many believe that the upper management (which is appointed by board members elected by delegates from the local chapters, not elected by members at large) may be out of step with its members. AARP's management consists overwhelmingly of former public employees who may be more disposed than the average member to support government spending programs. Although AARP is an aggressive recruiter, soliciting membership by mail as people turn 50, membership declined in 1993 for the first time.

WHEN

In 1955 Ethel Andrus, a retired Los Angeles high school principal and founder of the National Retired Teachers Association (NRTA, 1947), went looking for an insurance carrier for her group and could not find one, until she encountered insurance broker Leonard Davis. Davis found an insurance company in Chicago that would underwrite the group. Three years later, Andrus organized AARP to "enhance the quality of life . . . promote independence . . . lead in determining the role in society . . . and improve the image of aging" for older Americans.

Andrus offered members the same low rates for health and accident insurance enjoyed by NRTA members. Other services soon followed, including a mail order discount pharmacy and travel services. Andrus began publishing the organization's bimonthly magazine, *Modern Maturity,* in 1958, and AARP's first local chapter opened in Youngstown, Arizona, in 1960.

In 1963 Davis formed Colonial Penn Insurance to take over the AARP account and paid the organization royalties.

Andrus led AARP and its increasingly powerful lobby for the elderly until her death in 1967. In 1973 AARP endowed the Ethel Percy Andrus Gerontology Center (University of Southern California) for the study of aging.

During the 1970s criticism of Colonial Penn mounted, and finally in 1979, after a competitive bidding process, Prudential won AARP's insurance business.

The NRTA joined AARP in 1982, and AARP continued to expand. New services included the auto club, financial services such as mutual funds and expanded insurance policies, and hotel and motel discounts. In 1983 it lowered the eligibility age from 55 to 50 and raised its annual dues from \$3 to \$5. AARP membership grew phenomenally, up to 8,000 members per day, reaching over 33 million.

AARP acts as an agent between its members and service providers: Prudential for health insurance; Hartford for auto and home insurance; Scudder, Stevens & Clark for mutual fund investment services; and Amoco for auto club services. Revenues from these activities contributed approximately 29% of AARP's 1992 income, up from 25% in 1990.

In 1988 the AARP started a federal credit union for its members, but despite rosy projections, it ceased operations in 1990.

In 1988 AARP lobbied for reforms in Medicare that provided extended care benefits to Americans over 65, but when it became clear that this would require an increase in Medicare premiums, the hue and cry from members forced repeal of the legislation. Many took this as an example of how out of step the AARP was with its membership.

In 1992 the association raised its dues to \$8 per year, a reflection of the fact that revenues from membership dues have remained flat for several years.

In 1994 AARP refused to support the Clinton health insurance program.

HOW MUCH

	Annual Growth	1984	1985	1986	1987	1988	1989	1990	1991	1992	1993
Revenues ($ mil.)	6.1%	—	—	—	—	—	291	296	297	305	369
Membership (thou.)	7.0%	18,075	20,880	24,371	27,262	29,739	32,163	33,025	33,302	33,757	33,177
Employees	4.0%	—	—	—	—	—	1,532	1,593	1,635	1,718	1,793

Revenues ($ mil.) 1989–93

AARP

Association
Fiscal year ends: December 31

WHO

Chairman: Judith N. Brown
President: Lovola W. Burgess
Vice President: Margaret A. Dixon
Executive Director: Horace B. Deets
Treasurer: Allen W. Tull
General Counsel: Steven S. Zaleznick
Director Legislation and Public Policy: John C. Rother
Director Human Resources: Richard W. Henry
Auditors: Arthur Andersen & Co.

WHERE

HQ: American Association of Retired Persons, 601 E St. NW, Washington, DC 20049
Phone: 202-434-2277
Fax: 202-434-2525

AARP has over 33 million members worldwide.

WHAT

1992 Revenues	$ mil.	% of total
Membership dues	102	34
Group insurance administrative allowances	84	28
Publication advertising	40	13
Income from other programs & royalties	40	13
Interest income	38	12
Other	1	—
Total	**305**	**100**

1992 Assets	$ mil.	% of total
Cash	4	1
Investments committed to deferred dues	144	43
Receivables	35	10
Treasury bills & notes	107	32
Other	45	14
Total	**335**	**100**

Selected Periodicals
AARP Bulletin
Modern Maturity

Health and Insurance Services
Automobile (Hartford)
Health/Medigap (Prudential)
Homeowners (Hartford)
Mail order pharmacy service
Mobile Home (Foremost)

Financial Services
Credit cards (Bank One)
Mutual funds (Scudder, Stevens & Clark)

Travel Services
Auto club/road service (Amoco Motor Club)
Hotel, auto rental, and airline discounts (various providers)
Travel services (American Express)

Affiliated Entities
AARP Andrus Foundation
AARP Foundation

AMERICAN FINANCIAL CORPORATION

RANK: 74

OVERVIEW

Cincinnati-based American Financial (AFC) is a diversified holding company owned entirely by financier Carl Lindner and his family. AFC is primarily a supplier of property, casualty, and life insurance (through Great American Insurance). Other holdings include food distributors (Chiquita Brands International), broadcasting stations (Great American Communications), and magazines *(Financial World)*.

AFC uses cash from its insurance companies to invest in other businesses. The business is very much a family affair: Lindner's sons Carl III and Craig run AFC holdings, and his brother Robert is vice-chairman.

Great American Insurance offers multiline property and casualty coverage. Its life insurance unit, Great American Life, sells tax-sheltered annuities, mostly to schoolteachers. However, the insurance companies' results have been hurt by their investments in some of Lindner's more troubled operations.

Great American Communications is one of those troubled operations. In 1993, after having sold many of its nonbroadcasting operations (some to other Lindner companies), it went into a prepackaged Chapter 11 bankruptcy, i.e., one in which creditors agree to the restructuring terms before bankruptcy is declared.

AFC left the TV show production business in 1993 by swapping its 48% investment in Spelling Entertainment for 4% of Blockbuster Entertainment. Chiquita has also been hurt by European trade rules, oversupply, and a poorly timed expansion.

Private company
Fiscal year ends: December 31

WHO

Chairman and CEO: Carl H. Lindner, age 74
VC: Robert D. Lindner, age 73
President and COO: Ronald F. Walker, age 55
President, Great American Insurance Co.; President and COO, American Premier: Carl H. Lindner III, age 40
President, American Annuity Group: S. Craig Lindner, age 39
VP and General Counsel: James E. Evans, age 48
VP and Treasurer (Principal Financial and Accounting Officer): Fred J. Runk, age 51
VP Human Resources: Lawrence Otto
Auditors: Ernst & Young

WHEN

Carl Lindner, who had built his family's dairy business into the 220-unit United Dairy Farmers ice cream store chain, formed Henthy Realty (1955) and bought 3 S&Ls (1959). In 1960 the company's name became American Financial, to reflect the diversified financial services it offered. After a 1961 IPO American Financial bought United Liberty Life Insurance (1963) and Provident Bank (1966).

American Financial then diversified into several new areas. American Financial Leasing & Services Company was formed in 1968 to lease airplanes, computers, and other equipment to corporate customers, and in 1969 AFC acquired Phoenix developer Rubenstein Construction, renaming it American Continental. In 1971 American Financial bought several life, casualty, and mortgage insurance companies and entered publishing by purchasing a 95% stake in the *Cincinnati Enquirer*. In 1973 it bought National General, which owned the Great American Insurance Group; paperback publisher Bantam Books; and hardback publisher Grosset & Dunlap.

American Financial suffered during the mid-1970s when inflation grew faster than regulated insurance rates. In addition to selling its book publishers (1974), the company sold the *Enquirer* and American Continental (1975), leaving American Financial primarily an insurance and financial services company. The insurance companies were consolidated as Great American Insurance Company in 1976. AFC spun off Provident Bank as a special dividend to shareholders in 1980.

Lindner took AFC private in 1981. That year, subsidiary American Financial Enterprises acquired a 20% interest in Penn Central, the former railroad that had emerged from a 1970 bankruptcy as an industrial manufacturer. In 1984 American Financial sold convenience store chain UtoteM to Circle K for a minority interest in Circle K. Also in 1984, AFC increased its holdings in United Brands, renamed Chiquita Brands International, from 29% to 45%; Lindner installed himself as CEO of United Brands and reversed the company's losses. In 1990 after Circle K went bankrupt, AFC wrote off most of its investment in that company. AFC has since divested many holdings, including Hunter S&L, Kings Island amusement park, and its interest in Scripps Howard Broadcasting.

Part of the reason for this is the need to raise money to keep Great American Communications (formerly Taft Broadcasting) afloat. This business has done poorly since its purchase partly because of the recession but also because Lindner loaded it up with debt when he bought large portions of its stock in a $1.5 billion takeover. The company entered bankruptcy in 1992, but emerged the next year with a new focus (broadcasting to metropolitan markets) and a new name (Citicasters, Inc.) to reflect that focus. AFC steadily reduced its stake in the company during the 1990s and owned only 20% by 1994.

WHERE

HQ: One E. Fourth St., Cincinnati, OH 45202
Phone: 513-579-2121
Fax: 513-579-2580

American Financial has holdings that do business throughout the US.

WHAT

	1993 Sales $ mil.	1993 Sales % of total
Property/casualty insurance premiums	1,495	55
Investment income	602	22
Gains on sales of securities	82	3
Equity in earnings of investee corporations	70	2
Gains on sales of investee corporations	83	3
Gains on sales of subsidiaries	75	3
Sales of other products & services	152	6
Other income	163	6
Adjustments	(1)	—
Total	**2,721**	**100**

Subsidiaries and Affiliates

American Premier Underwriters (41%)
Leader National Insurance Company
Great American Holding Corporation
Great American Insurance Co. (100%)
American Annuity Group (80%)
Great American Life Insurance Co.
American Empire Surplus Lines Insurance Co.
American National Fire Insurance Co.
Great American Management Services, Inc.
Mid-Continent Casualty Co.
Stonewall Insurance Co.
Transport Insurance Co.

Publicly Traded Holdings

American Financial Enterprises, Inc. (83%)
Blockbuster Entertainment (4%)
Chiquita Brands International (46%)
General Cable (45%)
Great American Communications (20%)

KEY COMPETITORS

Aetna
Allstate
CIGNA
Cox
Equitable
GEICO
Kemper
MetLife
New York Life
Northwestern Mutual
Prudential
State Farm
Transamerica

HOW MUCH

	Annual Growth	1984	1985	1986	1987	1988	1989	1990	1991	1992	1993
Sales ($ mil.)	3.7%	1,959	2,310	2,791	2,588	6,814	7,038	7,761	5,219	3,929	2,721
Net income ($ mil.)	—	(40)	(23)	184	127	102	3	(6)	57	(162)	220
Income as % of sales	—	—	—	6.6%	4.9%	1.5%	0.0%	—	1.1%	—	0.8%
Employees	3.6%	—	45,800	44,300	52,800	52,000	53,000	54,000	54,000	69,200	60,790

1993 Year-end:
Debt ratio: 73.5%
Return on equity: —
Cash (mil.): $168
Assets (mil.): $10,078
Long-term debt (mil.): $1,054

Net Income ($ mil.) 1984–93

AMERICAN RED CROSS

RANK: 138

OVERVIEW

Headquartered in Washington, DC, the American Red Cross (ARC) is a member of the League of Red Cross and Red Crescent Societies. The movement, supported by more than 145 national societies, is an international humanitarian effort to alleviate all forms of human suffering. Although the ARC is chartered by Congress to provide relief services, it is not a government agency. It is a nonprofit organization staffed primarily by volunteers (50 volunteers to each paid employee) and funded by contributions, endowments, and income from its biomedical services unit.

The ARC is custodian of the largest blood supply in the US, collecting, handling, and delivering about 15 million units of blood a year. It also collects and delivers plasma and human tissues. Through its health and safety courses, it teaches CPR, first aid, water safety, and AIDS awareness. The ARC also provides services such as counseling and message transmission for US military personnel and aids in disaster relief efforts around the world. Nearly 93% of the ARC's annual expenditures go to its programs, with the remainder spent on administration and fund-raising.

During fiscal 1993 the ARC spent a record $248 million for disaster relief assistance as a number of major disasters, including flooding along the Mississippi River, hit the US.

WHEN

Clara Barton, who had become famous for her aid to soldiers on both sides during the US Civil War, first learned about the Red Cross when she assisted with relief efforts during the Franco-Prussian War (1870–71).

The Red Cross traces its beginnings to a trip made by Jean-Henri Dunant, a Swiss businessman, in 1859. Dunant was traveling in northern Italy when he saw the aftermath of the Battle of Solferino. Dunant published a pamphlet 3 years later calling for the formation of international volunteer societies to aid wounded soldiers. In 1863 a 5-member committee (including Dunant) formed the International Committee of the Red Cross (ICRC) in Geneva and called a conference that was attended by delegates of 16 countries. The conference resulted in the formation of national Red Cross societies across Europe. A red cross on a white background (the reverse of the Swiss flag) was chosen as the organization's symbol. (The Red Crescent symbol was added in 1876 by Muslim relief workers during the Russo-Turkish war.) In 1864 the ICRC principles were codified into international law through the Geneva Convention (the first of 4), which was initially signed by 12 nations.

After the Franco-Prussian War Barton returned home and worked to convince Congress to support the Geneva Conventions. In 1881 she and some friends founded the American Association of the Red Cross; the first chapter was established in Dansville, New York. In 1882 the US signed the Conventions, making the US the 32nd country to support the treaty.

Barton expanded the Red Cross's mission to include aiding victims of natural disasters. Among the ARC's first activities were relief efforts to aid forest fire victims in Michigan (1881) and flood victims along the Ohio River (1882). The ARC was granted a congressional charter in 1900 making it responsible for providing assistance to the US military and disaster relief in the US and overseas.

During WWI ARC membership soared as the number of chapters jumped from 107 to 3,864. ARC volunteers and Red Cross workers from other nations served beside the armed forces on the battlefields of Europe. After WWI the ARC helped refugees in Europe and recruited thousands of nurses to improve the health and hygiene of rural Americans. During the Depression the ARC provided food and shelter to millions in need.

In 1941 the organization established its first blood center in New York's Presbyterian Hospital. The ARC mobilized massive relief efforts again during WWII and again served beside the armed forces. At home volunteers taught nutrition courses, served in hospitals, and collected blood.

In 1956 the ARC began research to increase the safety of its blood supply. It also continued to provide assistance during natural disasters and during the Korean and Vietnam Wars and other US military conflicts.

During the 1980s the ARC was criticized for moving too slowly to improve testing of its blood supply for AIDS. After Elizabeth Dole was named head of the ARC in 1991, she reorganized the blood collection program. In 1993 the organization created Quick Response Teams, disaster units that can be deployed to a major disaster site on 4 hours notice.

HOW MUCH

	Annual Growth	1984	1985	1986	1987	1988	1989	1990	1991	1992	1993
Revenues	9.6%	787	851	973	972	1,000	1,140	1,466	1,410	1,568	1,796
Total assets ($ mil.)	8.6%	957	1,068	1,206	1,299	1,348	1,424	1,765	1,803	1,853	2,008
Expenditures ($ mil.)	10.0%	712	782	872	888	993	1,105	1,329	1,402	1,516	1,675
Employees	—	—	—	—	—	—	—	—	25,000	25,000	25,000

1993 Year-end:
Cash (mil.): $90
Long-term debt (mil.): $162

Revenues ($ mil.) 1984–93

American Red Cross

Nonprofit organization
Fiscal year ends: June 30

WHO

Chairman: Norman R. Augustine
President: Elizabeth Dole
EVP and COO Blood Services: Peter A. Tomasulo
Treasurer: Sarah A. Schwarz
Secretary and General Counsel: Karen Shoos Lipton
VP Finance/Comptroller: John D. Campbell
VP Human Resources: James E. Thomas III
Auditors: Deloitte & Touche

WHERE

HQ: 431 18th St. NW, Washington, DC 20006-5310
Phone: 202-737-8300
Fax: 202-639-3711

The American Red Cross has 2,624 chapters, 45 Blood Services regions, 23 Tissue Services centers, and 262 stations on military bases and in military hospitals worldwide.

WHAT

	1993 Revenues $ mil.	% of total
Contributions	499	28
Legacies & bequests	37	2
Biomedical services	956	53
Program materials	110	6
Contracts & grants	107	6
Investment income	42	2
Income from endowment funds	11	1
Other	34	2
Total	**1,796**	**100**

	1993 Expenditures $ mil.	% of total
Biomedical services	1,001	60
Disaster services	248	15
Health services	133	8
Services to members of the armed forces, veterans & their families	84	5
Community volunteer services	75	4
International programs	12	1
Membership & fund-raising	47	3
Management	75	4
Total	**1,675**	**100**

Activities

Biomedical services
- Blood services
- Plasma operations
- Research and development (Jerome H. Holland Laboratory)
- Tissue services

Disaster services
- Emergency assistance
- Long-term assistance
- Mass care

Health and safety education
- CPR courses
- First aid courses
- HIV/AIDS education
- Swimming and water safety courses

International services
- Disaster victim tracing and message service
- Refugee aid
- Relief aid

Military and social services
- Counseling
- Interest-free loans and grants for emergency travel
- Message service

AMERICAN STANDARD INC.

RANK: 47

OVERVIEW

The world's leading maker of plumbing fixtures, American Standard has seen its profits go down the tubes the last few years. Since the late 1980s the New York–based company has posted losses as it has struggled under the weight of more than $2 billion in debt from its 1988 LBO.

Besides plumbing products, the company also makes braking systems for heavy trucks and buses and air conditioning systems. Its plumbing products unit offers a wide selection of products designed to fit the consumer tastes of individual countries. Its air conditioning products unit makes products under the Trane brand name and emphasizes servicing, repair, and replacement over new construction. Its transportation products unit makes air brakes primarily for the commercial vehicle industries of Europe and Brazil.

American Standard is concentrating on increasing its overseas business, both in Europe and the Pacific Rim, and is also looking to increase its business in the growing retail home center market in the US.

Its stock is held by ASI Holding, which is owned by 3 groups: Kelso ASI Partners (the firm that bought the company in 1988, 73%), American Standard's employees (17%, through a stock ownership plan), and top executives and other employees (10%).

WHEN

In 1881 American Radiator was created in Buffalo to make steam and water heating equipment. J. P. Morgan acquired the company along with almost every other US heating equipment firm, consolidating them under the American Radiator name in 1899.

That same year Louisville-based Ahrens & Ott joined with Pittsburgh-based Standard Manufacturing to create Standard Sanitary. Standard Sanitary produced enameled cast-iron plumbing parts and developed the one-piece lavatory, built-in bathtubs, and single taps for hot and cold running water.

Both American Radiator and Standard Sanitary grew through numerous acquisitions in the early decades of the 20th century. In 1929 the 2 companies merged to form American Radiator & Standard Sanitary, headquartered in New York City, which later that year bought CF Church (toilet seats). During the next 3 decades the company expanded its operations across North and South America and into Europe. By the 1960s American Radiator & Standard Sanitary was the world's largest manufacturer of plumbing fixtures.

In 1967 the company changed its name to American Standard and then diversified out of the bathroom, acquiring a number of companies, the most important of which was Westinghouse Air Brake (WABCO, 1968). WABCO traces its history to Union Switch and Signal, begun in 1882. In 1917 Union Switch was acquired by Westinghouse Air Brake. George Westinghouse had invented the air brake before turning his attention to electricity. Union Switch merged with its parent company and adopted the WABCO name in 1951.

During the 1970s and 1980s American Standard consolidated its operations and sold off numerous businesses. It purchased Clayton Dewandre (truck brakes, 1977) and Queroy (faucets and fittings, 1982). In 1984 the company purchased Trane (air conditioners). In 1988 American Standard fought off a hostile takeover attempt by Black & Decker and then agreed to be purchased by ASI Holding (formed by the leveraged buyout firm Kelso & Co.) for $3 billion and taken private.

The transaction left American Standard deeply in debt. To raise cash in 1988, the company sold its Manhattan headquarters, its railway signal business ($105 million), and its Steelcraft division (steel doors, to Masco for $126 million). In 1989 the sale of American Standard's pneumatic controls business raised $102 million. The company sold its railway brake products operations to a group led by Investment AB Cardo (Sweden) in 1990. In 1991 it sold Tyler Refrigeration (commercial refrigerated display cases) to a Kelso affiliate for $82 million, losing $22 million in the deal.

California's attorney general filed suit against American Standard in 1992 for allegedly violating EPA lead limits. In 1993 Dan Quayle joined American Standard's board.

In 1994 American Standard, in a joint venture agreement, acquired 70% of German manufacturer Deutsche Perrot-Bremsen's brake business. That same year the company announced plans to expand its plumbing manufacturing business in China.

HOW MUCH

	9-Year Growth	1984	1985	1986	1987	1988	1989	1990	1991	1992	1993
Sales ($ mil.)	2.0%	3,215	2,912	2,998	3,400	3,716	3,334	3,637	3,595	3,792	3,830
Net income ($ mil.)	—	117	(3)	110	133	(26)	(34)	(54)	(111)	(57)	(209)
Income as % of sales	—	3.6%	—	3.7%	3.9%	—	—	—	—	—	—
Employees	(3.5%)	49,500	40,000	38,900	39,300	34,100	33,300	32,900	32,000	33,500	36,000

1993 Year-end:
Debt ratio: —
Cash (mil.): $54
Current ratio: 1.10
Long-term debt (mil.): $2,192
Total assets (mil.): $2,991

American Standard Inc.

Private company
Fiscal year ends: December 31

WHO

Chairman, President, and CEO: Emmanuel A. Kampouris, age 59, $1,162,500 pay
SVP Plumbing Products: George H. Kerckhove, age 56, $645,000 pay
SVP Transportation Products: Horst Hinrichs, age 61, $544,211 pay
VP and CFO: Fred A. Allardyce, age 52, $515,500 pay
VP, General Counsel, and Secretary: Frederick W. Jaqua, age 72
VP and Treasurer: Thomas S. Battaglia, age 51
VP Human Resources: Adrian B. Deshotel, age 48
Auditors: Ernst & Young

WHERE

HQ: 1114 Avenue of the Americas, New York, NY 10036
Phone: 212-703-5100
Fax: 212-703-5177 (Main Office)

The company operates 89 manufacturing facilities in 27 countries.

	1993 Sales		1993 Operating Income	
	$ mil.	% of total	$ mil.	% of total
US	2,096	54	125	44
Europe	1,315	34	118	42
Other countries	483	12	39	14
Adjustments	(64)	—	—	—
Total	**3,830**	**100**	**282**	**100**

WHAT

	1993 Sales		1993 Operating Income	
	$ mil.	% of total	$ mil.	% of total
Air conditioning	2,100	55	133	47
Plumbing	1,167	30	108	38
Transportation	563	15	41	15
Total	**3,830**	**100**	**282**	**100**

Products

Plumbing
Bathroom and kitchen fittings and fixtures
Bathtubs

Transportation
Air brake and related systems

Air Conditioning
Applied systems
Mini-split systems
Unitary systems

Major Brand Names

Plumbing
AMERICAN-STANDARD
AMERICAST (enameled steel composite)
IDEAL-STANDARD
STANDARD

Transportation
CLAYTON DEWANDRE
WABCO
WABCO WESTINGHOUSE

Air Conditioning
AMERICAN-STANDARD
TRANE

KEY COMPETITORS

AlliedSignal
American Brands
Black & Decker
Eaton
Electrolux
Eljer
Fedders
Kohler
Lennox
Masco
Tecumseh Products
United Technologies
Watsco
Whitman
York International

AMWAY CORPORATION

RANK: 41

OVERVIEW

Based in Ada, Michigan, near Grand Rapids, Amway is one of the world's largest direct sales businesses. It sells more than 5,000 products through more than 2 million independent representatives (called distributors) in nearly 60 countries. Distributors earn commissions not only on their own sales but also on sales of distributors they recruit. Amway is known for its evangelical promotion of free enterprise.

Its main product categories are health and beauty, home care, home tech, commercial/business-to-business, catalog merchandise, and education.

Amway has always been environmentally conscious (its first product, L.O.C., was a biodegradable household cleaner) and recycles much of its waste.

Amway is also notable for its degree of vertical integration. Operations include running the farms that produce the raw materials for its vitamins, R&D, production, packaging, printing, training, distribution, and delivery through its truck fleets.

Though part of its Japanese affiliate is public, Amway in the US and Europe is closely held and managed primarily by members of the founders' families, who hold all the seats on the company's policy board. In 1993 co-founder and president Richard DeVos retired and was replaced by his son Richard Jr.

Private company
Fiscal year ends: August 31

WHO

Chairman: Jay Van Andel, age 69
President: Richard M. DeVos, Jr., age 38
COO; EVP Worldwide Marketing: Thomas W. Eggleston, age 41
CFO: Lawrence Call
SVP and General Counsel: Craig Meurlin
SVP Operations: Roger E. Beutner
VP Catalog and Communications: Nan Van Andel
VP Human Resources: Dwight A. Sawyer

WHEN

Richard DeVos and Jay Van Andel were high school buddies who joined the Army Air Corps in WWII. After the war they tried several moneymaking projects together, and in the late 1940s, they became distributors for NutriLite, a California vitamin company that had pioneered network sales (in which distributors receive commissions on sales made by the people they recruit). After initial success, they branched out into other ventures, including a health-foods bakery. In 1958, when NutriLite's leadership was failing, DeVos and Van Andel decided to develop their own product line and founded the American Way Association (later shortened to Amway), working out of their Ada, Michigan, homes in 1959.

Amway's first product was a multipurpose liquid cleaner called L.O.C. (Liquid Organic Cleaner). The company then began making laundry detergent, other household cleaners, and personal grooming products. With the help of some of their NutriLite distributors, sales took off, reaching about $500,000 in 1960 and $10 million 4 years later. In 1963 the company established distributorships in Canada. Administration and sales support could hardly keep up with the growth of the distributor network: 70 building projects, including factories and warehouses, were undertaken between 1960 and 1978. The American way soon caught on in Australia and Europe and then in Asia in the 1970s and 1980s.

In 1972 the company bought NutriLite. Amway also bought the Mutual Broadcasting System (radio stations in Chicago and New York, 1977; sold in 1985 because of its unprofitability). In the 1970s Amway was hit by charges that it was a pyramid scheme. In 1979 the FTC exonerated the company, ruling that because distributors receive commissions only on actual sales of their recruit network (and because the company buys back excess inventory), the business was legitimate.

In 1982, after several years of investigation by Canadian authorities, the company was charged with defrauding the Canadian government of $22 million in import duties. Amway pleaded guilty and paid $20 million in fines.

From 1984 to 1986 the company experienced a sales slump in which revenues fell to about $800 million from $1.2 billion in 1982. Following several suits alleging abusive sales practices (primarily by overzealous, under-trained distributors), Amway brought in William Nicholson, a former assistant to President Gerald Ford, to help the company reorganize (he left in 1992). Nicholson beefed up training procedures and added new products and services, including MCI and a new car discount program. Sales rebounded to an estimated $1.5 billion in 1989. Also in that year Amway made a $2.1 billion buyout offer for Avon that was rejected.

Since its successful entry into Hong Kong in 1974, Amway has enjoyed particular strength in Asia, entering Japan, Taiwan, and Korea. In 1992 it entered into a $29 million joint venture in China to build a plant there (sales will commence in 1995). In 1993 Amway announced the IPO of Amway Asia Pacific, Ltd., a Bermuda company that will operate in 7 Pacific Rim nations.

Amway has also grown quickly in Eastern Europe, because the small initial capital investment ($110 per sales kit) has attracted more than 100,000 distributors in eastern Germany.

WHERE

HQ: 7575 Fulton St. East, Ada, MI 49355-0001
Phone: 616-676-6000
Fax: 616-676-7102 (public relations)

Amway operates in the following areas:

Australia	Indonesia	Poland
Canada	Japan	South America
The Caribbean	Korea	Taiwan
China	Malaysia	Thailand
Czech Republic	Mexico	UK
Hong Kong	New Zealand	US
Hungary	Pacific Islands	Western Europe

WHAT

Selected Products

Catalog Merchandise
- Furniture
- Luggage
- Stereo systems
- Watches

Commercial/Business to Business
- Institutional laundry products
- Janitorial supplies

Education
- Dictionaries
- *Encyclopedia Americana*
- *Rand McNally Atlas*

Health and Beauty
- Cosmetics
- Deodorant
- Diet products
- Hairspray
- Mouthwash
- Shampoo
- Sunscreens
- Toothpaste
- Vitamins

Home Care
- Air fresheners
- Car-care items
- Cleaning products
- Disinfectants
- Laundry products
- Vacuum cleaners

Home Tech
- Air purifiers
- Alarm systems
- Cookware
- Smoke detectors
- Water purifiers

Services
- Amway/MCI
- AMVOX Voice-Tel messaging service
- AMWAY Motoring Plan (auto and travel services)
- AMWAY Hospitality discounts by entertainment publications

Hotels
- Amway Grand Plaza Hotel (Grand Rapids, MI)
- Peter Island Resort (British Virgin Islands)

Subsidiaries
- Amway Hotel Corporation
- NutriLite Products, Inc.

HOW MUCH

	Annual Growth	1984	1985	1986	1987	1988	1989	1990	1991	1992	1993
Sales ($ mil.)	14.2%	—	1,200	800	550	1,477	1,513	1,842	2,550	3,069	3,465
Retail sales ($ mil.)	15.8%	1,200	1,200	1,300	1,500	1,800	1,900	2,200	3,100	3,900	4,500
Employees	5.2%	7,000	7,000	7,000	7,000	7,000	7,000	7,500	9,500	10,000	11,000

KEY COMPETITORS

American Home Products	Gillette	Mary Kay
Avon	Heinz	Maytag
Black & Decker	Henkel	Nu Skin
Brown-Forman	Herbalife	Owens-Illinois
Carter-Wallace	Hillenbrand	Premark
Casio	Jenny Craig	Procter & Gamble
Clorox	S.C. Johnson	Quaker Oats
Colgate-Palmolive	Johnson & Johnson	Royal Appliance
Corning	Johnson Publishing	Rubbermaid
Dial	L'Oréal	Schering-Plough
Dow Chemical	LVMH	Shiseido
Electrolux	MacAndrews & Forbes	Teledyne
Estée Lauder		Unilever
General Nutrition		Warner-Lambert

THE ARA GROUP, INC.

RANK: 38

OVERVIEW

Headquartered in Phildelphia, ARA is one of the largest food service companies in the world, serving more than 10 million people daily. Privately owned by ARA's management, the company is much more than a cafeteria business. It provides or manages an increasingly diverse range of service-related activities, including food and leisure services, textile rental and maintenance, health and education, and distributive services. Although the core of ARA's operations is the contract food business in the US, the company also has business concerns in 10 other countries.

One of the first US companies to begin operations in eastern Germany after the tearing down of the Berlin Wall, ARA has continued to expand into Eastern Europe, and in 1993 it moved into Spain with the purchase of 80% of Husa, S.L.

ARA is moving into the supermarket prepared food arena with its new in-store food court concept, Supreme Court, which offers a variety of ethnic foods to eat in or take out.

WHEN

In 1959 Davidson Automatic Merchandising, owned by Davre Davidson of California, merged with a midwestern vending company owned by William Fishman. Davidson became chairman and CEO and Fishman became president of the new company, Automatic Retailers of America (changed to The ARA Group, Inc., in 1969).

ARA serviced mainly candy, beverage, and cigarette machines and by 1961 operated in 38 states and ranked first in sales among vending companies. ARA moved into food vending in the early 1960s, with clients such as the Southern Pacific Railway. Between 1959 and 1963 ARA acquired 150 local food service companies, including Slater Systems in 1961, which gave ARA a top spot in operating cafeterias at colleges, hospitals, and work sites. Davidson and Fishman eased ARA into manual vending, despite the slimmer profit margins, because it was less capital-intensive and more responsive to price changes than machines, which required nickel increases. Growth was so rapid that the FTC stepped in, and the company agreed to restrict future vending acquisitions.

ARA began diversifying into other service businesses, such as publication distribution, in 1967 and in 1970 expanded into janitorial and maintenance services by buying Ground Services (airline cleaning and loading services, sold 1990). In 1968 ARA provided food service at the Mexico City Olympics. Since then the company has provided service and management at a number of Olympiads, including the Barcelona Olympics in 1992.

In 1973 ARA acquired National Living Centers (now Living Centers of America), which operates residential communities for the elderly. This acquisition also led to ARA's entry into emergency care, for which the company provides emergency room staff. A high percentage of revenues for these segments comes from Medicare and Medicaid payments. A 1976 joint venture with Mitsui & Company introduced ARA food services to Japan. ARA bought Work Wear (now ARATEX uniform rentals) in 1977 and National Child Care Centers in 1980.

In 1984 a former director, William Siegel, and 2 Texas-based partners offered chairman Joseph Neubauer $722 million for the company. Neubauer refused and, to avoid a hostile takeover, took the company private in a $1.2 billion deal. Since then ARA has repurchased shares from other investors (investment banks and employee-benefit plans) to increase management's stake to more than 90%. Stock ownership is an incentive award for more than 900 managers. ARA is known for the loyalty it commands from its employees.

The company acquired Szabo (correctional food services, 1986), Cory Food Services (1986), and Children's World Learning Centers (1987). In 1990 ARA divested its airport ground handling service and won the hospitality concessions for Olympic National Park.

In 1991 ARA targeted smaller clients and invested in the nation's largest stadium management company, SMG. ARA also expanded its textile rental and German food services operations. With sales slowing, ARA sold 90% of its nursing home business in 1992 and the remainder in 1993. That year the company bought Coordinated Health Services, a medical billing service, for $124 million.

HOW MUCH

	Annual Growth	1984	1985[1]	1986	1987	1988	1989	1990	1991	1992	1993
Sales ($ mil.)	4.1%	3,406	2,652	3,749	4,019	3,917	4,244	4,596	4,774	4,865	4,891
Net income ($ mil.)	2.1%	64	6	16	22	5	39	52	64	67	77
Income as % of sales	—	1.9%	0.2%	0.4%	0.5%	0.1%	0.9%	1.1%	1.3%	1.4%	1.6%
Employees	1.8%	—	112,000	115,000	119,000	120,000	125,000	134,000	135,000	124,000	131,000

1993 Year-end:
Debt ratio: 89.3%
Return on equity: 67.7%
Cash (mil.): $28
Current ratio: 1.1
Long-term debt (mil.): $1,020
Shareholder equity (mil.): $124

Net Income ($ mil.) 1984–93

[1] Nine-month period because of change in fiscal year-end.

Private company
Fiscal year ends: Friday nearest September 30

WHO

Chairman, President, and CEO: Joseph Neubauer, age 52, $1,310,000 pay
EVP; President, ARASERVE Sector: William Leonard, age 45, $515,000 pay
EVP; President, Leisure/International Sector: Richard H. Vent, age 52, $513,000 pay
EVP, Finance and Personnel and CFO: James E. Ksansnak, age 53, $510,000 pay
EVP; President, Health and Education Sector: Julian L. Carr, Jr., age 47, $505,000 pay
EVP, General Counsel, and Secretary: Martin W. Spector, age 55
Auditors: Arthur Andersen & Co.

WHERE

HQ: 1101 Market St., Philadelphia, PA 19107
Phone: 215-238-3000
Fax: 215-238-3333

ARA operates in the US, Belgium, Canada, the Czech Republic, Germany, Hungary, Japan, Korea, Mexico, Spain, and the UK.

	1993 Sales % of total
US	85
Other countries	15
Total	**100**

WHAT

	1993 Sales $ mil.	1993 Sales % of total	1993 Operating Income $ mil.	1993 Operating Income % of total
Food/leisure svcs.	3,150	64	137	48
Uniform services	731	15	88	31
Health & education	619	13	34	12
Distributive services	391	8	25	9
Adjustments	—	—	(15)	—
Total	**4,891**	**100**	**269**	**100**

Food, Leisure, and Support Services
Advertising Services, Ltd.
Aero Kitty Hawk, Inc.
ARA Coliseum Limited
ARA Consumer Discount Company
ARA Environmental Services, Inc. (janitorial)
ARA Facilities Management, Inc.
ARA Healthcare Nutrition Services, Inc.
ARA Leisure Services, Inc.
Lake Powell Resorts & Marinas, Inc.
Szabo Food Service, Inc. (correctional facilities)

Uniform Services
ARATEX Services, Inc. (uniform rental)

Health and Education Services
Children's World Learning Centers, Inc. (day care)
Spectrum Emergency Care, Inc. (physician staffing)

Magazine and Book Services
ARA Services Magazine & Book Company

KEY COMPETITORS

Accor
Amoskeag
Berkshire Hathaway
Carlson
Cintas
Corrections Corp. of America
Delaware North
Dial
Flagstar
W.R. Grace
Helmsley
Host Marriott
Matra-Hachette
McDonald's
Ogden
Pizza Hut
Schwan's Sales Enterprises
Uno Restaurant

ARMY & AIR FORCE EXCHANGE

RANK: 20

OVERVIEW

One of the largest retailers in the US, the Army & Air Force Exchange Service (AAFES) runs nearly 17,000 facilities, including retail stores, military clothing stores, food facilities, theaters, and vending centers, at post exchanges (PXs) and base exchanges (BXs) on army and air force bases around the world. AAFES also grants concessions to franchisers such as Burger King and Popeye's.

Headquartered in Dallas, AAFES is a government agency that operates under the Department of Defense. Although it receives no funding from the DOD, AAFES pays neither income taxes nor rent for US government property. AAFES passes these savings on to its customers: average prices are more than 20% less than competing retailers'. Eligible customers include active duty military personnel, National Guard members, reservists, and retirees, and their families. AAFES profits go into a capital improvements fund to refurbish the exchange stores and into a Morale, Welfare & Recreation fund to pay for things such as libraries, youth centers, and athletic equipment.

Although AAFES is headed by military personnel, it is staffed almost entirely by civilians, nearly half of whom are related to military personnel.

WHEN

The methods used to provide US military personnel with personal items has evolved since the American Revolution. During the Revolution peddlers, called sutlers, followed the army, selling items such as soap, razors, and tobacco. The practice lasted until after the Civil War, when sutlers were replaced by post traders. The post trader system was replaced in 1889 when the War Department authorized canteens at military bases.

The first US military exchanges were established in 1895, creating a system to supply military personnel with personal items on US Army bases around the world. The exchanges were run independently, with each division creating a PX to serve its unit. The post commander would assign an officer to run the PX (usually along with other duties) and would decide how profits were spent.

In 1941 the Army Exchange Service was created, and the system was reorganized. A 5-member advisory committee made up of civilian merchandisers was created to provide recommendations for the reorganization.

The restructuring made the system more like a chain store business. The independent PXs were bought by the War Department from the individual military organizations that ran them. Civilian personnel were brought in to staff the PXs, and a brigadier general was named to head an executive staff made up of army officers and civilians that provided centralized control of the system. The army also created a special school to train officers to run the exchanges.

During WWII the PXs' sales skyrocketed. The PXs also provided business for manufacturers who were unable to make certain products for civilian use because of rationing: a manufacturer making products for the PXs could get special permits to obtain materials that otherwise would have been rationed. Also during WWII the PXs added a catalog business so that soldiers could order gifts to send home to their families.

The exchange system has been run as a joint operation since 1947, when the Department of the Air Force was established. In 1948 the organization was renamed the Army & Air Force Exchange Service.

In 1960 the government decided to allow the overseas exchanges to provide more luxury items in an effort to keep soldiers from buying foreign-made goods. By the time the military had been cranked up again for the Vietnam War, big-ticket items such as televisions, cameras, and tape recorders were among the exchanges' hottest sellers. In 1967 AAFES moved its headquarters from New York to Dallas.

The number of people eligible to shop at the exchanges continued to grow. By 1991, with the military buildup for the Persian Gulf War and the passage of the National Defense Authorization Act, which opened up the exchanges to the National Guard and the Reserve, the number of eligible shoppers reached 14 million, not counting dependents.

When the military began downsizing in the 1990s, AAFES reorganized to streamline its operations. In 1993 AAFES began a pilot program at recently closed Carswell Air Force Base in Fort Worth to keep its stores open so it can provide goods for some 100,000 military retirees living in the Dallas–Fort Worth area.

HOW MUCH

	Annual Growth	1984	1985	1986	1987	1988	1989	1990	1991	1992	1993
Sales ($ mil.)	4.8%	4,770	4,881	4,918	5,187	5,855	6,195	6,777	7,422	7,501	7,263
Net income ($mil.)	3.5%	221	236	171	229	260	233	354	340	330	301
Income as % of sales	—	4.6%	4.8%	3.5%	4.4%	4.4%	3.8%	5.2%	4.6%	4.4%	4.1%
Employees	0.5%	—	—	—	70,385	78,823	—	—	79,609	75,584	72,562

1993 Year-end:
Return on assets: 14.4%
Cash (mil.): $333
Current ratio: 2.49
Total assets (mil.): $3,051

Net Income ($ mil.) 1984–93

Government instrumentality
Fiscal year ends: 4th Monday in January

WHO

Chairman: Lt. Gen. Merle Freitag
Commander and CEO: Maj. Gen. Albin G. Wheeler
Vice Commander: Brig. Gen. John L. Finan
COO: Paul E. Fromm
Chief of Staff: Col. Walter E. Cramer III
Acting Director, Marketing Directorate: Donald G. Smith
General Counsel: Lt. Col. D. Anthony Rogers
CFO: Martin R. Handel
Director, People Resources Directorate: Michael R. Cunningham
Auditors: Ernst & Young

WHERE

HQ: Army & Air Force Exchange Service, 3911 S. Walton Walker Blvd., Dallas, TX 75236
Phone: 214-312-2011
Fax: 214-312-3000

AAFES has operations in all 50 US states and in 26 countries and overseas areas.

	1993 Sales % of total
Continental US & Alaska	60
Europe	25
Pacific	14
Catalog sales	1
Total	**100**

	1993 Stores No.	1993 Stores % of total
Continental US & Alaska	179	66
Europe	76	28
Pacific	18	6
Total	**273**	**100**

WHAT

	1993 Sales $ mil.	1993 Sales % of total
Direct	6,561	90
Concession	702	10
Total	**7,263**	**100**

	1993 Sales % of total
Retail	80
Concessions	10
Food	7
Vending	2
Motion picture & services	1
Total	**100**

KEY COMPETITORS

50-Off Stores
Ames
Best Buy
Carter Hawley Hale
Circuit City
Dayton Hudson
Dillard
Edison Brothers
Federated
Fred Meyer
Home Depot
Ingram
Kmart
Kroger
Lechters
May
Meijer
Melville
Mercantile Stores
Merck
Montgomery Ward
Navy Exchange
J. C. Penney
Price/Costco
Sears
Service Merchandise
Walgreen
Wal-Mart
Woolworth

ARTHUR ANDERSEN & CO, S.C.

RANK: 27

OVERVIEW

The US's largest accounting firm for several years, Arthur Andersen passed KPMG in 1993 to become #1 in the world as well, but it wasn't just auditing and tax services that got the firm to the top. Its management consulting arm (also #1 in the world) has nearly tripled in size since 1988.

The company is composed of 2 distinct units (coordinated by a Swiss entity, Arthur Andersen & Co, S.C.): Arthur Andersen & Co., which provides auditing, business advisory services, tax services, and specialty consulting services; and Andersen Consulting, which provides strategic services and technology consulting.

Andersen Consulting is the world leader in systems integration, hardware configuration, software design, and operator training for clients that include half the *FORTUNE* 500. It hopes to edge out its consulting firm rivals by providing clients with a "one-stop shop" of integrated services.

The firm continues to expand its worldwide operations. A merger with Japan's Asahi Shinwa made Arthur Andersen the largest accounting firm in Asia.

WHEN

Arthur Andersen, an orphan of Norwegian parentage, worked in the Chicago office of Price Waterhouse in 1907. In 1908 at age 23, after becoming the youngest CPA in Illinois, he began teaching accounting at Northwestern University. Following a brief period in 1911 as controller at Schlitz Brewing, Andersen became head of the accounting department at Northwestern. In 1913 he formed a public accounting firm, Andersen, DeLany & Company, with Clarence DeLany.

Establishment of the Federal Reserve and implementation of the federal income tax in 1913 aided the firm's early growth by increasing demand for accounting services. The firm gained large clients, including ITT, Briggs & Stratton, Colgate-Palmolive, and Parker Pen, between 1913 and 1920. In 1915 it opened a branch office in Milwaukee. After DeLany left in 1918, the firm took its present name.

Andersen grew rapidly during the 1920s and added to its list of services financial investigations, which formed the basis for its future strength in management consulting. The firm opened 6 offices in the 1920s, including ones in New York (1921), Kansas City (1923), and Los Angeles (1926).

When Samuel Insull's empire collapsed in 1932, Andersen was appointed the bankers' representative and guarded the assets during the refinancing. Andersen opened additional offices in Boston and Houston (1937) and in Atlanta and Minneapolis (1940).

Arthur Andersen dominated the firm during his lifetime. Upon his death in 1947, new leadership was found in Leonard Spacek. Under Spacek (1947–63), the firm opened 18 new US offices and expanded outside the US by establishing an office in Mexico City, followed by 25 more in other countries.

An innovator among the major accounting firms, the company opened Andersen University, its Center for Professional Education, in the early 1970s in St. Charles, Illinois, and provided the first worldwide annual report in 1973. To broaden its scope, it transferred its headquarters to Geneva in 1977.

During the 1970s Andersen increased its consulting business, which accounted for 21% of revenues by 1979; by 1988 consulting fees made up 40% of revenues, making Andersen the world's largest consulting firm. Tension between the consultants and the auditors eventually forced a 1989 restructuring, which established Arthur Andersen and Andersen Consulting as distinct entities.

A rash of megamergers among the then–Big 8 accounting firms led Andersen and Price Waterhouse to flirt briefly with a merger (1989), but discussions broke down.

In 1992 the RTC sued Arthur Andersen for $400 million, alleging negligence in auditing failed Benjamin Franklin Savings. The firm paid the RTC $65 million in 1993 to settle the case as part of a "global" settlement, exempting it from any possible future government charges for its earlier role as auditor of failed US savings and loans.

However, the firm has gotten into other legal hot water. In 1994 Arthur Andersen and Deloitte & Touche were named in a $1.1 billion suit brought by investors who claim the 2 firms and Prudential Securities inflated the prices of several limited partnerships.

HOW MUCH

	9-Year Growth	1984	1985	1986	1987	1988	1989	1990	1991	1992	1993
Sales ($ mil.)	17.7%	1,388	1,574	1,924	2,316	2,820	3,382	4,160	4,948	5,577	6,017
Offices	7.0%	176	215	219	226	231	243	299	307	318	324
Partners	5.6%	1,528	1,630	1,847	1,957	2,016	2,134	2,292	2,293	2,454	2,487
Employees	11.6%	24,852	28,172	36,117	39,645	45,918	51,414	56,801	59,797	62,134	66,478

1993 Year-end:
Sales per partner: $2,419,381

ARTHUR ANDERSEN & CO.

International partnership
Fiscal year ends: August 31

WHO

Chairman, Managing Partner, and Chief Executive: Lawrence A. Weinbach
Managing Partner, Arthur Andersen: Richard L. Measelle
Managing Partner, Andersen Consulting: George T. Shaheen
CFO: John D. Lewis
Firm Secretary and General Counsel: Jon N. Ekdahl
Human Resources: Peter Pesce

WHERE

HQ: Arthur Andersen & Co, Société Coopérative, 18, quai Général-Guisan, 1211 Geneva 3, Switzerland
Phone: +41-22-214444
Fax: +41-22-214418
US HQ: 69 W. Washington St., Chicago, IL 60602-3094
US Phone: 312-580-0069
US Fax: 312-507-2548

Arthur Andersen & Co, S.C., maintains 324 offices in 72 countries.

Arthur Andersen	1993 Sales $ mil.	% of total
Americas	1,764	56
Europe, India, Africa & Middle East	1,127	35
Asia/Pacific	293	9
Total	**3,184**	**100**

Andersen Consulting	1993 Sales $ mil.	% of total
Americas	1,500	53
Europe, India, Africa & Middle East	1,094	39
Asia/Pacific	239	8
Total	**2,833**	**100**

WHAT

Operating Units

Arthur Andersen
Auditing
Business advisory and corporate specialty services
Tax services

Andersen Consulting
Application software products
Business process management
Change management services
FOUNDATION application development tools
Strategic services
Systems integration services
Technology services

Representative Clients

Blockbuster
First Chicago
GTE
Matra-Hachette
Olivetti
Tenneco
U.S. Shoe

KEY COMPETITORS

Bain & Co.
Booz, Allen & Hamilton
Boston Consulting Group
Coopers & Lybrand
DEC
Deloitte & Touche
Electronic Data Systems
Ernst & Young
H&R Block
IBM
KPMG
Marsh & McLennan
Perot Systems
Price Waterhouse

ASSOCIATED MILK PRODUCERS, INC.

RANK: 76

OVERVIEW

The cows may do the hardest part of the job, but Associated Milk Producers, Inc. (AMPI), is in there pulling, too. The US's largest milk cooperative, AMPI accounted for 12% of the country's milk supply in 1993. AMPI also produces generous shares of the nation's cheese, butter, nonfat dry milk, and dried whey.

The cooperative has 13,403 member farms in 3 operating regions. The North Central Region processes most of its milk into cheese, nonfat dry milk, and canned sauces under the name State Brand. The Morning Glory Farms Region supplies milk to the Chicago market and manufactures cheese, sour cream, and frozen yogurt. The Southern Region supplies Grade A milk to several markets but also operates 11 manufacturing plants.

Dairy farmers have been among the hardest hit of all of America's farmers. In the last 10 years, milk prices have actually declined, while overhead and taxes have risen sharply. Oversupply (3% in 1993) has consistently brought down prices despite sometimes drastic measures instituted by the US government, including the slaughter of more than 1.5 million dairy cows in 1985. There are about 220,000 dairy farms in the US at present, down from more than one million 30 years ago.

AMPI's lobby group, C-TAPE (Committee for Thorough Agricultural Political Education), is one of the largest agricultural PACs in the US. AMPI successfully lobbied the Department of Agriculture to strengthen dairy price supports in 1992.

WHEN

In 1969, faced with declining income and milk consumption, about 100 dairy cooperatives in the Midwest and the South merged to form Associated Milk Producers, Inc. The membership elected John Butterbrodt, from a Wisconsin cooperative, as the first president and established headquarters in San Antonio, home of the largest cooperative, Milk Producers Association. Cooperatives throughout the central US clamored to join, and AMPI became the largest US dairy cooperative within 2 years of its formation.

Almost from the beginning, AMPI became embroiled in the 2 main controversies involving dairy cooperatives: monopolistic practices and political contributions. In 1972 consumer advocate Ralph Nader alleged that the 3 main dairy cooperatives (AMPI, Dairymen, and Mid-America Dairymen) had illegally contributed $422,000 to President Nixon's re-election campaign in an attempt to obtain higher price supports (enacted in 1971) and an agreement that the administration would drop antitrust suits against the cooperatives. Watergate investigators subpoenaed Nixon's tapes, and AMPI was accused of bribery, destruction of evidence, and attempting to achieve "complete market dominance." In 1974 AMPI pleaded guilty to making illegal political contributions in 1968, 1970, and 1972. By 1975, 3 former AMPI employees had been convicted of various charges and Butterbrodt had resigned.

AMPI spent the last half of the 1970s quietly reorganizing; during this time it established its current regional management structure. In 1982 a suit for monopolistic practices, originally filed in 1971 by the National Farmers' Organization (NFO), finally reached the federal courts. The case was decided in favor of AMPI and 2 other large cooperatives, but before the year was out an appeals court reversed the decision, saying AMPI and its codefendants had conspired to eliminate competitive sellers of milk. In 1983 Congress rejected a bill to cut price supports for dairy farmers and instead adopted a program to pay farmers not to produce milk. Industry critics charged that the 3 major milk cooperatives had bought the legislation through large political contributions.

AMPI extended its dominance of the industry in 1985 by merging its central region, then called the Mid-States Region, with 2,200 members of Shawano, Wisconsin–based Morning Glory Farms Cooperative. In 1989 the US Supreme Court upheld the appeals court ruling in the NFO antitrust case.

In 1990 business soured for AMPI: it posted a $27 million loss. In 1991 dissatisfied Arkansas farmers threatened to bolt AMPI. Southern Region manager Noble Anderson replaced Ira Rutherford as general manager.

AMPI's membership has dropped (by 46% since 1984) because of the attrition of dairy farms.

HOW MUCH

	Annual Growth	1984	1985	1986	1987	1988	1989	1990	1991	1992	1993
Sales ($ mil.)	0.9%	2,485	2,416	2,489	2,710	2,777	2,987	3,063	2,768	2,835	2,692
Operating income ($ mil.)	—	6	—	—	7	4	12	(27)	1	(13)	11
Members	(6.5%)	24,600	23,300	23,500	22,400	20,800	19,400	18,478	16,321	14,729	13,403
Milk deliveries (mil. lbs.)	0.5%	15,050	15,700	15,900	17,200	17,700	17,300	17,700	17,100	16,500	15,700
Employees	0.0%	—	—	—	—	—	4,200	4,500	4,319	4,364	4,199

Sales ($ mil.) 1984–93

3,500
3,000
2,500
2,000
1,500
1,000
500
0

ampi

Mutual company
Fiscal year ends: December 31

WHO

President: Irvin J. Elkin
General Manager: Noble Anderson
Corporate Controller: Terry Krueger
Auditors: Deloitte & Touche

WHERE

HQ: 6609 Blanco Rd., San Antonio, TX 78216
Phone: 210-340-9100
Fax: 210-340-9158

AMPI is divided into 3 regions: North Central (Iowa, Minnesota, Missouri, Nebraska, South Dakota, and western Wisconsin); Morning Glory Farms (Illinois, Indiana, Michigan, Ohio, and eastern Wisconsin); and Southern (Arkansas, New Mexico, Oklahoma, and Texas and parts of Colorado, Kansas, Kentucky, Louisiana, Mississippi, Missouri, Nebraska, and Tennessee).

	1993 Milk Production	
	lbs. mil.	% of total
Morning Glory Farms	3,200	20
North Central	4,700	30
Southern	7,800	50
Total	**15,700**	**100**

WHAT

	1993 Sales	
	$ mil.	% of total
Milk product sales	2,652	98
Hauling & other	40	2
Total	**2,692**	**100**

	1993 Production
	lbs. mil.
Milk	15,700
Cheese	649
Dried whey	274
Nonfat dry milk	141
Butter	138

Dairy Activities

Grade A milk production

Production and packaging of dairy products, canned cheese sauces, and other milk-based goods under the State Brand, New Holstein, Morning Glory, and other labels

Major Subsidiaries, Affiliates, and Investments

Farm Credit System Banks
Land O'Lakes, Inc.
Northland Foods Cooperative
Prairie Farms Dairy, Inc.

Membership Services

AMPI Investment Corp.
Retirement plans and member insurance

Political Activities

Committee for Thorough Agricultural Political Education (C-TAPE)

State political committees in the Southern Region

KEY COMPETITORS

Alpine Lace
Atlantic Dairy Cooperative
Borden
Dairymen
Danone
Dean Foods
General Mills
Kellogg
Mid-America Dairymen
Philip Morris
RJR Nabisco

AVIS, INC.

RANK: 213

OVERVIEW

The #2 car rental and leasing company in the US (after Ford's Hertz unit), Avis says its competitive edge is its employee ownership. After years of being passed from company to company, Avis went private in 1987. In 1993 it was 74% owned by employees, 26% by General Motors.

Most of Avis's revenues come from its US Rent A Car Division. The company's International Division has corporate and joint venture holdings in 10 countries and licensed operations in another 60 countries. Avis Europe (8.8% owned by Avis) is the market leader in Europe. WizCom International, an Avis subsidiary created to provide Wizard computer technology to hotels and other travel-related businesses, has matured into a worldwide provider of technological products.

Avis's reputation for trying harder earned it recognition in 1993 editions of *The 100 Best Companies to Work For in America* and *The Best Companies for Minorities*.

In 1993 sales rose modestly but profits grew 48% after interest, despite auto makers' having increased prices by about 30%.

WHEN

A young Detroit car dealer by the name of Warren Avis noticed that no car rental agencies, including Hertz, had airport operations. A former army pilot, Avis believed air travel was the way of the future. In 1946 he invested his savings and $75,000 of borrowed funds to open Avis Airlines Rent-A-Car System outlets at Detroit's Willow Run Airport and Miami International Airport. Avis's idea was a success, and in 1948 his company opened inner city locations to serve hotels and office buildings.

By 1954 Avis had expanded to Mexico, Canada, and Europe. That year Warren Avis sold the company to Richard Robie, a Boston-based car rental agent, for $8 million. Robie planned to have a nationwide system of one-way car rentals and a company charge card but ran out of money and sold Avis to Boston investors in 1956. After forming a holding company (Avis, Inc.) with Avis Rent-A-Car System as its main subsidiary, the new owners instituted car leasing. In 1962 they sold Avis to investment bankers Lazard Frères, who named Robert Townsend (author of *Up the Organization: How to Stop the Organization from Stifling People and Strangling Profits*) president and moved Avis's headquarters to Garden City, New York. That was the year Avis first used the slogan "We're only No. 2. We try harder."

ITT bought Avis in 1965. Winston V. Morrow, Jr., replaced Townsend as CEO and focused the company on overseas expansion. A headquarters serving Europe, Africa, and the Middle East (now Avis Europe) was established in the UK. In 1972 Avis pioneered use of the Wizard System, now the industry's oldest and largest computer reservation system. That year, as part of an antitrust settlement, ITT sold 48% of the company to the public; the rest was held by a court-appointed trustee.

Within 5 years Avis once again had become privately owned; Norton Simon bought it for $174 million in 1977. In 1979 Avis's fleet started to feature GM cars.

Former Hertz executive Joseph Vittoria became president in 1982 and took 15 people with him when he went to Avis.

Over the next 4 years Avis was passed from owner to owner: Esmark bought Norton Simon in 1983 and, in turn, was bought by Beatrice in 1984. Kohlberg Kravis Roberts took Beatrice private through an LBO in 1985 and sold Avis to William Simon's Wesray Capital Corporation (an investment partnership) in 1986. That year Avis sold its leasing operations to PHH Group and most of Avis Europe to the public (on the London Exchange).

In 1987 Avis's employees, led by Vittoria, established an Employee Stock Ownership Plan (ESOP) and bought the company for $1.79 billion. Also in 1987 Avis established WizCom International, a subsidiary to sell the Wizard System to other industries. Avis then joined General Motors and Lease International to form Cilva Holdings, which bought Avis Europe in 1989.

In 1991 Hertz filed a lawsuit against Avis, alleging false advertising claims based on a survey Hertz believed used questionable methods. The suit was settled in early 1992 in Hertz's favor, but Avis paid no damages.

By March 1993 the company paid off over 82% of its ESOP acquisition debt. It plans to retire the debt completely before April 1995. Also in 1993 Avis promoted a sweepstakes ("Win Your Own Travel Agency") that caused established travel agencies to complain. Avis legally had to continue the contest but advised contestants, "do anything...but don't open your own agency."

HOW MUCH

	Annual Growth	1984	1985	1986	1987	1988	1989	1990	1991	1992	1993
Sales ($ mil.)	4.8%	—	—	916	813	1,060	1,100	1,159	1,205	1,222	1,260[1]
Employees	3.7%	—	—	10,500	10,500	14,000	14,000	13,000	13,000	13,000	13,500

1993 Year-end:
Long-term debt (mil.): $135

Sales ($ mil.) 1986–93

[1] Estimated.

AVIS

Private company
Fiscal year ends: Last day of February

WHO

Chairman and CEO: Joseph V. Vittoria
EVP and CFO: Lawrence Ferezy
EVP: Charles A. Bovino
EVP: James E. Collins
EVP: David P. McNicholas
SVP and General Manager: F. Robert Salerno
SVP Human Resources and Secretary to the Board: Donald L. Korn
VP, General Counsel, and Corporate Secretary: John J. Lynch
Auditors: Price Waterhouse

WHERE

HQ: 900 Old Country Rd., Garden City, NY 11530
Phone: 516-222-3000
Fax: 516-222-4381
Reservations: 800-331-1212

Avis's fleet of rental vehicles operates in 138 countries.

WHAT

	1993 Sales % of total
US Rent A Car	85
International	14
Other	1
Total	**100**

	1993 Rentals % of total
Commercial	39
Leisure	37
Associations/government	12
Telemarketing/direct mail	6
Other	6
Total	**100**

Major Subsidiaries and Affiliates
Avis Europe (8.8%)
  WizCom Europe
Avis International
  Avis Australia
  Avis Canada
Avis Rent A Car System, Inc.
  International Division
  US Rent A Car Division
  WizCom International, Ltd.

Services
Avis Cares safety and security services
Wizard System
  Inside Availability hotel reservations access
  Preferred Service rental check-outs
  Roving Rapid Return procedures
  Wizard Number customer profiles
  Wizard on Wheels computer terminal
Worldwide Reservation Center (Tulsa, OK)
  Tulsa Advanced Function Terminal

KEY COMPETITORS

Accor
Agency Rent A Car
Alamo Rent A Car
Budget Rent A Car
Chrysler
Enterprise Rent A Car
Ford
Mitsubishi
Sears
Volvo

BACARDI IMPORTS, INC.

RANK: 482

OVERVIEW

Miami-based Bacardi Imports is the US arm of the Bacardi family empire, which is held by some 500 descendants of founder Facundo Bacardi. Bacardi Imports markets Bacardi Rum, Bacardi Breezers, and other alcoholic beverages in the US. Maker of the world's best-selling liquor brand, Bacardi has sales estimated at $2.7 billion worldwide. Bacardi's trademark bat logo, said to have been inspired by a group of bats that lived in the first distillery, appears on every bottle of Bacardi rum.

Since 1992 Bacardi Imports and the other Bacardi companies have been controlled by Bacardi Ltd., a holding company in Bahamas. The restructuring, which made the US company a subsidiary of Bacardi Ltd., kept Bacardi Imports from being listed by *Hispanic Business* as the largest Hispanic-owned business in the US in 1993, a spot it had held since 1985.

Although Bacardi Rum is rated the most valuable spirits brand name in the world, the company has looked for ways to diversify. With sales of its Breezer fruit cocktail drinks falling, Bacardi switched the beverage from a rum-and-fruit juice concoction to a wine-and-fruit-juice one so it could sell them in stores barred from selling liquor. However, the company drew criticism for distributing a nonalcoholic version of the drink free to children at Bacardi-sponsored events.

Private company
Fiscal year ends: December 31

WHO

Chairman: Edwin H. Nielsen
President and CEO: Juan Grau
VC and VP: William A. Walker
VC and VP: Luis R. Lasa
EVP and COO: Eduardo M. Sardina
VP, Treasurer, and CFO: Rodolfo A. Ruiz
VP and Secretary: Robert B. White
VP and General Counsel: Steven Naclerio
VP Sales: Tom Valdes
VP Human Resources: Jose L. Aragon

WHEN

Facundo Bacardi y Maso immigrated to Cuba from Spain in 1830. He started in the liquor business as a rum salesman for John Nunes, an Englishman who owned a small distillery in Santiago, Cuba. In 1862 Facundo, his brother José, and a French wine merchant bought Nunes's distillery and began producing a smoother rum from a formula created by Facundo after years of trial and error. The gentler, more mixable quality of Bacardi's rum proved to be a key to its success.

In 1877 Facundo passed the running of the company on to his sons. Emilio, the eldest, took over leadership of the company (and spent some of his spare time in jail for his anti-Spanish activities).

Bacardi struggled during the 1890s as Cuba's economy foundered. The business was thrown into even greater turmoil when revolutionary leader José Martí began what would be the final fight for Cuban independence. One of Martí's biggest supporters was Emilio, who earned another stay in jail and then exile for his sympathies. After Cuba gained its independence in 1902, Bacardi grew rapidly, and the company got a further boost from Prohibition, as Havana became "the unofficial US saloon."

Bacardi moved into brewing in the 1920s and expanded its rum operations in the 1930s, opening a distillery in Mexico (1931) and another in Puerto Rico (1935). In 1944 it opened Bacardi Imports in the US. During the 1950s the company, led by Pepín Bosch, focused on building its overseas operations, including expanding its Mexican and Puerto Rican operations and building a new plant in Brazil.

Amid all its success, Bacardi again became embroiled in Cuban politics, with Bosch showing open opposition to Cuban leader Fulgencio Batista. However, it was not Batista but his successor, Fidel Castro, who would damage Bacardi. Castro seized Bacardi's assets in 1960, but while the expropriation was certainly a blow, it was not a fatal one. Both the Mexican and Puerto Rican operations had been out-earning the Cuban operations since the 1940s.

Bacardi continued to enjoy explosive growth during the 1960s and 1970s. In 1976 Pepín Bosch stepped down after having a dispute with the family, and in 1977 he and some other family members sold about 12% of the Bacardi empire to Hiram Walker.

By 1980 Bacardi was the #1 liquor brand in the US, but the 1980s brought problems — a series of family squabbles and bad decisions threatened the empire. In 1986 Bacardi Capital, set up to manage the empire's money, lost $50 million after some risky bond investments went sour. That same year the empire's leadership began a push to buy up shares in Bacardi companies, including those sold to Hiram Walker and the 10% of Bacardi Corporation that had been sold to the public in 1962. The companies spent more than $241 million to buy back their shares. A dissident faction of the family claimed the move was designed to keep financial information from the family.

In 1990, with liquor sales on the wane, Bacardi Imports introduced Bacardi Breezers. In 1992, in an effort to diversify and to increase its European markets, Bacardi paid $1.4 billion for a majority stake in Martini & Rossi.

In 1993 Bacardi threatened legal action against the Cuban government when the government put Bacardi's Cuban properties, seized in 1960, up for sale.

WHERE

HQ: 2100 Biscayne Blvd., Miami, FL 33137-5028
Phone: 305-573-8511
Fax: 305-573-0756

Bacardi sells rum in more than 175 countries. It has distilleries in the Bahamas, Brazil, Canada, Mexico, Panama, Puerto Rico, and Spain.

WHAT

Group Companies

Bacardi Limited (Bahamas; holding company)
- Bacardi Corp. (Puerto Rico; rum distillery and food distributor)
- Bacardi Imports (US; marketing and distribution)
- Bacardi & Co. (Bahamas; trademark ownership and rum distillery for Germany, UK, and the Caribbean)
- Bacardi International (Bermuda; trademark licensing; oversees rum distilleries in Spain, Canada, Brazil, and the Caribbean)
- Bacardi y Compania (Mexico; rum and brandy)

Brands

Fruit Cocktail Drinks

Breezer by Bacardi
- Calypso Berry
- Caribbean Key Lime
- Tahitian Tangerine
- Tropical Fruit Medley

Breezer by Bacardi Caribbean Classics
- Lemonade Daiquiri
- Piña Colada
- Rum Runner
- Strawberry Daiquiri

Rum

Bacardi Añejo
Bacardi Black
Bacardi Dark
Bacardi Light
Bacardi Reserve
Castillo Gold
Castillo Silver
Castillo Spiced

Other Brands

B&B
Benedictine
Calvados Boulard brandy
Gaston De LaGrange cognac
Martini & Rossi asti spumante
Martini & Rossi vermouth

HOW MUCH

	Annual Growth	1984	1985	1986	1987	1988	1989	1990	1991	1992	1993
Sales ($ mil.)	5.5%	—	—	—	419	433	515	500	398	580	578
Employees	—	—	—	—	—	—	—	—	—	300	—

Sales ($ mil.) 1987–93

0 100 200 300 400 500 600

KEY COMPETITORS

Allied-Lyons
American Brands
Anheuser-Busch
Brown-Foreman
Carlsberg
Gallo
Grand Metropolitan
Guinness
LVMH
Pearson
Seagram
Todhunter

BAKER & MCKENZIE

RANK: N/R

OVERVIEW

Chicago-based Baker & McKenzie, the largest of the "megafirms," is an international firm with 1,662 lawyers in most fields of law, who can meet their clients' complete legal needs in the US and abroad. In 1994 B&M had 54 offices in 31 countries, with representation in Brazil, Mexico, and Vietnam. B&M was one of the first US firms to practice in China.

The key to its success abroad has been its practice of employing local lawyers, which some have compared to fast-food chain franchising (one nickname was "McLaw"). Moreover, rather than sending billings back to the home office, local offices keep a large portion of their profits, a practice known among B&M lawyers as "eat what you kill." This approach, viewed by some as a weakness, allows B&M to offer its overseas clients an intimate knowledge of legal practices, business mores, and foreign cultures that is not easily accessible to the transplanted American.

B&M's smorgasbord approach allowed it to escape some of the worst effects of the recession of the late 1980s and early 1990s. Although revenue growth slowed (to under 2% in 1993, down from 18% in 1991) and with it the number of associates promoted to partner (20 in 1993 compared with 36 the year before), the firm at least has not experienced a drop in revenue, as have some of its rivals.

WHEN

Russell Baker came to Chicago from his native New Mexico on a railroad freight car to attend law school. Upon graduation in 1925 he started practicing law with his classmate Dana Simpson under the name Simpson & Baker. Inspired by Chicago's role as a manufacturing and agricultural center for the world and influenced by the international focus of his alma mater, the University of Chicago, Baker dreamed of developing an international law practice based in Chicago.

In his first cases Baker represented members of Chicago's growing Mexican-American community in a variety of minor criminal and civil matters. Since he frequently dealt with Mexican lawyers and issues involving multiple jurisdictions and legal systems, Baker developed an expertise in international law, which brought in other clients. In 1934 Abbott Laboratories retained him to handle its worldwide legal affairs, and Baker was on his way to fulfilling his dream.

In 1949 Baker joined forces with Chicago litigator John McKenzie, forming Baker & McKenzie. In 1955 the firm opened its first foreign office in Caracas to meet the needs of its expanding US client base and over the next 10 years opened offices in Amsterdam, Brussels, Zurich, São Paulo, Mexico City, London, Frankfurt, Milan, Tokyo, Toronto, Paris, Manila, Sydney, and Madrid. Another 23 offices were added in the Americas, Europe, and Asia between 1965 and 1990. Baker's death in 1979 did not slow the firm's growth nor change its international character.

To manage the sprawling law firm, B&M created the position of chairman of the executive committee (1984). Australian John McGuigan, former managing partner of the firm's Hong Kong office, was elected by his partners for a 5-year term as chairman starting in 1992. McGuigan cites the need to break down trade and commerce barriers between countries as one of the significant challenges facing the international financial and legal community in the 1990s.

A suit against B&M filed in late 1991 by Ingrid Beall, the firm's first female partner, charged B&M with sexual and age discrimination during her 33 years with the organization; it dragged on into 1993.

Also in late 1991 B&M dropped the Church of Scientology as a client, losing an estimated $2 million in business. It was speculated that pressure from client Eli Lilly (who makes the drug Prozac, which Scientologists actively oppose), influenced the decision.

In 1992 B&M was ordered to pay $1 million for wrongfully firing an employee who later died of AIDS. The firm is fighting the verdict.

In 1994 B&M will close its Los Angeles office (the former MacDonald, Halsted & Laybourne, acquired in 1988) amidst considerable rancor. In 1994 a former secretary at the firm received a $7.1 million judgment for sexual harassment by a partner.

HOW MUCH

	Annual Growth	1984	1985	1986	1987	1988	1989	1990	1991	1992	1993
Sales ($ mil.)	17.4%	—	—	—	196	261	341	404	478	504	512
Total lawyers	10.0%	704	755	908	946	1,179	1,339	1,522	1,580	1,604	1,662
Partners	7.7%	276	287	333	338	404	432	478	479	497	537
Associates	11.3%	428	468	575	608	775	907	1,044	1,101	989	1,125
Associates per partner	3.4%	1.55	1.63	1.73	1.80	1.92	2.10	2.18	2.30	1.99	2.09
No. of offices	6.0%	29	30	31	35	41	48	49	45	49	54
Employees[1]	1.9%	—	—	—	—	—	—	4,736	4,887	4,919	5,054

Starting Salaries for First-Year Associates:[2]
1980 — $32,000
1984 — $47,000
1986 — $65,000
1990 — $70,000
1992 — $70,000
1993 — $70,000

[1] Employee figures before 1990 include lawyers only [2] Chicago office

BAKER & McKENZIE

International partnership
Fiscal year ends: June 30

WHO

Chairman of the Executive Committee: John V. McGuigan, age 44
COO: Frank M. Wheeler
CFO: Robert S. Spencer
Director of International Administration: Teresa A. Townsend
Auditors: Arthur Andersen & Co.

WHERE

International Executive Offices: One Prudential Plaza, 130 E. Randolph Dr., Chicago, IL 60601
Phone: 312-861-8800
Fax: 312-861-8823

Office Locations

Amsterdam
Bangkok
Barcelona
Beijing
Berlin
Bogotá
Brasilia
Brussels
Budapest
Buenos Aires
Cairo
Caracas
Chicago
Dallas
Frankfurt
Geneva
Guangzhou
Hanoi
Ho Chi Minh City
Hong Kong
Juárez
Kiev
London
Madrid
Manila
Melbourne
Mexico City
Miami
Milan
Monterrey
Moscow
New York
Palo Alto
Paris
Prague
Rio de Janeiro
Riyadh
Rome
St. Petersburg
San Diego
San Francisco
São Paulo
Shanghai
Singapore
Stockholm
Sydney
Taipei
Tijuana
Tokyo
Toronto
Valencia
Warsaw
Washington, DC
Zurich

1993 Sales	$ mil.	% of total
North America	185	36
Europe & Middle East	165	32
Asia & Australia	122	24
Latin America	40	8
Total	**512**	**100**

WHAT

Areas of Practice
Antitrust
Banking/commercial lending/consumer finance
Bankruptcy
Corporate financings
Criminal law
Employee benefits
Environmental/land use/natural resources
Estate planning
Foreign trade
General corporate law
Government relations
Health and hospital law
Immigration
Insurance
Intellectual property
Labor/management relations
Maritime/shipping
Mergers and acquisitions
Oil and gas/mining
Real estate
Taxation

Selected Publications
Canadian Legal Report
China Law Quarterly
Colombian Newsletter
Computer & Software Update

KEY COMPETITORS

Cleary, Gottlieb, Steen & Hamilton
Cravath, Swaine & Moore
Jones, Day, Reavis & Pouge
Jenner & Block
Kirkland & Ellis
Mayer, Brown & Platt
Milbank, Tweed, Hadly & McCloy
Pillsbury Madison & Sutro
Shearman & Sterling
Sidley and Austin
Skadden, Arps, Slate, Meagher & Flom
Sullivan & Cromwell
Weil, Gotshal & Manges
White & Case

BAKER & TAYLOR INC.

RANK: 335

OVERVIEW

Baker & Taylor (B&T) is an international wholesaler of books, videotapes, audio products, and computer software. B&T, whose headquarters are in Stamford, Connecticut, was formed in 1992 after W. R. Grace sold its B&T Books subsidiary and 2 related companies to the Carlyle Group and B&T managers.

Baker & Taylor Inc.'s 3 divisions — B&T Books, B&T Video, and B&T Software — distribute 50 million books a year, plus software, videotapes, and audio products, to 100,000 retail stores and public and university libraries around the world. The book division, B&T's primary revenue earner, is the #1 book distributor in the US and dominates the US library book distribution market.

The company's Title Source, World Edition search-and-order system lists more than 2 million book, audio, and video titles all on one CD-ROM disc. The disc contains in-print, out-of-print, and forthcoming titles.

B&T has worked to integrate B&T Books and its 2 sister divisions, which Grace had operated as independent units. For example, in order to increase sales to the rapidly expanding CD-ROM market beyond traditional software dealers, the company coordinated its CD-ROM marketing strategy across all 3 divisions.

In 1994 the announced sale of Baker & Taylor to Follett Corp., a college bookstore operator, was called off.

WHEN

Baker & Taylor traces its roots back to a bindery founded by David Robinson and B. B. Barber in Hartford, Connecticut, in 1828. The company opened a bookstore a few years later and became a distributor for several publishers; in 1835 it moved to New York. After changing hands (and names) several times, the company became Baker & Taylor Co. in 1885 when James S. Baker and Nelson Taylor took over. After Nelson Taylor died in 1912, the company shifted its focus. It discontinued publishing, selling most of its book titles to Doubleday, Page and religious book publisher Revell and concentrated on wholesaling.

B&T moved its operations to New Jersey in 1950. In 1958 the company was acquired by the Parents' Institute, Inc., publisher of *Parents Magazine*. Parent's Institute sold B&T to W. R. Grace in 1969. In 1980 Gerald Garbacz, who had been with the company since 1974, became president of B&T's book division.

Under Grace, B&T developed a reputation for poor service, as librarians complained about incomplete orders, insufficient stock, and poor communication. B&T management complained that Grace placed too great an emphasis on short-term financial performance and not enough emphasis on developing markets.

In order to improve customer service, B&T Books introduced BT Link, an electronic ordering system for booksellers and libraries, in 1990. That same year B&T Books moved its headquarters from New Jersey to Charlotte, North Carolina.

In 1991 Grace began selling nonstrategic assets in order to specialize in the chemical and health care businesses. Garbacz brought B&T to the attention of The Carlyle Group, a Washington, DC–based investment company. Carlyle specialized in acquiring smaller firms from larger companies. Grace signed a deal to sell B&T Books, B&T Video, and Softkat to The Carlyle Group. The sale was completed in 1992, and B&T's new owners combined the 3 companies into a single company and named Garbacz chairman and CEO.

The company also began to concentrate on its global markets in 1992. It signed an agreement with UK library supplier T. C. Farries and Co., and, with Book Data, Ltd., a UK-based bibliographic and marketing information service, it released a World Edition of its Title Source CD. The World Edition was part of an updated version of the BT Link database.

In 1993 the company expanded its software offerings when it signed a deal to distribute software for the 3DO Interactive Multiplayer. It also entered agreements with a variety of retailers, including Blockbuster and Stop N' Shop, to distribute CD-ROM software. That same year Baker & Taylor reached an agreement with the British Library to develop a bibliographic CD-ROM database, using the library's extensive records.

In 1994, after the Northridge earthquake severely damaged its headquarters in Simi Valley, B&T Software moved its offices to Agoura Hills. Also in 1994 Garbacz resigned, and 3 people took his place: Patrick Gross and Joseph Wright as co-chairmen and Craig Richards as CEO.

HOW MUCH

	Annual Growth	1985	1986	1987	1988	1989	1990	1991	1992	1993	1994
Sales ($ mil.)	3.8%	—	—	—	722	767	784	780	838	872	900[1]
Employees	—	—	—	—	—	—	—	—	2,500	2,500	2,480

[1]Estimated

BAKER & TAYLOR

Private company
Fiscal year end: Last Friday in June

WHO

Co-Chairman: Patrick Gross
Co-Chairman: Joseph Wright
CEO: Craig M. Richards
President and COO: James B. Warburton
EVP and COO, B&T Books: James S. Ulsamer
SVP, Treasurer, and CFO: Edward H. Gross
SVP, Secretary, and General Counsel: Susan E. Backstrom
VP and Controller: David P. Finlon
VP Human Resources: Jeanne P. Rudell
Auditors: Arthur Andersen & Co.

WHERE

HQ: 300 First Stamford Place, Stamford, CT 06902
Phone: 203-462-7000
Fax: 203-961-8343

Baker & Taylor has offices and service centers in 14 states and in Australia, Japan, and the UK.

WHAT

Baker & Taylor Books (Charlotte, NC)

Products
Bargain books
Calendars
Children and young adult books
Hardcover books
Mass market paperbacks
Trade paperbacks
Spoken-word audio

Selected Services
B&T Link (title search and ordering system for bookstores and libraries)
B&T Consulting (technical services, library development, and training)

Baker & Taylor Video (Morton Grove, IL)

Products
Audio cassettes
Laser discs
Music CDs
Video and audio accessories
Video games
Videocassettes

Selected Services
Independents Days (incentive program featuring products from independent producers)
TalkVideo (24-hour touch-tone ordering and information service)

Baker & Taylor Software (Agoura Hills, CA)

Products
Educational software
Entertainment software
Home/office productivity software

Formats
CD-ROM
Disks
Expanded books
Videodiscs

Selected Services
Authorized Education Dealer Program (partnership program with educational software resellers)
Baker & Taylor Affiliated Labels (distribution, marketing, and sales support)

KEY COMPETITORS

Abco Distributors
Advanced Marketing
Blackwell Delaware
Bookazine
Brodart
Golden Lee
Handleman
Ingram
Kenfil
Koen
Merisel
Pacific Pipeline
Software Spectrum
Tech Data
Wal-Mart

BATTELLE MEMORIAL INSTITUTE

RANK: 347

OVERVIEW

Battelle

Battelle Memorial Institute is the world's largest and oldest contract research organization. The institute has developed a mind-boggling array of gadgets, from the ubiquitous (the copper/copper and nickel "sandwich" design of most US coins, plastic 6-pack holders, and cruise control) to the bizarre (a potato-peeling laser, heat-resistant chocolate bars that retain shape in temperatures as high as 140°F, and seat cushions that, if microwaved for 6 minutes, will stay warm for up to 8 hours). Although it is chartered as a nonprofit trust and reinvests all of its profits in technology, Battelle pays high taxes to Uncle Sam because of the taxability of some of its work.

Battelle contracts work from companies and the government in 6 major markets: commercial and industrial, environment, health, national security, technology development and transfer, and transportation. Among the institute's many government contracts is its important work for the DOE developing aluminum automobile parts (to replace the heavier steel).

Although the institute's scientists are surely pioneering, Battelle's employees do not like to think of themselves as futurists. The organization's general strategy is to develop technology that is applicable, affordable, and manufacturable. Recently Battelle has made a push to acquire more contracts from firms that find R&D too expensive or too problematic to handle.

Nonprofit charitable trust
Fiscal year ends: December 31

WHO

Chairman: Willis S. White, Jr.
First VC: Morris Tanenbaum
Second VC: John J. Hopfield
President and CEO: Douglas E. Olesen
SVP, CFO, and Treasurer: John H. Doster
SVP, General Counsel, and Secretary: Paul T. Santilli
SVP Corporate Development: John S. Christie
SVP and Director, Pacific Northwest Division: William R. Wiley
SVP and Gen Mgr, Health Division: Dennis B. Cearlock
SVP Human Resources: Robert W. Smith, Jr.
Auditors: KPMG Peat Marwick

WHEN

Battelle was founded with a $1.5 million trust (and a stipulation that the money was to be used to create an institute for "the encouragement of creative and research work and the making of discoveries and inventions") willed by Gordon Battelle, who died in 1923. Before taking his father's place as president of several Ohio steel mills, Battelle had funded a former university professor's successful work to extract useful chemicals found in mine waste. Though not a scientist, Battelle strongly believed in the value of research for the advancement of humankind. Battelle's mother, upon her death in 1925, left the institute a further $2.1 million.

The institute, which at first focused mainly on metallurgy, opened with about 30 employees in a research building across the street from Ohio State in Columbus in 1929. In its first year Battelle spent $71,000. By 1935 the institute's staff had increased more than threefold, and yearly spending was $198,000.

Battelle took on perhaps the most important project in its history when it decided to aid Chester Carlson, an electronics company's patent lawyer, in finding practical uses for xerography, an invention of his, in 1944. Eventually the team developed the first copying machine, and in 1955 Battelle sold the patent rights for the machine to Haloid, which went on to become Xerox, in exchange for royalties. In less than 20 years the value of Battelle's portfolio would rise to more than $225 million.

During WWII Battelle worked on uranium refining for the Manhattan Project, and in the early 1950s it established the world's first private nuclear research facility. It also set up facilities in Germany and Switzerland.

The tax man came knocking in 1961, questioning the taxability of some of Battelle's activities. The organization eventually had to pay $47 million. In 1965 Battelle developed a coin with a copper core and a copper and nickel alloy cladding for the US Treasury.

A reinterpretation of Gordon Battelle's will, concerning a clause that demanded that a share of profits be donated to charities, in 1975 resulted in a ruling that forced the institute to give $80 million to philanthropic enterprises. (Battelle continues to donate heavily to charities.) This ruling, coupled with the taxes that the organization was still unused to paying, forced Battelle to reexamine its strategy. The institute began to actively seek out contract work, revenues from which rose from $173 million in 1975 to $368 million in 1979.

In the 1970s Battelle codeveloped the Universal Product Code, the bar code symbol found today on the packaging of nearly all consumer goods; the institute also landed a lucrative contract from the DOE to manage its commercial nuclear waste isolation program.

In 1992 Battelle signed a 5-year extension with the DOE to run its Pacific Northwest Laboratory (which it has operated since 1965). The institute sold its Information Dimensions unit, maker of ZyIndex software, in 1993.

WHERE

HQ: 505 King Ave., Columbus, OH 43201-2693
Phone: 614-424-6424
Fax: 614-424-5263

Battelle manages programs in more than 30 countries.

WHAT

	1993 Sales	
	$ mil.	% of total
Government clients	767	88
Industrial clients	96	11
Other	6	1
Total	**869**	**100**

	1993 Sales	
	$ mil.	% of total
Pacific Northwest	517	60
Battelle Columbus	324	37
Other	28	3
Total	**869**	**100**

Selected Inventions
Copy machine (with Haloid, 1940s)
Cruise control (1960s)
Exploded-tip paint brush (nylon paint brush for Wooster Brush Company, 1950)
Golf ball coatings (1965)
Oil spill outline monitor (1992)
PCB-cleaning chemical process (1992)
Plastic breakdown process (1990s)
"Sandwich" coins (copper/copper and nickel alloy cladding design for US Treasury, 1965)
Smart cards (cards imbedded with tiny computers that store large amounts of information, 1980s)
SnoPake (correction fluid, 1955)
Universal Product Code (co-creator, 1970s)

Subsidiaries
Geosafe Corporation (Richland, WA)
Scientific Advances, Inc. (Columbus, OH)
Survey Research Associates (Baltimore, MD)

Strategic Alliances
Alternative Fuels Coalition
Gas Research Institute
U.S. Department of Energy
Vorwerk (European maker of appliances)

HOW MUCH

	9-Year Growth	1984	1985	1986	1987	1988	1989	1990	1991	1992	1993
Sales ($ mil.)[1]	7.1%	468	522	591	579	597	615	715	768	782	869
Net income ($ mil.)	11.6%	2	5	8	7	8	11	1	2	10	6
Employees	1.3%	7,487	7,716	7,939	7,600	7,546	7,477	7,791	8,398	8,553	8,400

1993 Year-end:
Debt ratio: 12.6%
Return on equity: 2.4%
Cash (mil.): $18
Long-term debt (mil.): $3
Total assets (mil.): $360

Net Income ($ mil.) 1984–93

[1] 1984–1991 not restated to reflect certain discontinued and divested operations.

KEY COMPETITORS

AT&T
Bellcore
Bolt Beranek and Newman
Cal Tech
Southwest Research Institute

L.L. BEAN, INC.

RANK: 346

OVERVIEW

Freeport, Maine–based L.L. Bean was the first national mail order house specializing in outdoor clothing, sporting goods, active wear, and household goods and furnishings. It makes 190 of its products (representing about 8% of sales), such as the Maine Hunting Shoe, in Brunswick, Maine, and sends over 130 million catalogs to more than 15 million people a year.

L.L. Bean is known for excellent customer service, exemplified by its unlimited return policy and its policy of perpetually replacing the rubber soles of its Maine Hunting Shoe.

L.L. Bean is owned and controlled by the family of its founder, Leon Leonwood Bean. There are 15 family members — Bean's grandchildren and great-grandchildren — but most are uninvolved in management.

Although the company underwent considerable modernization under the management of Bean's grandson Leon Gorman, its fulfillment and distribution systems are less automated than some competitors'. In recent years the company has been hit by rising shipping rates and in the 1990s began charging for shipping and handling.

The company is well known for its sponsorship of outdoor instructional activities, including an Outward Discovery Program, and for its ecological activism.

L.L. Bean has a growing presence in retailing (11% of sales), with 6 stores in the northeastern US. The performance of a 2nd store in Japan, opened in 1993, exceeded expectations, and a 3rd is planned for late 1994.

WHEN

Leon Leonwood Bean started out as a storekeeper in Freeport, Maine. Tired of wet, leaky boots, he experimented with various remedies and in 1911, when he was 39, came up with the Maine Hunting Shoe, a boot with rubber soles and feet and leather uppers. It became his most famous product.

From the outset in 1912, Bean's company was a mail order house. The first batch of boots was a disaster: almost all of them leaked. But Bean's personal touch and self-effacing willingness to correct his product's defects quickly at his own expense (the origin of the company's unlimited returns policy) saved the company. In 1918 Bean sold his store in order to concentrate on the mail order business; he was assisted by Maine's new hunting licensing system, implemented in 1917, which provided him with a mailing list of affluent, recreational hunters in the Northeast.

Thereafter, Bean cultivated the image of the folksy Maine guide, offering his clientele the sort of durable, comfortable, weather-resistant clothes and reliable camping supplies that would accompany any sensible Maine native into the woods.

In 1920 Bean built a store on Main Street in Freeport. The company continued to grow and add products, even during the Depression, and sales reached $1 million in 1937.

In 1954, recognizing women's growing interest in the outdoors, Bean added a women's department (a major portion of the customer base is now women).

Bean was not a driven businessman and resisted growing the business bigger, saying, "I'm eating 3 meals a day; I can't eat 4." Sales rose to $2 million in the early 1960s but increased at a rate slower than the US economic growth rate. Over one million mailing labels were typed by hand, and correspondence was filed in cardboard boxes. When Bean died in 1967, at the age of 94, sales were $4.8 million and the average age of employees was 60.

The new president was Bean's grandson Leon Gorman, who had started with the company in 1960. His early attempts at updating the mailing operations had been vetoed by his grandfather. When he took over in 1971, Gorman brought in new people and made improvements, including automating the mailing systems, updating distribution, improving the efficiency of the manufacturing systems, and enlarging and refining the mailing lists by targeting new, nonsporting markets, particularly women. By 1975 sales were $30 million, and the company had won a Coty Fashion Award.

That year Gorman hired Bill End as merchandise manager. Under End, L.L. Bean continued its transition to fashion-statement maker by targeting more of its classic customer profile: upper-middle-class college graduates — preppies.

For most of the 1980s sales grew about 20% annually. But by 1989 sales had slowed and growth flattened. In 1990 Bill End departed for Lands' End. The next year sales decreased slightly. In the early 1990s returns rose to 14% of sales, but the company's return policy remains unchanged. Since 1992 sales have increased over 17% annually.

L.L.Bean

Private company
Fiscal year ends: February 28

WHO

President and CEO: Leon A. Gorman, age 60
EVP and CFO: Norman A. Poole
SVP; General Manager, L.L. Bean, International: Scott Howard
SVP, Finance and Administration: Lee Surace
VP Marketing: Robert Frye
VP Human Resources: Bob Peixotto
Auditors: Coopers & Lybrand

WHERE

HQ: Casco St., Freeport, ME 04033
Phone: 207-865-4761
Fax: 207-865-6738

L.L. Bean sells sporting goods, accessories, and country classic clothes via direct mail catalogues, 6 stores in the US, and 2 retail stores in Japan.

WHAT

Subsidiaries
L.L. Bean Japan (joint venture of Seiyu Ltd. and Matsushita Electric Industrial Co., Ltd.)
Hurricane Island Outward Bound School, Inc.

Selected Products
Boat and Tote bags
Chamois cloth shirts
Handsewn footwear and specialties
Hudson Bay Point Blankets
The Maine Hunting Shoe
Soft luggage
Zipper duffle bags

	1993 Sales	
	$ mil.	% of total
Mail order sales	662	89
Retail sales	81	11
Total	**743**	**100**

	1993 International Sales
	% of total
Japan	70
Canada	20
UK	6
Other countries	4
Total	**100**

KEY COMPETITORS

Brown Group
Carter Hawley Hale
CML Group
Dayton Hudson
Dillard
Edison Brothers
Federated
Fieldcrest Cannon
Fruit of the Loom
The Gap
Hartmarx
Herman's Sporting Goods
Hudson's Bay
INTERCO
J. Crew
L.A. Gear
Lands' End
Levi Strauss
Liz Claiborne
Lost Arrow
Macy's
Marks and Spencer
May
NIKE
North Face
Oshkosh B'Gosh
Lost Arrow
J. C. Penney
Polo/Ralph Lauren
Recreational Equipment Inc.
Sears
Sharper Image
Spiegel
Springs Industries
U.S. Shoe
V. F.
Woolworth

HOW MUCH

	9-Year Growth	1985	1986	1987	1988	1989	1990	1991	1992	1993	1994
Sales ($ mil.)	14.7%	254	304	368	493	580	600	597	628	743	870
Employees	9.5%	1,550	1,775	2,300	2,800	3,000	3,200	3,200	3,300	3,500	3,500

BECHTEL GROUP, INC.

RANK: 19

OVERVIEW

Although it has been family-owned and -run for 4 generations, San Francisco–based Bechtel is no mom-and-pop store. It is the #1 US engineering and construction firm; has a worldwide work force of 29,400; and has worked on more than 15,000 projects in over 135 countries. In 1993, 44% of its $7.3 billion sales was earned outside the US.

With the US engineering industry's largest R&D staff, Bechtel designs and builds facilities in such fields as power, petroleum, chemicals, mining and metals, pipelines, surface transportation, aviation, space facilities, telecommunications, water management, environmental and pollution control, hazardous waste cleanup, and industrial and commercial construction. The firm is a leading environmental consultant in the US.

Bechtel was a manager of Kuwait Oil's post–Persian Gulf War reconstruction. Other high-profile overseas projects have included a Chinese nuclear power plant and major oil projects in the former Soviet Union.

Bechtel is a strong supporter of free trade and mobilized its work force to wage a vigorous campaign for the passage of NAFTA (the first such campaign in its history), which went into effect on January 1, 1994. One of its directors is Carla Hills, a former US trade representative.

Bechtel Group, Inc.

Private company
Fiscal year ends: December 31

WHO

Chairman Emeritus: Stephen D. Bechtel, Jr., age 68
President and CEO: Riley P. Bechtel, age 41
EVP: William L. Friend, age 58
EVP: Don J. Gunther, age 54
EVP: Cordell W. Hull, age 59
EVP: John Neerhout, Jr., age 62
Counsel: John W. Weiser, age 62
SVP, CFO, Treasurer, and Controller: V. Paul Unruh, age 44
VP, Manager of Human Resources: Shirley Gaufin, age 47
Auditors: Coopers & Lybrand

WHEN

In 1898, 26-year-old Warren Bechtel left his Kansas farm to grade railroads in the Oklahoma Indian territories, where he soon founded his own company. After Bechtel settled in Oakland, California, his engineering and management skills brought him large projects such as the Northern California Highway and the Bowman Dam. By the time of its incorporation in 1925, Bechtel was the West's largest construction company.

Stephen Bechtel (president after his father's death in 1933) weathered the Depression with huge projects like the Hoover Dam (where Bechtel supervised 8 companies) and the San Francisco Bay Bridge. WWII meant full recovery, with the company winning many contracts, including one to build 570 ships in Bechtel-built yards in California.

In the postwar years Bechtel expanded overseas, building pipelines (TransArabian, 1947; Canada's TransMountain, 1954; Australia's first, 1964) and numerous power projects, including one that doubled South Korea's energy output (1948). By the time Stephen Bechtel, Jr., became CEO in 1960 (when his father moved to chairman), the company was operating on 6 continents.

Bechtel built many nuclear power plants in the next 2 decades, including the world's first large one to be privately financed (Dresden, Illinois; opened 1960) and Canada's first (1962). Large transportation projects included San Francisco's Bay Area Rapid Transit system (BART, 1961–74) and Washington, DC's subway system (early 1970s). Work on Canada's James Bay hydroelectric project was begun in 1972 and completed in the mid-1980s; it supplies energy to 8 million people. Bechtel's Jubail project in Saudi Arabia, begun in 1976, will raise from the Arabian desert a city of 275,000 (projected completion date 1996).

With the attractions of nuclear power fading in the wake of the Three Mile Island accident (which Bechtel won the right to clean up, starting in 1979), Bechtel concentrated on less controversial markets such as mining in New Guinea (gold and copper, 1981–84) and China (coal, 1984).

Bechtel reeled under the general recession and rising Third World debt of the early 1980s. The company cut its work force by 22,000 (almost half the total) and stemmed losses by taking on plant modernizations and other small projects.

Under 4th-generation family member Riley Bechtel (CEO since 1990), Bechtel has won numerous contracts, including a $16 billion deal with Hong Kong for a new airport and transit system and project management of the channel tunnel between Britain and France.

Over the years Bechtel has built 50,000 miles of oil pipeline valued at over $20 billion. In 1992 and 1993 Bechtel signed deals to expand the former Soviet Union's crude oil pipeline network, to operate a series of new pipelines in Canada (with Interprovincial Pipe Line of Canada), and for a natural gas pipeline in Algeria.

In 1994 Bechtel won the contract for a new office complex in fast-growing Bangkok.

WHERE

HQ: 50 Beale St., San Francisco, CA 94105-1895
Phone: 415-768-1234
Fax: 415-768-0263 (Public Relations)

Bechtel operates worldwide with 4 regional offices in the US (Gaithersburg, MD; Houston; Los Angeles; and San Francisco) and offices in a number of other nations.

WHAT

Engineering, Construction, and Management
Civil projects
Food-processing plants
Microelectronics plants
Mining and metals plants
Missile launch complexes
Petroleum and chemical plants
Pipelines
Power plants
Pulp and paper mills
Weapons storage and security systems

Environmental
Environmental assessment
Hazardous waste cleanups
Regulatory compliance
Wastewater treatment

Operations
Nuclear and fossil fuel plants
Strategic oil reserves
Utilities

Operating Units
Bechtel Civil Co.
Bechtel Construction Co.
Bechtel Enterprises, Inc.
Bechtel National, Inc.
Bechtel Petroleum, Chemical & Ind. Co.
Bechtel Power Corp.
Becon Construction Co., Inc.

Selected Major Projects
Airport expansion (Miami)
Central Artery & Tunnel (Boston)
Chemical waste treatment center (Hong Kong)
Eurotunnel (England/France)
International airport (Hong Kong)
Jubail (Saudi Arabia)
Nuclear plant (Daya Bay, China)
Oil pipeline expansion (former Soviet Union)
Oil production facilities restoration (Kuwait)
PGT PG&E pipeline expansion (Canada/USA)
Trans National highway system (Turkey)

HOW MUCH

	9-Year Growth	1984	1985	1986	1987	1988	1989	1990	1991	1992	1993
Sales ($ mil.)	(1.7%)	8,600	6,891	6,679	4,501	4,472	5,096	5,631	7,526	7,774	7,337
New work booked ($ mil.)	7.3%	5,000	4,982	3,675	3,537	4,486	5,427	4,787	7,248	8,396	9,445
Number of clients	(1.7%)	700	750	—	800	900	950	900	850	750	600
Number of active projects	(1.0%)	1,200	1,300	—	1,350	1,450	1,600	1,700	1,750	1,400	1,100
Employees	(11.7%)	90,000	80,000	50,000	—	—	27,800	32,500	30,900	30,900	29,400

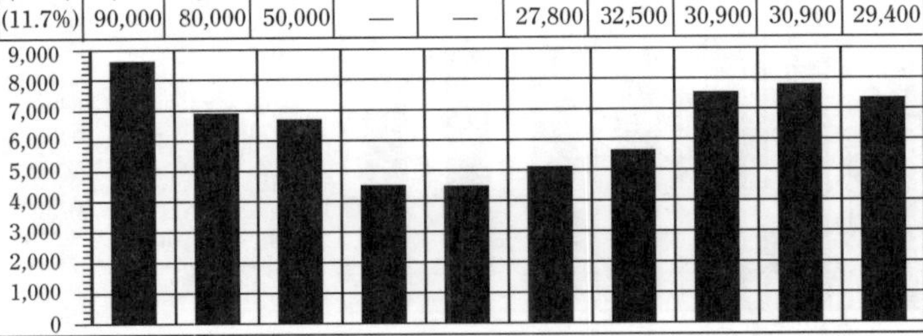

KEY COMPETITORS

ABB
Ashland
Baker Hughes
British Aerospace
CBI Industries
Consolidated Rail
Dresser
Duke Power
Fluor
Halliburton
Hanson
Jacobs Engineering
McCarthy Building
McDermott
Michael Baker Corp.
Mid-American Waste Systems
Morrison Knudsen
Parsons Corp.
Perini
Peter Kiewit Sons'
Raytheon
Safety-Kleen
TRW
Turner Industries
Union Pacific
USA Waste Services
WMX Technologies
Westinghouse

BLUE CROSS AND BLUE SHIELD

RANK: 1

OVERVIEW

The Blue Cross and Blue Shield Association is the national coordinating organization for 69 autonomous Blue Cross and Blue Shield prepaid health care plans. The "Blues," as they are called, are the US's oldest and largest health insurers and provide insurance plans for about 1/4 of the US population.

The Blues have traditionally been the insurers of last resort, often receiving state tax breaks as quasi-charitable institutions because they accept people who constitute the least desirable portion of the insurance market, such as those with preexisting conditions or past serious illnesses. This quasi-charitable status has led to allegations that some local Blues, especially Empire (New York) and the District of Columbia, abused their status.

In recent years many local Blues have gone out of business, become mutual companies, or consolidated. In 1994, Blue Cross announced that it would allow member organizations to sell stock and become for-profit companies so that they can better compete in the turbulent health care market. Blue Cross of California, a pioneer in this area, sold 20% of its Wellpoint Health Networks HMO to the public.

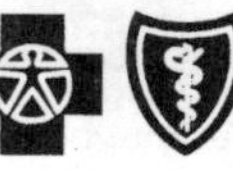

Association
Fiscal year ends: December 31

WHO

President and CEO: Bernard R. Tresnowski
EVP and COO: Thomas Kinser
General Counsel and Corporate Secretary: Roger G. Wilson
SVP Licensing, Finance, and Operations: David Murdoch
SVP Business Services: Harry P. Cain II
SVP Government Relations: Mary N. Lehnhard
VP Chief Administrative Officer: Kris Kurschner
Auditors: Coopers & Lybrand

WHEN

Blue Cross prepaid hospital plans were developed to provide working people with a means of paying for private hospitalization. The first plans were sponsored by hospitals in Texas, Iowa, and Illinois; premiums were as little as 50 cents per month. Fundamental to Blue Cross was its community rating system, which based premium amounts on the claims experience of the subscriber's community, rather than on his or her personal condition.

The idea spread to New Jersey, Cleveland, Chicago, and St. Paul, the last of which developed the Blue Cross name and symbol in 1934. By 1935 there were 15 Blue Cross plans in 11 states. In the late 1930s many states exempted plans from regulation and ratified their nonprofit status. In 1936 the American Hospital Association formed the Committee on Hospital Service (renamed the Blue Cross Association, 1948) to coordinate the plans.

As Blue Cross grew, state medical societies began sponsoring prepaid medical plans to cover physicians' fees. In 1946 they banded together under the guidance of the AMA as the Associated Medical Care Plans (which became the Association of Blue Shield Plans).

In 1948 the Blues decided to merge, but AMA opposition killed the plan. Despite this, the Blues cooperated on public policy matters (i.e., lobbying) while competing for members, and each Blue formed a nonprofit stock corporation to coordinate the activities of its plans.

Enrollment grew in the late 1940s and 1950s, despite competition from private insurers. In 1960 Blue Cross boasted almost 1/3 of the US population as members. The Blues started administering Medicare and other government health plans in the 1960s. By 1970 half of Blue Cross's $10 billion in premiums came from government sources.

Rapidly rising medical costs in the 1970s required the Blues to adopt such cost control measures as utilization review of hospital admissions to stem increasing premiums; many plans even abandoned the community rating system. Most began emphasizing preventive care in HMO or PPO environments.

The Blues joined forces in 1982, but this had little effect on the associations' bottom lines, as losses continued to grow.

By the 1990s the Blues had become big business, and some of the state associations had begun offering their officers the perks enjoyed by private-sector executives, while still insisting on special regulatory treatment. In 1992 this sparked a federal investigation.

In 1993 it was discovered that Empire Blue Cross of New York (which has received more than $100 million in state aid because of a $250 million loss) had overstated the amount of its losses attributable to its small-group and individual policyholders, who had been subject to repeated rate increases.

Although Blue Cross of California has pioneered in privatization, it has done so while benefiting from its nonprofit status. In 1994 the State of California demanded that Blue Cross give $100 million and 40% of its Wellpoint holdings to charity. That year the General Accounting Office declared that 11 local (mostly northeastern) Blues, insuring 16 million people, were in financial trouble.

WHERE

HQ: Blue Cross and Blue Shield Association, 676 N. St. Clair St., Chicago, IL 60611
Phone: 312-440-6000
Fax: 312-440-6609

The association has offices in Chicago and Washington, DC; 69 licensees operating in 50 states, Australia, Canada, Jamaica, and the UK; and more than 94 million private and Medicare subscribers.

WHAT

	1993 Enrollment % of total
Group subscribers	86
Individual subscribers	14
Total	**100**

	1993 Enrollment No. of subscribers (mil.)	1993 Enrollment % of total
Private	66	66
Medicare	36	34
Adjustment	(8)	—
Total	**94**	**100**

Policies and Programs
Group major medical insurance
Health maintenance programs (HMO–USA)
Individual major medical insurance
Medicare administration
Preferred-provider organizations

Organization Goals
Attainment of wide public acceptance of the principle of voluntary, nonprofit prepayment of health services
Betterment of public health
Cooperation with federal, state, and local governments for provision of health services
Development and maintenance of membership standards
Protection of Blue Cross and Blue Shield service marks

Publications
Building a Healthy America (series)
Your Healthy Best (health booklets)

HOW MUCH

	9-Year Growth	1984	1985	1986	1987	1988	1989	1990	1991	1992	1993
Net subscriptions revenue ($ mil.)	6.6%	39,954	41,508	43,526	46,345	51,249	56,040	62,566	67,068	70,913	71,161
Pvt. subscribers (mil.)	(2.1%)	80	78	77	76	74	73	70	68	68	66
HQ budget ($ mil.)	—	85	87	98	95	97	104	108	—	—	—
Employees	4.8%	89,000	98,000	110,000	118,000	125,000	129,000	133,000	138,000	143,000	135,883

Private Subscribers (mil.) 1984–93

0 10 20 30 40 50 60 70 80

KEY COMPETITORS

Aetna
CareNetwork
Chubb
CIGNA
Coventry
Employee Benefit Plans
Equitable
FHP International
Foundation Health
Gencare Health Systems
Healthsource
Health Systems
HMO America
Intergroup Healthcare
John Hancock
Kaiser Foundation Health Plan
MassMutual
Mediplex Group
MetLife
New York Life
Oxford Health Plans
PacificCare Health Systems
Prudential
Sierra Health Services
TakeCare
Travelers
UniHealth
Value Health

H. E. BUTT GROCERY COMPANY

RANK: 40

OVERVIEW

H-E-B, headquartered in San Antonio since 1985, is the largest (by revenues) food retailer based in Texas. But competitor Randalls is closing fast, with its 1993 acquisition of the AppleTree and Tom Thumb chains.

H-E-B operates more than 200 stores, including full-service groceries (which offer general merchandise, pharmaceuticals, housewares, party goods, and, at selected stores, craft supplies), Pantry Foods stores (which offer a relatively limited range of products at lower prices), and a new concept, the Marketplace and Central Market, which emphasize an upscale selection of foods. A prototype Central Market opened in Austin in 1994.

The company also operates videotape rental departments in 57 stores. In addition H-E-B operates several food processing plants that supply store-brand merchandise. Another venture, the Bodega warehouse club, which was aimed at luring Mexican shoppers to the US, ceased operations in April 1993 (8 months before NAFTA took effect) because of high Mexican tariffs.

H-E-B is currently managed by Charles Butt, the son of Howard E. Butt.

WHEN

Charles C. Butt and his wife, Florence, moved to Kerrville, in the Texas Hill Country, in 1905 in hopes that the climate would help Charles's tuberculosis. Since Charles was unable to work, Florence began peddling groceries door-to-door for A&P. Later that year she opened a grocery store, C. C. Butt Grocery, in Kerrville. Florence, a dyed-in-the-wool Baptist, refused to carry such articles of vice as tobacco, and she extended easy credit to fellow believers.

The family lived over the store, and all 3 of the Butt children worked there. The youngest son, Howard, began working in the store full-time in his teens. After a stint in the navy during WWI, he returned to take over the store.

At first Howard made little more profit than his mother, and his first attempt at expansion failed for want of capital. By adopting modern marketing methods like price tagging and by overcoming their moral objections to tobacco, the Butts earned enough to finance expansion. In 1927 Howard opened a 2nd store in Del Rio, in Southwest Texas. In the next few years, he bought 3 Piggly Wiggly stores in the Rio Grande Valley and opened new stores. He gained patron loyalty by making minimal markups on staples.

In 1935 Howard (who had adopted the middle name Edward) rechristened the chain the H. E. Butt Grocery Company, and in 1940, in view of the company's strength in South Texas, he moved the headquarters to Corpus Christi. Howard put his 3 children to work for the company.

Howard Jr. and his younger brother, Charles, were rivals for succession. But Howard decided that his interests lay in faith and philanthropy, and he took over the H. E. Butt Foundation from his mother while Charles was groomed for succession.

In the 1960s H-E-B seemed stuck in a time warp. While others followed up-to-the-minute targeting or decorating strategies, H-E-B plodded along with a down-market image.

In 1971 Howard Sr. resigned and Charles took over, bringing in new people with newer management styles. But this was not enough. Marketing studies showed that the greatest reasons for H-E-B's lagging market share figures were its refusal to stock alcohol and its policy of Sunday closing. In 1976 it abandoned these portions of Florence's principles. It also drastically lowered its prices, undercutting competitors. Many independents were driven out of business. Beginning in 1979 H-E-B fought off Kroger's entry into several Texas markets, allegedly by cutting its prices below cost in the affected markets and paying for it by raising prices in other markets. H-E-B won the price wars and emerged dominant in its major markets.

In the 1980s H-E-B concentrated on building superstores; the first, in Austin in 1979, was 56,000 square feet and offered a variety of general merchandise as well as such services as photofinishing and pharmacy. The company also added video rental centers in its stores and expanded to 35 freestanding locations called Video Central.

In 1993, 33 video stores were sold to Hollywood Entertainment, of Portland, Oregon, for $30.5 million. In another cost-cutting move, H-E-B closed its meat processing plant after 15 years of operation because of difficulty in securing a sufficient supply of carcasses (the industry trend is toward boxed beef).

In early 1994 the first Central Market store was opened in Austin with a splash of publicity, just as Randalls made its entry into that very competitive market.

HOW MUCH

	Annual Growth	1984[1]	1985[1]	1986	1987	1988	1989	1990	1991	1992[1]	1993
Sales ($ mil.)	10.9%	1,780	1,936	2,055	2,105	2,312	2,586	2,900	3,162	3,204	4,500
Employees	20.2%	—	—	—	—	—	9,485	10,000	12,000	12,000	19,772

Sales ($ mil.) 1984–93

[1] Estimated

H-E-B

Private company
Fiscal year ends: October 31

WHO

Chairman, President, and CEO: Charles C. Butt
EVP and COO: James F. Clingman
SVP Distribution: Ed Clark
SVP Marketing: Robert A. Neslund
SVP: Charles W. Sapp
VP and Secretary: Wesley D. Nelson
VP Store Operations, Northern Division: Hal Collett
VP Store Operations, San Antonio: Paul Madura
VP South Texas Division: Greg Souquette
VP Store Operations, Austin/North Central: John Butler
Chief Administrative Officer and CFO: Jack Brouillard
VP Human Resources: Louis M. Laguardia
Auditors: Arthur Andersen & Co.

WHERE

HQ: 646 S. Main Ave., San Antonio, TX 78204
Phone: 210-246-8000
Fax: 210-246-8169

H-E-B operates grocery and related stores throughout Texas and operates dairy and other food processing plants.

	1993 Stores	
	No. of stores	% of total
San Antonio area	138	65
Houston area	51	24
Dallas area	15	7
Other areas	9	4
Total	**213**	**100**

WHAT

	1993 Stores	
	No. of stores	% of total
H. E. Butt Food Stores	84	40
H. E. Butt Super Food/Drug Stores	74	35
Pantry Food Stores	54	25
Marketplace	1	—
Total	**213**	**100**

HEBCO (real estate and development operation)

KEY COMPETITORS

Albertson's
Army and Air Force Exchange
Blockbuster
Circle K
Fiesta Mart
Hastings
Homeland Holding
Jack Eckerd
Kmart
Kroger
Minyard Food Stores
National Convenience Stores
Randalls
Southland
Walgreen
Wal-Mart
Whole Foods Market
Winn-Dixie

CALTEX PETROLEUM CORPORATION

RANK: 9

OVERVIEW

Dallas-based Caltex Petroleum is a holding company for a collection of companies involved primarily in refining and marketing petroleum in Africa, Asia, and the Pacific Rim. Caltex is a 50-50 joint venture between Texaco and Chevron. Through its subsidiaries it markets petroleum products via a network of more than 18,000 retail outlets in 30 countries, including Japan, South Korea, the Philippines, Australia, and South Africa. Caltex holds average market shares of 18% in motor fuels and 20% in lubricants in its markets.

Caltex also holds interests in 14 refineries in 11 countries, with its largest concentration of refining capacity in Japan. Through P. T. Caltex Pacific Indonesia, it explores for and produces oil and gas in Sumatra, accounting for about half of Indonesia's oil production. Although its Japanese operations have suffered because of that country's weak economy, Caltex's overall refined product sales were up 7% in 1993.

With the economies in countries in the Asia/Pacific region expected to grow at more than twice the rate of Western countries' economies, Caltex is concentrating on increasing its refining and retailing capacity in that area. It is expanding its retail service network in southern China and is building a 130,000-barrel-a-day refinery in Thailand.

Joint venture
Fiscal year ends: December 31

WHO

Chairman, President, and CEO: Patrick J. Ward
VC and CFO: Charles A. Boyce
SVP: John McPhail
SVP: G. J. Camarata
SVP: Matt W. Saunders
SVP: David Law-Smith
Director Marketing: Bob Young
VP and General Counsel: Frank W. Blue
VP Human Resources: E. M. Schmidt
Auditors: KPMG Peat Marwick

WHEN

In the 1930s Standard Oil of California (Socal) had a problem most oil companies would only wish upon themselves: it had oil reserves in Bahrain with a potential 30,000-barrel-a-day production capacity. The problem was that Socal didn't have the marketing or refining network to sell the oil profitably.

While Socal's oil sat idly in the Bahrain soil, Texaco had problems of its own. It had set up a large marketing network in Asia and Africa but didn't have a crude supply in the eastern hemisphere; it was shipping its products from the US. Enter James Forrestal, head of the investment bank Dillon, Read, with plans for a little matchmaking. Forrestal brought together the 2 companies, and in 1936 they formed the California-Texas Oil Company.

The new company had barely taken its first steps when WWII disrupted operations. Before the war Caltex had moved drilling equipment into a promising field in Sumatra, but after the war started the Japanese took over the field and struck oil using Caltex's equipment.

Following the war Caltex grew rapidly as oil demand began to climb. It formed companies in Thailand, Malaysia, and Yemen. Caltex also increased its refining capacity in Bahrain (1945), began a refinery construction and expansion program in other areas (1946), and bought Texaco's European and North African marketing facilities (1947).

In 1951 the company formed the Nippon Petroleum Refining Company as a joint venture with Nippon Oil to refine crude oil, supplied by Caltex, in Japan. Caltex also bought 50% of Japan's Koa Oil Company.

Caltex sold its European operations, which it had served from Saudi Arabia, to Socal and Texaco in 1967, allowing it to concentrate on building its presence in Asia, Africa, and Australia. In 1968 Caltex entered Korea and formed the Honam Oil Refinery Company in a partnership with Lucky Chemical.

During the 1970s several of Caltex's Arab holdings were nationalized as an OPEC-spawned upheaval shook the oil industry, and in 1978 the Indian government nationalized Caltex Oil Refining (India) Ltd.

In 1982 the company moved its offices to Dallas from New York. In 1986 the company began a major modernization program of its refineries in Australia, Singapore, and the Philippines. That same year Caltex entered the real estate development business in Hong Kong when it began construction of a $176 million condominium and shopping complex, built on the site of a former petroleum products terminal. In 1988 the company created Caltex Services Corporation to provide technical support to Caltex companies.

P. T. Caltex Pacific Indonesia signed an agreement with the Indonesian government in 1992 to extend their production-sharing agreement in Sumatra through 2021.

In 1993, 3 Japanese refiners pulled out of a $9.5 billion joint venture with Caltex and Saudi Aramco, apparently because it would take at least 12 years to make a profit from the planned 3-refinery project. That same year Caltex formed a lubricants blending and marketing joint venture with Indian oil company IBP.

WHERE

HQ: 125 E. John Carpenter Fwy., PO Box 619500, Irving, TX 75602-2750
Phone: 214-830-1000
Fax: 214-830-1156

Caltex has operations in 63 countries, primarily in Africa, Asia, Australia, the Middle East, and New Zealand.

Refineries

Bahrain (40%)
Batangas (the Philippines)
Capetown (South Africa)
Karachi (Pakistan, 12%)
Kurnell (Australia, 75%)
Marifu (Japan, 50%)
Mombasa (Kenya, 11.75%)
Muroran (Japan, 50%)
Negishi (Japan, 50%)
Osaka (Japan, 50%)
Pualau Merilimau (Singapore, 33.3%)
Sriracha (Thailand, 4.75%)
Whangarei (New Zealand, 8.57%)
Yosu (South Korea, 50%)

WHAT

Selected Subsidiaries and Affiliates

American Overseas Petroleum Limited (coordinates activities of P. T. Caltex Pacific Indonesia)
Amoseas Indonesia Inc. (manages holdings in Indonesia)
Caltex Australia
Caltex Oil South Africa (refining and marketing)
Caltex Services Corporation (provides technical services to group companies)
Caltex Services Private, Ltd. (tanker operations, Singapore)
Honam Oil Refinery Company, Ltd. (refining and marketing, Korea)
Honam Tanker Company
Korea Tanker Company
Koa Oil Company, Ltd. (refining, Japan)
Nippon Petroleum Refining Company, Ltd. (refining, Japan)
P. T. Caltex Pacific Indonesia (oil and gas exploration)
Singapore Refining Company

Real Estate Holdings

Riviera Gardens (apartments, shopping, restaurants; Hong Kong)

HOW MUCH

	Annual Growth	1984	1985	1986	1987	1988	1989	1990	1991	1992	1993
Sales ($ mil.)	(1.6%)	17,753	14,784	9,526	10,186	10,277	11,507	15,147	15,445	17,281	15,409
Net income ($ mil.)	(2.8%)	928	701	568	472	471	609	601	839	720	720
Income as % of sales	—	5.2%	4.7%	5.7%	4.6%	4.6%	5.3%	4.0%	5.4%	4.2%	4.7%
Employees	0.4%	—	—	—	—	—	—	7,700	7,700	7,600	7,800

1993 Year-end:
Debt ratio: 11.3
Return on equity: 17.7%
Cash (mil.): $166
Current ratio: 0.88
Long-term debt (mil.): $497

Net Income ($ mil.) 1984–93

KEY COMPETITORS

Amerada Hess
Amoco
Ashland
Atlantic Richfield
British Petroleum
Broken Hill
Coastal
Elf Aquitane
ENI
Exxon
Hutchison Whampoa
Jardine Matheson
Koch
Mobil
Occidental
PDVSA
PEMEX
Petrobrás
Phillips Petroleum
Repsol
Royal Dutch/Shell
Swire Pacific
Total
USX–Marathon

CARGILL, INCORPORATED

RANK: 3

OVERVIEW

With revenues that topped $47 billion in 1993 and operations that span the globe, Cargill is the largest privately owned company in the nation and among the top dozen of all US companies in terms of sales. It is the #1 grain company and the #3 food company (after Philip Morris and ConAgra) in the US.

Cargill's success has been in trading commodities ranging from grain and seed to orange juice and coffee to petroleum products. In several countries — Venezuela and Brazil are examples — the company is known as a consumer products concern, selling everything from pasta to vinegar on supermarket shelves.

Despite the 1991 sale of 17% of the company's stock to its employees, Cargill is still a family-controlled company. However, the company went outside family ranks in June 1994 when it promoted Ernest Micek to the role of president and COO, positioning him to take over as Cargill's next CEO.

While the company's US operations are very strong, Cargill is facing an array of problems overseas. Although sales rose slightly in 1993, net income fell 22%. The company blamed the slide on major political changes, a continued weak global economy, policy reforms, and currency fluctuations, among other factors.

Private company
Fiscal year ends: May 31

WHO

Chairman and CEO: Whitney MacMillan, age 64
VC: Gerald M. Mitchell, age 64
President and COO: Ernest S. Micek, age 58
President, Trading Sector: David W. Raisbeck, age 44
President, Financial Markets: David W. Rogers
President, Food Sector: Guillame Bastianes
SVP and CFO: Robert L. Lumpkins, age 49
SVP Human Resources: Everett MacLennan
VP, General Counsel and Secretary: James D. Moe
Auditors: KPMG Peat Marwick

WHEN

William Cargill, the son of a Scottish immigrant sea captain, bought his first grain elevator in Conover, Iowa, shortly after the Civil War. He and his brother Sam bought grain elevators all along the Southern Minnesota Railroad in 1870, a time when Minnesota was becoming an important shipping route for grain. Sam and another brother, James, expanded the elevator operations while William worked with the railroads to monopolize grain transport to markets and coal transport back to the farmers.

Around the turn of the century, William's son, also named William, invested in a Montana irrigation project and other ill-fated ventures. William Sr. went to Montana to find that his name had been used to finance these undertakings and shortly afterward died of pneumonia. Cargill's creditors grew worried and started pressing for repayment, which threatened to bankrupt the company. John MacMillan, who had married William Sr.'s daughter Edna, took control and rebuilt Cargill. By the time the company recovered in 1916, it had been stripped of timber holdings and land in Mexico and Canada that William Sr. had collected. MacMillan opened offices in New York (1922) and Argentina (1929), expanding Cargill's grain trading and transport operations nationally and internationally.

During the Depression Cargill built the river barges necessary to transport its products. When the grain fields turned into the Dust Bowl, Cargill bought up all the corn futures on the Chicago exchange, prompting the Board to kick Cargill's broker off the floor. During WWII Cargill used its barge-building facilities to build ships for the navy.

After WWII North American wheat became an increasingly important product because of the ravages of war and a growing world population. In 1945 Cargill bought Nutrena Mills (animal feed) and entered soybean processing; corn processing began soon after and has grown with the demand for corn sweeteners. In 1954 the US began lending money to Third World countries to buy American grain, and Cargill was one of the main beneficiaries of the policy. Subsidiary Tradax, established in 1955, quickly became one of the largest grain traders in Europe. In 1965 Cargill entered sugar trading by buying sugar and molasses in the Philippines and selling it abroad.

As a requirement for a takeover bid of Missouri Portland Cement (the bid was unsuccessful), Cargill made its finances public in 1973, revealing itself as one of the US's largest companies ($5.2 billion in sales). In the 1970s Cargill expanded into coal, steel, and waste disposal and became a major force in metals processing, beef, and salt production.

In the early 1990s Cargill started selling branded meats and packaged foods directly to supermarkets and in 1992 bought a juice processing plant (its first) from Procter & Gamble. Former US VP Walter Mondale was elected to the board of directors in 1992.

In 1993 Cargill announced that it was pulling out of 2 offshore ventures: it will sell its meat plants in Japan and shelve plans for a salt plant in India. Record snowfall, however, boosted sales of Cargill's salt in 1994.

HOW MUCH

	Annual Growth	1984	1985	1986	1987	1988	1989	1990	1991	1992	1993
Sales ($ mil.)	5.8%	—	30,000	32,280	32,400	38,200	43,000	44,000	49,100	46,800	47,100
Net income ($ mil.)	(1.7%)	—	—	—	—	—	—	372	382	450	353
Income as % of sales	—	—	—	—	—	—	—	0.8%	0.8%	1.0%	0.8%
Employees	6.4%	40,202	41,738	46,351	51,600	55,020	53,710	55,200	60,000	63,500	70,000

Sales ($ mil.) 1985–93

50,000 / 45,000 / 40,000 / 35,000 / 30,000 / 25,000 / 20,000 / 15,000 / 10,000 / 5,000 / 0

WHERE

HQ: PO Box 9300, 15407 McGinty Rd., Minnetonka, MN 55440-9300
Phone: 612-742-7575
Fax: 612-742-6208

Cargill and its roughly 50 subsidiaries and affiliates have about 800 plants, 500 US offices, and 300 foreign offices in 60 countries.

Regional US Sales Offices
Northern and Central Region (Minneapolis)
North Atlantic Region (Watkins Glen, NY)
Central Atlantic Region (Baltimore)
Mideast Region (Cincinnati)
Midwest Region (Hutchinson, KS)
Southern Region (Breaux Bridge, LA)
Northwest Region (Portland)
Northern California (Newark, CA)
Southern California (Vernon, CA)

WHAT

Commodities Trading and Transport
Barges and vessels (Cargo Carriers, Inc.)
Coffee and cocoa
Cotton (Hohenberg Bros.)
Fertilizers
Grain and oilseeds
Iron and finished steel
Juice and fruit concentrates
Molasses and sugar
Oceangoing vessels
Petroleum products and petrochemicals
Rubber
Tallow

Industrial Products
Industrial chemicals
Scrap steel yards (Magnimet)
Steel and wire
Steel minimills (North Star)

Financial Operations
Equipment leasing
Futures trading and foreign exchange
Life insurance
Risk management

Food Production and Processing
Animal byproducts
Beef, pork, and chicken processing/packaging
Bulk commodities
Citric acid
Corn syrup sweeteners
Ethanol
Flour and corn milling
Salt (Leslie)
Starches

Agricultural Products
Animal feeds (Nutrena)
Feed supplements
Seed and fertilizer

KEY COMPETITORS

ADM
American President
Bethlehem Steel
Chiquita Brands
ConAgra
Continental Grain
CPC
CSX
General Mills
George Weston
W. R. Grace
Heinz
Hormel
IBP
IRI
Koch
LTV
Morton
Nippon Steel
Nucor
Occidental
Philip Morris
Ralston Purina
Salomon
Sara Lee
Thyssen
Tyson Foods
Universal Corp.
WMX Technologies

CARLSON COMPANIES, INC.

RANK: 97

OVERVIEW

In 56 years Minneapolis-based Carlson Companies has wandered far from its origins in a now-rare field (trading stamps) to become a major force in one of the fastest-growing fields — travel and tourism.

Carlson has 3 segments: travel, hospitality, and marketing and motivation. Most sales come from the Travel Group, which is a leading North American travel services provider.

Carlson Hospitality Group operates and franchises 345 Radisson Hotels, Colony Hotels & Resorts, and Country Inns. The company owns only 2 hotels outright. The group also oversees 235 Country Kitchens and 237 T.G.I. Friday's restaurants.

Carlson Marketing Group is the largest motivational company in the world, serving most of the *FORTUNE* 500 companies by providing employee training and incentives programs. It also administers Northwest Airlines's frequent flier program.

Carlson is aggressively expanding operations, opening a property every few days. A 1992 joint venture with Hospitality Franchise Systems is hastening the expansion of T.G.I. Friday's and Country Kitchen with a plan to open a restaurant adjacent to each of its partners' hotels.

In the 1990s Carlson's strategy has emphasized growth of its hospitality operations overseas, particularly in Asia and South America, in light of saturated markets in the US and Europe. To this end, in 1994 it entered into a 50-50 alliance with Accor's Wagonlit Travel of Paris, which gives Carlson a presence in more than 4,000 locations in 125 countries.

Carlson Companies Inc.

Private company
Fiscal year ends: December 31

WHO

Chairman, President, and CEO: Curtis L. Carlson, age 79
VC: Marilyn Carlson Nelson
CFO: Martyn Redgrave
EVP; President, Hospitality Group: Juergen Bartels
Co-EVP Marketing Group: Walt Erikson
Co-EVP Marketing Group: Mark Larson
EVP; President, Travel Group: Travis Tanner
VP Legal, Secretary, and General Counsel: Lee Bearmon
VP Human Resources: Terry M. Butorac
Auditors: Arthur Andersen & Co.

WHERE

HQ: Carlson Pkwy., PO Box 59159, Minneapolis, MN 55459
Phone: 612-540-5000
Fax: 612-540-5832

	1993 Sales % of total
US	67
Other countries	33
Total	**100**

WHEN

Curtis Carlson, the son of Swedish immigrants, graduated from the University of Minnesota in 1937 and went to work as a Procter & Gamble soap salesman in the Minneapolis/St. Paul area. In 1938 he borrowed $50 and formed Gold Bond Stamp Company to sell trading stamps to grocery stores in his spare time. His wife, Arleen, dressed as a drum majorette and twirled a baton to promote the concept. By 1941 the company had 200 accounts. In 1952 a large local chain, SUPERVALU, started using the stamps, boosting Gold Bond's sales to $2.4 million. By 1960 the trading stamps were generating so much capital that Carlson began investing in other enterprises: Ardan catalog and jewelry showrooms, travel agencies, and business promotion and employee motivation programs.

In 1962 Carlson bought the original Radisson Hotel in Minneapolis. He followed with 7 more hotels throughout the state and in 1970 expanded the Radisson chain outside Minnesota, buying the future Radisson Denver from Hyatt. By 1976 the majority of Radisson rooms were outside Minnesota. Carlson diversified into restaurants by buying the 11-unit T.G.I. (Thank God It's) Friday's, a dining and singles-bar chain, and Country Kitchen International (family restaurants).

By 1978 Radisson had 19 hotel properties, including one in the West Indies. Many of the Radissons were older hotels remodeled by Contract Services Associates, another Carlson company. In 1978 Carlson bought his first travel agency, Ask Mr. Foster (now Carlson Travel Network). In 1979 he bought Colony Resorts (hotel/condominium management company) from its founder, former baseball commissioner Peter Ueberroth.

Carlson Companies slowed the pace of its acquisitions in the 1980s. In 1984 Carlson hired Juergen Bartels to head its hospitality division. Bartels changed the division's growth strategy from one of building and owning hotels to one of franchising and managing them. This helped the company avoid the worst consequences of the 1980s hotel overbuilding boom. Carlson took T.G.I. Friday's public in 1983 (retaining 76% of the stock) to fund expansion of the chain but reacquired all outstanding shares in 1990. That year and the next year Carlson bought 2 UK travel agencies, A.T. Mays (1990) and Smith Travel (1991). The company entered the cruise ship business in 1992, launching the luxury liner SSC *Radisson Diamond*.

In the 1990s Carlson has been dogged by rumors that Curtis Carlson's health is failing and that there is a high turnover rate among its officers. In 1990 Carlson's son-in-law and heir-apparent, Edwin Gage, quit Carlson Marketing, taking with him a significant share of business. It is now believed that one of his 2 daughters, Marilyn Nelson, will succeed him.

WHAT

	1993 Systemwide Sales* $ mil.	% of total
Travel Group	6,100	67
Hospitality Group	2,900	32
Marketing Group	90	1
Total	**9,090**	**100**

* Includes franchisees

Carlson Travel Group
Carlson Travel Network (travel agents)
P. Lawson Travel (Canada)
A.T. Mays

Carlson Hospitality Group
Colony Hotels & Resorts
Country Lodging By Carlson
Country Kitchen International
Radisson Hotels International
SSC *Radisson Diamond*
T.G.I. Friday's Inc.

Carlson Marketing Group
Database management/learning systems
Direct marketing/direct mail/telemarketing
Event marketing and management
Frequency and partnership marketing
Marketing consultation and strategic planning
Meeting, convention, and trade show planning
Motivational programs
Quality service and productivity programs
Retail promotions/promotional merchandise

Carlson Real Estate Company

Carlson Investment Group

HOW MUCH

	Annual Growth	1984	1985	1986	1987	1988	1989	1990	1991	1992	1993
Estimated sales ($ mil.)	14.1%	700	900	1,300	1,500	1,800	2,000	2,200	2,300	2,900	2,295
Hotels and motels	27.2%	55	75	135	160	195	223	270	315	336	340
Hotel rooms	26.4%	14,000	20,000	32,000	38,000	47,000	50,000	60,000	69,000	76,000	73,000
Employees	(14.8%)	—	—	—	—	—	—	68,000	70,000	49,350	41,000

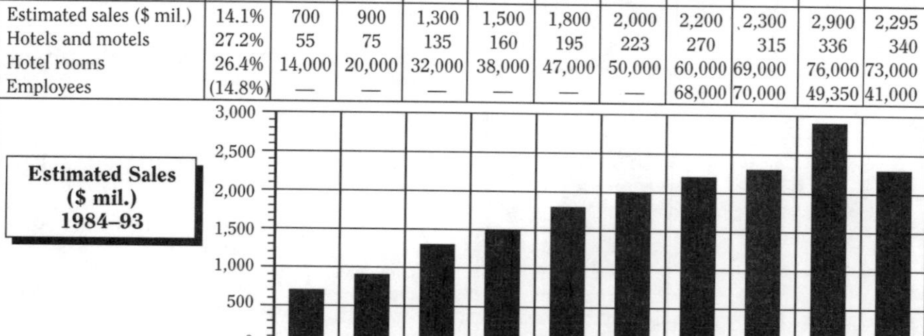

KEY COMPETITORS

AAA
American Express
Bass
Brinker
Canadian Pacific
Dun & Bradstreet
Edward J. DeBartolo
Flagstar
General Mills
Hilton
Hyatt
ITT
IVI Travel
Maritz
Marriott International
Metromedia
Rank
Reed Elsevier
Ritz-Carlton
Tennessee Restaurants
Thomson Corp.

CATHOLIC HEALTHCARE WEST INC.

RANK: 155

OVERVIEW

Headquartered in San Francisco, Catholic Healthcare West (CHW) is one of California's largest private nonprofit health care systems and the US's 10th largest nonprofit health organization. CHW runs a network of 17 hospitals in California, Arizona, and Nevada, including church-sponsored and community-sponsored acute care hospitals. It also operates clinics, long-term care facilities, and retirement residences and is affiliated with more than 3,100 doctors. CHW provides managed care to 225,000 enrollees in the Bay Area and Sacramento.

CHW, owned and run by the Roman Catholic Church, is sponsored by 2 California religious orders, the Regional Community of the Sisters of Mercy (Burlingame) and the Regional Community of the Sisters of Mercy (Auburn), and by the Sisters of St. Dominic of the Congregation of the Most Holy Rosary in Adrian, Michigan. CHW emphasizes care for poor, elderly, and HIV-infected patients and provides community services, including indigent programs and health education.

Under California state law, doctors cannot be employed directly by a hospital, so CHW acts as a legal connection to physician groups. CHW is concentrating on increasing its presence in the Bay Area by adding doctors to its network. In 1993 it formed Catholic Healthcare West Medical Foundation to oversee regional physician groups across the state of California. Also in 1993 CHW formed an alliance with Hill Physicians Medical Group, an 800-member physician group in Northern California.

WHEN

Catholic Healthcare West was formed in 1986 by the merger of 2 Roman Catholic health care systems: Mercy Health System of Burlingame, California (sponsored by the Sisters of Mercy of Burlingame), and Mercy Healthcare Organization of Sacramento, (sponsored by the Sisters of Mercy of Auburn, California). Mercy Healthcare had 4 hospitals in California, and Mercy Health System's facilities included 4 nursing homes and 2 residential units for the elderly, plus 4 hospitals in California and 1 in Arizona.

The newly formed organization faced tough times following the merger, with its net income dropping from nearly $58 million in 1986 to $28 million in 1988. Like others in the health care industry, CHW was hurt by rising costs and difficulty getting paid.

One of the hardest-hit CHW affiliates was Mercy Healthcare Sacramento, which lost $4.2 million between 1986 and 1987. In 1988 Mercy Healthcare restructured. A regional office was set up to take over Mercy's 3 hospitals' financial activities, and, to more easily coordinate capital allocation and to improve marketing efforts, Mercy consolidated its independent boards into one.

CHW added a 3rd sponsoring organization in 1989 when the Sisters of St. Dominic of Adrian, Michigan, joined. The alliance added 2 new hospitals, Dominican Santa Cruz Hospital in Santa Cruz, California, and St. Rose Dominican Hospital in Henderson, Nevada. That same year Richard Kramer, a former EVP of Minneapolis-based health services company LifeSpan, was named president and CEO, replacing Robert Densmore.

In 1990 CHW started its Community Economic Assistance Program to provide grants to human services and health care agencies. In its first year the program donated $220,000 to 16 organizations.

CHW continued to add new facilities to the fold. In 1990 it announced plans to acquire American River Hospital in Carmichael, California, and that same year CHW bought Santa Cruz's AMI Community Hospital. Since CHW already owned the area's only other acute care hospital, the FTC began an antitrust investigation and in 1993 ordered CHW not to acquire any more acute care hospitals in Santa Cruz County for 10 years without FTC approval.

By 1992 CHW had 14 hospitals and a retirement facility, with a total of more than 4,000 beds. While CHW's roster of hospitals continued to grow, the hospital system has maintained a strong financial commitment to programs for the poor, the elderly, and HIV-infected patients.

In 1993 CHW signed an alliance agreement with St. Francis Memorial Hospital in San Francisco. That same year CHW signed a prime distribution agreement with medical-surgical supplier Baxter Healthcare.

HOW MUCH

	Annual Growth	1984	1985	1986	1987	1988	1989	1990	1991	1992	1993
Sales ($ mil.)	14.3%	—	—	641	701	890	994	1,113	1,347	1,563	1,633
Net income ($ mil.)	(3.6%)	—	—	58	28	20	37	47	61	91	45
Income as % of revenue	—	—	—	9.0%	4.0%	2.2%	3.8%	4.3%	4.5%	5.8%	2.8%
Employees	(1.7%)	—	—	—	—	—	18,723	16,836	18,506	18,806	17,451

1993 Year-end:
Debt ratio: 47.9%
Cash (mil.): $50
Current ratio: 1.42
Long-term debt (mil.): $735
Total assets (mil.): $2,103

Net Income ($ mil.) 1986–93

0 20 40 60 80 100

Catholic Healthcare West 

Nonprofit organization
Fiscal year ends: June 30

WHO

Chairperson: Linda Bevilacqua
President and CEO: Richard J. Kramer
EVP and COO: Larry Wilson
VP Financial Services and CFO: John Burgis
VP Legal Services and General Counsel: Robert Johnson
VP Managed Care: David Hoskinson
VP Mission Services: Eileen Barrett
VP System Services: David Berg
Human Resources Director: Lawrence Kren
Auditors: Arthur Andersen & Co.

WHERE

HQ: 1700 Montgomery St., Ste. 300, San Francisco, CA 94111
Phone: 415-397-9000
Fax: 415-397-1823

Hospitals and Care Facilities
Dominican Santa Cruz Hospital (Santa Cruz, CA)
Mercy American River Hospital (Carmichael, CA)
Mercy General Hospital (Sacramento)
Mercy Healthcare (San Diego)
Mercy Hospital (Bakersfield, CA)
Mercy Hospital (Folsom, CA)
Mercy Medical Center (Mt. Shasta, CA)
Mercy Medical Center (Redding, CA)
Mercy Retirement and Care Center (Oakland, CA)
Mercy San Juan Hospital (Carmichael, CA)
Mercy Southwest Hospital (Bakersfield, CA)
Methodist Hospital (Sacramento)
St. Francis Memorial Hospital (San Francisco)
St. John's Pleasant Valley Medical Center (Camarillo, CA)
St. John's Regional Medical Center (Oxnard, CA)
St. Joseph's Hospital and Medical Center (Phoenix, AZ)
St. Mary's Hospital and Medical Center (San Francisco)
St. Rose Dominican Hospital (Henderson, NV)

WHAT

	1993 Sales $ mil.	1993 Sales % of total
Sales	1,577	97
Contributions	7	—
Investment earnings	48	3
Total	**1,633**	**100**

	1993 Sales % of total
Inpatient services	79
Outpatient services	21
Total	**100**

	1993 Sales % of total
Medicare	43
Medicaid	16
Contracted rate payors	28
Commercial insurance and other payors	13
Total	**100**

KEY COMPETITORS

Adventist Health Systems
Diversified Health Center
Foundation Health
Kaiser Foundation
PacifiCare Health Systems
Qual-Med
Sierra Health Services
Sutter Health Systems

THE CIRCLE K CORPORATION

RANK: 62

OVERVIEW

With 2,508 US units, located mostly in the Sunbelt, Phoenix-based Circle K is the US's #2 convenience store operator, after Ito-Yokado's Southland Corp. (owner of 7-Eleven). Via joint ventures Circle K also has interests in 2,474 convenience stores in 22 countries. Gasoline sales account for about half of the company's revenues.

After wildly expanding in the 1980s (at one time controlling over 5,700 stores worldwide) by issuing bonds by the wheelbarrowful, the company filed for bankruptcy protection in 1990. In 1993 Investcorp S.A., an international investment concern led by former Iraqi political prisoner Nemir Kirdar (and which also has interests in Saks Fifth Avenue and Gucci, among others), rescued Circle K from bankruptcy for $400 million and took it private.

Circle K has been busy widening its customer base and unloading unprofitable stores in the US (there are many; in its buying frenzy of the 1980s, Circle K bought several stores that turned out to be across the street from each other). However, the company has been growing rapidly overseas — its store count was up 49% to nearly 2,500 in 1993.

Circle K and National Convenience Stores agreed to swap several stores in 1994 so that each company can focus on important markets. Circle K will acquire 80 stores in California and Georgia and NCS will get 88 Texas stores.

Circle K is now trying new merchandising strategies to gain customers, including supermarket pricing and forays with fast food operators to open outlets within Circle K stores.

Private company
Fiscal year ends: April 30

WHO

Chairman: Bart A. Brown, Jr., age 60
President and CEO: John F. Antioco, age 43
EVP and COO: Mitch E. Telson, age 50
EVP Finance and CFO: Larry Zine, age 39
SVP and General Counsel: Gehl P. Babinec
VP Human Resources: Terry S. Broekemeier
Auditors: Arthur Andersen & Co.

WHERE

HQ: 3003 N. Central Ave., Phoenix, AZ 85012
Phone: 602-530-5001
Fax: 602-530-5278

Circle K operates 2,508 convenience stores in 28 US states, primarily in the Sunbelt, and 2,474 stores in 22 other countries.

	1993 US Stores	
Location	**No. of stores**	**% of total**
Arizona	543	22
Florida	436	17
California	303	12
Texas	271	11
Louisiana	190	8
Georgia	130	5
Oklahoma	87	3
North Carolina	66	3
Other US	482	19
Total	**2,508**	**100**

	1993 Total Stores	
Location	**No. of stores**	**% of total**
US	2,508	50
Japan	1,500	31
UK	200	4
Canada	194	4
Korea	177	4
Taiwan	155	3
Hong Kong	86	2
New Zealand	59	1
Argentina	25	—
Mexico	22	—
Guatemala	10	—
Costa Rica	7	—
Other countries	39	1
Total	**4,982**	**100**

WHEN

Circle K Corporation was formed in Texas in 1951 by Fred Hervey, a 2-term mayor of El Paso. Hervey bought the 3 locations of Kay's Food Stores in El Paso that year and soon extended the chain to 10 locations. In 1957 he expanded into Arizona, renamed the stores Circle K, and adopted the distinctive, western-style logo.

Circle K went public in 1963. During the 1960s and 1970s, the company expanded into New Mexico, California, Colorado, Montana, Idaho, and Oregon. In 1979 Circle K licensed UNY of Japan to operate Circle K stores there. UNY currently operates 1,586 Circle K stores in Japan and Hong Kong.

The corporation became a holding company in 1980, with its Circle K chain as a subsidiary, and began expanding through acquisitions. That year the company bought 13% of Nucorp Energy, an oil and gas developer. Nucorp filed for bankruptcy in 1982, and Circle K sold its remaining interest in 1983 at a large loss. Also in 1983 Circle K nearly doubled its size by acquiring the 960-store UtoteM chain from American Financial, headed by Cincinnati financier Carl Lindner. Hervey and Lindner's friend Karl Eller became chairman and CEO.

Eller initiated an aggressive growth plan aimed at quadrupling the number of stores by 1990. Through acquisitions Circle K grew from 1,221 stores in 1983 to 5,751 by the end of 1989, increasing its long-term debt from $40.5 million to $1.1 billion.

Circle K began having financial problems in 1989, owing in part to $96 million in annual interest payments. It put itself up for sale, but no buyers emerged. Lindner, whose American Financial owned 15% of Circle K's common stock (sold 1991) and was a major creditor, brought in Robert Dearth from his Chiquita Brands as Circle K's president in 1990. Shortly afterward, Eller left the company "to pursue personal business opportunities." Prices were cut and store managers were given more purchasing authority, but it was too late; in May Circle K declared bankruptcy. In June 1991 Dearth resigned.

In 1993, after losing nearly $1.3 billion since 1990, Circle K was sold to Investcorp for $400 million. The money went to pay off creditors, leaving many shareholders grumbling. Shortly after emerging from bankruptcy, the company changed its top executive as Bart Brown resigned as CEO (although remaining as chairman) and John Antioco, formerly COO, assumed this role.

Also in 1993 Circle K reached an agreement in federal court over ground contamination from leaking underground gasoline tanks and agreed to pay about $30 million in fines to 29 states. In 1994 rising crime against convenience stores prompted Circle K to begin staffing all of its stores with 2 clerks at all times.

WHAT

Selected Foreign Joint Venture Licensees
Royal Dutch/Shell (Argentina, Australia, Canada, and New Zealand)
UNY Co., LTD. (Japan)

HOW MUCH

	Annual Growth	1984	1985	1986	1987	1988	1989	1990	1991	1992	1993[1]
Sales ($ mil.)	13.2%	1,035	1,694	2,129	2,317	2,657	3,495	3,737	3,599	2,904	3,157
Net income ($ mil.)	—	22	33	40	49	60	15	(773)	(307)	(197)	(20)
Income as % of sales	—	2.1%	2.0%	1.9%	2.1%	2.3%	0.4%	—	—	—	—
Employees	5.4%	12,461	16,657	19,342	20,983	24,544	27,264	25,942	23,377	21,487	20,000

1993 Year-end:[2]
Debt ratio: —
Return on equity: (2.1%)
Cash (mil.): $166
Current ratio: 1.31
Long-term debt (mil.): $47

[1] Estimated. [2] As of March 31.

KEY COMPETITORS

ABCO Markets
Albertson's
Atlantic Richfield
Bashas'
British Petroleum
Bruno's
Chevron
Coastal
Exxon
Farmland Industries
Fiesta
Food 4 Less
Great A&P
H. E. Butt
Kroger
Lucky Stores
Mobil
National Convenience Stores
Pueblo International
Quik Trip
Racetrac
Randalls
Safeway
Southland
Star Enterprise
Sun
Texaco
Unocal
Vons
Wawa
Winn-Dixie

CONTINENTAL GRAIN COMPANY

RANK: 10

OVERVIEW

From its headquarters in New York City, Continental Grain oversees the world's 2nd largest grain and related commodities empire (Cargill is #1). With sales of about $15 billion, Continental is one of the nation's largest private companies. The company has additional operations in livestock, shipping, food processing, and oil. Continental also offers financial services ranging from non–currency-based trading to trade financing.

Through its various commodities groups, Continental serves customers in more than 100 countries. Each year the company stores, handles, and ships billions of bushels of wheat, sorghum, oilseeds, rice, feed grains, cotton, corn, and other products.

Although the company has offices and facilities in more than 50 countries, the majority of its revenues come from North America. Sales have remained flat since 1991.

Continental, in partnership with Huntsman Chemical, is building a plastic packaging manufacturing plant in China. The company will control 40% of the venture. Continental is also expanding ContiCotton, its cotton merchandising operations.

Chairman emeritus Michel Fribourg, great-great-grandson of Continental's founder, and his immediate family own 90% of Continental's stock. Other members of the Fribourg family own the rest. Fribourg also owns 8.6% of Overseas Ship Holding Co.

Private company
Fiscal year ends: March 31

WHO

Chairman Emeritus: Michel Fribourg, age 80
Chairman and CEO: Donald L. Staheli, age 62
President and COO: Paul J. Fribourg, age 40
President, Finagrain: Poul Schroeder
SVP Grain and Oilseeds Merchandising: John Laesch
SVP: Bernard Steinweg
VP Processing Division: Ronald Anderson
VP and General Counsel — Corporate: Lawrence G. Weppler, age 44
VP and General Counsel — Commodity Marketing: David G. Friedman, age 50
VP Public Affairs: Daryl Natz
General Manager, EEC: Charles Fribourg
General Manager, Europe: Rico Stroemer
VP Human Resources: Dwight Coffin

WHEN

In 1813 Simon Fribourg founded a commodity trading business in Belgium. The company operated there until 1848, when a severe drought in Belgium caused the company to buy large stocks in Russian wheat.

As the Industrial Revolution swept across Europe and populations shifted toward the cities, countries became more dependent upon traded grain. In the midst of such rapid changes, the company prospered.

After WWI, Russia, which had been Europe's primary grain supplier, ceased to be a major player in the trading game, and Western Hemisphere countries picked up the slack. Sensing the shift, Jules and René Fribourg reorganized the business as Continental Grain and opened the company's first US office in Chicago in 1921. In 1930 it leased a Galveston terminal from the Southern Pacific Railroad, and during the Depression the company bought US grain elevators wherever they could find them, often at low prices. Through its rapid purchases, the company built an elaborate North American grain network including such important locations as Kansas City, Nashville, and Toledo.

Meanwhile, in Europe the Fribourgs were forced to weather constant political and economic upheaval, often profiting from it (the Fribourgs supplied food to the Republican forces during the Spanish Civil War). When the Nazis invaded Belgium in 1940, the Fribourgs were forced to flee but reorganized the business in New York City after the war.

During the postwar years, Continental constructed a lucrative grain trade with the Soviets and expanded its international presence. During the 1960s and 1970s, the company went on a spree, buying Allied Mills (feed milling, 1965) and absorbing several agricultural and transport businesses, including feedlots in Texas, an English soybean producer (sold, 1986), a bakery, and Quaker Oats's agricultural products unit.

In 1979 the company found itself caught between US diplomacy and business when it tried to collect $80 million from Toprak Mahsulleri Ofisi, a state-owned Turkish grain company that had reneged on a contract to buy 385,000 tons of wheat from Continental.

During the 1980s the company slimmed down by selling its baking units (Oroweat and Arnold) as well as its commodities brokerage house. Michel Fribourg stepped down as CEO in 1988. Donald Staheli, the first nonfamily member to hold the position, succeeded him. Continental also realigned its international grain and oilseeds operations into the World Grain and Oilseeds Processing Group under the leadership of Paul Fribourg.

Because the company uses futures contracts, it was well insulated from price swings caused by Mississippi River basin flooding in 1993. Continental ran into opposition to several proposed Missouri pork-producing plants in 1994. Local citizens, holding signs that read, "Continental Grain, Go Home," were wary of land and air pollution and depressed land values.

In June 1994 the company named CEO Staheli as chairman and Michel's son Paul, widely seen as the next head of the company, as president and COO.

WHERE

HQ: 277 Park Ave., New York, NY 10172-0002
Phone: 212-207-5100
Fax: 212-207-5181

Continental Grain has offices and facilities in more than 50 countries.

WHAT

Commodity Marketing Group
Astral International Shipping (shipping agents)
ContiCarriers & Terminals (transport, Chicago)
ContiChem (liquefied petroleum gases, New York)
ContiCotton (cotton merchandising; Fresno, CA)
ContiLatin (Latin American trading unit, New York)
Continental Grain (Canada)
ContiQuincy Export (soybean merchandising partnership with Quincy Soybean)
Finagrain (European trading unit, Geneva)
North American Grain (Chicago)
Rice Division (rice trading, New York)
Stellar Chartering and Brokerage (ocean vessels)
World Grain and Oilseeds Merchandising (Chicago)
World Oilseeds Processing Division (New York)

Milling Group
Asian Agri Industries (China)
ContiMilling (New York)
International Designer Accessories (Secaucus, NJ)
Wayne Feed (Chicago)

Meat Group
Cattle Feeding Division (Chicago)
Dutch Quality House (poultry, GA)
Poultry Division (GA)

Financial Services Group
ContiFinancial Services (New York)
ContiTrade Services (New York)

HOW MUCH

	Annual Growth	1985	1986	1987	1988	1989	1990	1991	1992	1993	1994
Estimated sales ($ mil.)	0.9%	—	14,000	13,500	13,000	13,500	14,850	15,000	15,000	15,000	15,000
Employees	3.3%	—	12,000	12,000	12,000	12,000	14,500	14,500	14,750	14,700	15,500

Estimated Sales ($ mil.) 1986–94

16,000
14,000
12,000
10,000
8,000
6,000
4,000
2,000
0

KEY COMPETITORS

ADM
American Express
American President
Amoco
Ashland
Atlantic Richfield
Bear Stearns
Calcot
Cargill
CENEX
Central Soya
Charles Schwab
Chevron
Chiquita Brands
Coastal
ConAgra
Connell Co.
CPC
CSX
Dunavant Enterprises
Enron
Farmland Industries
W. R. Grace
Harvest States Cooperative
Hormel
IBP
King Ranch
Koch
Moorman
Morgan Stanley
Paine Webber
Perdue Farms
Pilgrim's Pride
Ralston Purina Group
Salomon
Scoular
Tyson Foods
Universal Corp.
USX-Marathon

COOPERS & LYBRAND L.L.P.

RANK: 36

OVERVIEW

One of the Big 6 accounting firms, Coopers & Lybrand is the world's 4th largest accounting firm and the 5th largest in the US. Besides auditing and tax preparation, the firm provides a variety of business services, including management consulting and human resource consulting. Coopers led the Big 6 in signing on new clients in 1993 after lagging behind its counterparts in the last few years.

Coopers has recently focused on expanding its Human Resource Advisory Group, acquiring several consulting firms, including Bufete Matemico Actuarial, the largest independent benefits and actuarial consulting firm in Mexico. The additions make the firm's human resource group the world's 5th largest.

In 1993 there was a downsizing of US operations, with over 90 partners laid off, and the firm experienced a decline in sales for the first time in 10 years. In 1994 Eugene Freedman said he would not seek another term as Cooper & Lybrand's chairman. The firm's partners elected Nicholas Moore to be its new chairman when Freedman's term ends.

WHEN

Coopers & Lybrand, the product of a 1957 transatlantic merger, literally wrote the book on auditing. Lybrand, Ross Bros. & Montgomery, as the US ancestor was known, had been formed in 1898 by 4 partners — William Lybrand, Edward Ross, Adam Ross, and Robert Montgomery. In 1912 Montgomery wrote *Montgomery's Auditing*, termed by many as the "Bible" of the accounting profession. The book is now in its 11th edition.

In the early years the accounting firm grew slowly, and the Ross brothers' sister served as secretary, typist, and bookkeeper. In 1902 the company opened a New York office at 25 Broad Street. Other offices across the country followed — Pittsburgh (1908), Chicago (1909), and Boston (1915).

WWI focused attention on Washington, DC, and the Lybrand firm opened an office there (1919) and then branched out to the new auto capital of Detroit (1920), to Seattle (1920), and to Baltimore (1924). A merger with the firm of Klink, Bean & Company gave the firm a window on California (1924). Another merger brought the firm into Dallas (1930), with an offshoot office in Houston a year later.

In Europe the Lybrand firm established offices in Berlin (1924, closed in 1938 as WWII loomed), Paris (1926), and London (1929). At the same time the UK firm of Cooper Brothers was also expanding in Europe.

Cooper Brothers had begun in 1854 when William Cooper, the oldest son of a Quaker banker, formed his accountancy at 13 George Street in London. He was quickly joined by his brothers, Arthur, Francis, and Ernest. The firm's name of Cooper Brothers & Company was adopted in 1861. After WWI Cooper Brothers branched out to Liverpool (1920), Brussels (1921), New York (1926), and Paris (1930). After WWII Cooper Brothers acquired 3 venerable firms — Alfred Tongue & Company; Aspell Dunn & Company; and Rattray Brothers, Alexander & France.

In 1957 Coopers & Lybrand was formed by the amalgamation of the international accounting firms, and by 1973 the affiliated partnerships had gravitated toward the Coopers & Lybrand name.

In the 1960s the company expanded into employee benefits consulting and introduced a new auditing method that included evaluating clients' systems of internal control. During the 1970s Coopers focused on integrating computer technology into the auditing process.

During the 1980s Coopers dropped from the top of the Big 8 to 5th in the Big 6 as several of its competitors paired off in a series of mergers. However, the firm unexpectedly became the refuge for partners defecting from other international mergers.

In 1991 Coopers and IBM formed Meritus, a consulting service for the health care and consumer goods industries. In 1992 the firm agreed to pay $95 million to settle claims of defrauded investors in now-defunct disk drive maker MiniScribe. In 1993 it hired former SEC chairman Richard Breeden as vice-chairman of its domestic and foreign financial service groups.

In 1994 Coopers & Lybrand introduced Telesim, a management simulation software package for the telecommunications industry. The software was developed with Pacific Telesis, NYNEX, and software maker Thinking Tools.

HOW MUCH

	9-Year Growth	1984	1985	1986	1987	1988	1989	1990	1991	1992	1993
Sales ($ mil.)	17.3%	1,243	1,414	1,780	2,076	2,520	2,977	4,136	4,959	5,350	5,220
Offices	4.7%	488	518	531	550	580	602	710	735	733	740
Partners	—	—	—	—	—	—	—	—	—	—	5,091
Employees	8.0%	33,055	36,243	38,520	41,134	45,486	50,636	63,300	67,175	66,600	66,300

1993 Year-end:
US sales per partner: $1,025,339

Sales ($ mil.) 1984–93

Coopers & Lybrand

International partnership
Fiscal year ends: September 30

WHO

Chairman and CEO: Eugene M. Freedman, age 62 (until October 1, 1994)
Chairman and CEO: Nicholas Moore (after October 1, 1994)
COO: Vincent M. O'Reilly
VC Coopers & Lybrand Consulting: John M. Jacobs
VC International: William K. O'Brien
VC Human Resources and Strategy: Anthony J. Conti
CFO: Frank V. Scalia
General Counsel: Harris J. Amhowitz

WHERE

HQ: 1251 Avenue of the Americas, New York, NY 10020
Phone: 212-536-2000
Fax: 212-536-3145

Coopers & Lybrand has offices in 125 countries.

	1993 Sales	
	$ mil.	% of total
US	1,640	31
Other countries	3,580	69
Total	**5,220**	**100**

WHAT

	1993 US Sales
	% of total
Accounting & auditing	56
Tax	19
Management consulting	25
Total	**100**

Selected Services

Business Assurance
Accounting and SEC
Auditing
Business investigation services
Business management for entertainers (Gelfand, Rennert & Feldman)
Emerging business services
Mergers and acquisitions

Tax
International tax
Personal financial services
Tax planning
Valuation

Coopers & Lybrand Consulting
Information technology
Resource management
Strategic management services

Human Resource Advisory
Benefit systems
Compliance
Executive compensation
Group health

Process Management
Business process assessment
Process improvement

Representative Clients

American Brands
AT&T
Burlington Northern
DEC
Glaxo
Ito-Yokado
Johnson & Johnson
The Limited
3M
Telmex

KEY COMPETITORS

Arthur Andersen
Bain & Co.
Booz, Allen & Hamilton
Boston Consulting Group
Deloitte & Touche
Delta Consulting
Electronic Data Systems
Ernst & Young
Gemini Consulting
H&R Block
Harcourt General
Hewitt
IBM
A.T. Kearney
KPMG
Marsh & McLennan
McKinsey & Co.
Price Waterhouse

COX ENTERPRISES, INC.

RANK: 77

OVERVIEW

One of the largest media conglomerates in the US, Cox Enterprises is looking to grow. The Atlanta-based company agreed to buy Times Mirror's cable television operations for $2.3 billion in cash and stock in 1994. Cox plans to fold Times Mirror's cable systems and its own into a new publicly traded company, Cox Cable Communications, which Cox will control. The new company will be the 4th largest cable system in the US.

Cox also agreed to a $4.9 billion cable television joint venture with Southwestern Bell, and it ponied up $500 million for QVC's bid to buy Paramount. However, both deals fell through: Viacom bought Paramount, and Southwestern Bell and Cox called off their deal after the 2 decided that new FCC rules would eat up profits.

All these moves are part of Cox's attempts to find the fast lane on the "information superhighway." It is investing in new technologies, including fiber optics, wireless communications, and interactive television.

Cox also publishes 18 daily newspapers, 7 weeklies, and one monthly magazine. It owns 6 broadcast TV stations and 14 radio stations. Cox's Manheim Auctions is the world's largest auto auction operator.

The company is owned by founder James Cox's daughters, Barbara Cox Anthony (mother of CEO Jim Kennedy) and Anne Cox Chambers.

COX ENTERPRISES, INC.

Private company
Fiscal year ends: December 31

WHO

Chairman and CEO: James Cox Kennedy, age 45
SVP and CFO: John R. Dillon
Secretary and VP Legal Affairs: Andrew A. Merdek
VP and Controller: John G. Boyette
VP Tax: Preston B. Barnett
VP Human Resources: Timothy W. Hughes
Auditors: Deloitte & Touche

WHERE

HQ: 1400 Lake Hearn Dr., Atlanta, GA 30319
Phone: 404-843-5000
Fax: 404-843-5142

Cox Enterprises has operations in 29 states and in Canada, Denmark, Poland, and the UK.

WHEN

James Middleton Cox dropped out of school in 1886 at 16 and worked as a teacher, reporter, and congressional secretary before buying the *Dayton Daily News* in 1898. He acquired the nearby *Springfield Press–Republican* in 1905 and soon took up politics. Cox served 2 terms in the US Congress (1909–13) and 3 terms as Ohio governor (1913–15; 1917–21). In 1920 he was the Democratic candidate for president, with Franklin D. Roosevelt as his running mate, but he lost to rival Ohio publisher Warren G. Harding. In 1923 Cox bought the *Miami Daily News* and formed WHIO, Dayton's first radio station. He bought Atlanta's WSB ("Welcome South, Brother"), the South's first radio station, in 1939 and expanded it in 1948 by starting WSB-FM and WSB-TV, the first FM and TV stations in the South. In 1949 Cox started WHIO-FM and WHIO-TV, the first FM and TV stations in Dayton. *The Atlanta Constitution*, now the company's flagship paper, joined Cox's collection in 1950. When Cox died in 1957, his company owned 7 newspapers, 3 TV stations, and several radio stations.

Cox Enterprises expanded its broadcasting interests by buying WSOC-AM/FM/TV (Charlotte, 1959) and KTVU-TV (San Francisco–Oakland, 1963). Cox became one of the first major broadcasting companies to enter cable TV when it purchased a system in Lewistown, Pennsylvania (1962). In 1964 the Cox family's broadcast properties were consolidated in publicly held Cox Broadcasting. Cox newspapers in 1968 were organized under the privately held Cox Enterprises. Also in 1968 the cable holdings became publicly held Cox Cable Communications, and by 1969 Cox was the #2 US cable operator. The broadcasting arm diversified, buying Manheim Services (the nation's largest auto auction operator, 1968) and Kansas City Automobile Auction (1969).

Cox Broadcasting bought TeleRep, a TV advertising sales representation firm, in 1972. Cox Cable was in 9 states and had 500,000 subscribers by 1977, when it rejoined Cox Broadcasting. The broadcasting company changed its name to Cox Communications in 1982; the Cox family took the company private again in 1985 and combined it with Cox Enterprises. James Kennedy, the founder's grandson, became chairman in 1987.

In 1991 Cox merged its Manheim unit with the auto auction business of Ford Motor Credit and GE Capital and bought Val-Pak Direct Marketing, a direct mail coupon company. In the same year Discovery Communications, 1/4-owned by Cox, bought The Learning Channel. In 1993 Cox started a cable and satellite television channel targeted at women in the UK called UK Living. BellSouth partnered with Cox in a venture to offer classified advertising and yellow pages–type information by phone, a service to be expanded to PCs and one that may use other technology. Cox also began providing news via a 511 phone number in Atlanta and South Florida.

In 1994 Cox teamed with Prodigy to put the *Atlanta Journal-Constitution* on-line.

WHAT

Daily Newspapers

The Atlanta Constitution
The Atlanta Journal
Austin American-Statesman
Chandler Arizonan Tribune
The Daily Sentinel (Grand Junction, CO)
The Daily Sentinel (Nacogdoches, TX)
Dayton Daily News
Gazeta Wyborcza (12%, Poland)
Gilbert Tribune (AZ)
Longview News-Journal (TX)
The Lufkin Daily News (TX)
Mesa Tribune (AZ)
Palm Beach Daily News
The Palm Beach Post
Scottsdale Progress Tribune
Springfield News-Sun (OH)
Tempe Daily News Tribune
Waco Tribune-Herald (TX)
The Yuma Daily Sun (AZ)

Radio Stations

KFI (AM), Los Angeles
KOST (FM), Los Angeles
WCKG (FM), Chicago
WCOF (FM), Tampa
WFLC (FM), Miami
WHIO (AM), Dayton
WHKO (FM), Dayton
WHQT (FM), Miami
WIOD (AM), Miami
WSB (AM/FM), Atlanta
WSUN (AM), Tampa
WWRM (FM), Tampa
WYSY (FM), Aurora-Chicago

Television Stations

KTVU (TV), San Francisco
WFTV (TV), Orlando
WHIO (TV), Dayton
WPXI (TV), Pittsburgh
WSB-TV, Atlanta
WSOC (TV), Charlotte

Cable and Other Television

Cox Cable Communications (3.1 million subscribers)
Fibernet (voice, data, video transmission; Norfolk, VA)
Innovative Media (majority interest; Atlanta, GA)
Rysher Entertainment (producer, distributor; Los Angeles)
SBC CableComms UK (25%; Woking, England)
StarSight Telecast (part owner, interactive TV guide)
STOFA A/S (50%; Horsens, Denmark)
TeleRep, Inc. (sales representation, New York)
UK Living (cable and satellite TV channel)

Manheim Auctions

50 auto auctions in the US and Canada

HOW MUCH

	9-Year Growth	1984	1985	1986	1987	1988	1989	1990	1991	1992	1993
Sales ($ mil.)	7.9%	1,347	1,471	1,569	1,665	1,816	1,973	2,094	2,323	2,495	2,675
Cable subscribers (thou.)	2.0%	1,494	1,511	1,372	1,442	1,442	1,555	1,616	1,678	1,722	1,784
Daily newspapers	—	19	19	20	20	20	18	17	17	18	18
Daily circulation (thou.)	—	1,236	1,210	1,250	1,275	1,310	1,306	1,320	1,283	1,256	1,241
Employees	8.4%	15,000	15,000	20,000	20,766	21,612	22,487	24,864	29,943	30,865	31,000

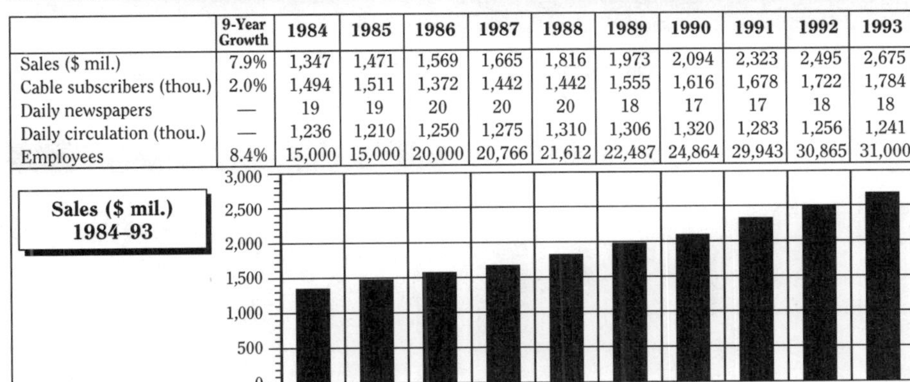

Note: Figures prior to 1985 are for the combined operations of the predecessor companies, Cox Enterprises and Cox Communications.

KEY COMPETITORS

Advance Publications
BET
Blockbuster
Cablevision
Carlson
CBS
Comcast
Continental Cablevision
Dow Jones
Dun & Bradstreet
Gannett
Hearst
Heritage Media
Knight-Ridder
Liberty Media
New York Times
News Corp.
E.W. Scripps
TCI
Thomson Corp.
Time Warner
Times Mirror
Tribune
Turner Broadcasting
Viacom
Washington Post

DEL MONTE FOODS COMPANY

RANK: 166

OVERVIEW

San Francisco–based Del Monte Foods is the country's #1 canner of fruits and vegetables (with 37% and 27%, respectively, of these markets, far ahead of its nearest competitors). Del Monte also cans stewed tomatoes (in which it holds a 36% market share) and makes ketchup, tomato sauce, and Snack Cups (single-serving fruit products and puddings).

In addition to its 14,000 staff members, Del Monte uses 12,000 seasonal employees and operates nearly 70 plants in the US and abroad. Del Monte grows very few of its own products, choosing to concentrate on processing instead. Del Monte buys about 1.2 million tons of produce annually.

Del Monte's food service business sells fruit and vegetable products for use by restaurants, schools, and government agencies. Its private label operations provide packaged food products to grocery chains for resale under their own labels. This business has prospered lately as food retailers have increasingly looked to private label goods to attract cost-conscious customers.

Merrill Lynch and Del Monte management, which had taken over the company in a 1990 LBO, agreed in June 1994 to sell Del Monte to Mexican company Grupo Cabal for roughly $1 billion. However, the deal fell into doubt later in 1994 when the head of Grupo Cabal, Carlos Cabal Peniche, became a fugitive from Mexican justice amid charges of illegal loans and improper financial practices.

Private company
Fiscal year ends: June 30

WHO

President and CEO: Robert W. D'Ornellas, age 43, $397,083 pay
EVP Administration: David M. Little, age 45, $280,629 pay
EVP International Operations: Norman S. Mackenzie, $377,700 pay
EVP Finance and CFO: David L. Meyers, age 47
EVP Sales: Michael J. Stieger, age 47
EVP US Operations: Michael G. Bingham, age 49
SVP, General Counsel, and Secretary: Phyllis Kay Dryden, age 46
VP Corporate Personnel: Mark J. Buxton
VP Corporate Affairs: William J. Spain
Auditors: Ernst & Young

WHEN

The Del Monte brand name was first used by the Oakland Preserving Company, founded in 1891. Uniform brand name labeling was just becoming a significant tool in marketing, and Del Monte, adopted from a coffee blend made for the Hotel Del Monte in Monterey, California, by Oakland Preserving employee Frederick Tillman, became known for high value.

In 1899 Oakland Preserving merged into California Fruit Canners Association (CFCA) with 17 other canneries (half of California's entire canning industry). The new company, the largest canner in the world, adopted Del Monte as its main brand name.

CFCA merged with other California canneries in 1916 to form Calpak. Calpak created national demand for Del Monte products through mass advertising. The company's first ad appeared in the *Saturday Evening Post* in 1917.

Calpak acquired Rochelle Canneries (Illinois), expanding into the Midwest in 1925. That same year it established British Sales Limited, its first overseas sales offices, and Philippine Packing Corporation.

The Depression had a disastrous effect on Calpak. Share prices fell from $6.16 in 1930 to $0.09 in 1931, and the decade was marked by labor unrest. In 1932 the company experienced its worst loss to date, $8.9 million, leading it to omit dividends and to cut salaries. Profits recovered in 1934, but the Depression slowed growth and spurred changes. In 1938 dividends were again halted and salaries cut.

Calpak benefited in several ways from WWII. The war provided a steady source of sales: in 1942 about 40% of the company's products went to feed US troops. Also, despite work stoppage at many overseas plants (including in the Philippines, where workers were interned by the Japanese), international expansion progressed as the US extended its reach, particularly into Asia, in the postwar era. In 1947 sales rose 35% over the previous year, and earnings increased nearly fourfold.

Calpak bought a majority stake in Canadian Canners Limited, the world's 2nd largest canner, in 1956, affording itself an entry into the heavily restricted (to US firms) British market. In the 1960s a venture into soft drink products ended in failure. Calpak changed its name to Del Monte Corporation in 1967.

RJR Industries bought Del Monte for $580 million in 1978. RJR eventually built up its food arm, acquiring Morton Frozen Foods, Heublein, and Nabisco Brands, and became one of the US's largest consumer products companies. Its extensive holdings proved too much, however, when KKR bought RJR in the largest LBO in corporate history in 1989. To reduce debt RJR sold Del Monte, which had been through at least 4 restructurings and a succession of management changes, to Merrill Lynch and Del Monte brass in 1990. A strategic change, to focus on marketing products under a single brand, bore positive results.

In 1993 the company sold its dried fruit operations to Yorkshire Food Group. In early 1994 A. Ewan MacDonald retired as chairman and CEO, and President Robert D'Ornellas assumed the duties of CEO.

WHERE

HQ: One Market Plaza, PO Box 193575, San Francisco, CA 94119
Phone: 415-247-3000
Fax: 415-247-3565

Del Monte has production operations in the US, Mexico, the Caribbean, the Philippines, and Central America and sells its products worldwide.

	1993 Sales		1993 Operating Income	
	$ mil.	% of total	$ mil.	% of total
US	1,380	86	(117)	—
Philippines	170	11	30	—
Latin America	60	3	4	—
Adjustments	(55)	—	—	—
Total	**1,555**	**100**	**(83)**	**—**

WHAT

Areas of Operation
Food service
Food ingredients
Private label
Export sales
Military food supply

Selected Products
Canned fruit
Canned vegetables
Single-serving products
- Fruit products
- Puddings

Tomato Products
Ketchup
Solid/stewed tomatoes
Tomato/spaghetti sauce

Brand Names
Argo
Bonanza
Chicken for Dippin'
Co-Va-Co
Del Monte
Del Monte Fruit Blends
Del Monte Lite
Deliwraps
Fresh Place
Fruit Blends
Fruit-in-Gel Cup
Fruit Naturals
Hometasting
La Costa
La Mesa
Milk Mate
Morton Munchwich
Orange Lane
Ortega
Pasta Classics
Snack Cups
Snap-E-Tom
Summer Crisp
Summer Isles
Sunkist Plus
Vegetable Classics
Yogurt Cup

HOW MUCH

	Annual Growth	1984	1985	1986	1987	1988	1989[1]	1990	1991	1992	1993
Sales ($ mil.)	(2.4%)	—	—	—	—	—	1,717	1,317	1,435	1,431	1,555
Net income ($ mil.)	—	—	—	—	—	—	56	(108)	(27)	(58)	(188)
Employees	(4.5%)	—	—	—	—	—	—	—	15,340	14,500	14,000

Net Income ($ mil.) 1989–93

[1] Fiscal year ending December 31, 1989

KEY COMPETITORS

ADM
Borden
BSN
Cadbury Schweppes
Campbell Soup
Cargill
Chiquita Brands
Coca-Cola
ConAgra
Dole
Fleming
Foster Farms
General Mills
Gold Kist
Grand Metropolitan
Heinz
Kellogg
PepsiCo
Perdue
Philip Morris
Quaker Oats
RJR Nabisco
Sara Lee
SUPERVALU
SYSCO
TLC Beatrice
Tyson Foods
Unilever
Verifine
Whitman

DELOITTE & TOUCHE

RANK: 37

OVERVIEW

The product of a 1989 merger of accounting firms Deloitte Haskins & Sells and Touche Ross, Deloitte & Touche is the 3rd largest of the Big 6 accounting firms in the US. Outside the US the company operates as Deloitte Touche Tohmatsu International, the 5th largest accounting firm in the world.

After a difficult 1992, Deloitte & Touche's worldwide revenues were up in 1993. The firm plans to emphasize its specialized service lines, including mergers and acquisitions, information technology, international tax, cost reduction, manufacturing technology, and employee benefits. The firm is also focusing on retaining and promoting more women. In 1993 it created the Advisory Council on the Advancement of Women, chaired by Lynn Martin, former secretary of labor.

Claims against Big 6 accounting firms have reached an estimated $30 billion in recent years. Deloitte, like its counterparts, has faced a continuing stream of lawsuits as plaintiffs' attorneys name the accounting firms in management fraud suits, blaming them for negligence in oversight.

In 1994 Deloitte was named in a $1.1 billion suit, along with Arthur Andersen and Prudential Securities, alleging that Prudential, with the accounting firms' help, inflated the prices of several limited partnerships.

WHEN

In 1845 — 3 years after the UK initiated an income tax — William Welch Deloitte opened his accounting office in London. Deloitte was the grandson of Count de Loitte, who had fled France during the Reign of Terror (1793–94), abandoned his title, and made a living as a French teacher.

In the early years of his accountancy, William Deloitte, a former staff member of the Official Assignee in Bankruptcy of the City of London, solicited business from bankrupts. During the 1850s and 1860s, Parliament established general rules for forming limited liability companies, which required companies to hire accountants. Deloitte performed accounting for the Great Western Railway and, later, for telegraph companies.

As the firm grew, Deloitte added partners, among them John Griffiths (1869). Griffiths visited the US in 1888, and in 1890 the firm opened a branch on Wall Street. Branches followed in Cincinnati (1905), Chicago (1912), Montreal (1912), Boston (1930), and Los Angeles (1945). In 1952 the firm formed an alliance with accounting firm Haskins & Sells, which operated 34 US offices.

Deloitte developed a reputation as a thorough, and therefore expensive, firm. In the late 1970s a partner proclaimed to *FORTUNE*, "We want to be the Cadillac, not the Ford, of the profession." But the firm, renamed Deloitte Haskins & Sells in 1978, began to lose its conservatism as competition became more intense. When government regulators nudged the profession to drop restrictions on advertising, Deloitte Haskins & Sells was the first Big 8 firm with aggressive ads extolling its virtues.

In 1984, in a move that foreshadowed the merger mania to come, Deloitte Haskins & Sells tried to merge with Price Waterhouse. However, British partners in Price Waterhouse objected to the deal, and it was dropped.

The Big 8 became the Big 6 in 1989. Ernst & Whinney merged with Arthur Young to become Ernst & Young, and Deloitte Haskins & Sells teamed up with Touche Ross & Company to form Deloitte & Touche. Touche Ross had been founded in New York in 1947 and had earned a reputation as the hard-charging, bare-knuckled bad boy of the Big 8, running into trouble over its role in junk-bond deals that turned sour during the 1980s. In 1992 California regulators sued Deloitte & Touche, claiming that it had been the "auditor of choice" of a "daisy chain" linking Drexel Burnham junk-bond king Michael Milken to failed Executive Life.

More legal grief came to Deloitte & Touche that year: the RTC sued the firm for $150 million in connection with its audits of the now-defunct Otero Savings. In 1994 Deloitte & Touche agreed to pay the US government $312 million to settle lawsuits brought by the RTC, the FDIC, and the Office of Thrift Supervision.

HOW MUCH

	Annual Growth	1984	1985	1986	1987	1988	1989	1990	1991	1992	1993
Sales ($ mil.)	11.7%	1,844	1,926	2,339	2,950	3,760	3,900	4,200	4,500	4,800	5,000
Deloitte Haskins & Sells	19.5%	940	953	1,188	1,500	1,920					
Touche Ross	19.4%	904	973	1,151	1,450	1,840					
Offices[1]	(5.3%)	185	192	205	195	196	125	125	116	116	113
Partners[1]	(1.4%)	1,614	1,619	1,600	1,590	1,600	1,652	1,670	1,525	1,472	1,426
Employees[1]	(0.1%)	16,009	17,253	17,521	18,252	19,276	19,668	19,500	16,500	15,300	15,800

1993 Year-end:
US sales per partner: $1,441,000

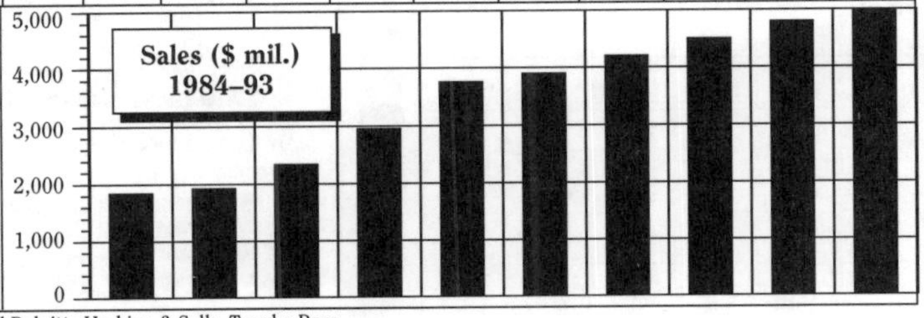

[1]US only; 1984–1988, combined Deloitte Haskins & Sells, Touche Ross

Deloitte & Touche

International partnership
Fiscal year ends: May 31

WHO

Chairman and CEO: J. Michael Cook
Managing Partner: Edward A. Kangas
CFO: Robert W. Pivik
National Director, Marketing and Communications: Gary Gerard
General Counsel: Howard J. Krongard
National Director, Human Resource Operations: James H. Wall

WHERE

HQ: 10 Westport Rd., Wilton, CT 06897
Phone: 203-761-3000
Fax: 203-834-2200

Deloitte & Touche operates offices in over 100 US cities and in over 108 countries worldwide.

	1993 Sales $ mil.	% of total
US	2,055	41
Other countries	2,945	59
Total	**5,000**	**100**

WHAT

	1993 US Sales % of total
Accounting & auditing	54
Tax	23
Management consulting	23
Total	**100**

Selected Services
- Accounting and auditing
- Information technology consulting
- Management consulting
- Mergers and acquisitions consulting
- Tax advice and planning

Representative Clients
- Bank of New York
- Boeing
- Chrysler
- Dow Chemical
- Equitable
- Flagstar
- Great A&P
- Litton Industries
- Mayo Foundation
- Merrill Lynch
- MetLife
- Mitsui
- PPG
- Macy
- RJR Nabisco
- Sears

Affiliated Firms
- Actuarial, Benefits, and Compensation Group (consultation on employee pay and benefits)
- Braxton Associates (strategic planning)
- Deloitte & Touche Eastern Europe
- Deloitte & Touche Valuation Group
- Douglass Group of Deloitte & Touche (health care facility planning and strategy)
- DRT Systems Ltd. (computer consulting)
- DTTI International
- Garr Consulting Group (consulting to retail and wholesale industries)
- Polaris Consulting Services (database, systems development)
- Tohmatsu & Co. (auditing, Japan)

KEY COMPETITORS

- Arthur Andersen
- Bain & Co.
- Booz Allen & Hamilton
- Boston Consulting Group
- Coopers & Lybrand
- Delta Consulting
- Electronic Data Systems
- Ernst & Young
- Gemini Consulting
- Hewitt
- H&R Block
- IBM
- A.T. Kearney
- KPMG
- Marsh & McLennan
- McKinsey & Co.
- Price Waterhouse

DHL WORLDWIDE EXPRESS

RANK: 68

OVERVIEW

DHL Worldwide Express is a major force in air express delivery. DHL operates as 2 separate entities, with DHL Airways (headquartered in Redwood City, California) servicing the US and its territories and DHL International (headquartered in Brussels, Belgium) servicing the rest of the world. In the early 1990s DHL International claimed a market share of 45–50% in the international market, while DHL Airways held a US market share of about 10%. DHL International and DHL Airways act as exclusive agents for each other, but they function as separate business entities. While formed about 3 years after DHL Airways, DHL International has about 5 times more offices than its US counterpart.

Japan Airlines, Lufthansa, and Nissho Iwai (a Japanese trading house) together own 2.5% of DHL Airways and have options to increase their interest to 22.5%. Japan Airlines and Lufthansa each hold 25% of DHL International, and Nissho Iwai has another 7.5%. This alliance provides DHL with a global network of air carriers and shipping facilities.

DHL has grown by being the first company to provide air express service in overseas markets (the Pacific Rim, Eastern Europe, and China). Its expertise in dealing with governments and customs has given it a competitive edge. Surveys of on-time deliveries have credited DHL with superior service. Unlike Federal Express, which seldom uses other airlines, DHL often places its shipments on other carriers, using the money it saves on airplanes to invest in technology and ground handling equipment. The company is currently in the midst of a 4-year, $1.25 billion capital investment program to improve its computer technology, communications, facilities, automation, and handling systems.

WHEN

In 1969 Adrian Dalsey (the D), Larry Hillblom (the H), and Robert Lynn (the L) formulated a long-term plan for success in the overnight delivery business. The 3 shipping executives were looking for a means of improving the turnaround time for ships in ports. Their concept was to fly shipping documents to ports so that they could be examined and processed before the ship arrived. This idea rapidly developed into an express delivery service between California and Hawaii. Bank of America became a primary customer because it wanted a single company to handle its letters of credit and other documents.

Service was expanded to the Philippines in 1971. The next year the 3 original investors asked Po Chung, a Hong Kong entrepreneur, to help them form DHL International, a global delivery network. Chung had no previous experience in the express delivery business, but he had a clear idea of what business wanted from express delivery. He pioneered a simplified rate structure and the single network concept, which required that his company take full responsibility for picking up and delivering the package. Also in 1972 service was extended to Japan, Hong Kong, Singapore, and Australia.

From its Pacific Basin origins, DHL expanded worldwide in the 1970s, moving into Europe in 1974, Latin America in 1977, and the Middle East and Africa in 1978.

An agreement with Hilton in 1980 to provide daily pickup and international delivery garnered new outlets for DHL. After focusing on the development of its international network during its early years, DHL invested heavily in the creation of a delivery network within the US during 1983. Point-to-point delivery was offered to 126 US cities, but DHL held less than 3% of the domestic market. Also in 1983 DHL extended its service to Eastern Europe. In 1985 DHL and Western Union entered a joint venture in which customers could transmit documents by electronic mail. That same year UPS and Federal Express began providing international express delivery in competition with DHL. In 1988 DHL established the first air express joint venture in China.

In 1990 DHL International sold 12.5% of the company to Japan Airlines (5%), Lufthansa (5%), and Nissho Iwai (2.5%). That same year those 3 companies obtained a 2.5% joint interest in the US operations of DHL. The transactions raised $500 million in capital for DHL. In 1992 Japan Airlines, Lufthansa, and Nissho Iwai increased their holdings in DHL International, and DHL and Emery Worldwide agreed to share European and transatlantic aircraft operations.

DHL expanded its operations in China in 1993 by increasing its offices from 3 to 18.

HOW MUCH

	Annual Growth	1983	1984	1985	1986	1987	1988	1989	1990	1991	1992
Estimated sales ($ mil.)	14.9%	—	—	—	—	1,400	1,600	1,900	2,100	2,300	2,800
Employees	9.7%	—	—	—	—	17,000	20,000	20,000	21,000	25,000	26,000

Estimated Sales ($ mil.) 1987–92

Private company

Fiscal year ends: December 31

WHO

Chairman and CEO, DHL International, Ltd.: Patrick Lupo

Group CFO, DHL International, Ltd.: Bob Parker

CEO Asia/Pacific, DHL International, Ltd.: Po Chung

Chairman, President, and CEO, DHL Airways, Inc.: Patrick Foley

COO, DHL Airways, Inc.: Vic Guinasso

SVP Operations, DHL Airways, Inc.: Stephen L. Waller

SVP Sales, DHL Airways, Inc.: Jim Tanchon

SVP Finance and CFO, DHL Airways, Inc.: William Smartt

General Counsel, DHL Airways, Inc.: Ted Orme

SVP Human Resources, DHL Airways, Inc.: Gary Sellers

WHERE

HQ: DHL Airways, Inc., 333 Twin Dolphin Dr., Redwood City, CA 94065

Phone: 415-593-7474

Fax: 415-593-1689

HQ: DHL International, Ltd., Rue du Noyer, 211, 1040 Brussels, Belgium

Phone: +32-2-735-7255

Fax: +32-2-733-2976

DHL Worldwide Express operates 14 hubs and 1,630 offices in 221 countries, including 272 offices in the US.

Hubs

Bahrain
Brussels
Cincinnati
Copenhagen
Frankfurt
Hong Kong
London
Los Angeles
Miami
New York
Panama City
Rio de Janeiro
St. Maarten
Singapore

WHAT

Services

Domestic
- USA Overnight

International
- DHL Worldwide Package Express
- International Airfreight
- International Document Service

Special
- Faxlynk (international facsimile service)
- On-Board Custom Courier Service
- "Same Day" Service (next-flight-out basis)
- Visa-Pak (passport and application pick up, delivery, and return)
- WorldMail

Subsidiaries and Affiliates

DHL Airways, Inc.
DHL International, Ltd.
DHL International de Mexico S.A. de C.V.
DHL International Express Ltd.
DHL International (UK) Ltd.
DHL South America, Inc.

KEY COMPETITORS

Air Express International
Airborne Freight
Consolidated Freightways
Federal Express
Harper Group
Pittston
Roadway
Skynet
UPS
U.S. Postal Service
Yellow Freight

DOMINO'S PIZZA, INC.

RANK: 99

OVERVIEW

Ann Arbor–based Domino's Pizza once dominated the delivery industry by offering nothing but pizza, Coke, and a 30-minute guarantee. The 5,269-store company is still #1 in delivery revenues, but in overall pizza sales it is behind PepsiCo's Pizza Hut and neck and neck with Little Caesar. Having sold more than 245 million pizzas in 1993, the company has about 2.8% of the fast-food market. The company has operations in more than 30 countries.

Domino's has followed 2 years of losses ($68 million in 1991 and $55 million in 1992) with record profits, despite declining sales. Domino's cites restructuring, cost-cutting measures, and the introduction of several new products as reasons for improved profits. A maturing pizza market, however, could hamper growth further and send Domino's into the red once again. The company also eliminated its famous 30-minute delivery guarantee after it drew criticism for allegedly leading delivery drivers to drive recklessly. In 1993 it was ordered to pay nearly $79 million to a St. Louis woman whose car was hit by a Domino's driver who had run a red light.

Devoutly Catholic founder and president Thomas Monaghan owns 98% of Domino's.

Private company
Fiscal year ends: December 31

WHO

Founder and President: Thomas S. Monaghan, age 56
VP Corporate Operations: Nickep Romyananda
VP Franchise Operations: Stuart Mathis
VP; Managing Director, Domino's Pizza International, Inc.: Gary McCausland
VP and CFO: Harry Silverman
VP Distribution: Mike Soignet
Director Human Resources: Mitch Srail
Auditors: Arthur Andersen & Co.

WHERE

HQ: 30 Frank Lloyd Wright Dr., PO Box 997, Ann Arbor, MI 48106-0997
Phone: 313-930-3030
Fax: 313-668-4614

	1993 Stores
US	4,616
Canada	161
Mexico	110
Japan	102
England	75
Australia	32
Puerto Rico	28
Taiwan	23
France	17
Israel	14
Saudi Arabia	10
Other	81
Total	**5,269**

WHEN

Thomas Monaghan's early life was one of hardship. After growing up in an orphanage and numerous foster homes, Monaghan spent his young adult life experimenting, trying everything from a Catholic seminary to a stint in the Marine Corps.

After dropping out of college for financial reasons, in 1960 he borrowed $900 and bought DomiNick's, a bankrupt pizza parlor in Ypsilanti, Michigan, which he operated with the help of his brother James. A year later Monaghan traded a Volkswagen Beetle for his brother's half of the company.

During the next several years, Monaghan learned the pizza business largely by trial and error. After a brief partnership with an experienced restaurateur with whom he later fell out, Monaghan developed a strategy to sell only pizza, to deliver it hot and fresh within 30 minutes, and to locate stores near colleges and military bases. In 1965 the company changed its name to Domino's.

In the 1960s and 1970s, Monaghan endured setbacks that almost ruined the growing company. Among these was a 1968 fire that destroyed Domino's headquarters and a 1975 lawsuit from Amstar Corporation (maker of Domino Sugar) for trademark infringement. After numerous legal battles, the company won, and by 1978 it operated 200 stores.

During the 1980s Domino's experienced phenomenal growth. In 1981 the company created regional offices in 6 cities to oversee its 500 units. Domino's went international 2 years later when it opened a store in Winnipeg, Canada. Between 1981 and 1983 Domino's doubled its number of US stores to 1,000. In 1984 Domino's moved its headquarters to Ann Arbor, Michigan.

The company's growth brought Monaghan a personal fortune. In 1983 he bought the Detroit Tigers baseball team for $53 million and amassed one of the world's largest collections of Frank Lloyd Wright objects (Monaghan had once aspired to be an architect). Monaghan also bought real estate and collected classic cars.

Domino's expansion continued during the mid-1980s. Sales topped $1 billion in 1985 and only 2 years later crossed the $2 billion mark. In 1989 the company introduced pan pizza, its first new product. Also that year Monaghan put the company up for sale. Unable to find a buyer, Monaghan installed a new management group and retired to pursue lay work for the Catholic Church. His religious stance on abortion put him at odds with the National Organization for Women, which urged a boycott of Domino's Pizza in the late 1980s.

When the company's market share began to slip in 1991, Monaghan returned and reorganized management. After his return the company instituted a plan to close the 100 worst-performing stores.

In light of liability problems relating to accidents allegedly arising from the 30-minute delivery guarantee, Domino's began to deemphasize speed and to stress quality.

In 1994 Domino's announced that it would open its first store in North Africa (probably in Cairo) the next year through an agreement with Specialized Catering Services.

WHAT

	1993 Sales % of total
US sales	86
Domino's Pizza International	14
Total	**100**

Major Products

Chicken wings	Salad
Garlic breadsticks	Submarine sandwiches
Pan pizza	Thin-crust pizza
Pizza	Soda

Ingredients Used in 1993	Amount
Bacon	2 million pounds
Beef	4.6 million pounds
Flour	156 million pounds
Green peppers	3.5 million pounds
Ham	4.3 million pounds
Hot peppers	44 thousand pounds
Mozzarella cheese	110 million pounds
Mushrooms	7 million pounds
Olives	151 thousand cases
Pepperoni	17 million pounds
Pineapple	85 thousand cases
Sausage	12 million pounds
Tomatoes	170 million pounds

KEY COMPETITORS

Accor	Papa John's
Buffets	PepsiCo
Flagstar	Rally's
Grand Metropolitan	Schwan's Sales Enterprises
International Dairy Queen	Sonic
Little Caesar	Subway Sandwiches
McDonald's	Uno Restaurant
	Wendy's

HOW MUCH

	Annual Growth	1984	1985	1986	1987	1988	1989	1990	1991	1992	1993
Sales ($ mil.)	15.0%	626	1,100	1,430	2,000	2,300	2,500	2,600	2,400	2,450	2,200
Stores	12.1%	1,887	2,841	3,610	4,279	4,858	5,185	5,342	5,571	5,264	5,269
Employees	5.9%	—	—	—	—	15,000	—	—	23,000	20,000	20,000

Sales ($ mil.) 1984–93

EDWARD J. DEBARTOLO CORPORATION

RANK: 136

OVERVIEW

Edward J. DeBartolo Corporation, based in the founder's hometown of Youngstown, Ohio, is a leading builder and operator of enclosed shopping malls in the US. Edward J. DeBartolo, Sr., and his children own the company. DeBartolo's son and company president Edward Jr. is the owner of the San Francisco 49ers. DeBartolo's daughter Marie Denise York is credited with developing employee programs that have become models for the industry.

Crumbling commercial real estate values and the credit crunch have hurt DeBartolo. With more than $4 billion in debt, the company, to appease creditors, issued an IPO in 1994 that left 48% of the company's retail operations in public hands. (The new subsidiary is called DeBartolo Realty.) DeBartolo had originally planned to sell a majority stake in 51 malls to the public in late 1993 but backed down when the market didn't seem eager enough. The final IPO included 51 malls and 11 community centers in 16 states. The company's take was approximately $575 million, over $150 million more than what the company might have realized from the earlier deal because of the more favorable market conditions.

Edward DeBartolo, now 84, has named his son as the next chairman and Richard Sokolov as his eventual replacement as CEO.

WHEN

Edward J. DeBartolo left his stepfather's paving business in 1948 to establish the company that bears his name. He built subsidized housing in Boardman, Ohio (near Youngstown), for young WWII veterans who were anxious to move to the suburbs. DeBartolo's foresight of the growth of the suburbs led him to build one of the first strip-style malls outside California in Boardman in 1950. Over the next 15 years the company built 45 more strip centers throughout the US.

DeBartolo also anticipated the real estate boom in Florida and bought large tracts of land there in the 1960s. Although the market developed later than DeBartolo had expected, the company had 1/3 of its holdings there when the boom did hit. Also in the 1960s DeBartolo became one of the first to develop large, covered regional malls in many parts of the nation.

DeBartolo opened Louisiana Downs, the first of his racetracks, in 1974; the track closed after 50 days of racing because it could not meet its payroll on time. However, the track prospered in the late 1970s. DeBartolo expanded his sports interests when he bought the San Francisco 49ers in 1977. The Pittsburgh Penguins came under DeBartolo ownership in 1978 when he received them as repayment for a debt.

In 1986 the management of Allied Stores asked DeBartolo to help fend off a bid by Campeau. DeBartolo, recognizing that control of Allied's department store chains would complement his mall development activities by providing anchor stores, instead loaned Campeau $150 million for the takeover. In 1988 he stepped in with a $480 million loan to Campeau for its acquisition of Federated Department Stores. In 1990 DeBartolo acquired a 60.3% stake in Ralphs Grocery Co., a successful Southern California supermarket owned by Campeau, in exchange for forgiveness of the Federated debt.

DeBartolo continued to expand its other interests, opening a new racetrack, Remington Park, in Oklahoma City in 1988. The $94 million racetrack's location was chosen because the company's research indicated that Oklahoma City had the highest number of horses per capita in the US (one horse for every 14 people); the location was a success, with 11,000 people going to the track each race day.

The Rivercenter (San Antonio) and Lakeland Square (Florida) malls also opened in 1988, with over one million square feet apiece; Chesapeake Square (Virginia) and Port Charlotte Town Center (Florida) opened in 1989. DeBartolo in 1991 opened malls in Texas, Virginia, Tennessee, and Illinois.

DeBartolo began unloading assets in 1991 to reduce its $4 billion debt, selling the Pittsburgh Penguins, a private jet, 3 malls, 2 office buildings, and, in 1992, its 50% interest in Higbee's department stores (to Dillard). Also in 1992 the company reached an agreement with its banks that provided it $300 million and a 5-year grace period before it must begin making most of its debt payments.

In 1993 the company sold its Rivercenter project in San Antonio to The L&B Group.

HOW MUCH

	Annual Growth	1984	1985	1986	1987	1988	1989	1990	1991	1992	1993
Estimated sales ($ mil.)	20.0%	—	—	500	650	1,066	1,189	1,350	1,378	1,500	1,800
Total sq. ft. under construction (thou.)	—	—	—	—	—	—	12,377	11,541	8,590	5,402	3,935
Employees	4.5%	—	—	11,000	12,000	12,000	15,000	15,000	15,000	14,000	15,000

Estimated Sales ($ mil.) 1986–93

DeBartolo

Private company
Fiscal year ends: June 30

WHO

Chairman and CEO: Edward J. DeBartolo, Sr., age 84
President and Chief Administrative Officer: Edward J. DeBartolo, Jr., age 45
EVP Corporate Marketing, Communications, and Personnel: Marie Denise DeBartolo York, age 40
SVP Development and General Counsel: Richard S. Sokolov
SVP Corporate Planning and Finance: Anthony W. Liberati
SVP Leasing and Operations: Willam D. Moses

WHERE

HQ: 7620 Market St., Youngstown, OH 44513-6085
Phone: 216-758-7292
Fax: 216-758-3598

DeBartolo maintains and operates 85.6 million square feet of retail space across the US. Branches are located in Cleveland; Dallas; Indianapolis; Miami; Mission Viejo, CA; Orlando; Paramus, NJ; Pittsburgh; South Bend, IN; and Tampa.

WHAT

	1993 Property Under Management % of total
Retail	93
Office	4
Sports	2
Hotel	1
Total	**100**

Major 1993 Projects Managed
Century III Mall, Pittsburgh
The Florida Mall, Orlando
New Orleans Centre, New Orleans
Randall Park Mall, Cleveland
West Town Mall, Knoxville

Major 1993 Development Projects
Brandon Town Center; Brandon, FL
Galleria Crossing, Nashville
Great Northern Mall, Cleveland
The Mall at Robinson Town Centre, Pittsburgh
Pembroke Lakes Mall; Pembroke Pines, FL
The Plaza at Brandon Town Center; Brandon, FL

Other Investments
Ralphs Grocery Co. (Los Angeles)
San Francisco 49ers (football team)
DeBartolo Realty (REIT; 52%)

KEY COMPETITORS

Albertson's
American Stores
Axiom Real Estate
Breslin Realty Development
Cafaro
Food 4 Less
Helmsley
Hines Interests
Hughes Markets
Hutensky Group
JMB Realty
L&B Group
LaSalle Partners
Lincoln Property
Longs
Melvin Simon & Assocs.
Olympia & York
PM Realty Group
Prudential
Rouse
Safeway
Sears
Stater Bros.
Taubman
Trammell Crow
Vons
Weingarten Realty
Zeckendorf

ENTERPRISE RENT-A-CAR

RANK: 152

OVERVIEW

Enterprise Rent-A-Car is not #1 and does not try harder to be #2 in the car rental industry. Instead, the St. Louis–based company avoids big competitors like Hertz and Avis in the travel segment of the industry, choosing to dominate the replacement end of the market. Replacement car renters include customers who temporarily need transportation after their cars are stolen or damaged. The company is one of the 5 largest car rental agencies in the US.

Founder Jack Taylor and his family own 85% of the company, with management owning the rest. His only son, Andrew, is CEO. In addition to renting cars, the company leases cars and light trucks (Enterprise Leasing); manages fleets of vehicles for other companies (Enterprise Fleets); and sells cars, both new (ELCO Chevrolet) and used (Enterprise Car Sales). As a service to property and casualty adjusters, Enterprise operates Claims Connection, which allows adjusters to arrange for rental cars with a single phone call. Through Enterprise Capital Group, the company owns Courtesy Products (a coffee, tea, and cocoa distributor for hotels in North America, Japan, and Europe), Crawford Supply (a provider of nonfood products, such as cards and writing supplies, to prison commissaries), and Monogramme Confections (a maker of candies and nuts).

Taylor has built Enterprise by emphasizing customer service (i.e., pickup and delivery of a car to the renter's home or office), helping adjusters whenever possible, promoting from within, and sharing profits with employees.

WHEN

In 1957 Jack Taylor, a veteran US Navy fighter pilot from WWII, hit on the idea that leasing cars might be an easier way to make money than selling them. At the time Taylor was the sales manager for a Cadillac dealership in St. Louis. Taylor's idea sounded good to his boss, Arthur Lindburg, who agreed to set Taylor up in the leasing business. In return for a 50% pay cut, Taylor received 25% of the new enterprise, called Executive Leasing, that began in the walled-off body shop of a car dealership.

In the early 1960s Taylor started renting cars for short periods of time as well as leasing them. When his leasing agents expressed annoyance with the rental operation, Taylor turned that business over to Don Holtzman. Holtzman realized that his 17-car rental operation was too little to take on industry giants like Hertz and Avis; instead, he concentrated on the "home city" or replacement market. He offered competitive rates to adjusters who needed to find cars for insureds whose cars were damaged or stolen. Propelled by court decisions that required casualty companies to pay for their insured's loss of transportation, Taylor expanded from his St. Louis base in 1969 with a branch office in Atlanta. Since another car leasing outfit in Georgia was already named Executive, Taylor changed the name of his company to Enterprise.

The company expanded into Florida and Texas in the early 1970s, targeting garages and body shops that performed repairs for insureds. Oil price shocks of that period compelled Taylor to diversify his operations. In 1974 the company acquired Keefe Coffee and Supply, a supplier of coffee, packaged foods, and beverages to prison commissaries. To service *FORTUNE* 1000 companies that lease or purchase more than 50 vehicles, the company started Enterprise Fleets in 1976.

In 1980 Enterprise acquired Courtesy Products. The following year sales reached the $100 million mark. In 1984 the company acquired Monogramme Confections, a supplier of candies and nuts. ELCO Chevrolet was acquired in 1986. That same year Enterprise formed Crawford Supply. The following year Taylor bought out the balance of the Lindburg family's interest in Enterprise.

In 1988 the company acquired Enterprise Cellular, and the following year Enterprise initiated a national television campaign that focused on an older and higher-income audience by showing its commercials exclusively on CBS. Also in the late 1980s, Enterprise began targeting "discretionary rentals"—families with visiting relatives or with children home for the holidays.

In 1990 Enterprise created adjuster referral service Claims Connection. Jack Taylor's son, Andrew, became CEO of the company in 1991, and Enterprise posted sales over $1 billion for the first time. In 1993 Enterprise began construction of a new $17 million, 210,000-square-foot, five-story corporate headquarters in St. Louis.

HOW MUCH

	9-Year Growth	1984	1985	1986	1987	1988	1989	1990	1991	1992	1993
Sales ($ mil.)	28.1%	179	237	329	402	500	687	889	1,022	1,124	1,659
Employees	24.2%	1,500	1,600	1,900	2,300	—	4,500	5,241	7,750	8,500	14,000

Private company
Fiscal year ends: July 31

WHO

Chairman: Jack Crawford Taylor, age 71
President & CEO: Andrew C. Taylor, age 45
EVP: Douglas S. Brown
SVP: Marcus T. Cohn
SVP: Wayne C. Kaufmann
SVP: Warren C. Knaup
SVP: Donald L. Ross
President, Enterprise Capital Group: Douglas A. Albrecht
EVP and General Manager, Enterprise Fleets, Inc.: Ernest C. Behnke
VP and General Manager, ELCO Chevrolet: Mark S. Hadfield
VP and General Manager, Enterprise Cellular: David W. Hermann
VP and General Manager, Keefe Coffee and Supply: David C. Kruse
VP and General Manager, Crawford Supply: Donald L. Marsh
VP and General Manager, Monogramme Confections: John A. Spesia
VP and CFO: John T. O'Connell
VP Human Resources: Jerry Spector

WHERE

HQ: 8850 Ladue Rd., St. Louis, MO 63124
Phone: 314-863-7000
Fax: 314-863-7621

Enterprise Rent-A-Car operates a fleet of more than 130,000 cars and trucks through more than 1,400 offices in the US.

WHAT

Subsidiaries

Claims Connection (adjuster referral service)
Courtesy Products (in-room coffee, cocoa, and tea for hotel patrons; Cafe Valet)
Crawford Supply (nonfood products such as cards, games, personal care items, stationery and writing supplies, dietary supplements, and apparel for prison commissaries)
ELCO Chevrolet Inc. (car dealership, St. Louis)
Enterprise Car Sales (used car sales)
Enterprise Cellular (cellular telecommunications)
Enterprise Fleets, Inc. (vehicle fleet management)
Enterprise Leasing (car and light truck leasing)
Keefe Coffee & Supply Company (packaged foods and beverages for prison commissaries, Keefe Kitchens)
Monogramme Confections (candies and nuts; Monogramme, Stoll's, and E.Z. Digby)

KEY COMPETITORS

Agency Rent-A-Car
Alamo Rent A Car
Avis
Budget Rent A Car
Chrysler
Dollar Rent A Car
Ford
General Motors
Mitsubishi
PepsiCo
Philip Morris
RJR Nabisco

ERNST & YOUNG LLP

RANK: 33

OVERVIEW

The 2nd largest accounting firm in the US after Arthur Andersen, Ernst & Young is the product of the 1989 merger of former Big 8 brethren Ernst & Whinney and Arthur Young. The firm provides accounting and auditing services as well as management consulting, human resources services, regulatory consulting, and other services.

The New York–based firm has been able to attract some hot new clients lately, leading the profession in signing on companies that have recently tendered initial public offerings. However, for the past 2 years it has also led the Big 6 in a dubious category, client defections.

Looking for ways to reduce costs, the firm is cutting its office space by allocating space only when it is specifically needed.

Ernst & Young, like its Big 6 counterparts, has faced mounting legal troubles recently, as investors and the government have brought suit against auditors of failed companies. In an effort to lower its litigation costs, the company continues to shed its riskier clients (such as real estate ventures and financial services companies).

In 1993 Philip Laskawy was picked to replace current chairman Ray Groves when Groves's term ends in October 1994.

WHEN

While the 1494 publication in Venice of Luca Pacioli's *Summa di Arithmetica* (the first published work dealing with double-entry bookkeeping) boosted the accounting profession, it wasn't until the Industrial Revolution in England that accountants developed their craft.

Frederick Whinney joined the UK firm of Harding & Pullein in 1849. R. P. Harding reputedly had been a hat maker whose business ended up in court. The ledgers he produced were so well kept that an official advised him to take up accounting.

Whinney's name was added to the firm in 1859. Later his sons became partners, and in 1894 firm's name changed to Whinney, Smith & Whinney, which became the longest-lived of the firm's many names, lasting until 1965.

After WWII, Whinney, Smith & Whinney formed an alliance with the US firm of Ernst & Ernst, which had been founded in Cleveland in 1903 by brothers Alwin and Theodore Ernst. The alliance, which recognized that the accountants' business clients were getting larger and more international in orientation, provided that each firm would operate in the other's behalf within their respective markets.

In 1965 the Whinney firm merged with Brown, Fleming & Murray to become Whinney Murray. The merger also included the fledgling computer department — the harbinger of electronic accounting systems — set up by Brown, Fleming & Murray to serve British Petroleum. Whinney Murray also formed joint ventures with other accounting firms to provide consulting services.

In 1979 Whinney Murray and Turquands Barton Mayhew — itself the product of a merger that began with a cricket match — united with Ernst & Ernst to form Ernst & Whinney, a firm with an international scope.

Ernst & Whinney still wasn't finished merging. Having grown to be the world's 4th largest accounting firm by 1989, it merged with the 5th largest, Arthur Young. Arthur Young had taken its name from the Scottish immigrant who had founded a partnership with C. U. Stuart in Chicago in 1894. When Stuart withdrew, Young took brother Stanley as a partner. The Arthur Young firm had long been known as the "old reliable" of the accounting giants. In 1984 the spotlight shone on it as vice-presidential candidate Geraldine Ferraro chose the firm to sort out her tax troubles.

The new firm of Ernst & Young faced a rocky start. At the end of 1990, it was forced to defend itself from rumors of collapse. In 1991 it pared back the payroll, thinning the ranks of partners and others. That same year it agreed to pay the RTC $41 million to settle claims stemming from its involvement with Charles Keating's Lincoln Savings and Loan.

The next year Ernst & Young agreed to pay $400 million for allegedly mishandling the audits of 4 failed S&Ls. In 1994 a federal judge in Rhode Island ordered Ernst & Young and the state to negotiate a settlement of a suit brought by Rhode Island, which claimed the firm's faulty audits had helped lead to the failure of Rhode Island's credit union system.

HOW MUCH

	Annual Growth	1984	1985	1986	1987	1988	1989	1990	1991	1992	1993
Sales ($ mil.)	12.1%	2,088	2,345	2,919	3,480	4,244	4,200	5,006	5,406	5,701	5,839
Arthur Young	—	1,060	1,160	1,427	1,702	2,053					
Ernst & Whinney	—	1,028	1,185	1,492	1,778	2,191					
Offices	1.1%	—	—	—	—	—	—	642	673	660	663
Partners	(0.6%)	—	—	—	—	—	—	5,609	5,665	5,300	5,318
Employees	(1.8%)	—	—	—	—	—	—	61,591	61,173	58,900	58,377

1993 Year-end:
Sales per partner: $1,097,969

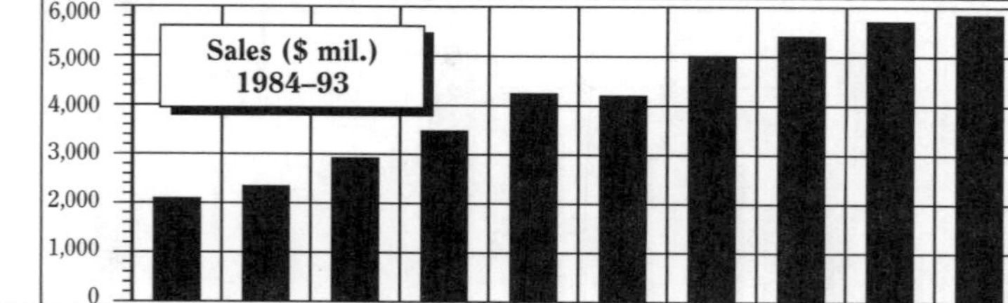

ERNST & YOUNG

International partnership
Fiscal year ends: September 30

WHO

Chairman: Philip A. Laskawy
Co-Chairman: William L. Kimsey
CEO, International: Michael A. Henning
VC Finance and Administration: Hilton Dean
VC Human Resources: Bruce J. Mantia
General Counsel: Carl D. Liggio

WHERE

HQ: 787 Park Ave., New York, NY 10019
Phone: 212-773-3000
Fax: 212-773-1996

Ernst & Young maintains more than 600 offices in over 100 countries.

	1993 Sales	
	$ mil.	% of total
US	2,351	40
Other countries	3,488	60
Total	**5,839**	**100**

WHAT

	1993 US Sales
	% of total
Accounting & auditing	51
Tax	22
Management consulting	27
Total	**100**

Selected Services

Human Resources Services
Actuarial, benefits, and compensation consulting
Personal financial counseling

Industry Services
Accounting, auditing, and tax services
Health care consulting

International Services
International tax compliance and consulting services
Investment services

Management Consulting
Organization alignment and change management
Performance measurement

Outsourcing Services
Corporate tax functions
Financial and accounting systems
Internal audit functions

Regulatory and Related Services
Environmental consulting
Health care legislative services
Insurance regulatory services
Tax policy and legislative services

Special Services
Capital markets services
Cash management services
Corporate finance services

Representative Clients

Apple Computer
BankAmerica
Coca-Cola
Eli Lilly
Hanson
Knight-Ridder
Martin Marietta
McDonald's
Mobil
Time Warner
USF&G
Wal-Mart

KEY COMPETITORS

Arthur Andersen
Bain & Co.
Booz, Allen & Hamilton
Coopers & Lybrand
Deloitte & Touche
Electronic Data Systems
H&R Block
Hewitt
KPMG
Marsh & McLennan
McKinsey & Co.
Price Waterhouse

ESTÉE LAUDER INC.

RANK: 81

OVERVIEW

Based in New York, Estée Lauder, described by *Forbes* as the largest privately held cosmetics and fragrances company in the world, is actually a group of companies, each with its own marketing and sales department. Group companies include Aramis, Clinique Laboratories, and Origins Natural Resources. The group focuses on higher-end products, sold only in top department and specialty stores.

The group's companies are controlled by the Lauder family, including Estée (who founded the company with her husband, Joseph) and her 2 sons, Leonard, the company's CEO, and Ronald. The group has no formal board of directors, preferring to keep all authority within the family.

Estée Lauder continues to break into new international markets ahead of its competitors. In 1992 it became the first US cosmetic company to open stores in Russia and Hungary, and in 1993 the company moved into Poland, China, and India.

WHEN

Estée Lauder (then Josephine Esther Mentzer) started her beauty career by selling skin care products formulated by her Hungarian uncle, John Schotz, during the 1930s. Eventually she packaged and peddled her variations of her uncle's formulas, which included an all-purpose face cream and a cleansing oil.

With the help of her husband, Joseph Lauder, she set up her first office in New York City in 1944 and added lipstick, eye shadow, and face powder to her line. Joseph oversaw production, and Estée sold her wares to beauty salons and department stores, using samples and gifts to convince customers to buy her products. At one Manhattan beauty salon, Estée Lauder asked the owner about her blouse: Where had she bought it? The owner replied that she didn't need to know, because she would never be able to afford it. Lauder has been driven ever since. Throughout the 1950s Lauder traveled cross-country, first to sell her line to high-profile department stores like Neiman-Marcus, I. Magnin, and Saks and later to train saleswomen in the same stores.

Estée Lauder created her first fragrance, a bath oil called Youth Dew, in 1953. In the late 1950s many of the large cosmetics houses in the US introduced "European" skin care lines, products that had scientific-sounding names and supposedly advanced skin repair properties. Estée Lauder's contribution was Re-Nutriv cream. It sold for $115 a pound in 1960, the same year the company hit the million-dollar profit mark. The advertising campaign for the cream established the "Lauder look": aristocratic, sophisticated, and tastefully wealthy, an image that Estée Lauder herself cultivated.

In 1964 the company introduced Aramis, a fragrance for men, and in 1968, with the help of a *Vogue* editor, launched Clinique, one of the first hypoallergenic skin care lines. In 1972 Estée Lauder's son Leonard became president, although Estée remained CEO.

By 1978 Aramis cologne and aftershave accounted for 50–80% of men's fragrance sales in some department stores. Also in 1978 the company put out 2 fragrances for women, White Linen and Cinnabar. In 1979 Estée Lauder introduced Prescriptives, a skin care and makeup line targeted at young professional women.

Much of Estée's work has been as a living symbol of the confident sophisticate, sharing meals with royalty and the rich. When Princess Diana was to be fêted at a White House dinner, she commanded the presence of Bruce Springsteen, Robert Redford, and Estée Lauder.

Between 1978 and 1983, the R&D budget for skin care products was increased, resulting in Night Repair, one of the company's largest-selling formulas. Leonard Lauder was named CEO in 1983. By 1988 the company had captured 1/3 of the US market in prestige cosmetics.

Leonard's brother, Ronald, had left the company in 1983 to become deputy assistant secretary for defense. He returned after losing an expensive bid to become mayor of New York in 1989 (reportedly spending $350 per vote).

During the early 1990s Estée Lauder unveiled its new Origins line of environmentally safe cosmetics. In 1990 the company recruited former Calvin Klein executive Robin Burns to head its domestic branch. Burns quickly made her mark at Estée Lauder by breathing life back into the company's traditionally conservative advertising. In 1991 the company launched the All Skins line of cosmetics.

In late 1993 the company introduced Resilience, a skin care product designed to combat signs of premature aging.

HOW MUCH

	9-Year Growth	1984	1985	1986	1987	1988	1989	1990	1991	1992	1993
Sales ($ mil.)	10.2%	1,200	1,200	1,350	1,600	1,730	1,865	2,010	2,160	2,420	2,614
Employees	2.3%	10,000	10,000	10,000	10,000	10,000	10,000	10,000	12,000	12,000	12,000

Sales ($ mil.) 1984–93

ESTĒE LAUDER

Private company
Fiscal year ends: December 31

WHO

Chairman: Estée Lauder, age 85
President and CEO: Leonard A. Lauder, age 61
Chairman, Estée Lauder International, Inc., and Clinique: Ronald S. Lauder, age 49
President and CEO, Estée Lauder U.S.A.: Robin Burns
President, Estée Lauder International, Inc.: Jeanette S. Wagner
EVP and COO: Fred H. Langhammer
SCVP: Evelyn H. Lauder
SVP and CFO: Robert J. Bigler
SVP Estée Lauder Product Development Worldwide: Dominique Szabo, age 53
SVP Public Relations: Rebecca C. McGreevy

WHERE

HQ: 767 5th Ave., New York, NY 10153-0002
Phone: 212-572-4200
Fax: 212-572-3941

Estée Lauder's products are sold worldwide.

Manufacturing Plants
Australia
Belgium
Canada
Spain
Switzerland
UK
US
Venezuela

WHAT

Group Companies

Aramis Inc.
Aramis Classic
Aramis 900
Lab Series
New West for Him
New West Skinscent for Her
Tuscany

Clinique Laboratories Inc.
(allergy-tested skin care and makeup)
Clinique skin care
Precision makeup
Skin Supplies for Men

Estée Lauder Inc.
(treatment, makeup, and fragrances)
Advanced Night Repair
Cinnabar
Lauder for Men
SpellBound
White Linen

Estée Lauder International, Inc.
(international marketing and sales for Lauder companies)

Origins Natural Resources Inc.
(natural skin care products with environmentally safe packaging and no animal testing)
Origins stores

Prescriptives, Inc.
(makeup and skin care for professional women)
All Skins (115 shades of foundation)
Calyx (fragrance)
Custom Blended Powder and Foundation
Exact skin care products

KEY COMPETITORS

Alberto-Culver
Allou
Amway
Avon
Body Shop
Colgate-Palmolive
Gillette
Helene Curtis
Jean Philippe Fragrances
Johnson & Johnson
Johnson Publishing
L'Oréal
LVMH
MacAndrews & Forbes
Mary Kay
Nature's Sunshine
Neutrogena
Procter & Gamble
Shiseido
Unilever

FARMLAND INDUSTRIES, INC.

RANK: 39

OVERVIEW

Kansas City–based Farmland is the largest agricultural cooperative in the United States. Its membership consists of other local cooperatives throughout the Midwest as well as individual pork and beef producers. In all, it serves the needs of more than 500,000 producers. As a cooperative it is owned by its members and exists to assist them in producing and marketing their products (output) and to provide them with many of the goods and services necessary for farm production (input). This gives them a combined market strength to compete with the public and private giants.

Products that Farmland manufactures and distributes include animal feed and nutritional supplements and petroleum products such as fuels and fertilizers. Farmland also provides informational services about animal nutrition and environmental regulations. Its profits are rebated to its members.

The co-op provides outlets for its members' products. Its beef and pork processing facilities produce fresh and cured meats under several brand names, adding value to these products and helping to shield members from the jolts of the commodities markets.

Farmland has significant trade with Japan and staunchly supported NAFTA because of its growing pork trade in Latin America. In 1993 it opened an office in Mexico City. Farmland hopes to achieve a 50–50 balance between input and output sales by the year 2000.

Farmland

Agricultural cooperative
Fiscal year ends: August 31

WHO

President and CEO: H. D. Cleberg
EVP and CFO: John F. Berardi
EVP Ag Input Operations: Robert W. Honse
EVP; Director General Farmland Industrias, S.A. de C.V.: Stephen P. Dees
SVP Ag Production Marketing/Processing: Gary Evans
Human Resources: Holly McCoy
Auditors: KPMG Peat Marwick

WHERE

HQ: 3315 North Oak Trafficway, Kansas City, MO 64116
Phone: 816-459-6000
Fax: 816-459-6979

Farmland operates in Illinois, Iowa, Kansas, Nebraska, Oklahoma, and South Dakota, and has an office in Mexico City.

WHEN

US agriculture has always been sensitive to boom and bust cycles and to the ups and downs of raw commodities prices.

After a golden age of supplying food for a world rent by WWI, US agriculture had a bad time of it during the 1920s. Many solutions were proposed, including the imposition of import/export tariffs. In 1929 the newly elected Herbert Hoover called a special session of Congress to deal with farm issues. The result was the Agricultural Marketing Act, which encouraged the formation of cooperatives. These were widely viewed as anticapitalistic.

One of the cooperatives formed was the Union Oil Company, Farmland's original predecessor. Union Oil was intended to provide petroleum supplies to farmers in a period of rapid agricultural mechanization.

But the Agricultural Marketing Act failed to improve conditions because 1928–29 grain production worldwide reached record levels. The glut ground down prices, and the Depression and drought dried up markets.

In the early 1930s, as the government sought to regulate supply by introducing payments for taking land out of production, Union Oil increased the range of its cooperative activities. It changed its name to Consumers Cooperative Association in 1935.

Farming did not revive until WWII, though price controls and supports remained an important feature of agricultural policy.

Throughout this period, the performance of Consumers Cooperative's growing membership of primary producers and local cooperatives remained tied to raw commodities prices, and the company's sales remained tied to the provision of fuels and other supplies, particularly fertilizers, to its members.

In 1959, however, to decrease its reliance on commodity prices, Consumers Cooperative bought a pork-processing plant in Denison, Iowa, and began making Farmbest meat products. It was a success, and 4 years later the company opened another plant in Iowa Falls. In 1966 Consumers Cooperative became Farmland Industries.

In the 1970s it expanded into beef production also, but when beef prices and consumption declined, it exited beef production.

As Farmland increased its output emphasis, it tried to decrease its input side, especially after the crash of oil prices in 1986 cost the company $90 million and almost bankrupted it. Since then the company has reduced the number and value of its petroleum and agricultural chemical production assets by selling refineries and other facilities.

Farmland has a flexible approach to marketing. After a period of volatile prices, the company stopped handling grains in 1985 but profitably reentered the market in 1992. In 1993 it resumed beef processing and expanded its pork-processing facilities. Farmland plans to expand its value-added product line. In 1993 it added a deli line and increased its business with restaurants and national accounts such as Pizza Hut, Subway, and Sam's Clubs.

WHAT

	1993 Sales		1993 Operating Income	
	$ mil.	$ of total	$ mil.	% of total
Petroleum	893	19	(7)	—
Chemicals	893	19	49	58
Feed	482	10	19	23
Foods	1,416	30	16	19
Grain	954	20	—	—
Other	105	2	—	—
Adjustments	(20)	—	—	—
Total	**4,723**	**100**	**77**	**100**

Feeds
Animal feed products
Liquid feed supplements

Fertilizer/Ag Chemicals
Fertilizers
Herbicides
Insecticides

Petroleum
Gas
Distillates
Fuels
Propane
Lube oils
Automotive parts and accessories

Brand Name Meats
Bavarian Ham
Brown Sugar Pit Ham
Extra Tender
Maple River
Marco Polo
Market Place
Premium Deli

Retail/Service
Business services
Convenience stores
Finance company
Fuel stations

HOW MUCH

	Annual Growth	1984	1985	1986	1987	1988	1989	1990	1991	1992	1993
Sales ($ mil.)	5.0%	3,042	2,967	2,703	2,590	2,817	2,975	3,378	3,638	3,429	4,723
Net income ($ mil.)	—	(11)	(60)	(152)	55	51	99	49	43	62	(30)
Members	—	2,277	2,269	2,265	2,186	2,123	2,068	2,002	1,820	—	—
Employees	—	8,217	8,256	7,495	6,246	5,670	6,372	6,691	7,126	7,616	8,155

1993 Year-end:
Debt ratio: 58.9%
Return on equity: —
Cash (mil.): $28
Current ratio: 1.40
Long-term debt (mil.): $486
Total assets (mil.): $1,720

Net Income ($ mil.) 1984–93

100
50
0
-50
-100
-150
-200

KEY COMPETITORS

ADM
Ag Processing
Agway
American Cyanamid
Amoco
Anheuser-Busch
Ashland
Campbell Soup
Cargill
Chevron
Circle K
Continental Grain
Dial
DuPont
General Mills
W. R. Grace
Grand Metropolitan
Hormel
IBP
Mobil
Monsanto
Pennzoil
Salomon
Southland
Tysons

FMR CORPORATION

RANK: 83

OVERVIEW

FMR is the holding company for Fidelity Investments, the largest family of mutual funds in the world, with $258 billion in assets, and Fidelity Brokerage Services, the #2 discount brokerage in the US (after Charles Schwab). Holding an 11% market share of the industry's assets, Fidelity's mutual funds own about 1% of all publicly traded stock in the US. FMR also has operations in insurance, credit cards, real estate, transportation, and publishing, among other things, and owns an art gallery. CEO Edward (Ned) Johnson and his family hold 81% of the company; management owns the rest.

To attain its dominant position in the investment business, FMR combined impressive investment performance, innovation, aggressive marketing, and swift adoption of technology. The company is known for giving its fund managers broad authority to invest assets of the funds. When account growth stalled beginning in the late 1980s, FMR responded by cutting prices and catering to beginning investors. The company mostly markets its funds directly to customers rather than through brokers and is one of the last direct-marketing mutual funds to charge a "load," or fee, for new investments.

FMR's Magellan is the world's largest mutual fund, with over $30 billion in assets distributed among over 600 stocks and 2 million shareholders. By investing in technology and energy companies while avoiding pharmaceutical and food companies, Magellan grew 24.7% in 1993, outperforming the S&P 500, which gained 10%.

WHEN

In 1930 Fidelity Fund was formed by Anderson & Cromwell, a Boston money management firm. Edward C. Johnson II became president of Fidelity Fund in 1943 when it had $3 million invested in Treasury bills. Johnson diversified into stocks, and by 1945 the fund had grown to $10 million. In 1946 Johnson established Fidelity Management and Research, the predecessor of Fidelity Investments, to act as investment advisor to Fidelity Fund.

In the early 1950s Johnson hired Gerry Tsai, a young immigrant from Shanghai, to analyze stocks. In 1957 Johnson put Tsai in charge of Fidelity Capital Fund. Tsai's investments in speculative stocks such as Xerox and Polaroid paid off, and within 10 years he was managing a portfolio of more than $1 billion.

The highly successful Magellan Fund was established in 1962. In subsequent years the company entered the markets for corporate pension plans (FMR Investment Management in 1964), retirement plans for self-employed individuals (Fidelity Keogh Plan in 1967), and investors outside the US (Fidelity International in 1968).

In 1972 FMR was formed. That same year Johnson turned control of Fidelity over to his son Ned. Ned initiated FMR's vertical integration by selling directly to customers rather than through brokers and assuming back-office accounting operations from banks. The next year he formed Fidelity Daily Income Trust, the first money market fund to offer check writing. Peter Lynch was hired as manager of the Magellan Fund in 1977. Under his management, Magellan grew from $20 million to $12 billion in assets and outperformed all other mutual funds. Fidelity Brokerage Services was established in 1978, making Fidelity the first major financial institution in the US to offer discount brokerage services.

In 1980 the company launched a nationwide network of branch offices, and it entered the credit card business in 1986. The Wall Street crash of 1987 hit Fidelity's Magellan Fund hard, forcing the liquidation of almost $1 billion in stock in a single day. That same year FMR moved into the insurance business by offering its customers variable life, single-premium, and deferred annuities policies. In 1989 the company introduced the Spartan Fund, targeted toward large, less active investors interested in lower expense charges.

In the early 1990s Magellan's performance sagged, and the fund dropped from the #1 spot in the industry to #3. Most of Fidelity's best performers were from its 36 "select" funds, which focus on narrow industry segments. Early in 1994 the SEC began an investigation of the personal trading accounts of FMR's portfolio managers to find out if they had profited from improper trading.

HOW MUCH

	9-Year Growth	1984	1985	1986	1987	1988	1989	1990	1991	1992	1993
Sales ($ mil.)	25.0%	344	470	804	1,075	872	1,083	1,272	1,474	1,824	2,570
Net income ($ mil.)	29.3%	22	39	87	81	24	53	32	89	125	225
Income as % of sales	—	6.5%	8.3%	10.8%	7.5%	2.8%	4.9%	2.5%	6.0%	6.9%	8.8%
Assets under mgmt. ($ bil.)	28.4%	27	39	65	75	84	109	119	156	181	258
Total accounts (mil.)	24.6%	2	3	5	6	6	7	6	7	13	17
Employees	21.1%	2,300	2,900	5,600	8,100	5,600	6,500	7,000	7,700	9,000	12,900

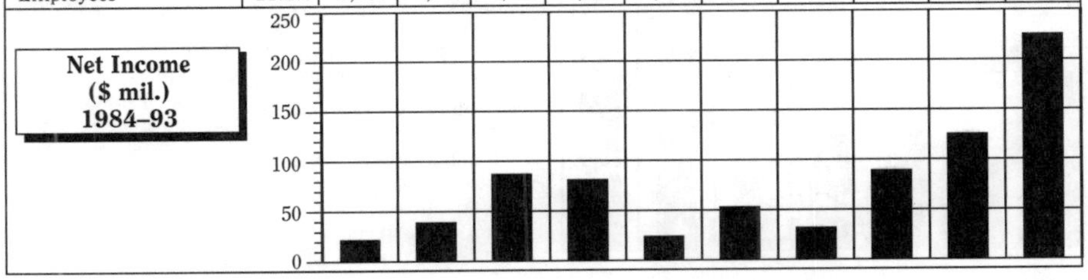

Fidelity Investments

Private company
Fiscal year ends: December 31

WHO

Chairman, President, and CEO: Edward (Ned) C. Johnson III, age 63
EVP: Mark A. Peterson, age 52
President, Fidelity Brokerage Services, Inc.: Roger T. Servison, age 48
SVP and CFO: Denis M. McCarthy
VP and Corporate Counsel: David C. Weinstein
Manager, Fidelity Magellan Fund: Jeff Vinik
Manager, Fidelity Dividend Growth Fund: Abigail P. Johnson, age 31
SVP Administration (Human Resources): Jerry Lieberman, age 46
Auditors: Coopers & Lybrand

WHERE

HQ: 82 Devonshire St., Boston, MA 02109
Phone: 617-570-7000
Fax: 617-720-3836

WHAT

Boston Coach Corp. (executive ground transportation)
Community Newspaper Co. (64 weekly suburban Boston newspapers)
Fidelity Brokerage Services, Inc.
Fidelity Investments (mutual funds)
- Aggressive growth equity (Advisor Growth Opportunity, Emerging Growth, Low-Priced Stock, Retirement Growth)
- Corporate fixed-income (Intermediate Bond, Short-term Bond)
- Flexible fixed-income (Advisor Short Fixed Income, Investment Grade Bond)
- Global equity (Emerging Markets, Europe, International Growth & Income, Overseas, Pacific Basin)
- Global fixed-income (Global Bond, Short-Term World Income)
- Gold equity (Select-American Gold, Select-Precious Metals & Minerals)
- Growth & income equity (Blue Chip Growth, Capital Appreciation, Contrafund, Convertible Securities, Destiny I & II, Disciplined Equity, Equity Income I, Growth Company, Growth & Income, Magellan, Market Index, Over-the-Counter, Stock Selector, Trend, Value)
- High yield fixed-income (Advisor High Yield, Capital and Income)
- Hybrid equity (Advisor Income and Growth, Asset Manager, Asset Manager-Growth, Balanced, Equity Income II, Puritan)
- Municipal fixed-income (Advisor High Income Municipals, Aggressive Tax-Free, Limited Term Municipals, Municipal Bond, Spartan Municipal Income, Spartan Short-Term Municipals)
- Sector equity (Select-Health Care, Select-Telecommunications, Select-Utilities, Utilities Income)
- US government fixed-income (GNMA Portfolio, Government Securities, Mortgage Securities, Spartan Government Income, Spartan Limited Maturity Government Income)

Fidelity Investments Life Insurance Company
Wentworth Gallery Ltd., Inc. (art galleries)
Worth (investment magazine)

KEY COMPETITORS

Aetna	Citicorp	Prudential
Alliance Capital	John Hancock	Merrill Lynch
American Express	Mellon Bank	New York Times
Bankers Trust	MetLife	Quick & Reilly
Blanchard	Oppenheimer Management	T. Rowe Price
Charles Schwab		Vanguard

FORD FOUNDATION

RANK: 388

OVERVIEW

The largest philanthropic foundation in the US, the nonprofit Ford Foundation gives millions of dollars annually in grants to organizations and institutions in the US and around the world. By the end of 1993, the foundation had given more than $7 billion in funding. In 1993 grant amounts ranged from $1,800 (Udayana University, Indonesia) to $5.4 million (National Academy of Sciences).

Education, research, and development grants focus on poverty, rights and justice, public policy, education and culture, international affairs, and population and health issues. Some grants also are awarded for media projects that focus on Ford Foundation interests. Overseas grants target developing countries. The foundation also makes investments (such as loans) in entities that further causes that the foundation supports.

A board of trustees sets broad policies, while foundation staff identifies and recommends worthy recipients and considers letters of application. The foundation's New York headquarters, completed in 1967, is noted for its award-winning architectural design.

The foundation no longer has stock in Ford Motor Co. or ties to the Ford family. Funds are derived solely from an internal stock and bond portfolio, which at year-end 1993 had a market value of more than $6.8 billion.

WHEN

Henry Ford and his son Edsel established the Ford Foundation in Michigan in 1936 with an initial gift of $25,000, followed the next year by 250,000 shares of nonvoting stock in the Ford Motor Co. The foundation's activities were limited mainly to Michigan until the deaths of Edsel (1943) and Henry (1947) made the foundation the owner of 90% of the automaker's nonvoting stock (catapulting the endowment to $474 million, the US's largest).

In 1951, under a new mandate and president (Paul Hoffman, formerly head of the Marshall Plan), the foundation made broad commitments to world peace, strengthening of democracy, and improved education. Early education program grants overseen by University of Chicago chancellor Robert Maynard Hutchins ($100 million in 1951–53 alone) helped establish major international programs (e.g., Harvard's Center for International Legal Studies) and the National Merit Scholarships.

Under McCarthyite criticism for its experimental education grants, the foundation in 1956 granted $550 million (after selling 22% of its Ford shares to the public) to noncontroversial recipients: 600 liberal arts colleges, 3,500 nonprofit hospitals, and 44 private medical schools. Foundation money set up the Radio and Television Workshop (1951). Public TV support became a foundation trademark.

Overseas work, begun in Asia and the Middle East (1950) and extended to Africa (1958) and Latin America (1959), focused on education and rural development; the foundation also supported the Population Council and research in high-yield agriculture with the Rockefeller Foundation. Other grants supported the arts and the upgrading of US engineering schools.

An emerging activism in the early 1960s (as the foundation spent $300 million a year and exceeded its income) targeted innovative approaches to employment, race relations, and minority voting rights. Grants to the arts included $80 million to numerous symphony orchestras. Assets were $3.7 billion by 1968.

McGeorge Bundy (formerly national security advisor to President Kennedy), named president in 1966, increased the activist trend with grants for direct voter registration; the NAACP and the Urban League; public interest law centers serving consumer, environmental, and minority causes; and housing for the poor.

The early 1970s saw support for black colleges and scholarships ($100 million) and women (child care, job training), but by 1974 inflation, weak stock prices, and overspending had eroded assets. Programs were cut.

Under lawyer Franklin Thomas (president since 1979) the foundation has kept expenditures in line with income. The resurgent assets in the 1980s allowed the foundation to help the homeless and, in cooperation with companies and local charities, to revitalize poor neighborhoods. A 1980s reorganization along program (rather than geographical) lines permitted greater sharing of solutions within fields and among countries.

In 1990 the foundation launched a $1.6 million program to fight racism on college campuses. In 1993 it began increasing its venture capital investments to 5% of assets.

FORD FOUNDATION

Nonprofit organization
Fiscal year ends: September 30

WHO

Chairman: Henry B. Schacht
President: Franklin A. Thomas
VP Program Division: Susan V. Berresford
VP and Chief Investment Officer: Linda B. Strumpf
VP, Secretary, and General Counsel: Barron M. Tenny
Treasurer and Director of Financial Services: Nicholas M. Gabriel
Director, Office of Human Resources: Bruce D. Stuckey
Auditors: Price Waterhouse

WHERE

HQ: 320 E. 43rd St., New York, NY 10017
Phone: 212-573-5000
Fax: 212-599-4584

The foundation has field offices in Bangladesh, Brazil, Chile, China, Egypt, India, Indonesia, Kenya, Mexico, Namibia, Nigeria, the Philippines, Senegal, South Africa, Sudan, Thailand, and Zimbabwe.

	1993 Program Approvals	
	$ mil.	% of total
Developing country programs	91	32
US & international affairs programs	197	68
Total	**288**	**100**

WHAT

	1993 Program Approvals	
	$ mil.	% of total
Education & Culture	54	19
Governance & Public Policy	39	13
International Affairs	34	12
Reproductive Health & Population	21	7
Rights & Social Justice	39	13
Rural Poverty & Resources	47	17
Urban Poverty	54	19
Total	**288**	**100**

Representative Programs

Education and Culture
Artistic creativity and resources
Curriculum development
Teaching and scholarship

Governance and Public Policy
Civic participation
Philanthropy
Public policy analysis

International Affairs
International human rights
Peace and security
US foreign policy/ international relations

Reproductive Health and Population
Community involvement
Dissemination of information
Ethics, law, and policy analysis

Rights and Social Justice
Access to social justice/ legal services
Refugees' and migrants' rights

Rural Poverty and Resources
Agricultural productivity
Employment generation
Land and water management
Rural community development

Urban Poverty
Physical, economic, and social revitalization
Welfare and teen pregnancy
Youth employment

HOW MUCH

	9-Year Growth	1984	1985	1986	1987	1988	1989	1990	1991	1992	1993
Revenues ($ mil.)[1]	1.5%	310	424	830	692	339	470	455	450	493	797
Assets ($ mil.)[2]	8.0%	3,418	3,831	4,646	5,304	4,940	5,672	5,291	6,158	6,367	6,821
Program expenditures ($ mil.)	8.7%	154	141	205	229	242	245	269	287	299	326
Administration ($ mil.)	5.4%	29	29	39	32	30	34	37	39	41	46
Program expenditures as % of assets	—	4.5%	3.7%	4.4%	4.3%	4.9%	4.3%	5.1%	4.7%	4.7%	4.8%
Employees	1.6%	511	530	534	535	568	561	559	568	590	590

1993 Year-end:
Return on investments: 12.1%

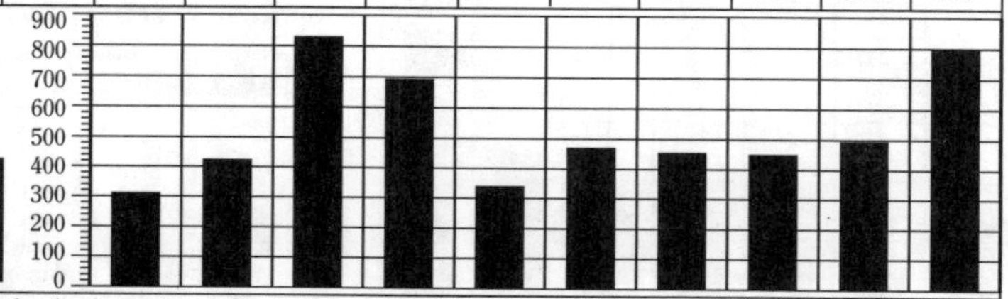

[1]Dividend & interest income and realized capital gains. [2]Investment assets only.

E. & J. GALLO WINERY

RANK: 252

OVERVIEW

Selling more than one out of every 3 bottles of wine bought in the US, E. & J. Gallo is the world's largest winemaker. Based in Modesto, California, and owned by the Gallo family, the company has over 1/4 of the domestic wine market selling key brands that include Carlo Rossi, Gallo, and Boone's Farm. Gallo markets more than 50 types of wine, including varietal wines, "jug" wines, fortified wines, wine coolers, and brandy.

Wine consumption is declining in most areas of the country, but Chairman Ernest Gallo, whose brother Julio died in 1993, is trying to maintain market share by broadening Gallo's product line. Gallo is offering new premium wines, a $30 chardonnay and a $50 cabernet sauvignon. The introduction of these much-heralded wines (one reviewer called the chardonnay "perfectly stylish") marks Gallo's entrance into the only wine market segment Gallo had not been in.

The sons of Ernest and Julio seem to be following closely in their fathers' footsteps. Ernest's sons are expected to take over the sales and marketing functions, and Julio's sons will control production and vineyard management. Ernest Gallo's fortune is valued at more than $300 million by *Forbes*.

Private company
Fiscal year ends: December 31

WHO

Chairman: Ernest Gallo, age 84
EVP: Albion Fenderson
VP Finance: Louis Freedman
VP: Joseph E. Gallo
VP: Robert J. Gallo
VP: James E. Coleman
VP: David Gallo
VP Human Resources: Robert Deitrich

WHEN

At the end of Prohibition in 1933, the Gallo brothers, Ernest and Julio, began making wine with a $200 grape crusher and redwood casks in a rented warehouse in Modesto, California. Ernest sold their first product, 6,000 gallons of table wine, to Pacific Wine Company (a Chicago distributor), which bottled the wine under several labels. The Gallos reported making a $34,000 profit their first year.

In the early 1940s the brothers began producing wine under the Gallo label from bottling plants in Los Angeles and New Orleans. In 1942 the Gallos got their first trademark, "Jolly Old Gallo." In the late 1940s Julio began experimenting with over 100 grape varieties to find those best for the Northern California climate. The company later led the industry in applying new technologies to the art of making wine. In the 1950s Gallo built its own bottle-making plant, becoming the first winery to do so. Thunderbird, a juice-flavored fortified wine introduced in 1957, was one of the company's first big successes, selling 2.5 million bottles in one year.

By the 1960s most small California vintners had folded or had been absorbed by larger wineries. Gallo, on the other hand, continued to grow as its wine gained in popularity. The company also spurred its growth by spending large amounts on advertising and keeping prices low. In 1964 Gallo introduced Hearty Burgundy, leading a trend in dry California jug wines. Even in the face of increasing European imports, Gallo was the US's #1 winemaker by the end of 1970, annually producing 66 million gallons of wine.

Gallo introduced the carbonated, fruit-flavored Boone's Farm Apple Wine in 1969, creating an interest in "pop" wines that lasted for a few years. In 1974 the company introduced its first premium varietal wines (an area in which Gallo leads today).

In the mid-1970s Gallo field workers switched unions, dropping the United Farm Workers in favor of the Teamsters. Repercussions included protests and boycotts, but sales were largely unaffected. From 1976 to 1982 Gallo was placed under an FTC order limiting its control over wholesalers. The order was lifted after heavyweight rivals entered the industry and changed the competitive balance. Gallo has, however, remained the country's top winemaker.

In 1988 Gallo started labeling all of its varietal wines with a vintage date. The company launched Eden Roc brand champagne in 1991. In 1992, as sales of wine coolers continued to decline, Gallo elected not to renew the contracts of the actors who played Frank Bartles and Ed Jaymes. That signaled the end of the well-known series of humorous TV ads touting Bartles & Jaymes wine coolers.

The 1993 book *Blood & Wine: The Unauthorized Story of the Gallo Wine Empire,* by Ellen Hawkes, paints an ugly portrait of the Gallos as obsessive protectors and promoters of the family business. The company called the book "contemptible and despicable."

Not long after the death of Julio in 1993, Ernest's wife, Amelia Franzia, died.

In 1994 the company introduced low-alcohol (4%) varieties of its Bartles & Jaymes wine coolers and a malt-based drink.

WHERE

HQ: 600 Yosemite Blvd., PO Box 1130, Modesto, CA 95353
Phone: 209-579-3111
Fax: 209-579-3249 (Public Relations)

Vineyards in California (Counties)
Fresno
Merced
Sonoma
Stanislaus

WHAT

Label Names
Andre
Ballatore
Bartles & Jaymes
Boone's Farm
Carlo Rossi
E & J Brandy
Eden Roc
Ernest & Julio Gallo
Gallo
Livingston Cellars
Night Train Express
The Reserve Cellars of Ernest & Julio Gallo
Thunderbird
Tott's
Wm. Wycliffe

Subsidiaries and Divisions
E & J Gallo Winery Europe (wholesale distributor in Europe)
Fairbanks Trucking Inc. (long-distance trucking)
Gallo Glass Co. (glass wine bottles)
Midcal Aluminum Inc. (metal bottle closures)
San Joaquin Valley Express (partnership, agricultural trucking)
United Packaging Co. (partnership, importer of wine bottle corks)
US Intermodal Services (partnership, freight brokerage)

HOW MUCH

	Annual Growth	1984	1985	1986	1987	1988	1989	1990	1991	1992	1993
Estimated sales ($ mil.)	6.1%	645	750	1,000	1,000	1,000	1,050	1,110	1,000	1,000	1,100
Wine shipments (gallons mil.)	—	143.6	154.3	169.2	166.0	165.4	169.2	156.8	—	150.0	—
Employees	4.5%	2,700	2,700	3,000	3,000	2,950	3,000	3,000	3,000	4,000	4,000

Estimated Sales ($ mil.) 1984–93

KEY COMPETITORS

Adolph Coors
Allied-Lyons
Anheuser-Busch
Bacardi
Bass
Brown-Forman
Canandaigua
Grand Metropolitan
Kendall-Jackson Winery
LVMH
Nestlé
Parducci
Robert Mondavi
Seagram
Sebastiani
Vintners International

THE GOLDMAN SACHS GROUP, LP

RANK: 12

OVERVIEW

Goldman Sachs is one of the largest investment banking companies in the world. The firm (which is the last major investment banking partnership on Wall Street) concentrates on a traditional group of blue-chip clients, which includes corporations, institutions, governments, and the wealthy in the US and, increasingly, abroad.

The firm's core areas are research, investment (trading and market making, derivatives), financing (underwriting equity and debt offerings), municipal finance (funding infrastructure and other civic improvements), mergers and acquisitions, foreign exchange and commodities, and real estate.

Though Goldman Sachs serves its own interests by serving those of its customers, behavior characterized by a former co-chairman as "long-term greed," the firm lost the underwriting business of some old clients (Ford and GTE) in the 1990s. Yet its star continues to rise overseas: it was the first non-German firm to colead an international share placement by a German company (Volkswagen), and in 1993 it managed Daimler-Benz's first US issue of shares on the NYSE.

Goldman Sachs

Private partnership
Fiscal year ends: Last Friday in November

WHO

Senior Partner and Chairman of the Management Committee: Stephen Friedman, age 54
Partner and Co–General Counsel: Robert J. Katz
Partner and Co–General Counsel: Gregory K. Palm
Partner, International Comptroller: David W. Blood
Partner, Personnel: Jonathan L. Cohen
Auditors: Coopers & Lybrand

WHEN

Philadelphia retailer Marcus Goldman moved to New York in 1869 and began to purchase customers' promissory notes from jewelry merchants and resell them to commercial banks. The business, renamed M. Goldman and Sachs in 1882 when Samuel Sachs, Goldman's son-in-law, joined the firm, became Goldman, Sachs & Company in 1885.

In 1887 Goldman Sachs, through British merchant bankers Kleinwort Sons, offered its clients foreign exchange and currency services between the New York and London markets. To serve clients such as Sears, Roebuck, the firm expanded to Chicago and St. Louis. In 1896 it joined the NYSE.

In the late 1890s and early 1900s, the firm increased its contacts in Europe. Goldman's son Henry made the firm a major source of financing for US industry. In 1906 the firm comanaged its first public offering, $4.5 million for United Cigar Manufacturers (later General Cigar). By 1920 the firm had arranged the IPOs of Sears, May Department Stores, Jewel Tea, B.F. Goodrich, and Merck.

Sidney Weinberg became a partner in 1927 and remained a leader until his death in 1969. In the 1930s the firm started a securities dealer (rather than agent) operation and opened sales departments. Since WWII it has been a leader in investment banking. In the 1950s it advised the Ford family on taking the auto company public and comanaged Ford's IPO (1956). In the 1970s Goldman Sachs was the first firm to buy blocks of stock for resale.

Under John L. Weinberg (co–senior partner with John Whitehead beginning in 1976, retired 1991), Goldman Sachs expanded its international operations, became a leader in mergers and acquisitions (M&A), and acquired First Dallas, Ltd. (1982, landed merchant banking). By 1982 it had become the largest M&A lead manager, with $24.7 billion in mergers, including U.S. Steel–Marathon Oil, Occidental Petroleum–Cities Service, and Connecticut General–INA. Another acquisition, J. Aron Co. (1981), the world's largest coffee trader, gave Goldman Sachs a significant presence in precious metals. Contacts made through Aron have been instrumental in the firm's recent growth in South America.

In the late 1980s Goldman Sachs sought capital, raising over $500 million from Sumitomo for a nonparticipatory 12.5% interest.

Goldman Sachs went into Russia in 1992 and also made Kamehameha Schools/Bishop Estate (a Hawaiian educational trust) a limited partner for a $250 million investment.

In 1993 the US Justice Department forced the firm, which owns 43% of US Gypsum, to divest its 20% interest in National Gypsum Co. because it was deemed monopolistic.

The public got a rare look at Goldman Sachs's financials in 1992 and 1993, as offering documents fell into the hands of the press. The documents revealed that the firm's pretax profits were $1.15 billion in 1991 and $1.5 billion in 1992. Its 1993 pretax earnings jumped to $2.7 billion on sales of $13.2 billion. Revenues from proprietary trading rose to $4 billion (about 30% of the total). In September 1994 chairman Stephen Friedman announced he would step down in November. The firm named a new leadership team from within the company: Jon Corzine as chairman and Henry Paulson, Jr., as VC and COO.

WHERE

HQ: 85 Broad St., New York, NY 10004
Phone: 212-902-1000
Fax: 212-902-3925

Goldman Sachs operates as an equities broker and underwriter, investment banker, asset manager, and commodities trader in the US and in other countries, including Belgium, France, Germany, Japan, Singapore, and the UK.

	1993 Office Locations	
	No. of offices	% of total
US	11	37
Asia & Pacific	8	27
Europe	7	23
Other	4	13
Total	**30**	**100**

WHAT

Selected Services
Asset Management
Investment Banking
- Advisory services
- Mergers and acquisitions
- Underwriting

Real Estate
Research
Trading

Subsidiaries
Goldman Sachs International Ltd. (UK)
Goldman Sachs (Japan) Corp.
Goldman Sachs (Asia) Ltd.
Goldman Sachs (Singapore) Pte. Ltd
Goldman, Sachs & Co. (Zurich)
Goldman, Sachs & Co. Finanz GmbH (Frankfurt)
Goldman Sachs (Australia) Ltd.

KEY COMPETITORS

AIG
Alex. Brown
Bankers Trust
Bear Stearns
Brown Brothers Harriman
CS Holding
Dean Witter Discover
Deutsche Bank
Equitable
General Electric
Hambrecht & Quist
KKR
Lehman Brothers
Merrill Lynch
J.P. Morgan
Morgan Stanley
Nomura Securities
Paine Webber
Prudential
Salomon
Travelers

HOW MUCH

	9-Year Growth	1984	1985	1986	1987	1988	1989	1990	1991	1992	1993
Estimated sales ($ mil.)	—	—	—	3,600	4,200	4,000	3,400	4,600	5,290	8,500	13,200
Pretax income	—	—	—	—	—	—	750	886	1,150	1,500	2,700
Pretax inc. as % of sales	—	—	—	—	—	—	22.1%	19.3%	21.7%	17.6%	20.5%
Partners' capital ($ mil.)	26.9%	585	868	1,104	1,656	1,876	2,145	2,477	3,010	3,714	5,008
Employees	6.7%	3,903	4,516	6,049	6,087	6,500	6,400	5,800	6,600[1]	6,733	7,000

1993 Year-end:
Debt ratio (mil.): 86.6%
Return on partners' equity: 61.9%
Cash (mil.): $5,273

Partners' Capital ($ mil.) 1984–93

GRAYBAR ELECTRIC COMPANY, INC.

RANK: 114

OVERVIEW

You may never have heard of Graybar Electric, but, if you have used the phone or turned on a light today, chances are you've used a product that has spent some time in one of their warehouses. Headquartered in St. Louis, Graybar is the largest independent electrical products distributor in the US.

Graybar sells more than 100,000 electrical and telecommunications products such as wiring devices, transformers, telephone equipment, fiber optic equipment, and voice data products from more than 1,000 manufacturers, including AT&T, General Electric, IBM, Motorola, and 3M. Graybar's customers include electrical contractors, industrial plants, telephone companies, and utility companies.

Graybar is owned by its current and retired employees. The company's voting shares are controlled by a 5-member board of senior officers. To prevent any hostile takeovers, the company has the right of first refusal on any shares. Working on narrow margins, Graybar has historically posted low profits.

With demand for new technologies increasing, Graybar is adding new voice and data communications products.

GraybaR

Private company
Fiscal year ends: December 31

WHO

President, CEO, and CFO: Edward A. McGrath
SVP Sales and Marketing: Aubrey A. Thompson
SVP Distribution: James R. Hade
VP and Treasurer: John W. Wolf
VP, Secretary, and General Counsel: George S. Tulloch
VP and Comptroller: John R. Seaton
VP Human Resources: Jack F. Van Pelt
Auditors: Price Waterhouse

WHEN

Following the Civil War, Enos Barton, who had served as a telegrapher during the war, joined with George Shawk to start an electrical equipment shop in Cleveland. In 1869 Elisha Gray, a professor of physics at Oberlin College who also had several inventions to his credit, including a printing telegraph, bought Shawk's interest in the shop. Later that same year the firm moved to Chicago and added a 3rd partner.

The fledgling company survived the Great Chicago Fire in 1871 (which stopped 2 blocks from its headquarters) and the following year was incorporated as the Western Electric Manufacturing Company, with 2/3 of the company's stock held by 2 Western Union executives. The company grew rapidly as the telegraph industry took off, providing equipment to the towns and the railroads in the burgeoning western US.

The invention of the telephone (1875) and the light bulb (1879) brought the company even more opportunities. The company began to grow into a major corporation, selling and distributing a variety of electrical equipment, including electric bells and batteries, telegraph keys, fire alarm boxes, and hotel annunciators. In 1885 Enos Barton became president of Western Electric.

One opportunity Gray and his company missed was credit for inventing the telephone. Gray's patent application for a "harmonic telegraph" reached the US Patent Office only a few hours after Bell's application for his telephone. (Maybe Gray should have faxed it.)

With demand for the telephone high, Western Electric increased its manufacturing business, and by 1900 it was the #1 telephone equipment manufacturer in the world.

Western Electric formed a new distribution company in 1926, Graybar Electric Company (from Gray and Barton). The new company was the largest electrical supplies merchandiser in the world.

In 1929 Graybar's employees bought the company from Western Electric for $3 million in cash and $6 million in preferred stock. During the 1930s the company marketed a line of appliances and sewing machines under the Graybar name. In 1941 Graybar bought the remaining outstanding shares of stock from Western Electric for $1 million.

During WWII Graybar worked with the US Navy to develop a distribution network for the Portsmouth Navy Yard. The company also provided men and equipment to wire the Panama Canal with telephone cable and continued to provide assistance to the US military during the Korean conflict and the Vietnam War.

By 1980 Graybar had reached nearly $1.5 billion in sales. In 1989 Edward McGrath succeeded James Hoagland as CEO. Graybar's business was hurt when construction business slowed in the late 1980s and the early 1990s. In response McGrath reorganized the company's management, closed regional offices, reduced work force, and centralized supervision of its service centers in 1991.

The company rebounded in 1992 as the US economy improved and that same year acquired New Jersey–based Square Electric Company. In 1994 Graybar celebrated its 125th anniversary and its 65th anniversary as an employee-owned company.

WHERE

HQ: 34 N. Meramec Ave., PO Box 7231, St. Louis, MO 63105-3874
Phone: 314-727-3900
Fax: 314-727-8218

Graybar has more than 220 offices in 15 countries.

WHAT

	1993 Sales % of total
Electrical contractors	41
Industrial plants	31
Telecommunication companies	19
Private & public power utilites	7
Other	2
Total	**100**

Selected Electrical Products	Selected Electrical Suppliers
Busways	Duracell
Controls	Emerson
Lamps	General Electric
Load centers	IBM
Motors	LTV
Timers	3M
Wire and cable	Motorola
	Zenith

Selected Communications Products	Selected Communications Suppliers
Computer network products	AMP
Fax machines	AT&T
Fiber optic products	Cray
Modems	IBM
Sound equipment	Motorola
Telephone systems	Northern Telecom
Testing and measurement instruments	Panasonic
	Zoom Telephonics

Selected Subsidiaries

ComMart, Inc.
Distribution Associates, Inc.
Graybar Electric de Mexico, S.A. de C.V.
Graybar Electric Limited (Canada)
Graybar Financial Services, Inc.
Graybar Foreign Sales Corporation (Virgin Islands)
Graybar Free Zone, S.A. (Panama)
Graybar Internationl Guam, Inc.

KEY COMPETITORS

ABB
Alcatel Alsthom
Arrow Electronics
Avnet
Cooper Industries
Dana
Eaton
Emerson
GEC
General Electric
General Signal
W. W. Grainger
Honeywell
Itel
Matsushita
Reliance Electric
Siemens
Toshiba
Westinghouse

HOW MUCH

	Annual Growth	1984	1985	1986	1987	1988	1989	1990	1991	1992	1993
Sales ($ mil.)	2.7%	1,600	1,600	1,625	1,645	1,795	1,894	1,885	1,735	1,894	2,033
Net income ($ mil.)	0.7%	—	—	14	17	10	13	12	10	10	15
Income as % of sales	—	—	—	0.9%	1.0%	0.6%	0.7%	0.6%	0.5%	0.5%	0.7%
Employees	1.4%	4,500	4,500	4,500	4,700	4,600	4,800	4,900	4,729	4,700	5,100

1993 Year-end:
Debt ratio: 52.5%
Return on equity: 9.2%
Cash (mil.): $17
Current ratio: 1.36
Long-term debt (mil.): $64
Total assets (mil.): $611

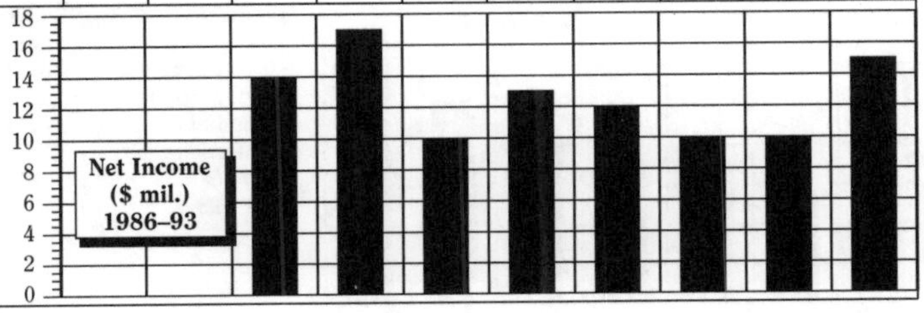

GUARDIAN LIFE

RANK: 22

OVERVIEW

Fundamentals never change. This is the theory by which New York–based Guardian Life Insurance operates. A tradition of conservative financial management has enabled the company to pay dividends for 126 consecutive years (since 1868) — one of the longest strings of dividend payment in the US.

Guardian, which operates in all 50 states and the District of Columbia, offers group and individual life and health insurance, disability and medical and dental coverage, and variable annuities. Its Guardian Asset Management and Investor Services corporations offer a variety of financial services to its customers, including the flagship Guardian Park Avenue Fund, Baillie Gifford International Fund (international investment fund), and a variety of other equity, money market, and bond funds. In 1993 total equities sales rose 82% and assets under management rose almost 54% to $2.4 billion.

Guardian resisted the temptation that struck most insurers in the 1980s to maximize returns by making risky, short-term investments. It avoided speculative real estate investments (its real estate delinquency rate is about 1/3 the industry average).

WHEN

Hugo Wesendonck made his way to Philadelphia in 1850, having escaped from Germany, where he had been sentenced to death for his part in the abortive revolution of 1848. After working in the silk business in Philadelphia, he moved to New York, which then had the largest percentage of German inhabitants in any city besides Berlin and Vienna.

In 1860 Wesendonck and several fellow expatriates formed an insurance company to serve the needs of the German American community. Germania Life Insurance was chartered as a mixed company, which paid dividends both to shareholders and policy owners. Wesendonck became the first president and led it through its formative years. The outbreak of the US Civil War blocked the company's growth among Germans in the South, but the company expanded within the rest of the US and its territories and, by 1867, even to South America.

After the Civil War many insurance companies foundered, victims of high costs. Wesendonck battled this problem by instituting strict cost controls and limiting commissions. This allowed the company to continue issuing dividends, which, in turn, kept shareholders happy and gave what amounted to a rebate on its policyholders' premiums.

In the 1870s Germania opened offices in Europe, and for the next decades much of the company's growth was concentrated in Europe. By 1910, 46% of sales originated in Europe. Germania's natural clientele decreased between the 1890s and WWI, as German immigration slowed, as Germans were assimilated into the population, and as the greatest influx of immigrants in US history brought in millions of people from eastern and southern Europe. During this period, Germania's market share dropped from 9th place in 1880 to 21st in 1910 because of the aforementioned demographic changes and the company's conservative management.

With the onset of WWI in Europe, the company lost contact with much of its business; in addition, American anti-German sentiment even before US entry into the war prodded Germania's officers to consider changing the company's name, which became The Guardian Life Insurance Company of America in 1917.

After the war the company began procedures to dispose of its German business, but the company did not completely disentangle itself until 1952, when it bought out its last policyholders.

In 1924 Guardian began mutualizing, but did not complete the process until 1944 because of the probate of a shareholder's estate.

After WWII Guardian began offering noncancellable medical insurance (1955) and group insurance (1957). In 1969 Guardian formed Guardian Investor Services to offer equity-based products. Two years later the company established Guardian Insurance & Annuity to sell variable contracts. In 1989 it organized Guardian Asset Management to handle pension funds.

In 1993 the company joined Private Health Care Systems, Inc., a consortium of commercial insurance carriers offering managed health care products and services. This allows Guardian to offer the services of 97,000 doctors at 1,035 hospitals throughout the US.

HOW MUCH

	Annual Growth	1984	1985	1986	1987	1988	1989	1990	1991	1992	1993
Assets ($ mil.)	17.1%	—	—	—	—	5,611	6,715	7,523	8,861	10,271	12,336
Net income ($ mil.)	34.3	—	—	—	—	57	134	236	186	132	249
Income as % of assets	—	—	—	—	—	1.0%	2.0%	3.1%	2.1%	1.3%	2.0%
Employees	—	3,500	4,472	4,930	3,149	4,704	3,420	6,845	7,175	7,502	—

1993 Year-end:
Equity as % of assets: 8.0%
Return on equity: 27.9%
Cash (mil.): $189
Sales (mil.): $7,069

Assets ($ mil.) 1988–93

The Guardian

Mutual company
Fiscal year ends: December 31

WHO

Chairman and CEO: Arthur V. Ferrara
President: Joseph D. Sargent
EVP and CFO: Peter L. Hutchings
SVP and Chief Investment Officer: Frank J. Jones
SVP and General Counsel: Edward K. Kane
VP and Comptroller: John R. Seaton
VP Human Resources and Administrative Support: Douglas C. Kramer
Auditors: Price Waterhouse

WHERE

HQ: The Guardian Life Insurance Company of America, 201 Park Avenue South, New York, NY 10003
Phone: 212-598-8000
Fax: 212-598-8813

Guardian has 513,983 life insurance policies in force in the US.

WHAT

	1993 Assets	
	$ mil.	% of total
Cash & equivalents	189	2
Bonds	5,644	45
Stocks	1,118	9
Mortgage loans	758	6
Real estate	128	1
Policy loans	714	6
Separate account assets	3,051	25
Other	734	6
Total	**12,336**	**100**

	1993 Sales	
	$ mil.	% of total
Premiums	6,314	89
Net investment income	574	8
Service fees	59	1
Other	122	2
Total	**7,069**	**100**

Services
Asset management
Group and individual disability insurance
Group and individual life insurance
Group and individual medical and dental coverage
Variable annuities

Subsidiaries
Guardian Asset Management Corporation
Guardian Baillie Gifford, Ltd. (UK)
Guardian Insurance & Annuity Company
Guardian Investor Services Corporation

KEY COMPETITORS

Aetna
Blue Cross
Charles Schwab
Chubb
CIGNA
Equitable
FMR
Health Systems International
Household International
Humana
John Hancock
Kemper
MassMutual
Merrill Lynch
MetLife
New York Life
Northwestern Mutual
Oxford Health Plans
Pacific Mutual
PacifiCare Health Systems
Paine Webber
Prudential
Salomon
T. Rowe Price
Transamerica
Travelers
United Health Care
U.S. Healthcare
USF&G
Wellpoint Health Networks

HALLMARK CARDS, INC.

RANK: 57

OVERVIEW

Hallmark is the world's biggest greeting card company. It commands 42% of the US market, offering 20,700 cards in over 20 languages and in more than 100 countries. Hallmark's Ambassador Cards, a separate division, is itself the #3 card maker in the US and accounts for 19% of the company's sales. In addition to cards, Hallmark is a leading producer of gift wrap, crayons, Christmas ornaments, wedding products, and related gift items. Employees own about 1/3 of the company; the Hall family owns the rest.

The company's personalized greeting card kiosks (about 4,000 across the US) have proved to be tremendously successful. Although American Greeting dominates the market (with 7,000 kiosks), Hallmark plans to install another 3,400. In order to focus more on its greeting card business, Hallmark sold its 15.5% stake in Heritage Media in early 1994. The company is now weighing whether or not to market its Hallmark brand cards in discount stores.

In 1994 Hallmark said it would buy RHI Entertainment, the #1 producer and distributor of TV movies and miniseries (including the heralded "Lonesome Dove") with 1993 sales of $120 million, for $365 million.

WHEN

Eighteen-year-old Joyce C. Hall started selling picture postcards from 2 shoeboxes in his room at the Kansas City, Missouri, YMCA in 1910. His brother Rollie joined him in 1911, and the 2 added greeting cards (made by another company) to their line in 1912. The brothers opened Hall Brothers, a store that sold postcards, gifts, books, and stationery, but it was destroyed in a 1915 fire (just before Valentine's Day). The Halls got a loan, bought an engraving company, and produced their first original cards in time for Christmas.

In 1920 a 3rd brother, William, joined the firm, which started stamping the backs of its cards with the phrase "A Hallmark Card." By 1922 Hall Brothers had salesmen in all 48 states and had begun offering gift wrap. Joyce Hall wrote the company's first national ad for the *Ladies' Home Journal* in 1928.

In 1936 Hall Brothers patented the "Eye-Vision" display case for greeting cards (which had previously been kept under counters or in drawers) and sold it to retailers across the country. The company aired its first radio ad in 1938. In 1939 Hall Brothers introduced a friendship card, showing a cart filled with purple pansies. The card became Hallmark's best seller and is still sold. In 1944 a Hallmark executive wrote the slogan, "When You Care Enough to Send the Very Best."

After WWII Hall Brothers grew rapidly. The company opened its first retail store in 1950 and in 1952 broadcast the first "Hallmark Hall of Fame," which became the longest-running dramatic series on television and has won more Emmy awards than any other TV show. Hall Brothers changed its name to Hallmark Cards in 1954 and 3 years later began selling overseas. Mass merchandising unit Ambassador Cards opened in 1959.

Hallmark introduced a line of paper party products and started putting "Peanuts" characters on cards in 1960. In 1973 Christmas ornaments were added to its product line.

In 1967 the company started constructing Crown Center, a privately financed redevelopment of 85 acres of formerly run-down properties surrounding the company headquarters in Kansas City. In 1981, 2 walkways collapsed at the Crown Center's Hyatt Regency hotel, killing 114 and injuring 225.

In 1982 Joyce Hall died; his son Donald became chairman in 1983. Hallmark acquired Binney & Smith (Crayola Crayons, Magic Marker) in 1984 and the Spanish-language Univision TV network in 1987 (sold 1992). In 1986 the company introduced Shoebox Greetings, a line of nontraditional cards.

In 1990 Hallmark acquired Willitts Designs (collectibles, sold 1993) and in 1991 entered the cable television industry by creating Crown Media and purchasing a controlling interest in St. Louis–based Cencom Cable, a transaction valued at about $1 billion. In 1993 Hallmark installed 1,600 "Touch-Screen Greetings" kiosks, which use computers to create cards with personal messages.

The company teamed up with Information Storage Devices in 1993 to test market recordable greeting cards. In 1994 Hallmark joined with Micrografx, a business software company, to develop children's computer programs.

Also in 1994 Hallmark announced the sale of Crown Media to Charter Communications and Marcus Cable. The $900 million deal is expected to close in December.

HOW MUCH

	9-Year Growth	1984	1985	1986	1987	1988	1989	1990	1991	1992	1993
Sales ($ mil.)	8.4%	1,640	1,833	1,882	2,102	2,358	2,487	2,742	2,850	3,100	3,400
Domestic employees[1]	(1.2%)	14,075	13,615	12,988	12,583	13,600	13,213	13,877	13,202	12,487	12,600

Sales ($ mil.) 1984–93

[1]Excludes Trifari, Burnes of Boston, Univision, and Willitts Designs, which were acquired and/or divested within this period; Litho-Krome, Evenson's, and Binney & Smith (acquired 1979, 1980, and 1984, respectively); and Crown Media (formed 1991).

Private company
Fiscal year ends: December 31

WHO

Chairman: Donald J. Hall, age 65
President and CEO: Irvine O. Hockaday, Jr., age 57
EVP Corporate Development & Strategy and CFO: Henry F. Frigon, age 59
President, Hallmark Brand: Bob Firnhaber
President, Ambassador Cards: Lanny Julian
VP Human Resources: Lowell J. Mayone
Auditors: KPMG Peat Marwick

WHERE

HQ: 2501 McGee St., Kansas City, MO 64108
Phone: 816-274-5111
Fax: 816-274-8513

Hallmark has production facilities in 3 cities in Kansas (Lawrence, Leavenworth, and Topeka) and in Kansas City, MO. It has distribution centers in Enfield, CT, and Liberty, MO. Products are distributed in more than 100 countries.

WHAT

Major Divisions
Ambassador Cards (cards, related products)
Hallmark International (global marketing)

Brand Names
Ambassador (cards, gift wrap, party goods)
Andrew Brownsword (greeting cards)
Crayola (crayons)
Hallmark (cards, gift wrap, party goods, Christmas ornaments, mugs, home decorations, plush toys, ribbon, writing paper, other goods)
Liquitex (art supplies)
Magic Marker (markers)
Shoebox Greetings (nontraditional cards)
Springbok (jigsaw puzzles)
Touch-Screen Greetings (computer-generated cards)
Valentines of Dundee

Subsidiaries and Affiliates
Binney & Smith Inc. (crayons, art products)
Crown Power and Redevelopment Corp.
Crown Center (Kansas City complex)
Evenson Card Shops, Inc.
Graphics International Trading Company
Hallmark Marketing Corp.
Halls Merchandising, Inc. (department stores)
Halls Crown Center (Kansas City)
Halls Plaza (Kansas City)
Litho-Krome Co. (lithography)
Mundi-Paper (cards, Spain)
RHI Entertainment, Inc. (TV miniseries, movies)
Signboard Hill Productions (TV, film)
Spanjersberg Group (cards, The Netherlands)
Verkerke Reprodukties (fine art reproductions)
W.N. Sharpe Holdings (cards, UK)

KEY COMPETITORS

American Greetings
Artistic Greetings
Artistic Impressions
Blockbuster
Brøderbund
Cox
Deluxe
Gibson Greetings
Gillette
Marvel
Microsoft
Pearson
Rank
TCI
Thomas Nelson
Time Warner
United Nations
Walt Disney

HARVARD UNIVERSITY

RANK: 203

OVERVIEW

Nearly all parents dream of sending their kids to Harvard University, the oldest and one of the most prestigious institutions of higher education in the US. Located across the Charles River from Boston, the private, coeducational school consists of Harvard College (the men's undergraduate college), Radcliffe (the women's undergraduate college), 10 graduate schools, and the Extension School. Harvard's $5.3 billion endowment is the nation's largest for a school.

Harvard's outstanding facilities and institutions include the Harvard University Library, the oldest US library and the largest university library in the world, with almost 12 million volumes, and a number of nontraditional educational progams, such as the Institute for Learning in Retirement.

Accepting only about 16% of freshman applicants, the university is among the US's most competitive. Harvard's alumni list reads like a *Who's Who of American History* and includes such notable figures as John Adams, John Quincy Adams, T. S. Eliot, Ralph Waldo Emerson, John Hancock, Oliver Wendell Holmes, Helen Keller, John F. Kennedy, Franklin D. Roosevelt, Theodore Roosevelt, and Gertrude Stein. Additionally, 33 Nobel laureates and 31 Pulitzer Prize winners have been associated with the university. The university pays its professors well: more than $70,000, on average, per 9-month contract.

Private university
Fiscal year ends: June 30

WHO

President, Harvard University: Neil L. Rudenstine, age 58
President, Radcliffe College: Linda Smith Wilson
VP Alumni Affairs and Development: Fred L. Glimp
VP Finance: Robert H. Scott
VP and General Counsel: Margaret Marshall
Treasurer: D. Ronald Daniel
Financial Systems Director: E. Lyndon Tefft
Dean of Faculty of Arts and Sciences: Jeremy Knowles
Human Resources Director: Diane Bemus Patrick

WHEN

In 1636 the General Court of Massachusetts appropriated £400 for the establishment of a college. The first building (Old College) was completed at Cambridge in 1639 and was named for John Harvard, who had willed his collection of about 400 books and half of his land to the school. Henry Dunster, a master of Old Testament languages, became the school's first president (and faculty) in 1640. The first freshman class consisted of 4 students.

During its first 150 years, Harvard adhered to the educational standards of European schools, with emphasis on classical literature and languages, logic, philosophy, and mathematics. Theology was studied only by graduate students (about half of the early graduates became ministers). The president and a small group of tutors (usually men who had just earned their bachelor's degrees) taught all of the subjects. Harvard's early presidents included Increase Mather and John Leverett.

In 1721 Harvard established its first professorship (the Hollis Divinity Professorship), which was quickly followed by professorships in mathematics and natural philosophy. In 1780 Harvard became a university and in 1783 appointed its first professor of medicine.

After Edward Everett (a Greek-literature professor) returned from studying abroad with reports of the modern teaching methods practiced at German universities in the early 1800s, the school updated its curriculum. Harvard established a Divinity School in 1816, a Law School in 1817, and 2 schools of science in the 1840s.

In 1869 Charles W. Eliot became president of Harvard and engineered a period of growth that included the development of graduate programs in arts and sciences, engineering, and architecture. Eliot also raised the standards of the schools of medicine and law and laid the groundwork for the graduate School of Business Administration (there is no undergraduate business instruction at Harvard) and the School of Public Health. In addition Eliot expanded the elective system to allow students to better design their own courses of study.

During the 20th century Harvard's enrollment, faculty, and endowment grew tremendously. The Graduate School of Education opened in 1920, and, in 1930, the first undergraduate residential house opened. In the 1930s and 1940s the school established a scholarship program as well as a General Education curriculum for undergraduates.

Since then the school has continued to grow, with new buildings, expanded programs, and a concerted effort to increase library holdings. In 1979 Harvard introduced its new core curriculum.

Neil Rudenstine took Derek Bok's place as Harvard's president in 1991 and has focused his efforts on bringing the university's distinct schools closer together, on integration rather than expansion. Rudenstine has also vowed to cut costs and to seek additional funding so that no one should be denied a Harvard education because of financial need. Currently, more than 70% of Harvard freshmen receive financial aid.

WHERE

HQ: 1350 Massachusetts Ave., Cambridge, MA 02138
Phone: 617-495-1000
Fax: 617-495-0754

Harvard University is located on more than 380 acres in Boston and Cambridge, MA.

WHAT

	1993 Income
	% of total
Tuition & fees	31
Research	25
Endowment	22
Gifts	6
Other	16
Total	**100**

	1993 Expenses
	% of total
Salaries	39
Building operation & depreciation	14
Equipment & supplies	12
Benefits	10
Scholarships	8
Other	17
Total	**100**

	1993 Admissions
	% of total
Caucasian	62
Nonresident alien	14
Asian	11
Hispanic	6
African American	6
Native American	1
Total	**100**

Schools and Colleges
- Harvard College
- Radcliffe College
- Graduate School of Arts and Sciences
- Medical School
- School of Public Health
- School of Dental Medicine
- Law School
- John F. Kennedy School of Government
- Graduate School of Design
- Graduate School of Education
- Graduate School of Business Administration
- Divinity School
- Extension School

Selected Affiliated Institutions
- Agassiz Theater
- Arnold Arboretum
- Carpenter Center for the Visual Arts
- Harvard University Museums of Natural History
- Houghton Library
- Loeb Drama Center
- Peabody Museum of Archaeology and Ethnology
- Semitic Museum
- Villa I Tatti (Florence, Italy)
- Widener Library

HOW MUCH

	9-Year Growth	1984	1985	1986	1987	1988	1989	1990	1991	1992	1993
Revenues ($ mil.)	9.3%	587	650	716	786	866	1,009	1,083	1,143	1,210	1,306
Enrollment	1.1%	16,781	16,871	17,298	17,419	17,454	17,762	18,179	18,283	18,273	18,556
Annual Tuition ($)	6.9%	9,035	9,800	10,590	11,390	12,015	12,715	14,450	14,860	15,410	16,454
Endowment ($ mil.)	11.2%	2,037	2,187	2,694	3,435	4,018	4,155	4,651	4,700	4,700	5,300
Faculty	2.2%	1,700	1,934	2,236	2,076	2,256	2,046	2,121	2,206	2,121	2,065

Annual Tuition ($) 1984–93

18,000
16,000
14,000
12,000
10,000
8,000
6,000
4,000
2,000
0

THE HEARST CORPORATION

RANK: 96

OVERVIEW

Owned by descendants of William Randolph Hearst, the Hearst Corporation is one of the world's largest diversified communication companies, with major stakes in newspapers, magazines, books, and broadcasting.

Hearst owns 17 newspapers; major US and UK magazines, including *Esquire* and *Good Housekeeping* (61 editions of its magazines are published in over 80 countries); and US and UK publications distributors. The company's entertainment and syndication properties range from cable TV networks to King Features Syndicate, the world's largest newspaper syndicate.

Former FCC chairman Alfred Sikes, hired in 1993 to head a New Media and Technology Group, is moving Hearst quickly onto the information superhighway. Sikes teamed Hearst with Le Groupe Vidéotron, a leading Canadian cable company, to provide on-line services in Quebec; bought a stake in a California company to electronically publish Hearst magazines; and made plans to launch HomeNet, which will offer interactive products for home repairs, design, and decorating. Sikes expects to open a new media center in early 1994 to showcase state-of-the-art multimedia and interactive technologies.

After considering the sale of its Avon and Morrow book publishing companies for 2 years, Hearst decided in 1994 to keep them for its growing multimedia interests.

WHEN

William Randolph Hearst, son of a California mining magnate, started his empire as a reporter, having been expelled from Harvard in 1884 for playing jokes on professors. He became editor of the *San Francisco Examiner,* which his father had obtained as payment for a gambling debt, in 1887. Hearst's sensationalist style brought financial success to the paper. In 1895 he bought the *New York Morning Journal* and competed against the *New York World*, owned by Joseph Pulitzer, Hearst's first employer. The "yellow journalism" resulting from that rivalry characterized American journalism at the turn of the century. Hearst used his newspapers as a forum for his personal and political views for more than 30 years.

The company branched out into magazines (1903), film (1913), and radio (1928). It owned 13 newspapers and 7 magazines by 1920 and pioneered film journalism with the Hearst-Selig News Pictorial. In 1935 the company was at its peak, with newspapers in 19 cities having nearly 14% of total US daily and 24% of Sunday circulation; the largest syndicate (King Features); international news and photo services; 13 magazines; 8 radio stations; and 2 motion picture companies. Two years later Hearst had to relinquish control to avoid bankruptcy. Movie companies, radio stations, magazines, and later most of his San Simeon estate, were sold to reduce debt. Hearst inspired Orson Welles's 1941 film *Citizen Kane*.

When Hearst died in 1951, control of the company fell to outsiders. Richard Berlin, who had been in charge since 1940, became CEO and sold off failing newspapers but also moved into television and acquired more magazines.

The Hearst family regained control of the company in 1974. Frank Bennack, Jr., president and CEO since 1979, expanded the company, acquiring newspapers (in Los Angeles, Houston, and Seattle, among others); publishing companies (William Morrow, 1981); 3 TV stations (1981, 1982, and 1986); magazines (*Redbook,* 1982; *Esquire,* 1986); and 20% of cable sports network ESPN (1991). Hearst branched into video via a joint venture with Capital Cities/ABC (1981) and helped launch the Lifetime and Arts & Entertainment cable channels (1984). It closed the Los Angeles *Herald Examiner* in 1989.

In 1992 Hearst and Dow Jones started *SmartMoney*, a personal finance magazine. In San Antonio Hearst closed the *Light* after buying its competitor, the *Express-News*. Hearst also teamed with *Izvestia* to start a newspaper in Russia and launched a New England news network with Continental Cablevision.

In 1993 the company bought Camdat (medical information); N-Squared (nutritional information); and Professional Drug Systems (drug pricing information). Founder Hearst's son and namesake, who was chairman of the executive committee, died in 1993 at 85.

HOW MUCH

	Annual Growth	1984	1985	1986	1987	1988	1989	1990	1991	1992	1993
Sales ($ mil.)	5.7%	1,400	1,540	1,529	1,886	1,986	2,094	2,138	1,888	1,973	2,300
Newspaper revenue ($ mil.)	10.3%	—	—	390	650	689	700	715	680	701	720
Magazine revenue ($ mil.)	5.3%	—	—	780	873	919	992	1,022	1,002	1,062	800
Broadcast revenue ($ mil.)	(4.7%)	—	—	280	262	263	270	290	206	210	219
Cable TV revenue ($ mil.)	—	—	—	9	11	15	21	—	—	—	—
Other revenue ($ mil.)	—	—	—	70	90	100	111	111	—	—	—
Employees	1.6%	13,000	12,000	12,000	15,000	15,000	14,000	13,950	14,000	13,000	15,000

Sales ($ mil.) 1984–93

The Hearst Corporation

Private company
Fiscal year ends: December 31

WHO

Chairman: Randolph A. Hearst, age 79
President and CEO: Frank A. Bennack, Jr., age 61
EVP and COO: Gilbert C. Maurer, age 66
SVP, CFO, and Chief Legal Officer: Victor F. Ganzi, age 46
VP, General Manager Hearst Broadcasting: John G. Conomikes
VP, General Manager Hearst Newspapers: Robert J. Danzig
Editor and Publisher, *San Francisco Examiner*: William Randolph Hearst III
VP and General Counsel: Jonathan E. Thackeray
VP Human Resources: Kenneth A. Feldman

WHERE

HQ: 959 Eighth Ave., New York, NY 10019
Phone: 212-649-2000
Fax: 212-765-3528 (Corporate Communications)

WHAT

US Magazines
Colonial Homes
Cosmopolitan
Country Living
Esquire
Good Housekeeping
Harper's Bazaar
House Beautiful
Motor Boating & Sailing
Popular Mechanics
Redbook
SmartMoney
Sports Afield
Town & Country
Victoria

Major Newspapers
Albany Times Union
Houston Chronicle
San Antonio Express-News
San Francisco Examiner
Seattle Post-Intelligencer

Broadcasting
KMBC-TV, Kansas City, MO
WBAL (AM), Baltimore
WBAL-TV, Baltimore
WCVB-TV, Boston
WDTN-TV, Dayton, OH
WISN (AM), Milwaukee
WISN-TV, Milwaukee
WIYY (FM), Baltimore
WLTQ (FM), Milwaukee
WTAE (AM), Pittsburgh
WTAE-TV, Pittsburgh
WVTY (FM), Pittsburgh

Book Publishing
Avon Books
United Technical
William Morrow & Co.

Business Publishing, Entertainment, Syndication, Software
American Druggist
Arts & Entertainment Network (37.5%)
Black Book series (auto guides)
Books That Work
Camdat Corp. (medical information software)
Cowles Syndicate
ESPN (20%)
First DataBank (drug database)
Hearst/ABC Video Services
Hearst Entertainment Distribution
Hearst Entertainment Productions
International Circulation Distributors
King Features Syndicate
Lifetime Television (33.3%)
Motor magazine
National Magazine Company, Ltd.
New England Cable News
North America Syndicate
N-Squared Incorporated
Professional Drug Systems
Retirement Advisors
UBI (with Le Groupe Vidéotron & 5 others)

Real Estate
Down East Timberlands
Hearst Realties
San Francisco Realties
Sunical Land & Livestock

KEY COMPETITORS

Advance Publications
Bertelsmann
Capital Cities/ABC
CBS
Chronicle Publishing
Cox
Enquirer/Star Group
Gannett
Heritage Media
King Ranch
Matra-Hachette
McGraw-Hill
MediaNews
New York Times
News Corp.
Reader's Digest
Reed Elsevier
E.W. Scripps
Time Warner
Times Mirror
Tribune
Viacom
Washington Post

HELMSLEY ENTERPRISES, INC.

RANK: 227

OVERVIEW

Leona may be out of the pokey, but things may never be the same at Helmsley Enterprises, a holding company owned by Harry and Leona Helmsley, which manages their real estate empire. Since its well-publicized brushes with the law, including Leona Helmsley's conviction on income tax evasion charges in 1989, the company has struggled. However, it still controls over 100 million square feet of commercial space, more than 100,000 apartments, and 13,000 hotel rooms across the US.

In addition to owning properties, the company's Helmsley-Spear and Helmsley-Noyes subsidiaries manage several hundred office and apartment buildings in New York and across the US, in most of which Harry Helmsley has an interest. Of these, the best known is the Empire State Building. Other subsidiaries include Deco Purchasing, the purchasing arm for Helmsley Hotels, and Owners Maintenance, which holds cleaning contracts with many Helmsley properties.

Although Harry Helmsley was declared mentally unfit to stand trial for 47 counts of fraud and tax evasion, the 84-year-old is still nominally in charge of the Helmsley empire. *Forbes* estimated his net worth at over $1 billion in 1993.

WHEN

Harry Helmsley began his career as a Manhattan rent collector in 1925. Rent collecting, then handled in person, gave Helmsley contact with building owners and an ability to evaluate a building. When the real estate market crashed in 1929, Helmsley obtained property at bargain prices. He paid $1,000 down for a building with a $100,000 mortgage and later quipped that he did so to provide employment for his father, whom he hired as superintendent. In 1946 he sold the building for $165,000.

In 1949 Helmsley teamed up with his lawyer, Lawrence Wien. Helmsley located property; Wien found financing. The deal they made on the Empire State Building in 1961 is typical of their tactics. They bought the building for $65 million and sold it to Prudential for $29 million, obtaining a 114-year leaseback. A public offering for the newly created Empire State Building Company made up the difference, and both men received stock for their efforts.

During the 1950s Helmsley bought into many noteworthy office buildings, including the Flatiron (1951), Berkeley (1953), and Equitable (1957). He bought the property management firm of Leon Spear in 1955. In the mid-1960s he began developing properties, beginning with a 52-story office tower on Broadway. By 1967 Helmsley was investing in shopping centers. In 1969 he bought the trust of Furman and Wolfson, which held about 30 buildings nationwide, for $165 million. To finance the trust, Helmsley borrowed $78 million in cash on his reputation — the largest unsecured signature loan ever.

Helmsley's association with Spear precipitated a meeting with successful real estate broker Leona Roberts, from whom Spear had purchased an apartment. Spear arranged for them to meet in 1969; Helmsley hired Leona, promoted her to SVP, and divorced his wife to marry her in 1971.

Helmsley became interested in hotels in the 1970s, although the Manhattan market for luxury hotels was considered saturated. In 1974 he leased a historical building (now called the Helmsley Palace) from the Catholic church and began renovation; the Palace opened in 1980. Leona's extravagance cost Harry millions on the venture. Beginning in 1979 Harry invested in Florida, first building Miami Palace and, in a later project that went bankrupt, Helmsley Center.

During the 1980s Harry's empire began to crumble as Leona gained control. Numerous lawsuits, lackadaisical bookkeeping, shoddy building maintenance (a ceiling collapsed at the Helmsley Windsor, killing a guest), and extravagant spending culminated in indictments for tax evasion. Harry was declared mentally incompetent to stand trial, but in August 1989 Leona was convicted, fined $7.1 million, and sentenced to 4 years in jail.

In 1990 the Helmsleys sold their Helmsley-Greenfield subsidiary. In 1991 the limited partners of the Helmsley Palace filed suit to remove the Helmsleys from control of the hotel, claiming that the Helmsleys' association with the hotel had caused many would-be customers to go elsewhere. In 1993 the Helmsleys gave up a battle for control of the hotel, renamed the New York Palace. The hotel was then sold by a receiver to a group of investors formed by the royal family of Brunei.

In 1994 Leona Helmsley fired several hotel executives. The hotels could lose their liquor licenses, since she is not allowed to have control over any business that serves liquor.

HOW MUCH

	Annual Growth	1983	1984	1985	1986	1987	1988	1989	1990	1991	1992
Estimated sales ($ mil.)	2.6%	—	—	1,000	1,700	1,430	1,400	1,480	1,435	1,327	1,200
Employees	3.8%	—	—	10,000	13,000	13,000	13,000	13,000	13,000	13,000	13,000

Estimated Sales ($ mil.) 1985–92

Private company
Fiscal year ends: December 31

WHO

Chairman, President, and CEO: Harry B. Helmsley, age 84
SVP: Joseph Licari
SVP: William La Blina
VP and Assistant Secretary: Alvin Schwartz
VP and Assistant Secretary: Irving Schneider
Treasurer, Secretary, and CFO: Martin S. Stone
Controller: Josephine Keenan
Manager Human Resources: Jennie Voscina
Auditors: Eisner & Lubin

WHERE

HQ: 60 E. 42nd St., New York, NY 10165-0001
Phone: 212-687-6400
Fax: 212-687-6437

Helmsley operates primarily in Manhattan but has holdings elsewhere across the US.

WHAT

Major Subsidiaries
Albert M. Greenfield & Co. (real estate)
Brown, Harris, Stevens, Inc. (real estate)
Deco Purchasing Co. (purchasing)
Helmsley Hotels Inc. (hotel management)
Helmsley-Noyes Co., Inc. (real estate)
Helmsley-Spear Conversion Sales Corp. (real estate)
Helmsley-Spear Inc. (restaurants, hotels, and other real estate)
John J. Reynolds, Inc. (real estate)
National Realty Corp.
Owners Maintenance Corp. (real estate services)

KEY COMPETITORS

Accor
Alexander's
American Express
Bass
Canadian Pacific
Carlson
Edward J. DeBartolo
Four Seasons
Hilton
Hyatt
ITT
JMB Realty
LaSalle Partners
Lefrak
Lincoln Property
Loews
Marriott International
Melvin Simon
Metromedia
Nestlé
Olympia & York
Promus
Rank
Ritz-Carlton
Rockefeller Group
Rouse
Taubman
Tishman Speyer Properties
Trammell Crow
Trump Organization
VMB Realty
Weingarten Realty
Zeckendorf

HUNTSMAN CHEMICAL CORPORATION

RANK: 131

OVERVIEW

Salt Lake City–based Huntsman Chemical is the largest privately held chemical business in the US. The company is one of several businesses owned by Jon Huntsman, a devout Mormon and father of 9. In addition to Huntsman Chemical, these businesses include Huntsman Polypropylene, General Electric Huntsman, Huntsman Packaging, and Polycom Huntsman, as well as foreign affiliates.

Once its acquisition of Texaco's petrochemical operations ($1.4 billion in annual sales) and of 2 of Monsanto's chemical lines ($200 million in annual sales; linear alkyl benzene surfactant and maleic anhydride) are completed, Huntsman Chemical will be one of the largest chemical producers in the US, with about $3.3 billion in sales. It is already the largest US maker of polystyrene (used to make items ranging from coffee cups to TV cabinets). The company also produces styrene monomer (raw material for making other plastics), expandable resins (packaging and insulation), and polypropylene (durable plastics).

Huntsman's strategy is simple: Buy when everyone else is selling, and then wait for market conditions to improve. He has acquired the chemical and plastic business of several major corporations as they have downsized their operations. After an acquisition Huntsman immediately closes inefficient plants, reduces staff positions, and cuts administrative costs to improve operating efficiency. Despite the huge Texaco transaction, Huntsman is looking for additional acquisitions as he seeks to expands and diversify within the chemical business.

WHEN

In the movie *The Graduate*, Dustin Hoffman's character was given one word of advice for achieving success in the business world: "Plastics." Jon Huntsman has taken that advice to heart. His first exposure to the use of plastics was in the manufacture of egg cartons. After 3 years of experience and frustration at Dow Chemical, Huntsman and his brother Blaine raised $300,000 and received a $1 million loan from Hambrecht & Quist to found Huntsman Container in 1970. The brothers used the money to buy a polystyrene plant in Ohio. To swing the deal Huntsman offered to buy $1.8 million of styrene monomer from ARCO over 13 years in exchange for a $10 million loan. With ARCO's $10 million Huntsman convinced Shell and a bank to lend him the balance of the purchase price and formed Huntsman Chemical to acquire the Ohio plant. Knowing the risks that Huntsman was taking, Shell executives presented him with a bronze sculpture entitled *The Riverboat Gambler*. Huntsman then hit the road and secured so many customers for his production that the Ohio plant was soon operating at 100% capacity. In 1985 the company formed a joint venture with Polycom to purchase Huntsman-Russtek Polymers, a maker of expandable polystyrene.

Despite a downturn in the chemical business in 1985, Huntsman acquired Hoechst-Celanese's polystyrene business, making Huntsman the largest producer of styrene in the US. The following year Huntsman formed 4 joint ventures with General Electric Plastics. In 1987 Huntsman sold 40% of Huntsman Chemical for $52 million and used some of the proceeds to acquire a New Jersey polypropylene plant from Shell. In 1989 Huntsman reentered the packaging business by acquiring Skelmersdale, a European packaging concern that had once been a part of Huntsman Container.

In 1991 Huntsman completed the construction of a plant in Armenia to manufacture prestressed extruded reinforced concrete. That same year McDonald's succumbed to environmental pressure and announced that it was curtailing its use of polystyrene clamshell containers. Almost overnight Huntsman lost about 10% of its business. That same year the company formed a joint venture called Huntsman-Styrol to construct a plant in Ukraine to make egg cartons, meat and vegetable trays, and food service containers. The following year the company added Mobil's polyethylene bakery bag manufacturing business. Also in 1993 Huntsman bought 50% of Chemplex Australia Limited from Consolidated Press Holdings (controlled by Australian tycoon Kerry Packer). Later in 1993 Huntsman and Packer joined forces again to bid $1.06 billion for Texaco's unprofitable petrochemical operations. Also that year Huntsman agreed to purchase Elf-Aquitaine's chemicals subsidiary in northern France.

HOW MUCH

	Annual Growth	1984	1985	1986	1987	1988	1989	1990	1991	1992	1993
Sales ($ mil.)	25.0%	—	310	—	—	1,389	—	1,325	—	—	1,850
Employees	24.0%	—	900	—	—	—	1,700	2,000	2,850	3,900	5,000

Private company
Fiscal year ends: December 31

WHO

Chairman and CEO: Jon Meade Huntsman, age 55
VC: Jake Garn
VC and CFO: Terry R. Parker
President and COO: Ronald A. Rasband
SVP: Randy Plant
VP and Treasurer: Lee S. Skidmore
VP Human Resources: Winston H. Conners
Auditors: Deloitte & Touche

WHERE

HQ: 2000 Eagle Gate Tower, Salt Lake City, UT 84111
Phone: 801-532-5200
Fax: 801-536-1581

The Huntsman companies operate 58 facilities at 46 sites in 15 countries.

WHAT

Subsidiaries and Affiliates

General Electric Huntsman
Huntsman AeroMar (joint venture, Russia)
Huntsman-Armenian Concrete Corporation (joint venture)
Huntsman Chemical Company Australia Limited (50%; joint venture with Consolidated Press Holdings)
Huntsman Chemical Company Limited (UK)
Huntsman Packaging Corporation (food service, fast food, grocery, and poultry/meat packaging)
Huntsman Polypropylene Corporation
Huntsman–Styrol LLC (joint venture, Ukraine)
Polycom Huntsman, Inc. (color and additive concentrates, reinforced compounds and toll compounding services for appliances, lawn and garden equipment, electronics, automotive parts, flexible and rigid packaging, and medical supplies)

Products

Expandable resins (molded polystyrene for residential, commercial, and industrial insulation; protective packaging; and insulated food containers)
Plastic compounds and colorants
Polypropylene (durable plastic used in the manufacture of automobiles, clothing, electronics, lawn furniture, and packaging materials)
Polystyrene (plastic used in appliances, disposable medical supplies, television cabinets, and toys)
Printed and laminated polyethylene and polypropylene films
Styrene monomer (primary raw material used in manufacture of polystyrene, expandable resins, and other thermoplastic resins and rubber-based products)

KEY COMPETITORS

Akzo Nobel
American Cyanamid
BASF
Bayer
Dow Chemical
DuPont
Eastman Chemical
Formosa Plastics
W. R. Grace
Hansen
Hercules
Imperial Chemical
Owens-Corning
Phillips Petroleum
Rhône-Poulenc
Union Carbide

HYATT CORPORATION

RANK: 85

OVERVIEW

Hyatt Corporation, the well-known hotel operator, is run by Chicago's wealthiest family, the publicity-shy Pritzker clan (net worth: over $4.4 billion), who own H Group Holding, the holding company of Hyatt Corporation.

While Hyatt's sales have been falling for several years, rising hotel occupancy rates (from 61.3% in 1991 to 63.9% in 1993) should help reverse this decline. But an improved market does not mean that Hyatt plans aggressive expansion: the chain opens only a few hotels each year.

Known for superlative service, Hyatt has introduced many amenities (free shampoo, restricted-access floors) that have been widely copied. Continuing that tradition, Hyatt in 1994 began offering business travelers rooms equipped with fax machines, work stations, enhanced lighting in the work area, and telephones with computer hook-ups, as well as 24-hour access to copy machines and printers. The company is experimenting with machines that dispense keys to preregistered guests who want to avoid check-in hassles.

WHEN

In 1881 Nicholas Pritzker left Kiev for Chicago, where he began his progeny's ascent to the ranks of America's wealthiest families.

Nicholas's son A. N. left the family law practice in the 1930s and began investing in a variety of businesses. He turned one 1942 investment (Cory Corporation) worth $25,000 into $23 million by 1967.

After WWII, A. N.'s son Jay followed in his father's wheeling-and-dealing footsteps. In 1953, with the help of his father's banking connections, Jay purchased Colson Company and recruited his brother Bob, an industrial engineer, to restructure a company that made tricycles and navy rockets. By 1990 Jay and Bob had added 60 industrial companies, with annual sales exceeding $3 billion, to the entity they called the Marmon Group.

In 1957 Jay bought a hotel called Hyatt House, located near the Los Angeles airport, from Hyatt von Dehn. Jay had added 5 locations by 1961 and brought his gregarious youngest brother, Donald, to California to manage the hotel company.

In 1967 the Pritzkers took the company public, but the move that opened new vistas was the purchase of an 800-room hotel in Atlanta that both Hilton and Marriott had turned down. John Portman's innovative design, incorporating a 21-story atrium, a large fountain, and a revolving rooftop restaurant, became a Hyatt trademark.

The Pritzkers formed Hyatt International in 1969 to operate hotels overseas, and the company grew rapidly during the 1970s in the US and abroad. Donald Pritzker died in 1972, and his successor ran up some questionable expenses. This prompted the family to move the corporate offices to Chicago in 1977 and to take the company private in 1979. In 1980 Hyatt built its first Park Hyatt, a European-style super-luxury hotel, near the Water Tower in Chicago. Six years passed before the company opened its next Park Hyatt, in Washington, DC.

Much of Hyatt's growth in the 1970s had come from contracts to manage, under the Hyatt banner, hotels built by other investors. In the 1980s Hyatt's cut on those contracts shrank, and it launched its own hotel and resort developments under Nick Pritzker, a cousin to Jay and Bob. In 1988, with US and Japanese partners, it built the $360 million Hyatt Regency Waikoloa on Hawaii's Big Island. At the time the resort was, according to *FORTUNE,* the most expensive hotel ever built.

Through Hyatt subsidiaries the Pritzkers bought bedraggled Braniff Airlines in 1983 as it emerged from bankruptcy. After a failed 1987 attempt to merge the airline with Pan Am, the Pritzkers sold Braniff in 1988.

In 1989 Hyatt launched Classic Residence by Hyatt, a group of upscale retirement communities. In 1993 Hyatt sold the majority of its 85% interest in Ticketmaster to Paul Allen, cofounder of Microsoft. That same year Donald Trump sued Hyatt, alleging that the hotelier was trying to squeeze him out of his 50% stake in New York City's Grand Hyatt. In 1994 Hyatt sued Trump, claiming that "The Donald" was trying to lessen his financial woes by blocking renovations on the Grand Hyatt and that he had turned over his share of the hotel to 2 of his creditors.

HOW MUCH

	Annual Growth	1984	1985	1986	1987	1988	1989	1990	1991	1992	1993
Estimated sales ($ mil.)	3.2%	—	—	2,000	2,300	2,330	2,400	3,101	2,915	2,400[1]	2,500[1]
Total hotels	11.0%	68	72	79	85	91	101	158	160	164	164
New hotels	—	4	4	7	6	6	10	57	2	4	—
Total rooms	—	39,081	40,715	44,409	47,124	50,396	54,127	57,137	55,000	55,562	—
New rooms	—	2,027	1,634	3,694	2,715	3,272	3,731	3,010	900	562	—
Employees	8.3%	—	—	30,000	30,000	40,000	40,000	55,195	49,820	51,275	52,275

Estimated Sales ($ mil.) 1986–93

3,500
3,000
2,500
2,000
1,500
1,000
500
0

[1]Does not include revenue for franchised or managed hotels

HYATT HOTELS & RESORTS

Private company
Fiscal year ends: January 31

WHO

Chairman and CEO: Jay A. Pritzker, age 71
President: Thomas V. Pritzker, age 43
SVP and CFO: Ken Posner
SVP Planning and Human Resources: Timothy Wolf
SVP Sales and Marketing: Jim Evans
President, Hyatt Hotels Corp.: Darryl Hartley-Leonard
President, Classic Residence: Penny S. Pritzker, age 34
President, Marmon Group: Robert Pritzker, age 67
General Counsel: Michael Evanoff
Auditors: KPMG Peat Marwick

WHERE

HQ: 200 W. Madison St., Chicago, IL 60606
Phone: 312-750-1234
Fax: 312-750-8550
Reservations: 800-233-1234

Through its domestic division Hyatt Corporation operates hotels across the US. Hyatt's international division is responsible for the company's network of foreign-based hotels, found worldwide.

	1993 Hotels	
	No. of hotels	% of total
US, Canada & Caribbean	105	64
Other countries	59	36
Total	**164**	**100**

WHAT

Subsidiaries
Hyatt Hotels Corp.
- Classic Residence by Hyatt (upscale retirement communities)
- Grand Hyatt
- Hyatt
- Hyatt Hotels International
- Hyatt Regency
- Park Hyatt

Spectacor Management Group (50%, arena management)

Related Pritzker Businesses
American Medical International (hospitals)
Conwood Co. (tobacco products)
Dalfort Corp. (aircraft maintenance)
Hawthorn Suites (lodging)
Itel Corp. (minority interest, railroad cars)
Marmon Group (over 60 industrial companies)
Penguin Realty Associates L.P.
Royal Caribbean Cruises Ltd. (50%, cruise line)
Tampa Bay Hockey Group (applicant for National Hockey League franchise)
Ticketmaster Corp. (minority interest, ticket sales)
Trans Union Corp. (credit reporting service)

KEY COMPETITORS

Accor
American Express
Bally
Bass
Canadian Pacific
Carlson
Carnival Cruise Lines
Circus Circus
Dial
Dole
Four Seasons
Helmsley
Hilton
ITT
Loews
Marriott International
Metromedia
Nestlé
Ogden
Promus
Rank
Ritz-Carlton
Trump Organization

INGRAM INDUSTRIES INC.

RANK: 26

OVERVIEW

Nashville-based Ingram Industries is the parent company of Ingram Distribution Group, the world's #1 seller of general interest books, microcomputer products, and prerecorded videos. Nearly all of company revenues come from book, video, and computer sales.

Ingram Distribution's 3 divisions are each market leaders. The largest, Ingram Micro, distributes computer hardware, software, and accessories from over 750 suppliers and has subsidiaries in Canada, Mexico, and 6 European countries. Ingram Book Company carries nearly 200,000 titles from more than 2,000 publishers. Ingram Entertainment is the world's largest seller of home entertainment products such as videos, laser discs, audio cassettes, video games, and musical tapes and CDs, with about 10% of the US videotape wholesale market.

Linwood Lacy, who is credited with transforming Ingram Micro — which now accounts for about 80% of the company's total sales — into the world's largest computer hardware and software distributor, was promoted to the post of president in late 1993. Ingram Micro has been experimenting with new ways to peddle, electronically, its products. The company now offers a catalog-on-a-disk, electronic data exchange, and its Customer-Assisted Purchasing System, an online interactive ordering service.

Ingram Industries, led by E. Bronson Ingram since 1963, also has interests in marine barging, aggregate supply, oil and gas wellhead equipment, and insurance.

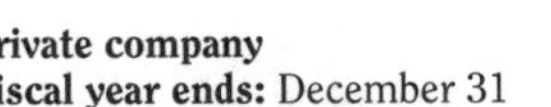

Private company
Fiscal year ends: December 31

WHO

Chairman and CEO: E. Bronson Ingram, age 61
President; Co-Chairman, Ingram Micro Inc.: Linwood A. Lacy, Jr., age 48
EVP; Chairman, Ingram Distribution Group Inc.: Philip M. Pfeffer
SVP: Roy E. Claverie
Co-Chairman, Ingram Micro Inc.: David R. Dukes
Chairman and COO, Ingram Book Co.: Lee Synnott
VP and Treasurer: Thomas H. Lunn
VP Human Resources: W. Michael Head

WHERE

HQ: One Belle Meade Place, 4400 Harding Rd., Nashville, TN 37205-2244
Phone: 615-298-8200
Fax: 615-298-8242

Ingram Book is headquartered in La Vergne, TN, with warehouses in Petersburg, VA; Avon, CT; Walnut, CA; Fort Wayne, IN; and Denver. Ingram Micro is headquartered in Santa Ana, CA, with warehouses in Cheshire, CT; Columbia, MD; Clarkston, GA; Buffalo Grove, IL; Carrollton, TX; and Fremont, CA.

WHEN

Bronson Ingram's great-grandfather, Orrin Ingram, was a New York farm boy who, in the late 1840s, took a job at a sawmill. He learned the business quickly and at age 21 began designing and operating mills in Ontario, Canada, for several owners. In 1857 Ingram and 2 partners founded a sawmill (Dole, Ingram & Kennedy) in Eau Claire, Wisconsin, on the Chippewa River, about 50 miles upstream from the Mississippi River. By the 1870s the company (renamed Ingram & Kennedy) was selling lumber as far downstream as Hannibal, Missouri.

Ingram's success was noticed by Frederick Weyerhaeuser, a German immigrant in Rock Island, Illinois, who, like Ingram, had worked in a sawmill before buying one of his own. In 1881 Ingram and 3 other companies formed Empire Lumber, with Orrin Ingram as president. That same year Ingram and Weyerhaeuser negotiated the formation of Chippewa Logging (35% owned by up-river partners, 65% owned by down-river interests), which controlled the white pine harvest of the Chippewa Valley.

In 1900 Ingram paid $216,000 for 2,160 shares in the newly formed Weyerhaeuser Timber Company. Ingram let his sons and grandsons handle the investment and formed O.H. Ingram Co. to manage the family's interests. He died in 1918.

Ingram's descendants founded the present conglomerate in 1946 by forming Ingram Barge, which hauled crude oil to the company's refinery near St. Louis. After buying and then selling other holdings, in 1962 the family formed Ingram Corp., which consisted solely of Ingram Barge. Brothers Bronson and Fritz Ingram bought the company from their father before he died in 1963. In 1964 they bought half of a textbook distributing company (Tennesee Book, founded 1935) and in 1970 formed Ingram Book to sell trade books to bookstores and libraries.

In 1982 Ingram formed a computer products distributor (Ingram Computer) and between 1985 and 1989 bought all the stock of Micro D, a Santa Ana–based computer wholesaler. Ingram merged Micro D with Ingram Computer to form Ingram Micro.

In 1990 Ingram Book opened 2 new warehouses. Ingram also gained a Denver warehouse 1991 through its purchase of Gordon's Books. In 1992 Ingram acquired Commtron, the world's #1 wholesaler of prerecorded video cassettes, and merged it into Ingram Entertainment. In late 1993 Ingram took Bantam Doubleday to court, charging unfair promotional practices and compensation to distributors.

Ingram said in 1994 that it was considering using Information Clearinghouse's Market/Net Online Catalog to market its products electronically. Also in 1994, Ingram Micro created a new subsidiary, Ingram Alliance Reseller Company, to service its high-volume resellers. The unit will provide deep discounting and specialty services to resellers who commit to buy at least $2 million of computer products each year. Initial customers include IBM, AST, and NEC.

WHAT

Ingram Book Publications and Services
Advance Magazine
Communique
Electronic ordering
Ingram Microfiche Service
Mac D Vision
Paperback Advance
Specialty magazines
Update
The Var Side
Videopedia

Ingram Distribution Group Inc.
Book Group
- Ingram Book Company
- Ingram International Inc.
- Ingram Library Services
- Ingram Periodicals Inc.
- Publisher Resources Inc.
- Tennessee Book Company

Entertainment Group
- Ingram Entertainment
- Ingram Merchandising Services Inc.

Microcomputer Group
- Ingram Alliance Reseller Co.

Ingram Micro Inc.
- Ingram Dicom S.A. de C.V. (Mexico)
- Ingram Micro Europe
- Ingram Micro Inc. (Canada)

Inland Marine Group
Ingram Barge Company (custom fuel services)
Ingram Materials Company

Energy Group
Ingram Cactus Company (66%; petroleum drilling equipment)
Ingram Coal Company
Ingram Production Company (owns 5% of an Indonesian oil field)

Insurance Group
Permanent General Companies (auto insurance)
Tennessee Insurance Company (insures Ingram affiliates)

HOW MUCH

	9-Year Growth	1984	1985	1986	1987	1988	1989	1990	1991	1992	1993
Estimated sales ($ mil.)	26.4%	750	900	1,000	1,170	—	2,090	2,677	3,422	4,657	6,163
Employees	17.9%	2,200	2,300	2,400	3,000	—	3,425	5,400	6,526	8,407	9,658

Estimated Sales ($ mil.) 1984–93

KEY COMPETITORS

Advanced Marketing
Atlantic Richfield
Baker & Taylor
Baker Hughes
BLOC Development
Bookazine
Brodart
Camco
Cargill
CIGNA
Coastal
Cooper Industries
CSX
Dresser
Egghead
W. R. Grace
Halliburton
Handleman
Kenfil
Lone Star Technologies
LTV
Merisel
Occidental
Otis Engineering
Pacific Pipeline
Software Spectrum
State Farm
Tech Data
USX-Marathon
Wal-Mart

IRVIN FELD & KENNETH FELD PRODUCTIONS

RANK: N/R

OVERVIEW

If there is one man in America who knows how many clowns can fit in a 1975 Pinto (and is working out a way to squeeze one more in), it is Kenneth Feld. Feld owns 82% of Irvin Feld & Kenneth Feld Productions, the largest live entertainment company in the world. Three company executives own the rest. The Vienna, Virginia–based company owns Ringling Brothers and Barnum & Bailey Circus and Walt Disney on Ice and produces a variety of other acts, including the Siegfried & Roy magic show.

Although Feld is closemouthed about how much the company takes in, *Forbes* estimates sales at about $500 million annually. The pretax profits of the company's concessioner, Sells-Floto, reportedly exceed 50%.

Feld is known in the industry for his tight-fisted ways. (He once challenged his sister's ownership of a house her father had given her.) He reportedly charges his circus performers, many of whom make about $20 a show, $10 a week to stay on the circus train and 25 cents a ride for a trip on the shuttle bus from the train to the arena.

With the collapse of communism threatening the state-supported circuses that had provided Feld with many of his performers, Feld is considering expanding the Ringling Clown College to include other circus performers.

Private company
Fiscal year ends: January 31

WHO

President: Kenneth Feld, age 45
SVP; VP and Treasurer, Ringling Brothers: Charles E. Smith
VP Marketing and Sales: Allen J. Bloom
Accounting Finance Manager: Joe Kobylski
Director Human Resources, Ringling Brothers: Connie Kepple

WHERE

HQ: Irvin Feld & Kenneth Feld Productions, Inc., 8607 Westwood Center Dr., Vienna, VA 22182-7506
Phone: 703-448-4000
Fax: 703-448-4100

Irvin Feld & Kenneth Feld Productions's shows are seen around the world by an estimated 25 million people per year.

WHEN

Legend has it when 5-year-old Irvin Feld found a $1 bill in 1923 he told his mother, "I'm going to buy a circus." It took him a few more years, and a few more dollars, but he did eventually fulfill his promise. He worked the sideshows of traveling circuses before settling in Washington, DC, in 1938, where he opened a novelty store. In 1940 Feld, who was white, opened the Super Cut-Rate Drugstore in a black section of segregated Washington with the backing of the NAACP.

Feld played gospel and popular music outside the pharmacy to attract customers, and later he began to stock records. In 1944 he opened the Super Music City record store and started his own record company, Super Disc. Feld and his brother Israel also began promoting outdoor concerts by Super Disc acts. When rock-and-roll became popular in the 1950s, Feld began promoting Chubby Checker and Fats Domino, among others.

In 1956 Feld began managing the Ringling Brothers and Barnum & Bailey Circus for majority owner John Ringling North. North's circus traced it roots back to promoter P. T. Barnum's circus, founded in 1871. In 1881 Barnum's circus merged with James Bailey's circus, creating Barnum and Bailey. In 1907 Bailey's widow sold Barnum and Bailey to North's uncles, the Ringling brothers, who had started their circus in 1884.

Among Feld's suggestions to North was moving the circus out from under the bigtop and into air-conditioned arenas, saving $50,000 per week because 1,800 roustabouts (who set up the tents) were no longer needed.

Feld continued to promote music acts, but he suffered a serious blow in 1959 when 3 of his stars — Buddy Holly, Ritchie Valens, and The Big Bopper — died in a plane crash.

Feld's dream of owning a circus came true in 1967 when he and a group of investors paid $8 million for Ringling Brothers. He fired most of the circus's performers and in 1968 opened his Clown College to train new ones. That same year Feld bought a German circus to get animal trainer Gunther Gebel-Williams. In 1969, in one of his most important innovations, Feld split the circus into 2 units so he could book it in 2 parts of the country at the same time and double his profits.

In 1971 Feld and the other investors sold the circus to Mattel for $50 million in stock, but Feld stayed on as manager. He held onto the lucrative concession business, Sells-Floto. In 1979 Feld convinced Mattel to buy the Ice Follies, Holiday on Ice, and the Siegfried & Roy magic show. When Mattel sold the circus back to Feld in 1982 for $22.6 million, he got the ice shows and the magic show, too.

When Irvin Feld died in 1984, his son Kenneth became head of the company. A chip off the old block, Kenneth fired almost all the circus performers when he took over. In 1985 Kenneth drew heat from the ASPCA when he introduced a new act to his circus — the Living Unicorn. Actually there were 2 living unicorns: each a goat with its horns laser grafted together by a Texas animal breeder.

In 1986 Kenneth took his Disney on Ice show to Japan, and in 1988 he started a 3rd circus unit for international touring.

In 1994 a Ringling Brothers circus train bound for a show in Orlando derailed near Lakeland, Florida; an animal trainer and a clown were killed.

WHAT

	1993 Estimated Sales % of total
Circus & ice show gate receipts	60
Concessions	40
Total	**100**

Attractions
American Gladiators Live
Fool Moon (touring Broadway show)
George Lucas's Super Live Adventure
Replica of the Space Shuttle
Ringling Bros. and Barnum & Bailey Circus
Siegfried & Roy magic show
Walt Disney's World on Ice

Selected Circus Acts
Amazing Españas Wheel of Death (motorcycle acrobatics)
Bamboo Balancers From The People's Republic of China
The Boger Buffaloes and Mountain Lions
Chepiakova & Kim (animal trainers)
Chinese Acrobatic Troupe
Crazy Clown Cavalcade
Johnny Peers' Muttville Comix (dogs)
Kaganovitch Flying Trapeze
The Lenz Chimpanzees
Mark Oliver Gebel (animal trainer)
Mednikov Highwire
Royal Bengal Tigers
Vivien Larible-Washington Trapeze

Subsidiaries
Feld Brothers Management (personal management)
Hagenbeck-Wallace (circus equipment)
Klowns Publishing Co. (show programs)
Sells-Floto (circus concessions)

HOW MUCH

	Annual Growth	1984	1985	1986	1987	1988	1989	1990	1991	1992	1993
Estimated sales ($ mil.)	—	—	—	—	—	—	—	—	—	—	494
Employees	—	—	—	—	—	—	—	—	—	—	2,500

Estimated Sales ($ mil.) 1993

KEY COMPETITORS

Anheuser-Busch
BET
Capital Cities/ABC
CBS
Cirque du Soleil
Clyde Beatty-Cole Brothers Circus
General Electric
Great American Circus
Hanneford Family Circus
Ice Capades
King World
Liberty Media
Metromedia
Pickle Family Circus
Sony
TCI
Thorn EMI
Time Warner
Turner Broadcasting
Viacom

J. CREW GROUP INC.

RANK: 460

OVERVIEW

Arthur Cinader, CEO of J. Crew Group, has captained a major success story in the mail order catalog business, but most of the credit should go to his daughter, Emily Woods. J. Crew Group is the parent company for 3 mail order catalogs: *J. Crew*, which markets to people in their thirties seeking a casual but elegant lifestyle; *Popular Club Plan*, which sells ladies' apparel, furniture, and kitchen supplies; and *Clifford & Wills*, which offers moderately priced clothing for career women. Father and daughter own the company.

The J. Crew subsidiary accounts for the bulk of company sales, and Woods, whose physical fitness regime includes weight lifting and boxing, is responsible for its rapid growth during the 1980s. Without any formal training in design, she masterminded the successful design and implementation of J. Crew's catalogs, retail stores, and clothing.

J. Crew sells more than just clothes; the company sells a lifestyle available to customers who buy and wear its clothing, which is designed and manufactured by J. Crew. Customers may buy the "J. Crew" look either in one of the company's 28 retail stores or from the catalog. Items available from the catalog are generally priced between $12 and $100, while the retail stores carry higher-priced clothing. Published 18 times a year with an average circulation of 4 million, the catalog is patterned after a magazine, with about 8,000 rolls of film exposed for each issue. Each week the company handles 50,000 catalog orders. A key to the success of J. Crew is its adoption of standardized sizing, which means that once a customer finds a size that fits, every other J. Crew item in that size will also fit.

Faced with increasing competition and rising postal rates, the company has initiated an ambitious international expansion of both its catalogs and its retail stores. It plans to have a strong foothold in Japan and Europe by 1995, as well as 50 retail stores in the US. Ventures into home furnishings and children's clothing are also being considered.

WHEN

Although J. Crew started in 1983, the Cinader family's participation in the mail order catalog business extends back to 1947, when Arthur Cinader's father, Mitchell Cinader, founded the *Popular Club Plan* with Saul Charles. The *Popular Club Plan* is a mail order catalog that sells ladies' apparel, furniture, and kitchen supplies.

After inheriting the *Popular Club Plan,* Arthur observed the remarkable growth in the late 1970s and early 1980s of *Talbots*, *L. L. Bean*, and other clothing catalogs. In 1983 he established his own women's classic apparel catalog as *J. Crew*, a name that connoted casual, collegiate clothing. First-year sales were about $3 million. The following year Arthur offered a job to his eldest daughter, Emily, who had recently graduated from the University of Denver. Her first decision was to ban polyester from all J. Crew clothes. Although early catalogs included clothing from a number of manufacturers, Emily moved the company to selling its own brand exclusively.

Also in 1984 Arthur started the *Clifford & Wills* catalog operation. J. Crew survived 2 major storms in the late 1980s. Executives Ted Pamperin and Jeff Aschkenes left J. Crew in 1987 to start *Tweeds*, a competing women's clothing catalog, and in 1989 the US Postal Service increased its rates by 30%.

Also in 1989 Emily became president of J. Crew at the ripe old age of 28. That same year the company launched a risky expansion into retail with its first store in the South Street Seaport area of New York City. Later that same year the company's 2nd retail store was opened in San Francisco a week before an earthquake struck the Bay Area. J. Crew has limited the cannibalization of its mail order sales by its retail operations by selling higher-priced goods in outlets and limiting inventory overlap. The retail operation has also provided a source of new customers for catalog sales.

In 1992 J. Crew licensed C. Itoh (the world's largest company, now known as ITOCHU) and Renown to market J. Crew apparel in Japan beginning in 1993. In 1993 J. Crew entered a licensing agreement with 3 Suisses International, France's 2nd largest mail order house, to market its lines of clothing in Europe. Also in 1993 Arnold Cohen stepped down as president and COO of J. Crew Group to become CEO of London Fog.

In 1994 Robert Bernard, former president of Liz Claiborne International, was named president and COO of J. Crew Group. Also in 1994 the company introduced a line of more sophisticated evening wear for women. The clothes will be sold in J. Crew's stores but will not be in its catalogs.

HOW MUCH

	Annual Growth	1985	1986	1987	1988	1989	1990	1991	1992	1993	1994
Sales ($ mil.)	24.0%	92	115	148	190	238	314	354	466	564	636
Number of stores	—	—	—	—	—	—	3	9	11	19	28
Employees	17.5%	1,500	1,750	2,100	2,550	2,300	2,700	3,670	4,479	5,413	6,400

J.CREW

Private company
Fiscal year ends: Last Saturday in January

WHO

Chairman and CEO: Arthur Cinader, age 65
VC and Head Designer; President, J. Crew Inc.: Emily Cinader Woods, age 33
President and COO: Robert Bernard, age 43
EVP: Keith Monda
VP Operations: Robert Paris
VP Finance and CFO: Michael P. McHugh
President, *Popular Club Plan*: Jim Northrop
President, *Clifford & Wills*: Alyce Goodman
VP Human Resources: Carol Dudgeon
Auditors: Deloitte & Touche

WHERE

HQ: 625 Sixth Ave., New York, NY 10011
Phone: 212-886-2500
Fax: 212-886-2666

J. Crew Group operates through 3 subsidiaries that sell clothing and other items throughout the US via mail order catalogs. One of those subsidiaries, J. Crew, Inc., also sells its apparel lines through 28 retail outlets in the US and has entered licensing agreements to sell its apparel in Japan and Europe.

	No. of Retail Stores
California	2
Illinois	3
Massachusetts	2
Michigan	1
Missouri	1
New Mexico	2
New York	1
Texas	2
Other states	14
Total	**28**

WHAT

	1994 Sales % of total
Mail order catalog & outlet stores	65
Retail stores	35
Total	**100**

	1994 Sales $ mil.	1994 Sales % of total
J. Crew, Inc.	350	55
Other operations	286	45
Total	**636**	**100**

Subsidiaries
Clifford & Wills (women's better-price career catalog)
J. Crew, Inc. (catalog and retail stores selling casually elegant clothing)
Popular Club Plan (moderate-price catalog offering ladies' apparel, furniture, and kitchen supplies)

KEY COMPETITORS

Ames
L. L. Bean
Benetton
Bombay Company
Broadway Stores
CML Group
Crate & Barrel
Dayton Hudson
Dillard
Federated
Fingerhut Cos.
The Gap
Harcourt General
Hartmarx
Lands' End
The Limited
Liz Claiborne
Loehmann's
Macy
Marks and Spencer
May
Melville
Men's Wearhouse
Montgomery Ward
Nordstrom
J. C. Penney
Sears
Spiegel
Talbots
Tweeds
U. S. Shoe

JM FAMILY ENTERPRISES INC.

RANK: 82

OVERVIEW

When auto enthusiasts think of a #1 family enterprise having to do with cars, they might mention the Pettys or the Unsers. At JM Family Enterprises, the car connection is showroom stock, not stock car racing. And its #1 ranking has to do with sales — its Southeast Toyota Distributors is the world's largest Toyota distributor, dealing in trucks and forklifts as well as cars, and JM Pontiac is the nation's #1 Pontiac dealer.

JM Family Enterprises's auto empire consists of its wholesale distributorship, 2 retail dealerships, leasing and financing through World Omni Finance, companies that process imported vehicles through Florida ports, a parts supplier, insurance companies, and a chemical company that makes auto protectants. In all, there are more than 20 companies owned by JM Family Enterprises.

The "JM" of the company name is Jim Moran, patriarch and company chairman. Moran, whose fortune is estimated at more than $600 million by *Forbes*, has passed on the presidency to his daughter Pat. Company sales put Pat at the top of the *Working Woman* magazine/National Foundation for Women Business Owners 1993 list of top female business owners.

Private company
Fiscal year ends: December 31

WHO

Chairman: James M. Moran, age 75
President: Patricia Moran, age 47
EVP: Lawrence Rich
EVP: L. Wayne McClain
SVP and CFO: Casey L. Gunnell
VP: Janice M. Moran
VP and General Counsel: Colin W. Brown
VP Human Resources: Rhonda B. Gallaspy
Auditors: Arthur Andersen & Co.

WHEN

Jim Moran first became visible as "Jim Moran, the Courtesy Man" in Chicago TV advertisements in the 1950s. At that time he ran Courtesy Motors, where he was so successful as the world's #1 Ford dealer that his picture was on the cover of *Time* magazine in 1961.

Moran had entered the auto sales business after getting more than 3 times the price he had paid for a car he fixed up. That profit was much better than what he made at the Sinclair gas station he had bought, so he opened a used car lot. Later, he moved to new car sales when he bought a Hudson franchise (Ford had rejected him). In 1948 Moran saw the promise of television advertising and pioneered the forum for Chicago car dealers, not only as an advertiser and program sponsor but as host of a variety show and a country-and-western music barn dance. The increased visibility positioned Moran as Hudson's #1 dealer, but the sales tactics at Courtesy Motors earned an antitrust suit that was settled out of court.

In 1955 Moran started with Ford, and, with his TV influence (at this time he was host of "The Jim Moran Courtesy Hour"), he became the world's #1 Ford dealer in his first month.

Moran moved to Florida in 1966 after being diagnosed with cancer and given one year to live. As he was successfully fighting the disease, he bought a Pontiac franchise and later started Southeast Toyota Distributors. In 1969 he formed JM Family Enterprises.

In 1973, legal problems set in when the Internal Revenue Service investigated a Nassau bank for serving as a tax haven for wealthy Americans and for its organized crime ownership. Moran's name, as well as the names of 3 Toyota executives, turned up. In 1978, Moran was indicted for tax fraud. Although Moran thought his attorney had worked out an exchange of testimony for immunity, the Justice Department refused to grant Moran immunity. In 1984 Moran entered a guilty plea to 7 tax charges and was sentenced to 2 years (suspended), fined more than $12 million, and ordered to perform community service. Moran's legal problems threatened his association with Toyota and were blamed for causing a stroke in 1983.

Legal problems continued in the 1980s, partly because of the imposition of auto import restrictions. To get more cars to sell, some managers at Southeast Toyota encouraged auto dealers to illegally file false sales reports. Some North Carolina dealers resisted, and one sued, settling out of court for $22 million. In the 1980s other dealers alleged racketeering and fraud on the part of Southeast, and by the beginning of 1994 JM had paid more than $100 million in fines and settlements for cases stretching back to 1988. However, JM's legal troubles did not drive Toyota away. Toyota did not exercise its option to withdraw its business from JM, and in 1993 Toyota renewed its contract with the company a year early.

Pat Moran succeeded her father as JM president in 1992 (the year her father was named the most admired car dealer in the US) after working her way through several executive positions. She started with the company as a clerk typist after working outside the family fold as a nurse and a travel agent.

JM Family Enterprises still faces some legal actions, and in 1994 the 3rd suit since 1991 alleging racism against blacks in establishing Toyota dealerships was filed against Jim Moran and Southeast Toyota (the first 2 were settled out of court).

WHERE

HQ: 100 NW 12th Ave., Deerfield Beach, FL 33442-1702
Phone: 305-429-2000
Fax: 305-429-2300

JM Family Enterprises operates its auto distribution, leasing, and financing businesses across the US, but its operations are concentrated in the Southeast, especially in Florida and Alabama .

WHAT

Selected Subsidiaries and Affiliates

Auction Enterprises, Inc.
Executive Incentives & Travel
JM Family Enterprises International Inc. (partnership in North American Vehicle Imports SA; GM vehicle and parts distributor; Europe)
JM Lexus (retail auto sales)
JM Pontiac & GMC Truck (retail auto sales)
JM&A Group (auto service contracts, insurance)
Courtesy Insurance Company
Fidelity Acceptance Corp.
Fidelity Insurance Agency, Inc.
Fidelity Warranty Services Inc.
JM&Associates
JMIC Life Insurance Co.
Joyserv Company, Ltd. (auto imports processor)
Distribution Center of Commerce (North American–made Toyota processor)
Petro Chemical Products
Southeast Industrial Equipment, Inc.
Southeast Toyota Distributors, Inc.
Carnett (data processing)
S.E.T. Parts (Toyota parts distributor)
S.E.T. Service (training)
World Cars (auto imports processor)
World Omni Finance Corporation (dealer financing, consumer auto leasing)

HOW MUCH

	Annual Growth	1984	1985	1986	1987	1988	1989	1990	1991	1992	1993
Estimated sales ($ mil.)	8.2%	—	—	1,500	2,100	2,400	2,134	2,295	2,400	2,600	2,600
Employees	(1.7%)	—	—	2,600	2,300	2,300	2,226	2,107	2,300	2,300	2,300

Estimated Sales ($ mil.) 1986–93

KEY COMPETITORS

BMW
Chrysler
Daimler-Benz
Fiat
Ford
General Motors
Honda
Island Lincoln Mercury
Isuzu
Mazda
Mid-Atlantic Cars
Morse Operations
Nissan
Peugeot
Potamkim Manhattan
Renault
Saab-Scania
Suzuki
Toyota
Volkswagen
Volvo

JOHN HANCOCK MUTUAL LIFE

RANK: 14

OVERVIEW

The US's 9th largest life insurer, John Hancock made a financial comeback in 1993, with income rising 41% from 1992. An increase in sales of life insurance was the primary driver behind this profit growth.

The company's international operations include associate insurers in 46 countries worldwide. In addition, John Hancock has acquired companies in emerging life insurance markets in Southeast Asia, such as Malaysia and Singapore.

John Hancock prefers to call itself a financial services company. In addition to traditional insurance and related products and services, the company offers brokerage and banking services (First Signature Bank, New Hampshire, 1985) and investment funds, especially in nontraditional areas: real estate syndicates, timber management (the world's largest timber management organization), and asset management.

In 1994 John Hancock Mutual Insurance Company (Massachusetts) and Cost Care, Inc. (acquired by John Hancock in 1990), formed TriState Network Services, a managed care referral service linking 20 hospitals and 2,100 doctors in the New York area.

John Hancock FINANCIAL SERVICES

Mutual company
Fiscal year ends: December 31

WHO

Chairman and CEO: Stephen L. Brown, age 56
President and COO: William L. Boyan, age 56
VC and Chief Investment Officer: Foster L. Aborn
EVP Corporate Sector: Diane M. Capstaff
SEVP Retail Sector: David F. D'Alessandro
SEVP Business Insurance: George F. Miller
Corporate Secretary: Bruce E. Skrine
General Counsel: Richard S. Scipione, age 56
CFO: Thomas E. Moloney
VP Corporate Human Resources: A. Page Palmer
Auditors: Ernst & Young

WHEN

In 1862 Albert Murdock and other Boston businessmen founded John Hancock Mutual Life Insurance Co., named after the signer of the Declaration of Independence. In 1865 the company added agents in Pennsylvania, Illinois, Connecticut, and Missouri.

In 1866 the company began making annual distributions of surplus to paid-up policyholders. In 1879 John Hancock became the first US mutual life insurance company to offer industrial insurance (weekly premium life insurance in small amounts). The company was also a pioneer in granting dividends and cash surrender values (the amount returned to the policyholder when a policy is canceled) with industrial insurance. In 1902 the company's weekly premium agencies began to sell annual premium insurance. By 1912 the company had more than $600 million worth of insurance in force.

John Hancock added annuities in 1922, group insurance in 1924, and individual health insurance in 1957. In 1968 the company formed John Hancock Advisers (mutual funds) and John Hancock International Group Program (group health and life insurance overseas). In the early 1970s it started property and casualty insurance operations in partnership with Sentry Insurance.

Despite these forays into new areas, John Hancock's mainstay was still whole life insurance, which was traditionally seen as a safe investment. In the late 1970s, as interest rates soared toward 20%, policyholders borrowed on their policies at low rates to invest at higher rates, draining company funds. Though interest rates later declined, the company was convinced that it had to diversify in order to survive and prosper.

Acquisitions included Tucker Anthony & R.L. Day (securities brokerage, Boston, 1982); Gabriele, Hueglin & Cashman (fixed-income securities, New York, 1985); and Sutro & Co. (investments, California, 1986). New product offerings included equipment leasing (1980), universal life (1983), and credit cards (1985).

Despite the proliferation of products, Hancock's position in the industry declined from 5th in 1978 to 9th. In the late 1980s Hancock became known for unusual investment vehicles. By 1990, of the $2.9 billion in nontraditional assets under management, 31% was in timber funds, 31% in venture capital funds, and the remainder in power, real estate, and agriculture. Because of its relatively large investment in real estate during the 1980s, Hancock established loss reserves to protect against potential defaults.

Insurers have generally found asset management a successful diversification, and John Hancock is aiming to become a major player in mutual funds.

The company expanded overseas with the acquisition of interests in insurers in Singapore and Thailand. In 1992 First Signature Bank sold its credit card operations to National Westminster Bank (UK) to concentrate on other business segments.

In 1994 John Hancock agreed to pay over $1 million in fines for making gifts (primarily entertainment costs) to Massachusetts state legislators over a period of 6 years. Of that sum, $900,000 was paid to the federal government and $110,000 to the state.

WHERE

HQ: John Hancock Mutual Life Insurance Company, PO Box 111, Boston, MA 02117
Phone: 617-572-6000
Fax: 617-572-6451

John Hancock is licensed in all 50 states, the District of Columbia, and Canada. It has subsidiaries and affiliates in Belgium, Indonesia, Malaysia, Thailand, and the UK and does business in 45 countries worldwide.

WHAT

	1993 Sales	
	$ mil.	% of total
Premiums	8,814	69
Net investment income	3,058	24
Other	860	7
Total	**12,732**	**100**

Selected Services
- Banking services
- Group life, accident, and health insurance
- Group retirement funds
- Guaranteed investment contracts
- Life insurance and annuities
- Long-term care insurance
- Mortgage loans
- Mutual funds
- Property and casualty insurance
- Securities brokerage and investment banking

Selected Subsidiaries
- P.T. Asuransi Jiwa Bumiputera John Hancock (Indonesia)
- British American Life Insurance Berhad (Malaysia)
- The Interlife Assurance Company Ltd. (Thailand)
- John Hancock Advisers International Ltd. (UK)
- John Hancock Intl. Holdings, Inc.
- John Hancock International Services Pte. Ltd. (Singapore)
- John Hancock International Services, S.A. (Belgium)
- John Hancock Life Assurance Company, Ltd.
- The Maritime Life Assurance Company (Nova Scotia)

HOW MUCH

	Annual Growth	1984	1985	1986	1987	1988	1989	1990	1991	1992	1993
Assets ($ mil.)	7.2%	24,840	26,594	27,808	28,211	29,461	32,344	35,332	38,105	41,242	46,468
Net income ($ mil.)	2.6%	158	108	134	132	171	232	224	233	141	199
Income as % of assets	—	0.6%	0.4%	0.5%	0.5%	0.6%	0.7%	0.6%	0.6%	0.3%	0.4%
Employees	1.3%	—	—	—	—	—	15,655	16,000	16,500	13,903	16,500

1993 Year-end:
Equity as % of assets: 3.9%
Return on equity: 11.2%
Cash (mil.): $1,076
Sales (mil.): $12,732

Assets ($ mil.) 1984–93

KEY COMPETITORS

Aetna
Allstate
Blue Cross
Charles Schwab
Chase Manhattan
Chemical Banking
Chubb
CIGNA
Citicorp
Conseco
Dean Witter, Discover
First Chicago
FMR
Kemper
Lehman Brothers
MassMutual
Merrill Lynch
MetLife
Morgan Stanley
New York Life
Northwestern Mutual
Oxford Health Plans
Prudential
Sierra Health Services
State Farm
T. Rowe Price
Teachers Insurance
Transamerica
Travelers
USF&G

JOHNSON PUBLISHING COMPANY

RANK: N/R

OVERVIEW

America's 2nd largest black-owned business (after TLC Beatrice), Johnson Publishing is the leading US publisher of black-oriented magazines, including *Ebony*, which reaches more than 11 million readers, and *Jet*, which reaches nearly 9 million. The Chicago-based company also publishes *EM*, a men's magazine, and owns 2 radio stations. The company also makes Duke and Raveen hair care products and produces cosmetics. Since 1978 the company has sponsored the "American Black Achievement Awards," a nationally syndicated TV special. Johnson's book division features works by black authors.

In 1993 Johnson added a new line of cosmetics to go with its Fashion Fair line. The new, lower-cost line, called Ebone, is targeted at younger black women and is designed to take on such lower-priced lines as Color Style, manufactured by Revlon, and Shades of You by Maybelline. Johnson also produces a fashion roadshow, Ebony Fashion Fair, which tours nearly 200 cities a year.

The company is owned by founder John Johnson, his wife, Eunice, and their daughter Linda Johnson Rice. John Johnson, who says he practices "hands-on, hands-in, hands-wrapped-around management," has served on the advisory board of the Harvard Business School and is a major contributor to black-oriented causes. He plans to pass control of the company to his daughter when he retires.

Private company
Fiscal year ends: December 31

WHO

Chairman and CEO: John H. Johnson, age 75
President and COO: Linda Johnson Rice, age 35
Secretary and Treasurer: Eunice W. Johnson, age 72
Controller: Gregory Robertson
Personnel Director: La Doris Foster

WHERE

HQ: Johnson Publishing Company, Inc., 820 S. Michigan Ave., Chicago, IL 60605
Phone: 312-322-9200
Fax: 312-322-0918

WHEN

John Johnson launched his publishing business in 1942 while still in college in Chicago. The idea for a magazine oriented to blacks came to him while working part-time for Supreme Life Insurance Co. of America, where one of his jobs was to summarize news about the black community from magazines and newspapers. With $500 his mother raised by mortgaging family furniture, Johnson mailed a $2 charter subscription offer to potential subscribers. He got 3,000 replies and with that $6,000 printed the first issue of *Negro Digest*, patterned after *Reader's Digest*. Within a year circulation was 50,000.

In 1945 Johnson started *Ebony* magazine, immediately popular in the black community and still Johnson's premier publication. *Ebony* (like *Life*, but focusing on black culture and achievements) and *Jet* (a celebrity-oriented magazine started in 1951) were the only publications for US blacks for 20 years.

In the early days Johnson was unable to obtain advertising, so he formed his own mail order business called Beauty Star and advertised its products (dresses, wigs, hair care products, and vitamins) through his magazines. Through persistence he won his first major account, Zenith Radio, by 1947.

By the 1960s Johnson had become one of the most prominent black men in America. In 1963 he posed with John F. Kennedy to publicize a special issue of *Ebony* celebrating the Emancipation Proclamation. *Negro Digest*, renamed *Black World*, became known for its provocative articles, but its circulation dwindled from 100,000 to 15,000. Johnson stopped publishing the magazine in 1975. In the meantime US magazine publishers named Johnson Publisher of the Year in 1972.

Unable to find the proper makeup for his *Ebony* models, Johnson founded his own cosmetics business, Fashion Fair Cosmetics, in 1973. Fashion Fair competed successfully against Revlon (who introduced cosmetic lines for blacks) and another black cosmetics company, Johnson Products (unrelated) of Chicago. By 1982 sales for the Fashion Fair division alone were more than $30 million.

In 1973 Johnson also launched *Ebony Jr!*, a magazine for black preteens, designed, like many of the company's ventures, to provide "positive black images." Johnson bought radio stations WJPC (Chicago's first black-owned station) and WLOU (Louisville, Kentucky) in 1974 and WLNR (Lansing, Illinois) in the mid-1980s (merged into WJPC in 1992). In 1984 Johnson Publishing passed Motown Industries to become the largest black-owned business in America. In 1987 TLC Beatrice passed Johnson to become #1. That same year *Black Enterprise* magazine selected John Johnson as Entrepreneur of the Decade.

In 1991 John Johnson and the company sold their controlling interest in Illinois's last minority-owned insurance company (and Johnson's first employer), Supreme Life Insurance, to Unitrin. That same year Johnson and Spiegel announced that they would jointly develop black women's fashions and an associated mail order catalog business.

The catalog, called *E Style*, was launched in 1993. It features clothing and home fashions. In 1994 Johnson and Spiegel introduced a credit card to go with the catalog.

WHAT

Business Lines

Beauty Aids
Ebone Cosmetics
Fashion Fair Cosmetics
Supreme Beauty Products Co.
Duke (hair care for men)
Raveen (hair care for women)

Books
Johnson Publishing Co. Book Division

Fashion
E Style (women's fashion catalog)
Ebony Fashion Fair

Magazines
Ebony
EM (Ebony Man)
Jet

Radio Stations
WJPC (AM/FM), Chicago
WLOU (AM), Louisville

Television Production
"American Black Achievement Awards"

KEY COMPETITORS

Advance Publications
Amway
Avon
BET
Capital Cities/ABC
Colgate-Palmolive
Cox Enterprises
Essence Communications
Estée Lauder
Gannett
Gillette
Hearst
Knight-Ridder
L'Oréal
Luster Products
MacAndrews & Forbes
Matra-Hachette
New York Times
Pavion
Procter & Gamble
Reader's Digest
Soft Sheen Products
Time Warner
Tribune
Unilever
Washington Post

HOW MUCH

	9-Year Growth	1984	1985	1986	1987	1988	1989	1990	1991	1992	1993
Sales ($ mil.)	8.7%	139	155	174	202	217	241	252	261	274	294
Employees	4.3%	1,786	1,802	1,828	1,903	2,364	2,370	2,382	2,710	2,785	2,600

Sales ($ mil.) 1984–93

S.C. JOHNSON & SON, INC.

RANK: 53

OVERVIEW

S.C. Johnson & Son is one of the largest makers of consumer chemical specialty products in the world. The Racine, Wisconsin–based company is a leader and innovator. Market-leading company products include Edge shaving gel (with a 27% market share), Raid household insecticide (about 33%), OFF! insect repellent (more than 50%), and Glade air freshener (32%).

Commonly known as Johnson Wax because of its popular floor wax products, the company also has interests in real estate, recreational products, sanitation services, over-the-counter drugs, commercial pest control, and venture capital financing.

Johnson has made several acquisitions recently, including Drackett, maker of Drano and Windex, but the added products have brought increased competition from heavyweights like Procter & Gamble and Clorox. In response, Johnson has raised its global advertising budget, stepped up product development, and increased its presence in the international market through acquisitions and alliances.

The company operates a charitable foundation and also gives 5% of pretax profits to charity. Chairman Samuel Johnson, whose great-grandfather founded the company, controls 60% of S.C. Johnson.

WHEN

S.C. Johnson & Son was founded in Racine, Wisconsin, in 1886 by Samuel C. Johnson, a carpenter whose customers were as interested in his floor wax product as in his parquet floors. Forsaking carpentry, Johnson began to manufacture floor care products. By the time his son and successor, Herbert Fiske Johnson, died in 1928, annual sales were $5 million. A dispute over Herbert's estate was later settled, with his son Herbert Jr. and his daughter Henrietta Louis receiving 60% and 40%, respectively, of the company.

In 1954, when annual sales were $45 million, Herbert Jr.'s son Samuel Curtis Johnson joined the company. As new products director, Samuel turned his attention in 1955 to insect control. In 1956 the company introduced Raid, the first indoor/outdoor insecticide, and soon thereafter an insect repellent, OFF!. Each became a leader in its market. The 1950s and 1960s saw unsuccessful diversification efforts into the paint, chemical, and lawn care businesses. The home care products section prospered, however, with the introduction of Pledge aerosol furniture polish and Glade aerosol air freshener.

Herbert Jr. suffered a stroke in 1965, and Samuel became president. Sales were $200 million that year. Herbert Jr. lived 13 more years, spending much of them ensuring continued family ownership of the business. Samuel, also determined to maintain family ownership, decided in 1965 to develop a recreational products business that could eventually be sold to pay estate taxes. This new company acquired boating, fishing, and camping gear companies and an ink stamping equipment maker. When the company went public in 1987 as Johnson Worldwide Associates, Inc., the family retained a large ownership interest and effective voting control. Johnson Worldwide had sales of $280 million in 1993.

In the 1970s successful product launches included Edge shaving gel and Agree hair products. In the 1980s, however, the company made few successful product launches.

In the 1970s the company moved into real estate with Johnson Wax Development (JWD). However, in 1989, with a portfolio worth $600 million, Johnson began winding JWD down, selling its portfolio.

S. Curtis Johnson, Samuel's son, joined Johnson in 1983 (all 4 of the chairman's children work there) and was instrumental in the company's investment in Wind Point Partners I, a $36 million venture capital fund, and, later, Wind Point Partners II. In 1986 Johnson bought Bugs Burger Bug Killers, moving into commercial pest control, and 4 years later entered into an agreement with Mycogen Corporation to develop biological pesticides for household use. Also in 1990 the company began selling a line of children's shampoos under the Fisher-Price (the toy maker spun off by Quaker Oats) label.

In 1993 the company sold the Agree and Halsa hair care lines to Dep Corporation. The next year Dep brought suit to make Johnson take the products back, charging that the company had altered its marketing efforts for these products during the sales negotiations.

HOW MUCH

	Annual Growth	1984	1985	1986	1987	1988	1989	1990	1991	1992	1993
Estimated sales ($ mil.)	7.4%	—	2,000	2,000	2,000	2,400	2,500	3,000	3,400	3,300	3,550
Employees	1.1%	—	12,000	11,000	11,000	11,500	12,000	13,000	13,600	13,400	13,100

SC Johnson wax

Private company
Fiscal year ends: Friday nearest June 30

WHO

Chairman: Samuel C. Johnson, age 65
President and CEO: William D. George, Jr., age 61
President and COO, Worldwide Consumer Products: William D. Perez
President and COO, Worldwide Professional: Barry P. Harris
EVP; Regional Director, Consumer Products, Europe: Gianni C. Montezemolo
EVP; Regional Director, Consumer Products, Asia/Pacific: Laurance R. Newman
SVP, Secretary, and General Counsel: Robert C. Hart
SVP and CFO: Neal R. Nottleson
SVP Human Resources and Corporate Communications Worldwide: M. Garvin Shankster
Auditors: Coopers & Lybrand

WHERE

HQ: 1525 Howe St., Racine, WI 53403-5011
Phone: 414-631-2000
Fax: 414-631-2133

S.C. Johnson has operations in the US and 46 foreign countries and distributors in over 20 countries.

	1993 No. of Employees	1993 % of Total
US	3,300	25
Other countries	9,800	75
Total	**13,100**	**100**

WHAT

Principal Subsidiaries

Johnson Venture Capital, Inc. (Chicago, IL; major limited partner in venture capital fund, Wind Point Partners LP)
Micro-Gen Equipment Corp. (San Antonio, TX; pest control equipment and chemicals)
PRISM (Miami, FL; sanitation services for restaurants and hotels)

Affiliated Enterprise

Johnson Worldwide (recreational products)

Principal US Brand Names

Home Care
Bathroom Duck
Brite
Drano
Favor
Fine Wood
Future
Glade
Glo-Coat
Glory
Jubilee
Klean 'n Shine
Klear
Pledge
Shout
Step Saver
Toilet Duck
Vanish
Windex

Insect Control
OFF!
Raid

Personal Care
Aveeno (bath products)
Edge (shaving products)
Rhuli (skin products)

KEY COMPETITORS

Amway
Bayer
Bristol-Myers Squibb
Carter-Wallace
Church & Dwight
Clorox
Colgate-Palmolive
Dial
Dow Chemical
DuPont
Eastman Kodak
First Brands
Gillette
Henkel
Johnson & Johnson
Pfizer
Procter & Gamble
Unilever

K-III COMMUNICATIONS CORPORATION

RANK: 359

OVERVIEW

K·III

Since 1989 K-III has spent over a billion dollars assembling a publishing and information empire. Led by CEO William Reilly, K-III continues to seek acquisitions that will place it among the major media conglomerates. Investment firm Kohlberg Kravis Roberts owns 88.4% of the New York–based company, and K-III management owns 9%.

K-III's Weekly Reader is the US's #1 publisher of student newspapers; Newfield is the largest direct marketer of children's book clubs in the US; and Krames is the largest provider of health care publications sold to US medical providers for distribution to patients. Funk & Wagnalls (*New Encyclopedia* and the *World Almanac*) is the #3 publisher of general reference encyclopedias in the US and Canada.

K-III's consumer magazines include *Automobile, New York, New Woman, Premiere, Seventeen, Soap Opera Digest,* and *Soap Opera Weekly* magazines. Through its Intertec subsidiary it publishes 28 trade magazines for specific markets, including agriculture, telecommunications, and automobiles.

K-III also publishes *Daily Racing Form*, a national Thoroughbred horse racing newspaper, and newsletters, service manuals, and directories for everything from the financial services industry to the music business.

In late 1993 K-III lost out to Paramount Communications in its bid to buy Macmillan. It was a major disappointment for Reilly, who had served as Macmillan's president for 9 years.

WHEN

In 1989, with several publishing properties up for grabs and most potential buyers burdened with heavy debt, Kohlberg Kravis Roberts & Co. zeroed in on the publishing industry as a solid investment opportunity. So KKR and several publishing executives, including future K-III CEO William Reilly, CFO Charles McCurdy, and General Counsel Beverly Chell, set up K-III Holdings to acquire Intertec Publishing and Newbridge Communications. The total price for Intertec (acquired from JW Corporation) and Newbridge (acquired from Macmillan) was $320 million.

Reilly and KKR had been buddies since KKR had backed him in his bid to buy Macmillan in 1988, a battle he lost to Robert Maxwell. But Reilly did get something from Macmillan: he brought 45 of the company's executives with him to K-III, including his entire management team. Reilly and his crew set about making K-III a major media player.

In 1991 KKR and K-III's management formed a 2nd partnership and paid $162 million for Weekly Reader, Newfield Publications, and Funk & Wagnalls. The deal doubled K-III's number of operating divisions at the time, but more targets were on the horizon.

Later that year the group formed a 3rd partnership and beat out a passel of rival bidders, including Condé Nast and Hearst, to pick up several publications from Rupert Murdoch's News Corp. K-III paid $675 million for 9 publications, including *Soap Opera Digest, Seventeen,* and the *Daily Racing Form.*

In 1992 the group paid $44 million for medical information publisher Krames Communications. Also in 1992 it consolidated the 3 partnerships into K-III Communications. By the end of 1992 K-III had spent a total of $1.3 billion on acquisitions.

In 1993 the group was outbid by Condé Nast when it tried to buy *Bon Appetit* and *Architectural Digest.* K-III also had trouble starting its own magazines; 2 publications test marketed in 1993, *Soap Opera Illustrated* and *True News* (celebrity and tabloid news), failed to win consumer support. *True News* was dropped and *Soap Opera Illustrated* was turned into a quarterly.

Those setbacks didn't slow down K-III's acquisitions department. In 1993 Funk & Wagnalls acquired the *World Almanac (*the #1 English language almanac) and the World Almanac Education division of United Media Publishing. Also in 1993 K-III acquired trade magazines *Soybean Digest* and *Stitches* and directory publisher Nelson Publications.

In 1994 the company acquired New York's B&B Enterprises, owner of Stagebill, the US's largest publisher of performing arts magazines. It also bought Whittle's Channel One education cable TV network, getting Chris Whittle in the bargain.

HOW MUCH

	Annual Growth	1984	1985	1986	1987	1988	1989	1990	1991	1992	1993
Sales ($ mil.)	8.4%	—	—	—	—	565	714	795	779	778	845
Net income ($ mil.)	—	—	—	—	—	23	(23)	(24)	(87)	(145)	(86)
Income as % of sales	—	—	—	—	—	4.0%	—	—	—	—	—
Employees	2.9%	—	—	—	—	—	—	3,300	3,473	3,445	3,600

1993 Year-end:
Debt ratio: 96%
Return on equity: —
Cash (mil.): $12
Current ratio: 1.01
Long-term debt (mil.): $661

Net Income ($ mil.) 1988–93

50
0
-50
-100
-150

Private company
Fiscal year ends: December 31

WHO

Chairman and CEO: William F. Reilly, age 55, $1,297,008 pay
President: Charles G. McCurdy, age 38, $795,322 pay
VC, General Counsel, and Secretary: Beverly C. Chell, age 51, $770,322 pay
VP and President, K-III Magazine Group: Harry A. McQuillen, age 47, $803,721 pay
VP and President, K-III Information Group: Jack L. Farnsworth, age 48, $687,326 pay
VP and President, Education Group: Peter J. Quandt, age 45, $544,901 pay
VP, Controller, and CFO: Curtis A. Thompson, age 42
VP Human Resources: Michaelanne C. Discepolo
Auditors: Deloitte & Touche

WHERE

HQ: 745 Fifth Ave., New York, NY 10151
Phone: 212-745-0100
Fax: 212-745-0169

WHAT

	1993 Sales		1993 Operating Income	
	$ mil.	% of total	$ mil.	% of total
Education	388	46	20	—
Magazine publishing	325	38	(4)	—
Information	132	16	(12)	—
Adjustments	—	—	(12)	—
Total	**845**	**100**	**(8)**	**—**

1993 K-III Magazines Circulation

	Avg. circulation (thou.)	Freq. of pub.
Automobile	566	monthly
New Woman	1,358	monthly
New York	434	50 issues per year
Premiere	605	monthly
Seventeen	1,907	monthly
Soap Opera Digest	1,443	bi-weekly
Soap Opera Weekly	520	weekly
Total	**6,833**	

Divisions

Education
Krames Communications, Incorporated (medical information booklets)
Newbridge Communications, Inc. (scientific and professional book clubs, educational programs, classic books, films)
Newfield Publications, Inc. (book clubs)
Weekly Reader Corporation

Magazine Publishing
K-III Magazines Corporation
Intertec Publishing Corporation (trade magazines, newsletters)

Information
Daily Racing Form
Funk & Wagnalls
K-III Directory Corporation
Nelson Publications, Inc.

KEY COMPETITORS

Advance Publications
Andrews and McMeel
Berkshire Hathaway
Bertelsmann
Capital Cities/ABC
Chronicle Publishing
Encyclopaedia Britannica
Hearst
Houghton Mifflin
John Wiley
Matra-Hachette
McGraw-Hill
New York Times
Pearson
Reader's Digest
Reed Elsevier
Scholastic
Thomson Corp.
Time Warner
Times Mirror
Tribune
TRW
Viacom

KAISER FOUNDATION, INC.

RANK: 15

OVERVIEW

The Kaiser Foundation Health Plan, more commonly known as Kaiser Permanente, is the umbrella organization for the Kaiser Foundation Hospitals and the Permanente Medical Groups. Kaiser Permanente is the largest managed health care system in the US, with nearly 6.6 million members, more than 9,300 physicians, and 29 medical centers throughout the US (although 25 of these are concentrated in California).

The Kaiser Foundation Health Plan (one of several charitable foundations established by the industrialist Henry J. Kaiser) exists to ensure the capitalization of the organization's health care and hospital systems. The health care system had revenues of $11.9 billion in 1993.

The Permanente Groups employ Kaiser's 9,308 physicians. However, the system's doctor/patient ratio is well below the nationwide ratio of 2.5, which often translates into lengthy waiting periods for nonemergency appointments.

However, the size of the system, which received 40 million outpatient visits in 1993, and the efficiency of its recordkeeping allow large-scale statistical studies of the efficacy of particular treatments or procedures. This makes Kaiser Permanente an important national force in clinical research.

Nonprofit organization
Fiscal year ends: December 31

WHO

Chairman and CEO: David M. Lawrence
President and COO: Wayne R. Moon
EVP and Regional Manager, Southern California Region: Hugh A. Jones
EVP and Regional Manager, Northern California Region: David G. Pockell
SVP Legal, General Counsel, and Secretary: Jerry J. Phelan
SVP Finance: Susan E. Porth
VP Human Resources Programs: Alfred Bolden
Auditors: Deloitte & Touche

WHEN

Henry J. Kaiser, builder of Hoover and Grand Coulee dams, shipbuilder, war profiteer, and founder of Kaiser Aluminum, was a bootstrap capitalist who did well by doing good.

In 1906 Kaiser, a high school dropout from upstate New York, moved to Spokane and went into road construction. During the Depression he was a leader in his field and headed the consortium that built the great WPA dams.

When WWII broke out, Kaiser moved into shipbuilding and steelmaking (the first steel plant on the West Coast), turning out more than 1,400 Liberty ships during the war. In his drive to turn out cargo ships at the rate of one per day, Kaiser noticed that healthy workers were more efficient and had lower levels of absenteeism. He therefore established clinics at his work sites, funded by the US government (through Kaiser's construction contracts) as part of legitimate operating expenses.

After the war the clinics became war surplus, and Kaiser and his wife bought them, through the newly founded Kaiser Hospital Foundation, at a 99% discount. Kaiser's vision was to provide the public with low-cost, prepaid medical care. To this end, he also created the Health Plan, the self-supporting entity that administers the system, and the Group Medical Organization, Permanente (named after the site of Kaiser's first cement plant). And he started the ball rolling by endowing the Health Plan with $200,000.

From the start, the Kaiser health plan, the first and most classic model of the HMO, was criticized by the medical establishment, which characterized the Kaiser plan as socialized medicine and scoffed at "employee" doctors.

The plan flourished, becoming California's largest system of hospitals and physicians. In 1958 Kaiser retired to Hawaii and started his health plan there. But national growth was limited by physician resistance — HMOs were outlawed in 38 states as late as 1978.

As health care costs rose in the 1980s, federal legislation legalized HMOs in all states. Kaiser began to expand, eventually going almost nationwide. As it expanded outside its traditional geographic areas, Kaiser began contracting for hospital space rather than building new hospitals. But the development of new HMOs and other health plans resulted in increased competition for Kaiser, forcing it to become more cost conscious, and slowing its growth rate. Kaiser's membership fell in the early 1990s, although members may have been lost to the California recession rather than to other providers.

Kaiser's strategy is to sharpen its focus in geriatrics (because of the aging population) and preventive and appropriate care.

In 1993 Kaiser's 30,000 unionized employees charged that Kaiser had cut back health benefits, but a strike was averted.

In 1994 Kaiser began letting members pay higher deductibles and premiums in order to choose doctors outside the system. This is expected to boost growth by attracting those who prefer to choose their own doctors.

WHERE

HQ: Kaiser Foundation Health Plan, Inc., One Kaiser Plaza, Oakland, CA 94612
Phone: 510-271-5910
Fax: 510-271-5917

	1993 Members		1993 Physicians	
	No.	% of total	No.	% of total
N. California	2,426,746	37	3,650	39
S. California	2,209,899	33	3,070	33
Northwest	378,567	6	548	6
Hawaii Region	190,680	3	292	3
Ohio Region	198,269	3	245	3
Colorado Region	289,259	4	407	4
Mid-Atlantic States Region	320,770	5	445	5
Texas Region	128,589	2	175	2
Northeast Region	115,904	2	117	1
N. Carolina Region	117,811	2	134	1
Georgia Region	165,015	2	171	2
Kansas City Region	45,082	1	54	1
Total	**6,586,591**	**100**	**9,308**	**100**

WHAT

	1993 Sales	
	$ mil.	% of total
Members' dues & supplemental charges	9,728	81
Other	2,202	19
Total	**11,930**	**100**

	1993 Assets	
	$ mil.	% of total
Property	6,452	66
Segregated securities	984	10
Cash & other current assets	1,747	18
Other	579	6
Total	**9,762**	**100**

Selected Services

Home health
Hospitals
Insurance
Support function

HOW MUCH

	Annual Growth	1984	1985	1986	1987	1988	1989	1990	1991	1992	1993
Sales ($ mil.)	14.6%	3,500	4,075	4,477	4,862	5,565	6,857	8,443	9,823	11,032	11,930
Net income ($ mil.)	22.8%	134	194	198	157	109	159	381	486	796	848
Income as % of sales	—	3.8%	4.8%	4.4%	3.2%	1.2%	2.3%	4.5%	4.9%	7.2%	7.1%
Employees	2.4%	—	—	—	—	—	—	—	—	82,858	84,885

Net Income ($ mil.) 1984–93

KEY COMPETITORS

Aetna
Blue Cross
Catholic Healthcare West
CIGNA
Foundation Health
Group Health Cooperative of Puget Sound
John Hancock
MassMutual
New York Life
PacifiCare Health Systems
Prudential
Qual-Med
Sierra Health Services
Travelers

KOCH INDUSTRIES, INC.

RANK: 7

OVERVIEW

KOCH

The 2nd largest privately held and family-run company in the US (after Cargill), Koch (pronounced "coke") Industries is an integrated petroleum company involved in all phases of the oil industry. The Wichita, Kansas–based company also has operations in chemical technology, agriculture, and minerals and has estimated sales of more than $20 billion.

Koch owns 2 refineries (Corpus Christi, Texas, and St. Paul, Minnesota; combined capacity of 340,000 barrels/day) that can produce a broad range of petroleum products. Koch operates a liquid pipeline network from Texas to Canada and a worldwide distribution system of storage facilities, terminals, trucks, and barges.

The company also manufactures equipment and systems for chemical processing and oil production and refining. Koch Membrane Systems is the world's #1 producer of membrane filtration systems that purify industrial wastewater. Koch's agricultural business controls 450,000 acres of ranchland in Montana, Texas, and Kansas and is one of the 10 largest calf producers in the US. Koch also makes building materials and specialty and commodity chemicals, sells fertilizers, and has operations in equipment leasing and real estate.

Koch is controlled by Charles and David Koch, survivors of a feud with their brother William, and owners of 80% of the company's stock. James Howard Marshall, a former executive at Ashland Oil and former partner of founder Fred Koch, owns approximately 15% of the company.

Private company
Fiscal year ends: December 31

WHO

Chairman and CEO: Charles G. Koch
President and COO: W. W. Hanna
EVP Chemical Technology Group: David H. Koch
EVP Finance and Administration: F. Lynn Markel
EVP and Chief Legal Officer: Donald L. Cordes
EVP Supply, Trading, and Transportation Group: Joe W. Moeller
Secretary and General Counsel: H. Allan Caldwell
Director Human Resources: R. A. Pohlman
Auditors: KPMG Peat Marwick

WHERE

HQ: 4111 E. 37th St. North, PO Box 2256, Wichita, KS 67220-3203
Phone: 316-832-5500
Fax: 316-832-5739 (Public Affairs)

WHEN

In 1928 Fred Koch developed a process to refine more gasoline from crude oil, but when he tried to market his invention, he was sued by the major oil companies for patent infringement. Although Koch eventually won the lawsuits, the controversy left him unable to attract many customers at home, so in 1929 he took his process abroad, to the USSR. Disenchanted with Stalin's brand of communism, he returned to the US and eventually became a founding member of the anticommunist John Birch Society.

Koch launched Wood River Oil & Refining in Illinois (1940) and bought the Rock Island refinery in Duncan, Oklahoma (1946). Though he would later sell the refineries, he folded the remaining purchasing and gathering network into Rock Island Oil & Refining.

After Koch's death in 1967, his 32-year-old son Charles took the helm and renamed the company Koch Industries. With the help of his father's confidant, Sterling Varner, Koch began a series of acquisitions, adding petrochemical and oil trading services operations.

During the 1980s Koch was thrust into various arenas, legal and political. Charles's brother David, also a Koch Industries executive, ran for US vice-president on the Libertarian ticket in 1980. Also in 1980 the other 2 Koch brothers, Frederick and William, launched a proxy fight for the company.

Charles, with the help of David, William's twin, retained control, and William was fired from his job as vice-president. The brothers traded lawsuits, and in a 1983 settlement Charles and David bought out the dissident family members, for just over $1 billion. William, though, continued to challenge his brothers in court, claiming he had been shortchanged in the deal. One 1987 suit listed his mother as a defendant.

Despite the family's legal wrangling, Koch Industries continued to expand. In 1981 it purchased Sun's Corpus Christi, Texas, refinery for $265 million, and its Massachusetts-based Koch Process Systems subsidiary purchased Helix Process Systems. It added to its large pipeline system by buying Bigheart Pipe Line in Oklahoma (1986) and 2 systems from Santa Fe Southern Pacific (1988).

In 1991 Koch purchased from Scurlock Permian (a unit of Ashland Oil) its Corpus Christi marine terminal, pipelines, and gathering systems for $21 million. The company bought United Gas Pipe Line (renamed Koch Gateway Pipeline Co.) and its 9,721-mile pipeline system, which extends from Texas to Florida, in 1992. In 1993 Koch bought Trident NGL's fractionation complex in Hutchison, Kansas.

In 1994 the Federal Energy Regulatory Commission gave permission to Koch Gateway Pipeline to charge market-based storage rates on its system, making it the first interstate pipeline to use such a rate system.

WHAT

Business Groups

Agriculture Group
Cattle ranches
Feedlots
Fertilizer and agricultural chemicals distribution
Grain storage and merchandising
Oil seed and feed processing

Chemical Technology Group
Automotive sealants
Combustion and vapor recovery equipment
Heat exchangers
Specialty coatings

Financial Services Group
Diversified real estate
Foreign exchange trading
Leasing

Hydrocarbon Group
Anhydrous ammonia
Carbon dioxide
Natural gas and gas liquids
Sulfur products

Materials Group
Asphalt
Recreational surfaces
Waterproofing products

Minerals Group
GranCem cement
Lime
Slag aggregate and slag-based specialty products

Refining and Chemical Group
Commodity and specialty chemicals
Crude oil
Sulfur and sulfur-based chemicals

Supply, Trading, and Transportation Group
Ammonia
Chemicals
Coal and petroleum coke
Crude oil
Intermediate feedstocks
Natural gas and gas liquids
Refined products

HOW MUCH

	Annual Growth	1984	1985	1986	1987	1988	1989	1990	1991	1992	1993
Estimated sales ($ mil.)	6.6%	—	12,000	16,000	13,000	16,000	16,000	17,190	19,250	19,914	20,000
Employees	8.0%	—	6,500	6,500	7,000	7,500	8,000	9,300	10,000	12,000	12,000

Estimated Sales ($ mil.) 1985–93

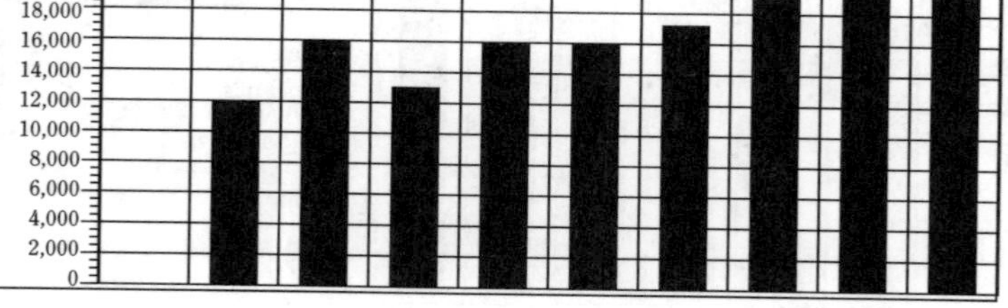

20,000
18,000
16,000
14,000
12,000
10,000
8,000
6,000
4,000
2,000
0

KEY COMPETITORS

Amerada Hess
Amoco
ASARCO
Ashland
Atlantic Richfield
British Petroleum
Broken Hill
Cargill
Chevron
Coastal
Continental Grain
DuPont
Elf Aquitaine
Enron
Exxon
General Dynamics
Hearst
Imperial Oil
King Ranch
Lyondell Petrochemical
Mobil
Norsk Hydro
Occidental
Oryx
PDVSA
PEMEX
Pennzoil
Petrobrás
Petrofina
Phillips Petroleum
PPG
Repsol
Royal Dutch/Shell
Salomon
Sun
Tenneco
Texaco
Total
Unocal
USX-Marathon
Vulcan

KOHLBERG KRAVIS ROBERTS & CO.

RANK: N/R

OVERVIEW

Since capping the LBO feeding frenzy of the 1980s with the $29.6 billion RJR Nabisco buyout in 1988, New York investment firm Kohlberg Kravis Roberts & Co. (KKR) has concentrated on managing its investments.

The company works with a "blind pool" of money from pension funds, insurance companies, and banks, which is used to secure bank loans for up to 90% of a deal's cost. KKR adds a stake of its own and shares the risk in return for the gain when (or if) the companies turn profitable or are sold. In the early 1980s return on equity peaked at 40%.

As the size of its deals has increased, the firm's own investments (and therefore risk) have remained low, an average of just 2% of each of the 6 pools raised since 1980, while profits from up-front fees (1.5% annual management fee, transaction fees, 1% investment banking fee, monitoring and consulting fees) have grown enormously. However, KKR's practice of collecting fees regardless of the outcome of the project (which is unusual) has become a sore point with some of its powerful institutional investors.

In the early 1990s some of KKR's LBOs proved to be less profitable than hoped, especially RJR. KKR and its investors have had to carry some of RJR's operating costs. This has dragged down earnings and made investing in KKR, by some estimates, no more profitable than investing in the stock market.

Private partnership

WHO

Founding Partner: Henry R. Kravis, age 49
Founding Partner: George R. Roberts, age 49
General Partner: James H. Greene, Jr.
General Partner: Robert I. MacDonnell
General Partner: Michael W. Michelson
General Partner: Paul E. Raether

WHERE

HQ: 9 W. 57th St., Ste. 4200, New York, NY 10019
Phone: 212-750-8300
Fax: 212-593-2430 (public relations firm)

WHEN

In 1976 Jerome Kohlberg left investment bank Bear Stearns, where he had orchestrated leveraged buyouts, to form his own firm. He brought with him Henry Kravis and Kravis's cousin George Roberts. They formed Kohlberg Kravis Roberts & Co. (KKR).

Kohlberg believed LBOs, by giving management ownership stakes in their companies, would result in greater efficiency and productivity. KKR put together friendly buyouts funded by investor groups and large amounts of debt. In 1979 KKR made the first buyout of an NYSE company, Houdaille Industries, a machine tool manufacturer, for $335 million.

In the purchase of the American Forest Products division of Bendix in 1981, KKR lost $93 million. By 1984 KKR had raised its 4th LBO fund and made the first $1 billion buyout, of Wometco Enterprises.

In 1985 KKR turned mean with a hostile takeover of Beatrice ($6.2 billion). The deal depended upon junk bond financing provided by Drexel Burnham Lambert's Michael Milken and on the sale of pieces of the company. KKR funded the acquisitions of Safeway Stores ($5.2 billion) and Owens-Illinois ($4.4 billion) in 1986 from the same investment pool. KKR bought out Jim Walter Homes (now Walter Industries, $2.4 billion) in 1987 and Stop & Shop ($1.2 billion) in 1988.

In 1987 Kohlberg, unhappy with the firm's hostile image, left to form Kohlberg & Co. His suit against KKR over alleged undervaluing of companies in relation to his departure settlement was settled for an undisclosed amount.

The Beatrice LBO had triggered a rash of LBOs as the financial industry sought fat fees. The frenzy culminated in the 1988 RJR Nabisco buyout, which provided KKR with $75 million in fees.

After 1989, as the US slid into recession, LBO activities died out, and KKR turned to managing its LBOs. RJR Nabisco, caught in a downturn of consumer brand loyalty and in tobacco price wars, required more cash. Investment of an additional $3 billion in RJR since the LBO doubled KKR's investors' equity stakes, halved return on equity, and necessitated the investment of over 50% of the 1987 investment pool (and 39% of all KKR investment funds) in a single company. Other troubled companies include Seamans furniture and Hillsborough Holdings, which went into Chapter 11 bankruptcy in 1989 after profitable operations were sold to service debt and the company was hit with asbestos claims.

In 1991, with banking partner Fleet/Norstar (now Fleet Financial Group), KKR bought the Bank of New England (assets of $12 billion) from the FDIC for $625 million. In the same year it made K-III Holdings one of the top consumer magazine publishers in the US with the purchase of 9 publications for $650 million. In 1992 KKR bought 47% of TW Holdings restaurant group (now Flagstar; Denny's and Hardee's) for $300 million and the refinancing of $950 million in old debt. KKR also bought reinsurer American Re from Aetna for $1.5 billion and profitably took it public in 4 months.

In one of its largest deals in years, KKR announced in September 1994 that it would acquire troubled food giant Borden in a $2 billion stock swap. KKR plans to use RJR Nabisco stock in the exchange, reducing its interest in that company by half.

WHAT

Largest LBO Deals	Value at Transaction Date ($ bil.)
RJR Nabisco	29.6
Beatrice	6.2
Safeway	5.2
Owens-Illinois	4.4

Selected Investment Holdings

Alden Press
American Re-Insurance Co.
Auto Zone (automotive parts retailer)
Bank of New England (in partnership with Fleet Financial Group)
Crossland Mortgage
Duracell (54.8%, batteries)
First Interstate (8.2%)
Flagstar (47.2%, restaurants)
Fred Meyer (51%)
IDEX Corp. (industrial products)
K-III (88.4%, publishing)
Marley Co. (water towers, heating systems)
Owens-Illinois (30%, glass containers)
PacTrust (Pacific Realty trust)
RJR Nabisco (35%, cigarettes, cookies, candy)
Safeway (66%, grocery stores)
Seaman Furniture
The Stop & Shop Cos. (63%)
Union Texas Petroleum
Walter Industries (construction products)
World Color Press

Investors in KKR Partnerships

Insurance companies
Nonprofit organizations
State pension funds
- Montana Investment Board
- Oregon Public Employees Retirement Fund
- Washington State Investment Board

KEY COMPETITORS

AEA Investors
American Financial
Apollo Advisors
Barclays
Bear Stearns
Berkshire Hathaway
Blackstone Group
Canadian Imperial
Clayton, Dubilier
Crédit Lyonnais
CS Holdings
Dai-Ichi Kangyo
Deutsche Bank
Forstmann Little
General Electric
Goldman Sachs
Hanson
Heico Acquisitions
Hicks, Muse, Tate & Furst
HSBC
Interlaken Capital
Jordan Co.
Lehman Brothers
Loews
MacAndrews & Forbes
Merrill Lynch
Morgan Stanley
National Westminster
Nomura Securities
Odyssey Partners
Paine Webber
Prudential
Royal Bank
Salomon
Thomas H. Lee
Union Bank of Switzerland

HOW MUCH

	Annual Growth	1984	1985	1986	1987	1988	1989	1990	1991	1992	1993[1]
Value of major new investments ($ mil.)	—	3,907	10,800	9,290	2,400	32,930	405	0	966	1,700	110
No. of major investments	—	5	3	2	1	4	2	0	3	2	2

Value of Major New Investments ($ mil.) 1984–93

[1]Complete value of investments not disclosed

KPMG PEAT MARWICK

RANK: 29

OVERVIEW

Once the world's largest accounting firm, Klynveld Peat Marwick Goerdeler (KPMG) fell to 2nd place (after Arthur Andersen) in 1993. The company's US practice, KPMG Peat Marwick, is the 4th largest accounting firm in the nation, after Arthur Andersen, Ernst & Young, and Deloitte & Touche.

KPMG blamed the drop on currency fluctuations, which lowered the value of its fees overseas, where it does 70% of its business. The firm continues to downsize; between 1990 and 1993 it cut more than 3,500 jobs, including those of more than 200 partners.

However, KPMG is expanding some of its services. In 1994, in an effort to increase its regulatory compliance business, it acquired Smith Banking Consultants, which helps financial institutions meet regulatory requirements such as the Community Reinvestment Act. KPMG also formed an alliance with Toshiba to provide hardware and software for sales force automation applications.

International partnership
Fiscal year ends: September 30

KPMG

WHO

Chairman: Hans Havermann
US Chairman and CEO: Jon C. Madonna
Administration and Finance Partner, KPMG Peat Marwick: Joseph E. Heintz
General Counsel, KPMG Peat Marwick: Ed Scott
Human Resources Partner, KPMG Peat Marwick: Mary L. Dupont

WHEN

KPMG was formed in 1987 when Peat, Marwick, Mitchell, & Copartners joined KMG, an international federation of accounting firms. The combined firms immediately jumped to #1 in worldwide revenues.

Peat Marwick traces its roots back to 1911, when William Peat, who had established a respected accounting practice in London, met James Marwick on a westbound crossing of the Atlantic. Marwick and fellow University of Glasgow alumnus S. Roger Mitchell had formed Marwick, Mitchell & Company in New York in 1897. Peat and Marwick agreed to join their firms, first under an agreement that terminated in 1919, and again in 1925 through a permanent merger to form Peat, Marwick, Mitchell, & Copartners.

In 1947 William Black became senior partner, a position he held until 1965. He guided the firm's 1950 merger with Barrow, Wade, Guthrie, the oldest and most prestigious US firm. He also built up the firm's management consulting practice. Peat Marwick restructured its international practice as PMM&Co. (International) in 1972 and reformed as Peat Marwick International in 1978.

In 1979 a group of European accounting firms led by the Netherlands's top-ranked Klynveld Kraayenhoff and Germany's 2nd-ranked Deutsche Treuhand discussed the formation of an international federation of accounting firms to aid in serving multinational companies. At that time 2 American firms that had been founded around the turn of the century, Main Lafrentz and Hurdman Cranstoun, agreed to merge in order to combat the growing reach of the Big 8. The Europeans needed an American member for their federation to succeed and had encouraged the formation of the new firm, Main Hurdman & Cranstoun. By the end of 1979, Main Hurdman had joined the Europeans to form Klynveld Main Goerdeler (KMG), named after 2 of the member firms and Deutsche Treuhand's chairman, Dr. Reinhard Goerdeler. Other members of the federation included C. Jespersen (Denmark), Thorne Riddel (Canada), Thomson McLintok (UK), and Fides Revision (Switzerland). KMG immediately became one of the world's largest accounting firms.

In 1987 Peat Marwick, then the #2 firm, merged with KMG to form Klynveld Peat Marwick Goerdeler (KPMG). In the merger KPMG lost 10% of its business owing to the departure of competing companies that had formerly been clients of Peat Marwick or KMG; the firm nevertheless jumped over Arthur Andersen into the #1 position worldwide.

In 1992 KPMG established the first joint accounting venture in China and opened an office in Estonia. In the same year the RTC sued KPMG for $100 million for alleged negligence and breach of contract in auditing Pennsylvania-based Hill Financial Savings Association. In 1993 the firm was named by the US Agency for International Development to head a consortium providing technical assistance to 12 countries of the former Soviet Union, as those countries attempt to privatize their economies.

In 1994 KPMG's Australian affiliate agreed to pay $97 million to settle a suit brought by the Australian state of Victoria. The state claimed that faulty audits were to blame in the collapse of Tricontinental Group, a subsidiary of the State Bank of Victoria.

WHERE

HQ: KPMG, PO Box 74555, 1070 BC Amsterdam, The Netherlands
Phone: 011-31-20-656-7890
Fax: 011-31-20-656-7000
US HQ: KPMG Peat Marwick, 767 Fifth Ave., New York, NY 10153
US Phone: 212-909-5000
US Fax: 212-909-5299

KPMG has offices in 131 countries. KPMG Peat Marwick has 135 offices in the US.

	1993 Sales	
	$ mil.	% of total
US	1,822	30
Other countries	4,178	70
Total	**6,000**	**100**

WHAT

	1993 US Sales
	% of total
Accounting & auditing	56
Tax	30
Management consulting	14
Total	**100**

Selected Services
Financial services
Government
Health care and life sciences
Information and communications
Manufacturing, retailing, and distribution

Representative Clients
Aetna
Apple Computer
BMW
Citicorp
Daimler-Benz
General Mills
Gillette
Kemper
Motorola
Nestlé
J. C. Penney
PepsiCo
Siemens
TCI
Texaco
Union Carbide
USAir
Xerox

Affiliated Firms
Century Audit Corp. (Japan)
KPMG Deutsche Treuhand-Gesellschaft (Germany)
KPMG Klynveld (Netherlands)
KPMG Peat Marwick (Belgium)
KPMG Peat Marwick (UK)
KPMG Peat Marwick (US)
KPMG Peat Marwick Huazhen (China)
KPMG Peat Marwick Thorne (Canada)
KPMG Reviconsult (Russia)

HOW MUCH

	9-Year Growth	1984	1985	1986	1987	1988	1989	1990	1991	1992	1993
Sales ($ mil.)	10.8%	1,340	1,446	1,672	3,250	3,900	4,300	5,368	6,011	6,150	6,000
Offices	14.3%	328	335	342	620	637	700	800	820	819	1,100
Partners	11.3%	2,326	2,507	2,726	5,150	5,050	5,300	6,300	6,100	6,004	6,100
Employees	11.9%	27,746	29,864	32,183	60,000	63,700	68,000	77,300	75,000	73,488	76,200

1993 Year-end:
Sales per partner: $983,000

Note: Figures prior to 1987 are Peat Marwick only; 1987 through 1993 are total figures for postmerger KPMG Peat Marwick.

KEY COMPETITORS

Arthur Andersen
Bain & Co.
Booz, Allen & Hamilton
Boston Consulting Group
Coopers & Lybrand
Deloitte & Touche
Delta Consulting
Electronic Data Systems
Ernst & Young
Gemini Consulting
H&R Block
IBM
A. T. Kearney
Marsh & McLennan
McKinsey & Co.
Perot Systems
Price Waterhouse

LAND O' LAKES, INC.

RANK: 72

OVERVIEW

Land O' Lakes, an agricultural cooperative based in Arden Hills, Minnesota, is the #1 marketer of butter, butter blends, and deli cheeses in the US and the #3 producer and marketer of all kinds of cheese. It produces the only national brand-name butter. Other products include milk, sour cream, yogurt, and ice cream. The co-op also conducts research on foods and packaging; supplies prepared sauces, dips, and puddings to restaurants and stores; and produces animal feeds and seeds for sale at wholesale prices to its member/owners. Its up-to-date agronomy research facilities provide a wealth of information to its members to help them boost production, cut costs, and run their farms and ranches more efficiently.

Land O' Lakes has always been an aggressive marketer (spending 4.5% of sales on advertising in 1993), creating a strong demand for its brand names and, therefore, for its members' products. Land O' Lakes is also a strong advocate for its members' interests in state and federal legislatures.

Since the early 1980s the co-op has received grants from industry and the US government to operate educational offices overseas, including offices in Russia, Bulgaria, Poland, Pakistan, West Africa, the Philippines, and Jamaica. These operations help teach modern farming methods and free market principles to farmers. They also provide contacts for possible future consumers of Land O' Lakes products.

In the US the co-op is a strong supporter of youth groups like the 4-H and Future Farmers of America. It is also a major contributor of food and funds to programs that feed the needy.

WHEN

In the good old days, the butter was bad and grocers sold it to their customers from communal tubs. The reason was largely technical: the distribution of dairy products had to await the invention of fast, reliable transportation.

By 1921 these technical feats had been achieved. That year more than half of the 622 dairy farmers in Minnesota formed the Minnesota Cooperative Creameries Association and launched a membership drive with $1,375 in seed money, most of it borrowed from the US Farm Bureau. Many believed the enterprise would fail because farmers were thought to be too individualistic to band together for their economic interest (it was also illegal for co-ops to sell farm merchandise until 1922).

The co-op arranged joint shipments for members, imposed strict hygiene and quality standards, and set out aggressively to market its members' "sweet cream butter" nationwide, packaged for the first time in the familiar box of 4 quarter-pound sticks. A month after the co-op's New York sales office opened, it was ordering 80 shipments a week.

In 1924 the co-op, as part of its promotional campaigns, ran a contest to name that butter. The result was Land O' Lakes. The distinctive Indian Maiden symbol was added about the same time. In 1926 the co-op was renamed Land O' Lakes Creameries. By 1929 its market share approached 50%.

The co-op weathered the Depression on the strength of its advertising. Much of its production was diverted to military use during WWII; civilian butter consumption dropped and many changed to margarine. During WWII the co-op increased production of dried milk (from a byproduct of butter-making used in animal feed), which was easily transported and provided food for soldiers and sailors and for newly liberated concentration camp victims.

In the 1950s and 1960s, the co-op added ice cream and yogurt makers to its membership and fought its archrival, margarine. Yet butter's market share continued to slide. In 1970 the co-op diversified through acquisitions, adding feeds and agricultural chemicals.

In 1972 Land O' Lakes threw in the towel and came out with its own margarine. Despite the decreasing use of butter nationally, Land O' Lakes's market share grew and the co-op began supplying individually wrapped pats to food service companies. As health consciousness grew in the 1980s, the co-op brought out reduced-fat and -cholesterol products, like Country Morning Blend (60% butter and 40% margarine) and Light sour cream. In 1993 Land O' Lakes brought out a light butter.

HOW MUCH

	Annual Growth	1984	1985	1986	1987	1988	1989	1990	1991	1992	1993
Sales ($ mil.)	4.3%	1,869	1,850	1,873	2,084	2,252	2,377	2,415	2,458	2,562	2,733
Net income ($ mil.)	18.8	10	12	10	12	30	34	37	54	57	47
Income as % of sales	—	—	—	—	—	1.3%	1.4%	1.5%	2.2%	2.2%	1.7%
Direct members	(3.0%)	10,736	9,120	9,176	9,619	7,101	6,885	7,323	8,605	8,155	8,188
Employees	1.1%	—	—	—	—	5,400	4,800	4,600	4,900	5,000	5,700

1993 Year-end:
Debt ratio: 37.6%
Return on equity: 14.5%
Cash (mil.): $1
Current ratio: 1.42
Long-term debt (mil.): $157
Equity as % of assets: 37.7%
Total assets (mil.): $866

Net Income ($ mil.) 1984–93

Agricultural cooperative
Fiscal year ends: December 31

WHO

Chairman: Stan Zylstra
President and CEO: Jack Gherty
EVP and COO: Duane Halverson
Group VP and CFO: Ron Ostby
VP and General Counsel: John Rebane
VP Public Affairs: Rita Reuss
VP Human Resources: Jack Martin
Auditors: KPMG Peat Marwick

WHERE

HQ: 4001 Lexington Ave. N., Arden Hills, MN 55126
Phone: 612-481-2222
Fax: 612-481-2022

Land O' Lakes has more than 1,000 member co-ops, serving 300,000 farmers and ranchers in 15 Midwest and Pacific Northwest states, and operates processing, manufacturing, warehousing, and distribution facilities across the US.

WHAT

	1993 Sales		1993 Pretax income	
	$ mil.	% of total	$ mil.	% of total
Dairy foods	1,474	54	6	13
Feed	696	25	29	57
Agronomy	478	18	14	27
Seed	85	3	2	3
Total	**2,733**	**100**	**51**	**100**

Selected Brands
Land O' Lakes
- Butter
- Light Butter
- Cheese

Lake to Lake Cheese
Bridgeman
- TLC Calci-Skim milk

TLC Light Egg Nog
Dairy Fresh
Lakeside

Agricultural supplies
Animal feeds
Seeds

Selected Services
Foodservice (service to restaurants and others)
Custom Products/Food Ingredients
Research, Technology and Engineering (product and packaging research)
Feeding programs
Dairy and other food processing

KEY COMPETITORS

ADM
Ag Processing
Alpine Lace
Associated Milk Producers
Borden
ConAgra
CPC
Dairy Gold Foods
Dannon
Darigold
Dean Foods
Grassland Dairy Products
Marathon Cheese
Mid-America Dairymen
PET
Philip Morris
Ralcorp
RJR Nabisco
Steuben Foods

LEFRAK ORGANIZATION INC.

RANK: 60

OVERVIEW

While everyone else in the 1980s was following the philosophy of buying high (with someone else's money) and selling higher, the Lefrak Organization stuck to its policy of buying low and selling high. That is why it is now stocking up on distressed real estate in New York and throughout the US while high-fliers like Donald Trump are borrowing tiaras for their fiancees to wear at their weddings.

The Lefrak Organization may be the US's largest private landlord; it owns more than 90,000 affordable apartments in the New York boroughs and controls millions of square feet of commercial space.

The company also has a significant presence in entertainment. Lefrak Entertainment operates LMR, the record label that launched Barbra Streisand. It also owns stage and movie theaters and produces television shows, movies, and Broadway shows (such as the 1982 Tony award winning musical *Nine*). Lefrak Oil & Gas Organization (LOGO) engages in petroleum exploration.

Samuel LeFrak (who in the 1970s capitalized the "F" in his own name but not his company's name) used the money he earned building low-cost housing in the postwar era to invest in a variety of other fields, including mining and forestry. He is also an active philanthropist, sponsoring oceanographic studies by Jacques Yves Cousteau and endowing a library at St. Cross College, Oxford. His personal net worth is estimated to be in excess of $1.6 billion.

WHEN

Harry Lefrak and his father, both builders, came to the US around the turn of the century and began building tenements to house the flood of immigrants then pouring into New York City. In 1905 they started what is now known as the Lefrak Organization. The company diversified into glass and for some time provided glass for the lamps of Louis Comfort Tiffany. After WWI, the glass factory was sold, and the organization expanded its scope to Brooklyn, where it developed housing and retail/commercial space in Bedford-Stuyvesant, among other areas.

Samuel, Harry's son, began working in the business early, assisting tradesmen at building sites. He then attended the University of Maryland and returned to the business.

After WWII, business took off as the company began providing low-cost housing for returning veterans and their burgeoning families. Samuel took over the company in 1948. To keep down expenses over the years, Samuel bought up clay and gypsum quarries, as well as forests, and operated his own lumber mills and cement plants, eventually achieving 70% vertical integration of his operations.

The 1950s building boom was in part spurred by new laws in New York authorizing the issue of state bonds dedicated to financing low-interest construction loans. Lefrak built more than 2,000 apartments in previously undeveloped coastal sections of Brooklyn. At its peak Lefrak could turn out an apartment every 16 minutes for projected rents as low as $21 per room.

In 1960 Lefrak began its greatest project to that date, Lefrak City, a 6,000 apartment development built on 40 acres in Queens. The privately financed development featured air-conditioned units at rents of $40 per room.

The next decade brought a real estate slump that endangered the organization's then-current project, Battery Park. In order to save it, Lefrak had to issue public bonds. In a time when all about him were losing their heads, Samuel LeFrak remained cool and solvent and picked up a few more properties.

In the Roaring '80s, while Donald Trump was fleeing his origins as the son of a builder of low-cost housing, LeFrak's son Richard was becoming increasingly involved in the business. The organization's big new project, Newport City, began going up on 400 acres along the Hudson River near Jersey City, New Jersey. The development, a partnership with the troubled Melvin Simon and Associates, was to include commercial and retail space and a marina, in addition to nearly 10,000 apartments. Newport ran into problems with local authorities. LeFrak refused to pay taxes related to the property because the community did not supply police and fire services for the facilities he had finished, which include more than 2,000 occupied apartments, and commercial and retail space. This sent him into technical default, which he disputed.

Richard LeFrak manages the organization on a daily basis and has begun to put his own imprint on the company, seeking properties out of state and overseas.

Private company
Fiscal year ends: Last Sunday in November

WHO

Chairman: Samuel J. LeFrak
President: Richard S. LeFrak
VP Finance: Arthur J. Phelan
VP and General Counsel: Howard Boris
Treasurer: Gerald Weinstein
VP Construction-Engineering: Anthony Scavo
Human Resources: Cheryl Jensen
Auditors: Lewis Goldberg

WHERE

HQ: 97-77 Queens Blvd., Rego Park, NY 11374
Phone: 718-459-9021
Fax: 718-897-0688

The company engages primarily in real estate development and management in the New York metropolitan area.

WHAT

Real Estate Developments
Residential (200,000 units built to date)
- Lefrak City (6,000 units, 1960)
- Battery Park City (2,200 units, 1973)
- Newport City (2,000 units, in progress)

Commercial (5 million square feet)
Retail (5 million square feet)

Energy
LOGO (Lefrak Oil & Gas Organization; 300 properties)

Entertainment
Lefrak Entertainment Co.

KEY COMPETITORS

Apache
Barrett Resources
Corporate Property Investors
Edward J. DeBartolo
Helmsley
Investment Properties Associates
JMB Realty
Lincoln Property
Melvin Simon & Associates
Nederlander Organization
Olympia & York
Pembrook Management
Rockefeller Group
Rouse
Rudin Management
Shubert Organization
Sony
Taubman Centers
Time Warner
Tishman Speyer Properties
Trammell Crow
Trump Organization
Zeckendorf

HOW MUCH

	Annual Growth	1983	1984	1985	1986	1987	1988	1989	1990	1991	1992
Estimated sales ($ mil.)	18.1%	—	—	1,000	2,000	2,600	3,000	2,875	2,900	3,100	3,200
Employees	0.0%	—	—	18,000	18,000	18,000	18,000	18,000	18,000	18,000	18,000

Estimated Sales ($ mil.) 1985-92

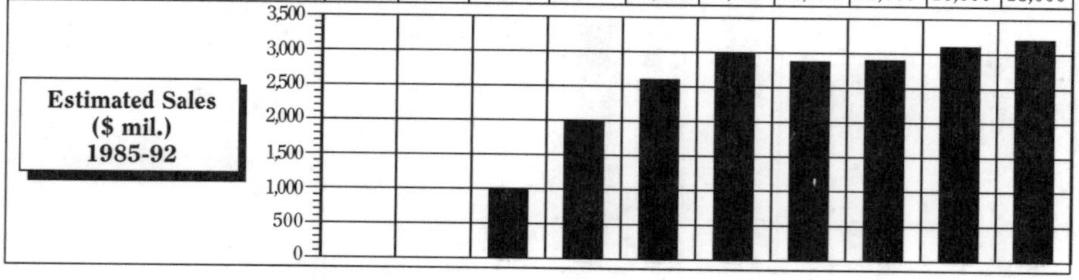

LEVI STRAUSS ASSOCIATES INC.

RANK: 31

OVERVIEW

Based in San Francisco but known around the globe, Levi Strauss is the world's #1 producer of brand-name clothing. Of the company's $5.9 billion in sales, approximately 70% comes from jeans and jean-related products under the brand names Levi's and Brittania. Levi Strauss ranks 2nd in US jean sales, after V. F. (Wrangler, Lee).

Levi Strauss has been losing US market share to V. F., which now has about 30% to Levi's 18% (from 21% in 1992). However, a renewed growth in the domestic jeans market (sales jumped 10% in 1992 over 1991) is encouraging. The company's real growth markets remain overseas, where American jeans are seen as glamorous and where a pair of 501s retail for as much as $80. The company is also pushing the sales of its domestically successful Dockers line (about 30% of US sales) in foreign markets. However, a continued poor global economy has Levi a little worried.

Haas family members, descendants of founder Levi Strauss, own more than 95% of the company, which is recognized for its ethnically and culturally diverse staff. The company has also gotten attention for stopping donations to the Boy Scouts because that organization excludes gays and atheists from its ranks.

WHEN

Levi Strauss arrived in New York City from Bavaria in 1847 to join his 2 brothers' dry goods business. In 1853 he moved to San Francisco to sell dry goods (particularly tent canvas) to the gold rush miners.

Shortly after Strauss arrived, a prospector told him of miners' problems in finding sufficiently sturdy pants. Strauss made a pair out of canvas for the prospector, and word of the sturdy pants spread quickly.

Strauss made a few more pairs of canvas pants before switching to a durable French fabric called serge de Nimes, soon known as "denim." Strauss colored the fabric with indigo dye and adopted the idea of Nevada tailor Jacob Davis of reinforcing the pants with copper rivets. In 1873 Strauss and Davis produced their first pair of Levi's Patent Riveted 501 Waist High Overalls (501 was the lot number). The pants, which soon became the standard attire of lumberjacks, cowboys, railroad workers, oil drillers, and farmers, are the same today as they were in 1873 (minus the rivets on the crotch and back pockets). The 2-horse logo was introduced in 1886.

Strauss continued to build his pants and wholesaling business until his death in 1902, when the company passed to his 4 nephews, who continued to produce their uncle's bluejeans (the term *jeans* traces its roots to the cotton trousers worn by ancient Genoese sailors) while maintaining the company's reputation for philanthropy.

After WWII Walter Haas, Jr., and Peter Haas (a 4th-generation Strauss family member) assumed leadership and in 1948 discontinued the wholesale segment (then most of the company) to concentrate solely on Levi's clothing.

Levi's jeans became popular in the 1950s and were soon the uniform of youth everywhere. In the 1960s the company branched into women's attire and overseas sales.

In 1971 Levi Strauss went public and diversified, buying Koret sportswear (sold 1984), adding a women's career line, and making a licensing agreement with Perry Ellis. By the mid-1980s profits had declined and the firm was losing its family business tradition. The Haas family took the company private again in 1985.

In 1987 the company acquired Brittania. In 1989 Levi Strauss publicly offered shares of Levi Strauss Japan (its subsidiary in Tokyo).

Although the basic jeans business declined in the 1980s, sales began rising again in 1991 as consumers forsook designer fashions for more traditional and practical clothes.

Levi, under Robert Haas (great-great-grandnephew of Strauss), is an innovator in employee-management relations. In 1991, in order to contain costs and keep jobs in the US, Levi Strauss instituted a team approach to production, in which the workers divide work within the unit. In 1993 Levi's sewing plants adopted Japanese-style production techniques that encourage more worker responsibility. These changes have increased flexibility and production and reduced errors.

In 1994 Heath Rackley won a Levi contest to find the oldest 501 jeans with a discarded pair of 1920s jeans he found in a mine shaft.

HOW MUCH

	9-Year Growth	1984	1985	1986	1987	1988	1989	1990	1991	1992	1993
Sales ($ mil.)	9.9%	2,514	2,584	2,762	2,867	3,117	3,628	4,247	4,903	5,570	5,892
Net income ($ mil.)	31.8%	41	(19)	49	116	85	272	265	367	362	492
Income as % of sales	—	1.6%	—	1.8%	4.0%	2.7%	7.5%	6.2%	7.5%	6.5%	8.4%
Employees	(0.2%)	37,000	—	—	—	—	31,000	31,000	32,100	34,200	36,400

1993 Year-end:
Debt ratio: 9.6%
Return on equity: 48.8%
Cash (mil.): $253
Current ratio: 1.95
Long-term debt (mil.): $81
Shareholders' equity (mil.): $1,251
Total assets (mil.): $3,109

Net Income ($ mil.) 1984–93

500
400
300
200
100
0
-100

Levi's

Private company
Fiscal year ends: Last Sunday in November

WHO

Chairman of the Executive Committee of the Board: Peter E. Haas, Sr., age 75
Chairman and CEO: Robert D. Haas, age 51, $3,538,982 pay
President and COO: Thomas W. Tusher, age 52, $2,926,614 pay
SVP, General Counsel, and Secretary: Thomas J. Bauch, age 50
SVP and CFO: George B. James, age 56, $1,324,695 pay
SVP; President, Levi Strauss North America: Robert D. Rockey, Jr., age 52, $1,285,058 pay
SVP Human Resources: Donna J. Goya, age 46
Auditors: Arthur Andersen & Co.

WHERE

HQ: 1155 Battery St., San Francisco, CA 94111-1230
Phone: 415-544-6000
Fax: 415-544-3939

The company has 44 production/warehouse and 8 distribution facilities in the US and 19 distribution and 22 production/warehouse facilities overseas.

	1993 Sales		1993 Operating Income	
	$ mil.	% of total	$ mil.	% of total
US	3,715	63	466	46
Europe	1,332	23	366	37
Other countries	845	14	171	17
Total	**5,892**	**100**	**1,003**	**100**

WHAT

	1993 Sales	
	$ mil.	% of total
Men's jeans (US)	1,970	33
Menswear (US)	733	12
Youthwear (US)	430	7
Womenswear (US)	415	7
Brittania (US)	157	3
Europe	1,332	23
Asia/Pacific	514	9
Canada	201	3
Latin America & other	140	3
Total	**5,892**	**100**

Brand Names
501 jeans
900 series (womenswear)
Brittania
Brittgear
Dockers
Levi's Action
Little Levi's
Orange Tab
Red Tab
SilverTab

Operating Divisions
Levi Strauss North America
- Brittania Sportswear Ltd.
- Canada
- Men's Jeans
- Menswear
- Mexico
- Womenswear
- Youthwear

Levi Strauss International
- Asia Pacific
- Europe
- Latin America

KEY COMPETITORS

L. L. Bean
Calvin Klein
Farah
Fruit of the Loom
The Gap
Guess?
Haggar
Hartmarx
J. Crew
Jordache
Lands' End
The Limited
Liz Claiborne
Oshkosh B'Gosh
J. C. Penney
Polo/Ralph Lauren
V. F.
YES

LEXMARK INTERNATIONAL INC.

RANK: 100

OVERVIEW

Described by *Newsweek* as the "model corporate structure for the 1990s," Lexmark has won praise for its entrepreneurial management style since breaking away from IBM in an LBO by investment firm Clayton, Dubilier & Rice in 1991. CD&R owns a controlling interest in the company, and Lexmark's employees own another 15%. IBM still owns 10% of the company (and is its biggest customer).

The Greenwich, Connecticut–based company makes and sells computer keyboards and printers, notebook computers, electric typewriters (a market IBM had pioneered in the 1930s and 1940s), and related supplies (such as printer cartridges and ribbons), under both its own name and the IBM logo, which it is licensed to use through 1996. It sells its products through independent dealers, OEMs, remarketers, distributors, and wholesalers as well as IBM marketing representatives and its own sales force.

Led by CEO Marvin Mann, the company has streamlined operations, improving product development cycle times and manufacturing processes. With profits exceeding expectations, Lexmark has been able to lower the debt left over from its LBO.

Lexmark is looking to fuel future growth in its printer and keyboard business by increasing its partnerships with OEMs. In early 1994 Lexmark postponed a planned initial public offering for at least a year.

WHEN

During the late 1980s, as a horde of Davids was taking aim at Goliath IBM, the computer giant began to downsize to compete. IBM cut its work force by 100,000 between 1986 and 1992 and also began to sell off its non-computer businesses, including Lexmark ("Lex" as in "lexicon" and "mark" as in "marks on paper," according to company literature).

In early 1991 IBM sold Lexmark to a group led by New York investment firm Clayton, Dubilier & Rice for $1.5 billion. Martin Dubilier, who helped to found the firm in 1978, had learned the LBO ropes as a turnaround expert for Jerome Kohlberg, founder of investment firm KKR, during the 1970s.

CD&R's LBO of Lexmark was financed primarily with bank loans, leaving the new company approximately $1.15 billion in debt. Marvin Mann, an IBM vice-president with 32 years at the company, became Lexmark's chairman.

Although no longer a part of IBM, Mann took a cue from his former bosses and did some downsizing of his own at Lexmark, cutting employees from 5,000 to 3,000, primarily in middle management. Along with cutting staff Mann also put more of the responsibility for running the company in the hands of his line managers, allowing them to come up with their own goals and business plans rather than hand down strategy from above.

While many employees were given their walking papers, Mann put up a "Help Wanted" sign in his sales department. The reason? He didn't have one. As an IBM subsidiary, Lexmark had relied on Big Blue's general sales force, which tended to focus more on the big ticket computer systems, so Lexmark had to create its own marketing operation. By the end of 1991, staff had risen to 4,000. As another sign of Lexmark's break from IBM, where it had sometimes got lost in the shuffle, Mann reorganized the company into 4 operating groups and made each group's financial information available to everyone in the company.

In 1992 Lexmark began to flex its independent muscles, introducing 2 laser printers for Macintosh. The company also introduced the first products (IBM PC-compatible keyboards) bearing its own name rather than the IBM logo. Also in 1992 Lexmark introduced its first color printer and began producing notebook computers for OEMs.

Lexmark's operating profits doubled in its 2nd year of operation and, using the additional cash flow, it reduced its debt ahead of schedule, to below $700 million.

In 1993 the company, through Lexmark Australia Pty Limited, made its first acquisition when it bought Australian printer maker Gestetner Lasers, increasing Lexmark's presence in the Pacific Rim. Lexmark continued to add new printer products during 1993, including a new series of network laser printers.

Also in 1993 Lexmark signed a licensing agreement with Interlink Electronics for joystick technology. That same year Lexmark and IBM/Canada sued Canadian office supply distributor Printech Ribbons, alleging that Printech had sold counterfeit ribbons with the IBM brand name.

HOW MUCH

	Annual Growth	1984	1985	1986	1987	1988	1989	1990[1]	1991	1992	1993
Estimated sales ($ mil.)	3.2%	—	—	—	—	—	—	2,000	2,000	2,200	2,200
Employees	(7.2%)	—	—	—	—	—	—	5,000	4,000	4,000	4,000

Estimated Sales ($ mil.) 1990-93

[1] As part of IBM

LEXMARK

Private company
Fiscal year ends: December 31

WHO

Chairman, President, and CEO: Marvin L. Mann
VP and CFO: Achim Knust
VP and General Manager: Paul Curlander
VP Sales and Support: Douglas R. LeGrande
VP Human Resources and Information Programs: A. Richard Murphy

WHERE

HQ: 55 Railroad Ave., Greenwich, CT 06836
Phone: 203-629-6700
Fax: 203-629-6725

Lexmark sells its products in over 100 countries in North and South America, the Caribbean, Europe, the Middle East, Africa, Asia, and the Pacific Rim.

Manufacturing Facilities
Boulder, CO
Lexington, KY
Orleans, France

WHAT

Products

Input Technologies
Keyboards

Printers
Dot matrix printers
- 2300 Plus family
- 4226

Ink-jet printers
- 4079
- ExecJet
- ExecJet II

Laser printers
- 4029 family
- 4037 family
- 4039 family

Network systems
- 4033 LAN Connection
- MarkNet Internal Network Adapters

Supplies
Laser printer cartridges
Ribbons

Typewriters
IBM Personal Typing System
IBM Personal Wheelwriter

KEY COMPETITORS

Apple
AST
Canon
Compaq
Gateway 2000
Hewlett-Packard
Key Tronic
Matsushita
NEC
Oki
Olivetti
Seiko
Smith Corona
Sony
Tandy
Xerox

LIBERTY MUTUAL INSURANCE

RANK: 32

OVERVIEW

Liberty Mutual is the leading insurer specializing in workers' compensation insurance. The company was formed specifically to insure in this field and has been an innovator in the related fields of loss prevention (which deals with the analysis of work sites and work practices to make them safer in order to prevent losses in the first place) and physical rehabilitation for injured workers.

Liberty Mutual also offers a variety of services in group health (the LibertyPREFERRED CARE PPO system, with more than 50,000 care providers in 34 states), group and individual life, property/casualty, reinsurance, and financial services (it had $30 billion in assets under management in 1993).

Though founded in Boston, the company has branched out to 46 states, Puerto Rico, and 3 Canadian provinces. Liberty Mutual also has operations in the UK, where it plans to expand, and in Mexico, where it opened an office in 1993. The company hopes to increase its share of sales attributable to overseas operations from roughly 5% to about 20% by the year 2000 because of the mature, fiercely competitive American insurance market and the burgeoning Latin American economies that are underserved by insurers.

Earnings were badly shaken by the recession in the Northeast, a string of natural disasters, and high workers' compensation costs. The high costs have prompted Liberty Mutual to begin reducing that segment, and, consequently, its premium income for that segment. With the easing of the recession, however, results have reached record levels.

WHEN

The idea of providing financial aid to workers injured on the job was recognized in Europe in the late 19th century but did not make its way to the US until a workers' compensation law for Federal employees was passed in 1908. The states did not begin passing such laws until 1911, and Massachusetts was one of the first. Liberty Mutual was founded in Boston in 1912 in response to this new legislation, which created an entirely new niche in the industry.

Liberty Mutual's founders followed the practice that had arisen in the fire insurance business of taking an active part in the prevention of loss. This involved making safety evaluations of clients' premises and procedures and making recommendations for the prevention of accidents. However, the company flew in the face of the budding industry practice of severely limiting medical fees. Rather, the company made a study of therapies and authorized payment therefor, in order to reduce the long-term cost of a claim by getting the injured party back to work as soon as possible.

In 1942 the company acquired the United Mutual Fire Insurance company (founded in 1908, which became the Liberty Mutual Fire Insurance Company in 1949). It also acquired a life insurance company that in 1963 became Liberty Life Assurance Company of Boston, a wholly owned subsidiary.

In 1943 the company founded a rehabilitation center in Boston to treat injured workers and to explore the efficacy of treatments.

In the 1960s and 1970s Liberty Mutual grew within its primary field and expanded into other areas of insurance to offer its customer/members a full range of insurance products. In 1970 it began offering group pensions and, in 1975, IRAs.

By 1983 the company sought to increase its presence nationally and formed Liberty Northwest Insurance Corporation (based in the northwestern US) and Liberty Insurance Corporation. Other new subsidiaries followed to increase the company's large commercial property, personal lines, and excess lines offerings. In the 1980s, following the lead of other insurance companies, Liberty Mutual branched into financial services by acquiring Stein Roe & Farnham (founded 1958).

This strategy seemed to be working. Between 1984 and 1986, earnings more than tripled on a total asset gain of 42%. Then came the downturn: recession followed by a string of natural disasters. Between 1986 and 1988 income fell 72% despite a 42% increase in assets. In 1992 and 1993 the company lost suits brought against it by Coors and Outboard Marine for failing to help them defend environmental litigation cases.

HOW MUCH

	Annual Growth	1984	1985	1986	1987	1988	1989	1990	1991	1992	1993
Assets ($ mil.)	10.7%	8,215	9,499	11,643	14,258	16,544	17,924	18,836	19,704	20,216	20,544
Net income ($ mil.)	14.8%	93	101	306	203	87	117	164	149	217	321
Income as % of assets	—	1.1%	1.1%	2.6%	1.4%	0.5%	0.7%	0.9%	0.8%	1.1%	1.6%
Employees	15.8%	—	—	—	—	—	—	—	—	19,000	22,000

1993 Year-end:
Equity as % of assets: 15.5%
Return on equity: 6.3%
Cash (mil.): $317
Sales (mil.): $5,859

Assets ($ mil.) 1984–93

Mutual company
Fiscal year ends: December 31

WHO

Chairman and CEO: Gary L. Countryman
President and COO: Edmund F. Kelly
SVP, CFO, and Treasurer: Robert H. Gruhl
SVP and General Counsel: Christopher C. Mansfield
Director Human Resources: Julie Baumgartner
Auditors: KPMG Peat Marwick

WHERE

HQ: Liberty Mutual Insurance Group, 175 Berkeley St., Boston, MA 02117
Phone: 617-357-9500
Fax: 617-350-7648

Liberty Mutual has over 450 offices in the US, Canada, Mexico, and the UK.

WHAT

	1993 Assets	
	$ mil.	% of total
Cash & equivalents	317	2
Government securities	2,137	10
State & municipal securities	3,070	15
Corporate bonds	1,682	8
Mortgaged-backed securities	7,242	36
Stocks	836	4
Other investments	905	4
Premiums receivable	3,375	16
Other	980	5
Total	**20,544**	**100**

	1993 Sales		1993 Net Income	
	$ mil.	% of total	$ mil.	% of total
Business lines	3,659	62	155	48
Personal lines	2,200	38	165	52
Total	**5,859**	**100**	**321**	**100**

Product Lines
Workers' compensation
General liability
Individual and group auto and property insurance
Individual and group life
Disability insurance
Annuities
Mutual funds
Investment advice and management

Selected Subsidiaries
First Liberty Insurance Corp.
Helmsman Management Services, Inc.
Keyport Life Insurance Co.
Liberty Financial Companies
Liberty Insurance Corporation
Liberty Life Assurance Co. of Boston
Liberty Mutual (Bermuda) Ltd.
Liberty Mutual Fire Insurance Company
Liberty Mutual Insurance Co. (U.K.) Ltd.
Liberty Mutual Property Casualty Holding Corp.
Liberty Northwest Insurance Corporation
Liberty Securities Corporation
LibertyPREFERRED CARE
LM Insurance Corporation
Stein Roe & Farnham

KEY COMPETITORS

Aetna
AFLAC
Allstate
AIG
Blue Cross
CIGNA
GEICO
ITT
John Hancock
Kemper
Lincoln National
Loews
MassMutual
MetLife
New York Life
Northwestern Mutual
Prudential
State Farm
Travelers
T. Rowe Price
Washington National

LITTLE CAESAR ENTERPRISES, INC.

RANK: 105

OVERVIEW

Private company
Fiscal year ends: December 31

"Pizza! Pizza!" is the war cry of Detroit-based Little Caesar Enterprises in the battle for pizza dominance. The husband-and-wife team of Michael and Marian Ilitch owns and operates one of the largest pizza chains in the US. Little Caesar claims to be the world's leading carry-out pizza provider and is growing faster than its 2 chief rivals, PepsiCo's Pizza Hut and Domino's.

Rather than emphasize speedy delivery the way fellow Detroiter Tom Monaghan did in building Domino's, Little Caesar focuses on carry-out and touts the quality of its pizza: grade A cheese, specially grown California tomatoes, and high-gluten flour. Since carry-out restaurants do not require waiters, bus-boys, dishwashers, or delivery personnel, they have lower overhead and maintenance costs than sit-down or delivery-only outlets. A high-powered, wacky advertising campaign featuring a toga-clad cartoon character who keeps repeating himself has been a driving force for sales.

In a joint venture with Kmart, the company opened 400 Pizza Stations inside Kmart stores in 1992 and intends to have 1,200 by 1996. The agreement has irked some franchisees who fear that the Pizza Stations will cannibalize sales of existing franchise operations.

The company is a family operation. All 7 of Mike and Marian's children work in the company, and about 85% of franchisees are relatives. Little Caesars Love Kitchen, a mobile pizza operation, has provided free pizza to over 935,000 needy people since 1985.

But Little Caesar is more than just pizza. The company also owns the Detroit Tigers Baseball Club, the Detroit Red Wings hockey team, Olympia Arenas (which manages Joe Louis, Cobo, and Glens Falls arenas), the Fox Theatre, and Blue Line Distributing (which distributes products to the pizza franchisees).

WHO

President and CEO: Michael Ilitch, age 64
VC: Charles P. Jones
President: David Deal
Treasurer, Secretary, and CFO: Marian Ilitch
SEVP: Denise Ilitch Lites
Senior Group VP: Kim Pollack
Group VP: Christopher Ilitch
Group VP: Michael Scruggs
VP Corporate Communications: Sue Sherbow
VP Marketing: Rob Elliot
Director Systems: Mike Breshears
VP, Olympia Arenas, Inc: Atanas Ilitch, age 30
Director Human Resources: Darrell Snygg

WHERE

HQ: 2211 Woodward Ave., Detroit, MI 48201
Phone: 313-983-6000
Fax: 313-983-6494

Little Caesar operates or franchises takeout-only stores in the US, Canada, England, and Puerto Rico.

WHEN

In 1959 Michael and Marian Ilitch sank $10,000 of their savings into their first pizza operation in Garden City, Michigan, a suburb on the west side of Detroit. Michael, the son of Macedonian immigrants, wanted to name the operation Pizza Treat, but Marian suggested that they name it after the way he acted (like a little Caesar). With Michael, who had grown up in a poor neighborhood on Detroit's west side, cooking pizza and Marian ringing up sales on the cash register, Little Caesar did well enough to open a 2nd location in 1961. The next year the company sold its first franchise.

Little Caesar grew to over 50 outlets during the 1960s. In 1971 the Ilitches eliminated delivery as a service, choosing to offer carry-out only. That same year the company initiated its 2-for-one marketing concept ("Pizza! Pizza! Two Great Pizzas! One Low Price!"). In 1977 Little Caesar installed drive-through windows at its quick-serve locations. Two years later the company introduced a pizza conveyor oven that increased the production of pizza and other baked products.

By 1980 Little Caesar sales had grown to $63.6 million and units numbered 226. During the 1980s Little Caesar opened the first college campus restaurant (at the University of Oklahoma) and the first hospital restaurant (at Mt. Carmel Mercy Hospital in Detroit). The 500th Little Caesar outlet was established by 1984 and the 1,000th by 1986. Sales really took off after a national ad campaign in 1988.

Profits from the sales of pizza allowed the Ilitches to expand the scope of their operations. They acquired the Detroit Red Wings hockey team for $8 million in 1982 and the Detroit Drive arena football team in 1988. Also that year the Ilitches reopened the renovated, 4,804-seat Fox Theatre in downtown Detroit as part of a $50 million complex that houses Little Caesar's executive staff.

In 1992 Mike Ilitch fulfilled a lifelong dream by acquiring the Detroit Tigers from Tom Monaghan for $85 million. Ilitch had played on a Tiger farm team from 1951 to 1955 until a leg injury sidelined him.

In 1993 *Financial World* magazine declared the Red Wings the most valuable team in the National Hockey League, estimating its value at $87 million. Also in 1993 some franchisees filed an antitrust action against Little Caesar, alleging that they were required to purchase supplies at artificially inflated prices from Blue Line Distributing. That same year Little Caesar introduced a promotion offering a bonus pizza for a buck with the purchase of 2 pizzas. TV ads featured Mike Ilitch driving a convertible behind a rickety truck full of chickens, trying to think of new ideas for selling pizza, when a bewildered bird is bumped off the truck and plops against his windshield, squawking "Buck, buck."

WHAT

Major Subsidiaries

America's Pizza Cafe (specialty pizzas)
Blue Line Distributing
Detroit Drive (arena football team)
Detroit Red Wings (hockey team)
Detroit Tigers Baseball Club
The Fox Theatre
Olympia Arenas
Second City–Detroit Comedy Theatre

Products

Baby Pan! Pan! (2 individual-sized pan pizzas)
Caesars Sandwiches (ham and cheese, turkey, Italian, tuna, and vegetarian)
Chocolate! Chocolate! Ravioli! Ravioli! (2-piece dessert filled with dark chocolate and covered with white chocolate)
Crazy Bread (bread brushed with garlic and sprinkled with Parmesan cheese)
Crazy Cheese (cheese spread)
Crazy Crust (pizza crust flavored with sesame seed, poppy seed, garlic, or Parmesan cheese)
Crazy Sauce (tomato sauce)
Pan! Pan! (deep-dish pizza)
Pasta
Pizza! Pizza! (small, medium, and large)
Salads
Slice! Slice! (2 slices equaling 1/3 of a large pizza)

HOW MUCH

	9-Year Growth	1984	1985	1986	1987	1988	1989	1990	1991	1992	1993
Sales ($ mil.)	28.4%	227	340	520	725	908	1,130	1,400	1,725	2,050	2,150
Number of Stores	28.0%	500	900	1,000	1,820	2,000	2,700	3,173	3,650	4,300	4,609
Employees	24.4%	12,900	18,000	26,160	36,400	43,600	54,000	63,460	73,000	86,000	92,000

Sales ($ mil.) 1984–93

KEY COMPETITORS

Buffets
Checkers Drive-In
Domino's Pizza
Flagstar
Grand Metropolitan
Imasco
International Dairy Queen
McDonald's
Papa John's International
PepsiCo
Philip Morris
Rally's
Schwan's Sales Enterprises
Sonic
Subway Sandwiches
Wendy's

MACANDREWS & FORBES

RANK: 70

OVERVIEW

New York–based MacAndrews & Forbes, led by financier Ronald Perelman, is the holding company for an eclectic collection of businesses ranging from Revlon cosmetics to Marvel Entertainment Group, the US's #1 comic book publisher. The company's other holdings include Coleman Company, the leading US maker of camping and recreational equipment, and Mafco Worldwide, a maker of licorice extract used in flavorings. It also has interests in banking through its First Madison Bank, which in 1994 bought Ford's First Nationwide, the 5th largest thrift in the US, with $15.5 billion in assets.

Revlon produces a large percentage of MacAndrews & Forbes's revenues but has lost money since 1991 because of debt incurred in its purchase. Perelman has sold several Revlon product lines and drastically cut its work force.

Perelman's focus lately, however, has been media. In 1993 he acquired 37.5% of Guthy-Renker, a TV infomercial producer, and 52% of SCI Television (7 TV stations; since raised to 100% and renamed New World Television). He bundled these together with Genesis Entertainment, a TV syndicator (also purchased in 1993) and TV producer New World Entertainment to create New World Communications, which went public in 1994. New World then bought 4 TV stations from Great American Communications, and, as part of a deal that brought a $500 million investment from Rupert Murdoch in exchange for switching its stations to Fox affiliates, bought 4 more stations from Argyle Television.

WHEN

Ron Perelman grew up working in his father's Philadelphia-based conglomerate, Belmont Industries, but left it at the age of 35 to seek his fortune in New York. In 1978 he bought 40% of jewelry store operator Cohen-Hatfield Industries. In 1979 Cohen-Hatfield bought a minority interest in MacAndrews & Forbes (licorice flavoring), acquired the rest of the company the next year, and then took MacAndrews & Forbes Group as its name.

In 1982 the company bought 82% of Technicolor, a motion picture processor (sold in 1988). After going private in 1983, MacAndrews & Forbes Group bought control of video production company Compact Video.

In 1984 Perelman reshuffled his assets, creating MacAndrews & Forbes Holdings and making it the owner of MacAndrews & Forbes Group. Perelman and his holding company then went on a shopping spree, acquiring Consolidated Cigar in 1984. In 1985 the company acquired control of Pantry Pride, a Florida-based supermarket chain. Pantry Pride had $400 million in tax credits, and Perelman planned to use the company as a tax shelter as he went on the prowl for a major acquisition. Later that year Pantry Pride announced a $1.8 billion hostile takeover bid for Revlon.

Revlon had been #1 in US cosmetics until 1975, when founder Charles Revson died. His successor, Michel Bergerac, cut R&D spending and used beauty division earnings to buy health care and pharmaceutical companies. Perelman acquired Revlon in 1985 and sold all its health care businesses, except for National Health Laboratories. In the late 1980s Perelman bought several other cosmetics companies (including Max Factor, Germaine Monteil, and Yves Saint Laurent's fragrance and cosmetic lines). MacAndrews & Forbes took Revlon private in 1987.

In 1988 MacAndrews & Forbes Holdings agreed to invest $315 million in 5 failing Texas S&Ls, which Perelman combined and named First Gibraltar (he sold it to BankAmerica in 1993, when Perelman sold 2.6 million shares of BankAmerica). The next year the company bought the Coleman Company for $545 million.

The company bought a controlling interest in Marvel Entertainment Group from New World Entertainment in 1988, agreeing to buy the rest of New World in 1989. Between 1988 and 1992 MacAndrews & Forbes sold 80% of National Health Laboratories. In 1991 Perelman took Marvel public and sold Revlon's Max Factor and Betrix units to Procter & Gamble for over $1 billion. In 1992 he sold the Halston and Princess Marcella Borghese brands to 4 unnamed Saudi brothers.

In 1993 the company increased its stake in Marvel from 60% to 80%, as part of its plan to crash big media's party (Marvel's characters could be used for cartoons for New World's production companies). Also in 1993 it bought Reebok International's Boston Whaler boat manufacturing subsidiary and closed all but its Florida facility. It then created a new subsidiary, Meridian Sports, to manage Boston Whaler and its other marine holdings.

HOW MUCH

	Annual Growth	1984	1985	1986	1987	1988	1989	1990	1991	1992	1993
Estimated sales ($ mil.)	17.6%	—	750	552	2,440	2,500	5,325	5,381	4,521	3,496	2,748
Employees	29.3%	—	3,000	3,000	28,000	24,582	44,000	44,000	38,100	25,700	23,500

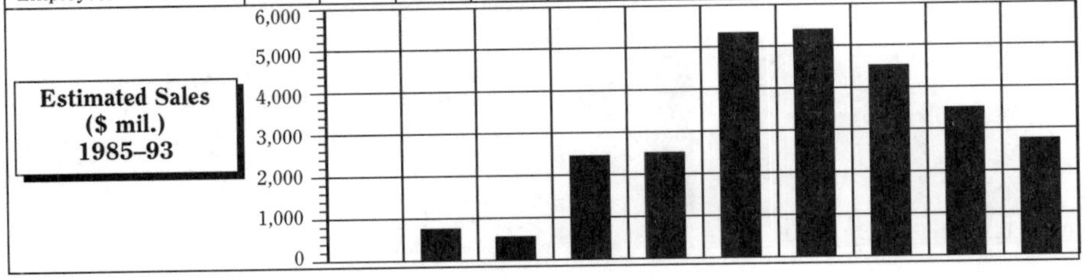

Estimated Sales ($ mil.) 1985–93

Private company
Fiscal year ends: December 31

WHO

Chairman and CEO: Ronald O. Perelman, age 51
VC: Howard Gittis, age 60
VC: Donald G. Drapkin, age 45
President: Bruce Slovin, age 59
EVP: Meyer Laskin
EVP and General Counsel: Barry F. Schwartz, age 43
CFO: Erwin Engelman
Auditors: KPMG Peat Marwick

WHERE

HQ: MacAndrews & Forbes Holdings Inc., 35 E. 62nd St., New York, NY 10021
Phone: 212-688-9000
Fax: 212-572-8400

MacAndrews & Forbes's entertainment, publishing, industrial, and consumer products operations are in the US.

WHAT

Entertainment and Publishing
New World Communications Group, Inc.
- Four Star International (film library)
- Genesis Entertainment (TV syndication)
- Guthy-Renker Corp. (37.5%, infomercial production)
- New World Entertainment, Ltd. (TV production, distribution)
- New World Sales and Marketing, Inc. (advertising representation)
- New World Television, Inc. (TV broadcasting)

Marvel Entertainment Group (80%, comic book publishing)
- Fleer Trading Cards

Industrial and Consumer Products
Coleman Co., Inc. (83%; camping equipment, power tools, and RV accessories)
Consolidated Cigar Corp.
MacAndrews & Forbes Group, Inc.
- Mafco Worldwide Corporation (flavorings)

Revlon Group, Inc.
- Almay, Inc. (cosmetics)
- Charles of the Ritz Group Ltd. (cosmetics and fragrances)
- Germaine Monteil Cosmetiques (cosmetics)
- National Health Laboratories (24%, medical testing services)
- Revlon, Inc. (cosmetics and fragrances)

Toy Biz (toys)

Marine Companies
Meridian Sports, Inc.
- Boston Whaler (boats)
- Mastercraft Boats
- O'Brien International
- Skeeter Products
- Wet Jet International

Financial Services
First Madison Bank
First Nationwide

KEY COMPETITORS

American Financial
Amway
Avon
Bayer
Black & Decker
Bristol-Myers Squibb
Brunswick
Colgate-Palmolive
Cox
Estée Lauder
Fleetwood
Gannett
General Electric
Hearst
IFF
Jean Philippe Fragrances
Johnson Publishing
Liz Claiborne
L'Oréal
LVMH
McGraw-Hill
Outboard Marine
Paramount
Procter & Gamble
RJR Nabisco
Roche
Rubbermaid
Score Board
Shiseido
Sony
Time Warner
Tribune
Turner Broadcasting
Unilever
Viacom
Warner-Lambert
Washington Post
Wrigley

R. H. MACY & CO., INC.

RANK: 24

OVERVIEW

Since going private in a 1986 LBO, New York City–based retailer R. H. Macy has faced crushing losses — almost $2.5 billion between 1987 and 1993. The company's financial woes forced it into bankruptcy in 1992.

Macy sells a wide variety of merchandise, including clothing and accessories (78% of sales) and furniture, home furnishings, housewares, and electronics (20%), usually in the middle-to-upper price range. The company's flagship store is the Macy's in Herald Square in midtown Manhattan. Since 1924 the store has been associated with some of New York's grandest traditions, including the Macy's Thanksgiving Day Parade.

The subject of repeated takeover and merger rumors in the past few years, Macy fought hard to maintain its independence, spurning the interest of such suitors as Dillard and the May Co. and unsuccessfully trying to float its own restructuring plan. However, after months of resistance, Macy agreed in July 1994 to merge with one of its largest creditors, retailer Federated Department Stores, to form the country's largest department store chain. The combined company will have sales of almost $14 billion and operate 450 stores in 35 states.

To get Macy out of bankruptcy protection, Federated will pay $4.1 billion (including almost $1.7 billion in stock of the new company) to settle the company's outstanding debts. Macy Chairman Myron Ullman is expected to be part of a 3-man office of the chairman in the merged company, along with Federated's chairman, Allen Questrom, and COO, James Zimmerman.

Private company
Fiscal year ends: Saturday nearest July 31

WHO

Chairman and CEO: Myron E. Ullman III, age 46, $1,080,000 pay
Chairman, Macy's East: Arthur E. Reiner, age 53, $705,000 pay
Chairman, Macy's West: Michael Steinberg, age 65
Chairman, I. Magnin, Inc.: Joseph Cicio, age 49, $578,125 pay
Chairman, R. H. Macy Product Development: Richard P. Crystal, age 48, $528,750 pay
SVP Finance: Diane Price Baker, age 39
SVP General Counsel: Herbert M. Hellman, age 50
SVP Human Resources: A. David Brown, age 51
Auditors: Deloitte & Touche

WHEN

Rowland H. Macy, a Nantucket Quaker and whaling captain, opened a store under his name in Manhattan in 1858. His policies of cash-only sales, setting fixed prices, advertising, and underselling the competition were uncommon at the time and quickly gained him customers. He added new lines constantly and gained a reputation for selling everything the housewife might need.

Macy hired Margaret La Forge, a distant relative, as the store's superintendent in 1866. She had started as his bookkeeper in 1860. Upon Macy's death in 1877, La Forge and her husband Abiel became co-owners of the store with Robert Macy Valentine, the founder's nephew. After the death of Abiel, Valentine bought out Margaret La Forge and brought in a new partner, Charles Webster. Valentine died shortly thereafter. His widow married Webster, who entered into a partnership with Isidor and Nathan Straus in 1887. The Straus family, New York china merchants, ran Macy's with Webster and finally bought him out in 1896. Macy's outgrew its site at 6th Avenue and 14th Street, moving to its present site in Herald Square at 34th and Broadway in 1902.

The Strauses expanded the company outside New York by buying Lasalle & Koch, a Toledo retailer (1923), and Davison-Paxon-Stokes of Atlanta (1925). The company then bought New Jersey–based L. Bamberger (1929) and O'Connor, Moffatt & Company (1945), a San Francisco department store, which became Macy's first West Coast location.

The company continued to build its reputation as a New York institution through such events as the Thanksgiving Day Parade (first held in 1924). Customers were encouraged to work around Macy's no-credit policy by depositing money with the company, against which they could debit purchases, and the company set up Macy's Bank in 1939 to manage these funds. In 1961 the company formed Macy's Credit.

The Straus family continued to run Macy into the 3rd and 4th generations. By 1986 the only Straus still in Macy's management was board member Kenneth Straus, a retired chairman of the Buying Division. That year Chairman Edward Finkelstein led a $3.5 billion buyout of the company. Macy lost its 1988 bid for Federated Department Stores to Campeau but was able to purchase California-based I. Magnin and Bullock's units of Federated, piling on more debt.

Until 1990 Macy held its own, but merchandising changes and a slowing retail environment took their toll. Macy cut its debt by buying back $300 million of its bonds in 1991 for less than half their face value; it also sold stock to outside investors and sold off its profitable credit card operation. But the debt load was ultimately too heavy, and Chapter 11 followed. Macy's management has moved to stem the cash drain by reorganizing the company along geographic lines. Macy lost a whopping $1.25 billion in 1992. In addition, 11 of its department stores were closed by 1994.

WHERE

HQ: 151 W. 34th St., New York, NY 10001-2101
Phone: 212-494-4249
Fax: 212-629-6814

Macy operates 122 Macy's, Bullock's, and I. Magnin department stores. Macy also operates 84 Aeropostale and Charter Club specialty stores and 15 inventory close-out centers.

WHAT

Store Divisions	1993 Sales $ mil.	1993 Sales % of total
Macy's East — 59 Macy's in Alabama, Connecticut, Delaware, Florida, Georgia, Louisiana, Maryland, New Jersey, New York, Pennsylvania & Virginia	3,438	55
Macy's West — 51 Macy's and Bullock's in Arizona, California, Minnesota, Nevada & Texas	2,388	38
I. Magnin — 12 I. Magnins in Arizona & California	329	5
Aeropostale/Charter Club — 84 stores	145	2
Total	**6,300**	**100**

	1993 Sales % of total
Apparel	78
Home furnishings	20
Other	2
Total	**100**

KEY COMPETITORS

Barney's
Benetton
Broadway Stores
Brown Group
Damark International
Dayton Hudson
Dillard
Edison Brothers
The Gap
Harcourt General
Lands' End
The Limited
May
Melville
Men's Wearhouse
Mercantile Stores
Montgomery Ward
Nordstrom
J. C. Penney
Saks
Sears
TJX
U.S. Shoe
Woolworth

HOW MUCH

	9-Year Growth	1984	1985	1986	1987	1988	1989	1990	1991	1992	1993
Sales ($ mil.)	4.4%	4,260	4,595	4,890	5,449	5,972	7,225	7,547	6,961	6,449	6,300
Net income ($ mil.)	—	222	189	221	(14)	(134)	(63)	(215)	(263)	(1,251)	(544)
Income as % of sales	—	5.2%	4.1%	4.5%	—	—	—	—	—	—	—
Employees	(0.6%)	54,000	57,000	55,000	56,000	70,000	78,000	76,000	69,500	60,000	51,000

1993 Year-end:
Debt ratio: 100.0%[1]
Return on equity: —
Cash (mil.): $42
Current ratio: 1.62
Long-term debt (mil.): $3,965
Debt in bankruptcy (mil.): $5,569

Net Income ($ mil.) 1984-93
500
0
-500
-1000
-1500

[1] In Chapter 11.

MAJOR LEAGUE BASEBALL

RANK: 142

OVERVIEW

The largest of the US's pro sports leagues (ranked by revenues), Major League Baseball (MLB) is made up of 28 franchises, divided into the American and National Leagues. The major league teams, and nearly 200 minor league teams, are organized under the Office of the Commissioner of Major League Baseball. The teams are run as separate businesses, but they share some broadcasting revenue, gate receipts, and licensing fees. In 1993 both leagues realigned into 3 divisions each and added an extra round of playoffs.

In 1994, to help small-market franchises, the owners agreed to a formula for overall revenue sharing. However, this deal is contingent on getting the players to agree to a salary cap, a contentious issue that, along with other matters, led the players to strike in August 1994.

Baseball's franchise values have soared in recent years. During the 1970s the average sale price for a team was $12.6 million; in 1993 *Financial World* estimated the average franchise value at $107 million. Players' salaries have also skyrocketed, rising from an average of $51,500 in 1976 (the year free agency was introduced) to more than $1.1 million in 1993.

During the 1993 season more than 70 million fans went to the ballpark. However, television ratings are down, and baseball's new national TV contract, with ABC and NBC, will pay the owners about $7 million less per team.

Since 1992, when Fay Vincent resigned, baseball has had no commissioner. Bud Selig, owner of the Milwaukee Brewers and chairman of MLB's executive council, has been the game's head since then.

Athletic association
Fiscal year ends: October 31

WHO

Commissioner: vacant
Chairman, Executive Council: Alan H. "Bud" Selig, age 59
Deputy Commissioner and COO: Steve Greenberg
President, American League: Bobby Brown
President, National League: Len Coleman, age 44
President, Major League Baseball Properties, Inc.: Richard White
General Counsel: Tom Ostertag
Director Human Resources: John Honor
Auditors: Ernst & Young

WHERE

HQ: Major League Baseball, Office of the Commissioner, 350 Park Ave., New York, NY 10022
Phone: 212-339-7800
Fax: 212-355-0007

WHEN

Most historians agree that baseball is a descendant of an English game known as rounders. Colonists brought the game to America in the 1700s, and Washington's troops played it at Valley Forge in 1778. (The myth that Abner Doubleday invented baseball was concocted in the early 1900s when Albert Spaulding, owner of the Chicago White Stockings, wanted proof that an American invented the game.)

Professional baseball began in the 1860s when teams began to pay some of their players. The first professional team was the Cincinnati Red Stockings, formed in 1869. In 1876 William Hulbert, owner of the Chicago White Stockings, formed the National League of Professional Baseball Clubs. The league sold 8 franchises for $100 each.

While several competing leagues sprang up and folded, the Western League, formed in 1892, was able to survive by luring away the National League's players by offering higher salaries. Renamed the American League before the 1900 season, the new league had spirited away more than 100 players, including star pitcher Cy Young, by 1901. By 1902 the American League was drawing more fans than the National League, and in 1903 the 2 sides agreed to work together, the champion of each league meeting in the World Series.

Baseball flourished in the early part of the century, attracting millions of fans, and, in 1920, scandal. That year 8 Chicago White Sox players were accused of accepting money to throw the 1919 World Series. Baseball's owners, looking to clean up the game's image, hired Judge Kenesaw Mountain Landis as its first commissioner.

In 1922 the Supreme Court upheld a lower court's ruling that baseball was protected from antitrust laws, giving it a position no other professional sport in the US enjoys.

In 1947 a joint committee of owners and players introduced a number of reforms, including a player pension fund. The players' unhappiness with the pension plan led to the formation of the Major League Baseball Players' Association (MLBPA) in 1954.

In 1968 the players and owners signed the first collective bargaining agreement, giving the players a voice in baseball policymaking for the first time. The players went on strike for the first time in 1972 for 13 days, winning an improved pension plan. During the 1970s the players began to gain more power, including the right to salary arbitration in 1973. In 1976, after the owners lost several appeals, the players won the right to free agency.

In the mid-1980s most free agents found the market for their services dried up, and salary increases slowed down. The MLBPA accused the owners of conspiring to keep the price of free agents down, and in 1990 the owners agreed to a settlement of $280 million in collusion damages. In 1993 the National League added 2 new teams, the Colorado Rockies and the Florida Marlins. And in 1994 the owners named Len Coleman to succeed Bill White as president of the National League.

WHAT

	1993 Sales	
	$ mil.	% of total
Media revenues	775	44
Gate receipts	698	39
Stadium revenues	253	14
Other	49	3
Total	**1,775**	**100**

Subsidiaries and Affiliates
The American League of Professional Baseball Clubs
The National League of Professional Baseball Clubs
The Baseball Network (TV partnership with ABC & NBC)
Major League Baseball Properties Inc.
Major League Scouting Bureau

Team	1993 Sales $ mil.	1993 Operating Income $ mil.
American League		
Baltimore Orioles	81	29
Boston Red Sox	77	7
California Angels	54	3
Chicago White Sox	79	11
Cleveland Indians	49	13
Detroit Tigers	56	(5)
Kansas City Royals	52	(6)
Milwaukee Brewers	46	(2)
Minnesota Twins	49	1
New York Yankees	108	18
Oakland Athletics	60	0
Seattle Mariners	51	(4)
Texas Rangers	60	1
Toronto Blue Jays	88	1
National League		
Atlanta Braves	79	(1)
Chicago Cubs	83	7
Cincinnati Reds	53	(5)
Colorado Rockies	52	13
Florida Marlins	45	12
Houston Astros	60	7
Los Angeles Dodgers	80	11
Montreal Expos	46	12
New York Mets	81	5
Philadelphia Phillies	61	1
Pittsburgh Pirates	43	4
St. Louis Cardinals	65	20
San Diego Padres	48	17
San Francisco Giants	69	(1)
Total	**1,775**	**169**

HOW MUCH

	9-Year Growth	1984	1985	1986	1987	1988	1989	1990	1991	1992	1993
Sales ($ mil.)	12.3%	624	718	792	911	1,008	1,241	1,337	1,537	1,663	1,775
Operating inc. ($ mil.)	17.0%	41	7	12	103	122	214	143	99	22	169
Attendance (mil.)	5.2%	44.7	46.8	47.5	52.0	53.0	55.2	54.8	56.9	55.9	70.3
Avg. salary ($ thou.)	14.7%	326	369	411	423	431	490	589	845	1,012	1,116
Employees	—	—	—	—	—	—	—	—	—	—	150

Sales ($ mil.) 1984–93

THE MARMON GROUP, INC.

RANK: 43

OVERVIEW

If variety is the spice of life, then The Marmon Group is a 3-alarm corporate gumbo. The manufacturing and services arm of the Pritzker family empire, The Marmon Group is made up of over 60 autonomous companies involved in everything from mining equipment to medical products. The Chicago-based group is owned by Chairman Jay Pritzker and his brother CEO Robert Pritzker. The Pritzkers, whose fortune is estimated at $4.4 billion by *Forbes*, also own hotelier Hyatt Corporation and tobacco company Conwood Co.

The Marmon Group boasts a number of leaders in their fields, including the world's #1 manufacturer of aircraft passenger seat belts (Am-Safe), the world's largest maker of residential water treatment systems (EcoWater Systems), the world's largest work and recreation glove manufacturer (Wells Lamont), and the US's #1 maker of copper plumbing tube (Cerro Copper Products). Other group companies include a poultry incubator manufacturer (Jamesway Incubator), a hatmaker (Kangol), and a consumer credit reporting service (Trans Union).

The group has expanded as the 2 brothers have worked their magic on troubled companies: dealmaker Jay buys them (usually for less than 80% of book value) and industrial engineer Robert finds a way to run them for a profit. The group has shown a profit every year since 1955.

Private company
Fiscal year ends: December 31

WHO

Chairman: Jay A. Pritzker, age 71
President and CEO: Robert A. Pritzker, age 67
EVP, Treasurer, and CFO: Robert C. Gluth
EVP: Sidney H. Bonser
SVP: Gerald T. Shannon
VP, General Counsel, and Secretary: Robert W. Webb
Personnel Director: George Frese
Auditors: Ernst & Young

WHERE

HQ: 225 W. Washington St., Chicago, IL 60606
Phone: 312-372-9500
Fax: 312-845-5305

The Marmon Group operates worldwide.

	1993 Sales % of total
US	74
Other countries	26
Total	**100**

WHAT

	1993 Sales % of total
Manufacturing	50
Services	50
Total	**100**

Manufacturing and Marketing
Automotive products
Building products
Consumer products
Electronic monitoring instruments
Industrial materials and components
Medical products
Mining equipment
Office equipment
Power protection equipment
Railroad equipment
Retail merchandising equipment
Water and industrial fluids treatment systems

Industrial and Commercial Services
Commercial and industrial equipment leasing and financing
Consumer credit information and telecommunications services
Liquified petroleum gas (LPG) storage facilities
Marketing and distribution of industrial, automotive, and consumer products
Metals trading
Rail car leasing
Sulfur processing plant construction and operation

KEY COMPETITORS

Astrum
Eaton
Equifax
Illinois Tool Works
Ingersoll-Rand
Itel
Manville
Masco
Met-Pro
Morgan Products
Owens-Corning
PACCAR
Peerless
Pullman
Robert Bosch
TRW

WHEN

Although the history of The Marmon Group officially begins in 1953, the company's roots are in the Chicago law firm started by Nicholas Pritzker in 1902. Through the firm, Pritzker and Pritzker, the family gained connections with the First National Bank of Chicago, which Nicholas's son, A.N., used to get a line of credit to begin acquiring real estate. By 1940 the firm had stopped accepting outside clients in order to concentrate on the family's growing investment portfolio.

In 1953 when A.N.'s oldest son, Jay, wanted to buy Colson Company, a small, money-losing manufacturer, he used his father's connections with the First National Bank to get the loan. Jay's brother, Robert, who had graduated from the Illinois Institute of Technology with a degree in industrial engineering, took charge of the company. Robert turned the company around and soon Jay began acquiring more companies for his brother to manage.

In 1963 the brothers paid $2.7 million for about 45% of the Marmon-Herrington Company (whose predecessor, Marmon Motor Car Company, built the car that, in 1911, won the first Indianapolis 500). The family now had a name for their industrial holdings — The Marmon Group.

The Marmon Group became a public company in 1966 when it merged with door- and spring-maker Fenestra Incorporated. However, Jay began to take greater control of the group through a series of stock purchases, and in 1971 The Marmon Group was private once again.

In 1973 the group began to acquire stock in Cerro Corporation, which had operations in mining, manufacturing, trucking, and real estate, and by 1976 had completed acquisition of the company. The brothers sold Cerro's trucking subsidiary, ICX, in 1977 and acquired organ manufacturer Hammond Corporation. The deal included Hammond's glove-making subsidiary, Wells Lamont.

In 1981 The Marmon Group acquired conglomerate Trans Union Corporation for $688 million. Trans Union brought the group a variety of businesses, including rail car and equipment leasing, credit information services, international trading, and water and waste water treatment systems.

While the company continued to grow, the Pritzkers made a foray into the airline business in 1984, buying Braniff Airlines. But after unsuccessfully bidding for Pan Am in 1987, they sold Braniff in 1988. Disappointments in other Pritzker businesses didn't slow down The Marmon Group. It added to its transportation equipment business in 1984 when it acquired Altamil Corporation, which made products for the trucking and aerospace industries. In 1990 The Marmon Group bought the Winamac Spring division from Masco Industries.

In 1993, in honor of its 40th anniversary, The Marmon Group and 10 member companies sponsored a car, the Marmon Wasp II, at the Indianapolis 500. In other family dealings that year, the Pritzkers sold Ticketmaster to Paul Allen, a cofounder of Microsoft, although they retained a minority interest.

HOW MUCH

	Annual Growth	1984	1985	1986	1987	1988	1989	1990	1991	1992	1993
Sales ($ mil.)	5.0%	2,783	2,767	2,878	3,239	3,507	3,841	3,846	3,867	4,008	4,319
Net income ($ mil.)	6.5%	118	114	116	144	204	206	125	126	145	207
Income as % of sales	—	4.2%	4.1%	4.0%	4.5%	5.8%	5.4%	3.3%	3.3%	3.6%	4.8%
Employees	0.3%	—	27,095	26,910	25,545	25,005	25,074	26,705	27,050	27,000	27,700

Net Income ($ mil.) 1984–93

250
200
150
100
50
0

MARS, INC.

RANK: 13

OVERVIEW

One of the largest private companies in the US, Mars fell behind #1 Hershey in the domestic candy market in 1992 (after see-sawing for the #1 spot for several years) and continued to fall behind in 1993. Mars now holds about 37% of the US chocolate candy market, to Hershey's 42%. Its well-known brands include M&Ms, Snickers, and Milky Way. Mars also produces pet food (Kal Kan), rice (Uncle Ben's), and electronic products.

Forrest E. Mars, Jr., and younger brother John F. set the pace for employees by punching the clock every day. Worth more than $9 billion, the Mars family is one of the richest in the country. It's also one of the most secretive, keeping a tight lid on information about the company's history and operations. Some say that the CIA, whose headquarters is located a scant 2 miles from Mars's own, is only the 2nd most mysterious organization in Virginia. However, the messy divorce of Jacqueline Mars Vogel, sister of Forrest and John, and Harry Vogel, who is asking for a share of his ex-wife's fortune, may reveal something of the company's workings.

Mars is doing a brisk business in Russia and other ex-Soviet states through Master-foods, its Russian arm. A gargantuan ad campaign has people of all ages desperate for Snickers bars — the most recent symbol of the new, modern Russia — and prompted one group to hijack a Mars delivery truck.

WHEN

Frank Mars, inventor of the Milky Way candy bar (1923), hired his son Forrest after the latter's Yale graduation to work at his candy operation. After arguments between the 2 men, Forrest moved to England and started his own Mars company in the 1930s. Forrest began making pet food and at one point controlled 55% of the British pet food market.

During WWII Forrest returned to the US and introduced Uncle Ben's rice and M&Ms. The idea for M&Ms was borrowed from British Smarties, for which Mars obtained rights (from Rowntree Mackintosh) by relinquishing similar rights for its Snickers bar in some foreign markets. The ad slogan "Melts in your mouth, not in your hand" elevated Mars to industry leader.

Little is known about Mars between the mid-1940s and 1964, when Forrest merged his operations with his deceased father's company after bitter family quarrels. In 1968 Mars bought Kal Kan and followed with Puppy Palace pet shops in 1969 (sold in 1976). During the 1970s Mars produced 5 of the country's top 10 candy bars.

Mars claims that Forrest (born in 1904) is still alive; likened to the late Howard Hughes, he is rumored to be living as a recluse in Las Vegas, having delegated responsibility for the company to his sons, Forrest Jr. and John, in 1973.

By 1978 the brothers, looking for snacks to offset dwindling candy revenues from a more diet-conscious America, brought out Twix, a chocolate-covered cookie. In 1987 they bought Dove Bar International, an ice cream bar manufacturer that had been started by Greek immigrant Leo Stefanos in his Chicago candy store in 1939 (to keep his children from buying ice cream bars from the passing ice cream trucks) and had grown to production of 40,000 per day by 1985.

Around 1988 the brothers purchased Ethel M Chocolates, producer of liqueur-flavored chocolates, a business their father had begun in his retirement. Unlike the other secretive Mars plants, the Ethel M plant is open to the public for conducted tours.

Hershey's passed Mars as the US's largest candy maker in 1988 when it acquired Cadbury Schweppes's US division (Mounds and Almond Joy). In 1989 Mars introduced Bounty Bars and PB Max. In response to the success of Hershey's Symphony Bar, Mars introduced a new dark chocolate candy bar, Dove, in 1991. Other recent introductions include peanut butter, mint, and almond M&Ms; Milky Way Dark; Peanut Butter Snickers; and Milky Way II, a reduced-calorie version of the company's famous candy bar.

In 1993 the company announced its entry into the Indian confectionery market with the establishment of a $10 million factory there. Also that year Procter & Gamble sued Mars for failure to meet a purchasing agreement (of caprenin, a low-calorie substance used in the poorly selling Milky Way II).

In 1994 Forrest Mars was named "Worst Marketer" by *The Delaney Report* for continuing to let Mars lose market share to Hershey.

HOW MUCH

	Annual Growth	1984	1985	1986	1987	1988	1989	1990	1991	1992	1993
Estimated sales ($ mil.)	10.5%	5,300	7,000	7,700	8,000	8,541	8,450	9,100	11,000	12,500	13,000
Ad expenses ($ mil.)	1.9%	276	313	379	340	293	272	254	255	320	—
Employees	2.6%	—	22,000	22,000	22,000	22,000	23,000	26,000	28,000	28,000	27,000

Private company
Fiscal year ends: December 31

WHO

Chairman, CEO, and Co-President: Forrest E. Mars, Jr., age 62
Co-President: John F. Mars, age 57
VP and CFO: Joseph Danvers
Director External Relations: Jim Conlan
Secretary: E. J. Stegeman
VP Marketing, M&M/Mars: Paul Michaels

WHERE

HQ: 6885 Elm St., McLean, VA 22101-3810
Phone: 703-821-4900
Fax: 703-448-9678

Mars owns candy plants in Albany, GA; Chicago, IL; Cleveland, TN; Hackettstown, NJ; Henderson, NV; and Waco, TX. It owns a pet food plant in Vernon, CA, and a rice plant in Houston, TX.

The company has over 50 global operating units.

WHAT

Brand Names

Candy
Bounty
Dove
M&Ms
Mars
Milky Way
PB Max
Skittles
Snickers
Starburst
3 Musketeers

Electronic Products
Coin changers
Hand-held scanning devices

Ice Cream Products
3 Musketeers
Dove
Milky Way
Snickers

Pet Food
Kal Kan
Mealtime
Pedigree
Sheba
Whiskas

Rice
Uncle Ben's Converted
Uncle Ben's Country Inn
Uncle Ben's Long Grain & Wild Rice

Other
Combos
Kudos
Twix

Major Subsidiaries

Kal Kan Foods, Inc.
M&M/Mars
Uncle Ben's, Inc.

KEY COMPETITORS

ADM
Allied-Lyons
Anheuser-Busch
Ben & Jerry's
Berkshire Hathaway
Borden
Cadbury Schweppes
Campbell Soup
Carter-Wallace
Colgate-Palmolive
ConAgra
General Mills
Grand Metropolitan
Heinz
Hershey
Hormel
Kellogg
Nestlé
PepsiCo
Philip Morris
Quaker Oats
Ralston Purina Group
Reynolds Metals
Riceland Foods
RJR Nabisco
Tootsie Roll
Tyson Foods
Unilever

MARY KAY COSMETICS INC.

RANK: 410

OVERVIEW

Mary Kay Ash, the 75-year-old matriarch of Mary Kay Cosmetics, the 2nd largest direct seller of cosmetics in the US (after Avon), is one of the only women to head a *FORTUNE* 500 company. Mary Kay makes about 200 products (120 million items are sold yearly), and total retail sales now surpass $1 billion.

Mary Kay cosmetics are sold only by the company's direct-sales consultants, who now number 325,000 in 21 countries. Upon signing up, consultants purchase a sales case containing sample wares and Ash's autobiography. Most of the consultants work part-time, and annual turnover hovers around 40% (far below Avon's 100–150% of its annual work force).

Ash, who believes that "Appreciation is the oil that makes things run," still stays up late at night signing birthday cards for her employees. Recognition, not necessarily just money, is the name of the game at Mary Kay. At the company's annual seminars, top saleswomen win diamonds, furs, lavish vacations, and, of course, the trademark pink Cadillacs. (Others win Buick Regals outfitted with a bumper sticker that reads: When I grow up, I'm going to be a Cadillac.)

Mary Kay boasts more women making over $50,000 per year than any other US company; it has made millionaires of about 50 women to date. Women make up 70% of its work force. Owned almost wholly by Ash and her family and considered a great employer, Mary Kay has outsourced employees to other companies during slow periods instead of laying them off.

WHEN

Before founding her own company in 1963, Mary Kay Ash worked as a salesperson for Stanley Home Products. Overcome with envy for the prize awarded the top saleswoman at a Stanley convention — an alligator handbag — Ash determined to win the next year's prize. She succeeded.

Tired of not receiving the recognition she deserved because of her sex, Ash used her life savings, $5,000, to go into business for herself. She bought a cosmetics formula invented years earlier by a hide tanner. (The mixture was originally used to soften leather, but when the tanner noticed how young the formula made his hands look, he began applying the mixture to his face, with great results.) Ash kept her first line simple — 10 products — and enlisted consultants, who were to hold "Beauty Shows" with 5 or 6 women in attendance. The idea was that, with such small numbers, consultants could spend more time with clients individually. With son Richard Rogers handling finances, the company grossed $198,000 in its first year.

In 1966 Ash bought a pink Cadillac that was much admired by employees. She began awarding the cars as prizes the next year. By 1981 orders had grown so large (almost 500) that GM dubbed a color "Mary Kay Pink."

When the company went public in 1968, Ash became a millionaire. The same year the company launched its first fragrance, Snare. In 1969 Mary Kay began foreign operations, in Australia. Over the next 20 years the company entered Argentina, Canada, West Germany, and the UK.

The company grew steadily through the 1970s. Ash published her autobiography in 1981, mainly as a motivational tool, complete with tips on how to save time (eat lunch in your office) and gain your husband's support (don't talk to him too much about your work) and favored words of wisdom ("Flowers leave their fragrance on the hand which bestows them").

In 1985 Ash and her family reacquired the company through a $315 million LBO. In the late 1980s the company, weighted with debt, lost money. A number of steps were taken to boost sales, income, and public image, including the introduction of recyclable packaging and empowerment groups (called Creative Action Teams). The company also began advertising in women's magazines (after a 5-year hiatus) to counter its old-fashioned image. In 1989 Avon rebuffed a buyout offer by Mary Kay, and both companies halted the practice of animal testing.

Mary Kay introduced a line of bath and body products in 1991, the result of a joint venture with International Flavors & Fragrances. The company's Skin Revival System, introduced in late 1993, raked in $80 million in its first 6 months on the market.

Private company
Fiscal year ends: December 31

WHO

Chairman Emeritus: Mary Kay Ash, age 75
Chairman and CEO: Richard R. Rogers, age 50
President and COO: Richard C. Bartlett
SVP, Secretary, and Legal Counsel: Bradley R. Glendening
CFO: John P. Rochon
SVP Human Resources: Amy Digeso
Auditors: Ernst & Young

WHERE

HQ: 8787 Stemmons Fwy., Dallas, TX 75247
Phone: 214-630-8787
Fax: 214-905-5699
Consultant Directory: 800-627-9529 (800-MARYKAY)

Mary Kay Cosmetics Inc. employs 325,000 direct-sales consultants who sell the company's merchandise in the US and 20 other countries. The company operates distribution centers in Atlanta, Chicago, Los Angeles, and Piscataway, NJ.

WHAT

	Types of Jobs % of total
Distribution	37
Manufacturing & research	35
Administration	12
Sales & marketing	10
Other	6
Total	**100**

Selected Products
Accessories
Bath and body products
Cleaning products
Clothing
Cosmetics
Fragrances
Hair care products
Jewelry
Luggage
Skin care products
Toiletries
Watches

Partnerships
Richmont Capital Partners (with New Arrow Corp. and J.R. Investments Corp.; owns 7.2% of Royal Appliance Manufacturing Co.)

KEY COMPETITORS

Alberto-Culver
Ames
Amway
Avon
Body Shop
Broadway Stores
Carter-Wallace
Chattem
Colgate-Palmolive
Cosmair
Dayton Hudson
Dillard
Edison Brothers
Estée Lauder
Gillette
Helene Curtis
Henkel
Hudson's Bay
Jack Eckerd
Jean Philippe Fragrances
Johnson & Johnson
S.C. Johnson
Kmart
Longs
L'Oréal
Macy
Marks and Spencer
May
Mercantile Stores
Montgomery Ward
Nature's Sunshine
Nordstrom
J. C. Penney
Procter & Gamble
Rite Aid
Schering-Plough
Shiseido
Unilever
Walgreen
Wal-Mart
Woolworth

HOW MUCH

	Annual Growth	1984	1985	1986	1987	1988	1989	1990	1991	1992	1993
Sales ($ mil.)	11.4%	278	249	255	326	406	450	487	520	613	737
Net income ($ mil.)	—	34	21	(33)	(3)	9	20	0	—	—	—
Income as % of sales	—	12.2%	8.4%	—	—	2.2%	4.4%	0.0%	—	—	—
Direct-sales consultants	7.3%	173,101	145,493	141,113	—	—	192,804	208,009	225,000	300,000	325,000
Employees	9.6%	—	—	1,265	—	—	1,400	1,722	1,900	2,100	2,400

Sales ($ mil.) 1984–1993

800
700
600
500
400
300
200
100
0

MASSACHUSETTS MUTUAL LIFE

RANK: 21

OVERVIEW

MassMutual, based in Springfield, Massachusetts, is the US's 12th largest life insurer, with $143 billion in life insurance in force.

MassMutual has 4 core business areas. Insurance and financial management includes investment and asset management services as well as life insurance. The life and health benefits management unit provides health coverage and managed care and case review services in over 100 major US markets. MassMutual's pension management services administer 401-K and other pension programs. The investment management unit (through its ownership of Concert Capital and a controlling interest in Oppenheimer Management) manages income from the company and outside clients.

The company stood aloof from the investment manias of the 1980s, practicing a policy of financial stewardship. This policy served MassMutual well in the recession of the late 1980s and early 1990s; after declines in 1990 and 1992, income rebounded in 1993. In that year MassMutual enlarged its group medical insurance sector by assuming ITT Hartford's benefits operations, worth about $820 million. It also increased capital by issuing notes against its surplus.

MassMutual

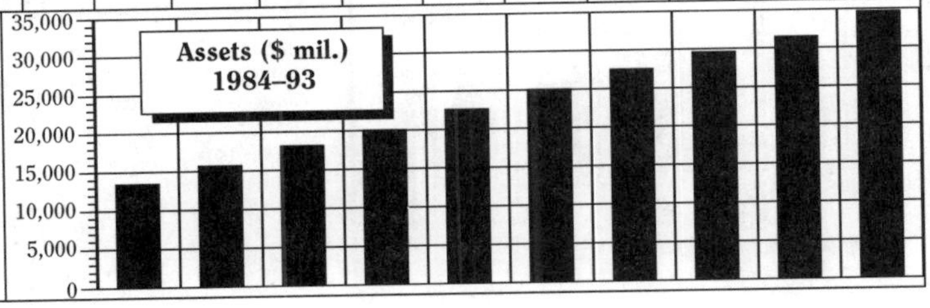

Mutual company
Fiscal year ends: December 31

WHO

President and CEO: Thomas B. Wheeler
EVP Corporate Financial Operations: Daniel J. Fitzgerald
EVP and Chief Investment Officer: Gary E. Wendlandt
EVP Insurance and Financial Management: Lawrence L. Grypp
EVP and General Counsel: Lawrence V. Burkett, Jr.
EVP Operations, Human Resources: John J. Pajak
Auditors: Coopers & Lybrand

WHEN

Massachusetts Mutual was formed in Springfield by George Rice, an insurance agent, in 1851. The company started as a stock company but in 1867 repurchased the stock and became a mutual company. By 1868 MassMutual had opened a San Francisco office. For its first 50 years the company sold only individual life insurance, but after 1900 it branched out, offering annuities (1917) and disability coverage (1918).

Though WWI brought a deluge of claims and forced the company to adopt higher premiums on new policies, the 1918 flu epidemic was much more costly. MassMutual endured the Great Depression despite policy terminations and expanded its products to include income insurance. In 1946 MassMutual wrote its first group policy, for Brown-Forman Distillers (Louisville), makers of Jack Daniel's. By 1950 the company had over 200 employees in its group sector and had diversified into medical insurance.

MassMutual began investing in stocks in the 1950s, switching over from reliance upon fixed-return bonds and mortgages, to receive a higher return. It also decentralized and began automating operations in 1961. By 1970 MassMutual had installed a computer network that linked it to its independent agents. In this period, whole life insurance remained the dominant product. The company was also responsive to social needs, investing in and anchoring commercial development that helped in the redevelopment of Springfield.

After the interest rate increases of the late 1970s, many insurers began to diversify, offering high-yield products, like guaranteed investment contracts, funded by high-risk investments. MassMutual resisted as long as it could, but as interest rates soared to 20%, the company experienced a rash of policy loans (policyholders taking low-rate loans on their policies to invest the money at higher rates), which led to a cash crunch. In 1981, with its policy growth rate trailing the rest of the industry, MassMutual sought new products. Fearing that a rush into universal life would hurt agents' earnings, the company instead developed UPDATE, which offered whole life holders higher dividends in return for adjustable interest on policy loans. Over 750,000 policyholders converted to UPDATE. Though the competition began diversifying into financial services, MassMutual stuck to its core business and avoided risky investments.

In the 1980s MassMutual reduced its investment in stocks (to about 5% of total investments by 1987), allowing the company to emerge virtually unscathed from the 1987 stock market crash.

In 1990 MassMutual bought a controlling interest in Oppenheimer Management, a mutual-fund manager, paying $21.6 million for stock in the parent company and loaning it $44.4 million.

In 1993 MassMutual announced that, because of state legislation limiting rates, it would stop writing new individual and small-group policies in New York.

The next year, in light of the slowing demand for insurance by large corporations, the company announced its plan to target the neglected niche of family-owned businesses.

WHERE

HQ: Massachusetts Mutual Life Insurance Company, 1295 State St., Springfield, MA 01111-0001
Phone: 413-788-8411
Fax: 413-744-8889

Massachusetts Mutual serves more than 2 million individual and group policyholders and other clients in the US.

WHAT

	1993 Assets	
	$ mil.	% of total
Cash & equivalents	2,253	6
Treasury & agency bonds	6,600	19
Mortgage-backed securities	1,928	6
Utility bonds	954	3
Corporate bonds	7,499	22
Stocks	143	—
Mortgage loans	3,767	11
Real estate	1,297	4
Policy loans	2,535	7
Receivables	932	3
Other investments	740	2
Other	6,051	17
Total	**34,699**	**100**

	1993 Sales	
	$ mil.	% of total
Individual policies	1,725	24
Life & health	275	4
Pension	1,041	15
Other premiums	1,788	25
Net investment income	2,280	32
Total	**7,109**	**100**

Subsidiaries
Concert Capital Management, Inc.
MML Bay State Life Insurance Co.
MML Pension Insurance Co.
Oppenheimer Management Corporation

HOW MUCH

	Annual Growth	1984	1985	1986	1987	1988	1989	1990	1991	1992	1993
Assets ($ mil.)	11.1%	13,449	15,716	18,182	20,042	22,589	25,062	27,507	29,582	31,495	34,699
Net income ($ mil.)	8.0%	—	75	288	51	50	142	101	180	116	139
Income as % of assets	—	—	0.5%	1.6%	0.3%	0.2%	0.6%	0.4%	0.6%	0.4%	0.4%
Employees	(4.6%)	9,816	10,007	9,860	10,515	10,947	11,244	11,000	10,463	9,314	6,428

1993 Year-end:
Equity as % of assets: 5.2%
Return on equity: 8.3%
Cash (mil.) $2,253
Sales (mil.): $7,109

Assets ($ mil.) 1984–93

35,000
30,000
25,000
20,000
15,000
10,000
5,000
0

KEY COMPETITORS

Aetna
AIG
Allianz
Allstate
American Financial
American General
Blue Cross
Charles Schwab
Chubb
CIGNA
Conseco
Dreyfus
Equitable
FMR
Foundation Health
Guaranty National
Jefferson-Pilot
John Hancock
Kaiser Foundation
Kemper
Liberty Mutual
Loews
Merrill Lynch
MetLife
New York Life
Paine Webber
Prudential
Sierra Health Services
State Farm
T. Rowe Price
Teachers Insurance
Torchmark
Transamerica
Travelers
USF&G

MAYO FOUNDATION

RANK: 163

OVERVIEW

The Mayo Foundation manages the world's largest private medical facility, the Mayo Clinic in Rochester, Minnesota; its branch facilities in Jacksonville, Florida, and Scottsdale, Arizona; and several Mayo Regional Practices in Iowa, Minnesota, and Wisconsin. It also operates Rochester's 2 formerly independent hospitals, Saint Marys and Rochester Methodist, and offers programs in medical education and research. Medical education is conducted by the Mayo Graduate School of Medicine (one of the nation's largest medical programs), Mayo Medical School, and the Mayo School of Health-Related Sciences.

The Mayo Clinic is known for its integrated approach to health care. The clinic's team of more than 1,000 physicians and scientists works together to provide some of the most comprehensive health care possible. Mayo is also known for its philanthropy, making health care available regardless of a patient's ability to pay.

The foundation offers services to other doctors and hospitals, including a lab service (doctors mail in blood samples for testing), Mayo Medical Ventures (publishes the *Mayo Clinic Health Letter* and the *Mayo Clinic Family Health Book*), and through a subsidiary runs the Rochester Airport.

Nonprofit organization
Fiscal year ends: December 31

WHO

Chair, Board of Trustees: Edson W. Spencer
President and CEO: Robert R. Waller
VP and Director for Education: Richard M. Weinshilboum
VP and Chief Administrative Officer: John H. Herrell
Secretary; Chair, Department of Planning & Public Affairs: Robert K. Smoldt
Treasurer; Chair, Department of Finance: David R. Ebel
HR: Gregory Warner
Auditors: Deloitte & Touche

WHEN

William W. Mayo emigrated to the US from England in 1845. After studying medicine at Indiana Medical College, Mayo practiced medicine in Indiana and Minnesota until finally settling in Rochester, Minnesota, in 1863. Twenty years later a tornado struck the town, and Mayo took charge of a makeshift hospital. Following the disaster, the Sisters of St. Francis (a Roman Catholic order) arranged for the construction of a permanent hospital and asked Mayo to assume leadership of the medical staff. Mayo reluctantly agreed (at that time hospitals were associated with the poor and the insane) and took charge when Saint Marys Hospital opened in 1889.

Mayo's 2 sons, William and Charles, had already joined their father's practice when Saint Marys opened, and they served with their father as the hospital's medical staff. After the elder Mayo retired, the sons ran the hospital by themselves, assisted only by a small group of Catholic sisters. The brothers accepted all medical cases, regardless of the patient's ability to pay, yet they were still able to make the hospital self-sufficient. Under the brothers' direction, Saint Marys was the first hospital in the US to implement the antiseptic surgical techniques developed by Joseph Lister.

By the turn of the century, the Mayos' expanding practice had helped thousands of patients. Physicians were added to the staff and a new wing was opened in 1905, at about the same time the present name was adopted (Saint Marys would remain one of the facilities under the Mayo umbrella). In 1915 the brothers established the Mayo Graduate School of Medicine in affiliation with the University of Minnesota. During WWI they served as the head surgical consultants to the US Army.

In 1919 the brothers organized the Mayo Properties Association, a self-perpetuating charity, to assume ownership of the clinic. Ten years later a new clinic building, with modern waiting rooms, laboratories, a library, and administrative offices, was opened. In 1933 the clinic established the first blood bank in the US and in 1938 saw its millionth patient. Both of the brothers died in 1939.

In 1950 scientists at the clinic won a Nobel Prize for their development of the drug cortisone. The clinic grew during the 1960s when it moved Rochester Methodist Hospital to a new building (1966) and completed a 10-story addition to the Mayo Building (1969).

In 1972 the Mayo Medical School (its 2nd medical school) was opened. The clinic's reputation for medical research and practice continued to grow, and it established satellite facilities in Jacksonville, Florida (1986), and Scottsdale, Arizona (1987). The clinic started its liver transplant program in 1985 and 3 years later performed its first coronary atherectomy (surgery for clogged arteries).

In 1993 Mayo experienced its first net operating loss, due primarily to reduced Medicare revenues and increased patient care expenses.

WHERE

HQ: Mayo Clinic, Rochester, MN 55905
Phone: 507-284-2511
Fax: 507-284-8713 (Communications)

The Mayo Foundation operates facilities in Rochester, Wabasha, and Plainview, MN; Jacksonville, FL; Scottsdale, AZ; Eau Claire and Alma, WI; and Decorah, IA.

	1993 Revenues % of total
Rochester	61
Mayo Clinic, Jacksonville	11
Mayo Regional Practices	7
Reference Laboratories	5
Mayo Clinic, Scottsdale	5
Research	5
Other	6
Total	**100**

WHAT

	1993 Donations $ mil.	% of total
Estates	19.2	36
Individuals	18.4	34
Personal/family foundations	6.2	11
Corporations	4.6	8
Philanthropic foundations	2.5	5
Alumni	1.1	2
Other	2.0	4
Total	**54.0**	**100**

	1993 Allocation of Donations $ mil.	% of total
Research	21.5	40
Medical education & research	16.9	31
Facilities	7.7	14
Education	5.6	11
Hospitals	0.5	1
Charity	0.5	1
Other	1.1	2
Total	**54.0**	**100**

HOW MUCH

	Annual Growth	1984[1]	1985	1986	1987	1988	1989	1990	1991	1992	1993
Operating rev. ($ mil.)	15.9%	418	658	761	836	965	1,058	1,181	1,323	1,490	1,579
Operating income ($ mil.)	—	—	49	65	26	38	42	42	35	45	(43)
Op. income as % of rev.	—	—	7.4%	8.5%	3.1%	3.9%	4.0%	3.6%	2.6%	3.0%	—
Patients (thou.)	3.8%	280	282	283	303	320	328	343	363	379	393
Donations ($ mil.)	15.3%	15	18	25	27	32	31	41	59	58	54
Employees	5.7%	—	—	—	—	16,524	17,165	17,836	18,775	20,615	21,770

1993 Year-end results:
Debt ratio: 24.9%
Cash (mil.): $23
Current ratio: 0.65
Long-term debt (mil.): $578
Investment assets (mil.): $1,163
Total assets (mil.): $2,796

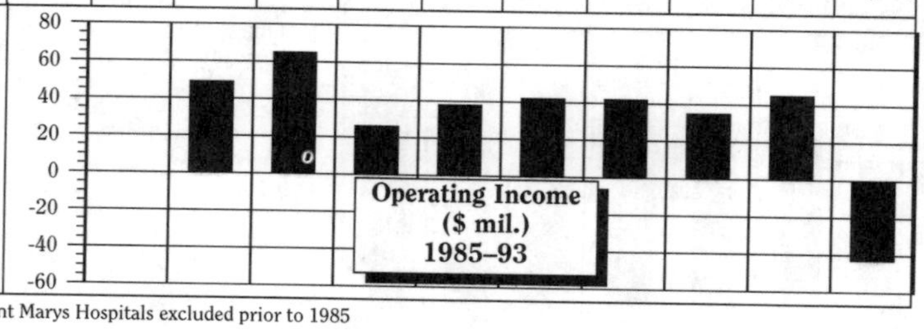

Operating Income ($ mil.) 1985–93
(Chart axis: 80, 60, 40, 20, 0, -20, -40, -60)

[1] Rochester Methodist and Saint Marys Hospitals excluded prior to 1985

KEY COMPETITORS

Allied Clinical Laboratories
Baylor College of Medicine
Columbia/HCA Healthcare
Detroit Medical Center
Harvard Medical School
Health Midwest
Johns Hopkins University
Lutheran Health Systems
Rush-Presbyterian-St. Luke's Medical Center
Unilab

MCKINSEY & COMPANY, INC.

RANK: 208

OVERVIEW

According to a partner of the world's largest independent management consulting firm, "There are only three great institutions left in the world: the Marines, the Catholic Church, and McKinsey."

As in the first 2 institutions, McKinsey's esprit de corps is maintained by a rigorous selection process, characterized as "up or out," which winnows out about 80% of the professional staff who don't make partner. Those not chosen may nevertheless go on to lead other companies and are a rich source of business and publicity for the firm. Alumni include business theorist Tom Peters, American Express chairman and CEO Harvey Golub, and IBM chairman and CEO Louis V. Gerstner, Jr.

McKinsey & Co. is one of the US's oldest consulting firms. Its meticulous methods of gathering data, its discretion, and its cultivated mystique have given it a reputation as the ultimate source of reliable, objective advice.

McKinsey has worked for many of the largest companies in America, including GM and IBM. Although the recent histories of these companies are hardly a recommendation, McKinsey maintains that the quality of its advice is tempered by the determination of the client to take it.

Companies pay about $1 million for a typical McKinsey study, during which 4 or 5 consultants camp out at company locations for several months and report on anything from general corporate strategy to specific company actions (such as a single acquisition).

McKinsey is owned by its partners and led by a managing director elected triennially. In 1994 the firm elected its first managing director of non-European descent — Indian born, US-educated Rajat Gupta. He is expected to streamline some of the firm's burgeoning bureaucracy and to bring a new perspective and style to its management.

McKinsey & Company, Inc.

Private company
Fiscal year ends: December 31

WHO

Managing Director: Rajat Gupta
CFO: James Rogers
General Counsel: Jean Molino
Director, Tokyo: Kenichi Ohmae
Director, London: Michael Patsalos-Fox
Director, Stockholm: Christian Caspar
Principal and Director of Personnel: Jerome Vascellaro

WHERE

HQ: 55 E. 52nd St., New York, NY 10022
Phone: 212-446-7000
Fax: 212-446-8575

McKinsey has 62 offices in 31 countries.

WHAT

Areas of Practice
Cost reduction and profit improvement
Electronic data processing
Management controls
Manufacturing and operations management
Marketing
Operations research
Organizational change
Strategic planning

Representative Clients
Alcoa
American Express
AT&T
British Airways
Citicorp
Deutsche Bank
Eastman Kodak
First Interstate Bank
Ford
General Electric
General Motors
Hewlett-Packard
IBM
Johnson & Johnson
Levi Strauss
LVMH
Merrill Lynch
Mobil
New York City Transit Authority
Nissan
Pacific Gas & Electric
PepsiCo
Royal Dutch/Shell
Sears
Time Warner
USF&G
The Vatican
Wells Fargo Bank

Pro Bono Clients
Cleveland Foundation
Golden Gate National Park Association
Greater Cleveland Regional Transit Authority
San Francisco Symphony

WHEN

McKinsey & Co. was founded in Chicago in 1926 by University of Chicago accounting professor James O. McKinsey, an early pioneer in the field of management. At first the firm did little more than audit clients' books, but this provided McKinsey and his partners, who included Marvin Bower and A.T. Kearney, with a wealth of basic information that they could use in their analyses of business and industry. Two years after McKinsey's death in 1937, Bower, who headed the New York office, and Kearney, in Chicago, split up the firm. Kearney renamed the Chicago office A.T. Kearney & Co. Bower kept the McKinsey name and built up a collegial practice structured like a law firm.

By 1950 billings were at $2 million, partly due to Bower's policy of emphasizing the "big picture" rather than specific operating problems. He hired staff straight out of the most prestigious business schools, a recruiting model still followed today by McKinsey. Bower also implemented the "up or out" policy that requires employees who are not continually promoted to leave the firm. Only 20% of associates become partners, and only 10% ever become directors.

Before becoming president in 1953, Dwight Eisenhower asked McKinsey to find what it was exactly that the government did.

By 1959 Bower had opened the first overseas office in London, followed by others in Europe. When Bower retired in 1967, sales were $20 million, and McKinsey was the preeminent management consulting firm. By 1976 the firm faced stiff competition from other firms with newer approaches. McKinsey lost market share until managing director Ronald Daniel instituted specialty practices and expanded McKinsey's foreign sales.

Much of the boom in consulting in the 1980s was spurred by the wave of corporate restructurings as executives looked to firms such as McKinsey to guide them through their transitions. By 1988, when Frederick W. Gluck, an engineer with no MBA, became managing director, the firm had 1,800 consultants, sales were $620 million, and 50% of billings came from overseas.

The recession of the early 1990s, however, hit white-collar workers, including business consultants. As McKinsey scrambled to upgrade its technical side, it bought the Information Consulting Group (ICG), its first acquisition. But there was a considerable clash of corporate cultures, and most ICG people left by September 1993. McKinsey has also begun to capitalize on its large store of consulting information through use of its internal database, PDNet.

KEY COMPETITORS

Arthur Andersen
Arthur D. Little
Bain & Co.
Booz, Allen & Hamilton
Boston Consulting Group
Carlson
Coopers & Lybrand
DEC
Deloitte & Touche
Earnings Performance Group
Electronic Data Systems
Ernst & Young
Gemini Consulting
Hewitt Associates
IBM
A.T. Kearney
KPMG
Maritz Communication
Marsh & McLennan
Measured Marketing Services
NYNEX
Perot Systems
Price Waterhouse
Richelieu Group
Towers, Perrin
Wyatt

HOW MUCH

	Annual Growth	1984	1985	1986	1987	1988	1989	1990	1991	1992	1993
Estimated sales ($ mil.)	17.8%	—	350	400	510	620	635	900	1,050	1,200	1,300
Employees	8.6 %	—	—	—	—	—	4,000	4,500	4,500	5,500	5,560

Estimated Sales ($ mil.) 1985–93

MEIJER, INC.

RANK: 44

OVERVIEW

With 85 Meijer combination stores (a kind of "Wal-Mart meets Safeway" blend), 69 gas stations, and more than 60,000 employees (up more than 17,000 from 1991), Grand Rapids–based Meijer is one of the largest food retailers in the US. The company was a pioneer of the American hypermarket in the 1960s. Today, its giant superstores often have as many as 24 departments and carry more than 100,000 items. The company operates in only 3 states, Michigan, Ohio, and now Indiana, which it aggressively entered in 1994, opening 8 stores.

Meijer, chaired by the founder's son, Fred Meijer, still operates under the standards and principles that transformed it into the retailing success it is today: high regard for both employees and customers (whom Meijer calls "guests"), a dedication to competitive pricing, and a strong focus on future growth.

Meijer abandoned its foray into the membership warehouse market in 1993, announcing that all 7 of its SourceClub warehouses would soon be closed. The company plans to use the resources freed up by this move to renovate its traditional combination stores. Plans call for larger stores with expanded produce, meat, and seafood sections.

Meijer continues to try to find new ways to bring in customers to its traditional stores. It has started placing company-owned eateries in some stores, including pizzerias and chinese restaurants, and reached an agreement with McDonald's that resulted in the opening of 2 restaurants in Meijer stores in 1994.

Readers of *Consumer Reports* rated Meijer the #1 grocer in competitive pricing in the US in 1993.

MEIJER

Private company
Fiscal year ends: December 31

WHO

Chairman of the Executive Committee: Fred Meijer, age 73
Co-Chairman: Doug Meijer
Co-Chairman: Hank Meijer
President: Earl Holton
EVP Retail Operations/Merchandising: Harold Hans
EVP: Paul Boyer
SVP Distribution, Properties, and Information Technology and Services: Jim McLean
SVP Finance and Administration: Fritz Kolk
SVP, General Counsel, and Secretary: Bob Riley
SVP Personnel: Windy Ray

WHERE

HQ: 2929 Walker Ave. NW, Grand Rapids, MI 49504-9428
Phone: 616-453-6711
Fax: 616-791-2572

Meijer operates 12 distribution centers, 11 in Michigan and one in Ohio.

	1993 Combination Stores
	Meijer Stores
Michigan	55
Ohio	23
Indiana	7
Total	**85**

WHEN

In 1934 Dutch immigrant and barber Hendrik Meijer opened Thrift Market in Greenville, Michigan, with the help of his wife, Gezina; son, Fred; and daughter, Johanna. Next to his barbershop was vacant storefront space that he owned but, because of the Depression, was unable to rent. He bought $338.76 worth of merchandise on credit and started his own grocery store.

Meijer had 22 competitors in Greenville alone, but his dedication to low prices (he and Fred often traveled long distances to find bargains) attracted customers. In 1935, to encourage self-service, Hendrik placed 12 wicker baskets at the front of the store and posted signs that read, "Take a basket. Help yourself."

A 2nd store was opened in 1942. The company continued to grow: 4 stores were opened in the 1950s. In the 1960s, Hendrik pioneered the one-stop shopping concept with the first Meijer Thrifty Acres stores. By 1964, the year that Hendrik died and Fred took over, 3 of these general merchandise stores were operating. In the late 1960s the company entered markets in Ohio.

In the 1970s many of the company's Meijer Thrifty Acres stores were equipped with gasoline pumps. However, a 1978 law that prohibited the sale of gasoline and alcohol at the same site forced the company to separate the 2 operations.

Meijer bought 14 Twin Fair stores in Ohio for more than $20 million in the early 1980s. The company renamed the stores, 10 of which were located in Cincinnati, Meijer Square. But in 1987 most of these stores were divested (Zayre was a major buyer) after disappointing results, signaling Meijer's egress from Cincinnati. The company had greater success in Columbus. It entered that city in 1987 and immediately captured 20% of the market with only one store. By 1993 Meijer was operating 4 stores in Columbus.

In 1988 the company began operating most of its stores on round-the-clock schedules. The next year Meijer instituted an environmental awareness program that emphasized recycling, among other earth-friendly measures.

In 1991 Meijer annihilated competitors in Dayton, Ohio, when it opened 4 stores in a one-year period. That same year the company reentered the Cincinnati area when 2 major competitors (including Ames) withdrew after declaring bankruptcy.

Rumors circulated about a possible Meijer/Kmart merger in 1992. Kmart has borrowed heavily from Meijer's concept in the development of its own superstores.

In 1993 Meijer entered the Toledo market with the opening of 2 stores there and plans for at least 2 more that year. In 1994 the company announced that it would try to open a $10 million store — which in 1993 neighbors had protested against — in the upscale Ethan's Green housing development area in Cleveland.

WHAT

	1993 Stores	
	No. of stores	% of total
Combination stores	85	55
Gas stations	69	45
Total	**154**	**100**

Selected Meijer Store Departments
Bakery
Bulk foods
Delicatessen
Food court
Pharmacy
Photo lab
Service meat and seafood
Video shop

Selected Departments, Services, and Programs
Associate Discount Days
Building Guest Relations
Catalina Coupons service (with Catalina Marketing)
Earth Friendly Program
Information Technology and Services
Private label program (as many as 10,000 products under more than 150 brand names)
Property Development
Property Management and Services

HOW MUCH

	Annual Growth	1984	1985	1986	1987	1988	1989	1990	1991	1992	1993
Estimated sales ($ mil.)	13.4%	—	—	—	—	2,000	3,000	3,700	5,370	5,390	4,250
No. of combination stores	9.9%	—	—	—	—	53	56	—	63	72	85
Employees	17.5%	—	—	—	—	—	—	37,000	42,700	50,000	60,000

Estimated Sales ($ mil.) 1988–93

6,000
5,000
4,000
3,000
2,000
1,000
0

KEY COMPETITORS

American Superstores
Ames
Amoco
Foodland Distributors
Great A&P
Kmart
Kroger
Marsh Supermarkets
Melville
Office Depot
Penn Traffic
J. C. Penney
Rite-Aid
Roundy's
Seaway Food Town
Spartan Stores
Sun
Walgreen
Wal-Mart
Woolworth

METROMEDIA COMPANY

RANK: 134

OVERVIEW

Eating and calling out are the primary businesses of Metromedia, one of the largest private partnerships in the US. Controlled by John Kluge, ranked the 3rd richest man in the US by *Forbes,* with an estimated fortune of $5.9 billion, Metromedia operates the Ponderosa, Bonanza, Steak and Ale, and Bennigan's restaurant chains. The restaurants, which account for about 60% of Metromedia's revenues, have been a major disappointment, however, losing over $190 million since 1989. The company is investing $26 million to improve the restaurants' decor and food quality.

Metromedia is in the process of merging its long-distance telecommunications subsidiary with 2 other long-distance carriers, Resurgens and LDDS. Once the merger is completed, the new entity (renamed LDDS Metro Communications) will be the 4th largest long-distance provider in the US (after AT&T, MCI, and Sprint), with estimated annual revenues of $3 billion. Kluge will own about 20% of the stock of the new company.

A 3rd interest of Metromedia and Kluge is troubled Orion Pictures. In an unusual attempt to revive Orion and build a major media and communications company, Metromedia announced in September 1994 that it would combine the Studio with Actava Group Inc. (Snapper lawn mowers) and 2 other concerns to form Metromedia International Group. The new venture will initially focus on programming and telecommunications and will be headed by Actava's flamboyant CEO Jack Phillips; Kluge will serve as chairman.

METROMEDIA

Private partnership
Fiscal year ends: December 31

WHO

General Partner, Chairman, President, and CEO: John W. Kluge, age 80
General Partner and EVP: Stuart Subotnick, age 51
SVP, Secretary, and General Counsel: Arnold L. Wadler, age 50
SVP Finance: Robert A. Maresca
President, Metromedia/ITT Long Distance: Howard Finkelstein
President, Metromedia Steakhouses: Michael Kaufman
President, Bonanza: Frank Steed, age 46
Chairman, S&A Restaurant Corporation: Steve Leipsner
President, Bennigan's: Bob Ferngren
President, Steak and Ale: John Underwood
President and CEO, Orion Pictures Corporation: Len White
General Manager; ESI Meats, Inc.: Curt Griggs
VP and Controller: David Gassler
Auditors: KPMG Peat Marwick

WHERE

HQ: 1 Meadowlands Plaza, East Rutherford, NJ 07073
Phone: 201-804-6400
Fax: 201-804-6540

WHAT

	1992 Restaurants No.
Ponderosa	770
Bonanza	310
Bennigan's	223
Steak and Ale	156
Total	**1,459**

Subsidiaries and Affiliates

Axon Systems (electronic brain monitoring equipment)
Bristol Valley Foods (meat processing)
LDDS Metromedia Communications (long distance telephone service; 20%)
Make Systems (software development)
Metbenale (holding company for Steak and Ale and Bennigan's restaurants)
Metromedia Steakhouses (Ponderosa and Bonanza family restaurants)
Metromedia Technologies (robotic painting)
MUZE, Inc. (music information technology; 80%)
North Communications (interactive multimedia)
Orion Pictures (56%, motion pictures)
Radisson Empire Hotel (New York)
Stanadyne Automotive (automotive equipment)

WHEN

Metromedia began when German immigrant John Kluge, fresh from a stint with US Army intelligence during WWII, bought WGAY radio station in Silver Spring, Maryland, in 1946. Kluge, born in 1914, had come to Detroit at age 8 with his mother and stepfather. At Columbia on scholarship, he studied economics and, to the chagrin of college administrators, poker. By graduation he had built a tidy sum with his winnings. After his release from the army, Kluge bought and sold small radio stations and dabbled in other enterprises.

A chance meeting on a Washington, DC, street led Kluge to investigate the possibility of buying television stations that were not affiliated with major networks. In 1959 he purchased control of Metropolitan Broadcasting, including TV stations in New York and Washington. The company was later renamed Metromedia, Inc.

Metromedia added independent stations — to the legal ceiling of 7— in other major markets, paying relatively little compared with what network affiliates could command. The stations struggled through years of Ginzu steak knife commercials but thrived in the late 1970s and early 1980s. Metromedia's stock price rose from $4.50 in 1974 to more than $500 in 1983. The company also acquired radio stations, the Harlem Globetrotters exhibition basketball team, and the Ice Capades.

In 1983 Kluge spurred Metromedia to pay $300 million for cellular telephone and paging licenses across the US. In 1984 Kluge took Metromedia private in a $1.6 billion buyout. The company began to sell off its assets in 1985. It sold a TV station in Boston to Hearst and sold the other 6 to Rupert Murdoch. The stations fetched $2 billion. The sell-off continued in 1986 with transactions involving Metromedia's outdoor advertising (sold for $710 million), 9 of 11 radio stations ($285 million), and the Globetrotters and Ice Capades ($30 million). Kluge also surprised industry analysts by selling most of the company's cellular properties to Southwestern Bell for $1.65 billion. In 1990 Metromedia sold its New York cellular operations to LIN Broadcasting for $1.9 billion and its Philadelphia cellular operations to Comcast for $1.1 billion.

Metromedia bought the Ponderosa Steakhouse chain in 1988 from Asher Edelman and later added Dallas-based USA Cafes (Bonanza steakhouses) and S&A Restaurant Corp. (Steak and Ale, Bennigan's). On another front, Metromedia integrated ITT's long-distance service into its operations in 1989.

In 1988 Kluge went to the rescue of friend Arthur Krim, whose Orion Pictures was threatened by Viacom. Metromedia paid $78 million for control of the filmmaker.

Early in 1990 Kluge bought into a partnership trying to set up cheaper wireless cable stations in Eastern Europe and a television station in Moscow. Krim retired from Orion in 1991 and it filed for bankruptcy protection in December of that year, emerging about one year later.

In 1993 Muze, an affiliate of Metromedia, formed a joint venture with IBM to make in-store music-information-retrieval systems.

HOW MUCH

	Annual Growth	1983	1984	1985	1986	1987	1988	1989	1990	1991	1992
Estimated sales ($ mil.)	15.1%	—	585	—	620	620	2,060	2,530	2,220	1,896	1,804
Employees	17.8%	—	5,500	—	3,000	3,000	18,732	18,732	24,652	20,252	20,400

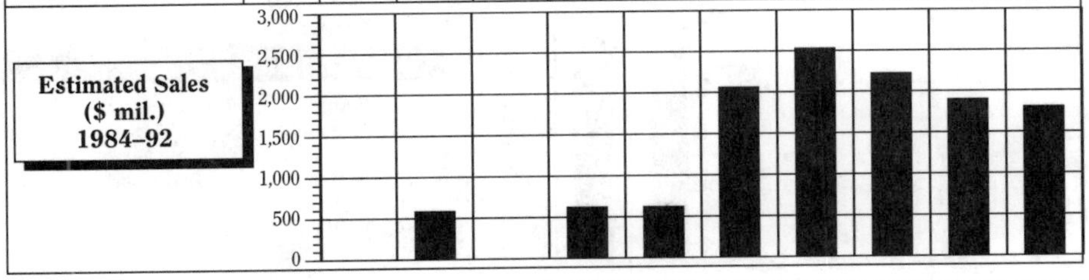

Estimated Sales ($ mil.) 1984–92

KEY COMPETITORS

AT&T
Brinker
Buffets
Cable & Wireless
Carlson
Crédit Lyonnais
Dial
Four Seasons
General Mills
Grand Metropolitan
GTE
Helmsley
Hyatt
Imasco
Loews
Lone Star Steakhouse
Matsushita
McDonald's
MCI
Outback Steakhouse
PepsiCo
Sony
Sprint
Time Warner
Turner Broadcasting
U. S. Long Distance
Viacom
Walt Disney
Wendy's

METROPOLITAN LIFE INSURANCE CO.

RANK: 5

OVERVIEW

MetLife

MetLife chairman Harry Kamen described 1993 as a roller coaster ride. While assets reached their highest level ever and operating earnings, at $265 million, equaled their best year, reported income fell by almost half, and MetLife was rocked by fraud accusations.

Metropolitan Life is the largest North American life insurer, with over $1.2 trillion of life insurance in force. Its Century 21 subsidiary is the largest real estate franchise sales organization in the world. Other real estate lines include real estate leasing, appraising, and mortgage banking subsidiaries and franchises. Metropolitan also offers financing, asset management, and investment services.

Metropolitan was not badly hurt by the collapse of the real estate and junk bond markets and has been able to capitalize on the misfortunes of defunct operations by acquiring assets and policyholders.

In 1993 MetLife issued notes against its surplus funds in order to raise capital. Despite uncertainty in insurance circles about the future of health care in the US, MetLife has discussed the possibility of a health care alliance with Travelers Insurance.

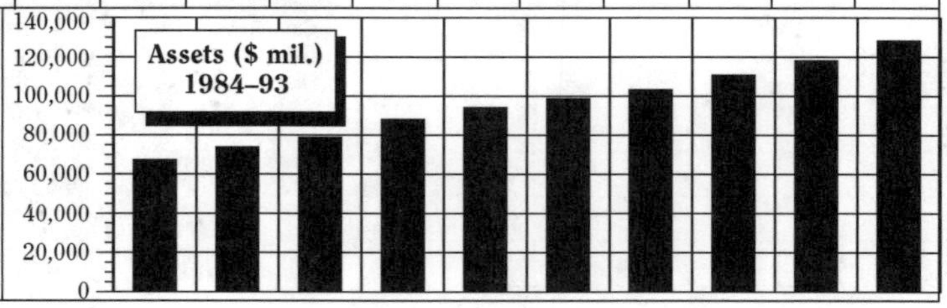

Mutual company
Fiscal year ends: December 31

WHO

Chairman and CEO: Harry Kamen, age 60
President and COO: Ted Athanassiades, age 54
SEVP and CFO: Stewart G. Nagler, age 49
EVP and Chief Investment Officer: Gerald Clark
EVP: Robert J. Crimmins
EVP: John D. Moynahan, Jr.
EVP: William G. Poortvliet
SVP and General Counsel: Richard M. Blackwell
SVP Human Resources: Anne E. Hayden
Auditors: Deloitte & Touche

WHEN

Simeon Draper, a New York merchant, tried to form National Union Life and Limb Insurance to cover Union soldiers in the Civil War, but investors were scared off by heavy casualties. After several reorganizations and name changes, the company emerged in 1868 as Metropolitan Life Insurance.

Sustained at first by business from mutual assistance societies for German immigrants, Metropolitan went into industrial insurance with workers' burial policies.

Aggressive sales became a Metropolitan hallmark. The company even imported polished British salesmen when no suitable Americans could be found.

Metropolitan became a mutual company, owned by policyholders, in 1915 and in 1917 offered group insurance. Metropolitan expanded to Canada in 1924.

After being led by the conservative Frederick Eckers and his son Frederick Jr. from 1929 to 1963, Metropolitan began to change, dropping industrial insurance in 1964. In 1974 Metropolitan began offering automobile and homeowner's insurance.

Metropolitan began to diversify in the 1980s (along with most insurers). It bought State Street Research & Management (1983), which founded the first US mutual fund; Century 21 Real Estate (1985); London-based Albany Life Assurance (1985); and Allstate's group life and health business (1988). In 1987 Metropolitan took over the annuities segment of the failed Baldwin United Co. and expanded into Spain and Taiwan in 1988.

In 1989 MetLife bought J. C. Penney's casualty insurance portfolio, United Resources Insurance Services (retirement and financial programs), and Texas Life Insurance. Metropolitan also launched a "Family Reunion" program to contact holders of old industrial insurance policies still in force.

With the economy in recession in the early 1990s, Metropolitan began to cut costs, trimming 1,000 jobs and transferring thousands of others from New York City. The company also reemphasized insurance products and added new ones, such as long-term care insurance, which is expected to grow in importance as the population ages.

In mid-1991 Metropolitan discussed merging with troubled Mutual of New York. Metropolitan offered instead to take over many of Mutual's pension contracts, but that was a deal so advantageous to Metropolitan that only 1/3 of the affected customers accepted.

In 1992 Metropolitan continued on its growth program despite the extra costs of natural disasters like Hurricane Andrew. In addition to joint ventures that took the company into Mexico and Portugal, MetLife added the 30,000 policyholders of United Mutual Life Insurance Company, which, until its merger into MetLife, was New York's only African-American life insurance company.

In 1993 Metropolitan was hit by charges of improper sales practices by agents in 13 states. Alleged improprieties included misrepresentation of life insurance policies as retirement accounts and churning (persuading policyholders to buy more expensive policies to replace old ones). Regulatory fines and refunds in these investigations exceeded $25 million by early 1994, and the bad publicity MetLife received contributed to a 23% decline in policy sales by May.

WHERE

HQ: Metropolitan Life Insurance Company, One Madison Ave., New York, NY 10010-3690
Phone: 212-578-2211
Fax: 212-578-3320

MetLife operates in the US, Canada, Mexico, South Korea, Portugal, Spain, Taiwan, and the UK.

WHAT

	1993 Assets	
	$ mil.	% of total
Cash & equivalents	1,372	1
Treasury & agency bonds	12,770	10
State & municipal bonds	1,464	1
Mortgage-backed securities	15,773	13
Corporate bonds	28,601	23
Other bonds	4,346	3
Stocks	3,191	2
Mortgage loans	15,460	12
Real estate	10,666	8
Policy loans	3,628	3
Separate account assets	25,375	20
Other	4,231	3
Total	**128,225**	**100**

	1993 Sales	
	$ mil.	% of total
Premiums & deposits	19,442	68
Supplementary contracts & dividends	1,654	6
Net investment income	7,356	25
Other	231	1
Total	**28,683**	**100**

Selected Affiliates
Albany Life Assurance Company Ltd. (UK)
Century 21 Real Estate Corporation
Farmers National Company
GFM International Investors Ltd. (UK)
Kolon-Met Life Insurance Company (Korea; joint venture with Kolon Group)
MetLife HealthCare Management Corporation
MetLife (UK) Limited
MetLife Securities, Inc.
Metropolitan Property and Casualty Insurance Company
Metropolitan Tower Life Insurance Company
Metropolitan Trust Company of Canada
Santander Met, S.A. (joint venture with Banco Santander, Spain)
Seguros Génesis, S.A. (Mexico)
Texas Life Insurance Company

HOW MUCH

	Annual Growth	1984	1985	1986	1987	1988	1989	1990	1991	1992	1993
Assets ($ mil.)	7.4%	67,354	73,803	78,773	88,140	94,232	98,740	103,228	110,799	118,178	128,225
Net income ($ mil.)	(26.0%)	—	—	—	809	836	494	360	237	225	133
Income as % of assets	—	—	—	—	—	0.9%	0.9%	0.5%	0.3%	0.2%	0.1%
Employees	4.8%	36,000	35,000	33,000	33,000	37,000	42,464	45,342	58,000	57,000	55,000

1993 Year-end:
Equity as % of assets: 5.0%
Return on equity: 2.3%
Cash (mil.): $1,372
Sales (mil.): $28,683

Assets ($ mil.) 1984–93

140,000
120,000
100,000
80,000
60,000
40,000
20,000
0

KEY COMPETITORS

Aetna
Allstate
Blue Cross
Equitable
GEICO
Guardian Life
John Hancock
Kemper
MassMutual
New York Life
Northwestern Mutual
Pacific Mutual Life
Prudential
RE/MAX
State Farm
Tokio Marine and Fire
Trammell Crow
Travelers
USAA

MILLIKEN & CO.

RANK: 78

OVERVIEW

Spartanburg, South Carolina–based Milliken is the largest privately held textile company in the US. The company's 57 plants sport the latest in mill technology and produce finished fabrics that are used in uniforms for Burger King, McDonald's, and other companies; swimsuits and sportswear (Lycra); braided polyester cords (Michelin tires); and clothes and tablecloths (Visa). Milliken holds about 40% of the market for acetate and acetate blends used in coat linings, 30% of the stretch fabric market, and 25% of the automotive fabric market.

Milliken Chemical produces chemicals for numerous applications, including dyes, plastics, petroleum products, and textiles.

The company has about 200 shareholders (most from the ranks of the Milliken family), but Roger "Big Red" Milliken, along with brother Gerrish and cousin Minot, control more than 50% of the company's stock. Roger Milliken, the company's stalwart leader since 1947, supports a variety of conservative political causes and is considered a living textile industry legend.

Although the company emphasizes R&D, customer satisfaction, and product quality, Milliken has fought hard to prevent any of its plants from being unionized and supports tariffs to keep out imports. The company has no significant debt.

WHEN

Seth Milliken and William Deering formed a company in 1865 to become selling agents for textile mills in New England and the South. Deering left the partnership and in 1869 founded Deering Harvester (later folded into International Harvester, now Navistar).

Milliken moved his operations to New York before the turn of the century, began buying the accounts receivable of cash-short textile mill operators, and invested in some of the companies. He also allied himself with leaders in the Spartanburg, South Carolina, area.

In his position as agent and financier, Milliken was able to spot failing mills. He bought out the distressed owners at a discount and soon became a major mill owner himself. In 1905 Milliken and his allies waged a bitter proxy fight and court case to win control of 2 mills, earning Milliken a fearsome reputation.

H. B. Claflin Co., a New York dry goods wholesaler who began operating retail stores, owed money to Milliken. After Claflin went bankrupt in 1914, Milliken won stores in the settlement. They became Mercantile Stores, and the Milliken family retains about 40% of the stock of the department store chain.

Roger Milliken, grandson of the founder, became the president of the company in 1947 and ruled with a firm hand. He fired his brother-in-law W. B. Dixon Stroud in 1955, and none of Roger Milliken's children, nephews, or nieces have ever been allowed to work for the company. In 1956 the workers at Milliken's Darlington, South Carolina, mill voted to unionize. The next day Milliken closed the plant. That began 24 years of litigation that ended at the US Supreme Court. Milliken settled with the workers for $5 million.

In the 1960s the company introduced Visa, a finish for easy-care fabrics. Milliken launched its Pursuit of Excellence program in 1981. The program stressed self-managed teams of employees and has since eliminated 700 management positions. Roger Milliken also emphasized research, training, and new technology. The company adapted quickly to automation, sometimes buying all the latest equipment a manufacturer could make, and competitors were left out in the cold. Tom Peters dedicated his 1987 bestseller, *Thriving on Chaos*, to Roger Milliken.The company's quality record — some clients are so confident about Milliken goods they don't even inspect for defects — earned a highly coveted Malcolm Baldrige National Quality Award in 1989. Roger Milliken is the only person to win *Textile World* magazine's Leader of the Year award twice — in 1986 and in 1990.

Away from that limelight, Milliken is and has always been a secretive, closely held business. In 1989 that secrecy and family control were threatened when members of the Stroud branch of the family sued the company in the Delaware courts and then sold a small number of shares to Erwin Maddrey and Bettis Rainsford, executives of Milliken competitor Delta Woodside. In 1992 the Delaware Supreme Court ruled in favor of the company; a lower court ruled that Maddrey and Rainsford be required to sign confidentiality agreements before receiving Milliken information.

In the meantime Milliken in 1991 introduced Fashion Effects, a new process that allowed it to customize drapery designs and textures. In 1993 Roger Milliken financially backed opponents of NAFTA.

HOW MUCH

	Annual Growth	1983	1984	1985	1986	1987	1988	1989	1990	1991	1992
Estimated sales ($ mil.)	2.3%	—	2,000	2,200	2,400	2,400	2,900	2,500	2,498	2,400	2,640
Employees	(13.6%)	—	45,000	45,000	20,000	20,000	20,000	14,000	14,000	14,000	14,000

Estimated Sales ($ mil.) 1984–92

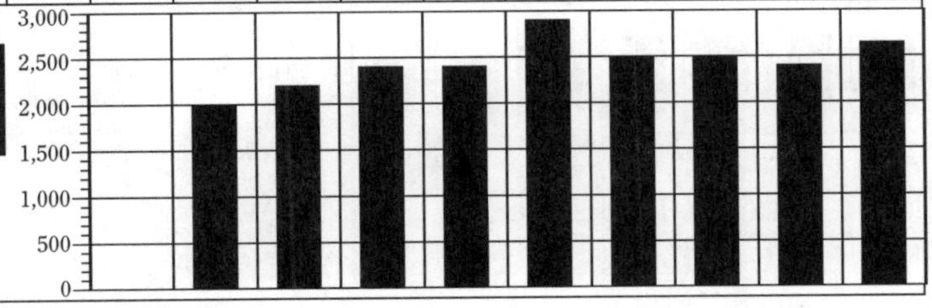

3,000
2,500
2,000
1,500
1,000
500
0

MILLIKEN

Private company
Fiscal year ends: November 30

WHO

Chairman and CEO: Roger Milliken, age 78
President and COO: Thomas J. Malone
VP and CFO: Minot K. Milliken, age 77
VP: Gerrish H. Milliken, age 76
VP and General Counsel: Bill Petry
Director of Marketing: Kay Shannon
VP Human Resources: Tommy Hodge
Auditors: Arthur Andersen & Co.

WHERE

HQ: 920 Milliken Rd., Spartanburg, SC 29303-9301
Phone: 803-573-2020
Fax: 803-573-2100 (Public Affairs)

Milliken operates manufacturing plants in North Carolina, South Carolina, and Georgia. It has international facilities in Canada, Belgium, France, Denmark, and the UK and sales offices in the US, Western Europe, Canada, and Japan.

WHAT

	1992 Estimated Sales % of total
Cotton broadwoven fabrics	75
Synthetic broadwoven fabrics & other	25
Total	**100**

Products

Area rugs (Milliken Modular Carpets)
Automotive air bag fabric
Automotive upholstery
Carpet and carpet tiles (Milliken Place Custom Carpets)
Carpet cleaner (Capture)
Colorants and tints (Versatint, Reactint, Blazon)
Duct tape reinforcement
Easy-care fabrics (VISA)
Elastic fabrics
Entrance mats (KEX)
Grass catcher bag fabric
Impression fabrics for computer printer ribbons
Knit and woven apparel fabrics
Lining fabrics
Machinery filters
Nylon fabric for sails
Packing reinforcement materials
Shop towels
Specialty chemicals
Stretch fabrics (Lycra)
Tennis ball felt
Textured yarns
Tire cord
Unfinished fabrics
Uniform fabrics

KEY COMPETITORS

Armstrong World
Burlington Industries
Dow Chemical
DuPont
Fieldcrest Cannon
Fruit of the Loom
Galey & Lord
W. R. Grace
Hercules
JPS Textile
Mohawk Carpet
Monsanto
R. B. Pamplin
Rhône-Poulenc
Samsung
Shaw Industries
Springs Industries
Union Carbide

MONTGOMERY WARD

RANK: 28

OVERVIEW

Chicago-based Montgomery Ward (affectionately known as Monkey Ward) is one of the US's largest department store operators. Ward, which is also one of the top 3 furniture sellers in the US, operates 364 stores in 39 states and also runs Montgomery Ward Direct (a catalog company) and 17 outlet stores.

CEO and firebrand Bernard Brennan, who owns about 30% of Ward's stock and whose brother chairs cross-town rival Sears, has been reformulating the company's strategy since the late 1980s, when insiders took the company private in a $3.8 billion LBO, one of the largest in US history. Brennan has introduced brand-name merchandise to the stores and established specialty departments. These departments are distinct and often have separate entrances. Nonetheless, profits have been dropping since 1990.

Ward's Electric Avenue department saw an 11% sales jump from 1992 to 1993. However, margins on electronic goods are being squeezed by price wars among leading consumer electronics/appliance chains, and sales of higher-margin items such as clothing are being won by more successful merchandisers like Sears. Ward recorded only a 2% rise in same-store sales growth in 1993.

In 1994 Ward agreed to buy Lechmere, an appliance and consumer electronics retailer, founded in 1913, with 24 stores in the Northeast and $800 million in annual sales.

Montgomery Ward

Private company
Fiscal year ends: Saturday nearest December 31

WHO

Chairman and CEO: Bernard F. Brennan, age 55, $3,459,849 pay
VC Operations and Specialty Catalogs: Richard M. Bergel, age 58, $747,387 pay
President and COO: Bernard W. Andrews, age 52
EVP and CFO: John L. Workman, age 42
EVP: Robert R. Schoeberl, age 58, $424,378 pay
EVP, Secretary, and General Counsel: Spencer H. Heine, age 51
EVP Human Resources, Montgomery Ward: Robert A. Kasenter, age 47
Auditors: Arthur Andersen & Co.

WHERE

HQ: Montgomery Ward Holding Corp., One Montgomery Ward Plaza, Chicago, IL 60671-0042
Phone: 312-467-2000
Fax: 312-467-3975

	No. of Stores
California	57
Texas	44
Illinois	36
Florida	21
Virginia	18
Maryland	16
Michigan	15
Pennsylvania	14
Colorado	13
New York	12
Arizona	11
Minnesota	10
Other states	111
Total	**364**

WHAT

	1993 Sales	
	$ mil.	% of total
Retail merchandising	5,602	93
Direct marketing	400	7
Total	**6,002**	**100**

Retail Specialties
The Apparel Store (includes The Kids Store)
Auto Express (tires, batteries, parts, and service)
Electric Avenue (electronics and major appliances)
Gold 'N Gems (jewelry)
Home Ideas (home furnishings and accessories)

Selected Consumer Services
Licensed operations (hair salons, optical shops, key shops, car rental agencies, tax services, portrait shops)

Subsidiaries
Lechmere, Inc. (24 stores in the Northeast)
Montgomery Ward Direct L.P. (partnership with Fingerhut Companies, Inc., specialty catalog)
Signature Financial/Marketing, Inc. (Montgomery Ward Auto Club, life/health insurance, direct-mail marketing)

WHEN

Aaron Montgomery Ward started the Chicago company that bears his name in 1872. It was the world's first general merchandise mail order concern. Before, farmers had bought goods from general stores or peddlers. Ward provided them with an inexpensive way to shop. In 1873 brother-in-law George Thorne became Ward's partner. In 1875 the company pioneered the "Satisfaction Guaranteed or Your Money Back" policy.

In 1893 Thorne bought a controlling interest in the company. By 1900 Ward's sales had fallen behind flamboyant Chicago rival Sears (founded in 1893). In 1904 Ward introduced what is believed to be the first company magazine edited by employees without a company-dictated policy. Profits surpassed $1 million for the first time in 1909, and the following year Thorne retired, leaving 5 sons in control of the company. In 1913 Ward died; Charles Thorne became president. He moved to chairman 3 years later, and his brother Robert became president. In 1919 Ward went public; Robert Wood took over.

From 1920 to 1924 Ward's sales grew by 48%, versus Sears's 16% decrease. Wood wanted Ward to develop retail stores, but the company wanted to remain in the mail order business, so in 1924 Wood left and went to work for Sears. In 1926 Ward opened its first retail store in Plymouth, Indiana. By the end of 1928 the company had 244 retail stores.

In 1931 Sewell Avery became CEO and ended 4 years of losses in 1934. Avery refused to turn Ward over to federal control during a WWII labor dispute, and President Franklin Roosevelt had National Guardsmen carry Avery out of his office. Having predicted the Great Depression, Avery was convinced a recession would follow WWII and canceled expansion plans; so Ward missed the postwar boom.

After Avery's departure (1955), Ward started an expansion program that included new stores in Alaska and the company's first major distribution center (1958). In 1968 the company merged with Container Corporation of America to form Marcor. In 1974 Mobil Oil acquired 54% control of Ward, acquiring 100% by 1976. Mobil made huge loans to the company in hopes of making Ward profitable.

In 1985 Mobil put Ward up for sale and brought in Bernard Brennan — who had left Sears by 1976, joined Ward in 1982, and quit after disputes with then-CEO Stephen Pistner in 1983 — to head the company. He and other top managers led a $3.8 billion LBO in 1988. Brennan sold Ward's credit card business to General Electric Capital for $716 million in cash and assumption of $1.7 billion in debt.

Between 1993 and 1994, 3 people held the post of president; Brennan's fiery temper is said to be the cause. Brennan talked Bernard Andrews into returning to Ward as president (from Circuit City) after a 3-year absence.

HOW MUCH

	Annual Growth	1984	1985	1986	1987	1988	1989	1990	1991	1992	1993
Sales ($ mil.)	(0.9%)	6,486	5,388	4,870	5,024	5,567	5,461	5,584	5,654	5,781	6,002
Net income ($ mil.)	4.5%	68	(298)	110	130	146	151	153	135	100	101
Income as % of sales	—	1.0%	(5.5%)	2.3%	2.6%	2.6%	2.8%	2.7%	2.4%	1.7%	1.7%
Earnings per share ($)	(3.5%)	—	—	—	—	2.74	2.71	2.79	2.40	2.01	2.29
Dividends per share ($)	—	—	—	—	—	—	—	—	—	0.25	0.50
Book value per share ($)[1]	24.1%	—	—	—	—	—	5.74	8.61	10.39	12.11	13.61
Employees	(4.6%)	78,300	71,200	56,300	52,300	65,000	67,000	66,300	62,400	62,300	51,350

1993 Year-end:
Debt ratio: 26.0%
Return on equity: 17.4%
Cash (mil.): $94
Current ratio: 0.73
Long-term debt (mil.): $213
No. of shares (mil.): 45
Dividend payout:
Class A: 21.8%
Class B: 24.5%
Total assets (mil.): $3,835

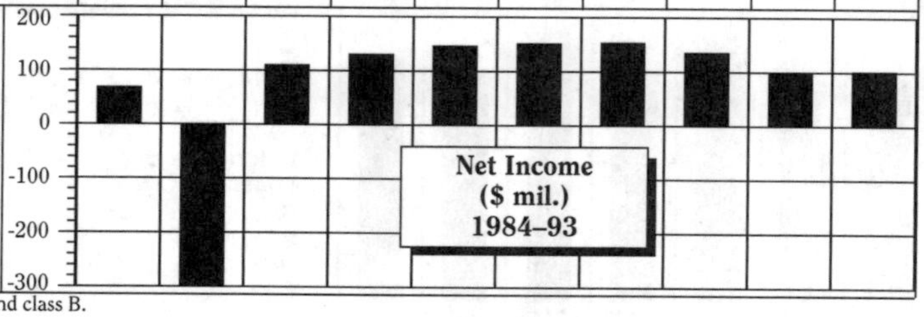

Net Income ($ mil.) 1984–93

[1] Approximate for both class A and class B.

KEY COMPETITORS

AAA
50-Off Stores
Ames
AutoZone
L. L. Bean
Best Buy
Circuit City
Damark International
Dayton Hudson
Dillard
Federated
The Gap
Good Guys
Kmart
Lands' End
May
Melville
Men's Wearhouse
J. C. Penney
The Pep Boys
Sears
Service Merchandise
Spiegel
Venture Stores
Wal-Mart
Woolworth

NATIONAL RAILROAD PASSENGER CORP.

RANK: 183

OVERVIEW

Although it is classified as a private, for-profit company and its employees are not part of the federal system, National Railroad Passenger Corporation, better known as Amtrak and almost wholly owned by the DOT, has lost more than $7 billion (on about $11 billion of revenue) in the last decade. Amtrak carries 51 million passengers over 25,000 miles of track, and controls 43% of all business travel in the northeast corridor.

Established by Congress in 1970, Amtrak (whose name is derived from "American travel by track") is heavily subsidized by both local and national governments: in its 24-year history it hasn't once turned a profit. Its 9-member board includes the secretary of transportation and 5 presidential appointees. Chairman W. Graham Claytor, Jr., retired in 1993 after a dozen years of service. During his tenure Amtrak's operating loss as a percent of revenue lessened considerably. The company's goal is to become profitable by the year 2000 — if it's around that long. Talk of privatization has surfaced, but the company's track record and fleet age have left Claytor shaking his head. "You couldn't give it away," he has said.

Add to that the 1993 wreck of the Sunset Limited: 47 people died near Mobile, Alabama, in the worst accident in Amtrak's history. Although a barge that had run into a bridge moments before the Sunset crossed it is thought to be at fault, the public remains jittery.

WHEN

US passenger train travel peaked in 1929. That year there were 20,000 passenger trains in operation. But the spread of automobiles, bus service, and air travel cut sharply into business, especially short-distance travel (the industry's most profitable), and by the late 1960s, there were only about 500 passenger trains operating in the US. CEOs who saw the demise of the industry looming let service and equipment decay dramatically. In 1970 the combined losses of all private train operations exceeded $1.8 billion in today's dollars. That year Congress passed the Rail Passenger Service Act, aimed to preserve America's passenger railroad system. Although railroads were offered stock in Amtrak for their passenger equipment, the majority of accepting companies just wrote off the loss. Track, stations, yards, and service staff remained with the individual railroads.

Amtrak began operating in 1971 with 1,200 cars, most of which had been built in the 1950s. Although Amtrak lost money from the get-go ($153 million in 1972), it continued to be bankrolled by Uncle Sam, despite much criticism. One economist claimed that there weren't enough train enthusiasts to support an operational museum line, let alone an entire national system.

Amtrak ordered its first new equipment in 1973; that year it also began taking over stations, yards, and service staff. By 1976 most of the staff that served Amtrak's passengers were the company's own. Amtrak didn't own any track until 1975, after 2 acts of Congress enabled it to purchase hundreds of miles of right-of-way track in several areas of the US.

In 1978 Amtrak lost $544 million. The following year Amtrak reduced its route mileage by 13% at the secretary of transportation's suggestion (although he had hoped for a greater reduction). After a 1979 study showed Amtrak passengers to be by far the most heavily subsidized travelers in the US, Congress mandated Amtrak to better maximize resources. This resulted in some diversification and better use of resources.

W. Graham Claytor, Jr., who had served as the navy secretary and the deputy defense secretary, took the helm in 1982. He has steadfastly maintained that profitability is attainable, despite never achieving it himself.

In 1992 Amtrak ordered new cars and locomotives to be delivered over the next several years. The following year the company reduced its work force and adjusted services in the name of cost cutting. But flooding in the Midwest during the peak travel season and continuing air fare wars hurt Amtrak. Adding insult to injury, just months after the Mobile derailment, a train near Kissimmee, Florida, derailed in December 1993, injuring 63.

Amtrak hopes the new, ultra-fast trains that will begin running in 1997 with service from New York to Boston (in 3 hours) will prove profitable. It has tested a Swedish X2000 trainset, which tilts at corners to offset the centrifugal force felt by passengers.

HOW MUCH

	Annual Growth	1984	1985	1986	1987	1988	1989	1990	1991	1992	1993
Sales($ mil.)	7.1%	759	826	861	974	1,107	1,269	1,308	1,359	1,325	1,403
Net income ($ mil.)	—	(763)	(774)	(702)	(699)	(650)	(665)	(703)	(722)	(712)	(731)
Ridership (mil.)	8.7%	—	21	21	31	37	39	40	40	42	51
Passenger miles (mil.)	3.2%	—	4,825	5,013	5,221	5,678	5,859	6,057	6,273	6,091	6,199
Employees	1.1%	—	—	—	—	—	23,000	—	23,741	24,000	24,000

Net Income ($ mil.) 1984–93

0
-100
-200
-300
-400
-500
-600
-700
-800

Amtrak

US government-owned corporation
Fiscal year ends: September 30

WHO

Chairman, CEO, and President: Thomas M. Downs
EVP and COO: Dennis F. Sullivan
EVP: William S. Norman
VP Finance and Administration: Norris W. Overton
VP Transportation: Robert C. VanderClute
VP Passenger Marketing and Sales: Robert E. Gall
VP Passenger Services: Arthur F. McMahon
VP Information Systems: Donald G. Gentry
Assistant VP Personnel: Neil D. Mann
Auditors: Arthur Andersen & Co.

WHERE

HQ: National Railroad Passenger Corporation, 60 Massachusetts Ave. NE, Washington, DC 20002
Phone: 202-906-3860
Fax: 202-906-3865

Amtrak operates trains in 45 states, running on 25,000 miles of track and through 535 stations.

WHAT

	1993 Sales % of total
Passenger related	69
Commuter contract services	17
Other contract services	5
Mail & express	4
Real estate & operations/corporate development	4
Other	1
Total	**100**

1993 Ridership	No. (mil.)	% of total
Amtrak system		
Northeast Corridor	10	20
Short Distance	6	11
Long Distance	6	12
Contract commuter	29	57
Total	**51**	**100**

1993 Fleet	No. passenger cars	% of total
Heritage	817	42
Amfleet I	491	25
Superliner	284	15
Amfleet II	149	7
Horizon	103	5
Turboliner	65	3
Low-level cab	30	2
Self-propelled	25	1
Total	**1,964**	**100**

KEY COMPETITORS

AMR
Continental Airlines
Delta
Greyhound
Peter Pan Bus Lines
USAir

NATIONWIDE INSURANCE ENTERPRISE

RANK: 11

OVERVIEW

Headquartered in Columbus, Nationwide Insurance Enterprise is one of the country's largest mutual multiline insurers, with more than 11 million active policies and certificates and combined assets of more than $42 billion. Through 130 companies Nationwide provides property/casualty insurance, life and health insurance, and financial services throughout the US and in more than 30 other countries.

The group's larger operating companies include Nationwide Mutual (automobile insurance), Nationwide Mutual Fire, and the Wausau Group. The company also has interests in communications (12 radio and 3 television stations in 12 states) and real estate.

The company experienced record profits (more than $500 million) in 1993, citing gains in its property and casualty businesses from growth in policy sales and better management of claims, among other factors.

After 43 years with Nationwide, John Fisher retired as chairman in 1994, relinquishing the post to CEO Richard McFerson. McFerson is focusing on loss reduction programs, keeping a lid on expenses, and installing state-of-the-art technology to improve customer service.

Mutual company
Fiscal year ends: December 31

WHO

Chairman, President, and CEO: D. Richard McFerson
EVP Investments; President and COO, Nationwide Life and Financial Horizons Life Insurance Companies: Peter F. Frenzer
EVP General Counsel and Secretary: Gordon E. McCutchan
SVP and CFO: Robert A. Oakley
SVP Business Operations: William P. DeMeno
VP Human Resources: Susan A. Wolken
Auditors: KPMG Peat Marwick

WHEN

Nationwide traces its origins to 1919, when members of the Ohio Farm Bureau Federation, a farmers' consumer group, decided to establish their own automobile insurance company. They assumed that because they were all rural drivers they shouldn't be made to pay the same for auto insurance as city drivers. In order to get a license from the state, the company had to have at least 100 policyholders. More than 1,000 policies were gathered by 1926 with only 3 employees and 20 volunteer agents. The company began as Farm Bureau Mutual. Murray D. Lincoln, a founder, headed the young company from its birth until 1964.

The company expanded across state lines in 1928 to Delaware, Maryland, North Carolina, and Vermont and in 1931 began selling auto insurance to city dwellers. The company expanded into fire insurance in 1934 and into life insurance in 1935 (buying American Insurance Union, which had been established in 1931) with $100,000 in capital and $50,000 in surplus.

During WWII growth slowed; nonetheless, the company had operations in 12 states and Washington, DC, by 1943. The company diversified out of insurance for the first time in 1946 when it bought a Columbus radio station. A few years later it moved into real estate. By 1952 the company had resumed expansion; to reflect this growth Farm Bureau Mutual changed its name to Nationwide. Nationwide was one of the first companies to have agents peddle life insurance and mutual funds at the same time (mid-1950s). Nationwide General, the country's first merit-rated auto insurance company, was formed in 1956.

Nationwide established Neckura, its first overseas venture, in Germany in 1965 to sell auto and fire insurance. Four years later the company bought GatesMcDonald, a provider of risk, tax, benefit, and health care management services. The company organized its property and casualty insurers into Nationwide Property & Casualty in 1979.

Nationwide experienced sold growth throughout the 1980s by establishing or purchasing insurance companies, among them Colonial Insurance of California (1980), Financial Horizons Life (1981; investment-oriented life insurance products), Scottsdale (1982; excess and surplus lines underwriter), and, the largest, Employer Insurance of Wausau (1985). Wausau, widely known for its "Spelling Bee" ("Wausau...it has a USA in the middle") and "Where's Wausau?" commercials and its sponsorship of the television program "60 Minutes," wrote the country's first workman's compensation policy in 1911. Nationwide has infused Wausau, which has been plagued by high loss ratios, with $400 million since 1985, including $100 million in 1992.

In 1994 the company issued $500 million in "surplus notes" (debt that is subordinate to policyholders' claims and other liabilities), which will be used to fuel growth in Nationwide's life and annuity arms and to beef up its property/casualty operations. It was the first move of its kind by a US property/casualty insurer.

WHERE

HQ: One Nationwide Plaza, Columbus, OH 43215-2220
Phone: 614-249-7111
Fax: 614-249-9071

WHAT

	1993 Sales $ mil.	1993 Sales % of total
Property & casualty	7,314	50
Health, life & family	5,100	34
Net investment income	2,275	15
Other	146	1
Total	**14,835**	**100**

Nationwide Life-Health Group
Financial Horizons Distributors Agency, Inc.
Financial Horizons Life
Nationwide Casualty/Hickey-Mitchell
Nationwide Communications
Nationwide Development Company
Nationwide Financial Services
Nationwide Life
NEA Valuebuilder Investor Services, Inc.
Public Employees Benefit Services Corporation
West Coast Life

Nationwide Property-Casualty Group
Colonial
Farmland Insurance Group/Nationwide Agribusiness
GatesMcDonald
Insurance Intermediaries, Inc.
Nationwide General
Nationwide Mutual
Nationwide Mutual Fire
Nationwide Property & Casualty

Wausau Group
American Marine Underwriters
Employers Insurance of Wausau
Employers Life of Wausau
Scottsdale
Wausau Business Insurance
Wausau General Insurance
Wausau Underwriters

HOW MUCH

	Annual Growth	1984	1985	1986	1987	1988	1989	1990	1991	1992	1993
Assets ($ mil.)	17.9%	9,600	14,700	17,500	—	22,349	25,044	27,848	32,779	37,582	42,213
Net income ($ mil.)	4.4%	—	—	—	—	403	261	148	393	69	501
Income as % of assets	—	—	—	—	—	1.8%	1.0%	0.5%	1.2%	0.2%	1.2%
Employees	8.1%	16,200	23,400	24,100	24,900	24,800	25,000	26,000	27,000	32,500	32,583

1993 Year-end:
Equity as % of assets: 9.5%
Return on equity: 13.0%
Cash (mil.): $393
Sales (mil.): $14,835

Assets ($ mil.) 1984–1993

45,000 / 40,000 / 35,000 / 30,000 / 25,000 / 20,000 / 15,000 / 10,000 / 5,000 / 0

KEY COMPETITORS

Aetna
AFLAC
Allianz
Allstate
American Financial
B.A.T
Blue Cross
CIGNA
Equitable
Foundation Health
Guardian Life
ITT
John Hancock
Kemper
Liberty Mutual
MassMutual
MetLife
New York Life
Northwestern Mutual
Oxford Health Plans
Pacific Mutual
PacifiCare Health Systems
Principal Financial Group
Prudential
Sierra Health Services
State Farm
Teachers Insurance
Tokio Marine and Fire
Transamerica
Travelers
USAA
USF&G

NEW UNITED MOTOR MANUFACTURING

RANK: 88

OVERVIEW

Fremont, California–based New United Motor Manufacturing, Inc. (NUMMI) is a 50-50 joint venture between General Motors and Toyota. NUMMI builds 3 vehicles: the Geo Prizm, the Toyota Corolla, and the Toyota half-ton pickup. About 74% of production goes to Toyota and about 26% to GM.

GM and Toyota entered the joint venture as an experiment, to see if Toyota's manufacturing techniques could be transplanted to the US. Toyota has responsibility for day-to-day management and appoints the company's top 2 executives. NUMMI uses Toyota's management and production systems as models, with workers divided into 4- to 8-member teams that are only 3 levels away from the vice-president of manufacturing. GM managers tour the plant almost every day to learn from NUMMI's managers.

Although the joint venture, formed in 1984, was originally designed to last only 12 years, in 1993 both companies agreed to continue it indefinitely, pending FTC approval. While NUMMI still imports its engines and transmissions from Japan, the company is focusing on cutting its reliance on imported parts. Toyota plans to use NUMMI to build an intermediate-size pickup truck.

WHEN

It's not only politics that makes strange bedfellows. General Motors, the lumbering Godzilla of the automaking world, and Toyota, one of the upstart Japanese companies that was carving US carmakers' market-share into sushi, weren't the most obvious possibilities for a joint venture. But in the early 1980s, GM was lagging in the small car market and was ready to learn from its Japanese rival, and Toyota, caught in the middle of tense US-Japanese trade relations, wanted to begin building cars in the US.

In 1982 GM head Roger Smith and Toyota chairman Eiji Toyoda met in New York to discuss the possibilities. After a year of negotiations the 2 companies announced their partnership in the cafeteria of the Fremont plant, which GM had closed down in 1982. Toyota put up $100 million and GM provided the plant (valued at $89 million) and $11 million cash. The companies also raised $350 million to build a stamping plant.

To gain FTC approval the companies agreed to limit the venture to 12 years, to make no more than 250,000 cars in a year for GM, and to refrain from exchanging strategic information. In 1984 the FTC approved the deal, and New United Motor Manufacturing, Inc., was born.

From the beginning the company was different. Management layers were limited to 5 rather than the normal 7, and the distinction between blue collar and white collar workers was blurred: there were no reserved parking places, everyone ate in the same cafeteria, and only the president had his own office, which he shared with the executive vice-president.

The Fremont plant had a reputation for poor labor relations before being closed down, and Toyota originally refused to rehire any of the workers from the plant, but, after prolonged negotiations with the UAW, the company agreed to hire 50% plus one of the former workers. When the plant began production, the actual number was over 80%.

NUMMI's first car, a Chevy Nova, rolled off the assembly line in December 1984. In 1986 the company began production of the Corolla FX, a 2-door version of the 4-door Nova. NUMMI earned kudos for high worker morale and productivity and in 1986 was selected as a case study on positive labor-management relations for the International Labor Organization Conference.

Despite its success on some fronts, NUMMI's sales slid during the late 1980s. It had earned a reputation for building high-quality cars, but was struggling because of high overhead and weak sales of the Nova. In 1988 NUMMI discontinued production of the Nova and the Corolla FX and began building the Geo Prizm and the Corolla sedan.

By the end of 1989, the company's production numbers had begun to rebound. In 1990 it began a $290 million expansion as it geared up to build Toyota's half-ton pickup. In 1991 NUMMI's first Toyota 4X2 pickup rolled off the assembly line, and in 1992 NUMMI began building the Toyota 4X4 pickup.

In 1993 NUMMI began building the Toyota Xtracab, an extended version of Toyota's pickup. That same year NUMMI began construction of a plastics plant to build bumper coverings for Prizms and Corollas.

HOW MUCH

	Annual Growth	1984	1985	1986	1987	1988	1989	1990	1991	1992	1993
Estimated sales ($ mil.)	13.6%	—	—	—	—	—	—	—	—	2,200	2,500
Annual vehicle production (thou.)	22.2%	—	65	206	187	128	192	205	209	256	323
Employees	22.1%	693	2,479	2,602	2,522	2,685	2,899	3,070	3,636	3,969	4,300

Vehicle Production (thou.) 1985–93

Joint Venture
Fiscal year ends: December 31

WHO

President and CEO: Iwao Itoh
SVP Manufacturing: Gary Convis
VP Corporate Planning/ External Affairs and Secretary: Dennis C. Cuneo
VP Production Control/ Quality Assurance: C. Mitsutoshi Sato
General Counsel and Assistant Corporate Secretary: Patricia Pineda
General Manager General Affairs: Harold Armstrong
General Manager Production Control: Bill Borton
General Manager Finance: Goro Ito
General Manager Quality Control: John Nogy
General Manager Engineering: Gary Twisselmann
General Manager Plant: Jesse Wingard
General Manager Purchasing: Noriyuki Yokouchi
VP Human Resources: D. William Childs

WHERE

HQ: New United Motor Manufacturing, Inc.
45500 Fremont Blvd., Fremont, CA 94538-6326
Phone: 510-498-5500
Fax: 510-498-1037

NUMMI's Fremont plant consists of 3.7 million square feet of covered space on 60 acres.

	1993 Parts Supplied	
	% domestic	% foreign
Geo Prizm	75	25
Toyota Corolla	75	25
Toyota trucks	60	40

WHAT

	1993 Vehicle Production	
	No. (thou.)	% of total
Geo Prizm	85	26
Toyota Corolla	122	38
Toyota trucks	116	36
Total	**323**	**100**

Products
Geo Prizm
Toyota Corolla
Toyota trucks
- 2-wheel-drive compact pickup
- 4-wheel-drive compact pickup
- Xtracab pickup

KEY COMPETITORS

BMW
Chrysler
Daimler-Benz
Fiat
Ford
Honda
Hyundai
Isuzu
Mazda
Mitsubishi
Nissan
Peugeot
Renault
Saab-Scania
Suzuki
Volkswagen
Volvo

NEW YORK LIFE INSURANCE COMPANY

RANK: 55

OVERVIEW

New York Life is the 5th largest US life insurance company, with $422 billion worth of life insurance in force. New York Life has insured the lives of 11 US presidents and such notables as George Custer and Susan B. Anthony. New York Life offers life, health, and disability insurance; annuities; mutual funds; and health care management services. It also provides brokerage services through an agreement with the M Financial Group.

Although the company remains strong in the US (1993 income rose 36% over the previous year on a 6% increase in sales), New York Life's Canadian business has slowed in recent years because of stagnating sales and increased competition that arose after Canada deregulated its financial markets. In 1994 the company sold most of its insurance business there to Canada Life Assurance; it will continue to do a small amount of Canadian group life business out of its New York office. New York Life's operations in Canada began in 1858.

Also in 1994, to improve its capitalization, the company issued notes on its surplus.

Mutual company
Fiscal year ends: December 31

WHO

Chairman and CEO: Harry G. Hohn
President: George A. W. Bundschuh
EVP and General Counsel: Alice T. Kane
VP and Treasurer: Jay S. Calhoun III
VP and General Auditor: Thomas J. Warga
SVP Human Resources: George J. Trapp
Auditors: Price Waterhouse

WHERE

HQ: 51 Madison Ave., New York, NY 10010
Phone: 212-576-7000
Fax: 212-576-6794

Operations are conducted in the US, Hong Kong, Indonesia, Korea, Mexico, Taiwan, and the UK.

WHEN

In 1841 actuary Pliny Freeman and 56 New York businessmen founded Nautilus Insurance Co., the 3rd US mutual (policyholder-owned) company. It began operating in 1845 and became New York Life in 1849.

In 1846 New York Life had the first life insurance agent west of the Mississippi River. Although cut off from its southern business by the Civil War, New York Life honored all its obligations and renewed former policies when the war ended. By 1887 the company had developed the branch office system that became an industry standard.

By 1900 the company had established the Nylic Plan for compensating agents, which features a lifetime income after 20 years of active service; it is still in use today. New York Life had expanded in Europe in the late 1800s but withdrew after WWI.

Much of the company's growth and product development has occurred since WWII. In the early 1950s the company simplified insurance policy forms, slashed premiums, and replaced mortality rates of the 1860s with a current rate table. These actions resulted in new company sales records and were widely copied by competitors. In 1956 the company became the first life insurance firm to use large-scale data processing equipment.

In the 1960s New York Life was instrumental in developing variable life insurance, a new product with variable benefits and level premiums. In 1968 the company began offering variable annuities. Steady growth continued until the late 1970s, when high interest rates led to heavy policyholder borrowing. Jarred by the outflow of money, the company sought to make its products more competitive as investments.

In 1981 the company offered single- and flexible-premium deferred annuities and in 1982 a universal life product. New York Life also formed New York Life and Health Insurance Co. in 1982.

The company acquired MacKay-Shields Financial Corp., which now oversees its MainStay mutual funds, in 1984. This acquisition, along with a modernization program, caused income to plummet. Also in 1984 NYLIFE Realty offered the company's first pure investment product, the real estate limited partnership.

Expansion continued in 1987 with the purchase of a controlling interest in Hillhouse Associates Insurance (3rd-party administrator of insurance plans) and Madison Benefits Administrators (group insurance programs). Also in 1987 New York Life acquired Sanus Corp. Health Systems, the largest privately held manager of health care programs in the US. In 1988 it returned to Europe, opening an office in Ireland.

In 1992 New York Life entered a joint venture to provide insurance in Indonesia and began operations in Korea and Taiwan. Another venture was the purchase of 83% of Magnus Software, which makes software for insurance, mortgage servicing, and claims and benefits uses. In 1993 New York Life bought Aetna UK's life insurance operations.

In 1993 and 1994, in a climate of increased scrutiny of insurance industry sales practices, New York Life was investigated by the state of Florida. The company was sued in Texas, in a case relating to the admitted illegal sales practices of one agent, and was slapped with a $21 million judgment, of which it paid an undisclosed amount in settlement.

WHAT

	1993 Assets	
	$ mil.	% of total
Cash & equivalents	1,537	2
Government bonds	17,534	26
Corporate bonds	23,770	36
Stocks	1,555	2
Mortgage loans	6,270	9
Real estate	1,243	2
Policy loans	5,409	8
Separate account assets	3,703	6
Other	5,770	9
Total	**66,791**	**100**

	1993 Sales	
	$ mil.	% of total
Premiums	10,288	66
Net investment income	4,615	30
Other	661	4
Total	**15,564**	**100**

Business Units
Asset Management
Group Operations
Individual Operations
Investments
New York Life Worldwide Holding, Inc.

Selected Subsidiaries
New York Life and Health Insurance Company
New York Life Capital Corp.
New York Life Insurance and Annuity Corp.
NYLIFE Securities Inc.
Sanus Corp. Health Systems (HMO)

Selected Products
Annuities
Disability insurance
Group pensions
Life insurance
Lifestyle Portfolios (retirement investing)
MainStay (mutual funds)

HOW MUCH

	Annual Growth	1984	1985	1986	1987	1988	1989	1990	1991	1992	1993
Assets ($ mil.)	10.1%	28,060	31,740	35,087	38,877	43,417	46,648	50,126	54,066	59,169	66,791
Net income ($ mil.)	8.9%	171	32	194	92	204	57	290	280	271	368
Income as % of assets	—	0.6%	0.1%	0.6%	0.2%	0.5%	0.1%	0.6%	0.5%	0.5%	0.6%
Employees	(3.1%)	—	—	—	—	—	19,438	18,200	18,848	17,406	17,169

1993 Year-end:
Equity as % of assets: 5.2%
Return on equity: 11.7%
Cash (mil.): $1,537
Sales (mil.): $15,564

KEY COMPETITORS

Aetna
Allstate
American National
Berkshire Hathaway
Blue Cross
Charles Schwab
CIGNA
Dreyfus
Equitable
Health Systems Inc.
ITT
John Alden
John Hancock
John Nuveen
Kaiser Foundation
Kemper
Loews
MassMutual
Merrill Lynch
MetLife
Mutual of Omaha
Northwestern Mutual
Oxford Health Plans
Paine Webber
Prudential
State Farm
T. Rowe Price
Transamerica
Travelers
USF&G

NORTHWESTERN MUTUAL LIFE

RANK: 17

OVERVIEW

Milwaukee-based Northwestern Mutual is the 8th largest life insurer in the US, with more than 2.5 million life and disability insurance policyholders and annuities investors and more than $313 billion of life insurance in force. Northwestern's policies have exceptional renewal rates of over 96%; average life policy longevity is over 40 years.

Northwestern markets its services through a network of 7,300 exclusive agents. The company is renowned for its agent retention rate and its training programs, which include college internships in which students represent the company on their campuses.

Northwestern has been one of the industry's lowest-cost providers for 50 years.

Although Northwestern bucked the 1980s trend to expand beyond core businesses and invest in risky, high-yield areas, it was forced to write down real estate losses and set aside loss reserves of more than $600 million in the 1990s, which had a depressing effect on net income. Northwestern is well capitalized, with a diverse, high-quality investment portfolio, and it saw income rise 14% in 1993.

The company has appeared on *FORTUNE*'s "most admired" list for 12 consecutive years.

WHEN

In 1854 at age 72 John Johnston, a successful New York insurance agent, moved to Wisconsin to become a farmer. Three years later Johnston returned to the insurance business when he and 36 leading Wisconsin citizens founded Mutual Life Insurance Co.

When the company became Northwestern Mutual Life Insurance Co. in 1865, it was already the 14th largest company in total amount of insurance in force. As early as the 1880s, however, Northwestern Mutual's commitment was to serve policyholders, rather than simply achieve size.

In 1907 Northwestern appointed policyholders to evaluate the entire company's operations. This 5-person committee, whose members change every year, still operates, and a summary of its report is published in the company's annual report.

The company continued to offer level-premium life insurance in the 1920s while competitors offered new types of products. As a result of its conservatism, Northwestern's insurance-in-force ranking fell from #6 in 1918 to #8 in 1946.

The company began to develop the most comprehensive computer system in the industry in the late 1950s. One result was the 1962 introduction of the Insurance Service Account (ISA), in which all policies owned by a family or business could be combined into one premium with monthly payments made by preauthorized checks.

Northwestern was one of the first life insurance companies to give women a lower premium rate than men because they live longer.

Northwestern in 1968 introduced Extra Ordinary Life (EOL), which combined whole life with term insurance, using dividends to convert term to paid-up whole life each year. In less than a year, EOL became the company's most popular policy.

Northwestern became a major advertiser in 1972 by spending $1.4 million on ABC's coverage of the summer Olympics to introduce "The Quiet Company" campaign. The result was a jump from 34th to 3rd place in public awareness of Northwestern.

In the 1980s Northwestern began financing leveraged buyouts. In return Northwestern gained ownership shares and stock options in addition to loan payments. The company and other insurers bought a 2/3 interest in Congoleum, a flooring manufacturer, and a majority interest in Robert W. Baird, a Milwaukee securities firm (1982), and in Mortgage Guaranty Insurance (1985).

Despite these modest purchases, the company remained largely immune to the 1980s mania for fast money and high-risk diversification. Northwestern has a very low level of below-investment-grade securities, and its real estate investment delinquency rate is less than 1/3 of the industry average.

Despite the 1982 purchase of a securities brokerage firm, Northwestern Mutual, unlike most insurers, has no aspirations to become a financial services supermarket. Instead, the company continues to devote itself, with an almost religious fervor, to its core business, despite predictions by some that it is a shrinking market.

HOW MUCH

	9-Year Growth	1984	1985	1986	1987	1988	1989	1990	1991	1992	1993
Assets ($ mil.)	11.9%	16,055	18,087	20,196	22,613	25,362	28,515	31,389	35,757	39,679	44,061
Net income ($ mil.)	20.6%	61	13	18	40	118	372	143	227	244	330
Income as % of assets	—	0.4%	0.1%	0.1%	0.2%	0.5%	1.3%	0.5%	0.6%	0.6%	0.7%
Employees	4.5%	2,357	2,432	2,468	2,761	2,840	2,970	3,050	3,100	3,298	3,500

1993 Year-end:
Equity as % of assets: 7.4%
Return on equity: 10.7%
Cash (mil.): $783
Sales (mil.): $8,778

Northwestern Mutual Life

Mutual company
Fiscal year ends: December 31

WHO

President and CEO: James D. Ericson, age 57
EVP: Robert E. Carlson, age 57
VP, General Counsel, and Secretary: John M. Bremer
VP and Treasurer: Mark G. Doll
VP New Business: Deborah A. Beck
SVP Human Resources and Administration: James W. Ehrenstrom, age 57
Auditors: Price Waterhouse

WHERE

HQ: Northwestern Mutual Life Insurance Company, 720 E. Wisconsin Ave., Milwaukee, WI 53202
Phone: 414-271-1444
Fax: 414-299-7022

Northwestern Mutual operates through 7,300 agents in all 50 US states and the District of Columbia, with more than 100 general agency offices.

WHAT

	1993 Assets	
	$ mil.	% of total
Cash & equivalents	783	2
Treasury bonds	2,372	5
Corporate bonds	13,180	30
Private placement bonds	4,897	11
Stocks	2,966	7
Mortgage loans	6,505	15
Real estate	1,216	3
Policy loans	5,846	13
Other investments	1,947	4
Separate account assets	3,483	8
Other	866	2
Total	**44,061**	**100**

	1993 Sales	
	$ mil.	% of total
Premiums	5,865	67
Net investment income	2,913	33
Total	**8,778**	**100**

Insurance Products
Annuities
Disability insurance
Mortgage insurance
Permanent and term life insurance
Securities brokerage

KEY COMPETITORS

Aetna
Alliance Capital Management
American Bankers Insurance Group
American Express
Berkshire Hathaway
Charles Schwab
Chubb
CIGNA
Colonial Group
Dean Witter Discover
Dreyfus
Eaton Vance
Equitable
FMR
GEICO
Guardian Life
John Hancock
John Nuveen
Kemper
MassMutual
Merrill Lynch
MetLife
Mutual of Omaha
New York Life
Prudential
Teachers Insurance
Transamerica
Travelers
USF&G

OCEAN SPRAY CRANBERRIES, INC.

RANK: 238

OVERVIEW

Headquartered in Lakeville-Middleboro, Massachusetts, Ocean Spray is the giant in the cranberry industry, holding 78% of the market. Marketing its products under its trademark blue-and-white wave logo, the company sells a wide variety of cranberry products, including juices (Cranberry Juice Cocktail), juice blends (Cranapple), cranberry sauce, and fresh cranberries.

One of the largest privately held food companies in the US, Ocean Spray is a marketing cooperative, owned by approximately 750 cranberry growers and 150 citrus growers. Ocean Spray provides its members with services such as agricultural research, pest management research, and environmental testing.

The company is concentrating on keeping its growers' returns stable by controlling prices, increasing efficiency, and keeping a hold on its leadership in the juice drink market. In 1994 Ocean Spray began a $35 million ad campaign with the slogan "Crave the Wave" in an effort to fend off inroads from private-label juice makers, who have cut into the company's market share. The company has also been hurt by independent buyers who have lured away some of its cranberry growers by offering up to 15% more per barrel.

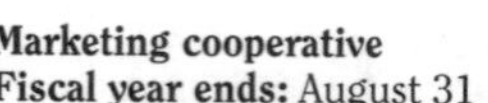

Marketing cooperative
Fiscal year ends: August 31

WHO

Chairman: Craige I. Scott
President and CEO: John S. Llewellyn, Jr., age 58
Group VP Sales and Marketing: Patrick M. McCarthy
SVP and CFO: Alexander W. Turnbull
SVP Retail Markets Division: Thomas E. Bullock
SVP Special Markets Division: Robert C. Zapletal
VP, General Counsel, and Secretary: Kenneth J. Beeby
VP Human Resources: Curtis L. Cowilson
Auditors: Deloitte & Touche

WHERE

HQ: One Ocean Spray Dr., Lakeville-Middleboro, MA 02349-0001
Phone: 508-946-1000
Fax: 508-946-7704

WHEN

Ocean Spray traces its roots to Marcus Urann, president of the Cape Cod Cranberry Company. In 1912 Urann, who became known as the "Cranberry King," began marketing a cranberry sauce he had developed that was packaged in tins and could be served year-round. Inspired by the sea spray that drifted off the Atlantic and over his cranberry bogs, Urann dubbed his concoction Ocean Spray Cape Cod Cranberry Sauce.

It didn't take long for other cranberry growers to make their own sauces, and rather than compete, the Cranberry King wanted to consolidate. In 1930 Urann merged his company with Makepeace Preserving and The Enoch F. Bills Co., forming a cooperative called Cranberry Canners, Inc.

Urann became president of the new company, and he set out to expand the demand for cranberries by introducing new products. In 1933 the company introduced Ocean Spray Cranberry Juice Cocktail, and in 1939 it introduced Ocean Spray Cran, a cranberry syrup. During the 1940s it added growers in Wisconsin, Oregon, and Washington and, to reflect its new scope, changed its name to the National Cranberry Association in 1946.

In 1950 the cooperative added Canadian growers to the fold. Urann retired in 1955, and in 1957 Ocean Spray introduced its first frozen products. To more closely associate itself with the Ocean Spray brand name, which had become increasingly well known, in 1959 the company changed its name again to Ocean Spray Cranberries, Inc.

Along with a name change, 1959 brought a serious crisis to the company. Two weeks before Thanksgiving the US Department of Health announced that aminotriazole, an herbicide used by some cranberry growers, was linked to cancer in laboratory rats. Sales of what consumers called "cancer berries" plummeted, and Ocean Spray nearly folded. The US government came to the rescue with subsidies in 1960, and the company stayed afloat.

The scare taught Ocean Spray that it was too dependent on one product line, so it began to diversify more aggressively into the juice business. The company sweetened its cranberry juice cocktail and also introduced a new line of juice blends, including Cranapple, Cran Grape, and Cran•Raspberry.

In 1976 the company expanded into grapefruit growing, allowing Florida grapefruit growers to join the co-op. The company continued to find new ways to sell its products. In 1981 it introduced the first brick-shaped juice container with attached straw.

Ocean Spray continued to add new products, and in 1985 it acquired Milne Food Products, a manufacturer of fruit concentrates and purées. In 1988 the company signed a deal with Japanese food company POKKA to distribute Ocean Spray products in Japan. That same year Ocean Spray was fined $400,000 for illegally dumping effluent into a Massachusetts river and Middleboro's sewer system.

In 1992 Ocean Spray expanded its distribution network when it signed a joint venture agreement with PepsiCo. In 1993 the 2 companies introduced a line of lemonades and Ocean Spray Splash sparkling fruit drinks for the "new age" beverage market. Also in 1993, in another agreement with a packaged foods giant, Ocean Spray and Nabisco introduced Cranberry Newtons cookies.

WHAT

	1993 Sales	
	$ mil.	% of total
Cranberry Division	880	75
Citrus Division	197	17
Ingredient Division	69	6
Other	22	2
Total	**1,168**	**100**

Subsidiary
Milne Fruit Products

Selected Products
Craisins (dried cranberries)
Cranapple juice drink
Cran•Cherry juice drink
Cran•Strawberry juice drink
Cranberry Juice Cocktail
Cranberry Newtons (in partnership with Nabisco)
Cranberry sauce
Fresh cranberries
Lemonade
- Cranberry
- Original
- Raspberry

Pink Grapefruit Juice Cocktail
Refills in PAPER BOTTLE (liquid concentrate)
Ruby Red Grapefruit Juice Drink
Splash Fruit Sparklers (in partnership with PepsiCo)
- Concord Grape
- Cranberry
- Cranberry Strawberry
- Raspberry Cranberry
- Ruby Red Grapefruit

Refreshers Juice Drink
- Citrus Cranberry
- Citrus Peach
- Orange Cranberry

Selected Member Services
Agricultural research
Pest management research
Wetlands management

HOW MUCH

	Annual Growth	1984	1985	1986	1987	1988	1989	1990	1991	1992	1993
Sales ($ mil.)	10.8%	466	542	636	736	781	889	942	974	1,091	1,168
Net income ($ mil.)	6.8%	147	170	197	207	204	245	211	210	260	266
Income as % of sales	—	31.6%	31.3%	30.9%	28.2%	26.1%	27.6%	22.4%	21.6%	23.8%	22.8%
Employees	7.2%	—	—	—	—	—	—	—	2,000	2,200	2,300

1993 Year-end:
Debt ratio: 45.4%
Return on equity: 122.1%
Cash (mil.): $4
Current ratio: 1.44
Long-term debt (mil.): $169
Total assets (mil.): $644

Net Income ($ mil.) 1984–93

KEY COMPETITORS

A.B.A. Holding
AriZona
Cable Car Beverage
Cadbury Schweppes
Celestial Seasonings
Chiquita Brands
Citrus World
Clearly Canadian
Coca-Cola
Del Monte
Dole
Dr Pepper/7Up
Lykes Bros.
National Grape Co-Operative
Nestlé
Northland Cranberries
Philip Morris
Seagram
Snapple
Veryfine Products

PACIFIC MUTUAL LIFE

RANK: 59

OVERVIEW

Pacific Mutual, based in Newport Beach, California, is the 25th largest life insurer in the US and the largest life and health insurer domiciled in California. The company has total assets and funds under management of $74.2 billion.

Pacific Mutual operates in 4 core business areas consisting of individual life insurance, pension investments, employee benefits (PM Group Life Insurance), and asset management (Pacific Financial Asset Management). Employee benefits include life, medical, dental, vision, prescription drug, disability, and stop-loss insurance as well as administrative and managed care services. In asset management the company offers stocks, bonds, index-enhanced portfolios, and real estate specialty funds and joint ventures to foundations, endowments, pension plan sponsors, and high-net-worth individuals.

In 1992 Pacific Mutual obtained approval to rehabilitate First Capital Life Insurance, which had been taken over by the California State Insurance Commissioner in 1991. Almost 90% of First Capital's customers elected to transfer their contracts to a newly created subsidiary of Pacific Mutual, Pacific Corinthian Life. When complete, the transaction should boost Pacific Mutual's assets 30% and double its individual insurance base.

In 1994 Thomson Advisory Group L.P., a publicly traded money-management firm with over $11 billion in managed assets, agreed in principle to merge with several of Pacific Mutual's investment management businesses.

The company's efforts to control health care costs include emphasizing managed care, reforming liability laws, reducing paperwork, and routing out fraud and abuse.

WHEN

Pacific Mutual began business in 1868 in Sacramento, California. Its board was dominated by prominent California business and political leaders, including 3 of the "Big Four" who created the Central Pacific Railroad (Charles Crocker, Mark Hopkins, and Leland Stanford) and 3 former governors (Newton Booth, Henry Huntley Haight, and Leland Stanford). Stanford served as the company's first president, bought the company's first policy, and later founded Stanford University.

Early company literature emphasized the flow of premium money to eastern life insurance companies and subtly hinted of the benefits of keeping the money in California. By 1870 Pacific Mutual was selling life insurance in Nevada, Idaho, the Dakotas, Utah, Oregon, and Illinois. Expansion continued in the early 1870s into New York, Ohio, Kentucky, Texas, Nebraska, and Colorado. The company ventured into Mexico in 1873 but sold few policies. It had more luck in Hawaii, where it started business in 1877. In 1881 Pacific Mutual moved to San Francisco.

The US was gripped by a financial panic in 1893, the year Leland Stanford died. Although rich in assets, his widow and Stanford University found themselves strapped for cash to meet their monthly obligations. The Pacific Mutual policy issued to Stanford had been forgotten, but its timely payment of the death benefit kept the doors of the university open until the estate could be settled.

In 1905 Conservative Life acquired Pacific Mutual but chose to retain the Pacific Mutual name. A severe earthquake shook San Francisco in 1906, and the fire that ensued leveled the city. Fortunately for Pacific Mutual, the new management from Conservative Life had installed fire vaults that saved the company's records. Shortly after the fire the company relocated to Los Angeles.

During the early 1930s a rise in claims on the company's noncancelable disability income policies forced Pacific Mutual into a reorganization plan initiated by the California Insurance Commissioner. After WWII, Pacific Mutual entered the group insurance and pension markets.

In 1957 Pacific Mutual became the first private company west of the Mississippi to install and use and UNIVAC I, one of the earliest computers.

The company relocated its headquarters to Newport Beach in 1972. By 1980 assets approached $3 billion.

In 1993 the company formed "Alliance for Choice" with Kaiser Permanente to provide flexible employer benefit programs. Under the company's plan to rehabilitate First Capital Life, Pacific Corinthian Life will be merged into Pacific Mutual in 1997.

PACIFIC MUTUAL

Mutual company
Fiscal year ends: December 31

WHO

Chairman and CEO: Thomas C. Sutton
VC and Chief Investment Officer: William D. Cvengros
EVP and CFO: Glenn S. Schafer
SVP and General Counsel: David R. Carmichael
SVP Corporate Services: Stephen T. O'Hare
President and CEO, PM Group Life Insurance Company: William L. Ferris
SVP Pension Investments: Daryle G. Johnson
SVP Investment Operations: Larry J. Card
SVP Real Estate Investments: Michael S. Robb
Auditors: Deloitte & Touche

WHERE

HQ: Pacific Mutual Life Insurance Company, 700 Newport Center Dr., Newport Beach, CA 92660
Phone: 714-640-3011
Fax: 714-640-7614

Pacific Mutual has more than $61 billion of life insurance in force in the US.

WHAT

	1993 Assets	
	$ mil.	**% of total**
Cash & equivalents	342	3
Bonds	5,901	44
Stocks	214	2
Policy loans	1,960	15
Mortgage loans	1,611	12
Real estate	134	1
Separate account assets	2,721	20
Other	463	3
Total	**13,346**	**100**

	1993 Sales	
	$ mil.	**% of total**
Premiums	2,325	73
Net investment income	880	27
Other	5	—
Total	**3,210**	**100**

Services
Asset management
Employee benefits
Individual life insurance
Pension investments

Subsidiaries
Pacific Corinthian Life Insurance Co.
Pacific Equities Network
Pacific Financial Asset Management Corp.
PM Group Life Insurance Co.

KEY COMPETITORS

Aetna
Blue Cross
Charles Schwab
CIGNA
Connecticut Mutual
Equitable
General American
Guardian Life
John Alden
John Hancock
Kemper
Liberty Mutual
Lincoln National
MassMutual
MetLife
Mutual of New York
New York Life
Northwestern Mutual
Principal Group
Provident Mutual
Prudential
State Farm
Transamerica
Travelers
USF&G

HOW MUCH

	Annual Growth	1984	1985	1986	1987	1988	1989	1990	1991	1992	1993
Assets ($ mil.)	15.3%	3,700	4,617	5,516	6,981	7,841	8,630	9,783	10,650	11,547	13,346
Net income ($ mil.)	30.0%	—	—	—	—	32	28	32	78	79	119
Income as % of assets	—	—	—	—	—	0.4%	0.3%	0.3%	0.7%	0.7%	0.9%
Employees[1]	2.8%	1,866	1,937	2,147	2,207	2,400	2,364	2,412	2,385	2,265	2,400

1993 Year-end:
Equity as % of assets: 4.4%
Return on equity: 24.8%
Cash (mil.) $342
Sales (mil.): $3,210

Assets ($ mil.) 1984–93

14,000
12,000
10,000
8,000
6,000
4,000
2,000
0

[1] Includes employees of subsidiary units; does not include sales associates.

THE PARSONS CORPORATION

RANK: 168

OVERVIEW

One of the largest firms of its kind in the world, The Parsons Corporation provides one-source design and engineering services to a wide array of customers, from government agencies to companies to cities and nations. Parsons has transformed a small fishing village into an industrial city of 100,000 in Saudi Arabia, built the first permanent oil and gas production facility in Arctic waters, built the first reef runway on a man-made island, and constructed the first modular mining facility in the world. A leader in the ground transportation, aviation, community and leisure, defense, power, and pulp and paper industries, Parsons is also one of the largest 100% employee-owned firms in the US.

Parsons's strategy, based on "diversity and global reach," insures the company against unfavorable trends in one geographic or business area. Revenues were flat in 1993 after showing strong growth in the previous few years.

In the US Parsons is building the nation's 2nd largest rail transit system, the Metro Red Line, in Los Angeles. Parsons is also steadfastly, if slowly, penetrating the Japanese market. It won part of an $18 million contract to build a research facility for the Japan Atomic Energy Research Institute in 1993. That year was also Parsons Environmental Services's first full year of operations.

PARSONS

Private company
Fiscal year ends: December 31

WHO

Chairman and CEO: Leonard J. Pieroni
President: Thomas L. Langford
SVP and CFO: Curtis A. Bower
VP, General Counsel, and Secretary: Gary L. Stone
Human Resources Director: Graydon Thayer
Auditors: Price Waterhouse

WHERE

HQ: 100 W. Walnut St., Pasadena, CA 91124
Phone: 818-440-2000
Fax: 818-440-2630

WHAT

Aviation Facilities
Airport expansion
Aviation services

Community and Leisure Facilities
Community and commercial facilities
Major infrastructure
Resorts and recreational facilities

Environmental Services
Air quality
Environmental planning
Hazardous, mixed, and nuclear waste
Solid waste
Water and waste treatment

Government Services
Defense and space
Demilitarization
Nuclear services

Ground Transportation
Bridges
Highways
Intelligent systems
Rail systems
Transit systems
Transportation planning

Petroleum and Chemical Facilities
Oil/gas production and gas treating
Petrochemical/chemical
Refining

Power Generation and Distribution Facilities
Cogeneration
Hydroelectric
Thermal power generation
Transmission and distribution

Pulp and Paper and Industrial Facilities
Industrial
Printing
Pulp and paper

Selected Subsidiaries
Barton-Aschman Associates, Inc.
Engineering-Science, Inc.
Harland Bartholomew & Associates, Inc.
Latinoamericana de Ingenieria, S.A. de C.V. (Mexico)
Parsons Construction Services, Inc.
Parsons Constructors Inc.
Parsons De Leuw, Inc.
Parsons Development Company
Parsons Engineering Gmbh (Germany)
Parsons Environmental Services, Inc.
Parsons International Limited (Philippines)
Parsons Overseas Company
Parsons Pacific Corporation (Korea)
Parsons Polytech Inc. (Japan)
Proyeparsons, C.A. (Venezuela)
The Ralph M. Parsons Company
The Ralph M. Parsons Company Limited (UK)
Saudi Arabian Parsons Limited (Saudi Arabia)
Steinman Boynton Gronquist & Birdsall

WHEN

Ralph M. Parsons, the son of a Long Island fisherman, was born in 1896. His first business venture, at age 13, was a garage and machine shop, which he operated with his brother. After a stint in the navy as an officer, Parsons joined Bechtel as an aeronautical engineer. The company changed its name to Bechtel-McCone-Parsons Corporation in 1938. However, Parsons later sold his shares in that company and left to start his own design/engineering firm in 1994 after differences with John McCone (who later headed the CIA) proved irreconcilable.

The company grew, expanding internationally to the Middle East, in the mid-1950s. In 1958 Parsons bought the *Argo*, then the world's largest yacht, entertaining some 2,000 people — many of them potential clients — on the vessel yearly.

In the early 1960s the company began working in Kuwait, which later proved to be one of its biggest markets, and by 1969 Parsons had built oil refineries for all of the major oil companies, designed launch sites for US missiles, and constructed some of the largest mines in the world. In 1969 — the year the company went public — annual sales were about $300 million, ranking it 2nd only to Bechtel in the design/engineering field. Ralph Parsons died in 1974.

Parsons had numerous projects in Alaska during the 1970s, at one time employing 2,000 in that state alone, building oil and gas treatment and production plants and other petroleum industry–related structures.

The company went private in 1985, taking advantage of a new tax law that favored ESOP-owned corporations. Employees weren't all happy, though. Several groups sued, and some workers maintained that they had little say in the decision to take Parsons private and that the ESOP was left with all the debt from the buyout and none of the decision-making power. (A large project in Mexico had kept many employees away from executive-led briefings in California that concerned the buyout.) A Labor Department investigation later exonerated Parsons executives.

Parsons had just completed work on a power plant in Kuwait when the Gulf War broke out in 1991. Several employees were detained by the Iraqis but were released shortly before the US entered the war. (Two years later the company would be hired by Kuwait Oil Co. to put back together some of the country's infrastructure that was destroyed in the war.)

In the early 1990s Parsons began modernizing sections of Amtrak's railroad track along the northeast corridor, between New York and Washington, DC. The company signed an agreement that allowed technology sharing between Parsons and Italy's Ente Nazionale per l'Energia Elettrica, the world's 3rd largest power company.

Parsons has had talks with the African National Congress in South Africa concerning city development work there and plans to enter the market.

HOW MUCH

	9-Year Growth	1984	1985	1986	1987	1988	1989	1990	1991	1992	1993
Sales ($ mil.)	7.0%	840	773	821	592	707	879	1,002	1,303	1,556	1,547
Employees	2.5%	8,000	8,000	7,000	7,000	8,000	8,000	9,500	10,000	10,000	10,000

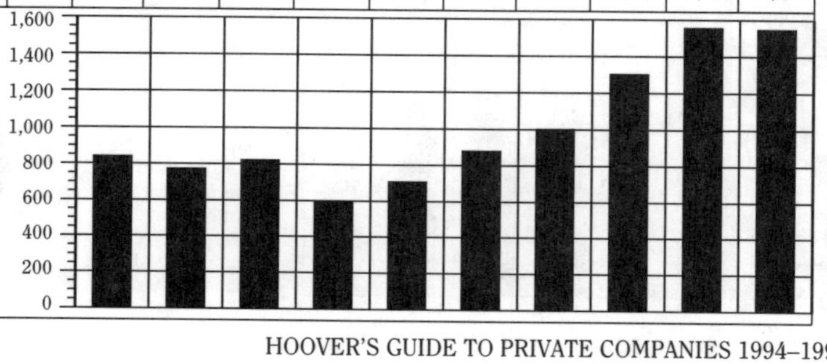

KEY COMPETITORS

ABB
Baker Hughes
Bechtel
British Aerospace
CBI Industries
Consolidated Rail
Dresser
Duke Power
Fluor
Gilbane Building
W. R. Grace
Halliburton
Hanson
McDermott
Morrison Knudsen
Peter Kiewit Sons'
Raytheon
Safety-Kleen
TRW
Turner Corp.
Union Pacific
Westinghouse
WMX Technologies

PATHMARK STORES, INC.

RANK: 45

OVERVIEW

Pathmark Stores, Inc., operator of Pathmark supermarkets and one of the leading grocery retailers in the northeastern US, became the successor company to Supermarkets General Corporation in 1993. It is also the #1 filler of prescriptions in New York City. The Woodbridge, New Jersey–based company operates 143 Pathmark supermarkets (of which 136 have in-house pharmacies) and 33 freestanding drugstores (which account for 4% of sales). The company believes it operates the largest private label program in the business, boasting more than 3,300 products and accounting for 23% of revenues.

A company plan to go public was shelved in 1993; executives did not believe the shares would garner a worthy price. Instead, the company was recapitalized, which resulted in a lower cost structure and improved cash flow.

Pathmark Stores plans to open 4 new supermarkets and one new drugstore in 1994 as well as renovate 27 older stores (at a cost of about $1 million per store). About 73% of the company's supermarket sales came from stores that were either built or renovated within the past 5 years.

Pathmark Stores attempts to take advantage of its large-store format to adeptly meet changes in the market. It now boasts a "Big Deals" program, for which products (currently more than 400) in large sizes are offered at warehouse membership club prices.

WHEN

After WWII, supermarket operators in New York and New Jersey banded together to form a cooperative to combat chain grocers, and the Wakefern Cooperative was born. Members enjoyed enhanced buying power and, with some stores sharing the name Shop-Rite, extended advertising reach.

Three participants in the cooperative — Alex Aidekman, Herbert Brody, and Milton Perlmutter — combined in a smaller group to form Supermarkets Operating Company in 1956. Supermarkets Operating's stores continued to use the Shop-Rite name and the Wakefern Cooperative's services.

In 1966 Supermarkets Operating merged with General Super Markets to become Supermarkets General Corporation.

Supermarkets General left Wakefern in 1968 and renamed its stores Pathmark. The company branched into small-town department stores by buying Genung's, which operated chains under the names Steinbach (New Jersey) and Howland (New York and New England). In 1969 the company added to its department store holdings with the purchase of Baltimore retailer Hochschild, Kohn & Co. and entered the home improvement market by purchasing the 6-store Rickel chain.

The company grew steadily in the 1970s, pioneering large supermarket and grocery/drug combinations in densely populated areas of New York, New Jersey, and Connecticut. The company's aggressive discounting and experimentation gained it a reputation as one of the best-run supermarket chains in the US.

Value House, a catalog showroom that grew to 20 locations, was sold in 1978. In 1983 Leonard Lieberman became CEO. Supermarkets General acquired Boston's Purity Supreme, operator of Purity Supreme and Heartland grocery stores and Li'l Peach convenience stores, for $80 million (1984; sold 1991). In 1985 the company opened superstores, under both the Pathmark and Purity Supreme names, which offered a great variety of merchandise. The company boosted its New England market share when it bought Angelo's Supermarkets in 1986. Also that year it sold its department store operations, and Aidekman stepped down as chairman.

Supermarkets General's expansion slowed when the Haft family's Dart Group made a $1.62 billion raid on the company in 1987. Merrill Lynch Capital Partners stepped in with an LBO, retaining control of Supermarkets General after the company was taken private. In 1989 CEO Kenneth Peskin, who had replaced Lieberman, resigned, and Jack Futterman took his place.

In December 1991 the company sold its Purity Operations to Freeman Spogli & Co. for about $265 million; it retains a 10% interest in Purity.

As part of its 1993 recapitalization, ownership of Pathmark was transferred to a newly formed holding company, Newco. As part of this transaction, Pathmark's Rickel Home Center chain was spun off to a new entity, Plainbridge Inc., which is also controlled by Newco.

HOW MUCH

	9-Year Growth	1985	1986	1987	1988	1989	1990	1991	1992	1993	1994
Sales ($ mil.)[1]	(0.4%)	4,347	5,123	5,508	5,767	5,962	5,475	4,481	4,378	4,340	4,207
Net income ($ mil.)[1]	—	52	64	63	(66)	(59)	(74)	(18)	(197)	(618)	(132)
Income as % of sales	—	1.2%	1.2%	1.1%	—	—	—	—	—	—	—
Employees[1]	(5.1%)	45,000	52,000	53,000	53,000	52,000	51,000	46,000	31,000	27,000	28,000

1993 Year-end:
Debt ratio: —
Return on equity: —
Cash (mil.): $5
Current ratio: 0.51
Long-term debt (mil.): $1,273
Shareholder deficit (mil.): $1,249
Total assets (mil.): $751

Net Income ($ mil.) 1985–94

[1] 1985–November 1990 includes certain discontinued operations.

Pathmark

Private company
Fiscal year ends: Saturday nearest January 31

WHO

Chairman and CEO: Jack Futterman, age 60, $601,301 pay
President and CFO: Anthony J. Cuti, age 48, $365,510 pay
SVP Retail Development: Harvey M. Gutman, age 48
SVP Administration: Robert Joyce, age 48
SVP Operations: Bernard Kenny, age 56, $221,992 pay
SVP Merchandising: Ronald Rallo, age 56, $220,100 pay
VP and Controller: Joseph W. Adelhardt, age 47
VP Operational Reporting and Planning: John Henry, age 44
VP, General Counsel, and Secretary: Marc A. Strassler, age 45
VP and General Counsel, Real Estate: Myron D. Waxberg, age 60
VP Human Resources: Maureen McGurl, age 46, $192,685 pay
Auditors: Deloitte & Touche

WHERE

HQ: 301 Blair Rd., Woodbridge, NJ 07095-0915
Phone: 908-499-3000
Fax: 908-499-3072

The company operates 143 Pathmark supermarkets (in Connecticut, Delaware, New Jersey, New York, and Pennsylvania) and 33 freestanding drugstores (in Connecticut, New Jersey, and New York). The company also has distribution processing facilities in the New Jersey cities of Avenel, Edison, Rockaway, Somerset, South Plainfield, and Woodbridge.

WHAT

Supermarkets and Drugstores
Pathmark
- Drugstores (31)
- Deep discount drugstores (2)
- Supermarkets (143)
  - Super Centers (126)
  - Pathmark 2000 (10)
  - Supermarkets (7)

Distribution Processing Facilities (7)

Trademarks
No Frills
Pathmark

KEY COMPETITORS

American Stores
Big V Supermarkets
Blockbuster
Circle K
Food Lion
Food Town
Golub
Grand Union
Great A&P
Imasco
Key Food Stores
King Kullen
Kmart
Mayfair Supermarkets
Melville
Merck
Penn Traffic
Red Apple
Rite Aid
Southland
Stop & Shop
Wakefern
Walgreen
Wal-Mart
Wegmans Food Markets

PERDUE FARMS INCORPORATED

RANK: 207

OVERVIEW

Perdue Farms of Salisbury, Maryland, produces more than chicken feed. With $1.3 billion in sales, it is the leading chicken producer in the northeastern US and the 4th largest in the country (after Tyson Foods, ConAgra, and Gold Kist). Principal markets for the company are located in the eastern half of the US.

The company's Fresh Poultry Division, its largest, produces chicken and turkey products, coordinating production and distribution. Through the Perdue Foods Division, it offers chicken and turkey products to delis, restaurants, and noncommercial establishments. The Grain and Oilseed Division provides the other 2 divisions with feeds, sells feeds to 3rd parties, and conducts international feed brokering. The company is vertically integrated, doing everything from hatching the eggs to feeding the chickens to processing the meat to shipping the final product.

Perdue Farms has risen in the chicken industry pecking order by emphasizing quality and introducing innovative customer services such as nutritional labeling and free food preparation tips. All Perdue chickens have a yellow color, which reflects a special diet that includes marigold petal extract. Frank Perdue, the family member most closely identified with the company, has made it famous by spouting slogans like "It takes a tough man to make a tender chicken," "My chickens eat better than you do," and "My breasts may be famous, but I've come a long way with my legs." To increase sales Perdue Farms is crossing the road to offer more turkey products as well as more convenience products.

Private company
Fiscal year ends: March 31

WHO

Chairman of the Executive Committee: Franklin Parsons Perdue, age 73
Chairman and CEO: James A. Perdue, age 44
President and COO: Robert A. Turley, age 54
CFO: George C. Reiswig
VP Sales: Roger Covey
VP: Dick Willey
Director Information Systems: Bob Cook
VP Human Resources: Tom Moyers

WHERE

HQ: Rt. 346, Salisbury, MD 21801
Phone: 410-543-3000
Fax: 410-543-3874

Perdue Farms owns processing plants in Salisbury, MD; Georgetown, DE; Accomac, Bridgewater, and Emporia, VA; Washington, IN; and Fayetteville, Lewiston, Robbins, Robersonville, and Rockingham, NC. It also operates a food service facility in Dillon, SC.

WHEN

If asked which came first, the eggs or the chickens, Frank Perdue will tell you the eggs did. His father, Arthur, a railroad express worker, bought 23 layer hens in 1920 and started supplying the New York City market with eggs from a henhouse in the family's backyard in Salisbury, Maryland. Frank joined the business in 1939.

The Perdues began offering broiling chickens to major processors such as Swift and Armour in the 1940s. They pioneered the crossbreeding of chickens to develop new breeds. In 1950 the Perdues started contracting with farmers in the Salisbury area to grow broilers for them. Frank became president of the company in 1952. The next year the company began mixing its own feed.

In 1961 Frank convinced his father to borrow money to build a soybean mill. Arthur had not willingly gone into debt in his previous 40-plus years in the poultry industry. The soybean mill was part of Frank's plan to vertically integrate the company — with grain storage facilities, feed milling operations, soybean processing plants, mulch plants, hatcheries, and 600 contract chicken farmers — to counter the threat of processors' buying chickens directly from farmers rather than through middlemen like the Perdues. To differentiate their products, the Perdue name was applied to packages on retail meat counters in 1968.

In 1970 the company began a breeding and genetic research program. During the following years Frank transformed himself from country chicken salesman to media poultry pitchman when the company decided to use him as spokesperson in print, radio, and television ads. Catchy slogans combined with Frank's whiny voice and sincere face drove sales. As Perdue Farms expanded geographically into new markets such as Philadelphia, Boston, Providence, Baltimore, Connecticut, and the District of Columbia, the company acquired the broiler facilities of other processors.

In an industry first, Perdue Farms added nutritional labels to its products in 1983. That same year James Perdue, Frank's only son, joined the company as a management trainee. The following year Perdue Farms acquired Shenandoah Valley Poultry (Virginia) and Shenandoah Farms (Indiana). Also in 1984 Perdue Farms began processing turkey products. In 1986 the company acquired Intertrade, a feed broker, and FoodCraft, a food equipment maker.

After enjoying rising demand for poultry by a health-conscious society in the 1970s and the early 1980s, the company found its sales leveling off in the late 1980s. After North Carolina fined Perdue Farms for unsafe working conditions in 1989, the company increased its emphasis on safety and quality. Perdue's sales dipped in 1991 as wholesale poultry prices fell; however, sales rebounded the following year. The company introduced Skinless Fresh Young Chicken Prime Parts in 1993.

In 1994 James Perdue, who had become chairman of the board in 1991, joined his father for the first time in a television ad as Frank passed the job of spokesman on to his son.

WHAT

Product Lines

Fit 'n Easy (skinless and boneless chicken, oven stuffer, and turkey products)
Freshly Sliced Deli Pick-Ups (8-ounce packs of turkey products)
Perdue Chicken Bologna
Perdue Chicken Franks
Perdue Cornish Game Hens (18 to 28 ounces, whole and split)
Perdue Oven Stuffer Parts
Perdue Oven Stuffer Roasters (5 to 7 pounds)
Perdue Done It! (fully cooked chicken products including oven-roasted whole chickens and Cornish game hens, oven-roasted and barbecued chicken parts, flavored chicken wings, breaded nuggets, fun-shaped nuggets, cutlets, and tenders)
Perdue Fresh Young Chickens (2-1/2 to 4 pounds)
Perdue Fresh Young Chicken Prime Parts
- Boneless breasts
- Breast tenders
- Drumsticks
- Legs
- Split breasts
- Thighs
- Whole breasts
- Wings

Perdue Skinless Fresh Young Chicken Prime Parts
Perdue's Soup & Stew Hen (4-1/2 to 7 pounds)

Other Products

Ground chicken
Ground turkey
Turkey parts
Turkey sausages
Young whole turkeys

HOW MUCH

	Annual Growth	1984	1985	1986	1987	1988	1989	1990	1991	1992	1993
Estimated sales ($ mil.)	7.3%	—	741	840	964	973	1,100	1,100	1,000	1,239	1,300
Employees	2.4%	—	11,000	12,000	13,000	12,700	12,080	12,080	12,500	12,500	13,300

Estimated Sales ($ mil.) 1985–93

1,400
1,200
1,000
800
600
400
200
0

KEY COMPETITORS

Cargill
ConAgra
Continental Grain
Farmland Industries
Foster Farms
Gold Kist
Hormel
Rocco Enterprises
Tyson Foods

PETER KIEWIT SONS', INC.

RANK: 103

OVERVIEW

Omaha-based Peter Kiewit Sons' is one of the nation's largest construction businesses and has built more miles of US interstate highway than any other contractor. Through its telecommunications and computer systems subsidiaries, Kiewit is also a player on the "information highway."

Kiewit has been owned by its employees since the death of the founder's son Peter Kiewit in 1979. Sales rose 8% in 1993.

Kiewit Construction, the company's original business, accounts for 80% of sales and serves as general contractor on many projects in North America (3/4 of them for the public sector), including highways, bridges, airports, railroads, and water treatment plants. Kiewit also manages projects in Taiwan and is building a railroad tunnel under Denmark's Great Belt Channel.

Kiewit mines coal (largely through 50% interests in Montana, Texas, and Wyoming mines) and owns a 21% interest in California Energy Company, which operates 5 geothermal power plants in the western US.

In 1993 Kiewit took its MFS Communications subsidiary (telecommunications services and network systems integration) public but retained a major stake. Kiewit also bought a controlling interest in C-TEC Corporation, a local phone and cable television provider.

WHEN

Peter Kiewit, the son of Dutch immigrants, founded a masonry in 1884 in Omaha, Nebraska. By 1912 several of the founder's 6 children were working at the company, and the name was changed to Peter Kiewit & Sons. One of the sons, Peter, started working at the company as a bricklayer at 19. After a year at Dartmouth, he grew bored and returned to work at the company full time. He changed its name to Peter Kiewit Sons' in honor of his father in 1931.

During the Depression, Peter Kiewit Sons' worked on huge public works projects begun by the Roosevelt administration to put jobless people back to work. In the 1940s Kiewit focused on wartime emergency projects, including 1,500 buildings at Fort Lewis (built in 90 days) and the Martin Bomber Plant in Omaha (built in 6 months in 1941). The company entered Wyoming coal mining in 1943.

One of Kiewit's most difficult projects was the construction of Thule Air Force Base in Greenland, above the Arctic Circle, where 5,000 men worked around the clock for more than 2 years beginning in 1951. During the 1950s and 1960s, Kiewit took on bigger projects. The company won the largest contract ever in the US, a $1.2 billion gas diffusion plant in Portsmouth, Ohio (1952), and became a contractor for the US interstate highway system (created in 1956).

Kiewit was fined $5 million for rigging bids on Army Corps of Engineers projects in 1970 and 1976.

Peter Kiewit died in 1979, leaving instructions that the company, which was already largely employee-owned, should remain under employee control and that no one employee could own more than 10% of the company. Kiewit's stock, when returned to the company, increased the value of all the other employees' holdings, making many of them millionaires.

Under Walter Scott, who became chairman and president in 1979, Peter Kiewit has continued to grow. In 1984 Kiewit and developer David Murdoch bought the Continental Group, a diversified company that made cans and boxes, ran timber operations, and owned gas and oil operations. Kiewit bought Murdoch's 20% stake the following year. In 1987 Kiewit spun off a communications subsidiary, creating MFS Communications.

In 1990 Kiewit agreed to pay $415 million to settle a lawsuit alleging that it used a secret computer program to identify and lay off workers just before they qualified for pensions. Kiewit sold most of Continental's packaging operations in 1991 and 1992 and bought an 18.8% stake (later increased to 36.3%) in geothermal energy developer California Energy.

In 1993 Kiewit took MFS Communications public but remained its main shareholder. Also that year MFS won a contract to install an electronic toll-tag system on a Southern California road. The system will use infrared beams to read windshield tags and will charge the tolls to commuters' accounts.

In 1994 Kiewit bought APAC-Arizona, a construction and construction materials business. Also in 1994 MFS agreed to buy Centex Telemanagement, a San Francisco–based telecommunications management company.

HOW MUCH

	Annual Growth	1984	1985	1986	1987	1988	1989	1990	1991	1992	1993
Sales ($ mil.)	7.7%	—	—	—	1,395	1,598	1,701	1,917	2,086	2,020	2,179
Net income ($ mil.)	22.3%	—	—	—	78	202	92	108	49	150	261
Income as % of sales	—	—	—	—	5.6%	12.6%	5.4%	5.6%	2.3%	7.4%	12.0%
Employees	15.2%	—	—	—	—	—	—	—	8,000	7,600	10,620

1993 Year-end:
Debt ratio: 22.2%
Return on equity: 16.7%
Cash (mil.): $1,378
Current ratio: 3.3
Long-term debt (mil.): $462

Net Income ($ mil.) 1987–93

Private company
Fiscal year ends: Last Saturday in December

WHO

Chairman and President: Walter Scott, Jr., age 62, $1,380,000 pay
VC: Charles H. Campbell, age 61, $510,500 pay
VC: William L. Grewcock, age 68
EVP: Kenneth E. Stinson, age 51, $753,500 pay
EVP and CFO: Robert E. Julian, age 54
VP Human Resources: Brad Chapman
Auditors: Coopers & Lybrand

WHERE

HQ: 1000 Kiewit Plaza, Omaha, NE 68131
Phone: 402-342-2052
Fax: 402-271-2829

	1993 Sales		1993 Operating Income	
	$ mil.	% of total	$ mil.	% of total
US	1,930	89	107	80
Canada	175	8	4	3
Other countries	74	3	22	17
Total	**2,179**	**100**	**133**	**100**

WHAT

	1993 Sales		1993 Operating Income	
	$ mil.	% of total	$ mil.	% of total
Construction	1,757	80	94	49
Mining	230	11	99	51
Telecommunications	189	9	(26)	—
Other	3	—	(34)	—
Total	**2,179**	**100**	**133**	**100**

Selected Subsidiaries and Affiliates

C-Tec Corporation (56.6%)
Telephone and cable television systems

Kiewit Coal Properties Inc.
Big Horn Coal Company
Black Butte Coal Company (50%)
Decker Coal Company (50%)
R-K Leasing Company (50%)
Rosebud Coal Sales Company
Walnut Creek Mining Company (50%)

Kiewit Construction Group Inc.
Buildings and highways
Dams, reservoirs, and power plants
Sewer, waste disposal, and water supply systems

Kiewit Energy Company
California Energy Company (21%, geothermal energy)

Kiewit Mining Group Inc.
Mine management services

MFS Communications Company, Inc.
MFS Network Technologies, Inc. (systems integration)
MFS Telecom, Inc. (telecommunication networks)

PKS Information Services, Inc. (96%)
Computer outsourcing

KEY COMPETITORS

AES
Amtech
Ashland
AT&T
Atlantic Richfield
Bechtel
BellSouth
British Aerospace
Cyprus Amax
Destec Energy
Dresser
Exxon
Fluor
General Motors
GTE
Halliburton
Kerr-McGee
Lockheed
Magma Power
Ogden
Parsons
Perini
Sprint
Turner Corp.
U S WEST

POLO/RALPH LAUREN

RANK: 137

OVERVIEW

Ralph Lauren is one of the world's most successful clothing designers. His women's and men's collections are distinguished for their classic elegance and air of exclusivity. Polo/Ralph Lauren Corporation, based in New York, is his mass marketing arm, which democratically allows Everyman, Everywoman, and Everychild to partake of that elegance and exclusivity, as long as they have the money.

Lauren's designs add distinctive details to classic clothing (and household furnishing) styles, but his genius lies as much in his feel for marketing as in his design and in his sure and early instinct that he is not merely selling clothes but a lifestyle as well.

Polo/Ralph Lauren operates primarily by licensing Ralph Lauren's designs. The big money comes from licensing — allowing other people to pay for the privilege of making and selling one's designs. The company has licensees throughout the US and in over 30 nations worldwide, selling through 140 independently licensed and company-owned Polo stores and through upscale department stores.

Polo/Ralph Lauren became wildly successful during the 1980s by appealing to free-spending Yuppies, but, as a portion of this clientele was victimized by the recession that began in the late 1980s, the company has sought to redefine its market in the subdued 1990s. The company is owned by Lauren (65%), partner Peter Strom (7%), and a Goldman Sachs investment fund (28%).

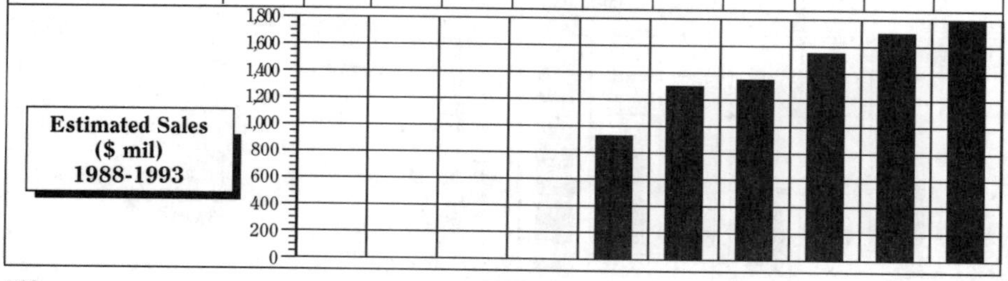

POLO RALPH LAUREN

Private company
Fiscal year ends: April 30

WHO

Chairman and CEO: Ralph Lauren, age 54
VC: Peter Strom
President: Cheryl Sterling
CFO: Michael J. Newman
VP Finance: Joanne Mandry
Director Marketing and Sales: Tracie Nelson
Director Human Resources: Karen Rosenback

WHERE

HQ: Polo/Ralph Lauren Corporation, 650 Madison Ave., New York, NY 10022
Phone: 212-318-7000
Fax: 212-318-5780

WHEN

Ralph was one of 4 children born to a Russian housepainter and muralist, Frank Lifschitz, and his wife, Frieda. Frank informally changed the family's name to Lauren and inspired his youngest son to recreate himself in the image of a member of the upper class.

After high school, Ralph Lauren worked as a salesman at Brooks Brothers and then as a sales representative for Rivetz, a Boston tie maker. His personal style helped him get a job as a tie designer for Beau Brummel, of New York, in 1967. Soon he was given his own style division, which he named Polo, because of the sport's image. There he invented the wide tie.

The next year Lauren started Polo Fashions, Inc., staked by Hilton Manufacturing (Norman Hilton became a 50% owner of Polo Fashions for his $50,000), to make tailored menswear. In 1971 the first licensed Polo store opened on Rodeo Drive in Beverly Hills.

In 1972 Lauren showed his first women's collection. That year, sales were $3.4 million.

Although Lauren's designs received critical acclaim, Polo Fashions had a bumpy start. Orders exceeded capacity, and making enough good clothes on time was difficult. Lauren did not yet fully grasp the business side and had difficulty finding someone who did. In 1972, when he and Norman Hilton parted, Lauren bought him out for $633,000, unaware that the company was deeply in debt. Business manager Michael Bernstein apparently didn't know either, and, when Lauren learned of it, he fired Bernstein. Bernstein sued Polo for back pay, the amount of loans to the company that he had personally guaranteed, and $1.2 million (Bernstein's valuation of his stock).

By the time the suit was settled in 1980 for $175,000, Polo Fashions had become Polo/Ralph Lauren and was a success. Lauren's profile rose in the 1970s when he won 3 Coty Awards for men's and women's designs and produced the men's costumes for the movie *The Great Gatsby*, with Robert Redford. Partner Peter Strom teamed up with Lauren in the early 1970s.

But one of the basic reasons for Polo's financial success was that the business side was finally brought under control. The company renegotiated its debt and licensed the unprofitable women's lines. Other licenses followed for Western wear, fragrances, sleepwear, boys' wear, and swimwear. Lauren also persuaded some of the largest upmarket department stores to open separate, distinctively decorated Polo/Ralph Lauren shops within their stores.

In 1982 Lauren added a line of home furnishings, which took off. In 1986 Lauren opened his flagship store in New York City, featuring merchandise in settings enhanced by antiques and mementos.

In 1993 Polo announced that it would stop making its tailored men's line and had licensed it to the Joseph J. Pietrafesa Company. A new product introduction, the Double RL line of western wear, was less successful than hoped, and $10 million worth of merchandise was taken off the market to prevent it from being discounted. In 1994 Lauren sold 28% of the company to a Goldman Sachs investment fund.

WHAT

Clothing and Accessories

Womenswear collections (seasonal and theme designs)
- Active wear (skiing and active sports wear)
- Classics/Country

Polo by Ralph Lauren (menswear)
- Sportswear (skiing and active sports)
- Tailored clothing and gentlemen's sportwear)

Polo for Boys

Ralph Lauren Girlswear

Ralph Lauren Footwear

Polo/Ralph Lauren
- Scarves
- Hosiery
- Eyewear
- Leathergoods (personal accessories)
- Luggage and handbags

Ralph Lauren Fragrances
- Polo (for men)
- Polo Crest (for men)
- Chaps (for men)
- Lauren (for women)
- Safari (scents for men and women)

Ralph Lauren Home Collection
- Bedding and blankets
- Draperies
- Flatware
- Floor coverings
- Furniture
- Dinnerware
- Giftware
- Glassware
- Table linens
- Towels

KEY COMPETITORS

AnnTaylor
Anne Klein
Bill Blass
Bombay Company
Broadway Stores
Calvin Klein
Dayton Hudson
Dillard
Estée Lauder
Federated
Fieldcrest Cannon
The Gap
Geoffrey Beene
Guess?
Hartmarx
INTERCO
Lands' End
Levi Strauss
Liz Claiborne
L.L. Bean
LVMH
MacAndrews & Forbes
May
Macy
Nordstrom
Sharper Image
Spiegel
Springs Industries
U.S. Shoe
V.F.

HOW MUCH

	Annual Growth	1984	1985	1986	1987	1988	1989	1990	1991	1992	1993
Estimated sales ($ mil.)	14.2 %	—	—	—	—	925	1,300	1,350	1,550	1,700	1,800
Employees	13.2%	—	—	—	—	1,500	2,000	3,000	3,000	3,000	2,800

Estimated Sales ($ mil) 1988-1993

PRICE WATERHOUSE LLP

RANK: 46

OVERVIEW

"As unapproachable as royalty" is how *FORTUNE* once described its reputation, but recently Price Waterhouse has lost a bit of its prestige. Once one of the top 3 accounting firms in the world, it is now last among the Big 6.

The firm is a worldwide organization of management consultants, accountants, tax advisors, and auditors and provides advisory services to businesses, individuals, government organizations, and nonprofit entities. PW's information technology services have spurred growth recently. In 1994 the firm introduced TeamMate, a Windows-based software package that provides audit preparation, review, report generation, and storage capabilities. PW is also expanding its services in Latin America to include privatization advisory, international valuations, and cross-border mergers and acquisitions services.

Price Waterhouse's reputation has been tarnished lately by a variety of financial scandals, including a damage suit brought by Deloitte & Touche, liquidators of failed Bank of Credit & Commerce International. PW had previously acted as BCCI's auditor.

WHEN

In 1850 Samuel Lowell Price founded an accounting firm in London, and in 1865 he took on Edwin Waterhouse as a partner. The firm quickly attracted several important accounts and a group of prestigious partners that included 4 Knights of the British Empire. Aided by the explosive industrial growth in Britain and the rest of the world, Price Waterhouse expanded rapidly (as did the accounting industry as a whole) and by the late 1800s had established itself as the most prestigious accounting firm, providing its services in accounting, auditing, and business consulting.

By the 1890s the firm's dealings in America had grown sufficiently to warrant permanent representation, so Lewis Jones and William Caesar were sent to open offices in New York City and Chicago. United States Steel chose the firm as its auditors in 1902.

Through the next several decades, Price Waterhouse's London office initiated tremendous expansion into other countries. By the 1930s, 57 Price Waterhouse offices boasting 2,500 employees operated globally. The growth of Price Waterhouse in New York was largely due to the Herculean efforts of partner Joseph Sterrett, and Price Waterhouse, along with other accounting firms, benefited from SEC audit requirements. The firm's reputation was enhanced further in 1935 when it was chosen to handle the Academy Awards balloting. Its prestige attracted several important clients, notably large oil and steel interests.

During WWII Price Waterhouse recruited and trained women with college experience to fill its depleted ranks for the duration; some remained with the firm after the end of the hostilities. In 1946 Price Waterhouse started a management consulting service.

While Price Waterhouse tried to coordinate and expand its international offices after the war, the firm lost its dominance in the 1960s, although by 1970 it still retained 100 of the *FORTUNE* 500 as clients. The company came to be viewed as the most traditional and formal of the major firms. PW tried to show more aggressiveness in the 1980s.

In 1989 the firm made plans to merge with Arthur Andersen, but the 2 managements were unable to agree on terms and style, and the merger was called off. When the deal fell through, the firm expanded internationally, merging with Swiss firm Revisuisse and opening a Budapest office (1989).

In 1992 Price Waterhouse lost a $338 million judgment in a suit brought by Standard Chartered PLC (UK). Standard Chartered had sued the firm for negligence in its audits of Arizona-based United Bank, which Standard Chartered had bought in 1987. However, the judgment was thrown out in late 1992 and a new trial was ordered.

In 1993 PW got into hot water with regulators when it was revealed that it had charged US thrift regulators 67 cents a page for copying more than 10 million documents in reviewing the assets of a failed S&L. Also in 1993 it was chosen by the People's Bank of China to act as special advisor.

In 1994 the firm was sued by a Spanish shareholders' association that claimed that PW had failed to alert Banco Español de Crédito stockholders to the bank's financial troubles.

HOW MUCH

	9-Year Growth	1984	1985	1986	1987	1988	1989	1990	1991	1992	1993
Sales ($ mil.)	15.3%	1,082	1,170	1,488	1,804	2,097	2,468	2,900	3,603	3,781	3,890
Offices	2.7%	354	360	381	400	412	420	448	458	453	448
Partners	5.6%	1,992	2,100	2,300	2,297	2,526	2,680	3,007	3,227	3,221	3,242
Employees	6.2%	28,300	30,372	32,794	33,236	37,120	40,869	46,406	49,461	48,600	48,781

1993 Year-end:
Sales per partner: $1,199,877

Price Waterhouse 

International partnership
Fiscal year ends: June 30

WHO

World and US Chairman: Shaun F. O'Malley, age 59
Chairman, Europe, and Deputy World Chairman: Jermyn Brooks
VC Human Resources: Richard P. Kearns
CFO: Thomas H. Chamberlain
General Counsel: Eldon Olson

WHERE

HQ: Southwark Towers, 32 London Bridge St., London SE1 9SY, UK
Phone: 011-44-71-939-3000
Fax: 011-44-71-378-0647
US HQ: 1251 Avenue of the Americas, New York, NY 10020
US Phone: 212-819-5000
US Fax: 212-790-6620

Price Waterhouse maintains 448 offices in 117 countries and territories.

	1993 Sales	
	$ mil.	% of total
US	1,430	37
Other countries	2,460	63
Total	**3,890**	**100**

WHAT

	1993 US Sales
	% of total
Accounting & auditing	44
Tax	26
Management consulting	30
Total	**100**

Selected Services
- Audit and business advisory services
- Employee benefits services
- Government services
- Industry services
- International business development services
- International trade services
- Inventory services
- Investment management and securities operations consulting
- Litigation and reorganization consulting
- Management consulting services
- Merger and acquisition services
- Partnership services
- Personal financial services
- Tax services
- Valuation services

Representative Clients
- AlliedSignal
- Amoco
- Anheuser-Busch
- Baxter
- Borden
- Bristol-Myers Squibb
- Campbell Soup
- Caterpillar
- Chase Manhattan
- Chemical Banking
- Chevron
- CIGNA
- Compaq
- Dresser
- DuPont
- Goodyear
- W. R. Grace
- Hewlett-Packard
- IBM
- Kellogg
- Kmart
- NIKE
- Scott
- United Technologies
- Walt Disney
- Warner-Lambert
- Washington Post
- Woolworth

KEY COMPETITORS

- Arthur Andersen
- Bain & Co.
- Booz Allen & Hamilton
- Boston Consulting Group
- Coopers & Lybrand
- Deloitte & Touche
- Electronic Data Systems
- Ernst & Young
- Gemini Consulting
- H&R Block
- Hewitt
- IBM
- A.T. Kearny
- KPMG
- Marsh & McLennan
- McKinsey & Co.
- Perot Systems

PRINCIPAL FINANCIAL GROUP

RANK: 23

OVERVIEW

Principal Financial Group is the parent company of Principal Mutual Life Insurance Company (The Principal), its flagship subsidiary and the largest life insurer headquartered west of New York City. Assets topped $40 billion in 1993. The company serves more than 8.4 million customers in all 50 states; Washington, DC; Puerto Rico; and Canada through 2,000 agents, 17,000 brokers, and 169 agencies.

The Principal operates in 3 core areas: group life and health insurance, individual insurance, and pension plans. Two of its insurance products, Adjustable Life and Adjustable Disability Income, have become industry standards.

The Principal experienced strong growth in 1993, particularly in net income and premiums and revenues. Chairman G. David Hurd credited heightened activity in the company's mutual funds, stock brokerage, residential mortgage banking, and pension businesses. In 1994 Hurd announced that he will step down sometime in 1995. President David Drury has been tentatively named as his successor.

WHEN

The Principal was founded as The Bankers Life Association in 1879 by Edward A. Temple, a Civil War veteran and banker. While life insurance gained in popularity in the years following the war, some insurers ran dishonest businesses, often canceling customers' policies before they had to pay out benefits. Temple set out to provide low-cost protection to bankers and their families. He based his system on one that was set up by a group of ministers, who would split the cost of benefits when one group member died. Soon after the incorporation of Bankers Life, the company began offering life insurance to nonbankers. Women, however, were not allowed to take out policies because of the high death rate during childbirth.

Bankers Life relied solely on volunteer labor until 1893. By 1900 it was operating in 21 states and had $143 million worth of life insurance in force. Temple died in 1909, and 2 years later the company was changed from an association to a legal reserve mutual life insurance company under a new name: The Bankers Life Company. The conversion scared many customers away, however. About 50,000 policies were lost over the next 3 years, and insurance in force dropped from $490 million to $398 million in 1915, the year Bankers Life began insuring women.

WWI slowed growth, but what hurt the young insurance company more was the 1918–1919 influenza epidemic, which struck (and killed) many of the company's policyholders. The Depression stunted company growth as well; insurance in force dropped about $220 million between 1930 and 1935. In 1941 the company began to offer group life insurance, and during WWII it became a major force in that area.

Bankers Life grew rapidly through the 1950s and 1960s. During this time it expanded its product line, adding, among others, individual accident and health insurance (1952). In 1968 it began offering variable annuities for pension profit sharing plans and mutual funds, forming what have since become Princor Financial Services and Principal Management. In 1977 Bankers Life made a splash when it introduced one of the first adjustable life insurance products, which allowed policyholders to change both premium costs and coverages.

In 1986 the company, which had long before outgrown the name Bankers Life, was renamed Principal Mutual Life Insurance. That same year it acquired Eppler, Guerin & Turner, the largest independent stock brokerage firm in the Southwest.

The Principal introduced annually renewable term and 10-year level term insurance products for individuals in 1992. That year it also overhauled some of its disability insurance policies. The Midwest floods of 1993 cost the company only $5.5 million, mostly from keeping its own employees who weren't able to make it to work on the payroll.

The Principal won the first new insurance license in Mexico in 50 years in 1993. It now owns 30% of a Mexican company that markets life insurance and pension plans. In 1994 the company ran a series of 30-second spots during the Winter Olympics to increase name recognition, with which it has been struggling since its name change in 1986.

HOW MUCH

	Annual Growth	1984	1985	1986	1987	1988	1989	1990	1991	1992	1993
Assets ($ bil.)	13.6%	12.7	14.9	17.0	19.0	22.0	24.8	27.5	31.5	35.1	40.1
Net income ($ mil.)	(19.8%)	—	—	—	—	—	—	—	330	237	212
Net income as % of assets	—	—	—	—	—	—	—	—	1.0%	0.7%	0.5%
Employees	6.5%	—	—	—	9,300	10,200	—	—	—	12,825	13,583

1993 Year-end:
Equity as % of assets: 4.1%
Return on equity: 13.8%
Cash (mil.): $470
Sales (mil.): 12,370

Assets ($ mil.) 1984–93

45
40
35
30
25
20
15
10
5
0

the Principal Financial Group

Private company
Fiscal year ends: December 31

WHO

Chairman and CEO: G. David Hurd, age 64
VC: Roy W. Ehrle
President: David J. Drury, age 49
EVP: Theodore M. Hutchinson
EVP: Ronald E. Keller
EVP: Charles C. Rohm
SVP: John Farrington
VP and General Counsel: Gregg R. Narber
VP and Secretary: Joyce N. Hoffman
VP and Controller: Harlan W. Bergman
VP Human Resources: Donald Keown
Auditors: Ernst & Young

WHERE

HQ: 711 High St., Des Moines, IA 50392-0001
Phone: 515-247-5111
Fax: 515-247-5930

The company's flagship subsidiary, Principal Mutual Life Insurance, serves more than 8.4 million customers through almost 250 satellite offices, claims centers, brokerage and sales offices, residential mortgage offices, and subsidiaries.

WHAT

	1993 Assets	
	$ mil.	% of total
Cash & equivalents	470	1
Government bonds	266	1
Corporate bonds	3,389	8
Private placements	12,631	31
Mortgage-backed securities	1,862	5
Stocks	858	2
Mortgage loans	9,458	24
Real estate	1,143	3
Policy loans	656	2
Separate account assets	7,809	19
Other	1,530	4
Total	**40,072**	**100**

Selected Products and Services
Annuities and IRAs
Corporate, mortgage, and real estate loans
Disability income insurance
Health insurance
Investment banking
Life insurance
Long-term care insurance
Mutual funds
Payroll deduction plans
Rehabilitation services
Retirement funding
Stock brokerage

Subsidiaries
Invista Capital Management, Inc.
Principal International, Inc.
Princor Financial Services Corp.

KEY COMPETITORS

Aetna
Allstate
American International Group
Blue Cross
Chubb
CIGNA
Equitable
GEICO
Guardian Life
John Hancock
Kemper
Liberty Mutual
MassMutual
MetLife
Nationwide
New York Life
Northwestern Mutual
Pacific Mutual
Prudential
State Farm
Teachers Insurance
Travelers
USF&G

THE PRUDENTIAL INSURANCE CO.

RANK: 4

OVERVIEW

Newark-based Prudential, the US's largest insurance company, had a great year in 1993, with net income more than doubling from 1992. But from a public relations perspective, the year was rockier than the company's Rock of Gibraltar logo.

Prudential Securities has operated under a cloud since 1991. In addition to the original allegations that the company misrepresented real estate partnerships as low-risk investments, 1993 saw widening investigations into the systematic misrepresentation of insurance benefits and into account churning. The eventual cost of these regulatory infractions may top $1 billion. The securities operations have been losing staff faster than they can be replaced. This has led the company to re-examine its quest for leadership in the worldwide financial services field.

Prudential now plans to concentrate on its core lines, which include individual and group life insurance and annuities, primary and secondary property/casualty insurance, individual and institutional asset management, investment advice and brokerage, and real estate sales and management.

Its health plans, enrolling 3.8 million people, include PruCare HMO and PruCare Plus. Prudential is also the primary underwriter for the health insurance products offered by the AARP, which is its largest group health client.

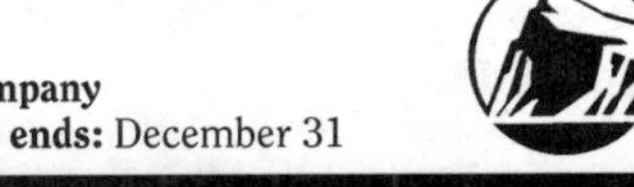

Mutual company
Fiscal year ends: December 31

WHO

Chairman, President, and CEO: Robert C. Winters
Chairman and CEO Group Operations: William P. Link
Vice Chairman: Garnett L. Keith Jr.
President and CEO, Prudential Securities Inc.: Hardwick Simmons
SVP and General Counsel: James R. Gillen
SVP, Comptroller, and CFO: Eugene M. O'Hara
SVP Human Resources: Donald C. Mann
Auditors: Deloitte & Touche

WHERE

HQ: The Prudential Insurance Company of America, 751 Broad St., Newark, NJ 07102-3777
Phone: 201-802-6000
Fax: 201-802-6092 (Human Resources)

Prudential operates throughout the US and in Canada, Italy, Japan, South Korea, Spain, Taiwan, and the UK.

WHAT

	1993 Sales	
	$ mil.	% of total
Premiums & annuities	29,982	65
Broker-dealer revenues	4,025	9
Net investment income	10,090	22
Other	1,877	4
Total	**45,974**	**100**

Product Lines
Annuities
Asset management
Credit card services
Deposit accounts
Estate and financial planning
Life, health, and property insurance
Reinsurance
Residential real estate services

Selected Subsidiaries
Pruco Securities Corporation
Prudential Asset Management Group
Prudential Bank and Trust Company
Prudential International Insurance
Prudential Investment Company
Prudential Preferred Financial Services
The Prudential Realty Group
Prudential Savings Bank, F.S.B.
Prudential Securities, Inc.

WHEN

In 1873 John F. Dryden founded the Widows and Orphans Friendly Society in New Jersey to sell workers industrial insurance (life insurance with small face values and premiums paid weekly). In 1875 he changed the name to the Prudential Friendly Society, naming it after the successful Prudential Assurance Co. of England. In 1876 he visited the English company and copied some of its methods, such as recruiting agents from neighborhoods where insurance was to be sold. In 1877 the company adopted its current name.

In 1886 Prudential began issuing ordinary life insurance (term or whole life) in addition to industrial insurance and by the end of 1890 was selling more than 2,000 ordinary life policies a year. By this time the company had 3,000 field agents in 8 states. In 1896 Dryden commissioned the J. Walter Thompson advertising agency to design a company trademark, its Rock of Gibraltar.

In 1928 Prudential introduced 3 new insurance policies. An Intermediate Monthly Premium Plan combined some features of the industrial and ordinary life policies. The Modified 3 policy was a whole life policy with a rate change after 3 years. The addition of an Accidental Death Benefit to weekly premium policies cost the company an extra $3 million in benefits in the next year alone.

Prudential issued its first group life insurance policy in 1916 and became a major group life insurer in the 1940s. In the 1920s it was a pioneer in shifting the burden of group life insurance record keeping from Prudential to the client company.

In 1943 Prudential became a mutual insurance company (owned by the policyholders). In the 1940s President Carroll Shanks began to decentralize the company's operations. When the system proved successful, other companies copied Prudential. Later the company introduced a Property Investment Separate Account (PRISA), which gave pension plans a real estate investment option. By 1974, 20 of the country's largest 100 corporations were PRISA contract holders, and Prudential was the US's group pension leader.

In 1981, at the dawn of the 1980s boom, Prudential acquired the Bache Group (renamed Prudential Securities), a securities brokerage firm, for $385 million. Bache's forte was retail investments, an area expected to blend well with Prudential's insurance business. Under George Ball the company tried to become a powerhouse investment banker — but failed. In 1991, after losing almost $260 million and facing lawsuits stemming from sales of real estate limited partnerships, Ball resigned.

In 1993 losses caused by Hurricane Andrew led Prudential to sue the state of Florida (which had declared a moratorium on policy cancellations), arguing for the right to allow 25,000 homeowners' policies to lapse.

Despite the 1992 settlement of a real estate partnership suit, Prudential found itself under increasing scrutiny in 1993 and 1994. It was hit with a $25.4 million judgment for benefits misrepresentation (which it will appeal), and it set aside $330 million to settle claims arising from the partnerships.

HOW MUCH

	Annual Growth	1984	1985	1986	1987	1988	1989	1990	1991	1992	1993
Assets ($ mil.)	11.9%	79,169	91,706	133,733	140,931	153,023	163,967	169,046	189,148	199,625	218,440
Net income ($ mil.)	(1.6%)	—	—	—	967	829	743	113	2,280	347	879
Income as % of assets	—	—	—	—	0.7%	0.5%	0.5%	0.1%	1.2%	0.2%	0.4%
Employees	3.4%	78,371	81,634	85,503	93,290	98,009	105,063	104,847	103,284	101,000	105,534

1993 Year-end:
Equity as % of assets: 3.7%
Return on equity: 11.4%
Cash (mil.): $1,666
Sales (mil.): $45,974

Assets ($ bil.) 1984–93

250
200
150
100
50
0

KEY COMPETITORS

Aetna
AIG
Alliance Capital Management
Allianz
Allstate
American Financial
Bankers Trust
Bear Stearns
Blue Cross
Canadian Imperial
Charles Schwab
Chase Manhattan
Chubb
CIGNA
Citicorp
Dreyfus
Equitable
First Chicago
FMR
Foundation Health
General Electric
General Re
Goldman Sachs
Guardian Life
ITT
John Hancock
John Nuveen
Kaiser Health Care
Kemper
Liberty Mutual
Marsh & McLennan
MassMutual
Merrill Lynch
MetLife
Morgan Stanley
New York Life
Northwestern Mutual
Oxford Health Plans
Paine Webber
RE/MAX
Salomon
Sierra Health Services
State Farm
T. Rowe Price
Trammell Crow Residential
Transamerica
Travelers
USF&G

PUBLIX SUPER MARKETS, INC.

RANK: 18

OVERVIEW

Lakeland, Florida–based Publix is the largest grocery chain in Florida, with almost 1/2 of the market in the state's heavily populated southeastern region and about 1/4 of the Gulf Coast market. Publix operates 425 supermarkets and is one of the largest employee-owned companies in the US, controlled by current employees, directors, and members of the founding Jenkins family. The company also makes dairy, deli, and bakery products, which it sells in its own stores.

In a very competitive and relatively poor domestic market for grocers, sales jumped by a surprising 12.1% in 1993, with over half of that increase (6.4%) from same-store sales.

With its leadership in Florida firmly in hand, Publix is now moving into adjacent markets. At year-end 1993, 5 stores in South Carolina and 21 in Georgia were under construction.

Publix's supermarkets were rated #1 in the US by *Consumers Digest* readers in terms of overall customer satisfaction. The company received top ratings in every survey category, which included cleanliness, courtesy, checkout efficiency, and brand variety — except prices. However, various consumer groups are unhappy with some of Publix's practices; the EEOC and several other groups are concerned with Publix's record of promoting women and minorities.

Private company
Fiscal year ends: Last Saturday in December

WHO

Chairman and CEO: Howard M. Jenkins, age 42, $370,000 pay
Chairman of the Executive Committee: Charles H. Jenkins, Jr., age 50, $283,000 pay
President and COO: Mark C. Hollis, age 59, $365,000 pay
EVP: Hoyt R. Barnett, age 50, $250,000 pay
EVP and Principal Financial Officer: William H. Vass, age 44, $280,000 pay
EVP: W. Edwin Crenshaw, age 44
VP: Jesse L. Benton, age 51
VP: Bennie F. Brown, age 52
VP: James J. Lobinski, age 54
VP Personnel: Edward H. Ruth, age 62
Auditors: KPMG Peat Marwick

WHEN

In 1930 George Jenkins, age 20, resigned as manager of the Piggly Wiggly grocery store in Winter Haven, Florida. With money he had saved to buy a car, he opened his own grocery store, the first Publix, next door to his old employer. Despite the Depression the small store prospered, and in 1935 Jenkins opened another Publix in Winter Haven.

In 1940 after the supermarket format became popular, Jenkins closed his 2 smaller locations and opened a new Publix Market, a modern marble, tile, and stucco edifice. With pastel colors and electric-eye doors, it was the first US store to feature air conditioning.

In 1944 Publix bought the All-American chain of Lakeland, Florida (19 stores), and moved its headquarters to Lakeland, where it also built a warehouse (1950). The company began offering S&H Green Stamps (1953) and replaced its original Winter Haven store with a mall featuring an enlarged Publix and a Green Stamp redemption center (1956). Publix expanded into southeastern Florida, opening a store in Miami and then buying and converting 7 former Grand Union stores (1959).

As Florida's population grew, Publix continued to expand and opened its 100th store in 1964. The company launched a discount chain, Food World, in 1970 (sold, mid-1980s).

Publix was the first grocery chain in Florida to use bar code scanners; all Publix stores had scanners by 1981. The company beat Florida banks in installing ATMs and during the 1980s opened debit card stations.

Publix continued to grow in the 1980s, safe from takeovers because of its employee ownership. In 1988 the company bought stores from takeover refugee Kroger and installed the first automated checkout systems in South Florida, giving patrons an always-open checkout lane.

The company completed its withdrawal from offering Green Stamps in 1989, and most of the $19 million decrease in Publix advertising expenditures was attributed to the end of the 36-year promotion. Also in 1989, after almost 60 years, "Mr. George" — as founder Jenkins is known — stepped down as chairman in favor of his son Howard.

In 1991 Publix opened its first store outside of Florida, in Savannah, Georgia, part of its plan to become a major player throughout the Southeast. The company's latest vehicle toward this end is a store prototype that offers ready-to-eat foods and a cafe. The chain is now designing other formats.

In 1992 Hurricane Andrew destroyed 3 of the company's stores. Publix entered South Carolina in 1993 with one supermarket; it also tripled its presence in Georgia to 15 stores. The 1993 edition of *The 100 Best Companies to Work for in America* named Publix as one of the top 10 US companies to work for. In 1994 *FORTUNE* ranked Publix #1 in terms of same-store sales and profits growth among grocers.

WHERE

HQ: PO Box 407, 1936 George Jenkins Blvd., Lakeland, FL 33801
Phone: 813-688-1188
Fax: 813-680-5257 (Public Relations)

Publix Super Markets operates 425 grocery stores in Florida, Georgia, and South Carolina. In Florida, the company also operates dairy processing plants at Deerfield Beach and Lakeland and bakery and deli plants in Lakeland. Publix also operates distribution centers in Boynton Beach, Deerfield Beach, Jacksonville, Lakeland, Miami, Orlando, and Sarasota.

	No. of Stores
Florida	409
Georgia	15
South Carolina	1
Total	**425**

WHAT

	1993 Sales	
	$ mil.	% of total
Existing stores	7,091	94
New/closed stores	382	5
Other	81	1
Total	**7,554**	**100**

Lines of Business

Food/drug supermarkets
- Bakery
- Deli
- Florist
- Groceries
- Health and beauty care
- Housewares
- Meat
- Pharmacy
- Produce
- Seafood

Food processing plants
- Dairy
- Baking (Danish Bakery brand)
- Delicatessen

KEY COMPETITORS

Affiliated Food Stores
Albertson's
American Stores
Associated Grocers
Bruno's
Fleming
Florida Supermarkets
Food Lion
Fred Meyer
Kash n' Karry
Kroger
Lil' Champ/Jiffy Stores
Melville
Pick Kwik Food Stores
Price/Costco
Pueblo Xtra International
Rite Aid
Sunshine JR. Stores
Wal-Mart
Winn-Dixie

HOW MUCH

	9-Year Growth	1984	1985	1986	1987	1988	1989	1990	1991	1992	1993
Sales ($ mil.)	10.0%	3,206	3,446	3,760	4,152	4,848	5,386	5,821	6,214	6,729	7,554
Net income ($ mil.)	10.3%	76	72	84	87	102	129	149	158	167	184
Income as % of sales	—	2.4%	2.1%	2.2%	2.1%	2.1%	2.4%	2.6%	2.5%	2.5%	2.4%
Employees	9.2%	37,042	40,098	44,813	50,123	57,791	64,037	66,756	68,606	73,000	82,000

1993 Year-end:
Debt ratio: 0.5%
Return on equity: 14.0%
Cash (mil.): $199
Current ratio: 1.23
Long-term debt (mil.): $5
No. of shares (mil.): 238
Total assets (mil.): $2,054

Net Income ($ mil.) 1984–93

0 20 40 60 80 100 120 140 160 180 200

RANDALLS FOOD MARKETS

RANK: 93

OVERVIEW

Houston-based Randalls Food Markets operates about 70 supermarkets in Texas, mostly in Houston (where it is first in the market), Austin, Dallas, San Marcos, and Killeen. The company's stores operate under the names Randalls Food Markets and Simon David. Randalls also makes its own line of foods, which includes milk, bread, and potato chips.

Now chaired by R. Randall Onstead, Jr., son of a cofounder, Randalls is working its way north across Texas, having already exhibited prowess in peddling to Houstonians. Exemplary services (hiring security guards to monitor parking lots, for example, to make customers feel safe) and innovation (the company was one of the first grocery store operators to allow customers to purchase goods with credit cards) are the operator's hallmarks.

Vicious Texas supermarket wars appear to be winding down as the economy picks up. And Randalls, which recently established its presence in Austin by purchasing Tom Thumb and AppleTree Market stores, has emerged as one of the state's top supermarkets. The AppleTree acquisition, coupled with Randalls's 1992 purchase of Tom Thumb from Cullum, should raise sales to about $3 billion in 1994.

Randalls

Private company
Fiscal year ends: June 30

WHO

Chairman, President, CEO, and COO: Robert Randall Onstead, Jr.
EVP Finance and Administration: Bob L. Gowens
EVP: Ronnie W. Barclay
SVP Marketing: Joseph Livorsi
VP and Division Manager: John Sullivan
VP, Randall's Properties Inc.: Joe Rollins
VP Marketing and Public Relations: Cindy Garbs
VP Human Resources: Jan Gillespie
Treasurer and Secretary: Jim Stiles
Auditors: Arthur Andersen & Co.

WHEN

The first Randalls store was opened in the late 1940s by Jack Randall under the name Randalls Super Valu. At first the venture was unsuccessful, and the small chain was sold in 1964.

In 1966 Robert Randall Onstead, Sr. (no relation to Jack Randall), Randall C. Barclay, and Norman Frewin, Sr., who had worked together for the previous Randalls chain, founded Randalls Food Markets with 2 Randalls food stores in Houston, Texas, and $85,000 in mostly borrowed money. Within 3 months sales at the 2 stores rose from $18,000 per week to $38,000 per week.

Onstead had first entered the business 11 years earlier, when he went to work for his father-in-law, who owned 3 Houston grocery stores. (Later, Onstead would steadfastly refuse to stock his stores with beer or wine, citing his father-in-law's alcoholism.)

Over the next few years, Randalls opened additional stores; by 1983 there were 25, and the company's market share in Houston had risen to 11% (from 4% in 1978). Randalls had blossomed during this time because of Onstead's strategy of copying the smaller gourmet stores then becoming popular in the eastern US, placing great service above all else, and locating his stores in upper- to upper-middle-class neighborhoods. In 1984 Onstead expanded into nearby Pasadena and Galveston, and Houston market share rose to 16%.

The store count reached 29 in 1985. That year the company also introduced its first of many "Flagship" stores, upscale, specialty groceries with amenities such as coffee bars.

By 1986 Randalls, with more than $600 million in annual sales, was 2nd in Houston only to Kroger. In 1987 the company debuted a "New Generation" concept store, more than tripling store size to 70,000–80,000 square feet. Having saturated the upscale markets in Houston, Onstead decided to lure fixed-income families with the new design and new locations. By 1991 the company had $1 billion in sales and, with a 21% market share and 44 stores (having taken advantage of a gutted Houston real estate market), had surpassed its main competitor.

In 1992 the company acquired Cullum Cos., the highly leveraged Dallas-based supermarket operator that ran 59 Tom Thumb, Simon David, and Page grocery/drug stores, among others, with a reputation very similar to Randalls's. By that time Onstead controlled 64% of Randalls, and the remaining shares were distributed among several other parties, including the families of the other company founders and certain company executives.

Also in 1992 Randalls embarked upon an aggressive push into the Austin area. Seven Tom Thumb stores were acquired there that year, and in 1993 the company bought 12 supermarkets from AppleTree, which was operating under Chapter 11. The company now has about 25% of the Austin market (ranking 2nd after H. E. Butt's H-E-B Stores), and a 27% share of the Houston market.

Also in 1993 the company sold a Dallas warehouse, acquired with the Cullum purchase, to Fleming for more than $50 million.

WHERE

HQ: 3663 Briarpark Dr., Houston, TX 77042
Phone: 713-268-3500
Fax: 713-268-3601

Randalls operates supermarkets in Austin, Dallas, Houston, Killeen, and San Marcos.

WHAT

Store Concepts
Conventional store (food and drug combination)
Flagship (upscale specialty goods, introduced 1985)
New Generation (large, open grocery stores, 70,000–80,000 sq. ft.; introduced 1987)

In-Store Services
Bakery
Bank
Coffee shop
Deli
Film developing
Florist
Gourmet counter
Pharmacies
Prepared food counter
Produce Row
Seafood market
Video rental shop

KEY COMPETITORS

Albertson's
Army & Air Force Exchange
Blockbuster
Circle K
Fiesta Mart
Food Lion
H. E. Butt
Jack Eckerd
Kmart
Kroger
McDonald's
Melville
Minyard Food Stores
National Convenience
Price/Costco
Southland
Walgreen
Wal-Mart
Whole Foods Market
Winn-Dixie

HOW MUCH

	Annual Growth	1984	1985	1986	1987	1988	1989	1990	1991	1992	1993
Estimated sales ($ mil.)	19.0%	500	600	650	675	800	900	1,000	1,100	2,250	2,400
Estimated employees	15.8%	—	—	2,800	7,500	2,331	2,250	2,991	3,385	8,102	7,800

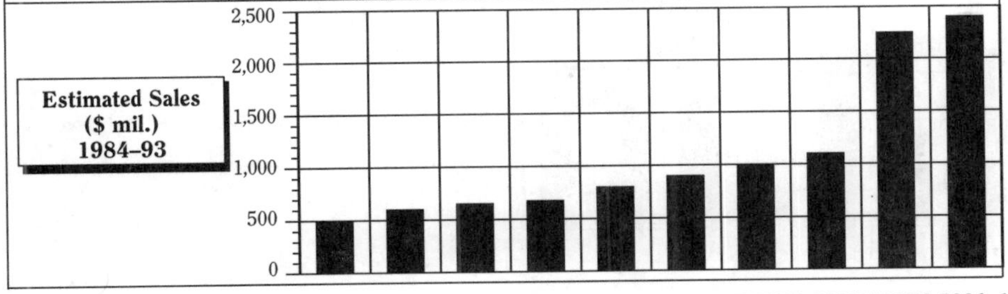

Estimated Sales ($ mil.) 1984–93

2,500
2,000
1,500
1,000
500
0

THE ROCKEFELLER FOUNDATION

RANK: N/R

OVERVIEW

Headquartered in New York, The Rockefeller Foundation is one of the oldest and largest private charitable organizations in the world. The foundation supports grants, fellowships, program-related investments, and conferences for activities in 3 areas: science-based development, the arts and humanities, and equal opportunity programs.

The foundation's science-based development programs focus on reducing poverty, disease, malnutrition, unwanted pregnancies, and illiteracy in developing nations and also seek to develop a global environmental strategy. Its arts and humanities programs focus on promoting international and intercultural understanding in the US. The equal opportunity programs provide litigation and advocacy support, promote voter registration, and support programs for the urban poor.

The foundation maintains no ties to the Rockefeller family or its other philanthropies. An independent board of trustees sets program guidelines and approves all expenditures. Three foundation presidents (John Foster Dulles, Dean Rusk, and Cyrus Vance) have gone on to become US secretaries of state.

Nonprofit organization
Fiscal year ends: December 31

WHO

Chairman: John R. Evans
President: Peter C. Goldmark, Jr.
SVP: Kenneth Prewitt
Acting VP Communications: Danielle Parris
VP: Hugh B. Price
Secretary: Lynda Mullen
Treasurer and Chief Investment Officer: David A. White
Director for Administration: Sally A. Ferris
Comptroller: Charles J. Lang
Manager Human Resources: Charlotte Church
Auditors: Ernst & Young

WHERE

HQ: 420 Fifth Ave., New York, NY 10018-2702
Phone: 212-869-8500
Fax: 212-398-1858

WHAT

	1993 Program Approvals	
	$ mil.	% of total
Equal Opportunity	24	22
Agricultural Sciences	17	16
Health Sciences	16	16
Arts & Humanities	15	13
Population Sciences	13	12
Global Environment	8	8
School Reform	8	7
African Initiatives	4	3
Special International Initiatives & Special Interests	5	5
Total	**110**	**100**

Divisions and Programs

Agricultural Sciences
Development and application of biotechnology to improve developing countries' food crops; improvements to food production systems in Africa; natural resource management studies

Arts and Humanities
Cross-cultural artistic experimentation; intercultural enrichment

Equal Opportunity
Basic rights protection; urban poverty programs

Global Environmental Program
Multilateral participation in environmental issues; energy efficiency and the use of renewable energy sources

Health Sciences
Development and implementation of low-cost, community-based disease prevention and control; disease prevention in developing countries through vaccinology and pharmacology

International Program to Support Science-Based Development
Promotion of modern science and technology to aid the developing world through Agricultural Sciences, Health Sciences, and Population Sciences divisions and global environmental program.

Population Sciences
Contraception development and application

School Reform
Improved public education for the poor

Special International Initiatives and Special Interests Grants
International Security, International Philanthropy, Rockefeller Foundation Archives, and other projects that do not fall within established program guidelines.

WHEN

Oil baron John D. Rockefeller, one of America's most criticized capitalists, was also one of its pioneer philanthropists. Before founding the Rockefeller Foundation in 1913, he funded the creation of the University of Chicago (with $36 million over a quarter century) and formed organizations for medical research (1901), the education of southern blacks (1903), and hookworm eradication in the southern US.

Rockefeller's faith in science's ability to cure all human ills was reflected in the foundation's early global campaigns to combat hookworm, malaria, and yellow fever (using his initial $35 million endowment); hookworm control alone spread to 62 countries on 6 continents. To ensure lasting effects on public health, Rockefeller gave another $50 million (1919) to strengthen medical schools in Europe, Canada, and Southeast Asia.

In the mid-1920s, the foundation started conducting basic medical research. In 1928 it absorbed several other Rockefeller philanthropies, adding programs in the natural and social sciences and the arts and humanities. During the 1930s the foundation developed the first effective yellow fever vaccine (1935), continued its worldwide battles against disease, and supported pioneering research in the field of biology. Other grants supported the performing arts in the US and social science research at various US research institutes.

During WWII the foundation supplied major funding for nuclear science, created new research tools (spectroscopy, X-ray diffraction), and stifled typhus epidemics.

After the war, with an increasing number of large public ventures modeled after the foundation (e.g., the UN's World Health Organization) taking over its traditional physical/natural sciences territory, the foundation dissolved its famed biology division (1951).

Emphasis swung to agricultural studies under chairman John D. Rockefeller III (1952). The foundation took wheat seeds developed at its Mexican food project (begun in 1942) to Colombia (1950), Chile (1955), and India (1956); a rice institute in the Philippines followed (1960). The resulting Green Revolution sprouted 12 more developing world institutes.

In the 1960s the foundation began dispatching expertise to African and Latin American universities in an effort to raise the level of training at those institutions. The long bear market of the 1970s caused the foundation's assets to drop to a low of $732 million (1977).

The foundation established the Energy Foundation in 1990, a joint effort with the MacArthur Foundation and the Pew Charitable Trusts, to explore alternate energy sources and promote energy efficiency.

In 1994 the foundation announced plans to award $1 million for the development of low-cost, easy-to-use diagnostic tests for sexually transmitted diseases for use in countries without easy access to medical testing.

HOW MUCH

	Annual Growth	1984	1985	1986	1987	1988	1989	1990	1991	1992	1993
Revenues ($ mil.)[1]	15.0%	59	206	367	288	157	305	33	211	198	208
Assets ($ mil.)	8.8%	1,109	1,354	1,615	1,676	1,845	2,152	1,972	2,172	2,152	2,375
Program expenditures ($ mil.)	12.5%	38	43	48	71	65	75	90	102	113	108
Program expenditures as % of assets	—	3.4%	3.2%	3.0%	3.5%	3.5%	3.5%	4.6%	4.7%	5.3%	4.5%
Employees	(2.1%)	—	—	—	—	—	160	151	142	142	147

1993 Year-end:
Return on investments: 9.4%

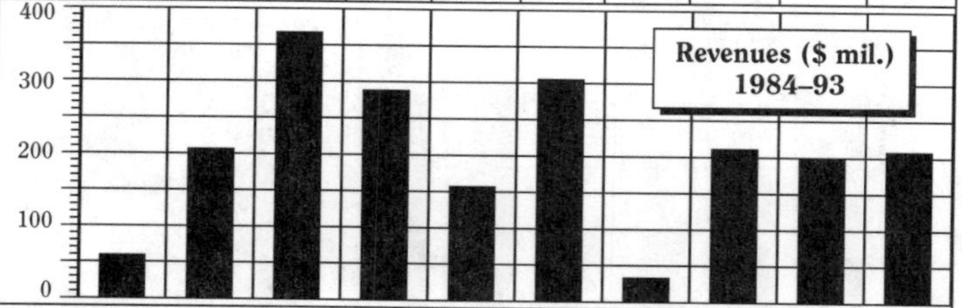

Revenues ($ mil.) 1984–93

400 / 300 / 200 / 100 / 0

[1]Net investment income. Includes realized gains.

ROTARY INTERNATIONAL

RANK: N/R

OVERVIEW

Rotary International is the oldest, most international service organization in the world. It has almost 1.2 million members in 26,474 clubs in 187 countries. Many other service clubs patterned themselves after the Rotary.

The organization's motto, "Service Above Self," exemplifies the Rotary's dedication to its "four avenues" of club, vocational, community, and international service. The organization promotes high ethical standards in business and international understanding, goodwill, and peace. Its immunization program (it is leading a drive to eradicate polio) and nutritional program have helped hundreds of thousands of people worldwide, and it runs the world's largest privately sponsored scholarship program through its Rotary Foundation.

The Rotary operates through local clubs, in which membership is by invitation only. These clubs are organized into 500 districts worldwide. The Rotary is governed by a 180-member elected board of directors. Although the executive officers are paid, the president performs his largely promotional duties at his own expense. About 4.5% of members are women.

Service organization
Fiscal year ends: June 30

WHO

General Secretary: Herbert A. Pigman
President: Robert R. Barth (1993–94)
President-Elect: Bill Huntley
Vice-President: Wilfrid J. Wilkinson
CFO: Mary Wolfenberger
Treasurer: Takuomi Matsumoto
Auditors: Deloitte & Touche

WHERE

HQ: One Rotary Center, 1560 Sherman Ave., Evanston, IL 60201
Phone: 708-866-3243
Fax: 708-328-8554

Rotary International has 26,474 clubs in 187 countries.

WHAT

	1993 Revenues	
	$ mil.	% of total
Dues	32	61
Magazine, publications & supplies	9	18
One Rotary Center tenants	4	8
Investments	3	6
Other	4	7
Total	**52**	**100**

	1993 Foundation Program Expenditures	
	$ mil.	% of total
Scholarships	24	36
PolioPlus (eradication program)	22	33
Matching grants	7	12
Health, hunger & humanity	6	10
Group study	6	8
Other	1	1
Total	**66**	**100**

Prominent Members

US Presidents
Dwight Eisenhower
Warren Harding
Herbert Hoover
John Kennedy
Richard Nixon
Franklin Roosevelt
Harry Truman
Woodrow Wilson

Politicians
Winston Churchill
J. William Fulbright
Mark Hatfield
Wayne Morse
Adlai Stevenson
Earl Warren

Literary Figures
Thomas Mann
Norman Vincent Peale
James Whitcomb Riley

Business Leaders
Frank Borman
Raymond Firestone
Connie Mack
Charles Walgreen

Royalty
Prince Bernhard (The Netherlands)
King Carl XVI Gustav (Sweden)
King Hassan II (Morocco)
Prince Philip (England)
Prince Rainier (Monaco)

Others
Neil Armstrong
Admiral Richard Byrd
Gordon Cooper
Albert Schweitzer
Alan Shepard

WHEN

On February 23, 1905, 4 small businessmen — a lawyer, a tailor, an engineer, and a coal dealer — met at Madame Galli's restaurant in Chicago. The lawyer, 37-year-old Paul Percy Harris, who was new to Chicago and pined for the close ties of his native Racine, Wisconsin, proposed that they form an organization dedicated to fellowship and the mutual business advantage of its members (no 2 of whom were to be from the same profession or business). The club soon assumed another objective, service, which now dominates its activities.

At first known as "the Conspirators," the club later took the name Rotary from the practice of rotating the meeting venue among members' places of business.

Harris refused to hold any office in the Rotary Club of Chicago until 1907, when he became president. By 1910 there were 16 clubs (including the first non-US one in Winnipeg) and 1,500 Rotarians. To reflect its wider geographical base, the club was renamed the National Association of Rotary Clubs. A London club opened in 1911, and 2 other UK clubs followed. In 1912 the organization became the International Association of Rotary Clubs, adopting its present name in 1922.

The Rotary Foundation was established in 1917 to further international understanding. It has since provided millions of dollars for scholarships and other worthy causes.

During WWI and WWII the Rotary aided war victims and helped establish UNESCO in 1945. The Rotary lost a number of clubs in Eastern Europe during and after WWII.

By the 1950s the Rotary was a fixture of American life. It excluded women because their presence at meetings was deemed a threat to the tranquility of its male members' marriages. The Rotary was also frowned upon by the Catholic Church, which deemed it a secret society like the Freemasons. So it was a club of Protestant, family businessmen, who, in the US, were mostly Republicans.

Membership continued to grow, to roughly 682,000 by 1970 and 876,000 by 1980. In 1986 the Rotary established the Village Corps to promote self-help community service projects.

In the 1980s a California club admitted a woman; the Rotary disciplined the club, which sued for the right to admit women under a California civil rights law — and lost. Upon appeal, the US Supreme Court ruled in 1987 that the Rotary is a business organization and must admit women. While many protested that this violated members' rights of free association, others believed it would revitalize the clubs. In 1989 the Rotary extended its welcome to women worldwide.

Also in 1989 the Rotary's board of directors fired the general secretary and eliminated 5 managerial positions to curb overspending and to reduce what had become a bureaucracy.

More management changes came in 1993 when Spencer Robinson, Jr., quit the general secretary post and was replaced by Herbert A. Pigman and when Mary Wolfenberger became the Rotary's first woman CFO.

In 1994 the Rotary continued to be active in relief efforts in the former Yugoslavia.

HOW MUCH

	Annual Growth	1984	1985	1986	1987	1988	1989	1990	1991	1992	1993
Revenues ($ mil.)	4.9%	—	36	34	—	—	36	40	46	51	52
Rotary Foundation assets ($ mil.)	5.2%	—	—	—	—	—	—	—	356	369	394
Foundation program expenditures ($ mil.)	0.8%	—	—	—	—	—	—	—	65	71	66
Membership (thou.)	2.3%	961	991	1,013	1,039	1,057	1,077	1,125	1,143	1,157	1,174
Employees	6.19%	—	—	—	—	—	487	532	—	554	617

1993 Year-end:
Cash (mil.): $6
Current ratio: 1.25
Total assets (mil.): $72

Revenues ($ mil.) 1985–93

THE SALVATION ARMY

RANK: 188

OVERVIEW

For thousands of Americans The Salvation Army spells relief. Most people are aware of the Army only around Christmas when they spot a lone soldier standing beside a kettle and hear a bell ringing for donations, but the Army is active year-round.

In 1992 the Army served more than 69 million meals, provided food and lodging for more than 6 million homeless persons, and visited more than 5 million persons in hospitals, nursing homes, and prisons. To provide these services, it raised more money from private donations ($726 million, $61 million of which came from the kettles) than any other nonprofit organization. The Army provides programs to assist alcoholics, drug addicts, battered women, the unemployed, pregnant women, AIDS victims, and teenagers through 118 medical clinics, 126 Adult Rehabilitation Centers, and 17 Harbor Light Centers throughout the US. About 87¢ of each donated dollar is spent on Army service programs.

Along with promoting charity, the Army seeks to save the souls of the persons it helps. The Army is an evangelic church that preaches the Christian message that salvation is possible only through the acceptance of Jesus Christ as savior. Toward that end the Army reported 133,833 Decisions for Christ in 1992.

Before joining the Army and becoming a soldier, one must sign an agreement known as the "Articles of War" that commits a person to the avoidance of gambling, debt, and profanity and abstention from alcohol, tobacco, and other recreational drugs. Officers are expected to wear their uniforms at all times and work full-time for the Army. They receive no salary; instead, they are compensated with a housing allowance, a car, a portion of the cost of their uniforms, 80% of their medical expenses, and a living allowance that never exceeds $282 a week. When a soldier or officer dies, the Salvationist is said to have been "promoted to Glory."

Nonprofit organization
Fiscal year ends: September 30

WHO

National Advisory Board Chairman: Arthur J. Decio
General: Bramwell H. Tillsley
National Commander: Kenneth L. Hodder
Central Territorial Commander: Harold D. Hinson
Eastern Territorial Commander: Ronald G. Irwin
Southern Territorial Commander: Kenneth Hood
Western Territorial Commander: Paul A. Rader

WHERE

HQ: 615 Slaters Ln., Alexandria, VA 22313
Phone: 703-684-5500
Fax: 703-684-5538

The Salvation Army operates community service centers and social services programs and facilities in almost 10,000 communities throughout the US.

WHEN

William Booth started preaching as a Wesleyan Methodist in the UK, but the church expelled him because he insisted on preaching outside and to everyone, including the poor. In 1865 he moved to the slums of London's East End and attracted large crowds with his volatile sermons. Opposition to his message of universal salvation for drunks, thieves, prostitutes, and gamblers often caused riots. At a meeting in 1878, a sign was used referring to the "Salvation Army." Booth adopted the reference as both the name and the style of his organization. Members became soldiers; evangelists were captains and majors; Booth was referred to as "General." Prayers became kneedrills, and contributions were called cartridges. "Blood and Fire" became the Army's motto.

The Army marched across the Atlantic to the US in 1880, led by 7 women and one man. All of the women except one were under the age of 20. Women have always played an active role in the Army, both as officers and soldiers, and have consistently outnumbered men. Booth's wife, Catherine Mumford, was a leading suffragette, and Booth advocated equal rights for women.

In 1891 a crab pot for donations was placed on a San Francisco street, with a sign reading "Keep the Pot Boiling." The idea became the genesis for the Army's annual Christmas kettle program. The Army provided relief for San Franciscans during the earthquake of 1906 that destroyed much of the city.

During WWI the Army became famous for the doughnuts that it served the doughboys fighting on the front lines. After some internal dissension, the Army took its only public political stance in 1928 with the endorsement of Herbert Hoover for his support of Prohibition during his presidential campaign. The Army opened its first home for alcoholics in 1939 in Detroit.

After WWII the Army began using radio and TV programs to spread its message, including "Heartbeat Theater," "The Living Word," and "Army of Stars."

In 1992 the Army provided assistance to victims of Hurricanes Andrew and Iniki. When an earthquake hit Los Angeles in 1994, the Army operated the tent cities that were set up to house thousands of residents who were left homeless by the disaster.

WHAT

	1992 Revenues	
	$ mil.	% of total
Contributions	517	37
Sales to the public	282	20
Hospital operations	181	13
Government funds	178	13
United Way	106	7
Program service fees	94	7
Other	40	3
Total	**1,398**	**100**

	1992 Program Expenditures	
	$ mil.	% of total
Corps Community Centers	334	27
Adult Rehabilitation Centers/ Corps Salvage/Thrift	318	26
Other social services	292	24
Hospitals	179	15
Residences & institutions	97	8
Total	**1,220**	**100**

Services
Adult rehabilitation centers
Christmas sharing (aids needy families, the elderly, and homeless people)
Correctional services (assists the incarcerated by offering spiritual material, Bible courses, and job training programs)
Day care centers
Disaster services
Homeless shelters
League of Mercy (distributes toilet articles, periodicals, and Bibles in institutions)
Maternal services
Missing persons assistance
Summer camps (for low-income children and senior citizens)
Youth services (Salvation Army Adventure Corps, Boys' Clubs, Girls' Clubs)
Other programs (Salvation Army Men's Fellowship Clubs, Red Shield Clubs, radio and television broadcasts)

HOW MUCH

	Annual Growth	1984	1985	1986	1987	1988	1989	1990	1991	1992	1993
Revenues ($ mil.)	7.3%	—	—	—	—	—	—	1,216	1,287	1,398	—
Program exp. ($ mil.)	—	—	—	—	—	—	—	—	1,145	1,220	—
Program expenditures as % of revenue	—	—	—	—	—	—	—	—	89.0%	87.3%	—
Membership	0.7%	—	—	—	434,002	433,443	445,556	445,991	446,403	450,028	450,312
Officers/cadets (clergy)	2.1%	—	—	—	5,211	5,322	5,413	5,707	5,876	5,770	5,842
Corps (churches)	1.3%	—	—	—	1,097	1,097	1,122	1,133	1,151	1,173	1,189

Revenues ($ mil.) 1990–92

SMITHSONIAN INSTITUTION

RANK: 413

OVERVIEW

Known as "the nation's attic," the Smithsonian Institution is the world's largest museum complex, holding over 130 million items in its 16 facilities. Some of the more well-known pieces include the Wright Brothers' *Kitty Hawk* and the flag that inspired Francis Scott Key's "Star-Spangled Banner." The Smithsonian's museums also house everything from plant specimens and fossils to paintings by Old Masters and collections of American folk art. The Smithsonian also runs the National Zoo, conducts research in its own laboratories and at locations around the world, and publishes the *Smithsonian* magazine.

Although it gets 47% of its funds from the US government, the Smithsonian is operated as a private foundation, taking private donations and raising revenue through its museum shops, food shops, and magazines. It is headed by a Board of Regents that includes the vice-president of the US, the chief justice of the Supreme Court, 3 senators, 3 representatives, and 8 private citizens. The secretary of the institution runs its day-to-day operations.

With government budget tightening leading to a slowdown in appropriations growth, the Smithsonian has begun to allow corporations to put their logos on the exhibits they underwrite. The first permanent exhibit to bear a corporate logo is the O. Orkin Insect Zoo, sponsored by Orkin Pest Control, which paid $500,000 to commemorate its founder.

WHEN

In 1826 James Smithson, an English chemist, wrote a proviso to his will that would lead to the creation of the Smithsonian Institution. When Smithson died in 1829, his will bequeathed his estate to his nephew, Henry James Hungerford, with the stipulation that if Hungerford died without heirs, the estate would go to the US to create "an Establishment for the increase and diffusion of knowledge among men." When Hungerford died in 1835 without any heirs, the US government inherited more than $500,000 in gold.

Although the 105 bags of gold coins didn't arrive in the US until 1838, Congress still hadn't decided exactly what to do with them. While they were deciding they invested most of the money in State of Arkansas bonds. When Arkansas defaulted, Congress, perhaps feeling pangs of guilt for having lost the "increase of knowledge" endowment, made an appropriation to cover the loss.

In 1846 Congress finally created the institution and named Princeton physicist Joseph Henry as its first secretary. That same year the Smithsonian established the Museum of Natural History, the Museum of History and Technology, and the National Gallery of Art. In 1855 the Smithsonian's first building, a red stone "medieval-style" castle designed by Thomas Renwick, was completed.

In 1858 the collection of the US Patent Office was turned over to the Smithsonian, and Stephen Baird, who succeeded Henry in 1878, developed the National Museum around the Patent Office's collection. The Smithsonian continued to expand, adding the National Zoological Park in 1889 and the Smithsonian Astrophysical Observatory in 1890.

The Freer Gallery, a gift of industrialist Charles Freer, opened in 1923. In 1937 the National Gallery was renamed the National Collection of Fine Arts. A new National Gallery, created with Andrew Mellon's gift of his art collection and a building, opened in 1941. In 1946 the Air and Space Museum was established, and the Smithsonian began directing the Tropical Research Bureau in Panama.

More museums were added in the 1960s, including the National Portrait Gallery (1962) and the Anacostia Museum (exhibits and materials on African-American history, 1967). The Kennedy Center for the Performing Arts was opened in 1971. In 1980 the Collection of Fine Arts was renamed the National Museum of American Art, and the Museum of History and Technology was renamed the National Museum of American History.

In 1992 a scandal erupted when the institution paid $351,000 in legal fees for a zoologist affiliated with the organization who was charged with helping hunters stalk endangered species. The Smithsonian broke from tradition in 1993 when it placed contribution boxes in 4 of its museums. Also in 1993 Secretary Robert Adams announced plans to retire; in 1994 the Board of Regents named Ira Michael Heyman, former chancellor of the University of California, to replace him.

HOW MUCH

	9-Year Growth	1984	1985	1986	1987	1988	1989	1990	1991	1992	1993
Revenues ($ mil.)	8.2%	360	430	443	501	506	578	595	656	706	729
Assets ($ mil.)[1]	8.0%	539	595	644	732	777	838	887	941	1,030	1,077
Appropriations ($ mil.)	8.3%	168	191	191	211	230	246	267	326	332	344
Employees	(0.2%)	6,900	6,900	6,800	7,100	—	6,000	6,300	6,700	6,800	6,800

1993 Year-end:
Debt ratio: 1.3%
Return on trust fund: 8.8%
Cash (mil.): $60
Long-term debt (mil.): $12

Revenues ($ mil.) 1984–93

[1]Not including collections.

Nonprofit organization
Fiscal year ends: September 30

WHO

Secretary: I. Michael Heyman, age 63
Under Secretary: Constance B. Newman
Treasurer: Sudeep Anand
General Counsel: Peter G. Powers
Assistant Secretary for Finance and Administration and CFO: Nancy D. Suttenfield
Director of Planning and Budget: L. Carole Wharton
Personnel Director: Marilyn Marton
Auditors: KPMG Peat Marwick

WHERE

HQ: 1000 Jefferson Dr. SW, Washington, DC 20560
Phone: 202-357-2700
Fax: 202-786-2515

The Smithsonian Institution runs museums, publishing operations, and a zoo in the US and oversees research projects around the world.

WHAT

	1993 Revenues	
	$ mil.	% of total
Appropriations	344	47
Government grants & contracts	44	6
Investment gains & income	37	5
Gifts, bequests & private grants	43	6
Auxiliary activities	191	26
Other	70	10
Total	**729**	**100**

Selected Organizations

Arts and Humanities
Anacostia Museum
Archives of American Art
Arthur M. Sackler Gallery
Cooper-Hewitt, National Museum of Design
Freer Gallery of Art
Hirshhorn Museum and Sculpture Garden
International Gallery
National Air and Space Museum
National Museum of African Art
National Museum of American Art
National Museum of American History
National Museum of the American Indian
National Portrait Gallery

Education and Public Service
Center for Folklife Programs and Cultural Studies

Publishing
Air & Space/Smithsonian magazine
Smithsonian magazine

Sciences
National Museum of Natural History/ National Museum of Man
National Zoological Park
Smithsonian Astrophysical Observatory
Smithsonian Environmental Research Center

Independently Governed Organizations

John F. Kennedy Center for the Performing Arts
National Gallery of Art
Woodrow Wilson International Center for Scholars

STAR ENTERPRISE

RANK: 25

OVERVIEW

Barely 5 years old, Star Enterprise is a big kid with some big parents. A joint venture between Texaco, the US's 3rd largest oil company, and the state-owned Saudi Arabian Oil Company (Saudi Aramco), the world's largest crude oil producer, the company is the 4th largest branded gasoline retailer in the US (ranked by outlets).

Headquartered in Houston, Star acts as Texaco's refining and marketing arm for 9,500 Texaco brand retail outlets, including StarMart convenience stores, in 26 states in the eastern and southern US and in the District of Columbia, the majority of which are independently owned. As part of the joint venture agreement, Saudi Aramco provides crude oil for Star's 3 refineries, which produce gasoline, home heating oil, petrochemical feedstocks, and other petroleum products.

To keep prices low, Star is working with a limited number of convenience store suppliers to improve its buying power, and it is also upgrading many of its refining facilities to comply with stricter emission standards.

WHEN

Texaco and Saudi Aramco had been doing business together in various ventures since 1936, but they had never tried anything on the scale of the joint venture signed in London by Texaco CEO James Kinnear and Saudi Oil Minister Hisham Nazer in late 1988. The deal, valued at nearly $2 billion, was the largest joint venture of its kind in the US.

The agreement to create Star Enterprise sprang, in part, from Texaco's tumultuous ride following its acquisition of Getty Oil in 1984. After acquiring Getty, Texaco was sued by Pennzoil for preempting Pennzoil's bid for Getty. A Texas court ordered Texaco to pay Pennzoil $10.5 billion in 1985, the largest damage award ever. After losing an appeal, Texaco filed for bankruptcy in 1987 and eventually settled with Pennzoil for $3 billion.

In 1988 Texaco emerged from bankruptcy after announcing a reorganization. However, corporate raider Carl Icahn had begun buying up Texaco's stock in a bid to take control of the company. Icahn wanted 5 seats on Texaco's board, but he was narrowly defeated in a proxy vote after Texaco's management announced the deal with Saudi Aramco at a stockholder meeting.

Texaco got a much needed injection of cash, and Saudi Aramco got a steady US outlet for its supply of crude. The Saudis had been at odds with their OPEC partners for several years, and in late 1985 Saudi oil minister Sheikh Yamani and Saudi Aramco began increasing production, leading to an oil price crash in 1986. Nazer replaced Yamani and changed Saudi Aramco's strategy. In order to secure market share, the Saudis began signing long-term supply contracts.

The deal with Texaco gave Saudi Aramco a 50% interest in Texaco's refining and marketing operations in the East and Gulf Coast—about 2/3 of Texaco's US downstream operations—including 3 refineries and its Texaco brand stations. In return the Saudis paid $812 million cash and provided 75% of Star's initial inventory, about 30 million barrels of oil. It also agreed to a 20-year, 600,000- barrel-a-day commitment of crude. Each company named 3 representatives to Star's management committee, and Donald Schmude, a VP of manufacturing for Texaco, was named CEO.

The new company officially began operation on January 1, 1989. It soon began a modernization and expansion program, acquiring 65 stations, building 30 new outlets, and remodeling another 172 during 1989.

The company continued to upgrade its retail outlets in 1990 and announced it would spend $300 million over 5 years to build approximately 300 new System 2000 stations. In 1991 Lester Wilkes became president and CEO of Star after Schmude was named president of Texaco Refining & Marketing.

In 1992 Star settled a dispute with homeowners near a tank farm it operated with 3 other companies in Fairfax, Virginia, after an estimated 100,000 to 200,000 gallons of refined products leaked from the facility. In a settlement estimated at $200 million, Star agreed to pay cleanup costs, buy homes near the spill, and pay compensation to homeowners. Also in 1992 Star completed construction of a delayed coker unit, which aids in the refining of low-grade crude, at its Port Arthur, Texas, refinery.

In 1993 Texaco and Star formed a cooperative association, Star Marketers Acceptance Corporation, to provide loans to Texaco brand marketers.

StarEnterprise

Joint venture
Fiscal year ends: December 31

WHO

President & CEO: Lester A. Wilkes
VP Finance and CFO: William J. Mathe
VP Marketing: Joseph W. Bernitt
VP Refining: Reidar O. Fauli
Treasurer: Michael V. Carlucci
General Counsel and Secretary: Clydia J. Cuykendall
Director Public and Government Affairs: Paul B. Doucette
Manager, Southeastern Region: Frank H. Van Dyke
Manager, Northeastern Region: Michael S. Mattingly
Manager, Southwestern Region: E. V. Don Becker
Director Human Resources: Floyd Chaney
Auditors: Arthur Andersen and Deloitte & Touche

WHERE

HQ: 12700 Northborough Dr., Houston, TX 77067-2508
Phone: 713-874-7000
Fax: 713-874-7760 (Public Relations)

Star operates refineries in Delaware City, DE; Convent, LA; and Port Arthur, TX. It sells its products in Texaco brand stations in the eastern and southern US.

WHAT

	1993 Retail Outlets	
	No.	% of total
Company owned & leased	700	7
Independently owned	8,800	93
Total	**9,500**	**100**

Refinery Products
Asphalt
Aviation fuel
Butane
Diesel fuel
Gasoline
Home heating oil
Lubricant base oils
Natural gas liquids
Petrochemical feedstocks
Propane

KEY COMPETITORS

Amoco
Ashland
British Petroleum
Circle K
Coastal
Cumberland Farms
Dairy Mart Convenience Stores
Diamond Shamrock
DuPont
Exxon
Kerr-McGee
Marathon Oil
Mobil
National Convenience
PDVSA
Racetrac
Petrofina
Phillips Petroleum
Royal Dutch/Shell
Southland
Sun
Wawa

HOW MUCH

	Annual Growth	1984	1985	1986	1987	1988	1989	1990	1991	1992	1993
Sales ($ mil.)	(1.1%)	—	—	—	—	—	6,522	8,067	7,165	6,825	6,252
Net income	(1.7%)	—	—	—	—	—	135	249	175	29	126
Income as % of sales	—	—	—	—	—	—	2.1%	3.1%	2.4%	0.4%	2.1%
Employees	—	—	—	—	—	—	—	—	—	5,000	5,000

1993 Year-end:
Return on equity: 5.4%
Current ratio: 1.57
Net assets (mil.): $2,395

Net Income ($ mil.) 1989–93

250
200
150
100
50
0

STATE FARM

RANK: 6

OVERVIEW

State Farm Mutual Automobile Insurance of Bloomington, Illinois, has been the nation's largest auto insurance company for more than 50 years. Owned by policyholders, the company has been run since its beginning by 2 families, the Mecherles (1922–54) and the Rusts (1954–present). Its Fire and Casualty Company affiliate is also the largest US homeowners' insurer. Other affiliate companies offer life and health insurance. A new affiliate, State Farm Indemnity Company, was created in 1992 to segregate New Jersey auto insurance policies while the company evaluates the regulatory and market conditions in that state. It had already begun shrinking its Pennsylvania business and in 1993 stopped writing new auto policies in Texas.

All of this is due to spiraling claims and increased regulation. In addition, the company's fire affiliate was hit by $3.6 billion in claims relating to Hurricane Andrew. However, one bright spot in the company's profit picture was life insurance. State Farm is reassessing its premium structures and underwriting policies in order to try to reduce future risks to profitability. It also believes that the federal government should share in catastrophe risks.

Mutual company
Fiscal year ends: December 31

WHO

Chairman, President, and CEO: Edward B. Rust, Jr., age 43
EVP and COO: Vincent J. Trosino, age 53
SVP and Treasurer; Chairman, State Farm Fire and Casualty: Roger S. Joslin, age 57
Senior Agency VP: Chuck Wright
VP and General Counsel: Cranford A. Ingham
VP Investments: Kurt Moser
VP Personnel: John Coffey
Auditors: Coopers & Lybrand

WHEN

Retired farmer George Mecherle founded State Farm Mutual Automobile Insurance Co. in Bloomington, Illinois, in 1922. State Farm restricted membership, primarily to members of farm bureaus and farm mutual insurance companies, and charged a one-time membership fee and a premium to protect an automobile against loss or damage.

From the beginning State Farm, unlike most of its competitors, offered 6-month premium payments. State Farm also billed and collected renewal premiums from its home office, relieving the agent of the task. Another State Farm feature was a simplified 7-class system for charging auto rates instead of charging separate rates for each auto model, as most other companies did.

Before the end of its first year, State Farm had placed policies in 46 Illinois counties. To insure nonfarmers' autos, the company in 1926 started City and Village Mutual Automobile Insurance, which became part of State Farm in 1927. Between 1927 and 1931 State Farm introduced borrowed-car protection, wind coverage, and insurance for buses or cars used in transporting schoolchildren.

State Farm expanded to Berkeley, California, in 1928; started State Farm Life Insurance, a wholly owned subsidiary, in 1929; and established State Farm Fire Insurance in 1935. George Mecherle moved up to chairman in 1937, and his son Ramond assumed the presidency. Yet George remained active, challenging agents in 1939 to write "A Million or More (auto policies) by '44." Agents met the deadline with a 110% increase in policies.

In the 1940s State Farm began to focus on metropolitan areas after most of the farm bureaus formed their own insurance companies. By 1941 State Farm was the largest auto insurer in total automobile premiums written. In the late 1940s and 1950s, it moved to a full-time agency force.

Adlai Rust led State Farm from 1954 to 1958, when Edward Rust took over and ran the company until his death in 1985. Edward's son now holds the top spot.

Between 1974 and 1987 the company was hit by several sex discrimination suits (a 1992 settlement awarded $157 million to 814 California women). The company has since tried to hire more women and minorities.

Facing increasing state regulation, the company in 1990 stopped writing new auto business in Pennsylvania. After legislation in other states prompted some insurers to stop insuring in those states, State Farm faced the dilemma of either using the exodus to pick up market share or avoiding risk. By 1993 it seemed to be resolving the problem in favor of the bottom line.

Also in 1991 State Farm was identified as one of several auto insurers failing to give state-mandated discounts for air bags and automatic safety belts. The company estimated that it owed $10 to $15 in rebates to each of about 2.5 million customers.

Although the Los Angeles riots of 1992 and a series of major fires, floods, and earthquakes threw the company's consolidated results into the red, State Farm remains the most strongly capitalized insurance company in the US.

WHERE

HQ: State Farm Mutual Automobile Insurance Company, One State Farm Plaza, Bloomington, IL 61710-0001
Phone: 309-766-2311
Fax: 309-766-6169

State Farm has operations in all 50 states, the District of Columbia, and Canada.

WHAT

	1993 Auto Company Assets	
	$ mil.	% of total
Cash & equivalents	772	2
Bonds	22,865	48
Stocks	11,637	25
Equity in subsidiaries	6,373	13
Other	5,890	12
Total	**47,537**	**100**

	1993 Auto Company Sales	
	$ mil.	$ of total
Premiums & membership	21,972	90
Investments	2,349	10
Other	142	—
Total	**24,463**	**100**

Lines of Business
Automobile insurance
Fire insurance
Health insurance
Homeowners insurance
Inland marine insurance
Life insurance

Subsidiaries
State Farm County Mutual Insurance Co. of Texas
State Farm Fire and Casualty Co.
State Farm General Insurance Co.
State Farm Indemnity Co. (New Jersey)
State Farm Life & Accident Assurance Co.
State Farm Life Insurance Co.
State Farm Lloyds

HOW MUCH

	9-Year Growth	1984	1985	1986	1987	1988	1989	1990	1991	1992	1993
Assets ($ mil.)	12.4%	16,671	19,695	23,679	27,101	30,922	35,493	37,508	42,676	43,603	47,537
Net income ($ mil.)	8.9%	808	666	1,033	1,041	721	419	372	1,317	1,780	1,742
Income as % of assets	—	4.8%	3.4%	4.4%	3.8%	2.3%	1.2%	1.0%	3.1%	4.1%	3.7%
Employees	7.3%	34,160	37,543	40,748	44,086	48,082	52,236	55,133	58,113	60,786	64,520

1993 Year-end:
Equity as % of assets: 22.5%
Return on equity: 3.8%
Cash (mil.): $772
Sales (mil.): $24,463

Assets ($ mil.) 1984–93

50,000
45,000
40,000
35,000
30,000
25,000
20,000
15,000
10,000
5,000
0

KEY COMPETITORS

Aetna
AFLAC
Allstate
Chubb
CIGNA
Equitable
GEICO
ITT
John Hancock
Kemper
Liberty Mutual
Loews
MassMutual
MetLife
Nationwide
New York Life
Northwestern Mutual
Prudential
Travelers
USAA

STEELCASE INC.

RANK: 87

OVERVIEW

Headquartered in Grand Rapids, Michigan, Steelcase is the world's largest office furniture manufacturer. The company provides a wide variety of products — from swivel tilt chairs and filing cabinets to entire office furniture systems.

Listed in *The 100 Best Companies to Work for in America*, Steelcase pays profit-sharing bonuses to all its employees. The company is owned by about 100 descendants of the company's founders, including Chairman Robert Pew and William Crawford, president of Steelcase Design Partnership.

Steelcase, credited with creating "the look of the modern office," continues to unveil new designs. In 1993 it introduced the Personal Harbor, a semi-enclosed workstation that gives a worker control over his or her own heat, light, and air conditioning.

Steelcase suffered its first-ever loss in 1994 on slightly lower revenues. The company blamed the loss on weak overseas sales and restructuring changes associated with its wood furniture business.

WHEN

In the early 1900s offices were still heated with wood stoves and lit with gas lamps, so when a pensive executive leaned back in his wooden chair and put his feet up on his wooden desk, he was taking a calculated risk. Enter Peter M. Wege, a sheet-metal designer who espoused the fireproof benefits of steel furniture. Wege persuaded a group of investors, led by Grand Rapids banker Henry Idema, to sink $75,000 into his idea, and in 1912 the Metal Office Furniture Company was born.

The company's first big hit, however, wasn't a desk or a chair; it was a metal wastepaper basket, much less flammable than the wicker wastebaskets popular at the time.

Despite the company's innovative ideas, businesses were slow to switch from wood to the more expensive metal furniture. However, US government architects, concerned with fire safety, began specifying metal furniture in their designs, and in 1915 the company won the first of many government contracts.

In 1921 Wege hired media consultant Jim Turner to tout the benefits of metal furniture. Turner came up with a trademark to describe the indestructible nature of the company's products — Steelcase. During the 1930s Metal Office Furniture continued to create innovative designs, patenting the suspension cabinet in 1934 and teaming with Frank Lloyd Wright in 1937 to create office furniture for the Johnson Wax headquarters building.

WWII brought a cutback in steel available for use by furniture manufacturers, but the company was able to weather the storm thanks to a contract to provide the US Navy with shipboard furniture. After the war the company introduced modular furniture based on designs learned in building furniture with interchangeable parts for the navy.

The company changed its name to Steelcase Inc. in 1954 and in 1959 introduced Convertibles and Convertiwalls, a system of frames, cabinets, and panels that could tailor a work area to an individual worker's needs. By 1968 the company had become the largest metal office furniture maker in the world.

During the early 1970s Steelcase entered into a pair of joint ventures in order to boost its presence overseas, signing deals with Kurogane Kosakusho (creating Steelcase Japan) in 1973 and Strafor Facom (creating Steelcase Strafor) in 1974. In 1978 Steelcase began a series of acquisitions, fueling growth that helped to triple its sales during the 1980s.

In 1987, in an effort to position itself as a more design-oriented company, Steelcase created the Steelcase Design Partnership, made up of 7 companies providing products for special market niches such as wood office furniture (Stow Davis) and fabrics (DesignTex).

Steelcase was hit hard by the early 1990s recession as many businesses postponed buying new office furniture. The company, long known for its job security, was forced to fire 300 salaried employees and lay off hourly workers, but by 1992 it was able to recall all the hourly employees.

Also in 1992 Steelcase fought off an effort by outsiders — who had obtained company stock after it had passed to a brokerage firm following the death of an heiress of one of the founders — to force the company to go public. Through a reverse stock split, the outsiders were forced to sell their stock to Steelcase.

Steelcase launched 2 new companies in 1993: Turnstone, which serves small businesses and home office workers; and Continuum, which commissions work from minority designers.

In 1994 the company shuffled its management after Robert C. Pew III, grandson of one of the founders, resigned as president of Steelcase North America, for personal reasons.

HOW MUCH

	9-Year Growth	1985	1986	1987	1988	1989	1990	1991	1992	1993	1994
Sales ($ mil.)	7.6%	1,186	1,393	1,506	1,624	1,810	1,896	1,945	2,300	2,400	2,500
Employees	4.4%	12,000	15,000	16,000	14,000	18,500	21,500	21,000	20,500	19,000	17,800

Sales ($ mil.) 1985–94

2,500
2,000
1,500
1,000
500
0

Steelcase

Private company
Fiscal year ends: Last day of February

WHO

Chairman: Robert Pew, age 70
President and CEO: Jerry K. Myers
EVP; President, Steelcase Design Partnership: William P. Crawford, age 51
EVP Operations: William S. Elston, age 53
EVP and CFO: William Williams, age 40
SVP Sales: Lawrence F. Leete
EVP Sales and Marketing: Roger L. Choquette, age 46
EVP Ventures Group and President, Turnstone: James P. Hackett, age 38
VP, Secretary, and General Counsel: David S. Fry
Director Human Resources: Dan Wiljanen
Auditors: BDO Seidman

WHERE

HQ: 901 44th St. SE, Grand Rapids, MI 49508-7575
Phone: 616-247-2710
Fax: 616-246-9015

Steelcase has manufacturing plants in Belgium, Canada, France, Germany, Japan, Ivory Coast, Morocco, Portugal, Spain, the UK, and the US. It sells its products worldwide through a network of over 900 independent dealers.

WHAT

Products

Desks and Tables
Chancellor
Edgewood
Ellipse
Paladin

Filing and Storage
Bookcases
Lateral files
Modular storage cabinets
Vertical files

Seating
Criterion
Player
Protegé
Rally
Sensor

Systems Furniture
Activity
Avenir
Context
Elective Elements
Valencia

Other Operations

Selected Subsidiaries
Attwood Corporation
Continuum Inc.
Steelcase Design Partnership
- Atelier International, Ltd.
- Brayton International, Inc.
- DesignTex Fabrics, Inc.
- Details
- Health Design (subsidiary of Brayton International)
- Metropolitan Furniture Corporation
- Stow Davis
- Vecta

Steelcase Export
Steelcase North America
Turnstone

Joint Ventures
Steelcase Japan Ltd. (with Kurogane Kosakusho)
Steelcase Strafor (with Strafor Facom)

KEY COMPETITORS

Allsteel
American Brands
Globe Business Furniture
Hanson
Haworth
Herman Miller
Hon Industries
Krueger International
Masco
O'Sullivan Industries
Shelby Williams Industries
Westinghouse

THE STROH COMPANIES INC.

RANK: 289

OVERVIEW

Stroh is the #4 US brewer (after Anheuser-Busch, Miller, and Coors), with less than 1/6 the market share of Anheuser-Busch, and the world's #12 beverage company. Old Milwaukee, Stroh's leading brand, is the #10 beer, but for 6 years its sales have shrunk. The company has lost money for 9 years, but it has eliminated all debt.

Stroh produces beers and malt liquors, including the fire-brewed Stroh's brand, Schlitz, Schaefer, and Old Milwaukee. Other operations include real estate, malt cooler production, and a new iced tea venture. Since its 1850 founding the brewery has rested completely in the hands of the descendants of founder Bernhard Stroh.

Once a regional operation, Stroh rose to prominence during the 1980s through aggressive marketing and the acquisition of brewers F&M Schaefer and Schlitz. Stroh's domestic future might require a return to regional marketing — accepting that Stroh is an also-ran nationally but earning strong sales as a "local" beermaker wherever its brands are sold.

Overseas, the company has fared much better. Stroh's brands have posted double-digit growth rates in the more than 50 countries where they are sold.

WHEN

Bernhard Stroh fled Germany in 1848 to escape the German Revolution. In 1850 he settled in Detroit, establishing a brewery to make Bohemian-style beer. Stroh expanded his operation and named it the Lion's Head Brewery, adopting a logo from the Kyrburg Castle in his native town of Kirn.

When Stroh died in 1882, his son Bernhard Stroh, Jr., took charge. Bernhard operated the company until 1908, when management passed to his brother Julius, who renamed the brewery the Stroh Brewing Company.

Julius Stroh embarked on a tour of European breweries in 1912 and brought back the fire-brewing process that is still a hallmark of the company. To survive Prohibition, Stroh shifted production to alcohol-free beer, malt products, soft drinks, and ice cream.

Following Julius's death in 1939, the company's management passed from one family member to the next, with little change except the 1964 purchase of the Goebel Brewery (which was across the street from Stroh in Detroit). Peter Stroh, great-grandson of the company's founder, became president in 1968 and shifted away from the company's previously conservative pattern.

During the early 1970s the local market was ailing alongside the auto industry, and Anheuser-Busch and Miller were making life miserable for many regional brewers; subsequently, Peter Stroh made the decision to go national. He hired a team of savvy marketers and in 1978 launched Stroh's Light, the company's first new product in 128 years. By 1979 Stroh's was sold in 17 states.

In 1981 Stroh acquired the F&M Schaefer Brewing Corporation in New York and became the 7th largest brewer in the US. The company jumped into the 3rd largest spot the following year by acquiring the Schlitz brewing company, which was founded in Milwaukee in 1849 by August Krug. Joseph Schlitz, formerly Krug's bookkeeper, named the brewery for himself after Krug died. After Schlitz's death, the company was managed by Krug's descendants (the wealthy Uihlein family) and became the nation's leading brewery for a short time during the 1950s, although it had sunk to the #3 spot at the time Stroh bought it.

In 1985 Stroh closed its original Detroit brewery. That year the company introduced White Mountain Cooler and Sundance (a sparkling-water fruit drink; sold to a partnership that included a 44% Stroh interest in 1989 and again sold to Everfresh Beverages in 1992). In 1989 Adolph Coors proposed to buy Stroh, but the 2 companies could not reach an agreement. Stroh then made an unsuccessful try for Heileman.

In 1991 Stroh sold its 31.6% interest in Spanish brewer Cruzcampo to Guinness and used the proceeds to retire its debt and introduce new brands. That same year Stroh's advertisements for Old Milwaukee, depicting a "Swedish Bikini Team" descending on groups of male beer drinkers (intended as parody), became fodder for a sexual harassment suit from several female Stroh employees. (The suit was settled out of court in 1993.)

Stroh sold its last remaining packaging plant in 1993 in a move to keep the brewer's focus on beer. Stroh followed an industry trend and went for draft beer in a big way that year, introducing 6 different packaged draft beers and a draft malt liquor.

HOW MUCH

	Annual Growth	1984	1985	1986	1987	1988	1989	1990	1991	1992	1993
Estimated sales ($ mil.)	(5.6%)	—	1,600	1,500	1,500	1,450	1,300	1,293	1,116	1,150	1,010
US sales (thou. of barrels)	(6.7%)	24,300	23,900	23,400	22,400	20,100	18,500	16,300	15,000	14,200	13,000
US market share (%)	—	13.7	13.4	13.1	12.6	11.9	11.3	8.6	7.9	6.9	6.9
Employees	(7.6%)	—	6,000	6,000	5,000	5,000	3,500	3,732	2,700	3,500	3,200

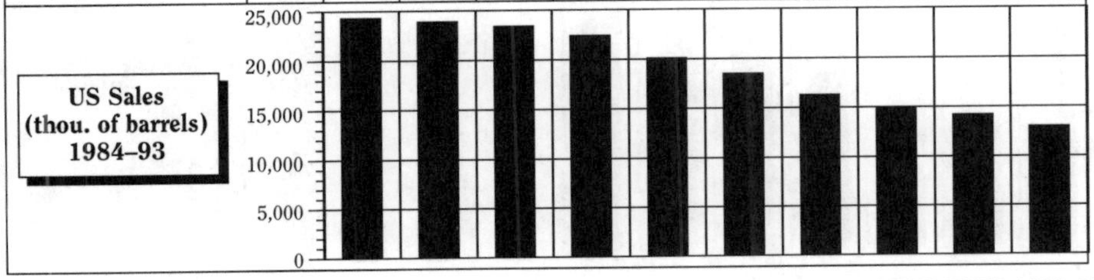

STROH

Private company
Fiscal year ends: March 31

WHO

Chairman and CEO: Peter W. Stroh
VC: John W. Stroh, Jr.
VC: Harold A. Ruemenapp
VC: Gari M. Stroh
President and COO: William L. Henry
SVP, General Counsel, and Secretary: George E. Kuehn
SVP Operations: James R. Avery
SVP Customer Marketing and Administration: Joseph J. Franzem
SVP and CFO: Christopher T. Sortwell
Director Human Resources: Glen Korzin
Auditors: Deloitte & Touche

WHERE

HQ: 100 River Place, Detroit, MI 48207-4225
Phone: 313-446-2000
Fax: 313-446-2206

The company operates breweries in Allentown, PA; Longview, TX; St. Paul, MN; Tampa, FL; and Winston-Salem, NC. The company's real estate unit is in Detroit.

WHAT

Brands
Augsburger
Augsburger Dobbelbock
Augsburger Oktoberfest
Augsburger Weiss
Bull Ice
Chaos (iced teas)
  Cinnamon Spice
  Lunar Lemon
  Rad Berry
Goebel
Goebel Light
Old Milwaukee
Old Milwaukee Genuine Draft
Old Milwaukee Genuine Draft Light
Old Milwaukee Light
Old Milwaukee N.A.
Piels
Piels Light
Primo
Red Bull Malt Liquor
Schaefer
Schaefer Genuine Draft
Schaefer Light
Schaefer Light Draft
Schaefer Premium Light
Schlitz
Schlitz Genuine Draft
Schlitz Ice Premium
Schlitz Light
Schlitz Malt Liquor
Schlitz Malt Liquor Genuine Draft
Signature
Silver Thunder Malt Liquor
Stroh's
Stroh's Draft Light
Stroh's Light
Stroh's Non Alcoholic
White Mountain Cooler (malt-based cooler)
  Cranberry Splash
  Original Citrus
  Tropical Orange
  Wild Raspberry

Subsidiaries and Affiliates
Calamitea Beverage Co. (iced teas)
Colorado Cooler Co. (wine coolers)
Stroh Brewery Company (beer, malt liquor, and nonalcoholic beer)
Stroh Properties Inc. (industrial and commercial real estate)
Stroh International (beer export)

KEY COMPETITORS

Adolph Coors
Allied-Lyons
Anheuser-Busch
Bacardi
Bass
Boston Beer
BSN
Carlsberg
Celestial Seasonings
Foster's Brewing
Gallo
Genesee
Guinness
Heileman
Heineken
John Labatt
Kirin
Molson
Nestlé
Ocean Spray
Philip Morris
S&P Co.
San Miguel
Seagram
Snapple

TEACHERS INSURANCE

RANK: 16

OVERVIEW

New York–based Teachers Insurance and Annuity Association–College Retirement Equities Fund (TIAA–CREF) is one of the US's largest insurance companies and the world's largest private pension system, providing pensions and life, disability, and long-term care insurance to 1.7 million people at 5,200 educational and research organizations. TIAA provides annuities and insurance, while CREF offers a variety of investment funds.

Because its clientele is so targeted, TIAA–CREF gains new clients primarily through the adoption of its services by new institutions, as part of an increasing menu of benefit plans available to a formerly underserved group.

One of TIAA–CREF's strengths is its unusually low overhead: about 0.25% for TIAA and 0.4% for CREF. This is largely attributable to the association's size, nonprofit status, and, in the past, to its long-term and somewhat monolithic investment strategy. Increasing investment options and fewer restrictions on funds withdrawals may impede the association's ability to make very long-term investments.

For now, TIAA–CREF's size is its major asset. It is a financier of large real estate projects (such as the Mall of America in Minneapolis), and it owns about 1% of all US stocks.

WHEN

The Carnegie Foundation for the Advancement of Teaching established TIAA in New York City in 1905 with an endowment of $15 million to provide retirement benefits and other forms of financial security to employees of educational and research organizations. The original endowment was found to be insufficient, and in 1918 the fund was reorganized into a defined contribution plan with another $1 million from Carnegie. TIAA, now the major pension system of higher education in the US, was the first portable pension plan, allowing participants to move between institutions without losing retirement benefits and offering a fixed annuity. But the fund kept requiring cash from the foundation until 1947.

In 1952 CEO William Greenough pioneered the first variable annuity, based on common stock investments, and established the College Retirement Equities Fund (CREF) to offer it. Designed to supplement TIAA's fixed-dollar annuity, CREF invested participants' premiums in stocks. CREF, like TIAA, was subject to New York insurance regulation but not SEC regulation.

In the 1950s TIAA led the fight for Social Security benefits for university employees and began offering group total disability coverage (1957) and group life insurance (1958).

In 1971 TIAA–CREF established The Common Fund to help colleges boost investment returns from their endowments; TIAA went on to help manage endowments. In 1972 TIAA facilitated the establishment of the Investor Responsibility Research Center, which provides objective information on making socially responsible investments.

For 70 years TIAA–CREF members had no way to exit the system other than retirement. Members had only 2 investment choices: stocks through CREF or a one-way transfer into TIAA's long-term bond, real estate, and mortgage accounts. In the 1980s CREF indexed its funds to the S&P average. By the 1987 stock crash, the organization had one million members, many of whom wanted protection from stock market fluctuations and more investment options. In 1988 CREF added a money market fund, but this required SEC oversight, and the SEC required complete transferability, even outside of TIAA–CREF.

Since transferability made TIAA–CREF vulnerable to competition, it began to add investment options: the TIAA Interest Payment Retirement Option, CREF Bond Market and Social Choice (for politically correct investing) accounts, and a Global Equities, Growth, and Equity Index accounts. It expanded life eligibility to public school teachers and staff and began offering long-term care plans.

With about 40% of its investments in mortgages real estate, TIAA has been somewhat affected by the problems of the commercial real estate sector, but less so than other insurers because of its policy of direct investment.

In 1993 Chairman and CEO Clifton F. Wharton resigned his post after being named US deputy secretary of state.

HOW MUCH

	9-Year Growth	1984	1985	1986	1987	1988	1989	1990	1991	1992	1993
TIAA assets ($ mil.)	15.0%	19,205	23,159	27,887	33,210	38,631	44,374	49,894	55,576	61,777	67,483
TIAA sales ($ mil.)	9.4%	4,643	5,774	6,839	7,735	8,414	9,046	9,370	10,067	10,300	10,400
TIAA net income ($ mil.)	11.2%	1,956	2,472	3,032	3,375	3,778	4,145	4,473	4,672	5,060	5,074
Income as % of assets	—	10.2%	10.7%	10.9%	10.2%	9.8%	9.3%	9.0%	8.4%	8.2%	7.5%
CREF assets ($ mil.)	15.7%	16,308	21,651	26,191	25,510	31,700	39,515	38,055	48,450	52,064	60,737
Employees	5.8%	2,400	2,600	2,800	3,200	3,500	3,500	3,700	3,800	3,800	4,000

1993 Year-end:
TIAA only
Equity as % of assets: 7.1%
Sales (mil.): $11,900

TIAA Assets ($ mil.) 1984–93

Nonprofit organization
Fiscal year ends: December 31

WHO

Chairman and CEO: John H. Biggs
President and COO: Thomas W. Jones
EVP Finance and Planning: Richard L. Gibbs
EVP Law and General Counsel: Charles H. Stamm
EVP TIAA Investments: J. Daniel Lee, Jr.
EVP CREF Investments: James S. Martin
EVP External Affairs: Don W. Harrell
EVP Human Resources: Matina S. Horner
Auditors: Deloitte & Touche

WHERE

HQ: Teachers Insurance and Annuity Association–College Retirement Equities Fund, 730 Third Ave., New York, NY 10017-3206
Phone: 212-490-9000
Fax: 212-916-6231 (chairman's office)

TIAA–CREF is licensed in 33 states, is exempt from licensing in 17 states, and is licensed in Canada.

WHAT

	1993 TIAA Assets	
	$ mil.	% of total
Cash & equivalents	1,516	2
US, Canadian & other government bonds	1,810	2
Utility bonds	7,119	11
Corporate bonds	18,032	27
Mortgage- & asset-backed securities	9,917	15
Stocks	299	—
Mortgage loans	20,035	30
Real estate	7,093	11
Other	1,662	2
Total	**67,483**	**100**

	1993 CREF Assets	
	$ mil.	% of total
Stock Account	55,319	91
Money Market Account	2,576	5
Bond Market Account	620	1
Social Choice Account	713	1
Stock Account	1,509	2
Total	**60,737**	**100**

TIAA Insurance Products
Group life insurance
Group total disability insurance
Individual life insurance
Long-term care insurance
Retirement and group retirement annuities

CREF Investment Accounts
Bond Market Account
Global Equities Account
Money Market Account
Social Choice Account
Stock Account

KEY COMPETITORS

Aetna
American Express
Berkshire Hathaway
Chubb
CIGNA
Equitable
Fleet
FMR
John Hancock
Kemper
Loews
MassMutual
Merrill Lynch
MetLife
New York Life
Northwestern Mutual
Prudential
T. Rowe Price
Transamerica
Travelers
USAA

TEAMSTERS

RANK: N/R

OVERVIEW

Based in Washington, DC, the International Brotherhood of Teamsters is the nation's largest and most diverse labor union. With approximately 1.4 million members, the Teamsters represent truckers, United Parcel Service workers (UPS is the union's largest employer, with 165,000 members), warehouse employees, cab drivers, airline workers, and factory and hospital employees.

The Teamsters have 620 local chapters in the US and Canada. The union's political action committee (DRIVE) lobbies federal and state lawmakers on such issues as striker replacement, foreign trade and health care.

Ronald Carey, the first president elected directly by the rank and file, has sought to reform the union, which has been plagued with corruption and links to organized crime for over 40 years. Carey has named trustees to oversee mismanaged locals, sold the union's limos and 5 jets, and cut his own salary. Still his reign has been tumultuous.

Members rejected Carey's proposal to hike dues despite his insistence that the general fund could dry up by 1995. Since 1991 the union has been spending far more than it has been taking in. Carey has denied charges by foes that he once had ties to "the mob." Rivals have questioned how Carey, who has lived in a modest duplex for 36 years, bought condos in Florida and Arizona in the 1980s with only his $45,000 salary as head of a New York City local.

WHEN

In 1903, 2 rival team-driver unions, the Drivers International Union and the Teamsters National Union, merged to form the International Brotherhood of Teamsters. Led by Cornelius Shea, the Teamsters established headquarters in Indianapolis.

Daniel Tobin (president for 45 years from 1907) demanded that union locals obtain executive approval before striking. Membership expanded from the team-driver base, prompting the union to add Chauffeurs, Stablemen, and Helpers to its name (1909).

Following the first transcontinental delivery by motor truck (1912), the Teamster deliverymen traded their horses for trucks. The union then recruited food processing, brewery, farm, and other workers to augment Teamster effectiveness during strikes; jurisdictional disputes with other unions soon became a Teamster trademark. In 1920 the Teamsters joined the American Federation of Labor.

Until the Depression era the Teamsters were still a relatively small union (about 100,000 members) of predominantly in-city deliverymen. Then a Teamster Trotskyite from Minneapolis, Farrell Dobbs, organized the famous Minneapolis strikes in 1934 to protest local management's refusal to allow the workers to unionize. Workers clashed with police and National Guard units for 11 days before management conceded to the workers' demands. The strikes demonstrated the potential strength of unions, and Teamsters membership swelled. Although union power ebbed during WWII, the Teamsters continued to grow. In 1953 the union moved its headquarters to Washington, DC.

The AFL–CIO expelled the Teamsters in 1957 when its ties to "the mob" became public during a US Senate investigation. New Teamsters boss Jimmy Hoffa eluded indictment and took advantage of America's growing dependence on trucking to negotiate the powerful National Master Freight Agreement (1964). Hoffa organized industrial workers and added enticements such as medical programs and a strong political voice (DRIVE, 1963). Hoffa also used a union pension fund to make mob-connected loans. He was later convicted of jury tampering and sent to prison. In 1975, after his release, Hoffa disappeared.

The Teamsters rejoined the AFL–CIO in 1987. The union settled a 1988 lawsuit filed by the Justice Department's antiracketeering forces by agreeing to allow government appointees to discipline corrupt union leaders, help run the union, and oversee its elections.

In 1991 Ronald Carey's election with 48.5% of the vote seemed to portend real changes for the union. However, membership dropped 40,000 in both 1991 and 1992, resulting in loss of income. In 1993 Carey led negotiations with UPS for a new 4-year contract, which gave UPS Teamsters a 3% wage hike. In 1994, however, the Teamsters struck UPS after the company lifted its weight limit for packages from 70 to 150 pounds. The one-day strike disrupted deliveries, and UPS sued the union for $50 million. Also in 1994, 70,000 Teamsters struck 22 US freight carriers for 24 days.

HOW MUCH

	Annual Growth	1984	1985	1986	1987	1988	1989	1990	1991	1992	1993
Revenues ($ mil.)	(6.2%)	—	—	—	—	—	—	—	83	78	74
Expenses ($ mil.)	1.1%	—	—	—	—	—	—	—	123	136	126
Assets ($ mil.)	(6.1%)	194	199	199	198	194	192	207	176	138	110
Membership (thou.)	4.8%	—	—	—	—	—	1,161	1,419[1]	1,379	1,339[1]	1,400[1]

Assets ($ mil.) 1984–93

[1]Estimated

Labor union
Fiscal year ends: December 31

WHO

General President: Ronald Carey, $150,000 pay
General Secretary-Treasurer: Tom Sever
General Counsel: Richard Gilberg
Auditors: Grant Thornton

WHERE

HQ: International Brotherhood of Teamsters, 25 Louisiana Ave. NW, Washington, DC 20001
Phone: 202-624-6800
Fax: 202-624-6918

The Teamsters have 620 local unions in the US and Canada. The union also maintains 43 joint councils and 10 state conferences to provide an additional level of administrative support.

State Conferences
Arkansas-Oklahoma Conference
Georgia-Florida Conference
Illinois Conference
Indiana Conference
Iowa Conference
Kentucky–West Virginia Conference
Missouri-Kansas Conference
Ohio Conference
Pennsylvania Conference
Texas Conference

WHAT

	1993 Revenue $ mil.	% of total
Dues	68	92
Investment income	5	7
Initiation fees & other sources	1	1
Total	**74**	**100**

	1993 Expenses $ mil.	% of total
Out-of-work benefits	29	23
Divisional & departmental	21	17
Administrative, office & general expenses	17	13
Teamster Affiliates Pension	16	13
Affiliation fees	7	6
Organizing expenses	6	5
National headquarters building	5	4
Civil RICO	4	3
Legal fees, judgments, suits & settlements	4	3
Per capita area conferences	4	3
Legislative & political education	3	2
Magazine	3	2
Post-retirement benefits	3	2
Communications	2	2
Officers & employees retirement	2	2
Total	**126**	**100**

Trade Divisions
Airline Division
Automotive, Petroleum, and Allied Trades Division
Building Material and Construction Division
Freight Division
Household Goods, Moving and Storage Trade Division
Industrial Trade Division
Laundry Division
Newspaper Drivers Division
Public Employees' Trade Division
Trade-Show and Movie-Making Trade Division
Warehouse Division

TENNESSEE VALLEY AUTHORITY

RANK: 35

OVERVIEW

Headquartered in Knoxville, Tennessee, the Tennessee Valley Authority (TVA) is a federally owned corporation set up by Congress as part of the New Deal to provide power and nonpower programs to the Tennessee River Valley. Nonpower programs, including flood control and river management, agricultural and industrial development, and forestry services, are funded primarily by congressional appropriations ($135 million in 1993).

The TVA's power programs, although originally financed by congressional appropriations, are now required to be self-supporting. The TVA supplies electricity to power companies serving 7 million people in an 80,000-square-mile region covering Tennessee and parts of Alabama, Georgia, Kentucky, Mississippi, North Carolina, and Virginia through a power network consisting of nuclear, coal-fired, and hydroelectric plants.

The agency is run by a 3-member board, appointed by the US president and approved by the Senate. Facing mounting debt brought on, in part, by an expensive foray into nuclear power (estimated cost: $20 billion), the TVA has cut employment by 14,000 since 1987.

WHEN

In 1924 the Army Corps of Engineers completed construction (begun in 1918) of the Wilson Dam on the Tennessee River at Muscles Shoals, Alabama. The dam was built to provide power for 2 nitrate plants that were to manufacture munitions for WWI. With the war long since ended, the question of what to do with the facilities became a favorite political football during the 1920s.

Senator George Norris, head of the Senate Committee on Agriculture and Forestry, got 2 bills to create a regional federal agency to take control of the plants and to manage the waterways of the Tennessee Valley through Congress (1928 and 1931), but both were vetoed. It wasn't until 1933, after Franklin Roosevelt became president, that the Tennessee Valley Authority was created by an act of Congress. Seen by New Dealers as a way to revitalize the economy of the region, the TVA's goals included providing flood control, improving navigation, and generating electricity.

From the beginning the TVA faced opposition. Power companies claimed the agency was unconstitutional, but in 1939 a special 3-judge federal court ruled against them. By 1939 the agency had 5 hydroelectric facilities in operation and 5 others under construction. That same year the TVA bought the Tennessee Electric Power Company's power plants and transmission lines.

During the 1940s the TVA supplied power for the war effort, including the Manhattan Project in Oak Ridge, Tennessee. Between 1945 and 1950 power usage in the Tennessee Valley nearly doubled as postwar industries sprang up in the region, but even though it continued to add dams to provide hydroelectric power, it couldn't keep up with demand, so in 1949 it began construction of its first coal-fired plant.

The TVA's move into coal-fired power generation brought more controversy as some members of Congress questioned whether the new (nonhydroelectric) plants fit in with the agency's mission. In 1955 a task force headed by former President Herbert Hoover recommended the TVA be dissolved. The agency survived that salvo but saw its funding cut back.

In 1959 the TVA Act was amended so that the TVA could sell bonds. It no longer received government appropriations and was also required to pay back the funds it had received from the government.

During the 1960s the TVA passed 2 million in electric customers. As its customer base grew, it continued to add generating capacity. In 1967 it began construction of its first nuclear plant, Browns Ferry in Alabama. The agency undertook an ambitious nuclear program, planning a total of 17 units. However, costs skyrocketed, forcing the TVA to raise rates and cut maintenance to its coal-burning plants, which led to breakdowns. Construction on 8 of the units was canceled, and in 1985, 5 reactors that had come on-line had to be shut down because of safety concerns.

In 1988 former auto industry executive Marvin Runyon was appointed chairman of the agency. Nicknamed "Carvin'" Marvin, he eliminated layers of management, sold 3 airplanes, and got rid of peripheral businesses, saving $400 million a year. Runyon left the TVA to become US postmaster general in 1992. He was replaced by Craven Crowell in 1993. In 1994 the White House budget office began a review to see if the TVA was too close to its $30 billion debt ceiling set by Congress.

US government-owned corporation
Fiscal year ends: September 30

WHO

Chairman: Craven Crowell, $123,100 pay
Director: William H. Kennoy, $115,700 pay
Director: Johnny H. Hayes, $115,700 pay
President, Generating Group: Oliver D. Kingsley, Jr.
President, Customer Group: Mary Sharpe Hayes
President, Resource Group: Norman A. Zigrossi
EVP and CFO: William F. Malec
EVP: Mary Cartwright
SVP and General Counsel: Edward S. Christenbury
Employment Services Manager: Kathleen Branson
Auditors: Coopers & Lybrand

WHERE

HQ: 400 W. Summit Hill Dr., Knoxville, TN 37902-1415
Phone: 615-632-2101
Fax: 615-632-6783

The Tennessee Valley Authority operates through 160 municipal and cooperative power distributors in 7 states.

Major Substations

- Alcoa SW Sta. (TN)
- Bowling Green (KY)
- Charleston (TN)
- Clarksville (TN)
- Columbia (TN)
- Columbus (MS)
- Cordova (TN)
- Corinth (MS)
- Covington (TN)
- Davidson (TN)
- Decatur (AL)
- Franklin (KY)
- Franklin (TN)
- Freeport (TN)
- Harriman (TN)
- Holly Springs (MS)
- Jackson (TN)
- Lawrenceburg (TN)
- Lebanon (TN)
- Madison (AL)
- Manchester (TN)
- Marshall (KY)
- Maury (TN)
- Mayfield (KY)
- McMinnville (TN)
- Milan (TN)
- Montgomery (TN)
- Morristown (TN)
- Murfreesboro (TN)
- North Nashville (TN)
- Philadelphia (MS)
- Phipps Bend (TN)
- Pigeon Forge (TN)
- Radnor (TN)
- Roane (TN)
- Rockwood (TN)
- Shelby (TN)
- Starkville (MS)
- Sullivan (TN)
- Trinity (AL)
- Tupelo (MS)
- Union (MS)
- Volunteer (TN)
- Weakley (TN)
- West Nashville (TN)
- West Point (MS)
- Wilson (TN)

WHAT

	1993 Power Generation
	% of total
Coal	76
Hydro	15
Nuclear	9
Total	**100**

	1993 Electricity Sales	
	$ mil.	% of total
Municipalities & cooperatives	4,479	85
Federal agencies	254	5
Industries	472	9
Other	71	1
Total	**5,276**	**100**

Nonpower Programs

- Coal gasification
- Land Between the Lakes (national outdoor recreation center in Kentucky and Tennessee)
- National Fertilizer and Environmental Research Center
- Rural development
- Water quality programs

HOW MUCH

	Annual Growth	1984	1985	1986	1987	1988	1989	1990	1991	1992	1993
Sales ($ mil.)	1.9%	4,453	4,547	4,639	5,156	5,322	5,287	5,339	5,136	5,065	5,276
Net income ($ mil.)	—	(134)	426	274	451	413	559	(387)	286	120	311
Income as % of sales	—	—	9.4%	5.9%	8.7%	7.8%	10.6%	—	5.6%	2.4%	5.9%
Employees	(6.6%)	35,213	33,238	31,189	33,031	30,131	26,700	28,392	24,870	19,493	18,974

1993 Year-end:
Debt ratio: 83.1%
Cash (mil.): $236
Current ratio: 0.30
Long-term debt (bil.): $21

Net Income ($ mil.) 1984–93

THRIFTY PAYLESS INC.

RANK: 42

OVERVIEW

The 2nd largest drugstore chain in the US, after Walgreen, and the largest on the West Coast, Thrifty PayLess was formed in 1994 when Los Angeles–based Thrifty Drugs and Oregon-based PayLess Drug Stores Northwest merged. TCH Corp., Thrifty's parent, bought PayLess from Kmart for $595 million in cash, $100 million in debt securities, and a stake in the new holding company, Thrifty PayLess Holdings. Investment firm Leonard Green & Partners owns approximately 53% of the company's stock, and Kmart owns the rest.

Based in Wilsonville, Oregon, Thrifty PayLess has nearly 1,100 stores, two combined revenues of $4.6 billion, and employs 30,000 people.

The new company's 2 drug chains continue to operate under their respective names in their markets. Thrifty PayLess also operates Bi-Mart, a discount membership drug and general merchandise chain that was formerly part of Thrifty's holdings. The company plans to close some of its stores as part of its reorganization, and it is concentrating on developing its pharmacy and 3rd-party drug programs.

Private company
Fiscal year ends: Last Saturday in September

WHO

President and CEO: Tim R. McAlear
SEVP: Gordon Barker
EVP & CFO: Dave Jessick
EVP Merchandising and Marketing: Gary Rocheleau
EVP Store Operations: Ken Flynn
SVP Human Resources: Jeannette Stone
Auditor:

WHERE

HQ: 9275 SW Peyton Ln., Wilsonville, OR 97070
Phone: 503-682-4100
Fax: 503-685-6140

Thrifty PayLess operates 576 PayLess Drug Stores in Alaska, Arizona, California, Colorado, Hawaii, Idaho, Nevada, Oregon, Utah, Washington, and Wyoming; 492 Thrifty Drugs in California; and 42 Bi-Mart stores in Oregon and Washington.

WHAT

Retail Operations
Bi-Mart (discount membership store)
PayLess Drug Stores
Thrifty Drugs

KEY COMPETITORS

A and H Stores
Albertson's
American Stores
Baxter
Bill's Drugs
Circle K
Fred Meyer
Gavin Herbert
Kmart
Kroger
Longs
McKesson
Medi-Mail
Melville
Merck
J. C. Penney
Price/Costco
Publix
Safeway
Southland
Vons
Walgreen
Wal-Mart
Whole Foods Market
Winn Dixie

WHEN

In 1919 Harry and Robert Borun and their brother-in-law, Norman Levin, opened a wholesale drug business called Borun Brothers. In 1929, with many of their retail customers struggling, they decided to move into retailing. That year the company opened its first Thrifty Cut Rate drugstore in Los Angeles. To draw customers to its stores, the company heavily advertised loss leaders. Thrifty Cut Rate became famous for its 29-cent chicken dinners, and the company grew rapidly. By the 1940s Thrifty Cut Rate had 17 stores in the Los Angeles area and 58 total.

During the 1950s, as strip shopping centers began to dot the Southern California landscape, the company moved into the super drugstore retailing category. Led by CEO Leonard Straus, Thrifty signed long-term leases at low rates for large stores and offered broad merchandise lines. Between 1952 and 1966 Thrifty added nearly 200 stores.

However, competition from other discount retailers began to take its toll. Rather than open new stores, Straus focused on remodeling Thrifty's existing stores. The process moved slowly because it was financed on a pay-as-you-go basis from retained earnings. Thrifty also began a diversification into sporting goods.

In 1986 Thrifty was acquired by Pacific Lighting Corporation (renamed Pacific Enterprises, 1988). Pacific paid over $800 million in stock for Thrifty's 594 Thrifty Drug Stores and 94 Big 5 Sporting Goods stores. Between 1986 and 1989 Thrifty acquired 12 retailers, including 110 Pay 'n Save drugstores and 37 Bi-Mart discount memberships stores.

However, Thrifty began struggling as competition and the recession cut into its profits. It had also shifted its focus away from pharmacy and health care and was instead developing a prototype modeled after specialty boutiques. In 1991 Bill Yingling was named CEO. He concentrated on rebuilding the drug chain's image as a neighborhood pharmacy.

In 1992, 4 Thrifty stores were burned to the ground and another 19 were looted during the Los Angeles riots, causing $8–10 million in damage. That same year, as part of a strategy to focus on its utility business, Pacific Enterprises sold Thrifty to Leonard Green & Partners and Thrifty's management.

In late 1993 Thrifty announced plans to merge with PayLess Drug Stores Northwest. PayLess was founded by Peyton Hawes and William Armitage in 1939, when the 2 acquired 5 drugstores in Washington and Oregon. The company concentrated on building a chain in the Northwest's smaller towns. By 1960 it had 13 stores. PayLess went public in 1967.

The company began a rapid expansion during the late 1960s and 1970s, acquiring House of Values (1969) and Value Giant (1976), but its biggest acquisition came when it won a battle with Jewel to buy Pay Less Drug Stores of California (an unrelated company) in 1980, adding 60 stores to boost its total to 149.

In 1985, as part of a diversification strategy, Kmart bought PayLess for about $500 million. PayLess bought 25 Osco stores in Washington and Idaho in 1987 and 52 Osco stores in Colorado, Utah, and Wyoming in 1991.

In 1992, 2 months before it sold Thrifty to Leonard Green's group, Pacific Enterprises sold 124 Pay 'n Save drugstores to PayLess. In 1994 Tim McAlear, CEO of PayLess, was named CEO of Thrifty PayLess.

HOW MUCH

	Annual Growth	1984	1985	1986	1987	1988	1989	1990	1991	1992	1993
Thrifty sales ($ mil.)	(11.7%)	—	—	—	—	—	—	—	2,715	2,661	2,119
PayLess sales ($ mil.)[1]	16.4%	—	—	—	—	—	—	1,480	1,642	1,892	2,335
PayLess net income ($ mil.)[1]	12.1%	—	—	—	—	—	—	38	47	53	64
PayLess income as % of sales[1]	—	—	—	—	—	—	—	2.6%	2.8%	2.8%	2.8%

PayLess Sales ($ mil.) 1990–93

2,500
2,000
1,500
1,000
500
0

[1]End-of-January fiscal year.

TLC BEATRICE INTERNATIONAL

RANK: 154

OVERVIEW

TLC Beatrice International Holdings is an international food distribution and grocery manufacturing company operating primarily in Western Europe, although headquartered in New York City. Business is conducted through 19 operating companies, with sales in over 20 countries, and manufacturing facilities in 8. Founder, chairman, CEO, and principal stockholder Reginald F. Lewis, at 50, died of brain cancer in 1993.

The company's food distribution holdings include Baud, which distributes products to nearly 500 independent grocers operating in the Paris area under the names Franprix and Leader Price. In addition, TLC Beatrice owns and operates 35 Franprix and 49 Leader Price stores (featuring limited selection, lower prices, and private label goods) in France.

The grocery products segment makes ice cream, dairy, and dessert products under names including La Menorquina (Spain), Interglas (Canary Islands), Sanson (Italy), Artic (Belgium and France), and Premier Is (Denmark). The Tayto subsidiary is the leader in the Irish potato chip market, and TLC Beatrice bottles soft drinks under several names.

Reginald Lewis's widow, Loida Nicolas Lewis, a lawyer and the majority shareholder (55%) of TLC Beatrice, was named chairman in 1994. The remaining 45% is held by various individuals and investment groups.

WHEN

Reginald F. Lewis played quarterback for Virginia State in the mid-1960s and hoped for a pro career. After a shoulder injury ended his future in sports, Lewis concentrated on his studies and graduated from Harvard Law School in 1968. He worked briefly for the New York law firm of Paul, Weiss, Rifkind, Wharton & Garrison but left in 1970 to form Lewis and Clarkson, a firm specializing in providing venture capital to growing companies. Lewis then decided to move into the world of high finance. In 1983 he started TLC Group as a holding company.

The first move by TLC Group was the purchase of McCall Pattern Company for $24.5 million (only $1 million of which was Lewis's money; the rest was borrowed) in 1984. McCall, a Manhattan, Kansas–based sewing pattern company founded in 1871, had stagnated, but under TLC sales increased from $6.5 million in 1984 to $14 million in 1986 (the 2 most profitable years of the company's history despite a declining market for home sewing products). Lewis raised the company's net worth by shuffling assets (he bought McCall's Manhattan factory through an affiliate and leased it back to the company) and was able to raise an additional $22 million through the bond market. At the end of 1986, TLC sold McCall to Britain's John Crowther Group for $95 million ($63 million cash and $32 million of assumed debt) — a return of 9,000%.

In 1987 the breakup of Beatrice by Donald Kelly and the buyout firm of Kohlberg Kravis Roberts provided Lewis with another opportunity. Lewis arranged for a $495 million junk bond financing through Drexel Burnham Lambert's Michael Milken and purchased the international holdings of Beatrice (Beatrice International Companies) for $985 million. Lewis assumed the positions of chairman and CEO of Beatrice International. The acquisition increased TLC's sales from $63 million in 1986 to almost $1.5 billion in 1987.

Soon after the Beatrice purchase, TLC changed its name to TLC (rumored to stand for The Lewis Company) Beatrice International Holdings. Lewis retained his position as head of the company and, to pay down the acquisition debt, began selling off assets, including operations in Latin America and Canada.

In 1992 the company began operating Boissons du Monde, which distributes Anheuser-Busch's BUD beer and other beverages to French supermarkets. In 1993 a preliminary prospectus to sell $150 million in 10-year notes revealed a weakening financial performance (operating profits down 52% in 1992).

Shortly before his death Lewis handpicked his successor, half-brother Jean S. Fugett, Jr., a lawyer and former tight end for the Washington Redskins and Dallas Cowboys. After just a year Fugett was replaced as chairman by Loida Nicolas Lewis, and a search began for a CEO.

In 1994 the company sold its Choky powdered drinks division (based in France) to pay down debt.

HOW MUCH

	Annual Growth	1984	1985	1986	1987	1988	1989	1990	1991	1992	1993
Sales ($ mil.)	2.3%	—	—	—	1,446	1,639	1,141	1,496	1,542	1,664	1,656
Net income ($ mil.)	(45.7)	—	—	—	39	(8)	16	46	51	(17)	1
Income as % of sales	—	—	—	—	2.7%	—	1.4%	3.0%	3.3%	—	0.1%
Employees	(6.4%)	—	—	—	7,000	7,300	4,500	4,500	5,000	4,700	4,700

Net Income ($ mil.) 1987–93

Private company
Fiscal year ends: December 31

WHO

Chairman: Loida Nicolas Lewis
EVP Finance and CFO: John R. Ranelli, age 47
EVP Legal Affairs: Albert M. Fenster, age 41
EVP Operations: Dennis P. Jones, age 41
SVP Strategic Planning and Project Finance: David A. Guarino, age 29
SVP, General Counsel, and Secretary: W. Kevin Wright, age 39
VP (Personnel): Rene S. Meily, age 39
Auditors: Deloitte & Touche

WHERE

HQ: TLC Beatrice International Holdings, Inc., 9 West 57th St., New York, NY 10019
Phone: 212-756-8900
Fax: 212-888-3093

The company operates principally in Western Europe.

WHAT

Food Distribution Operations
Boissons du Monde (distributes Anheuser-Busch's BUD beer, France)
Dairyworld (dairy products broker, Switzerland)
Distribution Leader Price (grocery wholesaler, France)
Etablissements Baud (supplies Franprix grocery stores, France)
Minimarché Group (operates Franprix and Leader Price grocery stores, France)
Retail Leader Price (operates Leader Price grocery stores, France)
Sodialim (institutional distribution of dry grocery and baked goods, France)

Grocery Products Operations
Artic and Artigel (ice cream and desserts, Europe)
Bireley's (beverages, Thailand)
Gelati Sanson (ice cream and desserts, Italy)
Interglas (ice cream, Canary Islands)
La Menorquina (ice cream and desserts, Spain)
Premier Is (ice cream, Denmark)
Sunco (beverages, Belgium)
Tayto (potato chips and snacks, Ireland)
Winters (beverages, the Netherlands)

KEY COMPETITORS

Allied-Lyons
American Brands
Borden
Cadbury Schweppes
Chiquita Brands
Coca-Cola
CPC
Dannon
Dole
General Mills
Grand Metropolitan
John Labatt
Mars
Nestlé
PepsiCo
Philip Morris
Sara Lee
Source Perrier
Unilever

TRUMP ORGANIZATION

RANK: 113

OVERVIEW

"When you're negotiating with people who've been promised the world a half dozen times and gotten nothing, credibility is critical." So spake Donald Trump in his *Art of the Deal* (1987). This was when Trump could pick up a phone and get financing for a project on the strength of his name alone. In addition to acquiring equity interests in his projects, generally for no personal investment, Trump received management fees for his projects.

By the mid–1980s Trump was everywhere. He owned the Plaza Hotel, 3 Atlantic City casinos, the Eastern air shuttle, the world's largest private yacht (formerly owned by Adnan Khashoggi), a mansion in Palm Beach, and part of the Grand Hyatt Hotel in Manhattan and Alexander's Department Store.

As the 1990s dawned, people finally looked at his balance sheet, finding it loaded with debt that could not be serviced from cash flow. Bankruptcies followed, from which Trump emerged focused on gambling and debt repayment. Simultaneously, his marriage to the flamboyant Ivana broke up in a splash of publicity. In 1993 Trump married Marla Maples, mother of his daughter Tiffany.

In 1994 Trump sought a comeback, announcing his intentions to proceed with the development of a 75-acre tract along the Hudson River at 59th Street. But his future remained in doubt when it was announced that Citibank and other creditors were exploring the possibility of selling the Plaza Hotel, as allowed under their settlement agreement.

WHEN

Donald Trump was the 2nd-to-last of 5 children born to Fred Trump, a successful builder in Queens and Brooklyn, New York, and his wife, Mary. Donald was an aggressive boy who claims to have blackened a teacher's eye in 2nd grade. When he was 13 his parents sent him to New York Military Academy. Trump graduated from the Wharton School of Finance in 1968.

His first job concerned a 1,200-unit foreclosed apartment building in Cincinnati with a 75% vacancy rate. Fred Trump bought it for $6 million with no money down and had Donald turn it around.

Seeing his father's experience with low-cost housing and managing the Cincinnati job gave Donald a distaste for the nonaffluent. He wanted to get out of the boroughs and into Manhattan to meet all the right people.

In 1973 Trump, working as the Trump Organization, which had no legal existence, contacted Victor Palmieri, who was selling Penn Central Railroad's real estate assets. In 1974 Trump took options on 2 Hudson River sites, at 34th and 59th Streets, for no money down. He began lobbying the city to finance his construction of a convention center at 34th Street.

The center was built, but not by Trump. He received about $800,000 in connection with the center, but of greater importance was the publicity he received.

Working with Palmieri, he got control of a site near Grand Central Station. With the support of the Pritzker family and financing from Equitable Life and the Bowery Savings Bank, Trump began his first Manhattan job, the Grand Hyatt Hotel, in which he had a 49% interest with no money down.

Trump was launched. His next project, Fifth Avenue's Trump Tower, was built under a tax abatement program for moderate-income housing. Yet his market was "the wealthy Italian with the beautiful wife and the red Ferrari." "The Donald" had his own beautiful wife, "top fashion model" Ivana.

In the mid-1980s Trump joined with Holiday Inn, for no money down, to build a casino (the Trump Plaza), using public issue bonds. He bought out Holiday Inn's interest and then did the unthinkable: he personally guaranteed a loan to acquire the Trump Castle from Hilton. Trump then began a battle with Merv Griffin for Resorts International. When the dust cleared, Griffin had Resorts International and Trump had the unfinished Taj Mahal, the world's largest casino. Trump overspent, vastly exceeding cost estimates, and made it the world's glitziest. Returning to Manhattan, Trump bought the Plaza Hotel, for which he had always had great affection, in 1988.

Back in Atlantic City, the Taj was a sensation, but it cannibalized business from Trump's other casinos and still could not make interest payments to its bondholders. Trump took the Taj into Chapter 11 bankruptcy, from which he emerged in nominal control. The other casinos also flirted with default. In 1990 Trump's 70 creditor banks consolidated and restructured his debt and put him on a monthly allowance. In 1991 they reduced his personal recourse debt to $155 million. Since then he has worked to reduce that debt and regain his credibility so that he can go on to even greater success.

HOW MUCH

	Annual Growth	1983	1984	1985	1986	1987	1988	1989	1990	1991	1992
Estimated sales ($ mil.)	10.7%	—	—	1,000	850	700	1,359	1,494	1,340	1,400	2,037
Employees	1.0%	—	—	14,000	14,000	20,000	25,000	25,000	20,000	17,000	15,000

Estimated Sales ($ mil.) 1985–1992

Private company
Fiscal year ends: December 31

WHO

Chairman: Donald J. Trump, age 48
President: Nicholas Ribis
VP Finance: John Burke

WHERE

HQ: 725 Fifth Ave., New York, NY 10022-2519
Phone: 212-832-2000
Fax: 212-935-0141

Plaza Hotel (51%, New York City)
Trump Castle casino (50%, Atlantic City, NJ)
Trump Plaza casino (Atlantic City, NJ)
Trump Regency Hotel (Atlantic City, NJ)
Trump Taj Mahal casino (50%, Atlantic City, NJ)
Trump Tower (New York City)

WHAT

	Primary Deals	
	Year	$ mil.
Grand Hyatt Hotel (49%)*	1979	100
Trump Tower	1982	190
Trump Plaza Hotel & Casino	1984	218
59th St. Railyard	1984	100
Trump Castle casino	1985	320
Mar-A-Lago	1985	8
Plaza Hotel	1988	408
Trump Princess*	1988	29
Trump Shuttle*	1989	365
Trump Taj Mahal	1989	230

* repossessed

	1993 Hotel Rooms	
	No. of rooms	% of total
Trump Taj Mahal	1,250	31
Plaza Hotel	896	23
Trump Castle	723	18
Trump Regency	563	14
Trump Plaza	556	14
Total	**3,988**	**100**

Operating Units
Land Corporation of California
Park South Co.
The Trump Corporation
Trump Development Co.
Trump Enterprises Inc.
Wembly Realty Inc.

KEY COMPETITORS

Bally
Bass
Carlson
Circus Circus
Four Seasons
Helmsley
Hilton
Hyatt
ITT
Lefrak
Lincoln Property
Loews
Marriott International
MGM Grand
Mashantucket Pequot Gaming
Olympia & York
Promus
Resorts International
Ritz-Carlton
Tishman Speyer
Zeckendorf

U-HAUL INTERNATIONAL, INC.

RANK: 278

U-HAUL

OVERVIEW

U-Haul International, based in Phoenix, was the pioneering company in the truck and trailer rental business. In recent years its market share has fallen behind that of Ryder.

The 13 battling Shoens (founder L. S. and his 12 children) own the company, which has 1,030 outlets and 10,400 franchisees. AMERCO, U-Haul's parent, was formed in 1969 to facilitate diversification into consumer rentals, self-storage facilities (#3 in the industry), real estate, and insurance (primarily to serve the company's own real estate holdings and insurance needs).

U-Haul's history in the 1980s was dominated by family infighting, which culminated in 1986 when several children combined to wrest control of the company from their other siblings and their father, who had distributed 94% of the company's stock to his children, retaining only 2% for himself, with the rest going to employees.

Family and management discord brought decreasing profits and delayed investment in capital improvements, particularly in the replacement of aging truck and trailer fleets. This is currently being remedied, but the company has been forced recently to seek outside investors. In 1993 the company made a public offering of $600 million in nonvoting stock and debt. A simultaneous increase in the proportion of stock owned by employees may shift the balance of control among various family factions.

Private company
Fiscal year ends: March 31

WHO

Chairman, President, and CEO: Edward J. (Joe) Shoen, age 44, $244,970 pay
EVP: Harry B. DeShong, Jr., age 44, $132,710 pay
VP: James P. Shoen, age 33, $211,017 pay
VP: John M. Dodds, age 56, $185,679 pay
Treasurer: Gary B. Horton, age 49
Secretary and General Counsel: Gary V. Kleinefelter, age 45
VP Human Resources: Dick Renckly
Auditors: Price Waterhouse

WHEN

Leonard Samuel (L. S.) Shoen earned his nickname, "Slick," as a poor kid trying to make a buck in the Great Depression.

L. S. started U-Haul after leaving the navy in 1945. He saw a niche serving long distance do-it-yourself movers who could not return a truck to its origin. L. S. bought used equipment and began years of travel, convincing gas station owners to act as agents. By the late 1950s U-Haul had over 250,000 rentals a year.

L. S. and his first wife, Anna Mary, who died in 1957, had 6 children, each of whom received nearly 10% of U-Haul's stock. In 1958 L. S. remarried and with his 2nd wife, Suzanne (19 years his junior), had 5 children, each of whom received lesser amounts of stock. It was not a happy household, rent by jealousy between siblings and dislike for the young stepmother, who was left alone with the children while L. S. traveled ceaselessly.

As the company kept growing in the 1960s, L. S. brought his sons into it by having them do maintenance work on the trailers.

By the early 1970s U-Haul had 14,000 outlets and business was booming. Then came the oil crunch of 1973. Many of U-Haul's outlets closed, and it was forced to open its own rental agencies. U-Haul also began facing competition from other truck and trailer rental companies, including Ryder and Jartran. U-Haul's market share began dropping to barely more than 50%.

Shoen's response was to use debt to diversify into general consumer rentals, locating agencies in more than 900 former Chrysler dealerships, which he bought outright. Profits dropped. During this time AMERCO established real estate and insurance subsidiaries.

Shoen's 2nd wife divorced him following the out-of-wedlock birth of his 12th child in 1977. After a brief marriage to the mother, they divorced, and he remarried again.

Meanwhile, L. S. had tapped his eldest son, Sam, to help plot the company's new course. In 1979, 2 younger sons, Joe and Mark, disapproving of their father's and brother's actions, left the company. Sam became president.

Earnings roller-coastered for the next few years. In 1986 Joe and Mark got the support of enough siblings to gain a voting majority and ousted their father and brother. L. S. and Sam almost regained control in 1988 but were outmaneuvered by Joe, who issued enough stock to loyal employees to shift the balance again. Then the family went to court. Annual meetings became slugfests. In 1990 Sam's wife was murdered in a professional-style hit in their home that is still unsolved.

Joe began to divest the consumer rental business and to upgrade U-Haul's fleet, reducing the fleet's average age from 11 years to 5, and to restructure AMERCO. This led to a 1991 loss. In the 1990s the company diversified into self-storage warehouses; a 1993 attempt to buy a majority interest in some real estate trusts managed by Shurgard, the #2 self-storage company, was rebuffed and withdrawn in early 1994.

WHERE

HQ: 2727 N. Central Ave., Phoenix, AZ 95004
Phone: 602-263-6011
Fax: 602-277-4329

	1993 Sales		1993 Operating Income	
	$ mil.	% of total	$ mil.	% of total
US	1,013	97	50	—
Canada	27	3	(1)	—
Total	**1,041**	**100**	**49**	**—**

WHAT

	1993 Sales		1993 Operating Income	
	$ mil.	% of total	$ mil.	% of total
U-Haul	888	78	860	80
AMERCO	21	2	9	1
Amerco Real Estate	64	5	63	6
Ponderosa	170	15	141	13
Adjustments	(102)	—	(81)	—
Total	**1,041**	**100**	**992**	**100**

	1993 U-Haul Sales	
	$ mil.	% of total
Rentals	743	84
Sales	145	16
Total	**888**	**100**

AMERCO Operating Units

- Amerco Real Estate
- Ponderosa Holdings, Inc.
  - Oxford Life Insurance Co.
  - Republic Western Insurance Co.
- U-Haul International, Inc.

HOW MUCH

	Annual Growth	1984	1985	1986	1987	1988	1989	1990	1991	1992	1993
Sales ($ mil.)	4.5%	—	731	783	820	795	928	951	987	972	1,041
Net income ($ mil.)	(2.9%)	42	—	9	2	—	42	18	(10)	21	32
Income as % of sales	—	—	—	—	—	—	4.5%	1.9%	—	2.1%	3.1%
Employees	(0.3%)	—	11,200	12,500	12,100	13,000	12,000	13,600	10,000	9,300	10,900

1993 Year-end:
Debt ratio: 59.2%
Return on equity: 22.3%
Cash (mil.): $21
Current ratio: —
Long-term debt (mil.): $571

Net Income ($ mil.) 1984–93

KEY COMPETITORS

Berkshire Hathaway
Budget Rent a Car
Chancellor
Hillenbrand
Mayflower Group
Norfolk Southern
Penske
PHH
Public Storage
Rollins Leasing
Ryder
Shurgard
Unigroup
UPS

UNIHEALTH AMERICA

RANK: 204

OVERVIEW

UniHealth is the 5th largest nonprofit health care organization in the US and the 2nd largest in the Los Angeles area (after Kaiser Permanente). Headquartered in Burbank, the company operates 11 hospitals with nearly 3,000 beds and approximately 4,000 doctors. Its other operations include CliniShare, a home health care service; ElderMed America, a senior medical service; and the UniHealth America Foundation, which conducts educational and research programs.

UniHealth also owns CareAmerica Health Plans, which serves more than 3,000 employer groups in Southern California, and 49% of publicly traded PacifiCare Health Systems. The 3rd largest HMO in California, PacifiCare also has operations in Oklahoma, Oregon, Texas, and Washington and serves 925,000 members.

In order to survive in the competitive Southern California market, UniHealth is looking for growth from its payor division, from its physician network, and from new product development. A proposed merger with Blue Shield of California to create a $6.5 billion managed-care company fell through, although the companies have not ruled out some sort of collaboration in the future.

UniHealth America

Nonprofit organization
Fiscal year ends: September 30

WHO

Chairman: David R. Carpenter
President and CEO: Terry Hartshorn, age 48
EVP and COO: Gary L. Leary
SVP and CFO: Eric S. Benveniste, age 45
SVP Medical Affairs: Edward C. Geehr
SVP Corporate Development: Dennis W. Strum
SVP Human Resources: Stanley M. Croonquist, Jr.
Auditors: Ernst & Young

WHERE

HQ: 4100 W. Alameda Ave., Burbank, CA 91505-4153
Phone: 818-566-6300
Fax: 818-566-7070

WHEN

UniHealth was formed by the 1988 merger of the Los Angeles area's 2 largest secular, nonprofit health systems: LHS Corp. (formerly Lutheran Hospital Society, founded in 1920), headquartered in Los Angeles, and HealthWest Foundation (founded in 1979), based in Woodland Hills. UniHealth's formation came as many hospitals and health care systems were joining together to weather increased competition and take advantage of government deregulation. The 2 systems hoped that by joining together they could compete more effectively for Los Angeles–area employers' and insurers' contracts by blanketing the region with care facilities.

HealthWest's operations included 9 hospitals, CareAmerica, ElderMed, and several home-care programs. LHS owned 5 hospitals and a majority interest in PacifiCare Health. Samuel Tibbitts, president of LHS and founder of PacifiCare Health, became the new company's chairman, and Paul Teslow, who had served as HealthWest's CEO, became UniHealth's CEO.

To reduce costs UniHealth cut its corporate staff by 125, saving $5 million annually. It also sold nonstrategic assets, including St. Luke's General Hospital in Bellingham, Washington; Pasadena Community Hospital; Golden Triangle Medical Center, a nursing home in Murrieta, California; and Morningside Hospital in Los Angeles. The new company spent $15 million to upgrade its computer system and earmarked $250 million for capital improvements.

In 1990 it launched QUEST, a program designed to improve the company's service by developing a database of statistics such as common diagnoses, death rates, lengths of stay, and return visits. Also in 1990 UniHealth created physician network UniMed America.

As part of its strategy to cover the Los Angeles area, UniHealth added 2 hospitals to its roster in 1991: Glendale Memorial Hospital and Health Center and San Gabriel Valley Medical Center.

In 1992 UniHealth signed a 5-year supply contract, estimated at more than $200 million, with Baxter Healthcare. The contract gave its hospitals access to Baxter's stockless inventory program, ValueLink, which provides daily delivery of medical supplies, allowing hospitals to reduce inventories. At the end of 1992 CEO Paul Teslow retired. He was replaced, in early 1993, by PacifiCare CEO Terry Hartshorn. Also in 1993 UniHealth sold 4% of Pacific Health, reducing its stake to 49%.

Continuing to look for ways to integrate its health care system, UniHealth bought Facey Medical Group, a 78-member multispecialty physicians group, for $8.9 million in 1993. In 1994 UniHealth announced plans to acquire the 70-physician multispecialty Harriman-Jones Medical Group for $19.1 million.

Also in 1994, to focus on its California market, UniHealth sold its New Jersey–based Meadowlands Hospital Medical Center. That same year CareAmerica bought C. E. Heath International Holdings' US workers' compensation business. David Carpenter, chairman and CEO of Transamerica, was named to replace Samuel Tibbitts as chairman of UniHealth after Tibbitts's death in 1994.

WHAT

Subsidiaries and Affiliates
Arroyo Seco Medical Group
Bellflower Medical Group
CareAmerica Health Plans
CaseCARE
CliniShare
ElderMed America
Facey Medical Group
Harriman Jones Medical Group
Hunington Provider Group
Medical Communication Networks, Inc.
Pacific Health Resources
Pacific Media Associates
PacifiCare Health Systems Inc. (49%)
PPO Alliance
UniHealth America Foundation
UniMed America
VertiHealth

Hospitals and Care Facilities
California Medical Center-Los Angeles
Glendale Memorial Hospital and Health Center
La Palma Intercommunity Hospital
Lindsay Hospital Medical Center
Long Beach Community Hospital
Martin Luther Hospital
Northridge Hospital Medical Center
San Gabriel Valley Medical Center
Santa Monica Hospital Medical Center
Valley Hospital Medical Center

HOW MUCH

	Annual Growth	1984	1985	1986	1987	1988	1989	1990	1991	1992	1993
Sales ($ mil.)	20.1%	—	—	—	—	—	626	704	878	1,141	1,303
Net income ($ mil.)	86.1%	—	—	—	—	—	5	40	19	61	60
Income as % of sales	—	—	—	—	—	—	0.8%	5.7%	2.2%	5.4%	4.6%
Employees	11.0%	—	—	—	—	—	7,500	7.859	8,950	10,978	11,367

1993 Year-end:
Debt ratio: 46.0%
Current ratio: 1.42
Long-term debt (mil.): $466

KEY COMPETITORS

Adventist Health System
Aetna
Blue Cross
Catholic Healthcare West
Chubb
CIGNA
Columbia/HCA Healthcare
Equitable
Foundation Health
Health Systems
John Hancock
Kaiser Foundation Health Plan
MassMutual
Maxicare
MetLife
National Medical
New York Life
Northwestern Mutual
Prudential
St. Joseph Health System
Sierra Health Services
Travelers

UNITED PARCEL SERVICE

RANK: 8

OVERVIEW

Although it still makes deliveries in its familiar chocolate-colored trucks, UPS is adding a few modern touches to hold off some hard-charging competitors. The world's #1 package delivery company, Atlanta-based UPS delivered nearly 3 billion packages and documents in 1993. But the loss of business to rivals such as Federal Express and Roadway Package System has inspired "Big Brown" to establish UPSnet, a cellular network covering the entire US, the first nationwide system of its kind. The system provides the company with instant tracking information.

UPS has been shifting its focus from the residential deliveries that originally fueled its growth toward the more profitable commercial business. It has won new business by creating customized shipping programs and by offering price breaks to corporate shippers.

Continuing to look overseas for new opportunities, UPS has expanded its air service to 185 countries (from 41 in 1988). However, its foreign operations still suffer, particularly in Europe, where recession has hurt profits. In 1993 overseas operations lost $267 million.

UPS stock is owned primarily by employees and their families and heirs. The company is noted for philanthropy and for 25 years has assigned managers to 30-day community service projects in poor neighborhoods.

Private company
Fiscal year ends: December 31

WHO

Chairman and CEO: Kent C. Nelson, age 56
EVP and COO: James P. Kelly, age 50
SVP, Treasurer, and CFO: Robert Clanin
SVP Legal and Regulatory: Joseph Moderow, age 45
SVP: Charles L. Schaffer
SVP Human Resources: John J. Kelley, age 58
Auditors: Deloitte & Touche

WHERE

HQ: United Parcel Service of America, Inc., 55 Glenlake Pkwy., Atlanta, GA 30328
Phone: 404-828-6000
Fax: 404-828-6593

UPS operates in over 185 countries and territories and owns and operates 128,000 vehicles.

Air Hub Locations

Cologne/Bonn, Germany
Dallas, TX
Hamilton, Ontario
Hong Kong
Louisville, KY
Miami, FL
Montreal, Quebec
Ontario, CA
Philadelphia, PA
Singapore

	Airports Served
US	391
Other countries	219
Total	**610**

	1993 Sales		1993 Operating Income	
	$ mil.	% of total	$ mil.	% of total
US	15,822	89	1,698	—
Other countries	1,960	11	(267)	—
Total	**17,782**	**100**	**1,431**	—

WHEN

Seattle teenagers Jim Casey and Claude Ryan started American Messenger Company, a telephone message service, in 1907. They were soon making small-parcel deliveries for local department stores and in 1913 changed the company's name to Merchants Parcel Delivery. By 1915 the company had 20 messengers and 2 important events had already occurred — Casey, who led the company for the next 47 years, had established a policy of manager-ownership, and Charlie Soderstrom (one of the 4 stockholders) had chosen the brown paint still used on company delivery trucks.

Service expanded outside Seattle in 1919 when Merchants Parcel bought Oakland-based Motor Parcel Delivery. Renamed United Parcel Service, the company by 1930 served residents in New York City (its headquarters from 1930 to 1975), Newark, and Greenwich.

UPS expanded small-package delivery to include addresses within a 150-mile radius of certain city centers, starting with Los Angeles in 1952. Expanding westward from the East Coast and eastward from the West, UPS slowly blanketed the US mainland by 1975.

In 1972 the US Postal Service, in an effort to improve its own public image, cited UPS as a competitor. Up to this time UPS had developed in relative obscurity, with most of its stock owned by managers, their families, heirs, or estates.

After moving to Greenwich in 1975, UPS expanded to Europe in 1976 with service to West Germany and in the late 1970s set up a base at Standiford Airfield in Louisville, Kentucky, to start an air express delivery service. By 1982 UPS Blue Label Air Service (now UPS 2nd Day Air) guaranteed delivery anywhere on the mainland US and Oahu, Hawaii, within 48 hours. Overnight service (UPS Next Day Air) began in 1982, expanding nationwide and to Puerto Rico by 1985. In the late 1980s, when UPS adopted the slogan "We run the tightest ship in the shipping business" for its first TV ad campaign, it was one of the US's most profitable transportation companies.

To ensure a market for its services, in 1990 UPS bought 9.5% (since upped to 14.8%) of Mail Boxes Etc., America's leading neighborhood mailing and business service center franchise. Also that year UPS expanded service into Eastern Europe and, with Japan's Yamato Transport, formed a joint venture (UniStar Air Cargo) to gain a foothold in the Japanese market. To cut costs UPS moved its headquarters from Greenwich to Atlanta in 1991.

To expand its presence in Europe, the company acquired Prost Transports (France) in 1991 and, in 1992, Carryfast (UK), Star Air Parcel (Austria), and Beemsterboer (the Netherlands). In 1993 UPS announced plans to spend $400 million to lower the noise levels of its fleet of 727-100s.

In 1994 UPS and the Teamsters traded lawsuits after the union staged a one-day strike to protest UPS's new per-package weight limit, raised from 70 to 150 pounds. UPS claimed the walkout cost it over $50 million.

WHAT

Major Subsidiaries and Affiliates

Mail Boxes Etc. (14.8%)
Martrac (refrigerated transport)
Roadnet Technologies (technological support)
II Morrow (technological support)
UniStar Air Cargo, Inc.
UPS Inventory Express
UPS Properties, Inc.
UPS Telecommunications (cellular network)
UPS Truck Leasing, Inc.
UPS Worldwide Logistics, Inc.

Selected Services

2nd Day Air
3 Day Select
Customs & brokerage
GroundSaver (package delivery)
GroundTrac (electronic tracking)
Hundredweight Service
Next Day Air
On Call Air Pickup

HOW MUCH

	Annual Growth	1984	1985	1986	1987	1988	1989	1990	1991	1992	1993
Sales ($ mil.)	11.2%	6,833	7,687	8,620	9,682	11,032	12,358	13,606	15,020	16,519	17,782
Net income ($ mil.)	6.1%	477	568	669	625	759	693	597	700	765	810
Income as % of sales	—	7.0%	7.4%	7.8%	6.5%	6.9%	5.6%	4.4%	4.7%	4.6%	4.6%
Earnings per share ($)	7.0%	—	—	—	—	—	1.07	0.95	1.14	1.29	1.40
Dividends per share ($)	1.0%	—	—	—	—	—	0.48	0.48	0.48	0.50	0.50
Book value per share ($)	5.6%	—	—	—	—	—	—	5.77	6.29	6.25	6.80
Employees	8.2%	141,000	152,400	168,200	191,600	219,400	237,700	246,800	256,000	267,000	286,000

1993 Year-end:
Debt ratio: 8.2%
Return on equity: 8.7%
Cash (mil.): $281
Current ratio: 1.00
Long-term debt (mil.): $852
No. of shares (mil.): 580
Total assets (mil.): $9,574

KEY COMPETITORS

Air Express International
Airborne Freight
American Freightways
American President
AMR
Consolidated Freightways
Continental Airlines
Delta
DHL
Federal Express
Harper Group
Heartland Express
KLM
Lufthansa
Northwest Airlines
Pittston
Qantas
Roadway
Ryder
SAS
Singapore Airlines
Skynet
UAL
USAir
US Postal Service

UNITED STATES POSTAL SERVICE

RANK: 2

OVERVIEW

Each day the United States Postal Service processes and delivers more than 550 million pieces of mail. The service is the biggest US government agency in the executive branch and boasts the nation's largest civilian work force. An 11-member board of governors sets policy, and a 5-member Postal Rate Commission recommends postage rates.

Competition from an increasing number of communication services and devices (fax, telephone, overnight services, electronic transfers, video shopping, and telemarketing) contributed to losses of more than $4.6 billion from 1990 to 1993. The service is also struggling under the weight of retirement benefit costs that total more than 10% of sales. CEO Marvin Runyon, known variously as "Onion Runyon" (he peels until you cry) and "Carvin' Marvin" from his reputation for cutting costs, is reducing head count, eliminating bureaucracy, and focusing on customer service. A proposal to increase postal rates across the board in 1995 (including a 3-cent increase for first-class stamps) is before the Postal Rate Commission.

Despite the huge volume of mail that the service handles each year (171 billion pieces in 1993), 95% of local and 90% of cross-country first-class mail is delivered on time.

Government agency
Fiscal year ends: September 30

WHO

Chairman: Bert H. Mackie
VC: Tirso del Junco
Postmaster General and CEO: Marvin Runyon
Deputy Postmaster General: Michael S. Coughlin
EVP and COO: Joseph R. Caraveo
SVP Finance and CFO: Michael J. Riley
SVP and General Counsel: Mary S. Elcano
VP Employee Relations: Suzanne J. Henry
Auditors: Ernst & Young

WHEN

The 2nd oldest agency of the US government (after Indian Affairs), the Post Office was created by the Continental Congress in 1775, with Benjamin Franklin as its first postmaster general. Since then, the postal system has played a vital role in the development of transportation in the US.

When the Post Office first began operation, mail service consisted of men riding on horses on muddy roads delivering letters with no stamps and no envelopes. Postal rates varied, depending on distance and number of pages in a letter. Letters were taken to the post office for mailing and picked up at the recipient's post office. Congress approved the first official postal policy in 1792: rates ranged from 6¢ for less than 30 miles to 25¢ for more than 450 miles. Letter carriers began delivering mail in cities in 1794. Instead of a salary, they collected 2¢ from each recipient.

Along with the rest of the government, the Post Office was headquartered in Philadelphia until 1800. That year, all postal records, furniture, and supplies were loaded into 2 wagons and transferred to Washington, DC. In 1829 Andrew Jackson elevated the postmaster general to cabinet rank and transformed the office into a means for rewarding political cronies. The first adhesive postage stamp appeared in the US in 1847. Mail contracts subsidized the early development of US railroads.

Uniform postal rates that did not vary with distance were instituted in 1863. That same year free city delivery began. Rural free delivery started in 1896, and its implementation stimulated the construction of roads for the delivery of mail to isolated parts of the US.

Parcel post was inaugurated in 1913, providing the means for mail order houses such as Montgomery Ward and Sears, Roebuck to flourish. Scheduled airmail service between Washington and New York began in 1918, stimulating the development of commercial air travel.

The ZIP Code was introduced in 1963. In 1966 the Chicago post office, then the world's largest postal facility, ceased to function for 3 weeks until a backlog of 10 million pieces of mail was eliminated. Postal workers grew increasingly militant under the stress of the working environment. A work stoppage in the New York City post office in 1970 spread within 9 days to 670 other post offices, and the US Army was deployed to handle the mail. Later that year the Postal Reorganization Act was passed. The new law pulled the postmaster general out of the president's cabinet and made the position the CEO of an independent agency, the US Postal Service. The next year the new agency entered the first US government labor contract negotiated through collective bargaining. Express Mail Service, which guaranteed either same day or next day delivery, was instituted in 1977 to counter the growth of Federal Express and similar businesses. In 1978, 4 digits were added to existing ZIP codes.

In 1991 the cost of mailing a first-class letter was raised from 25¢ to 29¢. In 1992 the service began a reorganization that included a streamlining of management. In 1994 Postmaster Marvin Runyon proposed an overhaul of the service's classification system based on speed of delivery and level of service.

WHERE

HQ: 475 L'Enfant Plaza SW, Washington, DC 20260-0010
Phone: 202-268-2000
Fax: 202-268-2175

The US Postal Service is the largest independent agency of the executive branch of the US government.

WHAT

	1993 Sales	
	$ mil.	% of total
First-Class	28,828	61
Second-Class	1,740	4
Third-Class	9,817	21
Fourth-Class	1,183	2
Priority Mail	2,300	5
Express Mail	627	1
Mailgram	7	—
International Surface	211	1
International Air	1,196	2
Special services	1,509	3
Total	**47,418**	**100**

Services

First-Class Mail (letters)
Second-Class Mail (classroom, nonprofit, and regular-rate publications)
Third-Class Mail (nonprofit, regular bulk, and single-piece)
Fourth-Class Mail (bound printed matter, library materials, and parcels)
Priority Mail (2-day delivery between major business centers in the US)
Express Mail (overnight delivery every day of the year)
Mailgram (combination letter-telegram)
International Surface
International Air
Special Services
- Box rentals
- Certified mail
- Collection-on-Delivery
- Insurance
- Money orders
- Registry
- Special Delivery
- Stamped envelopes

HOW MUCH

	9-Year Growth	1984	1985	1986	1987	1988	1989	1990	1991	1992	1993
Sales ($ mil.)	6.7%	26,474	28,956	31,021	32,297	35,036	37,979	39,201	43,323	46,151	47,418
Net income ($ mil.)	—	117	(251)	305	(223)	(597)	61	(874)	(1,469)	(536)	(1,765)
Income as % of sales	—	0.4%	(0.9%)	1.0%	(0.7%)	(1.7%)	0.2%	(2.2%)	(3.4%)	(1.2%)	(3.7%)
Pieces of mail (mil.)	6.7%	131,500	140,098	147,400	153,900	160,954	161,603	166,301	165,851	166,443	171,220
Employees	(0.2%)	702,000	744,000	785,000	791,000	779,083	777,715	760,668	748,961	725,290	691,723

1993 Year-end:
Cash (mil.): $3,222
Current ratio: 0.44
Long-term debt (mil.): $8,686
Total assets (mil.): $47,281

Net Income ($ mil.) 1984–93

500
0
-500
-1,000
-1,500
-2,000

KEY COMPETITORS

Airborne Freight
Consolidated Freightways
DHL
Federal Express
Harper Group
Pittston
Roadway
Skynet
UPS

UNITED WAY OF AMERICA

RANK: N/R

OVERVIEW

United Way of America (UWA), a nonprofit service agency that provides assistance to local United Way chapters across the country, is recovering from a scandal in which its president resigned, its CFO was fired, and public confidence in its charitable function was tested. UWA responded to the controversy by increasing local United Way representation on its voluntary board of governors, adding several committees (including ethics and budget and finance committees), and hiring a new president, Elaine Chao, formerly director of the Peace Corps. The amount of funds raised in 1992 decreased following the scandal, but UWA's increased focus on finances and accountability saved it from a disastrous slide.

Each of the nearly 2,100 local United Way chapters coordinates its own charitable fund-raising campaigns. The autonomous local United Way chapters choose whether to affiliate with UWA; in 1993, 1,214 member charters joined, an increase of 13.5% over 1992.

UWA also raises funds through private sources, such as NFL Charities; the NFL donated $45 million in TV advertising time to UWA in 1993.

WHEN

United Way traces its origins to the Charity Organizations Society, which was founded in Denver in 1887 to help coordinate the services of 22 local charitable agencies. The society raised $21,700 at its first fund-raiser in 1888.

Other associations of charitable organizations were formed in Boston (1885) and Pittsburgh (1908). In 1911 the National Association of Societies for Organizing Charity was established in Columbus, Ohio to provide a channel of communication among social agencies. In 1913 the Federation for Charity and Philanthropy was created in Cleveland; its practice of raising funds from all social classes and allocating them according to need would serve as a model for United Way.

In 1918 representatives from 12 fund-raising organizations met in Chicago and established the American Association for Community Organizations (AACO), which changed its name to the Association of Community Chests and Councils (ACCC) in 1927 (shortened to CCC in 1933). By 1929 there were 353 Community Chest organizations in the US.

In 1943 the government introduced payroll deductions for charitable contributions, which allowed every worker to become a philanthropist. By 1948 there were more than 1,000 Community Chests, raising almost $182 million. Community Chests formed a cooperative relationship with the AFL and CIO in 1946, and in 1955 the AFL-CIO Services Committee was created. In 1949 the Detroit organization adopted the name United Fund.

In 1963 Los Angeles became the first city to adopt the United Way name, when over 30 local Community Chests and United Funds merged. By 1967, 31,300 agencies serving 27.5 million families were affiliated with United Way. The CCC reorganized as United Way of America in 1970; established its headquarters in Alexandria, Virginia, in 1971; and in the early 1970s introduced its distinctive person/hand/rainbow logo.

UWA established a set of operating standards for community service agencies in 1973. The next year it launched the largest public service campaign in US history (which included its first public service announcements in conjunction with the National Football League) and established United Way International to facilitate the formation of United Way organizations worldwide. That year UWA became the first single organization to raise over $1 billion in an annual fund-raising campaign.

When Congress made its first emergency food and shelter grant to the private sector in 1983 ($50 million), UWA was selected as the fiscal agent. As a result of the grant, over 51 million meals and almost 7 million nights' shelter were provided to the needy. In 1990 the organization published its 6 Principles for the 1990s, which it listed as: providing leadership on urgent needs, supporting self-sufficiency, building coalitions, exploring new forms of access, empowering people with knowledge, and providing choice.

In 1991 UWA's president since 1970, William Aramony, came under fire for alleged mismanagement and living more extravagantly than the head of a nonprofit organization should. Some local organizations withheld 1992 dues, and that year the organization experienced its first downturn in giving since WWII. Other charitable organizations took advantage of UWA's troubles by increasing their own fund-raising efforts, and local United Ways gave more to groups not associated with UWA .

Nonprofit organization
Fiscal year ends: December 31

WHO

Chairman: Thomas F. Frist, Jr., M.D. (Chairman, Columbia/HCA Healthcare Corp.)
VC: Mort Bahr (President, Communication Workers of America, AFL-CIO • CLC)
VC: Edward A. Brennan (Chairman and CEO, Sears, Roebuck and Co.)
VC: Paul J. Tagliabue (Commissioner, National Football League)
President: Elaine L. Chao, $195,000 pay
Secretary: Cathleen P. Black (President and CEO, Newspaper Association of America, Inc.)
Treasurer: Ragan A. Henry (Chairman and CEO, US Radio, L.P.)
Auditors: Arthur Andersen & Co.

WHERE

HQ: 701 N. Fairfax St., Alexandria, VA 22314-2045
Phone: 703-836-7100
Fax: 703-836-7840 (Public Relations)

UWA operates from its headquarters and 6 regional offices in the US. There are approximately 2,100 local chapters coast to coast.

WHAT

	1993 Revenues	
	$ mil.	% of total
Conferences	0.5	2
Contributions	2.2	8
Investment income	0.3	1
Membership support	16.8	63
Program service fees	2.0	8
Promotional material sales	4.5	17
Rental & service income	0.2	—
Other	0.2	—
Total	**26.7**	**100**

	1993 Program Expenses	
	$ mil.	% of total
Campaign/resource development	4.2	18
Communication & advertising	5.5	24
Community partnerships & national initiatives	3.1	14
Cost of goods sold	3.0	13
External services	2.0	9
Field relations	1.9	9
Sales-related expenses	0.6	2
Training & conferencing	2.5	11
Total	**22.8**	**100**

Representative Recipients of United Way Funds

- Agencies for the Aged
- American Heart Association
- American Red Cross
- Association for Retarded Citizens
- Big Brothers/Big Sisters
- Boy Scouts
- Boys Clubs
- Camp Fire
- Catholic Charities
- Cerebral Palsy Associations
- Child Welfare League
- Easter Seal Societies
- Girl Scouts
- Girls Clubs
- Goodwill Industries
- Jewish Federations
- Lutheran Services
- National Council on Alcoholism
- National Recreation and Park Association
- Planned Parenthood
- Salvation Army
- Urban League
- Visiting Nurse Associations
- YMCA
- YWCA

HOW MUCH

	Annual Growth	1984	1985	1986	1987	1988	1989	1990	1991	1992	1993
Revenues ($ mil.)	(1.5%)	—	—	—	—	28.8	31.9	33.2	33.3	25.4	26.7
Program expenses	(2.8%)	—	—	—	—	26.2	30.6	30.4	30.4	23.3	22.7
Amount raised ($ mil.)	3.8%	2,145	2,330	2,440	2,600	2,780	2,980	3,110	3,170	3,040	3,050

1993 Year-end:
Cash (mil.): $3
Current ratio: 1.02
Assets (mil.): $35

Amount Raised ($ mil.) 1984–93

3,500 · 3,000 · 2,500 · 2,000 · 1,500 · 1,000 · 500 · 0

UNIVERSITY OF CALIFORNIA

RANK: 319

OVERVIEW

The University of California (UC) is the largest public university in the country, with 9 main campuses — among them Berkeley, Davis, Los Angeles (UCLA), Irvine, Santa Barbara, and San Diego — and accommodates more than 162,000 students. Offering a place to every California high school student who graduates in the top 1/8 of his or her class, UC doesn't have much room for out-of-staters. UC/Berkeley has the highest percentage of non-Californians enrolled (about 18%).

Headed since 1992 by US Constitution–specialist Jack Peltason, UC has endured severe cutbacks in state funding as California shakes its way through recession. The state cut UC's budget by almost 7% for both the 1991–92 and 1992–93 school years; the next year saw a 4% drop. However, an increase promised for 1994–95 is feared to be too little too late. Horror stories about large classes and ever-increasing student fees are scaring some students away. Peltason says he will not skimp on research programs, considered to be UC's forte. Plans for another campus have been put off indefinitely. Says Peltason, "We're hanging on the edge of a cliff."

UC is a leader in the fields of engineering and physical sciences. For the DOE, UC manages Los Alamos National Laboratory, where the atom bomb was developed during WWII; Lawrence Livermore Laboratory, where the world's first "atom smasher" was used; and Lawrence Berkeley Laboratory. All 3 have been managed by UC for more than 40 years. UC has a strong reputation in medical research as well (owning and operating a number of hospitals and clinics); it had a hand in the development of the nicotine patch and is working on a cure for AIDS.

Public university
Fiscal year ends: December 31

WHO

President: Jack W. Peltason, age 69
Chancellor: Chang-Lin Tien
SVP Academic Affairs and Provost: Walter E. Massey
SVP Business and Finance: Wayne Kennedy
SVP: William R. Frazer
SVP: Ronald W. Brady
VP: Kenneth R. Farrell
VP: William B. Baker
Director Personnel: Alice Gregory
Auditors: KPMG Peat Marwick

WHEN

In 1849 the founders of California's government provided for a state university (via a clause in the state's constitution) 19 years before one even existed. The origins of the College of California, opened in Oakland in 1869, date back to the Contra Costa Academy, a small school established by Yale alumnus Henry Durant in 1853. Durant ran Contra Costa, and then the college, until 1872. Women were allowed to enter the school in 1870. The college moved to Berkeley and graduated its first class (12 men) in 1873.

Renamed University of California in 1879, UC had 1,000 students enrolled by 1895. Agriculture, mining, geology, and engineering were among UC's first important faculties. A 2nd campus was established at Davis in 1905, followed by campuses in San Diego (1912), Los Angeles (1919), and Santa Barbara (1944). With the US government, UC runs the Los Alamos National Laboratory, which, under Robert Oppenheimer, tested the first atomic bomb on July 18, 1945.

Between 1945 and 1965, enrollment quadrupled, spurred by G.I. Bill–sponsored servicemen and a population exodus to the West. The state legislature formulated the Master Plan for Higher Education in 1960, which reorganized university administration and established admission requirements. In 1965 campuses at Irvine and Santa Cruz were established.

UC/Berkeley's first important demonstration of the 1960s came in 1964 over the university's attempts to ban political activity on a strip of UC-owned land. Berkeley quickly became famous for its radical activists. The "People's Park" riot of 1969, started when UC tried to close a parcel of land in Berkeley that students had turned into a kind of playground for the counterculture, left one dead and more than 50 wounded.

Aware of the changing demographics of its student body, especially its growing Asian enrollment (28% in 1990), UC named Chang-Lin Tien chancellor in 1990.

Strapped for cash, UC launched a for-profit concern in 1992 to tap, through license agreements, its extensive library of patents.

In 1993 Lawrence Livermore Lab, fearing for its future in the wake of the cold war's demise, teamed up with Fischer Imaging to develop a digital mammography device. With Samsung and the University of Colorado, UC has also developed a device that emits infrared rays for agricultural use. Ameritech donated $700,000 to a university consortium, which includes UC, to form a communications network allowing universities to more effectively share technologies in 1994.

WHERE

HQ: 300 Lakeside Dr., 22nd Fl., Oakland, CA 94612-3550
Phone: 510-987-0700
Fax: 510-987-0894

UC has 9 undergraduate and graduate campuses in California, 16 foreign campuses, and about 150 institutes, bureaus, centers, and laboratories throughout California.

Main Campuses

UC/Berkeley
110 Sproul Hall
Berkeley, CA 94720

UC/Davis
Davis, CA 95616

UC/Irvine
Irvine, CA 92717

UC/Los Angeles (UCLA)
405 Hilgard Ave.
Los Angeles, CA 90024

UC/Riverside
900 University Ave.
Riverside, CA 92521

UC/San Diego
9500 Gilman Dr.
La Jolla, CA 92093

UC/San Francisco (medical school)
MU-200 Box 0244
San Francisco, CA 94143

UC/Santa Barbara
1210 Cheadle Hall
Santa Barbara, CA 93106

UC/Santa Cruz
Santa Cruz, CA 95064

Affiliated Institutions

Lawrence Berkeley Laboratory
One Cyclotron Rd.
Berkeley, CA 94720

Lawrence Livermore Laboratory
3000 Lakeside Dr., Ste. 21
Oakland, CA 94612-3524

Los Alamos National Laboratory
PO Box 1663
Los Alamos, NM 87545

WHAT

	1993 Sources of Revenue	
	$ mil.	% of total
State of California and general fund	2,006	26
Teaching hospitals	1,729	22
Federal government	1,195	16
Student fees and tuition	725	10
Educational activities	584	8
Auxiliary enterprises	498	7
Private gifts, grants, and contracts	377	5
Endowments	86	1
Local government	71	1
Other	277	4
Total	**7,548**	**100**

HOW MUCH

	9-Year Growth	1984	1985	1986	1987	1988	1989	1990	1991	1992	1993
Revenues ($ mil.)[1]	8.9%	3,495	3,988	4,450	4,860	5,353	5,847	6,443	6,993	7,394	7,548
Enrollment	1.6%	140,141	143,247	148,151	152,090	156,795	156,357	161,391	162,700	162,500	162,064
Faculty (est.)	—	10,800	14,900	15,200	15,000	15,200	7,900[2]	8,400[2]	8,900[2]	9,000[2]	10,700
Employees	2.9%	101,991	105,008	109,273	114,042	118,768	124,958	124,329	129,946	132,279	131,661

Enrollment 1984–93

180,000
160,000
140,000
120,000
100,000
80,000
60,000
40,000
20,000
0

[1] Does not include affiliated institution laboratories. [2] Does not include UC/Berkeley faculty.

USAA

RANK: 30

OVERVIEW

San Antonio–based USAA is the nation's 4th largest home insurer and its 5th largest automobile insurer. USAA's membership is limited to active and retired military officers, Secret Service and FBI agents and other selected government officials, and their families. It has 2.5 million members, including more than 95% of active-duty US military officers.

The company dropped its full name, United Services Automobile Association, because it has evolved from an auto insurer into a full-fledged financial services company. It provides a variety of products and services, including property, casualty, life, and health insurance; discount brokerage; banking; mutual funds; credit cards; a travel agency; and a buying service that allows members to buy discount merchandise. The property and casualty insurance and the buying service are sold only to members, but most of USAA's other products are available to nonmembers.

USAA's corporate headquarters (at 5 million square feet) is billed as the largest private office building in the world. The company is listed in *The 100 Best Companies to Work For in America* as one of the 10 best employers in the US.

The company, which has no field agents, has become known for its customer service and its use of high technology, conducting almost all of its business by telephone or mail. Although USAA's net income was up in 1993 (after being hurt by claims from Hurricane Andrew the previous year), the company faces shrinking military budgets that could cut into its customer base.

WHEN

In 1922 a group of US Army officers gathered at the Gunter Hotel in San Antonio and formed their own automobile insurance association. The reason? As military officers they often moved from one post to another and had a hard time getting insurance because they were considered "transient." So the 26 officers who met that day decided to insure each other. Led by Major William Garrison, who became the company's first president, they formed the United States Army Automobile Insurance Association.

In 1924, when navy and marine corps officers were allowed to join, the company changed its name to United Services Automobile Association. By the mid-1950s the company had over 200,000 members.

During the 1960s the company added to its insurance lines when it formed USAA Life Insurance Company (1963) and USAA Casualty Insurance Company (1968).

In 1969 Robert McDermott, a retired air force brigadier general and a former dean of the Air Force Academy, became president. McDermott cut employment through attrition (USAA has never had a layoff), established education and training seminars for employees, and invested heavily in technology. A computer system McDermott installed cut automobile policy processing time from 13 days to 3 days.

McDermott also added new products and services, such as mutual funds, real estate investments, and banking services. Under McDermott, USAA's membership grew from 653,000 in 1969 to over 2.5 million in 1993.

In 1974 USAA began its move into its huge new headquarters facilities on a 286-acre campus, featuring subsidized cafeterias, 2 walk-in medical clinics, and 2 physical fitness centers.

During the 1970s, as part of McDermott's goal to make USAA a completely paperless company, USAA switched most of its business from mail to toll-free telephone, becoming one of the insurance industry's first companies to use 800 numbers.

In the early 1980s the company introduced USAA Buying Services, allowing members to buy merchandise at a discount. In 1985 it opened the USAA Federal Savings Bank next door to its headquarters. In the late 1980s USAA automated some customer service operations by installing an optical storage system.

In 1993 McDermott retired and was succeeded by Robert Herres, a former vice-chairman of the Joint Chiefs of Staff. USAA continues to add new services. In 1994 USAA Federal Savings Bank was developing a home banking system, providing members with information and services over advanced screen telephones provided by IBM. Also that year the company sued a Los Angeles Avis franchisee for credit card fraud losses. An employee of the rental agencies had recorded the account numbers of customers paying with USAA MasterCard and VISA cards and sold them to counterfeiters. Over $900,000 of illegal charges were eventually recorded.

HOW MUCH

	9-Year Growth	1984	1985	1986	1987	1988	1989	1990	1991	1992	1993
Assets ($ mil.)	20.5%	3,455	4,121	5,740	7,168	8,866	10,562	12,258	14,520	16,235	18,494
Net income ($ mil.)	12.6%	230	207	294	482	430	424	321	413	140	671
Income as % of assets	—	6.7%	5.0%	5.1%	6.7%	4.8%	4.0%	2.6%	2.8%	0.9%	3.6%
Employees	9.5%	7,020	7,896	8,355	9,274	11,226	12,515	13,884	14,222	14,667	15,905

1993 Year-end:
Sales (mil.): $5,990

Assets ($ mil.) 1984–93

Mutual company
Fiscal year ends: December 31

WHO

Chairman and CEO: Robert T. Herres, age 60
VC: H. T. Johnson
EVP and Chief Administrative Officer: Herbert L. Emanuel
EVP and Chief Information Officer: Staser Holcomb
SVP, CFO, & Controller: Josue Robles
SVP and Chief Communications Officer: John R. Cook
SVP, General Counsel, & Secretary: William McCrae
SVP Human Resources: William B. Tracy
President, Property and Casualty Division: Charles Bishop
President, Life Company: Ed Rosane
President, Investment Management Division: Mickey Roth
Auditors: KPMG Peat Marwick

WHERE

HQ: 9800 Fredericksburg Rd., USAA Building, San Antonio, TX 78288-0001
Phone: 210-498-2211
Fax: 210-498-9940

USAA provides services worldwide.

Regional Offices
Colorado Springs, CO
Norfolk, VA
Sacramento, CA
Tampa, FL
London, England
Frankfurt, Germany

WHAT

	1993 Sales $ mil.	% of total
Property & casualty	4,517	76
Life insurance	619	10
Investment management	79	1
Other	775	13
Total	**5,990**	**100**

Products and Services
Alliance Services
- USAA Floral Service
- USAA Road & Travel Plan
- USAA/Sprint Long-Distance

Annuities
Auto insurance
Banking
Car rental discounts
Credit card services
Health insurance
Homeowners'/property insurance
Investments
- Brokerage services
- Mutual funds
- Tax deferred plans

Life insurance
Merchandise
- Electronics
- Jewelry
- Furnishings

Real estate limited partnerships
Retirement services
- USAA Parklane West (health care facility)
- USAA Towers (retirement community)

Travel services

KEY COMPETITORS

AAA
Aetna
AFLAC
Allstate
American Express
American Financial
American General
Charles Schwab
Chubb
CIGNA
Dean Witter, Discover
Equitable
FMR
GEICO
Guardian Life
ITT
John Hancock
Kemper
Liberty Mutual
MassMutual
MetLife
Nationwide
New York Life
Northwestern Mutual
Pacific Mutual
Paine Webber
Prudential
Sharper Image
State Farm
T. Rowe Price
Transamerica
Travelers
USF&G

VANSTAR, INC.

RANK: 101

OVERVIEW

In 1994 Pleasanton, California–based ComputerLand (the US's #1 personal computer retailer) pulled off a repositioning coup, becoming Vanstar, the country's largest reseller of personal computers and provider of related services.

The company accomplished this feat by selling its 224 US franchise operations (including the US rights to the ComputerLand name), its Distribution Division, and Datago operations (a chain of value-added resellers) to Merisel for $110 million. The name Vanstar was chosen to convey the new company's position in the vanguard of providing integrated services to clients.

Although the operations sold to Merisel account for about half of company sales, Vanstar was able to announce, along with its name change, 2 lucrative outsourcing agreements, one with ISSC, an IBM subsidiary, and one with Microsoft, which will add more than $200 million in sales. It will also continue to provide services on a contract basis to the operations sold to Merisel.

Vanstar is owned by an investor group led by E.M. Warburg, which bought the company in 1987 when its founder, William Millard, sold his 53% share after an adverse judgment in a stockholder's suit.

Private company
Fiscal year ends: September 30

WHO

Chairman, President, and CEO: William Y. Tauscher
SVP Operations: Robert C. Kuntzendorf
SVP and Financial Controller: Michael Fung
SVP and General Counsel: Richard F. Vitkus
SVP and Chief Information Officer: Michael J. Moore
VP International: Peter C. Alexander
Director Human Resources: Judith Marshall
Auditors: Ernst & Young

WHERE

HQ: 5964 W. Las Positas Blvd., PO Box 9012, Pleasanton, CA 94588-8540
Phone: 510-734-4000
Fax: 510-734-4802

Vanstar sells computers and accessories and provides networking and other services through 250 service and sales offices in the US and in 50 other nations in Eastern and Western Europe, North America, South America, and Asia.

WHAT

Manufacturers Represented
Apple
Compaq
Epson
Hewlett-Packard
IBM
Intel
Lotus
Microsoft
NEC
Novell
Okidata
Sun
SynOptics
Toshiba

Services
LANs (local area networks)
- LAN monitoring
- LAN interconnection
- LAN diagnostics

WANs (wide area networks)

Systems Consulting

Service/Support
- National Help Desk
- Multinational account service
- Centralized service dispatch

Training
- 150 Learning Centers
- 300 course offerings

WHEN

In 1973 William Millard, a computer consultant working under the name IMS Associates, had already lost one company, System Dynamics, to bankruptcy. That year Philip Reed's car dealership was so successful that he needed a computer program to track sales and inventory. The 2 men met and agreed that Millard would develop and Reed would finance the software.

The software was never developed, but, in their quest to salvage their investments, the men decided to sell a do-it-yourself computer kit through magazine ads. It was a hit, and they followed it with a preassembled computer called the IMSAI 8080.

But they remained strapped for cash and in 1976 received a $250,000 loan from Reed's father's company, Marriner & Co., of Boston. As part of the loan terms, Marriner received a note convertible into 20% of IMS stock.

Reed left in 1976, after differing with Millard on the direction and management of the company. Millard, a follower of the est movement, insisted on running the company according to est principles.

Also in 1976 franchise consultant John Martin-Musumeci sold Millard on the idea of franchise retailing for the 8080. The operation, Computer Shack, was a hit because it sold the new Apple computer as well.

Millard reshuffled the businesses to try to limit the Marriner note to IMS (and its successor company, IMSAI), but failed. He succeeded in shielding Computer Shack from IMSAI's debts, and in 1979 IMSAI went bankrupt, wiping out Reed's $149,000 investment.

Renamed ComputerLand in 1977, the company prospered after the 1981 introduction of the IBM PC. In the early 1980s the novelty of PCs drove sales to ever greater heights, and Millard steadily raised franchise fees, causing friction with the franchisees.

In 1981 Martin-Musumeci, through his new company, Micro/Vest, bought the Marriner note and split it with Philip Reed. When Millard refused to recognize his right to the stock, Martin-Musumeci sued.

Micro/Vest won the stock plus punitive damages in 1985. Unable to pay for the appeal of the $141 million award, Millard sold out to Warburg for $81 million in 1987.

The new management, led by William Tauscher, intended to go public in 1988, but the market was unenthusiastic. Instead ComputerLand began to reposition itself as a reseller to business and as a provider of service and support and began buying out some of its franchisees. In 1991, to build its customer service base, it bought NYNEX Business Centers for $150 million in cash and a 21% interest in the company. In 1992 it bought TRW's customer service division.

The repositioning was expensive; sales fell in the early 1990s, and the cost of the acquisitions dragged down earnings. But these acquisitions provided the basis for the company's new service orientation. By 1993 ComputerLand was in the midst of a credit crunch that resulted in shipment restrictions by Compaq and Toshiba but was eased by the sale of its franchise operations. The company changed its name to Vanstar in March 1994.

HOW MUCH

	Annual Growth	1984	1985	1986	1987	1988	1989	1990	1991	1992	1993
Estimated sales ($ mil.)	6.0%	1,300	1,400	1,400	1,700	2,039	2,630	3,000	1,500	2,000	2,200
Employees	—	—	—	—	—	—	—	—	2,069	3,763	3,295

Estimated Sales ($ mil.) 1984–93

0 – 500 – 1,000 – 1,500 – 2,000 – 2,500 – 3,000

KEY COMPETITORS

Apple
Best Buy
Circuit City
Commodore
Compaq
CompuCom Systems
Coopers & Lybrand
DEC
Dell
Egghead
Electronic Data Systems
Gateway 2000
Good Guys
Hewlett-Packard
IBM
InaCom
Intelligent Electronics
Litton Industries
MicroAge
Montgomery Ward
NYNEX
Office Depot
Price-Costco
Random Access
Sears
Service Merchandise
Tandem
Tandy
Technology Solutions
Unisys

VOUGHT AIRCRAFT COMPANY

RANK: 383

OVERVIEW

Vought Aircraft Company is one of the oldest aircraft manufacturers in the US. The bulk of the company's current projects are subcontracting jobs, building airplane parts for industry giants like Boeing and McDonnell Douglas. The 75-year-old company had been a part of the conglomerate LTV since 1961, but bankruptcy and reorganization forced LTV to sell Vought to the Carlyle Group (investment bank; 51%) and Northrop (49%) in 1992. In July 1994 the two companies reached an agreement for Northrop Grumman to buy Carlyle's remaining interest for $130 million.

Vought expects to lay off some 2,000 workers in 1994 and 1995 because of cutbacks in defense spending, specifically on the B-2 bomber and C-17 airlifter programs, as well as a weak commercial market. The company already reduced its work force by 3,500 in 1992 and 1993. Like many other defense contractors, Vought, headed by Frank Carlucci, a Carlyle officer and secretary of defense under Ronald Reagan, is carving itself a bigger niche in commercial aviation. In 1993 it signed a revenue-sharing agreement with Gulfstream Aerospace to make the wings for a new commercial plane. However, about 50% of its revenues still come from military contracts.

Vought is now developing the Pampa 2000, a training plane that will compete for acceptance by the navy and air force in a $4 billion Pentagon program.

WHEN

Chance Vought, an aeronautical engineer, founded his own aircraft company on Long Island in 1917. Vought had been taught to fly 7 years earlier by aviator Max T. Lillie and went on to become a flight instructor. His first plane, the VE-7, became in 1922 the first aircraft to take off from a carrier. Vought debuted its first biplane, the O2U-1, in 1926.

In the 1920s one of Vought's major engine suppliers was Pratt & Whitney (P&W). Vought joined with Bill Boeing and Fred Rentschler of P&W to form the United Aircraft and Transportation Company in 1929, providing P&W with steady customers and Boeing and Vought with a reliable engine supply. Chance Vought died in 1930, and his company became part of United Aircraft Company, along with P&W, Sikorsky, Ham Standard, and Northrop; headquarters were moved to Connecticut.

Vought supplied the navy with the successful F4U Corsair, a bent-wing plane that boasted an 11:1 victory ratio, during WWII. The company's first entry into commercial markets came in 1946 when it built the F-24 passenger plane for Fairchild and 200 "Swift" airplanes for Globe. In 1948 the company relocated to Dallas in the largest industrial move in US history at that time. In 1954 United Aircraft (which later became United Technologies) sold Vought, which eventually merged with Ling-Temco, one of the world's largest diversified conglomerates, in 1961.

Vought began making the A-7 Corsair II in 1964. Navy and air force pilots flew these planes in more than 100,000 combat sorties in many countries, including Vietnam and Libya. A variation of the A-7 was used as a munitions carrier in the Persian Gulf War. In 1967 Boeing chose Vought to make the tail sections for its new 747s; the next year McDonnell Douglas tapped Vought to manufacture the tail sections for its DC-10 passenger aircraft.

Vought lost many lucrative Pentagon contracts in the mid-1970s, which forced it to delve more deeply into commercial markets. Its first large commercial project was a ground transportation system for the Dallas/Ft. Worth airport, which was plagued with problems from the start. The company took a $23 million loss on the project.

In 1983 Rockwell chose Vought to build the B-1B bomber's aft and aft intermediate fuselage sections. The same year Vought began producing parts for the C-17 transport plane for McDonnell Douglas. In 1991 the company was awarded a $1.5 billion renewal contract from Boeing to make sections of its 747, 757, and 767 airliners. It received another $700 million contract from Boeing in 1992.

Former defense secretary Les Aspin put the C-17 airlifter program on probation in late 1993 because of problems with expense and performance. Although Vought's parts are not to blame, the company still stands to lose a substantial portion of its business.

In 1993 Vought joined with Boeing in a government-backed project to develop materials to be used to make a supersonic aircraft available sometime in the early 21st century. The company completed the first flight tests of its Pampa 2000 in 1994; delivery isn't expected until 1996 or 1997.

HOW MUCH

	Annual Growth	1984	1985	1986	1987[1]	1988[1]	1989[1]	1990[1]	1991[1]	1992[1]	1993
Estimated sales ($ mil.)	(4.1%)	—	—	—	1,026	867	673	797	994	691	800
Employees	(13.2%)	—	—	—	—	11,800	—	—	9,500	9,000	5,800

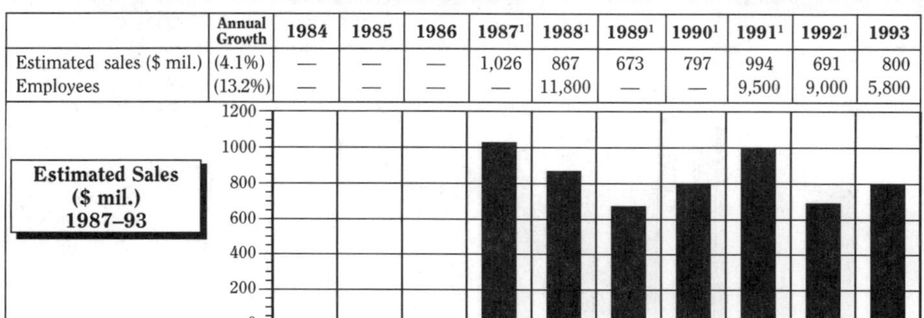

[1] Aerospace division of LTV

Vought aircraft company

Joint venture
Fiscal year ends: December 31

WHO

Chairman: Frank Carlucci
President: Gordon L. Williams
SVP and CFO: W. J. McMillan
SVP Administration and Support (Human Resources): Jerry P. Carr
VP, Secretary, and General Counsel: W. B. White
VP Corporate Communications: Lynn J. Farris
VP General Manager, Military Programs: Henry Spence
VP General Manager, Commercial Programs: Jim McConnell
VP Product Operations: Cliff Harris
Assistant Treasurer: B. B. Blocker
Auditors: Ernst & Young

WHERE

HQ: PO Box 655907, Dallas, TX 75265-5907
Phone: 214-266-2446 **Fax:** 214-266-4140

Vought has manufacturing, engineering, wind tunnel, structure testing, airport, subassembly, assembly, tool fabrication, and warehousing facilities in the Dallas–Ft. Worth area.

WHAT

Commercial Operations
Boeing
- Horizontal stabilizer (767)
- Tail sections (747)
- Vertical and horizontal stabilizers (757)

Canadair
- Engine nacelles (CL 601-3A and Regional Jet)

Gulfstream
- Wing design and manufacture (Gulfstream V)

Military Operations
B-2 Stealth Bomber
- Intermediate sections

C-17 Globemaster III
- Engine nacelles
- Universal aerial refueling receptacle slipway
- Vertical and horizontal stabilizers

Pampa 2000

Facilities
Airport operations
Detail manufacturing
Engineering laboratories
Subassembly and assembly operations
Tool fabrication
Warehousing

Products
Buried propulsion systems
Contoured co-cured composite sandwich structures
Engine nacelles
Integrally stiffened skin panels
Pressure bulkheads
Smart skins
Tail sections

KEY COMPETITORS

AlliedSignal
BF Goodrich
Coltec Industries
EG&G
Fairchild
InterTech Group
Kaman
Lockheed
Lucas Industries
Martin Marietta
McDonnell Douglas
Moog
Northrop Grumman
Sundstrand
Textron

YOUNG & RUBICAM INC.

RANK: 290

OVERVIEW

Young & Rubicam's new CEO, Peter Georgescu, is looking to put Y&R back on top by putting more people on top. Formerly the US's largest consolidated advertising agency, Y&R fell to #2 (ranked by worldwide income, after McCann-Erickson) in 1994. Its sales and billings have been falling since 1990. In order to make Y&R more productive, Georgescu, who succeeded Alex Kroll as CEO in 1993, plans to add more senior-level management while cutting the agency's overall work force.

Y&R's 5 main divisions provide advertising, public relations, sales promotion/direct marketing, corporate and product identity consulting, and health care communications.

The employee-owned agency, which has 304 offices in 64 countries, is focusing on making its operations more client-driven by getting its offices to work together to win new accounts. Y&R added an estimated $350 million in new billings in the last half of 1993 but lost Johnson & Johnson's media buying account, valued at $200 million.

Also, as part of its effort to expand its Latin American business, Y&R consolidated its Latin American headquarters in Miami.

WHEN

In 1923 Raymond Rubicam and John Orr Young founded their Philadelphia advertising agency literally on a shoestring: their first client was Presto Quick Tip Shoelaces. Y&R got its first major client, General Foods, when it obtained the account for the company's least successful product, Postum. Success in increasing Postum's sales led to more business with General Foods and to a 1926 move to New York at that client's request. With its informal atmosphere and tolerance for eccentric behavior, the agency became a haven for the top creative people in the industry.

In 1931 the firm opened an office in Chicago. In the early 1930s Rubicam, who by then dominated the firm, recruited George Gallup to create advertising's first research department. In 1934 Young was forced out; the firm, despite its unconventional working environment, had become a hard-driving place.

The Depression put many agencies out of business, but Y&R billings grew from $6 million in 1927 to $22 million in 1937. Y&R became the #2 agency, after J. Walter Thompson.

WWII brought surprising prosperity to the industry. By 1945 Y&R billings had reached $53 million. Rubicam retired in 1944 at 52.

During the 1950s the agency prospered; billings reached $212 million in 1960. In the 1960s Y&R produced the first color television commercials and a series of notable campaigns. Rubicam's emphasis on creativity, teamwork, and group management continued to work. During this period, however, growth slowed, and expenses and staff grew.

In 1970 Edward Ney became CEO, cut staff, and installed Alex Kroll as creative director. Kroll required that creativity be controlled, disciplined, and quantifiable by sales results. Ney expanded the agency through acquisitions, which included Wunderman Worldwide (direct marketing, 1973), Cato Johnson (sales promotion, 1976), and Burson-Marsteller (public relations, 1979).

By 1975, when Kroll became president of US operations, billings of $477 million had made Y&R the #1 US agency. Since 1979 it has been the largest independent agency in the US. The 1980s saw challenges to Y&R's dominance from such huge holding company agencies as the UK's Saatchi & Saatchi. Y&R's size and bureaucracy also threatened its reputation for creativity. Kroll became CEO in 1985.

In 1990 Y&R pleaded guilty to bribery charges in connection with a Jamaican tourism account. HDM Worldwide, a partnership with Dentsu (Japan) and Eurocom (France), fell apart when Eurocom withdrew. Y&R and Dentsu, partners for 30 years, regrouped as Dentsu, Young & Rubicam Partnerships.

In 1993 Y&R announced its 4th restructuring in 8 years, spending $50–$80 million on a new communications system. That year the managing director of Y&R's Italian subsidiary was arrested for allegedly giving a government official a kickback to win a government-sponsored anti-AIDS campaign contract.

In 1994 Y&R's Dentsu, Young & Rubicam Partnerships announced plans to buy 40% of Bombay-based Rediffusion Advertising.

HOW MUCH

	9-Year Growth	1984	1985	1986	1987	1988	1989	1990	1991	1992	1993
Total billings ($ mil.)	10.0%	3,202	3,575	4,191	4,905	5,390	6,251	8,001	7,840	7,781	7,559
Total sales ($ mil.)	8.6%	480	536	628	736	758	865	1,074	1,057	1,059	1,009
Sales as % of billings	—	15.0%	15.0%	15.0%	15.0%	14.1%	13.8%	13.4%	13.5%	13.6%	13.3%
US billings ($ mil.)	6.1%	2,155	2,272	2,389	2,577	2,792	3,115	3,937	3,739	3,637	3,670
US sales ($ mil.)	3.6%	323	341	358	386	373	410	487	466	458	445
Employees	1.8%	8,418	9,030	10,844	11,634	12,311	10,473	11,133	10,324	10,122	9,846

Total Sales ($ mil.) 1984–93

1,200
1,000
800
600
400
200
0

Young&Rubicam Inc.

Private company
Fiscal year ends: December 31

WHO

Chairman: Alexander S. Kroll, age 56
VC and Worldwide Creative Director: Ted Bell
President and CEO: Peter A. Georgescu, age 54
CEO, Worldwide Advertising Operations: John McGarry, age 54
EVP and CFO: Dave Greene
EVP and General Counsel: R. John Cooper
Director Human Resources: Raquel Suarez
Auditors: Price Waterhouse

WHERE

HQ: 285 Madison Ave., New York, NY 10017-6486
Phone: 212-210-3000
Fax: 212-210-9073

	1993 Total Billings		1993 Total Sales	
	$ mil.	% of total	$ mil.	% of total
US	3,670	49	445	44
Other countries	3,889	51	564	56
Total	**7,559**	**100**	**1,009**	**100**

WHAT

	1993 Total Billings		1993 Total Sales	
	$ mil.	% of total	$ mil.	% of total
Advertising, PR & identity consulting	6,026	80	792	79
Sales promotion & direct marketing	1,076	14	148	15
Direct mail	166	2	25	2
Health care comm.	291	4	44	4
Total	**7,559**	**100**	**1,009**	**100**

Divisions
Young & Rubicam Advertising
Burson-Marsteller (public relations)
The Advocacy Communications Team
Black, Manafort, Stone & Kelly (lobbying, public affairs)
City & Corporate Counsel Ltd. (UK)
Cohn & Wolfe (public relations)
Executive Consultants Limited (Canada, public affairs)
Gold & Liebengood (lobbying, public affairs)
Robinson Linton Associates (Belgium, gov't. relations)
Chapman Direct Advertising
The Muldoon Agency (catalogs)
DecisionBase Resources (database/mktg. consulting)
Landor Associates (corporate identity management)
Sudler & Hennessey (health care communications)
Wunderman Cato Johnson (sales promotion)

Joint Ventures
Dentsu/Burson-Marsteller (public relations)
Dentsu Wunderman Direct (Japanese direct marketing)
Dentsu, Young & Rubicam Partnerships (advertising)
Y&R/Sovero (marketing, with Sovero of Moscow)

Representative Clients
American Express
AT&T
Clorox
Dr Pepper/7Up
DuPont
Ford
MetLife
PepsiCo
Sears
Tandy
Time Warner
Xerox

KEY COMPETITORS

N. W. Ayer
Bozell
Carlson
D'Arcy Masius Benton & Bowles
Grey Advertising
Heritage Media
Interpublic Group of Companies
Leo Burnett
Omnicom Group
Saatchi & Saatchi
WPP Group

ZIFF COMMUNICATIONS COMPANY

RANK: 297

OVERVIEW

Ziff Communications

Ziff Communications is the leading US publisher of computer magazines, with a total circulation of 3.2 million. The company produces such magazines as *PC Magazine*, Ziff's flagship monthly and the 9th largest US magazine; *PC WEEK; PC Computing; MacUser;* and *Computer Shopper*. Ziff also publishes computer magazines in Europe. *Forbes* estimates the Ziff family fortune at more than $1.5 billion.

Ziff's current strategy of focusing on computer magazines has proved remarkably savvy. Bill Ziff, Jr., who retired as chairman in 1993, had realized the growing need for specialized information in publishing. Ziff, known for his dazzling intellect and eccentric style of management, built up a publications portfolio by forming or acquiring magazines to fill each computer niche. Most have prospered.

In addition to its publishing unit, the company has operations in electronic information, computer trade shows, and book and newsletter publishing. Ziff also operates the largest independent testing facility in the industry.

In 1994 Bill Ziff's 3 sons, who own the company, decided that the market was at its peak and put the company up for sale. Potential bidders include McGraw-Hill, K-III, and Reed Elsevier.

Private company
Fiscal year ends: December 31

WHO

Chairman and CEO: Eric Hippeau, age 42
VP and Publisher, *PC Magazine*: Jim Stafford
VP: Jeff Ballowe
SVP and CFO: Bruce Barnes
VP Operations, Domestic Publications Group: Dirk Ziff
Chairman and CEO, Interop Co.: Dan Lynch
President and COO, Seybold: Aymar de Lencquesaing
President, Information Access: Robert Howells
VP and Assistant to the Chairman, Ziff-Davis: Sam Huey
VP, Ziff Desktop: James Reilly
VP, Ziff Desktop: John Dickinson
VP Human Resources: Fred Staudmyer

WHEN

William Ziff, a famed WWI flyer, author, and lecturer, and Bernard Davis founded Ziff-Davis Publishing in 1927 with the publication of *Popular Aviation* (now *Flying*). The pair concentrated on hobby- and leisure-related publications. When Ziff died of a heart attack in 1953, Ziff-Davis was publishing *Modern Bride*, *Popular Electronics*, and *Popular Photography*, among others.

Ziff's son Bill, Jr., was just 24 when his father died. He shocked his family by giving up a promising career in academia to take over the company, saying, "I didn't grow up with businessmen as my heroes, but my dad died and I wanted a piece of him." In 1956 Ziff bought out Davis and began an unprecedented buying spree. He sought out, as his father had, niche markets, where a steady supply of new products and services would keep readers interested.

In 1973 Ziff acquired the publishing arm of Boise Cascade, inheriting, among other titles, *Psychology Today*. By the mid-1980s his enterprise published about 35 magazines, including *Car & Driver*, *Boating*, *Yachting*, *Cycle*, *Travel Weekly*, and *Hotel & Travel Index*, and owned 6 television stations.

In the 1980s, however, Ziff's battle with prostate cancer slowed, then reversed, company growth. Ziff began selling practically all of the company's holdings. The television stations were sold for $100 million in 1983. In 1985, 12 trade magazines went to Rupert Murdoch for $350 million, and 12 consumer magazines went to CBS for $363 million. (CBS later sued the company, claiming that it was given misleading financial information. The suit was eventually dismissed.) Ziff also passed ownership of the company on to his 3 sons and 3 nephews, 4 of whom are now VPs.

What the company did keep was its computer magazines, which were already among the strongest in the industry, if not the most profitable. *PC Magazine*, acquired in 1982, didn't turn a profit for 3 years. In 1985 the company lost over $10 million on $100 million in sales. Reasoning that there would eventually be a healthy market for computer magazines because of the high price of computers, the growing availability of computers to the average American, and the upgradability of computers, the company began building up its holdings in computer publishing.

In 1988, having beaten cancer, Ziff resumed the chairmanship; by the early 1990s the company was the US's #1 publisher of computer magazines. In 1990 *Forbes* estimated the Ziff family fortune at over $1 billion.

The company shut down 2 of its magazines, *PC Sources* and *Corporate Computing*, in 1993. Seeing signs of a slowdown of the industry, Ziff decided to expand into other businesses: trade shows, newsletters, and electronic services. Also in 1993 Bill Ziff, at 63, retired.

The company acquired *Computer Gaming World*, launched *Window Sources*, and worked with Disney on a family-oriented computer magazine in 1993. The next year Ziff Communications announced plans to form a new on-line services network, Interchange Online Network. It also acquired SandPoint Corp., a marketer of Lotus Notes-based software products designed to access on-line databases for corporate users.

WHERE

HQ: One Park Ave., New York, NY 10016-5801
Phone: 212-503-3500
Fax: 212-503-4599

Ziff Communications publishes magazines in the US and Europe and licenses the rights to publish its titles in Asia, Australia, Europe, and Latin America.

WHAT

Selected Operating Groups and Subsidiaries
Information Access (electronic information)
Ziff-Davis Exhibitions
- Interop Co. (trade shows and newsletters)
- MicroDesign Resources (newsletters)
- Seybold (computer conferences and newsletters)

Ziff-Davis Publishing Company
Ziff Desktop Information (electronic information and publishing)
Ziff Technology Group
- Bendata Management Systems (software)
- Help Desk Institute (training and customer support)
- Logical Operations (training manuals)
- Ziff Technologies (training and customer support)

Selected Publications
Computer Gaming World
Computer Shopper
MacUser
MacWEEK
PC Computing
PC Magazine
PC WEEK
Windows Sources

Electronic Information Services
Interchange Online Network
SandPoint Corp.
Ziffnet

HOW MUCH

	Annual Growth	1984	1985	1986	1987	1988	1989	1990	1991	1992	1993
Estimated sales ($ mil.)	32.1%	—	100	175	—	—	—	500	600	792	925
Employees	10.0%	—	—	2,200	—	—	—	2,300	3,100	4,100	4,300

Estimated Sales ($ mil.) 1985–93

KEY COMPETITORS

Advance Publications
America Online
Apple
AT&T
CMP Publications
H&R Block
Hearst
IBM
International Data Group
Matra-Hachette
McGraw-Hill
Meckler
New York Times
Pittway
Prodigy
Reed Elsevier
Scholastic
Sears
Sierra On-Line
Thomson Corp.
Time Warner
Times Mirror
Wired Ventures

THE
Private 500

"21" INTERNATIONAL HOLDINGS, INC. RANK: 205

153 E. 53rd St., Ste. 5900
New York, NY 10022
Phone: 212-230-0400
Fax: 212-593-1363

1992 Est. Sales: $1,301 million
FYE: December
Employees: 4,500

Key Personnel
Chm & CEO: Marshall S. Cogan
CFO: Robert H. Nelson
VP & Managing Dir: Barry Zimmerman
Gen Counsel: Philip N. Smith, Jr.

Business Lines
Bedding & home furnishings
Carpet & rug cushions
Insulation & cushioning material
New & used cars (Emco Motor)
Packaging & shipping material
Plastics foam products
Polyurethane foam
Restaurants (The "21" Club)

Key Competitors
BASF
Carpenter Co.
Dow Corning
ICI
Monsanto
New York Restaurant Group
Rhône-Poulenc
Union Carbide

Industry
Diversified operations

Overview
Owned by Marshall Cogan, "21" International includes the legendary "21" Club in New York; some auto dealerships; and a substantial interest in publicly traded Foamex International (1993 revenues of $696 million), the #1 U.S. maker of polyurethane foam. Foamex, of which Cogan is CEO, has in recent years bought companies that make bedding and home furnishing products. In 1994 Foamex bought JPS Automotive, an interior auto trim products maker. Cogan and Stephen Swid formed the company in 1974 (they parted in 1986). The "21" Club ranks among the top 10 restaurants in the US, with $12.5 million of sales in 1993.

84 LUMBER CO. RANK: 268

Rt. 519
Eighty Four, PA 15384
Phone: 412-228-8820
Fax: 412-225-2530

1993 Sales: $1,060 million
FYE: December
Employees: 3,500

Key Personnel
CEO: Joseph A. Hardy, Sr.
Pres: Margaret H. Magerko
CFO: Sid McAllister
EVP: Dennis Brua
Dir HR: Steve Cherry

Major Products
Bathroom fixtures
Construction material
Fencing
Flooring material
Insulation
Lumber
Windows

Key Competitors
Ace Hardware
Cotter & Co.
Hechinger
Home Depot
Kmart
Lowe's
McCoy
Waban

Industry
Building products - retail

Overview
With 350 stores in 31 states across the US, 84 Lumber is the largest privately held building products company in the country. Founded in 1956 by Joseph A. Hardy, the company caters to do-it-yourselfers and contractors, ignoring casual retail shoppers, and locates in small towns. Hardy is grooming daughter Maggie Hardy Magerko as heir apparent to this home improvement retail giant. In 1991 Hardy gave his daughter 40% of the company.

ABCO MARKETS INC. RANK: 467

3001 W. Indian School
Phoenix, AZ 85017
Phone: 602-222-1600
Fax: 602-222-1473

1994 Sales: $625 million
FYE: January
Employees: 6,000

Key Personnel
Pres & CEO: Edward G. Hill, Jr.
CFO & Sec: David Walters
SVP & Asst Sec: Edward A. Gast
VP Mktg: Leslie H. Knox
VP Info Sys: Jerry Johnson
Dir HR: Dennis Williams

Selected Services
Bakery & deli departments
Dairy departments
Floral departments
General merchandise departments
Gourmet coffee departments
Liquor departments
Meat & seafood departments
Ready-to-go food

Key Competitors
Albertson's
Bashas'
Circle K
Kroger
Safeway
Smith's Food & Drug
Southland
Steinberg

Industry
Retail - supermarkets

Overview
ABCO Markets competes in the intense Phoenix grocery wars by pampering its customers and stressing neighborhood convenience, not low prices. ABCO was founded in 1984 as the result of an LBO of 33 Alpha Beta Stores from American Stores by investment firm Odyssey Partners and wholesaler Fleming Companies. The chain, with its 77 stores (all but one located in Phoenix and Tucson), treats shoppers to environmental sounds, textured walls modeled after southwestern terrain, and waterfalls. Retail Bakers of America named ABCO the best bakery operation in the western region.

ACE HARDWARE CORPORATION RANK: 115

2200 Kensington Ct.
Oak Brook, IL 60521
Phone: 708-990-6600
Fax: 708-573-4894

1993 Sales: $2,018 million
FYE: December
Employees: 3,405

Key Personnel
Chm: Richard E. Laskowski
Pres & CEO: Roger E. Peterson
EVP & COO: David F. Hodnik
VP Fin: Rita D. Kahle
VP, Gen Counsel & Sec: David W. League
VP HR: Fred J. Neer

◀ See page 18 for full-page profile.

Selected Services
Advertising
Fixtures & equipment
In-store displays
Insurance
Retail computer services
Store planning & development
Training

Key Competitors
84 Lumber
Ames
Cotter & Co.
Hardware Wholesalers
Home Depot
Menard
SERVISTAR
Sherwin-Williams

Industry
Building products - retail & wholesale

Overview
Ace Hardware is the 2nd largest hardware cooperative wholesaler in the US, after Cotter & Co. (True Value Hardware). Founded in 1924, Ace is owned by its more than 4,100 dealers. Ace acts as middleman between manufacturers and dealers, distributing products through 14 Retail Support Centers, and also makes its own brand-name paint. Ace dealers receive dividends from the company's net profits and from paint manufacturing profits.

ADVANCE PUBLICATIONS, INC.

RANK: 34

950 Fingerboard Rd.
Staten Island, NY 10305
Phone: 718-981-1234
Fax: 718-981-1415

1993 Est. Sales: $5,320 million
FYE: December
Employees: 19,000

Key Personnel
Chm & CEO: Samuel I. "Si" Newhouse, Jr.
Pres: Donald E. Newhouse
Publisher: Richard Diamond
Chm, Pres & CEO, Random House: Alberto Vitale
Pres, The Condé Nast Publications: Steven T. Florio
Pres, Newhouse Newspapers: Edwin F. Russell

◀ **See page 19 for full-page profile.**

Principal Subsidiaries
The Condé Nast Publications Inc.
The New Yorker
Parade
Newhouse Broadcasting (cable)
Newhouse Newspapers
Random House (books)
Alfred A. Knopf
Ballantine Books

Key Competitors
Gannett
Hearst
New York Times
TCI
Time Warner
Tribune
Viacom
Washington Post

Industry
Publishing - newspapers, magazines, books

Overview
Advance Publications is the holding company for the largest privately held media conglomerate in the US. Its newspaper chain (Newhouse) and magazine publisher (Condé Nast) are both in the top 5 of their fields, and its book arm is the US's biggest trade book publisher (Random House). Brothers Si and Donald Newhouse control the company's 10 shares of voting stock. Si is known for big personnel shakeups, typified by his 1994 promotion of James Truman (the 35-year-old editor of *Details*), whom he dubbed the new editorial director for Condé Nast's vast periodical empire.

ADVANTIS

RANK: 253

231 N. Martingale Rd.
Schaumburg, IL 60173
Phone: 708-240-3000
Fax: 708-240-3857

1993 Est. Sales: $1,100 million
FYE: December
Employees: 3,200

Key Personnel
Chm & CEO: Syd N. Heaton
Pres & COO: Gary R. Weis
VP Fin & Planning, & CFO: Patrick M. Kerin
VP Mktg, Partnership Accounts: J.F. "Fritz" Skeen
VP & Gen Counsel: Joel A. Stern
VP Human Relations & Admin: Jim P. Doyle

Selected Services
Bulletin board services
Custom-designed LANs & WANs
Electronic data interchange
Electronic mail network
High-speed data networks
Terminal emulation software
Time sharing of network facilities

Key Competitors
AT&T
Electronic Data Systems
General Electric
LDDS
MCI
Sprint
Sterling Software

Industry
Telecommunications services

Overview
Advantis, founded in 1992, is a joint venture between IBM and Sears, Roebuck and Co. It is a networking technology company that manages IBM's global network operations. Services include network outsourcing; leased line, dial, and wireless connections, electronic mail, and electronic data interchange (EDI). Advantis systems serve a customer base of 23,000 who in turn support more than 1.5 million users worldwide.The company offers services in 700 cities. From its marketing headquarters in Tampa, Florida, Advantis sells both customized and value-added networking technology packages.

ADVENTIST HEALTH SYSTEM/WEST

RANK: 193

2100 Douglas Blvd.
Roseville, CA 95661-9002
Phone: 916-781-2000
Fax: 916-783-9146

1993 Sales: $1,350 million
FYE: December
Employees: 13,000

Key Personnel
Chm: Thomas J. Mostert
Pres: Frank F. Dupper
EVP : Donald R. Ammon
SVP S. California Healthcare: Robert G. Carmen
SVP Fin: Douglas E. Rebok
Dir HR: Roger Ashley

Selected Services
24-hour emergency services
Acute care hospitals
Community health education
Home health agencies
Intermediate care nursing facilities
Pharmacies

Key Competitors
Alta Bates
Baptist Hospitals and Health Systems
Catholic Healthcare West
Columbia/HCA
Kaiser Foundation Health Plan
Memorial Health
Samaritan Foundation
Summit Health

Industry
Hospitals

Overview
Founded in 1980 when the Seventh-Day Adventist Church merged the operations of its 2 western health care facilities, Adventist Health System/West is a nonprofit organization that operates 18 health care institutions (with about 2,800 beds), as well as outpatient facilities and home health services, in 10 western states, including Hawaii and Alaska. It admits more than 90,000 patients yearly. AHS/West is trying to keep costs down by organizing a network of primary care physicians and by developing partnerships with other health care organizations.

AECTRA REFINING & MARKETING INC.

RANK: 175

3 Riverway, Ste. 800
Houston, TX 77056
Phone: 713-629-7563
1992 Est. Sales: $1,500 million
Employees: 75

Key Personnel
Pres & CEO: Mois Mottale
Treas & CFO: Anthony J. Voigt
VP: Henry Tepper
Controller: Joe Kocurek

Selected Products
Fuel oil
Gasoline
Jet fuel
Liquid natural gas

Key Competitors
Coastal
Enron
George E. Warren
Global Petroleum
Salomon
Wyatt Inc.

Industry
Oil refining & marketing

Overview
Established in 1980, Aectra Refining & Marketing is a wholesale distributor of petroleum products through its system of petroleum bulk stations and terminals. The company experienced some expensive skirmishes with the EPA over excess lead in its gasoline in the mid-1980s. In 1991 Aectra increased its liquid natural gas extraction capacity through a pipeline acquisition in Louisiana. The company also sells naphtha and other petroleum products in Northern Germany.

AG PROCESSING INC

RANK: 223

12700 W. Dodge Rd.
Omaha, NE 68154
Phone: 402-496-7809
Fax: 402-498-2215

1993 Sales: $1,219 million
FYE: August
Employees: 2,128

Key Personnel
CEO & Gen Mgr: James W. Lindsay
VP Fin & CFO: Kenneth S. Grubbe
Grp VP Soy Ops: Anthony L. Porter
Grp VP Veg Oils & Pet Foods: Joseph L. Meyer
VP Admin: Kenneth J. McQueen
VP HR: Gordon Dorff

Business Lines
Cat & dog foods
Farm supplies
Grain storage
Poultry hatcheries
Prepared feeds
Soybean processing

Key Competitors
Bartlett
Cargill
Ferruzzi
Grand Metropolitan
Harvest States Co-ops
Mars
Moorman
Southern States Coop

Industry
Food - flour & grain

Overview
Ag Processing, an agricultural cooperative founded in 1943, with operations spanning 15 states in the Midwest, Texas, and Canada, is the 4th largest private food company and the 2nd largest soybean processor in the US, producing, at its own mills, lecithin, flour, and soybean oil, cake, and meal. These items are used in human and animal food products. The company also operates poultry hatcheries and farm supply stores, and through a joint venture with ADM, bought International Multifoods's animal feed and grain operations.

AGWAY INC.

RANK: 147

333 Butternut Dr.
DeWitt, NY 13214
Phone: 315-449-7061
Fax: 315-449-6078

1993 Sales: $1,711 million
FYE: June
Employees: 6,600

Key Personnel
Chm: Ralph H. Heffner
Pres, CEO & Gen Mgr: Charles F. Saul
SVP Fin: Peter J. O'Neill
SVP Planning/Ops: Bruce D. Ruppert
SVP Corp Svcs: David M. Hayes
VP HR: Robert T. Engfer

Operating Units
Agriculture Group
  Farm production supplies
Consumer Group
  Retail stores
Energy Group
  Farm & home heating fuels
Financial Services Group
  Insurance & leasing services

Key Competitors
Ag Processing
Andersons
ConAgra
Deere
Farmland Industries
Global Petroleum
Kmart
Wal-Mart

Industry
Agricultural operations

Overview
Founded in 1964, Agway is the largest agricultural cooperative in the Northeast and the 2nd largest in the US (after Farmland), with operations in 12 states and more than 90,000 members. Facing a rapidly declining number of farms in the Northeast, Agway embarked upon a 3-year reengineering program in 1992. The cooperative has announced plans to divest its food operations, Agway's largest operating division, which had been providing almost 50% of net sales.

◀ **See page 20 for full-page profile.**

AID ASSOCIATION FOR LUTHERANS, INC.

RANK: 65

4321 N. Ballard Rd.
Appleton, WI 54919
Phone: 414-734-5721
Fax: 414-730-4757

1993 Sales: $2,885 million
FYE: December
Employees: 3,959

Key Personnel
Chm: Henry F. Schieg
Pres & CEO: Richard L. Gunderson
SVP, CFO & Treas: Roger J. Johnson
SVP & Chief Investment Officer: John H. Pender
SVP, Sec & Gen Counsel: William R. Heerman
SVP Member Field Svcs: Kevin J. Van Eron

Business Lines
Disability income policies
Health insurance
IRAs & annuities
Life insurance
Medicare supplemental insurance
Mutual funds

Key Competitors
American Express
John Hancock
Lutheran Brotherhood
MetLife
New York Life
Northwestern Mutual
Prudential
Teachers Insurance and Annuity

Industry
Insurance - life

Overview
Founded in 1902, the Aid Association for Lutherans (AAL) is one of the nation's largest fraternal benefits societies. Not officially affiliated with the Lutheran Church, the society provides insurance, retirement, and investment products to 1.6 million Lutheran members through more than 8,600 local volunteer groups, called branches. A nonprofit organization, the society channels its profits directly to insurance holders and uses them to finance more than $50 million worth of charitable activities, such as college scholarships and an alcohol and drug abuse prevention program.

ALAMO RENT A CAR, INC.

RANK: 262

110 SE Sixth St.
Ft. Lauderdale, FL 33301
Phone: 305-522-0000
Fax: 305-468-2184

1993 Sales: $1,080 million
FYE: December
Employees: 7,500

Key Personnel
Chm & CEO: Michael S. Egan
EVP Mktg & Sales: Macdonald Clark
SVP Fin & Admin: Bob Pickup
Senior Dir Public Affairs: Liz Clark
Exec Dir HR Devel: Connie Hoffmann

Selected Services
Car rental
Financial services
Truck rental

Key Competitors
Agency Rent-A-Car
Avis
Budget Rent A Car
Chrysler
Enterprise Rent-A-Car
Ford
General Motors
Mitsubishi

Industry
Leasing - autos

Overview
Alamo is the US's 3rd largest car rental company, with 151 locations in the US, UK, Switzerland, Ireland, The Netherlands, Germany, and Belgium. The company is noted for the zeal of its employees, whose practices sometimes opened the company to FTC criticism of their bait-and-switch tactics and failure to disclose extra charges. The company has moved to correct these problems through increased training. Alamo was started in 1974 by insurance magnate John MacArthur to target vacationers. Michael Egan and several others bought it in 1978, and since the mid-1980s Egan has pursued the business market.

ALCO HEALTH SERVICES CORPORATION

RANK: 49

300 Chesterfield Pkwy.
Valley Forge, PA 19482
Phone: 215-296-4480
Fax: 215-647-0141

1993 Sales: $3,719 million
FYE: September
Employees: 2,403

Key Personnel
Chm, Pres & CEO: John F. McNamara
Group Pres, Central Reg: R. David Yost
Group Pres, Eastern Reg: David M. Flowers
VP Fin & Treas: Kurt J. Hilzinger
VP, Legal Counsel & Sec: Teresa T. Ciccotelli
VP HR & Asst Sec: Robert D. Gregory

◄ **See page 21 for full-page profile.**

Selected Services
Family Pharmacy (merchandising)
Income Pax (promotional aid)
Income RePax (bulk purchasing)
Income Rx (generic sales)
Partner Pak (promotional aid)
Pharmaceuticals wholesaling
PrimeNet (hospital purchasing)

Key Competitors
American Home Products
Baxter
Cardinal Health
Eli Lilly
Merck
National Intergroup
Pharmacy Direct Network
Price/Costco

Industry
Drugs & sundries - wholesale

Overview
Alco Health Services is one of the largest pharmaceuticals wholesalers in the US; it also provides distribution for a variety of health and beauty products to independent pharmacies, chains, nursing homes, and hospitals. Spun off as a public company from Alco Standard in 1985, Alco Health went private in a 1988 management-led LBO with the investment assistance of Citicorp Venture Capital Corp. Since then it has concentrated on paying down its debt.

ALEX LEE INC.

RANK: 264

120 Fourth St. SW
Hickory, NC 28602
Phone: 704-323-4424
Fax: 704-323-4435

1993 Sales: $1,073 million
FYE: September
Employees: 4,500

Key Personnel
Chm, Pres & CEO: Boyd Lee George
SVP, Sec & Treas: Ronald W. Knedlik
VP; Pres & CEO, Lowe's Food Stores: Dennis G. Hatchell
VP; Pres, Institution Food House: Frank Sherman
VP; Pres, Merchants Distributors: Gerald Davis
VP HR: Glenn Debiasi

Operating Units
Alex Lee Inc.
Institution Food House Inc.
Lowe's Food Stores Inc.
Merchants Distributors, Inc.

Key Competitors
Fleming
Food Lion
Kroger
K-Va-T
SUPERVALU
SYSCO
US Foodservice
Winn-Dixie

Industry
Food - wholesale to grocers

Overview
Alex Lee was created in 1992 as a holding company for 3 existing companies that are located primarily in the Southeast: a wholesale food and merchandise distributor, a supermarket and convenience store operator, and a food service distributor. With the consolidation, Lee serves its own as well as other independent retail operations, supermarkets, and convenience stores and is a food service provider for restaurants, schools, and other institutions. Its service area consists of North Carolina, South Carolina, Virginia, West Virginia, Tennessee, and Georgia.

ALLEGHENY HEALTH, EDUCATION AND RESEARCH FOUNDATION

RANK: 314

320 E. North Ave.
Pittsburgh, PA 15212
Phone: 412-359-3131
Fax: 412-359-6606

1993 Sales: $938 million
FYE: June
Employees: 14,018

Key Personnel
Chm: W. P. Snyder III
VC & VP: Douglas Danforth
Pres & CEO: Sherif S. Abdelhak
Treas & CFO: David W. McConnell
SVP: Stephen H. Spargo
Sec: Nancy A. Wynstra

Principal Members
Allegheny General Hospital
Hahnemann School of Medicine
Hahnemann University Hospital
Medical College Hospitals
Medical College of Pennsylvania
St. Christopher's Hospital

Key Competitors
American Healthcare
Brim
Franciscan Health
Legacy Health System
National Medical
Presbyterian Medical
Universal Health Services
Voluntary Hospitals of America

Industry
Hospitals

Overview
Pittsburgh-based Allegheny Health, Education and Research Foundation (AHERF) is a statewide alliance of hospitals and medical schools in eastern and western Pennsylvania that together have over 3,000 beds, more than 2,800 students, and 3,220 faculty members. The 1993 addition of Hahnemann University merges 2 of Philadelphia's 6 medical schools and is one of the more visible efforts of consolidation in the health care industry. The new organization is looking for ways to combine services and reduce costs.

ALLINA HEALTH SYSTEM

RANK: 313

2810 57th Ave. North
Minneapolis, MN 55430
Phone: 612-574-7800
Fax: 612-574-7953

1993 Sales: $948 million
Employees: 15,600

Key Personnel
Exec Officer: Gordon M. Sprenger
Pres: K. James Ehlen
SVP Fin, HealthSpan: David B. Jones
Fin Officer: Richard Blair
Legal Officer, HealthSpan: Mark G. Mishek
HR Officer, HealthSpan: Mike Howe

Selected Services
Acute & long-term care facilities
Home care
Home medical equipment services
Hospice services
Long-term care & living facilities
Managed care health plans
Medical transportation services
Preferred provider plans

Key Competitors
Blue Cross
Columbia/HCA
Employee Benefit Plans
Family Health Plan
Mayo Foundation
PreferredOne
Prudential
United HealthCare

Industry
Hospitals

Overview
Allina, formed by a 1994 merger of HealthSpan Health Systems Corporation (integrated health services) and Medica (managed care), is a nonprofit health care delivery system serving Minnesota and regions of Wisconsin and North and South Dakota. The new system includes HealthSpan's 3,200 affiliated physicians and its hospitals, clinics, and health-related services as well as Medica's managed care health plans (with over 550,000 enrollees), services, and network of over 5,000 physicians.

ALLING AND CORY COMPANY

RANK: 489

25 Verona St.
Rochester, NY 14602-0403
Phone: 716-454-1880
Fax: 716-454-6169

1993 Sales: $557 million
FYE: December
Employees: 1,150

Key Personnel
Chm: Richard M. Harris
Pres & CEO: Samuel T. Hubbard, Jr.
Treas: James W. Stenger
Sec: R. Macy Harris
VP Fin: John B. Henderson
Dir HR: Margaret Supinski

Major Locations
Baltimore, MD
Buffalo, NY
Cleveland, OH
Harrisburg, PA
New York, NY
Philadelphia, PA
Pittsburgh, PA
Rochester, NY

Key Competitors
Alco Standard
Avery Dennison
Boise Cascade
Georgia-Pacific
International Paper
Mead
Moore
Office Depot

Industry
Paper & paper products

Overview
Alling and Cory, the nation's oldest and largest independent paper distributor, was founded in Rochester, New York, in 1819 when Thomas Jefferson was US president. The company was originally a stationery, book selling, and publishing business. In 1834 founder Elihu Marshall sold his company to William Alling, who was joined by partner David Cory in 1859. It has remained under the control of the Alling and Cory families ever since. Alling and Cory supplies paper, business products, and packaging supplies to some 15,000 customers and has 16 sales and distribution centers in the northeastern US.

ALLISON ENGINE CO.

RANK: 408

5601 Fortune Circle South
Indianapolis, IN 46421-5530
Phone: 317-230-2000
Fax: 317-230-3562

1993 Sales: $740 million
FYE: December
Employees: 4,100

Key Personnel
Chm & CEO: F. Blake Wallace
EVP: Wilson Burns
EVP: Frank Verkamp
EVP: Mike Hudson
CFO: Joe Doyle
VP HR: Barry Smith

Major Products
Commercial aircraft engines
Helicopter engines
Industrial engines
Marine engines
Tiltrotor aircraft engine
Transport aircraft engines
Turboprop engines
Turboshaft engines

Key Competitors
AlliedSignal
Briggs & Stratton
Cummins Engine
General Electric
Penske
Rolls-Royce
Stewart & Stevenson
United Technologies

Industry
Aerospace - aircraft equipment

Overview
Formerly the Allison Gas Turbine Division of General Motors, Allison Engine Co. went private when New York buyout firm Clayton, Dubilier & Rice and members of Allison's management paid GM $313 million in December 1993. Most engines Allison makes are for aircraft. Founded by James A. Allison, cofounder of the Indianapolis Motor Speedway, as the Allison Speedway Team Co. in 1913, the company began overhauling aircraft engines for the army in WWI. GM bought the company in 1929. Allison later specialized in turboprop and turbojet engines.

ALLMERICA FINANCIAL

RANK: 75

440 Lincoln St.
Worcester, MA 01653
Phone: 508-855-1000
Fax: 508-853-6332

1993 Sales: $2,705 million
FYE: December
Employees: 3,429

Key Personnel
Pres & CEO: John F. O'Brien
SVP & Gen Counsel: John F. Kelly
VP HR: Bruce C. Anderson
VP & CFO: Eric A. Simonsen
VP & Chief Investment Officer: James R. McAuliffe
VP Govt Affairs & Sec: Richard J. Baker

Business Lines
Employee benefit products
Insurance products
Investment products
Mutual fund services
Retirement plans

Key Competitors
Aetna
Allstate
Equitable
John Hancock
MetLife
New York Life
Northwestern Mutual
Prudential

Industry
Insurance - life

Overview
Allmerica Financial, a holding company for insurance and financial service companies, began as State Mutual Life Assurance Company of America in 1844. Recently, Allmerica has focused on variable annuities and variable life insurance. Allmerica's 2 newest companies provide securities and custodial services to banks, brokers, and institutional investors and sell nonmedical insurance products. The company operates in all 50 states, DC, US Virgin Islands, Puerto Rico, and Canada through 1,280 agents. Presently a mutual company, Allmerica is becoming a stock company.

A-MARK FINANCIAL CORPORATION

RANK: 301

100 Wilshire Blvd., 3rd Fl.
Santa Monica, CA 90401
Phone: 310-319-0200
Fax: 310-319-0279

1993 Est. Sales: $1,000 million
FYE: July
Employees: 60

Key Personnel
Chm & Pres: Steven C. Markoff
SVP & Chief Admin Officer: John B. Fern
Sec & Treas: Joseph Pozaki

Selected Services
Gold trading
  Coins, bullion, bars & wafers
Platinum trading
  Coins, bars & plates
Silver trading
  Coins, bars, ingots & medallions
  Coin bags
Storage programs

Key Competitors
Citra Trading
Donald Bruce
Harlan J. Berk
Harry Winston
William J. Kappel Wholesale

Industry
Precious metals & jewelry - wholesale

Overview
A-Mark Financial is the holding company of A-Mark Precious Metals. Founded in 1965, the subsidiary trades coins, bars, grain, and ingots on behalf of dealers, bankers, miners, refiners, jewelers, investment advisors, and others worldwide. A-Mark boasts the industry's largest trading and depository network and also offers a wide range of customer service programs, including marketing support, consignment, and metal refining. A-Mark is owned by Chairman Steven Markoff, who founded the company at age 16.

AMERICAN ASSOCIATION OF RETIRED PERSONS

RANK: N/R

601 E St. NW
Washington, DC 20049
Phone: 202-434-2277
Fax: 202-434-2525

1993 Sales: $369 million
FYE: December
Employees: 1,793

Key Personnel
Chm: Judith N. Brown
Pres: Lovola W. Burgess
Exec Dir: Horace B. Deets
Treas: Allan W. Tull
Dir Legislation & Public Policy: John C. Rother
Dir HR: Richard W. Henry

◀ **See page 22 for full-page profile.**

Selected Services
Auto club
Auto insurance
Health insurance
Homeowner insurance
Informational publications
Mail order pharmacy
Travel discounts

Industry
Membership organization

Overview
The American Association of Retired Persons (AARP) is a service and advocacy group open to all Americans over age 50. It provides information on issues of importance to older people, lobbies for legislation on behalf of its more than 33 million members, provides insurance at attractive rates, and offers travel and entertainment discounts in cooperation with nationally known providers. Founded in 1958 by Ethel Andrus, AARP also sponsors community volunteer programs for its members.

AMERICAN CRYSTAL SUGAR COMPANY

RANK: 494

101 N. Third St.
Moorhead, MN 56560
Phone: 218-236-4400
Fax: 218-236-4422

1993 Sales: $543 million
FYE: August
Employees: 1,500

Key Personnel
Chm: E.N. "Cactus" Warner
Pres & CEO: Joseph P. Famalette
VP Agriculture: Robert W. Levos
VP Fin: James J. Horvath
VP Mktg: Jack G. Lackman
VP HR: Larry L. Mathias

Selected Services
Molasses production
Seed marketing
Seed production
Sugarbeet marketing
Sugarbeet pulp marketing
Sugarbeet pulp refining
Sugarbeet refining
Sugarbeet storage

Key Competitors
ADM
Connell
Contran
Imperial Holly
King Ranch
Monsanto
Savannah Foods
Spreckels Industries

Industry
Food - sugar & refining

Overview
Incorporated in 1973, American Crystal Sugar is owned by its approximately 2,000 members, all of whom are sugarbeet growers in North Dakota and Minnesota. The largest producer of beet sugar in the US, American Crystal also processes sugarbeet pulp, molasses, and seed and markets all these products. The cooperative operates processing facilities in Crookston and East Grand Forks, Minnesota, and in Drayton and Hillsboro, North Dakota. Recently American Crystal agreed to invest with another agricultural cooperative in a wet corn processing plant that is expected to become the 4th largest producer of high fructose corn syrup in the US.

AMERICAN FAMILY MUTUAL INSURANCE COMPANY

RANK: 67

6000 American Pkwy.
Madison, WI 53783
Phone: 608-249-2111
Fax: 608-243-4921

1993 Sales: $2,818 million
FYE: December
Employees: 6,373

Key Personnel
Chm & CEO: Dale F. Mathwich
Pres & COO: Harvey R. Pierce
EVP Admin: James R. Klokner
EVP Fin & Treas: Paul L. King
VP & Corp Legal: James F. Eldridge
VP HR: Vicki L. Chvala

Major Products
Business insurance
Financial services
Health insurance
Home & property insurance
Life insurance
Vehicle insurance

Key Competitors
Aetna
AFLAC
Allstate
Equitable
GEICO
MetLife
State Farm
Travelers

Industry
Insurance - multiline

Overview
Founded in 1927, Madison, Wisconsin–based American Family Insurance represents 6 insurance-related companies that provide property, casualty, life, fire, health, and marine insurance, as well as annuities and financial services, primarily to individuals. Chairman Dale Mathwich attributes the company's success to the loyalty of its employees (most of whom have been with the company 10–15 years).

AMERICAN FINANCIAL CORPORATION

RANK: 74

One E. Fourth St.
Cincinnati, OH 45202
Phone: 513-579-2121
Fax: 513-579-2580

1993 Sales: $2,721 million
FYE: December
Employees: 60,790

Key Personnel
Chm & CEO: Carl H. Lindner
Pres & COO: Ronald F. Walker
Pres, Great American Ins: C.H. Lindner III
VP & Treas: Fred J. Runk
VP & Gen Counsel: James E. Evans
VP HR: Lawrence Otto

◀ **See page 23 for full-page profile.**

Investments
American Financial Enterprises
American Premier Underwriters
Blockbuster Entertainment
Chiquita Brands International
Citicasters Inc.
General Cable Corp
Great American Insurance

Key Competitors
Aetna
Allstate
MetLife
New York Life
Northwestern Mutual
Prudential
State Farm
Transamerica

Industry
Diversified operations

Overview
Founded in 1955, Cincinnati-based American Financial Corp. oversees the diverse holdings of financier Carl Lindner and his family. It supplies property, casualty, and life insurance through its Great American Insurance Co. subsidiary. But Lindner's shakier investments, like Chiquita Brands International, have hurt the company's operations. Another troubled investment is Citicasters, Inc., a broadcasting company in which AFC owns 20%. Citicasters emerged from bankruptcy reorganization in 1993.

AMERICAN RED CROSS

RANK: 138

431 18th St. NW
Washington, DC 20006
Phone: 202-737-8300
Fax: 202-639-3711

1993 Sales: $1,796 million
FYE: June
Employees: 25,000

Key Personnel
Chm: Norman R. Augustine
Pres: Elizabeth Dole
Treas: Sarah A. Schwarz
Sec & Gen Counsel: Karen Shoos Lipton
VP Fin & Comptroller: John D. Campbell
VP HR: James E. Thomas III

◀ See page 24 for full-page profile.

Selected Services
Blood collection & delivery
Disaster services
Health & safety education
Military & social services
Plasma collection & delivery
Refugee aid
Tissue collection & delivery
Victim tracing & message services

Industry
Nonprofit organization

Overview
Founded in 1881 by a group led by Clara Barton, the American Red Cross is a member of the League of Red Cross and Red Crescent Societies, which is made up of more than 145 societies around the world. Although the American Red Cross is chartered by Congress, it is not a government agency. It is a nonprofit organization staffed primarily by volunteers (at a ratio of 50 volunteers to one paid employee). It is funded by contributions, endowments, and income from its biomedical services unit, the custodian of the largest blood supply in the US.

AMERICAN RETAIL GROUP, INC.

RANK: 107

1114 Avenue of the Americas
New York, NY 10036
Phone: 212-391-4141
Fax: 212-302-4381

1992 Est. Sales: $2,120 million
FYE: December
Employees: 17,000

Key Personnel
Pres: Roland Brenninkmeyer
EVP Fin: Jim Painter
VP HR: Tom Elliott

Operating Units
Byrons
EMS (Eastern Mountain Sports)
Maurices
Miller's Outpost
Modern Woman
Steinbach
Uptons
Women's World

Key Competitors
L.L. Bean
Dayton Hudson
The Gap
Kmart
Merry-Go-Round
Melville
One Price Clothing
Wal-Mart

Industry
Retail - apparel

Overview
American Retail Group (ARG), once known as Amcena Corp., is a holding company for 8 chains of low- to moderately priced apparel stores. Founded in 1963, ARG is owned by the secretive Brenninkmeyer family, which rules one of the world's largest apparel retailing empires. The company began by acquiring smaller apparel chains and later moved into specialty department stores, like the landmark retailer Orhbach's and the Howland-Steinbach chain, which was converted to Steinbachs. ARG owns groups of stores from Florida to New Hampshire as well as in California, Minnesota, and Canada.

AMERICAN STANDARD INC.

RANK: 47

1114 Avenue of the Americas
New York, NY 10036
Phone: 212-703-5100
Fax: 212-703-5177

1993 Sales: $3,830 million
FYE: December
Employees: 36,000

Key Personnel
Chm, Pres & CEO: Emmanuel A. Kampouris
SVP Plumbing Products: George H. Kerckhove
SVP Transportation Products: Horst Hinrichs
VP & CFO: Fred A. Allardyce
VP, Gen Counsel & Sec: Frederick W. Jaqua
VP HR: Adrian B. Deshotel

◀ See page 25 for full-page profile.

Major Products
Air brakes
Bathroom fittings & fixtures
Bathtubs
Custom-engineered AC parts
Field-installed air conditioning
Kitchen fittings & fixtures
Mini-split air conditioning systems
Unitary air conditioning systems

Key Competitors
AlliedSignal
American Brands
Black & Decker
Eaton
Eljer Industries
Kohler
Masco
United Technologies

Industry
Building products - plumbing fixtures

Overview
Products, if not profits, are flowing at American Standard, the world's #1 plumbing fixture manufacturer, founded in 1929. The company claims to have increased the inventory turnover rates of all its items with its production-on-request strategy. But it hasn't washed its hands of old debts: to fend off a hostile takeover by Black & Decker in 1988, American Standard deeply plumbed the money well, leaving its profits drowning in an ocean of interest expense. It is concentrating on expanding its international business and its US retail home center business.

AMERICAN UNITED LIFE INSURANCE COMPANY

RANK: 248

One American Sq.
Indianapolis, IN 46204
Phone: 317-263-1877
Fax: 317-236-1931

1993 Sales: $1,103 million
FYE: December
Employees: 864

Key Personnel
Chm, Pres & CEO: Jerry D. Semler
EVP: R. Stephen Radcliffe
SVP Corp Fin: James Murphy
SVP Investments: G. D. Sapp
Gen Counsel & Sec: William R. Brown
SVP HR: Gerald L. Plummer

Business Lines
Annuities
Credit life insurance
Group insurance
Individual insurance
Medical and disability insurance
Pension products
Reinsurance

Key Competitors
Aetna
Equitable
General Re
John Hancock
MetLife
New York Life
Prudential
Travelers

Industry
Insurance - multiline

Overview
American United was formed as the result of a merger between American Central Life Insurance and United Mutual Life Insurance companies in 1936. Owned by its policyholders, the Indiana-based company operates in 45 states and the District of Columbia. American United specializes in pension products but offers an array of insurance products, including individual and group life, medical, disability, and credit insurance, and annuities. The oldest life reinsurer in the US, the company still has a presence in the field of reinsurance, accepting risks written by more than 140 other companies.

AMERISERV FOOD CO.

RANK: 365

13355 Noel Rd., Ste. 2225
Dallas, TX 75240
Phone: 214-385-8595
Fax: 214-702-7391

1993 Sales: $833 million
FYE: December
Employees: 1,200

Key Personnel
Chm: John P. Lewis
Pres & CEO: William R. Burgess
VP & COO: Jim Fenner
VP Fin & CFO: A. Scott Letier

Principal Subsidiaries
Alpha Distributors
First Choice Food Distributors
Food Service Systems
Interstate Distributors
Post Food Service
The Sonneveldt Co.

Key Competitors
Ben E. Keith
Gordon Food Service
Heinz
Philip Morris
Quaker Oats
Sara Lee
SYSCO
US Foodservice

Industry
Food - wholesale to restaurants

Overview
AmeriServ is one of the fastest-growing commercial foods distributors in the US, handling more than 2,500 food items for over 5,000 restaurants and fast-food outlets (including Dairy Queen and Wendy's) in more than 35 states. Founded in 1989 by John P. Lewis (and owned by his The Lewis Company), AmeriServ has grown primarily via the acquisition of 6 food distribution companies throughout the US. Debt associated with these acquisitions led management to consider going public in the early 1990s, but the issue was withdrawn after the prospectus was published.

AMI COS.

RANK: 486

46 W. Boylston St.
Worchester, MA 01605
Phone: 508-852-5311
Fax: 508-856-9354

1993 Sales: $561 million
FYE: March
Employees: 650

Key Personnel
Pres: Eugene J. Ribakoff
Treas: Charles K. Ribakoff II
HR: Gloria Labovitz

Selected Services
Automobile leasing & rentals
Automobile parts
Automobile sales
Automobile service
Equipment leasing & rentals
Truck leasing & rentals

Key Competitors
Alamo Rent A Car
Avis
Enterprise Rent-A-Car
Holman Enterprises
Lily Transportation
Ryder
UB Vehicle Leasing
U-Haul

Industry
Retail - new & used cars

Overview
AMI, incorporated in 1952, began when Eugene Ribakoff purchased a small Ford dealership with a 2-car showroom in Worcester, Massachusetts. AMI is now a holding company for 7 car dealerships, a car rental corporation, a Budget Rent A Car franchise, a truck leasing corporation, and an equipment leasing corporation that operate in Connecticut, Maryland, Maine, Massachusetts, New Hampshire, New Jersey, New York, Ohio, Rhode Island, and Vermont. The 7 automobile dealerships owned by AMI sell Buicks, Dodges, Fords, Lincolns, Mercurys, and Toyotas. AMI also exports vehicle parts and markets vehicles to municipalities.

AMICA MUTUAL INSURANCE COMPANY

RANK: 344

10 Weybosset St.
Providence, RI 02903
Phone: 401-521-9100
Fax: 401-453-3463

1993 Sales: $871 million
FYE: December
Employees: 2,900

Key Personnel
Chm & CEO: Joel N. Tobey
Pres & COO: Thomas A. Taylor
EVP: Andrew M. Erickson
SVP, CFO & Treas: Harold Hitchen, Jr.
SVP & Gen Counsel: Kenneth H. Nails
SVP HR: Kenneth M. Moffat Jr.

Business Lines
Automobile insurance
Flood insurance
Homeowners insurance
Life insurance
Marine insurance
Personal excess liability insurance
Renters insurance
Workers' compensation insurance

Key Competitors
Aetna
Allstate
CIGNA
GEICO
Kemper
Liberty Mutual
Prudential
State Farm

Industry
Insurance - property & casualty

Overview
Amica began operation in 1972 when Automobile Mutual Insurance Company of America and Factory Mutual Life Insurance Company of America, founded in 1907, merged. A mutual company, Amica offers a broad range of personal insurance products. The company consistently wins high ratings from consumer groups for its customer service, boasts of low employee turnover, and has paid annual dividends since 1972. Amica spurns costly advertising campaigns, counting on referrals for most of its business. Amica is in good financial shape, emerging relatively unscathed from a series of natural disasters, such as the 1994 Los Angeles earthquake.

AMSTED INDUSTRIES INCORPORATED

RANK: 349

205 N. Michigan Ave., 44th Fl.
Chicago, IL 60601
Phone: 312-645-1700
Fax: 312-819-8425

1993 Sales: $868 million
FYE: September
Employees: 7,900

Key Personnel
Pres & CEO: Gordon R. Lohman
VP & CFO: Gerald K. Walter
VP: Warren W. Rasmussen
VP: David B. Whitehurst
VP, Gen Counsel & Sec: Thomas C. Berg
Dir Personnel: Arthur M. Meske

Major Products
Cooling towers
Conveyor belt chains
Evaporative cooling equipment
Piston pins
Powder metal products
Railroad car components
Steel cable
Water & sewer pipe

Key Competitors
Bethlehem Steel
Duchossois Industries
Ingersoll-Rand
Morrison Knudsen
Newcor
Nordson
Traco Manufacturing
United Rail Car Manufacturing

Industry
Metal products - fabrication

Overview
AMSTED Industries makes a wide variety of products for 3 main markets: railroad, construction and building, and general industry. Founded in 1902 as American Steel Foundries, this employee-owned company focused on products for railroads during its early years. In the 1940s it began venturing into nonrailroad manufacturing and took the name AMSTED Industries in 1962. AMSTED operates globally through 7 divisions: American Steel Foundries, Baltimore Aircoil, Burgess-Norton, Diamond Chain, Griffin Pipe Products, Griffin Wheel, and Macwhyte.

AMWAY CORPORATION

RANK: 41

7575 Fulton St. East
Ada, MI 49355
Phone: 616-676-6000
Fax: 616-676-7102

1993 Sales: $3,465 million
FYE: August
Employees: 11,000

Key Personnel
Chm: Jay Van Andel
Pres: Richard M. DeVos, Jr.
COO & EVP: Thomas W. Eggleston
SVP & Gen Counsel: Craig Meurlin
CFO: Lawrence Call
VP HR: Dwight A. Sawyer

◀ **See page 26 for full-page profile.**

Major Products
Health & beauty supplies
Home care & cleaning products
Housewares
Janitorial supplies
Reference books
Watches

Key Competitors
American Home Products
Avon
Carter-Wallace
Herbalife Industries
Home Interiors & Gifts
Mary Kay
Premark
Warner-Lambert

Industry
Retail - direct

Overview
One of the leading direct sales businesses in the world, Amway was founded in 1959 by high school friends Jay Van Andel and Richard DeVos, Sr., who, with their families, own and control the company. Amway makes a wide variety of personal care, household, and cosmetic products and distributes them through its network of more than 2 million independent distributors throughout the world. Amway is noted for its high degree of vertical integration; it owns everything from the farms that produce raw materials for vitamins to trucking fleets that deliver its products.

ANDERSEN CORP.

RANK: 298

100 Fourth Ave. North
Bayport, MN 55003
Phone: 612-439-5150
Fax: 612-430-5107

1993 Sales: $1,000 million
FYE: December
Employees: 3,600

Key Personnel
VC, Pres & CEO: Jerold W. Wulf
VP, Treas & CFO: Michael O. Johnson
EVP & Sec: Alan H. Johnson
VP Business Planning: Donald Garofalo
VP Eng: Jerry Larson
Mgr HR: Paul Wiemerslage

Major Products
Custom-built window units
Insulated windows
Patio doors
Standard window units
Window frames

Key Competitors
Boise Cascade
Bright Wood
Jeld-Wen
Jim Walter
Mervin Lumber
Pella Corp.
Weyerhaeuser

Industry
Building products - windows

Overview
Hans Jacob Andersen, the Danish immigrant who founded the predecessor to Andersen Corp. in 1903 with his sons, revolutionized the building industry by standardizing the size of wooden window frames and using interchangeable parts. Now his company is the world's top maker of wooden windows and patio doors, accounting for about 10% of the market. Known for its benefits and incentive programs, Andersen has some of the highest-paid factory workers in the US, and employees own 27% of its stock; the Andersen family, no longer active in management, owns the rest.

THE ANDERSONS MANAGEMENT CORP.

RANK: 406

1200 Dussel Dr.
Maumee, OH 43537
Phone: 419-893-5050
Fax: 419-891-6655

1992 Sales: $747 million
FYE: December
Employees: 886

Key Personnel
Chm: Thomas H. Anderson
Pres & CEO: Richard P. Anderson
VP: Joseph Braker
CFO: Dick George
Gen Counsel: Dale Fallet
HR: Joe Christen

Business Lines
Crop preparation services
Department stores
Farm product warehousing
Farm supplies
Grains & field beans
Management services

Key Competitors
Bunge Corp.
Cargill
Continental Grain
Countrymark Co-op
General Mills
GROWMARK
Midwest Co-ops
Sears

Industry
Food - flour & grain

Overview
Andersons is an Ohio-based partnership whose primary business is grain sales and storage facilities in Ohio, Michigan, Indiana, and Illinois. Founded in 1947, Andersons also operates Andersons General Stores in Columbus, Lima, Maumee, Northwood, and Toledo, Ohio, in addition to a smaller store in Delphi, Indiana. The department stores reflect Andersons's agricultural background by specializing in lawn and garden products, building supplies, and hardware, as well as offering pet care products, workwear, office products, and food.

THE ANSCHUTZ CORPORATION

RANK: 63

555 17th St., Ste. 2400
Denver, CO 80202
Phone: 303-298-1000
Fax: 303-298-8881

1992 Sales: $3,134 million
FYE: December
Employees: 23,000

Key Personnel
CEO: Philip F. Anschutz
VP Fin: Douglas L. Polson
Treas: Tom Kundert
Sec: Craig Slater
VP & Gen Counsel: Richard M. Jones

Business Lines
Building contracting
Freight car leasing
Industrial land development
Oil & gas extraction
Rail transportation
Railroad bridge operation
Real estate investing
Trucking

Key Competitors
Belgian Oil
Burlington Northern
Consolidated Freightways
Santa Fe Pacific
Schneider National
Sinclair Oil
Union Pacific
Yellow Corporation

Industry
Diversified operations

Overview
The Anschutz Corporation, founded in 1958, acts primarily as a holding company for the interests of Philip F. Anschutz, a Denver billionaire whose personal fortune gushes from oil on his Utah/Wyoming ranch. In 1993 he ended a 5-year stint as sole owner of the debt-ridden Southern Pacific Railroad by taking the company public, retaining an interest (now at 42%) in the historic railway. He also owns the Denver & Rio Grande Western Railroad, an oil and gas exploration company, and real estate.

APOLLO ADVISORS

RANK: N/R

2 Manhattanville Rd.
Purchase, NY 10577
Phone: 914-694-8000
Fax: 914-694-8067

Employees: 25

Key Personnel
Owner: Leon Black
Partner: Craig Cogut

Selected Investments
Astrum Inc. (47%)
Gillett Holdings (61%)
Interco (68%)
McCrory Corp.
New York Law Publishing (65%)
Restaurant Enterprises (41%)
Salant Corp. (41%)
Walter Industries

Industry
Financial - investors

Overview
Often referred to as a "vulture investor," financier Leon Black and his staff at Apollo Advisors specialize in buying distressed assets. A former Drexel Burnham mergers specialist, Black is the head of a group of partnerships that have significant ownership stakes in as many as 100 companies. Founded in 1990, with about a dozen other former Drexel bankers, the group started by investing in distressed junk bond issues. The company has flourished by reviving bankrupt or near-bankrupt companies, and it is now focusing on media and apparel businesses.

THE ARA GROUP, INC.

RANK: 38

1101 Market St.
Philadelphia, PA 19107
Phone: 215-238-3000
Fax: 215-238-3333

1993 Sales: $4,891 million
FYE: October
Employees: 131,000

Key Personnel
Chm, Pres & CEO: Joseph Neubauer
EVP & Pres, ARASERVE: William Leonard
EVP & Pres, Leisure/Intl : Richard H. Vent
EVP; Pres, Health & Educ: Julian L. Carr Jr.
EVP Fin & Personnel & CFO: James E. Ksansnak
EVP, Gen Counsel & Sec: Martin W. Spector

◀ See page 27 for full-page profile.

Operating Units
ARA Coliseum Limited
ARA Environmental Services, Inc.
ARA Facilities Management, Inc.
ARA Services Magazine & Book
ARATEX Services, Inc.
Children's World Learning Centers
Lake Powell Resorts & Marinas
Szabo Food Service, Inc.

Key Competitors
Accor
Berkshire Hathaway
Corrections Corp. of America
Delaware North
Dial
Helmsley
Host Marriott
Ogden

Industry
Food services

Overview
Formed from a 1959 merger, Philadelphia-based ARA is one of the largest food service companies in the world, serving more than 10 million clients daily, many of whom are long-term patrons. The company provides or manages an increasingly diverse range of service-related activities, including food and leisure services, uniform rental and maintenance, health and education services, and distribution services. The company went private in 1984 to avoid a hostile takeover, and management has since acquired over 90% of ARA stock.

ARMY & AIR FORCE EXCHANGE SERVICE

RANK: 20

3911 S. Walton Walker Blvd.
Dallas, TX 75236
Phone: 214-312-2011
Fax: 214-312-3000

1993 Sales: $7,263 million
FYE: January
Employees: 72,562

Key Personnel
Chm: Lt. Gen. Merle Freitag
Commander & CEO: Maj. Gen. Albin G. Wheeler
COO: Paul E. Fromm
Gen Counsel: Lt. Col. D. Anthony Rogers
CFO: Martin R. Handel
Dir, People Resources Directorate: Michael R. Cunningham

◀ See page 28 for full-page profile.

Selected Services
Clothing stores
Food facilities
Personal services concessions
Retail stores
Theaters
Vending centers

Key Competitors
Ames
Dayton Hudson
Kmart
Montgomery Ward
NEX
J. C. Penney
Sears
Wal-Mart

Industry
Retail

Overview
Established in 1895, the Army & Air Force Exchange (AAFES) is one of the nation's largest retailers, operating post exchanges (PXs) and base exchanges (BXs) at military bases around the world. AAFES operates under the Department of Defense but receives no funding from it. The exchange provides its customers — active duty military personnel, National Guard members, reservists, and retirees, and their families — with savings of around 20% off normal retail. Although it is headed by military personnel, AAFES is staffed almost entirely by civilians.

ARTHUR ANDERSEN & CO, SOCIÉTÉ COOPÉRATIVE

RANK: 27

69 W. Washington St.
Chicago, IL 60602
Phone: 312-580-0069
Fax: 312-507-2548

1993 Sales: $6,017 million
FYE: August
Employees: 66,478

Key Personnel
Chm, CEO & Mng Part: Lawrence A. Weinbach
Mng Part, Arthur Andersen: Richard L. Measelle
Mng Part, Andersen Consulting: George T. Shaheen
Firm Sec & Gen Counsel: Jon N. Ekdahl
CFO: John D. Lewis
HR: Peter Pesce

◀ See page 29 for full-page profile.

Operating Units
Arthur Andersen
- Auditing
- Business advisory
- Tax services

Andersen Consulting
- Application software products
- Business integration services
- Systems integration services

Key Competitors
Coopers & Lybrand
Deloitte & Touche
Electronic Data Systems
Ernst & Young
IBM
KPMG
Marsh & McLennan
Price Waterhouse

Industry
Business services - accounting & consulting

Overview
Formed by a 28-year-old Illinois CPA in 1913, Arthur Andersen now ranks as the world's largest accounting firm. The company split into 2 distinct entities in 1989, Arthur Andersen & Co. (accounting) and Andersen Consulting. The aggressive consulting arm quickly stole the spotlight, helping Andersen's total revenue nearly double in 5 years. Like many accounting firms in the early 1990s, Andersen was sued for negligence in auditing a failed S&L. The firm, however, agreed to a "global" settlement with the RTC, exempting Andersen from further charges.

ASPLUNDH TREE EXPERT CO. — RANK: 487

708 Blair Mill Rd.
Willow Grove, PA 19090
Phone: 215-784-4200
Fax: 215-784-4493

1992 Est. Sales: $560 million
FYE: December
Employees: 14,500

Key Personnel
Chm: Robert H. Asplundh
Pres & CEO: Christopher B. Asplundh
Treas & Sec: Joseph P. Dwyer
EVP: Paul S. Asplundh
Gen Counsel: Philip Tatoian
HR: William Hughes

Operating Units
Asplundh Aviation
Asplundh Manufacturing
Asplundh Pipeline Services
Asplundh Pole Treating
Asplundh Railroad
Asplundh Street Lighting
Asplundh Tree

Key Competitors
ARC Tree Service
Country Club Tree Service
Davey Tree Expert
Lewis Tree Service
Trees Inc.
Wright Tree Service

Industry
Business services - tree pruning

Overview
Founded in 1928, family-owned Asplundh is the nation's largest tree-trimming and weed-clearing operation. Its tree division works for utilities to keep power lines clear of tree limbs and bushes. Its rail division (founded in 1975) has been a major revenue earner and has done work for both the Union Pacific and Southern Pacific railroads, cutting and trimming trees and clearing weeds from tracks. Asplundh's other divisions perform similar services for the aviation, construction, and pipeline industries, among others. The company has come under fire recently for its use of herbicides, although it maintains that the chemicals are safe.

ASSOCIATED FOOD STORES, INC. — RANK: 394

1812 Empire Rd.
Salt Lake City, UT 84104
Phone: 801-973-4400
Fax: 801-973-2158

1993 Sales: $787 million
FYE: March
Employees: 1,300

Key Personnel
CEO, Pres & Gen Mgr: Richard A. Parkinson
SVP & CFO: S. N. Berube
VP Ops & Sec-Treas: Stanley R. Brewer
VP: Kerry Atkins
VP: Gary Angel
VP HR: Larry O. Rowe

Selected Services
In-store, radio & TV advertising
Marketing assistance
Newspaper ad preparation
Retail pricing assistance
Store development financing
Wholesale groceries

Key Competitors
Albertson's
Fleming
Fred Meyer
Kroger
Smith's Food & Drug
SUPERVALU
Waremart
Yucaipa

Industry
Food - wholesale to grocers

Overview
Associated Food Stores is a regional cooperative wholesaler owned by the independent supermarkets and convenience stores it serves in Arizona, Colorado, Idaho, Montana, Nevada, Oregon, and Utah. Donald E. Lloyd, former manager of the Utah Retail Grocers Association, persuaded 23 small retailers to invest in the fledgling co-op in 1940; there are now more than 700 members. Based in Salt Lake City, the company also has distribution centers in Montana and Idaho.

ASSOCIATED GROCERS, INCORPORATED — RANK: 265

PO Box 3763
Seattle, WA 98124
Phone: 206-762-2100
Fax: 206-764-7731

1993 Sales: $1,073 million
FYE: September
Employees: 1,381

Key Personnel
Pres & CEO: Donald W. Benson
SVP Mktg: Frank M. Johnson
SVP Warehouse Ops: Dennis Stalder
SVP Retail Programs: Arthur L. Jones
VP HR: Angelo Bruscas
Controller: Maureen Murphy

Selected Services
Advertising
Computer services
Distribution
Marketing
Wholesale purchasing

Key Competitors
Albertson's
Fleming
Fred Meyer
Safeway
Save Mart Supermarkets
United Grocers
West Coast
Wal-Mart

Industry
Retail - supermarkets

Overview
Associated Grocers was formed in 1934 by 11 independent retailers who were trying to save money by buying items in bulk. Based in Seattle, Associated Grocers is now owned by some 200 independent retailers, who run about 360 grocery stores in the Northwest, Hawaii, and the Pacific islands. The company ranks #1 in wholesale food distribution in the Seattle area. Associated Grocers recently adopted a just-in-time inventory system that it hopes will allow its members to compete on price and availability with national retailers doing business in its market.

ASSOCIATED MILK PRODUCERS, INC. — RANK: 76

6609 Blanco Rd.
San Antonio, TX 78216
Phone: 210-340-9100
Fax: 210-340-9158

1993 Sales: $2,692 million
FYE: December
Employees: 4,199

Key Personnel
Pres: Irvin J. Elkin
Gen Mgr: Noble Anderson
Corp Controller: Terry Krueger

Major Products
Butter
Cheese
Dried whey
Milk
Nonfat dry milk

Key Competitors
Atlantic Dairy Co-op
Borden
Dairymen
Danone
Darigold
Dean Foods
Mid-America Dairymen
Wisconsin Dairies Co-op

Industry
Food - dairy products

Overview
The largest US milk cooperative, formed in 1969 from old farm collectives dating back to the 1870s, AMPI accounts for 12% of the US milk supply and also takes a hunk of the cheese, butter, and nonfat dry milk markets. The group has 13,403 member farms and offers credit, life insurance, and retirement programs. In 1990 the company posted a $27 million loss, souring members' confidence. AMPI successfully lobbied the government for stronger price supports in 1992, but oversupply is still consistently bringing down prices.

◀ See page 30 for full-page profile.

ASSOCIATED WHOLESALE GROCERS INC. RANK: 84

5000 Kansas Ave.
Kansas City, KS 66106
Phone: 913-321-1313
Fax: 913-573-1508

1993 Sales: $2,540 million
FYE: December
Employees: 1,900

Key Personnel
Pres & CEO: Mike DeFabis
Pres, Supermarket Insurance Agency: Lanny Riedel
EVP Mktg: Douglas Carolan
SVP, Kansas City Div: Tom Williams
VP, Treas, Sec & CFO: Joseph L. Campbell
Dir HR, Kansas City Div: Frank Tricamo

Selected Products
Bagels
Cheese
Detergent
Frozen vegetables
Paper goods
Poultry
Soft drinks
Spreads

Key Competitors
Affiliated Foods
Albertson's
Aldi
Fleming
Hy-Vee Food Stores
Schnuck Markets
SUPERVALU

Industry
Food - wholesale to grocers

Overview
Founded in 1926, Associated Wholesale Grocers is one of the largest and most successful wholesale cooperatives in the US, with some 400 members who operate about 700 stores. The cooperative's 2 distribution centers supply food products to grocers in the nation's heartland, with most items going to stores in Kansas, Missouri, Arkansas, and Oklahoma. AWG members boast market shares as high as 60% in many areas. The company was named one of the nation's 10 largest cooperative businesses in a recent National Cooperative Bank report.

ASTRUM INTERNATIONAL CORP. RANK: 288

600 Madison Ave., Ste. 11
New York, NY 10022
Phone: 212-307-8100
Fax: 212-307-8115

1994 Sales: $1,013 million
FYE: January
Employees: 10,000

Key Personnel
Chm & CEO: Steven J. Green
VP & CFO: Joseph Dempsey
VP & Treas: Gregory Hunt
VP Gen Counsel: Jacob Hollander

Major Brands
American Tourister
Anvil (T-shirts)
Botany 500
Culligan
MacGregor (clothing)
Pet Specialties (pet food)
Samsonite

Key Competitors
Brown-Forman
Clorox
Hartmarx
Hartz
LVMH
Oxford Industries
Polo/Ralph Lauren
Sun Sportswear

Industry
Diversified operations

Overview
Investor Leon Black and his Apollo Advisors partners own a majority of Astrum International, a holding company for several manufacturers. Incorporated in 1987 as E-II Holdings from the nonfood divisions of the dissected Beatrice empire, the company spiraled into bankruptcy after Meshulam Riklis bought it in 1988 and promptly transferred $925 million to his ailing McCrory Corp. The company changed its name to Astrum when it emerged from Chapter 11 in 1993 with Black in control. Samsonite Luggage produces a lion's share of Astrum's revenues; water softener company Culligan is the #2 revenue producer.

AURORA EBY-BROWN CO. RANK: 279

1001 Sullivan Rd.
Aurora, IL 60506
Phone: 708-897-8674
Fax: 708-897-8677

1993 Sales: $1,040 million
FYE: May
Employees: 1,300

Key Personnel
Chm & CEO: William S. Wake , Jr.
Co-Pres & COO: Richard Wake
Co-Pres & Sec: Thomas Wake
CFO: Jeff Adams
EVP Fin: Barbara G. Wake
Dir Personnel: Rodney Kapanash

Major Products
Cigarettes
Cigars
Confectioneries
Cosmetics
Food products
Snuff
Sundries
Toiletries

Key Competitors
S. Abraham and Sons
C&S Wholesale Grocers
Core-Mark
Farmer-Bocken
Flue-Cured Tobacco Co-op
Imperial Trading
Republic Tobacco
Weeke Wholesale

Industry
Wholesale distribution - consumer products

Overview
Aurora Eby-Brown is a wholesale distributor of tobacco and tobacco products, including cigarettes, cigars, and snuff. The company also distributes confectioneries, food products, and various toiletries. The Wake family owns the company, and members are also top officers. Founded in 1956, the company's philosophy calls for focusing on its customers and using "family style" management. Many high-level employees come up through the company ranks. Because of the uncertain state of the domestic tobacco market, the company has increased its distribution of milk and dairy products.

AVIS, INC. RANK: 213

900 Old Country Rd.
Garden City, NY 11530
Phone: 516-222-3000
Fax: 516-222-4381

1993 Est. Sales: $1,260 million
FYE: February
Employees: 13,500

Key Personnel
Chm & CEO: Joseph V. Vittoria
EVP & CFO: Lawrence Ferezy
EVP: Charles A. Bovino
EVP: James E. Collins
EVP: David P. McNicholas
SVP HR & Board Sec: Donald L. Korn

◀ **See page 31 for full-page profile.**

Selected Services
Avis Cares
Inside Availability
Preferred Service
Roving Rapid Return
Wizard on Wheels
Worldwide Reservation Center

Key Competitors
Agency Rent-A-Car
Alamo Rent A Car
Budget Rent A Car
Chrylser
Enterprise Rent A Car
Ford
Mitsubishi
Volvo

Industry
Leasing - autos

Overview
Avis, the #2 car rental and leasing company in the US (after Ford's Hertz unit), was started in 1946 by a former army pilot who noticed there were no car rental agencies at airports. After years of being bought and sold, Avis went private in 1987 through an employee stock ownership plan. In 1993 employees owned 74% of Avis, with General Motors owning the rest. The company now has holdings in 10 countries and licensed operations in another 60. Avis's reputation for trying harder earned it recognition in the 1993 edition of *The 100 Best Companies to Work For in America* .

BACARDI IMPORTS, INC. — RANK: 482

2100 Biscayne Blvd.
Miami, FL 33137
Phone: 305-573-8511
Fax: 305-573-0756

1993 Sales: $578 million
FYE: December
Employees: 300

Key Personnel
Chm: Edwin H. Nielsen
Pres & CEO: Juan Grau
EVP & COO: Eduardo M. Sardina
VP, Treas & CFO: Rodolfo A. Ruiz
VP & Gen Counsel: Steven Naclerio
VP HR: Jose L. Aragon

◀ **See page 32 for full-page profile.**

Major Products
B&B
Bacardi rums
Benedictine
Breezer by Bacardi
Calvados Boulard brandy
Castillo rum
Gaston De LaGrange cognac
Martini & Rossi asti spumante

Key Competitors
Allied-Lyons
American Brands
Brown-Forman
Carlsberg
Grand Metropolitan
LVMH
Pearson
Seagram

Industry
Beverages - alcoholic

Overview
Founded in 1944, Bacardi Imports is the US arm of the Bacardi family empire, which is held by some 500 descendants of Facundo Bacardi, who founded a rum company in Cuba in 1862. Bacardi Imports acts as the US importer for all Bacardi products, including Bacardi rum, the world's best-selling liquor brand. The company is a subsidiary of Bacardi Limited, a Bahamian holding company. Bacardi has distilleries in 7 countries and sells its rum in 175 countries.

BAKER & MCKENZIE — RANK: N/R

One Prudential Plaza, 130 E. Randolph Dr.
Chicago, IL 60601
Phone: 312-861-8800
Fax: 312-861-8823

1993 Sales: $512 million
FYE: June
Employees: 5,054

Key Personnel
Chm Exec Committee: John V. McGuigan
COO: Frank H. Wheeler
CFO: Robert S. Spencer
Dir Intl Admin: Teresa A. Townsend
Dir Intl Sys: Thomas R. Potter

◀ **See page 33 for full-page profile.**

Business Lines
Bankruptcy law
Corporate finance law
Employee benefits law
Environmental/land use law
Government relations
Intellectual property law
Oil & gas/mining law
Real estate law

Key Competitors
Cleary, Gottlieb
Cravath, Swaine
Jones, Day
Kirkland & Ellis
Mayer, Brown
Skadden, Arps

Industry
Law firm

Overview
Baker & McKenzie is a prime example of the "megafirm," whose practice includes virtually every field of domestic and international law. The firm operates 54 offices in 31 nations, including China, Vietnam, and Russia, hiring locals and allowing the offices to keep most of their own profits. The strategy worked well during the recession of the late 1980s and early 1990s. Although overall revenue growth and the promotion of associates to partner have slowed, Baker & McKenzie still continues to grow.

BAKER & TAYLOR INC. — RANK: 335

300 First Stamford Place
Stamford, CT 06902
Phone: 203-462-7000
Fax: 203-961-8343

1994 Est. Sales: $900 million
FYE: June
Employees: 2,480

Key Personnel
Co-Chm: Patrick Gross
Co-Chm: Joseph Wright
CEO: Craig M. Richards
Pres & COO: James B. Warburton
SVP, Treas & CFO: Edward H. Gross
VP HR: Jeanne P. Rudell

◀ **See page 34 for full-page profile.**

Major Products
Audiocassettes
Calendars
Hardcover books
Mass market paperbacks
Music CDs
Software
Trade paperbacks
Videocassettes

Key Competitors
Advanced Marketing
Blackwell Delaware
Bookazine
Brodart
Handleman
Ingram
Merisel
Pacific Pipeline

Industry
Wholesale distribution - books & software

Overview
Founded in 1828, Baker & Taylor is an international wholesaler of books, videotapes, audio products, and computer software. The company consists of 3 divisions — B&T Books, B&T Video, and B&T Software — which distribute their products to more than 100,000 retail stores and public and university libraries. B&T's book division is the #1 book distributor in the US and dominates the library book distribution market. In 1994 the Carlyle Group, B&T's majority owner, broke off negotiations to sell the company to Follet Corporation, a textbook distributor and college bookstore operator.

BARTLETT AND COMPANY — RANK: 421

4800 Main St., Ste. 600
Kansas City, MO 64112
Phone: 816-753-6300
Fax: 816-753-0062

1993 Sales: $708 million
FYE: April
Employees: 525

Key Personnel
Chm: Paul D. Bartlett, Jr.
VC: W. Robert Berg
Pres: James B. Hebenstreit
Pres, Grain Div: Bernard F. Walch
Dir Transportation: Tom Overacker
Dir Personnel: J. Timothy Crouch

Business Lines
Cattle feed lots
Flour milling
Grain elevator storage
Grain mills
Grain wholesaling

Key Competitors
ADM
Ag Processing
Cargill
Continental Grain
Farmland Industries
GROWMARK
Harvest States Co-ops
Scoular

Industry
Food - flour & grain

Overview
Founded in 1907, Bartlett & Co. is a wholesaler, distributor, and trader of grains, flour, and cattle feed. The company, owned by Paul D. Bartlett, Jr., also trades in commodities futures. Bartlett & Co.'s 17 grain storage facilities include 4 river facilities (Kansas City, Kansas; St. Joseph and Waverly, Missouri; and Nebraska City, Nebraska), 2 terminals (Council Bluffs, Iowa; Kansas City, Missouri), and 11 country elevators. The operation's total licensed grain storage capacity is over 31 million bushels.

BASHAS' INC.

RANK: 479

22402 S. Alma School Rd.
Chandler, AZ 85248
Phone: 602-895-9350
Fax: 602-895-1206

1992 Est. Sales: $586 million
FYE: December
Employees: 4,500

Key Personnel
Chm & CEO: Edward N. Basha , Jr.
Pres & COO: Wayne C. Manning
VP Fin & CFO: Darl J. Andersen
Treas: Karen Rishwain
Sec: Edward R. Felix
VP HR: Fred Felix

Operating Units
A.J.'s Fine Foods
Bashas' Bargain Basket
Bashas' Mercado
Food City
Prototype 6

Key Competitors
ABCO Markets
Albertson's
Affiliated Foods
Circle K
Megafoods
Safeway
Smith's Food & Drug
Southland

Industry
Retail - supermarkets

Overview
Founded in 1932, Bashas' is a 68-unit grocery chain that operates primarily in Arizona (there is one store each in New Mexico and California). The only family-owned chain in the state includes upscale, gourmet-style supermarkets, neighborhood groceries, superstores, and warehouse stores, many of these in the Phoenix area. Six of its supermarkets (including its New Mexico store) serve the Navajo Nation and have tailored their products specifically to the Navajo's lifestyle, stocking mutton instead of beef and no frozen products (many Navajos do not have freezers). Bashas' also operates a supermarket on a Papago reservation.

BASIN ELECTRIC POWER COOPERATIVE

RANK: 403

1717 E. Interstate Ave.
Bismarck, ND 58501
Phone: 701-223-0441
Fax: 701-224-5336

1993 Sales: $764 million
FYE: December
Employees: 2,002

Key Personnel
Gen Mgr: Robert L. McPhail
CFO: Clifton T. Hudgins
Asst Gen Mgr Mktg: Howard Easton
Asst Gen Mgr Ops: Richard B. Fockler
Gen Counsel: Michael J. Hinman
Asst Gen Mgr Mgmt Svcs/HR: Richard W. Weber

Principal Subsidiaries
Basin Cooperative Services
  Property
Dakota Gasification Company
  Synfuels plant & pipeline
Dakota Coal Company
  Coal
  Lignite
  Lime

Industry
Utility - electric power

Overview
Founded in 1961, Basin Electric is a nonprofit regional cooperative, headquartered in Bismarck, North Dakota, that supplies wholesale electricity to 118 member systems in Colorado, Iowa, Minnesota, Montana, Nebraska, North Dakota, South Dakota, and Wyoming. With 3 subsidiaries, Basin Electric is a diversified energy corporation that generates and transmits electricity from coal- and lignite-fired generating plants, including the Great Plains Synfuels Plant — the US's only commercial-scale plant producing synthetic natural gas from coal. The co-op purchased this $2.1 billion plant from the US government in 1988.

BATH IRON WORKS CORPORATION

RANK: 380

700 Washington St.
Bath , ME 04530
Phone: 207-443-3311
Fax: 207-442-1567

1992 Est. Sales: $800 million
FYE: December
Employees: 9,000

Key Personnel
Pres: Duane D. Fitzgerald
SVP & CFO: Howard J. Yates
Dir Mktg: Winn W. Price
VP Info Sys: John Parker
HR: Stephen Wilson

Business Lines
Dry dock facilities
Ship building
Ship maintenance
Ship repair

Key Competitors
American Ship Building
Avondale Industries
Litton Industries
General Dynamics
McDermott
Southwest Marine
Tenneco
Todd Shipyards

Industry
Boat building

Overview
Founded in 1884, Bath Iron Works is a defense contractor that builds destroyers. The company is the largest single employer in Maine. Bath has a navy contract to build 3 Aegis guided missile destroyers, which will carry a mix of Standard surface-to-air and Tomahawk surface-to-surface missiles and antisubmarine rockets. The company's future is questionable because the end of the Cold War is limiting new defense spending. Bath is in a government program designed to help it convert to private ship making by 1997. The majority shareholder is an investment partnership made up of Gibbons, Goodwin, and Amerongen LP (a firm doing LBOs) and Fulcrum III.

BATTELLE MEMORIAL INSTITUTE

RANK: 347

505 King Ave.
Columbus, OH 43201
Phone: 614-424-6424
Fax: 614-424-5263

1993 Sales: $869 million
FYE: December
Employees: 8,400

Key Personnel
Chm: Willis S. White, Jr.
Pres & CEO: Douglas E. Olesen
SVP & Gen Mgr, Health Div: Dennis B. Cearlock
SVP, CFO & Treas: John H. Doster
SVP, Gen Counsel & Sec: Paul T. Santilli
SVP HR: Robert W. Smith, Jr.

Areas of Research
Commercial & industrial research
Environment
Health
National security
Technology development
Technology transfer
Transportation

Key Competitors
AT&T
Bellcore
Bolt Beranek and Newman
Cal Tech
Southwest Research Institute
Science Applications

Industry
Engineering - R&D services

Overview
Founded in 1923, Battelle Memorial Institute, chartered as a nonprofit trust, is the world's largest and oldest contract research organization. Its résumé is mind-boggling: company scientists have invented thousands of products, from cruise control to the copper/copper-nickel "sandwich" design of most US coins to the copying machine. Battelle does work for both companies and governments; important customers include the DOE and the DOD.

◀ **See page 35 for full-page profile.**

L.L. BEAN, INC.

RANK: 346

Casco St.
Freeport, ME 04033
Phone: 207-865-4761
Fax: 207-865-6738

1994 Sales: $870 million
FYE: February
Employees: 3,500

Key Personnel
Pres & CEO: Leon A. Gorman
EVP & CFO: Norman A. Poole
SVP & Gen Mgr, L.L. Bean Intl: Scott Howard
SVP Fin & Admin: Lee Surace
VP Mktg: Robert Frye
VP HR: Bob Peixotto

◀ **See page 36 for full-page profile.**

Selected Products
Boat & Tote bags
Chamois cloth shirts
Handsewn footwear
Hudson Bay Point blankets
The Maine Hunting Shoe
Soft luggage
Zipper duffle bags
Miscellaneous sporting goods

Key Competitors
CML Group
Gander Mountain
INTERCO
J. Crew
Lands' End
Lost Arrow
North Face
REI

Industry
Retail - mail order

Overview
L.L. Bean, founded in 1912, is one of the largest specialty mail order houses. It sells camping gear, shoes, country classic fashions, and home accessories. Since founder Leon Leonwood Bean's grandson Leon Gorman took over in 1967, he has modernized the mailing and distribution systems and refined the mailing and product lists to transform L.L. Bean from camping goods purveyor to lifestyle merchant.

BECHTEL GROUP, INC.

RANK: 19

50 Beale St.
San Francisco, CA 94105
Phone: 415-768-1234
Fax: 415-768-0263

1993 Sales: $7,337 million
FYE: December
Employees: 29,400

Key Personnel
Chm Emeritus: Stephen D. Bechtel, Jr.
Pres & CEO: Riley P. Bechtel
EVP: William L. Friend
SVP, CFO, Treas & Controller: V. Paul Unruh
Counsel: John W. Weiser
VP, Mgr HR: Shirley Gaufin

◀ **See page 37 for full-page profile.**

Business Lines
Construction
Engineering
Environmental cleanup, treatment
Fossil fuel plant operation
Nuclear fuel plant operation
Pipeline operation
Project management
Utility plant operation

Key Competitors
Fluor
Halliburton
McCarthy Building
McDermott
Morrison Knudsen
Parsons
Peter Kiewit Sons'
Turner Industries

Industry
Engineering and construction services

Overview
The Bechtel Group, incorporated in 1925, is the #1 US engineering and construction firm. Owned and run by descendants of Warren Bechtel, the company has worked on more than 15,000 projects in over 135 countries and boasts the largest R&D staff in US engineering. Bechtel's reputation has won it key projects like the cleanup of Three Mile Island and Kuwait's postwar oil field devastation and the construction of the Eurotunnel.

BEEFAMERICA, INC.

RANK: 228

14748 W. Center Rd., Ste. 201
Omaha, NE 68144
Phone: 402-330-1899
Fax: 402-330-2684

1992 Sales: $1,200 million
FYE: October
Employees: 1,500

Key Personnel
Pres & CEO: Robert R. Norton
VP Fin: Roger McConnell
Dir HR: Dean Miller

Selected Services
Gelatin production
Hide processing
Meat fabrication
Meat packing
Meat processing
Meat slaughtering operations
Meat trucking

Key Competitors
Cargill
ConAgra
GFI America
Gillett Holdings
IBP
Seaboard

Industry
Food - meat products

Overview
BeefAmerica Inc. was founded in 1988 when a group of investors bought Beef Nebraska, Dubuque Packing, and Nebraska Boxed Beef. Operating primarily in Iowa and Nebraska, BeefAmerica is the 5th largest beef packer in the US, slaughtering about 5,000 head of cattle a day. The company is owned by the investment firm Thomas H. Lee Company and New York businessman Eli S. Jacobs. BeefAmerica is facing tough times because of the steady decline in consumer demand for beef. In 1993 the company closed 3 plants in Omaha as it moved to consolidate operations at its Norfolk, Nebraska, plant.

BELK STORES SERVICES, INC.

RANK: 143

2801 W. Tyvola Rd.
Charlotte, NC 28217
Phone: 704-357-1000
Fax: 704-357-1876

1994 Sales: $1,774 million
FYE: January
Employees: 19,000

Key Personnel
Chm: John M. Belk
Pres: Thomas M. Belk
SVP HR: Thomas M. Belk, Jr.
Treas: William L. McGill
Gen Counsel: Leroy Robinson

Selected Services
Accounting services
Centralized purchasing
Data processing
Development planning
Legal planning
Market research
Training

Key Competitors
Dillard
Federated
Kmart
Mercantile Stores
Montgomery Ward
J. C. Penney
Sears
Wal-Mart

Industry
Retail - regional department stores

Overview
Tracing its origins to a single store opened by William Henry Belk in 1888, Belk Stores Services (BSS) has grown into the US's largest family-owned department store organization. Spun off from the family's department store chain in 1955, BSS provides centralized services to 300 independently owned and operated Belk and Leggett stores in 14 states, located mostly in the South.

BELL COMMUNICATIONS RESEARCH INC.

RANK: 260

290 W. Mt. Pleasant Ave.
Livingston, NJ 07039
Phone: 201-740-3000
Fax: 210-740-6877

1993 Sales: $1,086 million
FYE: December
Employees: 6,624

Key Personnel
Pres & CEO: George H. Heilmeier
VP & COO: George C. Via
SVP & CFO: Edward G. Grogan
VP & Gen Counsel: N. Michael Grove
VP Research: Robert W. Lucky
VP HR: Robert A. Meese

Selected Services
Emergency comm. coordination
Industry standards development
Research & development
Systems integration & development
Technical consulting
Training

Key Competitors
Arthur Anderson
AT&T
Battelle
Electronic Data Systems
GTE
Southwest Research Institute

Industry
Engineering - R&D services

Overview
An umbrella group owned by the 7 regional Bell operating companies, Bellcore was founded in 1984 to perform telephone system integration, research, and training. CEO George H. Heilmeier, a pioneer in liquid-crystal displays, wants to become a major player in the development of the "information superhighway," but funding is a problem. The prospect of future competition has made the Baby Bells (currently responsible for 83% of Bellcore's revenues) less willing to cooperate on research. Therefore, Bellcore is concentrating on developing new services and a broader customer base. Sprint received permission to join Bellcore in 1993.

BELL & HOWELL CO.

RANK: 441

5215 Old Orchard Rd.
Skokie, IL 60077
Phone: 708-470-7100
Fax: 708-470-9825

1993 Sales: $676 million
FYE: December
Employees: 5,770

Key Personnel
Chm, Pres & CEO: William J. White
EVP & CFO: Nils A. Johansson
VP & Controller: Stuart Lieberman
VP & Treas: Patrick J. Graver
Sec & Corp Counsel: Gary S. Salit
VP HR: Maria T. Rubly

Major Products
Binding equipment
Computerized filing equipment
Database publishing products
Electronic auto parts catalogs
Magazine databases
Mail-handling equipment & software
Microfiche & microfilm equipment
Scanners

Key Competitors
AM International
Business Records
General Binding
GEC
IBM
3M
Siemens
Thomson SA

Industry
Office automation

Overview
Once known for its movie cameras, Bell & Howell is now a leader in information management technology. The company produces mail processing and document handling equipment; it also makes microfiche equipment and provides recording services. Founded in 1907 and owned by investor Robert Bass and management, the company licenses its name to Montgomery Ward, which sells a line of Bell & Howell camcorders, televisions, and VCRs. In 1993 Bell & Howell acquired an equity interest in Blue Lake Software, which produces software for mail processing, along with exclusive distribution rights.

BIG V SUPERMARKETS INC.

RANK: 427

176 N. Main St.
Florida, NY 10921
Phone: 914-651-4411
Fax: 914-651-7048

1992 Sales: $700 million
FYE: December
Employees: 4,500

Key Personnel
Chm & CEO: David Bronstein
Pres & COO: Stuart A. Rosenthal
SVP, Treas & CFO: Gary Koppele
SVP, Sec & Gen Counsel: Cornelius Madera
VP & Controller: Duane Wilkes
VP HR: Tom Hoskison

Selected Services
Bakery
Delicatessen
Frozen food, grocery & dairy
Health & beauty department
Membership club store
Pharmacy
Produce department
Video department

Key Competitors
Associated Food
American Stores
C&S Wholesale Grocers
Golub
Great A&P
Grand Union
Pathmark
Wal-Mart

Industry
Retail - supermarkets

Overview
Big V Supermarkets, founded in 1942, owns 29 ShopRite grocery stores (the retailing arm of New Jersey's Wakefern Food Cooperative), primarily in New York, and is the market leader in the mid-Hudson Valley. Big V was publicly held until 1987, when affiliates of Metropolitan Life Insurance and CS First Boston Inc. took it private in a friendly LBO. In 1991 the company was sold to investment firm Thomas H. Lee Company and 3 affiliates. Faced with increased competition from warehouse clubs and other food retailers, Big V has experimented successfully with in-store video rentals and unsuccessfully with a membership club format, PriceRite.

BLACK AND VEATCH

RANK: 434

8400 Ward Pkwy.
Kansas City, MO 64114
Phone: 913-339-2000
Fax: 913-339-3817

1993 Sales: $693 million
FYE: December
Employees: 4,900

Key Personnel
Chm & CEO: P. J. Adam
CFO: Wayne F. Hall
Managing Partner: Patrick G. Davidson
Managing Partner: Ronald D. Hardten
Gen Counsel: F. E. Schoenlaub
Dir HR: Dave H. Lillard

Selected Services
Architectural services
Construction management
Environmental engineering
Financial services
Management services
Process engineering

Key Competitors
ABB
Bechtel
Halliburton
Hensel Phelps
Fluor
Parsons
Raytheon
H. B. Zachry

Industry
Construction - heavy

Overview
With international business accounting for almost 50% of Black & Veatch's revenues, the 79-year-old partnership is a major player in the global construction and engineering market and the worldwide leader in project awards for electricity generation. The company's 350-plus international projects have included power plants, wastewater treatment systems, and hydrocarbon processing facilities. In an attempt to increase profits, the partnership is putting more of an emphasis on building projects, instead of just designing them.

BLUE CROSS AND BLUE SHIELD ASSOCIATION — RANK: 1

676 N. St. Clair St.
Chicago, IL 60611
Phone: 312-440-6000
Fax: 312-440-6609

1993 Sales: $71,161 million
FYE: December
Employees: 135,883

Key Personnel
Pres & CEO: Bernard R. Tresnowski
EVP & COO: Thomas Kinser
Gen Counsel & Corp Sec: Roger G. Wilson
SVP Licensing, Fin & Ops: David Murdoch
SVP Business Svcs: Harry P. Cain II
VP Chief Admin Officer: Kris Kurschner

◀ See page 38 for full-page profile.

Selected Services
Group medical insurance
Health maintenance programs (HMO-USA)
Individual major medical insurance
Medicare administration
Preferred-provider organizations
Publications

Key Competitors
Aetna
CareNetwork
Kaiser Foundation Health Plan
MetLife
PacifiCare Health Systems
Prudential
Sierra Health Services
UniHealth America

Industry
Insurance - prepaid health care plans

Overview
Tracing its roots back to a health plan created in Dallas in 1929, Blue Cross Blue Shield is the nonprofit national coordinating organization for 69 autonomous Blue Cross and Blue Shield prepaid health care plans. The Blues have often been seen as the insurers of last resort, but they insure about 25% of the US population. The organizations have enjoyed a quasi-charitable status in many states. Some local plans, notably Empire (New York) and one in Washington, DC, have come under fire for abuse of their status. As costs have climbed, many Blues have gone out of business, consolidated, or turned into for-profit plans.

BOOZ, ALLEN & HAMILTON INC. — RANK: 428

101 Park Ave.
New York, NY 10178
Phone: 212-697-1900
Fax: 212-551-6732

1993 Est. Sales: $700 million
FYE: March
Employees: 3,700

Key Personnel
Chm, Pres & CEO: William F. Stasior
CFO & Treas: Frank Matteotti
SVP, Sec & Counsel: Daniel R. Idzik
Controller: Kevin Cook
Controller: Doug Swenson
Personnel Dir: Susan Galager

Selected Services
Business information management
Computer systems integration
Defense & aerospace consulting
Management consulting
Marketing consulting
New product management
Retailing & financial management
Technological consulting

Key Competitors
Arthur Andersen
Arthur D. Little
Bain & Co.
Boston Consulting Group
Electronic Data Systems
IBM
McKinsey & Co.
Towers, Perrin

Industry
Consulting

Overview
The grandfather of consulting partnerships, Booz, Allen & Hamilton was founded in 1914 and provides management and technology consulting services to clients worldwide. Teaming technical specialists with management experts, the firm helps clients deal with complex business problems that often involve technology. Best customer Uncle Sam provides 1/3 of Booz, Allen's revenues. Other customers include many leading industrial companies, banks, and insurance firms.

BOSTON UNIVERSITY — RANK: 411

147 Bay State Rd.
Boston, MA 02215
Phone: 617-353-2000
Fax: 617-353-2053

1993 Sales: $736 million
FYE: June
Employees: 14,859

Key Personnel
Chm: Earle Cooley
Pres: John R. Silber
EVP & Provost: Jon Westling
SVP: Joseph P. Mercurio
VP Fin & Treas: Kenneth Condon

Schools & Colleges
College of Communication
College of Engineering
College of General Studies
College of Liberal Arts
Henry M. Goldman School of Graduate Dentistry
Sargent College of Allied Health Professions
School for the Arts
School of Law
School of Management
School of Medicine

Industry
Schools

Overview
Founded in 1839, Boston University is a private institution with 10 undergraduate and 15 graduate schools. It boasts a diverse student body, with 4,000 of the 29,000 students coming from 125 countries. Among its faculty are 3 Nobel laureates — Elie Wiesel, Derek Walcott, and Saul Bellow. Since 1971 the university has been guided by John Silber, who turned around the school's financial fortunes, transforming a $9 million deficit into a streak of surpluses. As part of an experiment in education reform, the university has signed a 10-year contract to manage the public schools in Chelsea, Massachusetts, in conjunction with local authorities.

BRENLIN GROUP — RANK: 439

670 W. Market St.
Akron, OH 44303
Phone: 216-762-2420
Fax: 216-762-4604

1993 Est. Sales: $680 million
FYE: October
Employees: 4,000

Key Personnel
CEO & Chm: David L. Brennan
VC: Richard M. Hamlin
Pres: James P. McCready
Treas & CFO: James D. Vantiem
VP Ops & Fin: James F. Gaul
VP HR: Stephen J. Tomasko

Major Products
Axles
Bearings
Brakes
Bumpers
Gaskets
Industrial wheels
Stampings
Steel

Key Competitors
Acme Metals
Bethlehem Steel
Chrysler
Dana
FMC
Eaton
Inland Steel
SIFCO

Industry
Metal products - fabrication

Overview
The #1 producer of iron and steel forgings, the Brenlin Group was founded in 1975 by partners David Brennan and Richard Hamlin, who were joined in 1976 by James McCready. Still owned by its 3 partners, the group consists of 18 companies that primarily produce steel, metal stampings, axles, and brakes. Brenlin companies employ 4,000 people in 9 states. The group recently announced that Richard Hamlin would buy out Brennan's and McCready's interests, thus becoming sole owner.

BROOKSHIRE GROCERY COMPANY

RANK: 429

1600 SW Loop 323
Tyler, TX 75701
Phone: 903-534-3000
Fax: 903-534-2206

1993 Est. Sales: $700 million
FYE: September
Employees: 3,700

Key Personnel
Chm: Bruce G. Brookshire
Pres & CEO: James Hardin
EVP & COO: Charles E. Davis
Treas: Marvin Massey
VP & Controller: Preston Triplett
EVP HR: Tim Brookshire

Operating Units
Brookshire Grocery Stores
 Full-service supermarkets
Super 1 Stores
 Bulk merchandise
 Groceries
 Self-service supermarkets

Key Competitors
Albertson's
H. E. Butt
Food Lion
Kroger
Minyard
Randalls
Whole Foods Market
Winn-Dixie

Industry
Retail - supermarkets

Overview
Founded in 1928, Tyler, Texas–based Brookshire Grocery has 2 main operations. It runs 84 full-service (and some say elegant) supermarkets and 18 no-frills self-service (but upscale) food warehouse stores in Texas, Arkansas, and Louisiana. Brookshire is increasing its presence in the northern suburbs of the Dallas–Ft. Worth metroplex with its largest warehouse store to date, which will include such specialty departments as a delicatessen, bakery, seafood counter, and pharmacy.

BROWN BROTHERS HARRIMAN & CO.

RANK: 189

59 Wall St.
New York, NY 10005
Phone: 212-483-1818
Fax: 212-493-8526

1992 Sales: $1,390 million
FYE: December
Employees: 1,650

Key Personnel
Managing Partner: Terence M. Farley
Controller: George Gage
Personnel Mgr: Allan B. Wechsler
Gen Partner: Walter H. Brown
Gen Partner: Peter B. Bartlett
Gen Partner: J. E. Banks

Business Lines
Banking
Security brokers
Security dealers
Trust facilities

Key Competitors
Bank of New York
Bankers Trust
Bear Stearns
Chase Manhattan
Chemical Banking
Goldman Sachs
Lehman Brothers
J.P. Morgan

Industry
Financial - investment bankers

Overview
Founded in 1818, Brown Brothers Harriman is one of the oldest private banks in the US and also one of the most prestigious. It is owned by 35 partners, all of whom have unlimited liability, and is known for following a conservative strategy. Nonetheless, the company has an enviable return on equity and has avoided the financial imbroglios some other firms faced in the 1980s. Brown Brothers specializes in global custody and private banking, 2 sectors that are expected to grow in the 1990s.

BUDGET RENT A CAR CORPORATION

RANK: 287

4225 Naperville Rd.
Lisle, IL 60532
Phone: 708-955-1900
Fax: 708-955-7799

1993 Sales: $1,018 million
FYE: December
Employees: 10,400

Key Personnel
Pres & CEO: William N. Plamondon
EVP & CFO: Kevin M. McShea
SVP Ops: Herbert V. Luckwaldt
SVP & Gen Counsel: Robert Aprati
VP Info Sys: Don Savlic

Selected Services
Automobile rental
Financial services
New & used car sales
Truck rental

Key Competitors
Agency Rent-A-Car
Alamo Rent A Car
Avis
Chrysler
Enterprise Rent-A-Car
General Motors
Mitsubishi
Volvo

Industry
Leasing - autos & trucks

Overview
Founded in 1958 in Los Angeles by Morris Merkin to meet the needs of nonbusiness renters, Budget Rent A Car is a leading world provider of rental cars and trucks, with a fleet of about 233,000 and a presence in all 50 states and more than 100 countries. Owned by Beech Holdings, a firm controlled by Budget management and investment banker Gibbons, Green, Van Amerongen, the company made a name for itself by catering to the budget-conscious leisure traveler. In the early 1990s, however, Budget began broadening its client base, becoming more service-oriented and offering more upscale rentals.

H. E. BUTT GROCERY COMPANY

RANK: 40

646 S. Main Ave.
San Antonio, TX 78204
Phone: 210-246-8000
Fax: 210-246-8169

1993 Sales: $4,500 million
FYE: October
Employees: 19,772

Key Personnel
Chm, Pres & CEO: Charles C. Butt
EVP & COO: James F. Clingman
Chief Admin Officer & CFO: Jack Brouillard
VP & Sec: Wesley D. Nelson
VP HR: Louis M. Laguardia

Operating Units
HEBCO
H. E. Butt Food Stores
H.E. Butt Super Food/Drug Stores
Marketplace
Pantry Food Stores

Key Competitors
Albertson's
Fiesta Mart
Kroger
Megafoods
Minyard Food Stores
Randalls
Whole Foods Market
Winn-Dixie

Industry
Retail - supermarkets

Overview
H-E-B is the largest food retailer based in Texas, with 213 stores in the state. Owned and managed by the descendants of the woman who founded the company in 1905, H-E-B is noted for its competitive pricing policies and the breadth and variety of its merchandise and services. Many stores contain pharmacies and video rental units. It is highly vertically integrated and processes many of its own products. H-E-B launched a new concept store, Central Market, in Austin in 1994.

◀ See page 39 for full-page profile.

C&S WHOLESALE GROCERS INC.

RANK: 129

Old Ferry Rd.
Brattleboro, VT 05301
Phone: 802-257-4371
Fax: 802-257-6727

1993 Sales: $1,867 million
FYE: September
Employees: 1,300

Key Personnel
Chm, Pres & CEO: Richard B. Cohen
CFO: William Hamlin
VP Warehousing & Distrib: George McGraw
VP Mktg & Chain Sales: Dick Geary
VP Mktg & Indep Sales: Larry Newton
VP HR: Mitchell Davis

Major Products
Beverages
Frozen foods
Groceries
Meats
Produce
Tobacco products

Key Competitors
Aurora Eby-Brown
Di Giorgio
Fleming
Hannaford Bros.
SUPERVALU
United Grocers
Wakefern Food
Wegmans Food Markets

Industry
Food - wholesale

Overview
C&S Wholesale Grocers, founded in 1919, distributes groceries, frozen foods, meats, produce, beverages, and tobacco products to chain and independent grocery stores. C&S also delivers groceries to military bases in New England and on the upper East Coast. Owned by Richard Cowen, the company operates in Connecticut, Maine, Massachusetts, New Hampshire, New Jersey, New York, Rhode Island, and Vermont.

CALCOT, LTD.

RANK: 473

1601 E. Brundage Ln.
Bakersfield, CA 93307
Phone: 805-327-5961
Fax: 805-861-9870

1993 Sales: $600 million
FYE: August
Employees: 200

Key Personnel
Pres: Thomas W. Smith
Treas: Larry Nickols
SVP Fin & Admin: Robert W. Norris
SVP Sales: Bruce Groefsema
VP & Corp Sec: Gene Lundquist
Mgr HR: Mary Joe Pasek

Selected Services
Cotton marketing
Cotton transportation
Cotton warehousing
Members' credit

Key Competitors
Cargill
Continental Grain
Dunavant Enterprises
Natural Cotton Colours
Plains Cotton Co-op
Southwestern Irrigated Cotton Growers
Staple Cotton Co-op
Weil Brothers Cotton

Industry
Agricultural operations

Overview
Calcot, Ltd., is the largest cotton cooperative in the US. Founded in 1927, Calcot markets 89% of the cotton grown in Southern California, 42% of the cotton grown in the San Joaquin Valley, and 46% of the cotton grown in Arizona. Much of the cotton produced by Calcot's 3,000 members is Acala, a premium grade. The majority of the co-op's cotton (65–70%) is sold overseas, mainly to the Far East. Calcot is strictly a marketing organization and offers no fertilizers or ginning services. Calcot and the 3 other regional cotton cooperatives organized Amcot to market their cotton. Amcot controls 30% of the US market.

CALIFORNIA STATE LOTTERY COMMISSION

RANK: 145

600 N. 10th St.
Sacramento, CA 95814
Phone: 916-323-0400
Fax: 916-322-6768

1993 Sales: $1,760 million
FYE: June
Employees: 900

Key Personnel
Exec Dir: A. A. "Del" Pierce
Gen Counsel: Cathy Van Aken
Dir Fin & Admin: Dennis Sequeira
Dir Sales: Al Frazier
Dir Mktg: Dennis Kimes
HR: Elaine Chiao

Selected Games
Break the Bank
Daily 3
Fantasy 5
Instant Millionaire
Keno
Lotto
Power Hitter
World Cup

Industry
Leisure & recreational services - lottery

Overview
Created by voters in November 1984, the California Lottery sells lotto tickets and scratcher cards in that state. By law, 50% of the proceeds of sales must be returned to lottery players as prizes and 34% is dedicated to public education. The remaining 16% of lottery revenue may be spent on administration of the games, with retailers who offer the games receiving a 6.5% commission.To increase sales, lottery officials contracted with GTECH to install and operate a new $203 million on-line gaming system that will include 13,000 new vendor-supplied terminals. Since the lottery's inception, players have gambled away nearly $18 billion.

CALTEX PETROLEUM CORPORATION

RANK: 9

125 E. John Carpenter Fwy.
Irving, TX 75602
Phone: 214-830-1000
Fax: 214-830-1156

1993 Sales: $15,409 million
FYE: December
Employees: 7,800

Key Personnel
Chm, Pres & CEO: Patrick J. Ward
VC & CFO: Charles A. Boyce
SVP: John McPhail
Dir Mktg: Bob Young
VP & Gen Counsel: Frank W. Blue
VP HR: E. M. Schmidt

◀ **See page 40 for full-page profile.**

Business Lines
Exploration
Marketing
Production
Real estate
Refining
Storage
Technical services
Transportation

Key Competitors
Amoco
British Petroleum
Broken Hill
Exxon
Mobil
Phillips Petroleum
Royal Dutch/Shell
TOTAL

Industry
Oil refining & marketing

Overview
Caltex Petroleum Corporation is a holding company for a collection of petroleum refining and marketing businesses with operations in 63 countries, primarily in Africa, Asia, and Australia. Founded in 1936, Caltex is a joint venture between Chevron and Texaco. Caltex companies operate a network of more than 18,000 retail outlets in 30 countries. Caltex also owns interests in 14 refineries and explores for oil in Indonesia. Caltex is concentrating on increasing its refining and retailing efforts in the booming Pacific Rim region.

CARGILL, INCORPORATED

RANK: 3

15407 McGinty Rd.
Minnetonka, MN 55440
Phone: 612-742-7575
Fax: 612-742-6208

1993 Sales: $47,100 million
FYE: May
Employees: 70,000

Key Personnel
Chm & CEO: Whitney MacMillan
VC: Gerald M. Mitchell
Pres & COO: Ernest S. Micek
SVP & CFO: Robert L. Lumpkins
SVP HR: Everett MacLennan
VP, Gen Counsel & Sec: James D. Moe

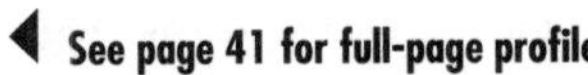
See page 41 for full-page profile.

Business Lines
Agricultural products (feeds, seed)
Commodities trading & transport
Equipment leasing
Food production & processing
Futures trading, foreign exchange
Industrial chemicals
Life insurance
Steel yards & mills

Key Competitors
ADM
Continental Grain
CPC
General Mills
Hormel
Koch
Nucor
Philip Morris

Industry
Food - trading & processing

Overview
Cargill has grown from a string of grain elevators, purchased by founder William Cargill in 1870, into a diversified global operation. It is the #1 grain company in the US and ranks among the top dozen of all US companies (public and private) in terms of sales. Despite the 1991 sale of 17% of Cargill's stock to its employees, descendants of the Cargill and MacMillan families still run the company. The company blamed a 22% drop in net income between 1992 and 1993 on major political changes, a weak global economy, policy reforms, and currency fluctuations.

CARLSON COMPANIES, INC.

RANK: 97

Carlson Pkwy.
Minneapolis, MN 55459
Phone: 612-540-5000
Fax: 612-540-5832

1993 Est. Sales: $2,295 million
FYE: December
Employees: 41,000

Key Personnel
Chm, Pres & CEO: Curtis L. Carlson
VC: Marilyn Carlson Nelson
EVP & Pres, Hospitality Group: Juergen Bartels
CFO: Martyn Redgrave
VP Legal, Sec & Gen Counsel: Lee Bearmon
VP HR: Terry M. Butorac

See page 42 for full-page profile.

Business Lines
Database mgt./learning systems
Direct marketing/telemarketing
Hotel operation (Radisson)
Investments
Motivational programs
Real estate
Restaurant franchise (TGI Friday's)
Travel agencies

Key Competitors
AAA
American Express
Bass Enterprises
Flagstar
Hilton
Hyatt
Maritz
Marriott International

Industry
Travel services, hospitality & restaurants

Overview
Carlson is owned and run by Curtis Carlson, who started out selling Gold Bond trading stamps in 1938. The company has 3 segments: travel, hospitality, and marketing. Carlson Marketing Group provides employee training and incentive plans and runs Northwest Airlines's frequent flier program. Carlson's hospitality segment franchises 345 Radisson Hotels worldwide and manages other hotels but owns very few outright. Carlson Travel operates travel agencies worldwide and in 1994 announced a joint venture with Accor's Wagonlit Travel of Paris.

THE CARLYLE GROUP L.P.

RANK: N/R

1001 Pennsylvania Ave. NW
Washington, DC 20004
Phone: 202-347-2626
Fax: 202-347-1818

Employees: 25

Key Personnel
Chm: Frank Carlucci
Managing Dir: Edward J. Mathias
Partner: Richard Darman
Partner: James Baker III
Dir Fin: Ann Montgomery

Selected Investments
Baker & Taylor (book wholesaler)
BDM International (def. consult.)
Caterair Intl (in-flight catering)
CB Commercial (R.E. brokers)
Fresh Fields Markets
GDE Systems (def. electronics)
Magnavox Electronics (defense)
Sage Hospitality (hotel mgmt.)

Industry
Financial - investors

Overview
With former Defense Secretary Frank Carlucci at the helm and a raft of Republican notables as mates, this investment firm, not surprisingly, likes defense companies. However, Carlyle has eclectic tastes — it owns pieces of a book and software wholesaler, an organic grocery chain, and a commercial real estate brokerage and has interests in hotels and the #1 in-flight caterer. Carlyle partners include George Soros and the Mellon family. Carlyle likes to buy divisions from big companies (General Dynamics, Ford, Marriott, Sears, W.R. Grace) but usually partners with management to run them.

CARNIVAL HOTELS AND CASINOS

RANK: 366

3250 Mary St.
Miami, FL 33133
Phone: 305-445-2493
Fax: 305-858-6239

1992 Est. Sales: $830 million
FYE: December
Employees: 12,000

Key Personnel
Chm & CEO: Sherwood M. Weiser
CFO: Peter Temling
Pres, Dev & Capital Group: Peter L. Sibley
Pres, Hospitality Group: Thomas F. Hewitt
VP: Donald E. Lefton
HR: Harry Spicer

Selected Operating Units
Carnicon Resort
Golden Rainbow Balcones
Grand Bay Hotels
Hilton franchises
Louisiana Casino Cruises, Inc.
Metro Hotels
Morichal Largo
Sheraton franchises

Key Competitors
Bally Entertainment
Fairmont Hotel Management
Four Seasons
Hyatt
Marriott International
Rank
Ritz-Carlton
Wyndham Hotel

Industry
Hotels & motels

Overview
Carnival Hotels and Casinos is a hotel management group that resulted from the 1994 merger of the privately held The Continental Companies (TCC, founded in 1970) and certain casino and management assets of the publicly traded Carnival Corporation. In its early years TCC operated primarily east of the Mississippi, but at the time of the merger the company managed more than 63 hotels and resorts all over the US and in 7 countries. Franchise affiliations include Hilton, Sheraton, Omni, Radisson, Holiday Inn, and Ramada. Overseas, the company is focusing on Latin America, Mexico, and the Caribbean. Plans are to take the company public in the near future.

CARPENTER CO. — RANK: 469

5016 Monument Ave.
Richmond, VA 23261
Phone: 804-359-0800
Fax: 804-353-0694

1993 Sales: $619 million
FYE: December
Employees: 6,905

Key Personnel
Chm & CEO: Stanley F. Pauley
Pres & COO: William R. Easterling
VP Fin & CFO: A. F. Markey
VP Mktg & Sales: Lonnie Scheps
Sec & Corp Counsel: Herbert A. Claiborne III
Dir Personnel: David Harned

Major Products
Bedding
Carpet underlay
Comforters
Furniture cushioning
Insulation
Medical products
Packaging material
Pillows

Key Competitors
Aladdin Industries
Foamex
James River
Monsanto
Gates Corp.
Sealed Air
Spartech
Tuscarora Plastics

Industry
Rubber & plastic products

Overview
Established in 1948 as a latex foam rubber distributor, Carpenter Co. is a *FORTUNE* 500 company that manufactures polyurethane foam and polyester fibers used as cushioning for the automotive, bedding, floor covering, and furniture industries, among others. Along with manufacturing facilities in the US, Canada, Mexico, France, and the UK, the company has pouring plants and over 60 satellite branches throughout the US. Carpenter plans to expand its line of comfort-sleep retail products (comforters, mattress pads, and pillows), which are sold through department stores and account for roughly 20% of revenues.

CATALYST ENERGY CORPORATION — RANK: 425

250 Park Ave., 20th Fl.
New York, NY 10022
Phone: 212-867-3800
Fax: 212-867-2955

1992 Est. Sales: $705 million
FYE: December
Employees: 1,400

Key Personnel
Chm & CEO: Ronald W. Cantwell III
VP Fin & Controller: Jack R. Sauer
Asst Controller: Bill Gendron

Business Lines
Electrical generation
Power plant construction
Power plant leasing
Power sales to end users
Power sales to utilities

Industry
Energy - alternate sources

Overview
Catalyst Energy, wholly owned since 1988 by Thomas Pickens III's Merrimac Corporation, sells power to utilities and end users from power plants and hydroelectric dams that it leases, buys, or builds. The company was founded in 1982 to take advantage of laws designed to encourage new power sources, which required utilities to buy power from independent producers. Many utilities use such producers because they are reluctant to face the expense and public outcry that normally accompany proposals for new power projects.

CATERAIR INTERNATIONAL CORP. — RANK: 272

6550 Rock Spring Dr.
Bethesda, MD 20817
Phone: 301-897-7800
Fax: 301-897-7893

1993 Sales: $1,050 million
FYE: December
Employees: 21,000

Key Personnel
Chm, Pres & CEO: Daniel J. Altobello
EVP & COO: Angelo D. Bizzarro
EVP & CFO: Harry J. D'Andrea
SVP Corp Comm: Robert J. Dunn
SVP, Gen Counsel & Sec: John C. Carr
SVP HR: David B. Workman

Selected Clients
Aeroflot
Aerolineas Argentinas
Air France
All Nippon Airways
Canada 3000 Airlines Ltd.
KLM Royal Dutch Airlines
United Airlines
Varig

Key Competitors
ARA
Continental Airlines
Dial
Lufthansa
Ogden
Sky Chefs

Industry
Food services

Overview
Caterair International, the largest US airline catering company in the US, was Marriott's In-Flite Services division until it went private in a management-led LBO in 1989. It controls about 27% of the US airline catering market and 14% of the international in-flight food service market. It services 200 airlines worldwide, operating 118 flight kitchens on 6 continents. The largest shareholders are former Marriott executives Daniel Altobello and Frederic Malek, a group of 40–50 former executives, institutional investors, and the Carlyle Group.

CATHOLIC HEALTHCARE WEST INC. — RANK: 155

1700 Montgomery St., Ste. 300
San Francisco, CA 94111
Phone: 415-397-9000
Fax: 415-397-1823

1993 Sales: $1,633 million
FYE: June
Employees: 17,451

Key Personnel
Chm: Linda Bevilacqua
Pres & CEO: Richard J. Kramer
EVP & COO: Larry Wilson
VP Fin Svcs & CFO: John Burgis
VP Legal Svcs & Gen Counsel: Robert Johnson
Dir HR: Lawrence Kren

◀ **See page 43 for full-page profile.**

Selected Care Facilities
Mercy General Hospital
Mercy Healthcare
Mercy Medical Center
Mercy San Juan Hospital
Methodist Hospital
St. Francis Memorial Hospital
St. Mary's Hospital & Med. Ctr.

Key Competitors
Adventist Health
Diversified Health Center
Foundation Health
Kaiser Foundation Health Plan
PacifiCare
Qual-Med
Sierra Health Services
Sutter Health System

Industry
Hospitals

Overview
Catholic Healthcare West (CHW) is the US's 10th largest nonprofit health organization. Formed by the merger of 2 Roman Catholic health care systems in 1986, CHW now runs a network of 17 hospitals in California, Arizona, and Nevada. The system, which is still owned and run by the Catholic Church, also operates clinics, long-term care facilities, and retirement residences. CHW emphasizes care for poor, elderly, and HIV-infected patients and provides community services, including indigent programs and health education.

CAWSL CORP.

RANK: 132

7 E. Wynnewood Rd.
Wynnewood, PA 19096
Phone: 215-647-2701
Fax: 215-889-9250

1992 Est. Sales: $1,846 million
FYE: December
Employees: 5,835

Key Personnel
Chm & CEO: Paul E. Kelly
Pres: Paul E. Kelly Jr.
VP Fin: Philip Howse
VP: Andrew J. Bozzelli
Treas: Joseph Klock

Principal Subsidiaries
Anchor Darling Industries Inc.
Anchor Darling Valve Co.
Delta Government Options (81%)
Pressure Products Industries
Williams & Company, Inc.
Williams House of Metals, Inc.

Key Competitors
Aarque
Centerline Piping
L. B. Foster
Lone Star Technologies
Quanex
Southwire
Sumitomo

Industry
Steel - pipes & tubes

Overview
Founded in 1981, Cawsl Corp. is a holding company with interests in metal products and financial services. The company's Anchor Darling Industries manufactures engineering valves, industrial machinery, metal stampings, and steel pipes and tubes and operates more than 10 full-line metals service centers. Cawsl also owns 81% of Delta Government Options, a computer system for trading options on government securities.

CERTIFIED GROCERS OF CALIFORNIA, LTD

RANK: 116

2601 S. Eastern Ave.
Los Angeles, CA 90040
Phone: 213-723-7476
Fax: 213-724-7667

1993 Sales: $2,007 million
FYE: August
Employees: 2,500

Key Personnel
Chm: Everett W. Dingwell
Pres & CEO: Alfred A. Plamann
SVP Admin: Donald W. Dill
SVP HR: Donald G. Grose
CFO: Daniel Bane
Sec & Treas: David A. Woodward

Principal Subsidiaries
Grocers & Merchants Insurance
Grocers Capital Company
Grocers Equipment Company
Grocers General Merchandise Co.
Grocers Specialty Company
Hawaiian Grocery Stores

Key Competitors
Farmer Bros.
Fleming
Nash Finch
Select Foods
Services Grocers of America
Young's Market

Industry
Food - wholesale to grocers

Overview
Founded in 1922 by 15 independent grocers in Southern California, CERGRO is a grocery wholesaling cooperative that supplies food products and related nonfood items to over 3,000 member-owners in California, Nevada, Arizona, and Hawaii. CERGRO also provides its members with services such as site selection and design, insurance, advertising, merchandise distribution, and financing. CERGRO, the 2nd largest retailer-owned co-op in the US, is the leading wholesale distributor to independent retail grocers in Southern California and the #2 distributor in Northern California.

CF INDUSTRIES, INC.

RANK: 331

One Salem Lake Dr.
Long Grove, IL 60047
Phone: 708-438-9500
Fax: 708-438-0211

1993 Sales: $906 million
FYE: December
Employees: 1,478

Key Personnel
Chm: Gene A. James
Pres & CEO: Robert C. Liuzzi
SVP & CFO: Stephen R. Wilson
VP Mktg & Sales: John H. Sultenfuss, Jr.
VP, Gen Counsel & Sec: Paul R. Obert
VP HR: William G. Eppel

Major Products
Ammonia
Nitrogen fertilizer
Phosphate fertilizer
Potash fertilizer
Urea granules

Key Competitors
Arcadian
Farmland Industries
Freeport-McMoRan
IMC Fertilizer
JR Simplot
Nu-West
Transammonia
Unocal

Industry
Fertilizers

Overview
Organized in 1946, CF Industries is an interregional agricultural cooperative that manufactures and markets plant food products to its members in 46 states and 2 Canadian provinces. CF is owned by 12 regional agricultural co-ops, including Land O' Lakes and CENEX, who own 38%. The co-op operates 2 nitrogen plants, 2 phosphate plants, a phosphate mine, and a network of distribution terminals and storage facilities. Expansion of its Donaldsonville, Louisiana, plant has increased the co-op's ability to upgrade ammonia into higher-priced granular urea.

CHEMCENTRAL CORPORATION

RANK: 443

7050 W. 71st St.
Bedford Park, IL 60499
Phone: 708-594-7000
Fax: 708-594-6328

1993 Sales: $675 million
FYE: December
Employees: 900

Key Personnel
Chm: R. T. Hough
Pres & CEO: H. Daniel Wenstrup
VP & Sec: William D. Mulliken
VP Environmental: Robert J. Garner
VP Fin: Arlen L. Haines
VP Mktg: David W. Courtney

Business Lines
Adhesives
Coatings
Consumer specialties
Printing & graphics
Rubber & plastics compounding

Key Competitors
Ashland Oil
Concord UXCO
W. R. Grace
ICI
Stinnes
Texaco
Union Carbide
Univar

Industry
Chemicals - distribution

Overview
Founded in 1926 as William J. Hough Co., a supplier of naval stores, Illinois-based Chemcentral has grown to be one of the top 3 chemical distribution companies in North America. Through acquisitions the company has expanded from the Chicago area into the mid-Atlantic and southeastern states, as well as New England and the Pacific Northwest. It also has a limited presence in Canada and Mexico. Since the 1960s the company has carved a niche for itself in 5 specialty chemical markets as well as in electronics, oil-field chemicals, and urethanes.

THE CIRCLE K CORPORATION

RANK: 62

3003 N. Central Ave.
Phoenix, AZ 85012
Phone: 602-530-5001
Fax: 602-530-5278

1993 Est. Sales: $3,157 million
FYE: April
Employees: 20,000

Key Personnel
Chm: Bart A. Brown, Jr.
Pres & CEO: John F. Antioco
EVP & COO: Mitch E. Telson
EVP & CFO: Larry Zine
SVP & Gen Counsel: Gehl P. Babinec
VP HR: Terry S. Broekemeier

◀ **See page 44 for full-page profile.**

Major Brands
Aero K gasoline
Dairy Fair dairy products
Delifresh pizza
DeliPride frozen sandwiches
Dip 'N Snack
Fairmont popcorn, corn chips
Giant meat snacks
Nice 'N Natural yogurt, ice cream

Key Competitors
Chevron
Mobil
National Convenience
QuikTrip
Racetrac
Southland
Texaco
Unocal

Industry
Retail - convenience stores

Overview
Launched by a former mayor of El Paso in 1951, Phoenix-based Circle K is the nation's #2 convenience store chain (after Ito-Yokado's 7-Eleven), with 2,435 units in the US and 2,461 abroad. After wildly expanding in the 1980s, the company labored under heavy debt and filed for bankruptcy protection in 1990. In 1993 investment group Investcorp S.A. bought Circle K for $400 million, rescuing it from Chapter 11. The company is now trying to unload unprofitable stores (of which there are many) and is widening its customer base through innovative merchandising tactics and joint ventures.

THE CITY UNIVERSITY OF NEW YORK

RANK: 110

535 E. 80th St.
New York, NY 10021
Phone: 212-794-5555
Fax: 212-794-5397

1993 Est. Sales: $2,050 million
FYE: June
Employees: 27,001

Key Personnel
Chancellor: W. Ann Reynolds
Dep Chancellor: Laurence Mucciolo
Fin Mgr: Gerald Glick
Comptroller: Anthony Hladek
Dep Comptroller: Helen Woo

Schools & Colleges
Baruch College
Brooklyn College
City College
College of Staten Island
Herbert H. Lehman College
Hunter College
John Jay College of Criminal Justice
Medgar Evers College
New York City Technical College
Queens College
York College

Industry
Schools

Overview
Founded in 1847, CUNY is a public university system of 20 campuses in the New York City metropolitan area. Eleven campuses offer 4-year undergraduate programs and 3 offer doctoral programs. Enrollment stands at 200,000; the faculty numbers 7,000. The university focuses on providing education to nontraditional students, such as minority and commuter students. Its City College campus is one of the US's largest sources of black and Hispanic engineers. Few campuses offer residential housing or off-campus dormitories. Because of severe financial difficulties, CUNY is reducing course offerings and costs, by, for example, delaying maintenance expenditures.

CLARK ENTERPRISES, INC.

RANK: 158

7500 Old Georgetown Rd.
Bethesda, MD 20814
Phone: 301-657-7100
Fax: 301-657-7263

1993 Est. Sales: $1,600 million
FYE: December
Employees: 5,000

Key Personnel
Chm & CEO: A. James Clark
CFO & COO: Lawrence C. Nussdorf
VP: Robert J. Flanagan
VP & Gen Counsel: Kathy Taub
Dir Corp Comm: Louise E. Pulizzi
Dir Comp & Benefits: Andrea Danko-Koenig

Principal Subsidiaries
Clark Broadcasting Co. (radio)
Clark Construction Group
Clark Transportation Co. (freight)
Seawright Corp. (real estate)

Key Competitors
Bechtel
Bovis
CRSS
Fluor
Jacobs Engineering
Peter Kiewit Sons'
Perini
Turner Industries

Industry
Construction - heavy

Overview
Clark Enterprises is the parent of Clark Construction Group, which itself is parent to George Hyman Construction, HRW (precast concrete), Omni Construction, and TTW (retaining walls). Hyman, founded in 1906, is the centerpiece of Clark Enterprises. Owner A. James Clark began his career with Hyman in 1950 as an engineer, became president in 1969, and took Hyman under Clark Construction's wing in 1982. Other subsidiaries include Clark Transportation, a coastal and air freight shipper, and Seawright Corp., a real estate developer. Hyman and Omni specialize in heavy construction, and each has office building subsidiaries.

CLAYTON, DUBILIER & RICE, INC.

RANK: N/R

126 E. 56th St., 25th Fl.
New York, NY 10022
Phone: 212-355-0740
Fax: 212-752-7629

Key Personnel
Pres: Joseph L. Rice III
Principal: Richard S. Braddock
Principal: Alberto Cribiore
Principal: Donald J. Gogel
Principal: Hubbard C. Howe
Principal: Andrell Piarson

Selected Investments
Allison Engine Co. (jet engines)
APS (auto parts)
Homeland Stores (supermarkets)
Kendall (medical products)
Lexmark Int'l (office equipment)
Remington Arms (rifles)
Van Kampen Merritt (invest.)
Wesco (elec. equip. distribution)

Industry
Financial - investors

Overview
Clayton, Dubilier & Rice, formed in 1978, is an investment firm specializing in turn-around situations. Mostly targeting underachieving units of large corporations, Clayton, Dubilier traditionally structures an LBO and works to improve operations. The investment firm's partners, many of whom are former CEOs or COOs, have gained a reputation as hands-on managers of the acquisitions they oversee. Since 1978 Clayton, Dubilier has purchased at least 18 businesses with combined sales of over $11 billion, resulting in an estimated 40% annual return for investors in its $1 billion fund.

CLUB CORPORATION INTERNATIONAL

RANK: 226

3030 LBJ Fwy., Ste 700
Dallas, TX 75234
Phone: 214-888-7308
Fax: 214-888-7583

1993 Est. Sales: $1,200 million
FYE: December
Employees: 25,000

Key Personnel

Chm & CEO: Robert H. Dedman
Pres & COO: Robert H. Dedman Jr.
EVP & Chief Admin Officer: John H. Gray
SVP Accounting & CFO: R. Michael Carroll
SVP, Gen Counsel & Sec: Terry A. Taylor
SVP HR: Dorothy Lawrence

Principal Subsidiaries

CCA International, Inc.
Club Corporation of America
Club Resorts Inc.
ClubCorp Consulting
ClubCorp Financial Mgmt.
ClubCorp Realty
Franklin Federal Bancorp
GolfCorp

Key Competitors

Capital City Club
Club Mark
Cullen/Frost Bankers
Marriott International
McAuley LCX
NationsBank
Texas Commerce Bancshares

Industry

Leisure & recreational services - club management

Overview

Club Corporation International is a holding company for hospitality and financial service companies, including flagship ClubCorp of America and Franklin Federal Bancorp, and is the world's largest private club and golf course operator. Attorney Robert Dedman founded the company in 1957 as a sideline. Now Club Corporation owns real estate, provides financial services, and caters to 400,000 members. Sitting out the 1980s real estate boom, Dedman picked up property at rummage-sale prices during the bust.

COCA-COLA BOTTLING CO. OF CHICAGO

RANK: 391

7400 N. Oak Park Ave.
Niles, IL 60714
Phone: 312-775-0900
Fax: 708-647-7104

1993 Sales: $793 million
FYE: December
Employees: 2,400

Key Personnel

Chm: Marvin J. Herb
Pres & COO: William F. O'Rourke
VP Fin: Jerry Moza
Mgr Adv & Promotions: Robert McCabe
VP HR: Robert T. Palo

Major Products

Barq's Root Beer
Caffeine-free Coca-Cola
Cherry Coke
Coca-Cola
Coca-Cola Classic
Diet Coke
Minute Maid
Sprite

Key Competitors

Cadbury Schweppes
Dr Pepper/7Up
National Beverage
PepsiCo
Royal Crown Bottling (Chicago)
Seagram
Snapple
Whitman

Industry

Beverages - soft drinks

Overview

Purchased by Marvin Herb from the Coca-Cola Company in 1981, Coca-Cola Bottling Co. of Chicago is the 3rd largest Coca-Cola bottling plant in the country, selling 90 million cases in 5 states. Also a bottler and distributor for Barq's Root Beer, Coca-Cola Bottling of Chicago is responsible for more than 12% of Barq's sales. Owner Herb, who is frugal and intensely publicity-shy, is reportedly a tough negotiator and manager who does not believe in discounts.

COLUMBIA UNIVERSITY IN THE CITY OF NEW YORK

RANK: 280

Broadway & W. 116 St.
New York, NY 10027
Phone: 212-854-1754
Fax: 212-749-0397

1993 Sales: $1,033 million
FYE: June
Employees: 6,430

Key Personnel

Pres: George Rupp
Provost: Jonathon R. Cole
EVP Fin: John Masten
VP Investments: Bruce M. Dresner
Treas & Controller: Patricia Francy
Gen Counsel: Elizabeth Head

Schools & Colleges

Barnard College
College of Physicians & Surgeons
Columbia College
Graduate School of Arts & Sciences
Graduate School of Business
Graduate School of Journalism
School of Dental & Oral Surgery
School of Engineering & Applied Science
School of General Studies
School of Law
School of Public Health
School of Social Work
School of the Arts
Teachers College
Union Theological Seminary

Industry

Schools

Overview

Located on the former site of the Bloomingdale Insane Asylum, Columbia University today is an academic asylum to 19,900 students. The school was founded in 1754 as King's College; the name was patriotically changed after the American Revolution. Columbia offers 348 degree programs through its 15 schools; 2 of the schools are Barnard (an independent women's college) and Columbia College (smallest of the Ivy League schools). The university's endowment is $1.9 billion. George Rupp, who had been Rice University president, succeeded Michael Sovern as Columbia's president in 1993.

CONNECTICUT MUTUAL LIFE INSURANCE COMPANY

RANK: 95

140 Garden St.
Hartford, CT 06154
Phone: 203-987-6500
Fax: 203-987-6532

1993 Sales: $2,310 million
FYE: December
Employees: 5,000

Key Personnel

Chm: Denis F. Mullane
Pres & CEO: David E. Sams, Jr.
SVP & CFO: J. Brinke Marcuccilli
SVP HR: David J. Beed
Chief Invest Officer: Anne Melissa Dowling
Sec: Ann F. Lomeli

Operating Units

CM Advantage
CM Asset Advisors
C.M. Life Insurance Company
Connecticut Mutual Financial Svcs.
State House Capital Management

Key Competitors

Aetna
CIGNA
Equitable
John Hancock
MetLife
New York Life
Northwestern Mutual
Prudential

Industry

Insurance - life

Overview

Chartered in 1846, Hartford-based Connecticut Mutual Life is one of the largest and most respected mutual insurance companies in the US. It is one of a few insurance companies to operate in all 50 states, the District of Columbia, Puerto Rico, and Guam. Through more than 3,000 agents and brokers, the company offers a complete portfolio of individual, term, permanent, and universal life insurance; individual variable annuities; group pension plans; and disability income insurance. "The CM Alliance" is a corporate signature for Connecticut Mutual and its associates and affiliates.

CONNELL CO.

RANK: 274

45 Cardinal Dr.
Westfield, NJ 07090
Phone: 908-233-0700
Fax: 908-233-1070

1992 Est. Sales: $1,050 million
FYE: December
Employees: 200

Key Personnel
Chm & Pres: Grover Connell
EVP: Ted Connell
EVP: George Alayeto
EVP: Ron C. Connolly
SVP & Treas: Terry Connell

Business Lines
Equipment leasing
Processed food importing
Real estate development
Rice & sugar brokerage
Rice & sugar trading

Key Competitors
Cargill
ConAgra
Continental Grain
GPA
Imperial Holly
Itel
Riceland Foods
Savannah Foods

Industry
Food - brokerage

Overview
Founded in 1912, Connell is the largest independent rice and sugar trader/broker in the US, with an export share estimated at over 20%. The company also imports processed foods from the Orient. Connell also leases heavy equipment to the railroad, airline, and utility industries and develops real estate. Owner Grover Connell keeps a low public profile and lives modestly but has a penchant for big political contributions. The well-connected Democrat is known for spending heavily on speaking honoraria for politicians, which he believes is more effective than hiring lobbyists.

CONNELL LIMITED PARTNERSHIP

RANK: 324

One International Place, 31st Fl.
Boston, MA 02110
Phone: 617-737-2700
Fax: 617-737-1617

1993 Sales: $913 million
FYE: December
Employees: 3,054

Key Personnel
Chm & CEO: William F. Connell
Pres & COO: Robert E. Brooker
VP & CFO: Kathleen A. Murphy
VP & Sec: Edward J. Joyce
VP: Maurice R. Heller
Asst Controller: John J. Kwiatek

Major Products/Services
Boilers
Die sets
Machine tools
Scrap handling equipment
Scrap metal
Smelting of aluminum & steel

Key Competitors
Alcan
Alcoa
Autodie
Bethlehem Steel
Commercial Metals
Cyprus Amax
Inland Steel
USX - U.S. Steel

Industry
Metal products - fabrication

Overview
Connell LP recycles metal and manufactures industrial products, including specialty dies, tools, and pressure vessels. Headed by William Connell, former chairman and CEO of shipyard operator Avondale Industries, Connell LP is a closely held partnership formed in 1987 to buy 6 Avondale divisions. The purchase settled Avondale's lawsuit with its former parent company, Ogden Corp.; the lawsuit had charged Ogden with overvaluing assets spun off to create employee-owned Avondale in 1985.

CONSOL ENERGY INC.

RANK: 122

1800 Washington Rd.
Pittsburgh, PA 15241
Phone: 412-831-4000
Fax: 412-831-4916

1993 Sales: $1,927 million
FYE: December
Employees: 10,036

Key Personnel
Pres & CEO: B. R. Brown
VP & Treas: M. F. Nemser
VP & Controller: W. D. Welch
Asst Sec: J. P. Garniewski
Asst Sec: M. G. McClure
Treas Coord/Admin: Marsha Spear

Principal Subsidiaries
CONSOL Inc.
Consolidation Coal Company
McElroy Coal Co.
Quarto Mining Co.

Key Competitors
Cyprus Amax
Hanson
Kerr-McGee
Pittston
Rochester & Pittsburgh Coal
Walter Industries
Westmoreland Coal
Zeigler Coal

Industry
Coal

Overview
CONSOL Energy Inc. operates as a joint venture between DuPont and Rheinbraun AG, a subsidiary of RWE AG, the dominant electricity producer in Germany, with each owning 50%. Called by its trade name, CONSOL, the venture, founded in 1991, includes a 34% interest in DuPont's Consolidation Coal Co., one of the largest coal producers in the US, as well as some of DuPont's other coal businesses. Rheinbraun contributed its stake in coal reserves and mines, located in southwestern Pennsylvania, which had been acquired from DuPont in 1981. CONSOL mines bituminous coal, which is a major fuel used by US electric utilities.

CONTINENTAL CABLEVISION, INC.

RANK: 237

The Pilot House, Lewis Wharf
Boston, MA 02110
Phone: 617-742-9500
Fax: 617-742-0530

1993 Sales: $1,177 million
FYE: December
Employees: 7,000

Key Personnel
Chm & CEO: Amos B. Hostetter, Jr.
VC: Timothy P. Neher
Pres & COO: Michael J. Ritter
SVP & Treas: Nancy Hawthorne
SVP HR: Andrew J. Dixon, Jr.
VP & Gen Counsel: Margaret A. Sofio

Investments
CableLabs (R&D)
C-SPAN
E! Entertainment Network
New England Cable NewsChannel
Turner Broadcasting System
Viewer's Choice (pay-per-view)

Key Competitors
Advance Publications
Cablevision Systems
Comcast
Cox
Jones Intercable
TCI
TeleCable
Time Warner

Industry
Cable TV

Overview
Founded in 1963 by 2 fraternity brothers, Amos Hostetter and Irving Grousbeck, Continental Cablevision is now among the top 5 cable companies in the US. The company has 2.9 million subscribers in those 16 states, mostly in New England and the Midwest, as well as California and Florida. Hostetter, who helped create C-SPAN in 1979, is principal owner (Grousbeck left in 1981), having purchased a sizable stake from Dow Jones in 1989. Through a partnership with Performance Systems International, the company is offering subscribers in Massachusetts access to the Internet at higher speeds than conventional telephone lines.

CONTINENTAL GRAIN COMPANY

RANK: 10

277 Park Ave.
New York, NY 10172
Phone: 212-207-5100
Fax: 212-207-5181

1994 Sales: $15,000 million
FYE: March
Employees: 15,500

Key Personnel
Chm & CEO: Donald L. Staheli
Pres & COO: Paul J. Fribourg
Pres Finagrain: Poul Schroeder
SVP: Bernard Steinweg
VP & Gen Counsel: Lawrence G. Weppler
VP HR: Dwight Coffin

Business Lines
Commodity Marketing Group
Financial Services Group
Meat Group
Milling Group
World Grain Group

Key Competitors
Ashland Oil
Cargill
Chevron
ConAgra
Harvest States Co-ops
Koch
Pilgrim's Pride
Salomon

Industry
Food - brokerage

Overview
Continental was founded in Belgium by Simon Fribourg in 1813 to trade commodities, but a severe drought sent the company expanding into the wheat business. Now the company oversees the world's #2 grain and related commodities empire (after Cargill), with offices and facilities in more than 50 countries. Continental boasts operations in livestock, shipping, food processing, and oil as well as financial services. Michel Fribourg, Simon's great-great-grandson, and his family own 90% of the company's stock.

◀ See page 45 for full-page profile.

CONTRAN CORPORATION

RANK: 243

5430 LBJ Fwy., Ste. 1700
Dallas, TX 75240
Phone: 214-233-1700
Fax: 214-385-0586

1993 Sales: $1,147 million
FYE: December
Employees: 1,500

Key Personnel
Chm, Pres & CEO: Harold C. Simmons
VC: Glenn R. Simmons
VP & Contoller: J. Thomas Montgomery
VP & Sec: Steven L. Watson
VP Fin & Admin, Treas: William C. Timm
Dir Personnel: Keith Johnson

Business Lines
Chemicals
Fast food
Forest products
Hardware
Locks
Steel
Sugar
Titanium products

Key Competitors
Connell Co.
DuPont
Imperial Holly
Louisiana-Pacific
Savannah Foods
Spreckels Industries
Stanley Works
Tate & Lyle

Industry
Diversified operations

Overview
Founded by Texas billionaire Harold Simmons in 1964, Contran is a holding company controlling 90% of Valhi, Inc., a publicly traded company with diversified operations ranging from sugar to titanium. Valhi's holdings include Amalgamated Sugar Co., Medite Corp. (fiberboard), Sybra (Arby's fast food franchises), and National Cabinet Lock. Valhi also owns almost 50% of NL Industries (titanium pigments) and Tremont Corp. (titanium products). All of the shares of Contran are owned by the Harold C. Simmons Family Trust, established for the benefit of Simmons's children and grandchildren.

COOPERS & LYBRAND L.L.P.

RANK: 36

1251 Avenue of the Americas
New York, NY 10020
Phone: 212-536-2000
Fax: 212-536-3145

1993 Sales: $5,220 million
FYE: September
Employees: 66,300

Key Personnel
Chm & CEO: Eugene M. Freedman
VC Intl: William K. O'Brien
VC HR & Strategy: Anthony J. Conti
COO: Vincent M. O'Reilly
CFO: Frank V. Scalia
Gen Counsel: Harris J. Amhowitz

Selected Services
Auditing
Benefit systems
Group health
Information technology (programming)
International tax
Mergers & acquisitions
Personal financial services
Resource management

Key Competitors
Arthur Andersen
Deloitte & Touche
Ernst & Young
Hewitt Associates
KPMG
Marsh & McLennan
McKinsey & Co.
Price Waterhouse

Industry
Business services - accounting & consulting

Overview
Formed by a transatlantic merger in 1957, Coopers (UK) & Lybrand (US) is the world's 4th largest accounting company and the 5th largest in the US. Its forebears wrote *Montgomery's Auditing*, an accounting bible. Like its Big 6 brethren, Coopers & Lybrand has faced legal costs as investors in failed companies have brought suit against auditors. The company has resisted the industry's "megamerger" trend, becoming a haven for accountants fleeing from coupling firms. The company has focused recently on expanding its Human Resource Advisory Group.

◀ See page 46 for full-page profile.

COOPERSMITH INC.

RANK: 310

3500 One Peachtree Center
Atlanta, GA 30308
Phone: 404-581-8354
Fax: 404-581-8330

1992 Est. Sales: $952 million
Employees: 12,250

Key Personnel
Chm: Frederick E. Cooper
EVP & COO: John C. Johnson
Sec: Cindy Herndon

Principal Subsidiaries
American Bread
Kern's Bakeries, Inc.
Smith's Bakery
- Holsum bread
- Roman Meal bread
- Smith's bread

Key Competitors
Anheuser Busch
Campbell Soup
CPC
Flowers Industries
Interstate Bakeries
Ralston Continental Baking
Philip Morris
Tasty Baking

Industry
Food - baked goods

Overview
Formed in 1990, CooperSmith is the holding company for 3 bread, cake, and rolls companies. The company was created by Frederick Cooper after the FTC denied a request by *FORTUNE* 500 company Flowers Industries to acquire Smith's Bakery. Cooper, formerly Flowers's vice chairman and general counsel, left to become chairman of the new company, but he remains a Flowers director. With a service area that includes Alabama, Florida, Georgia, Louisiana, Kentucky, Mississippi, Tennessee, and Virginia, the bakery conglomerate is considered a major regional player.

CORE-MARK INTERNATIONAL, INC.

RANK: 127

395 Oyster Point Blvd.
South San Francisco, CA 94080
Phone: 415-589-9445
Fax: 415-952-4284

1993 Sales: $1,900 million
FYE: December
Employees: 1,700

Key Personnel
Chm, Pres & CEO: Gary L. Walsh
VP, Asst Sec & CFO: Leo F. Korman
SVP Distribution: Robert A. Allen
SVP Mktg & Sales: Leo Granucci
SVP Ops: Michael Walsh
Dir HR: Henry Hautau

Major Products
Candy
General merchandise
Grocery products
Health & beauty care products
Tobacco products

Key Competitors
Aurora Eby-Brown
Fleming
GSC Enterprises
McDonald Candy
Nash Finch
Rykoff-Sexton
Southland
Wal-Mart

Industry
Food & sundries - wholesale to convenience stores

Overview
Founded in 1973, Core-Mark is a convenience store distributor, operating in an area that stretches from western Canada, south to Mexico, and west to the Pacific. Majority-owned since 1989 by investment firms Dyson-Kissner-Moran and Bessemer Securities, Core-Mark has streamlined its operations by selling its nondistribution businesses, a foam rubber producer, and a furniture company, and divesting its distribution operations in the Midwest. Core-Mark is reducing its reliance on tobacco products and expanding its health and beauty care, general merchandise, and food service programs.

CORNELL UNIVERSITY

RANK: 201

Cornell University Campus
Ithaca, NY 14853
Phone: 607-255-2000
Fax: 607-255-0327

1993 Sales: $1,315 million
FYE: June
Employees: 9,500

Key Personnel
Pres: Frank H. Rhodes
SVP: James E. Morley
VP Fin & Treas: Frederick A. Rogers
VP Academic Planning: John R. Wiesenfeld
Dean of Faculty: Peter Stein
Assoc VP HR: Beth Warren

Colleges & Schools
Agriculture & Life Sciences
Architecture, Art & Planning
Arts & Sciences
Engineering
Hotel Administration
Human Ecology
Industrial & Labor Relations
Veterinary Medicine

Industry
Schools

Overview
Founded in 1865 as a land-grant college, Cornell University has 19,000 students, almost half of them from the state of New York. This Ivy League university supports 7 undergraduate and 4 graduate schools. While the university is under private control, 4 of the schools are statutory colleges of the State University of New York. The university fields 20 intercollegiate sports teams for men and 15 for women. Cornell's recently constructed Carl A. Kroch Library for rare books was built underground (at a cost of $18.6 million) to allow proximity to the graduate school library while maintaining the aesthetics of the historic campus.

COTTER & COMPANY

RANK: 94

2740 N. Clybourn Ave.
Chicago, IL 60614
Phone: 312-975-2700
Fax: 312-975-1712

1993 Sales: $2,356 million
FYE: December
Employees: 4,400

Key Personnel
Pres & CEO: Daniel A. Cotter
EVP & COO: Steven J. Porter
VP Fin, Sec ,Treas & CFO: Kerry J. Kirby
VP & Gen Counsel: Daniel T. Burns
VP Distribution: John P. Semkus
Dir HR: Pat Kelley

Major Products
Brooms & brushes
Farm machinery
Hardware
Home furnishings
Lawn & garden equipment
Lawnmowers
Painting supplies
Snowblowers

Key Competitors
84 Lumber
Ace Hardware
Hardware Wholesalers
Home Depot
Kmart
Menard
SERVISTAR

Industry
Building products - retail & wholesale

Overview
Founded in 1948, Cotter & Company is the world's largest hardware wholesaler. Cotter is a cooperative owned by the 7,500 dealers who buy into the co-op and agree to make it their sole supplier. Some 6,500 of Cotter's members are True Value Hardware dealers, while 1,000 are V&S Variety Stores. In an attempt to thwart the customer-gobbling menace from warehouse chains such as Home Depot, Cotter recently persuaded 100 of its members to invest in rental programs for customers.

COULTER CORPORATION

RANK: 461

11800 SW 147th Ave.
Miami, FL 33196
Phone: 305-380-3800
Fax: 305-380-8312

1993 Est. Sales: $635 million
FYE: March
Employees: 5,000

Key Personnel
Chm: Wallace Coulter
Pres: Joseph Coulter, Jr.
CFO: Sue Van
Dir Product Dev: Edward Doty
Dir Ops: Joseph Coulter III
Dir HR: James Ring

Major Products
Diagnostic equipment
Industrial process analyzers
Laboratory apparatus
Laboratory furniture
Process control instruments

Key Competitors
Abaxis
Abbott Labs
Baxter
Becton, Dickinson
Corning
Miles
Technicon
Trimedyne

Industry
Medical instruments

Overview
A manufacturer and distributor of medical equipment, Coulter was organized in Chicago as Coulter Electronics in 1958. The principal owners — Wallace Coulter, who invented the Coulter Principle of counting and sizing particles by volume, and his brother Joseph — moved the company to Florida in 1960. Known primarily for its automated blood-cell counters (an estimated 95% worldwide are Coulter-made or clones), Coulter has sold equipment to 80% of the world's clinical laboratories. The company also is developing a drug to fight lymphoma, a form of cancer.

COUNTRYMARK COOPERATIVE, INC.

RANK: 118

950 N. Meridian St.
Indianapolis, IN 46204
Phone: 317-685-3000
Fax: 317-685-3191

1993 Est. Sales: $2,000 million
FYE: August
Employees: 750

Key Personnel
Chm: Larry Curless
Pres & CEO: Philip F. French
SVP & Sec: William F. Paddack
VP Fin: Robert Werner
VP Planning & Mktg: Paul Weinstein
VP HR: P. D. Denhart

Business Lines
Animal feeds
Farm supplies
Fertilizer
Grain handling
Petroleum
Seeds

Key Competitors
ADM
Andersons
Cargill
ConAgra
Continental Grain
EDI International
Ferruzzi
GROWMARK

Industry
Food - flour & grain

Overview
Countrymark was formed in 1991 when the Indiana Farm Bureau Cooperative Association, created in 1926, merged with its counterparts in Ohio and Michigan. Owned by local agricultural cooperatives, Countrymark provides feeds, fuels, and fertilizers to farmers in addition to helping them bring their grains to market. Countrymark is Indiana's largest private company and, according to CEO Philip French, serves 8 out of every 10 farmers in its territory in one way or another.

COX ENTERPRISES, INC.

RANK: 77

1400 Lake Hearn Dr.
Atlanta, GA 30319
Phone: 404-843-5000
Fax: 404-843-5142

1993 Sales: $2,675 million
FYE: December
Employees: 31,000

Key Personnel
Chm & CEO: James Cox Kennedy
SVP & CFO: John R. Dillon
Sec & VP Legal Affairs: Andrew A. Merdek
VP Tax: Preston B. Barnett
VP & Controller: John G. Boyette
VP HR: Timothy W. Hughes

◀ **See page 47 for full-page profile.**

Selected Operations
The Atlanta Constitution
Cox Cable (22 cable systems)
Dayton Daily News
Fibernet
Manheim Auctions (auto auctions)
Radio stations (13)
Rysher Entertainment
TV stations (6)

Key Competitors
Advance Publications
Gannett
Hearst
Knight-Ridder
TCI
Time Warner
Turner Broadcasting
Viacom

Industry
Publishing - newspapers

Overview
Cox Enterprises was formed in 1968 to operate the media empire created by newspaperman and politico James Middleton Cox, who bought his first newspaper in 1898. It is now one of the world's largest media companies, with 18 daily newspapers; 7 weeklies; one monthly magazine; and, with the purchase of Times Mirror's cable systems, the 3rd largest cable system in the US. Cox also owns the world's largest auto auction operator. The company is investing in a number of new technologies, including fiber optics and interactive television. It is owned by Barbara Cox Anthony and Anne Cox Chambers, daughters of the founder.

CRAWFORD FITTING COMPANY INC.

RANK: 476

29500 Solon Rd.
Solon, OH 44139
Phone: 216-248-4600
Fax: 216-349-5970

1992 Est. Sales: $594 million
FYE: December
Employees: 5,000

Key Personnel
Chm: Fred A. Lennon
Pres: F. J. Callahan
Treas: Norge Tobbe
VP: Alice Lennon
Personnel Mgr: Richard Mach

Principal Subsidiaries
Alfred Machine Co.
Central Swagelok Company Inc.
Colony Tool Inc.
Falon Co. Inc.
Kenmore Research Company Inc.
Solex Corp.
Valport Co.
Whitey Co. Inc.

Key Competitors
Amcast Industrial
American United Global
BWIP Holding
Crane
Dresser
FMC
Henry Vogt Machine
Wheatley TXT

Industry
Pumps & seals

Overview
Crawford Fittings is a Cleveland, Ohio–based manufacturer of valves and pipe fittings with a reputation for quality and secrecy. Its reclusive owner, Fred A. Lennon, started the company in 1947 with partner Cullen Crawford, a designer of high-pressure pipe fittings. Lennon eventually bought out Crawford and made the company a market leader both in the US and abroad. The company is one of only a handful nationwide that manufacture seals for high-pressure hydraulic systems. These are marketed under several brand names, such as Swagelok and Cajon. Despite its success, the company maintains a low profile.

CROWLEY MARITIME CORPORATION

RANK: 251

155 Grand Ave.
Oakland, CA 94612
Phone: 510-251-7500
Fax: 510-251-7625

1993 Sales: $1,100 million
FYE: December
Employees: 5,000

Key Personnel
Chm & CEO: Thomas B. Crowley, Sr.
Pres & COO: Thomas B. Crowley, Jr.
SVP & CFO: Robert C. Hood
SVP Gen Counsel: William P. Verdon
SVP & Chief Info Officer: Robert P. Andres
SVP HR: William A. Pennella

Selected Services
Barge services
Cargo services
Environmental cleanup
Ferry and passenger operations
Marine salvage operations
Stevedoring
Trucking services
Tugboat operations

Key Competitors
American President
CSX
International Shipholding
Lykes Bros.
OMI Corp.
Overseas Shipholding
Totem Resources
Zapata

Industry
Transportation - shipping

Overview
Ninety percent–owned by CEO Thomas Crowley, his family, and his employees, Crowley Maritime, founded in 1892, operates 2 main subsidiaries dealing in marine transportation and related services. The company has more than 100 offices dotting the world's major ports and cities in the US, Latin America, and the Caribbean. It offers such services as cargo and passenger transport, barge and trucking services, oil transportation, and environmental cleanup. Crowley's fleet consists of over 400 vessels.

CROWN HOLDING COMPANY

RANK: 466

Pasquerilla Plaza
Johnstown, PA 15901
Phone: 814-536-4441
Fax: 814-535-9343

1993 Sales: $626 million
FYE: January
Employees: 9,000

Key Personnel
Chm & CEO: Frank J. Pasquerilla
Pres: Mark E. Pasquerilla
CFO: Patrick Miniutti
EVP: Nicholas O. Antonazzo
EVP: Marlin R. Havener
Dir of Admin: Donato Zucco

Business Lines
Hess Department Stores
Hotels & motels
Malls
Office buildings

Key Competitors
Dayton Hudson
Edward J. DeBartolo
Equitable
Prudential
Simon Property
Weingarten Realty

Industry
Real estate operations

Overview
Department store and mall operator Crown oversees a group of related companies that originated as Crown Construction in 1950. The company is owned by Frank Pasquerilla, who became president in 1956 and later bought out his partners. Through its subsidiaries (including publicly traded Crown American Realty Trust) Crown owns hotels, office buildings, and 23 shopping malls in 7 states. Although the company also owns 30 Hess Department Stores, it announced plans in August 1994 to sell them to focus on its mall operations and other real estate holdings. Bon-Ton Stores plans to buy 20 of the stores and The May Co. will purchase the rest.

CUMBERLAND FARMS INC.

RANK: 261

777 Dedham St.
Canton, MA 02021
Phone: 617-828-4900
Fax: 617-828-5246

1993 Est. Sales: $1,085 million
FYE: September
Employees: 3,800

Key Personnel
Pres: Lily H. Bentas
CFO: Arthur Koumantzelis
SVP Mfg: Donald Holt
VP Mktg: Henry Brenner
VP HR: Foster G. Macrides
Company Atty: Lena Goldberg

Business Lines
Bakery
Beverage factory
Convenience stores
Dairies
Gulf gasoline stations
Oil terminals

Key Competitors
Circle K
Dairy Mart Convenience Stores
Exxon
Racetrac
Southland
Sunshine-Jr. Stores
Uni-Marts
Wawa

Industry
Retail - convenience stores

Overview
Founded in 1938 as a one-cow dairy, Cumberland Farms is one of the nation's largest privately owned convenience store chains, with over 900 locations in the Northeast and Florida, 2,400 Gulf gas stations, and other related properties. The company, 100%-owned by the Haseotes family, was involved in a 1970s milk scam and a 1980s environmental regulatory action. In 1993 the company emerged from a 19-month bankruptcy (stemming from losses in real estate and a Canadian oil refinery) with an outsider-controlled board that will oversee plans to close stores, reduce staff, and repay creditors.

DAIRYMAN'S COOPERATIVE CREAMERY ASSOCIATION

RANK: 475

400 S. M Street
Tulare, CA 93274-5431
Phone: 209-685-6800
Fax: 209-685-6911

1993 Sales: $595 million
FYE: December
Employees: 570

Key Personnel
Pres: Jack Prince
SVP Operations: Lee Blakely
SVP: Gary Gilman
VP Fin.: Alan Pierson

Major Products
Butter
Cottage cheese
Cream cheese
Fluid milk
Hard cheeses
Nonfat dry milk powder
Whey products

Key Competitors
Associated Milk Producers
California Co-op
Dairymen
Darigold
Land O' Lakes
Mid-America Dairymen
Schreiber Foods
Wisconsin Dairies Co-op

Industry
Food - dairy products

Overview
Milk has always been the name of the game at Dairyman's Cooperative Creamery Association. Since its founding with a single plant in 1909, Dairyman's has grown into one of the nation's largest dairy cooperatives, handling over 9 million pounds of milk each day. Rather than producing branded products, Dairyman's focuses on the private label market. It converts milk produced by its members into a variety of products and then enters into joint ventures with other firms who packge and market them. Dairyman's has seen some unfamiliar controversy lately as some of its members have begun using the growth hormone BST to increase milk production.

DAIRYMEN, INC.

RANK: 395

10140 Linn Station Rd.
Louisville, KY 40223
Phone: 502-426-6455
Fax: 502-423-6739

1993 Sales: $784 million
FYE: August
Employees: 3,000

Key Personnel
CEO & EVP: James E. Mueller
Pres: Buckey M. Jones
SVP & CEO, Flav-O-Rich: Steve G. Conerly
VP Mktg: George Jung
VP & Controller: Dale A. Yost
VP HR Dev: Gerald L. Roadcap

Major Products
Butter
Cheese
Dry milk powder
Raw milk
Whey powder

Key Competitors
Associated Milk Producers
Borden
Dairyman's Co-op Creamery
Dean Foods
Finevest
Land O' Lakes
Mid-America Dairymen
Prairie Farms Dairy

Industry
Food - dairy products

Overview
Dairymen, founded in 1968, is a cooperative of milk farmers in 16 US states and Puerto Rico. In 1993 it sold the Ehrler's Dairy Store chain and Ehrler's Candies, and it almost sold its chief subsidiary, Flav-O-Rich (milk, ice cream), to Dean Foods, but Dean canceled the deal in early 1994. The cooperative is restructuring to focus on marketing, trucking, and storage of its 3,500 members' raw milk. Dairymen continues to operate 5 dairy products plants. The cooperative has been recovering from antitrust legal troubles, and a price-fixing scandal has cost Dairymen more than $20 million.

D'ARCY MASIUS BENTON & BOWLES, INC.

RANK: 499

1675 Broadway
New York, NY 10019
Phone: 212-468-3622
Fax: 212-468-4385

1993 Sales: $531 million
FYE: December
Employees: 5,904

Key Personnel
Chm & CEO: Roy J. Bostock
EVP & CFO: Craig D. Bowen
Creative Dir: John Nieman
Dir Planning: Joseph Plummer
Sec: Michael S. Moore
Dir Personnel: Judith Kemp

Selected Clients
Amoco
Anheuser-Busch
Blockbuster Entertainment
Coca-Cola
Dow Chemical
General Motors
Mars
Procter & Gamble

Key Competitors
Foote, Cone & Belding
Grey Advertising
Interpublic Group
Leo Burnett
Omnicom Group
Saatchi & Saatchi
WPP Group
Young & Rubicam

Industry
Advertising

Overview
D'Arcy Masius Benton & Bowles (DMB&B), among the world's largest privately owned advertising and communications firms, provides advertising, promotional marketing, public relations, and health care communications through 100 offices in 50 countries. The company is the result of a 1985 merger between D'Arcy MacManus Masius (St. Louis) and Benton & Bowles (New York) — the largest merger in the history of the advertising business. Billings in 1993 were $4.8 billion. DMB&B business units include AdVista (software); Feldman & Associates (infomercials); and Manning, Selvage & Lee (public relations).

DARIGOLD INC.

RANK: 340

635 Elliott Ave. West
Seattle, WA 98119
Phone: 206-284-7220
Fax: 206-281-3456

1993 Sales: $882 million
FYE: March
Employees: 1,750

Key Personnel
Pres & CEO: Wesley Eckert
Treas: Ron Furrer
Dir Mktg: James Robson
Dir Data Processing: Oscar Ringness
Dir HR: Veseth Yates

Major Products
Butter
Cheese
Dry, condensed & evaporated milk
Fresh milk
Ice cream
Low-cholesterol milk
Low-fat ice cream
Protein-fortified milk

Key Competitors
Borden
California Co-op
Dairyman's Co-op Creamery
Dean Foods
Dreyer's Grand Ice Cream
Land O' Lakes
PET
Philip Morris

Industry
Food - dairy products

Overview
Formed by 5 Puget Sound–area cooperatives in 1918 to fight arbitrary pricing, Darigold consists of 3 companies: Darigold Farms, a milk marketing cooperative owned by about 1,400 dairy farmers in the northwestern US; Darigold Inc., the Seattle processing and marketing manager for the organization; and Dairy Export Co., which operates retail farm stores in Washington, Oregon, and Idaho. The co-op sold 120 million pounds of dried milk to 13 countries in 1992 and sells its products in the Pacific Northwest and in California. The co-op hopes to put the squeeze on international markets with new items like low-fat ice cream.

DAY & ZIMMERMANN INCORPORATED

RANK: 423

1818 Market St.
Philadelphia, PA 19103
Phone: 215-299-8295
Fax: 610-975-6666

1993 Sales: $706 million
FYE: December
Employees: 12,000

Key Personnel
Chm, Pres & CEO: Harold L. "Spike" Yoh, Jr.
SVP Fin & CFO: John P. Follman
VP Admin & Sec: William R. Hamm
Gen Counsel: James Goodman
VP HR: Anthony G. Natale

Principal Subsidiaries
Barry Services, Inc.
D&Z Inc.
Day Products Inc.
Mid-Atlantic
H.L. Yoh Company

Key Competitors
Bechtel
Fluor
Halliburton
McCarthy Building
McDermott
Parsons
Peter Kiewit Sons'
Raytheon

Industry
Construction - heavy

Overview
Founded in 1901, Day & Zimmermann is one of Philadelphia's largest engineering firms. While its corporate headquarters are located in Philadelphia, the company has regional offices in the Delaware Valley and New Jersey. This consulting company, with clients in the US and 75 other countries, has 30 operating units that provide, among other services, construction management, marine, transportation, maintenance, security, and technical personnel services. Day & Zimmermann has also been one of the top 10 suppliers of ordnance to the Army.

DEL MONTE FOODS COMPANY

RANK: 166

One Market Plaza
San Francisco, CA 94119
Phone: 415-247-3000
Fax: 415-247-3565

1993 Sales: $1,555 million
FYE: June
Employees: 14,000

Key Personnel
Pres & CEO: Robert W. D'Ornellas
EVP Fin & CFO: David L. Meyers
EVP Admin: David M. Little
EVP Sales: Michael J. Stieger
SVP, Gen Counsel & Sec: P. Kay Dryden
VP Corp Personnel: Mark J. Buxton

◀ **See page 48 for full-page profile.**

Major Products
Canned fruit
Canned vegetables
Fruit products
Ketchup
Private label goods
Puddings
Spaghetti sauce

Key Competitors
ADM
Campbell Soup
Dole
General Mills
Heinz
Kellogg
RJR Nabisco
Unilever

Industry
Food - canned

Overview
Del Monte, founded in 1899 when 18 California canneries merged, is the largest canner of fruits and vegetables in the US. It also operates exporting, food service, and private label businesses. RJR Nabisco, owners from 1978 to 1990, blurred the company's focus; Merrill Lynch and Del Monte brass took over in a 1990 LBO and changed the strategy to emphasize sales and advertising of products under the Del Monte brand name. The company agreed to be acquired by Mexican investment firm Grupo Cabal in June 1994. That deal fell into doubt when the head of Grupo Cabal became a fugitive from Mexican justice later in 1994.

DELAWARE NORTH COMPANIES INC.

RANK: 206

438 Main St.
Buffalo, NY 14202
Phone: 716-858-5000
Fax: 716-858-5479

1993 Est. Sales: $1,300 million
FYE: December
Employees: 20,000

Key Personnel
Chm & CEO: Jeremy M. Jacobs
Pres, COO & Acting CFO: Richard T. Stephens
VP Public Affairs: Samuel L. Gifford II
Chief Counsel: Bryan Keller
VP HR: Marlene Jennings-Galla

Business Lines
Airport concessions
Hotels (Australia)
Metals processing
Parimutuel racetracks
Park concessions
Publishing & typography
Riding stables
Sports concessions

Key Competitors
ARA
Dial
Flagstar
General Electric
Host Marriott
Hyatt
Ogden
Volume Services

Industry
Diversified operations

Overview
Founded in 1915 when Marvin Jacobs began hawking peanuts at sports events, Delaware North provides food service for dozens of sports facilities, including Comiskey Park in Chicago. Owned by Jeremy Jacobs, the founder's nephew (who also owns the Boston Bruins hockey team), the company has diversified into metals processing, publishing, hotels, and riding stables. Delaware North now has the concession rights for Yosemite National Park and The Ballpark in Arlington, Texas.

DELOITTE & TOUCHE

RANK: 37

10 Westport Rd.
Wilton, CT 06897
Phone: 203-761-3000
Fax: 203-834-2200

1993 Sales: $5,000 million
FYE: May
Employees: 15,800

Key Personnel
Chm & CEO: J. Michael Cook
Managing Partner: Edward A. Kangas
CFO: Robert W. Pivik
Gen Counsel: Howard J. Krongard
Natl Dir Mktg & Comm: Gary Gerard
Natl Dir HR Ops: James H. Wall

◄ See page 49 for full-page profile.

Selected Services
Accounting & auditing
Computer consulting
Employee benefits service
Health care facility planning
Information technology consulting
Management consulting
Mergers/acquisitions consulting
Tax advice & planning

Key Competitors
Arthur Andersen
Coopers & Lybrand
Ernst & Young
Hewitt Associates
KPMG
Marsh & McLennan
McKinsey & Co.
Price Waterhouse

Industry
Business services - accounting & consulting

Overview
Partner-owned Deloitte & Touche, the 3rd largest accounting firm in the US, began in a small London office opened by William Welch Deloitte in 1845. By 1978, as Deloitte Haskins & Sells, the venerable company had earned a reputation for being pricey and conservative, but new competition demanded more aggressive marketing strategies. In 1989 Deloitte merged with Touche Ross, a hard-charging firm that had run into junk bond trouble. The firm is emphasizing its specialized service lines, including information technology and employee benefits.

DELTA DENTAL PLAN OF CALIFORNIA

RANK: 139

100 First St.
San Francisco, CA 94105
Phone: 415-972-8300
Fax: 415-972-8366

1993 Sales: $1,792 million
FYE: December
Employees: 1,200

Key Personnel
Chm: R. Jerome Ennis
Pres & CEO: William T. Ward
SVP & CFO: Joseph C. Jaeger
SVP Public & Professional Svcs: John F. Field
SVP Comm Ops & Corp Svcs: Jerry R. Holcomb
Dir HR: Sandra J. Boros

Selected Services
Dental care insurance
Fee audits
Post-treatment reviews
Preset fee agreements

Key Competitors
Aetna
Aon
CIGNA
ITT
Pac Rim Holding
Prudential
Transamerica
Travelers

Industry
Insurance - health

Overview
Founded in 1955, Delta Dental Plan of California (Delta is the Greek symbol for dentistry) is the nation's largest dental insurer, providing benefits in every state, the District of Columbia, Puerto Rico, Guam, and the Virgin Islands. With over 100,000 dental offices, this nonprofit organization has experienced rapid growth over the past several years while its industry grew only modestly. Much of Delta Dental's boost is due to alliances formed with major HMOs (a strategy the company intends to continue) and recently awarded government contracts. Among the company's managed-care features within its plans are predetermined fee levels.

DEMOULAS SUPER MARKETS INC./MARKET BASKET INC.

RANK: 214

875 East St.
Tewksbury, MA 01876
Phone: 508-851-8000
Fax: 505-851-3942

1992 Est. Sales: $1,260 million
FYE: December
Employees: 9,000

Key Personnel
Pres, Demoulas Super Markets: Telemachus A. Demoulas
Pres, Treas & CEO, Market Basket: Arthur T. Demoulas
EVP: James D. Miamis
EVP Mktg: Julien J. Lacourse
VP Fin & Treas: D. H. Sullivan
VP Store Ops: William F. Marsden

Operating Units
Demoulas Super Markets
Market Basket supermarkets
Real estate (47 shopping malls)
Resort hotel & golf course

Key Competitors
Cumberland Farms
Great A&P
Freeman Spogli
Shaw's Supermarkets
Star Market
Stop & Shop
Sweet Life Foods
Whole Foods Market

Industry
Retail - supermarkets

Overview
Founded in 1955 by brothers George and Telemachus ("Mike") Demoulas, Market Basket and Demoulas Super Markets make up one of the largest supermarket chains in New England, with about a 10% share of the regional market. The chain, which has 45 stores in the New England area, is controlled by the Demoulas family and has been run by Mike since George's death in 1971. However, George's wife and children have taken Mike to court, claiming he has systematically stripped them of most of their stock in the company.

THE DETROIT MEDICAL CENTER

RANK: 126

4201 St. Antoine Blvd.
Detroit, MI 48201
Phone: 313-745-5051
Fax: 313-993-0438

1993 Sales: $1,900 million
FYE: December
Employees: 14,384

Key Personnel
Pres & CEO: David J. Campbell
EVP & COO: Robert B. Johnson
SVP & CFO: Guy J. LaPrad
SVP Medical Affairs: Robert J. Sokol,
VP Legal Affairs: Robert Yelan
VP HR: Dan Zuhlke

Selected Care Facilities
Children's Hospital of Michigan
Detroit Receiving Hospital
Grace Hospital
Harper Hospital
Huron Valley Hospital
Hutzel Hospital
Kresge Eye Institute
Rehabilitation Institute of Michigan

Key Competitors
Bronson Healthcare
Columbia/HCA
Mayo Foundation
Mercy Health Services
National Medical
Oakwood Health Services
Sinai Health Care

Industry
Hospitals

Overview
The Detroit Medical Center originated in 1955, when 4 Detroit hospitals joined efforts to provide nonprofit, coordinated medical services. Now the medical center is one of the largest multihospital complexes in the US, with almost 2,600 beds. It includes 7 Detroit-area hospitals, 31 outpatient facilities, and a nursing home and convalescent center. Detroit Medical Center fosters medical education and research through an affiliation with Wayne State University School of Medicine.

DHL WORLDWIDE EXPRESS

RANK: 68

333 Twin Dolphin Dr.
Redwood City, CA 94065
Phone: 415-593-7474
Fax: 415-593-1689

1992 Est. Sales: $2,800 million
FYE: December
Employees: 26,000

Key Personnel
Chm & CEO, DHL Intl, Ltd.: Patrick Lupo
Group CFO, DHL Intl, Ltd.: Bob Parker
Chm, Pres & CEO, DHL Airways: Patrick Foley
SVP Fin & CFO, DHL Airways: William Smartt
Gen Counsel, DHL Airways: Ted Orme
SVP HR, DHL Airways: Gary Sellers

◀ **See page 50 for full-page profile.**

Selected Services
DHL Worldwide Package Express
Faxlynk
International Airfreight
International Document Service
On-Board Custom Courier Service
USA Overnight
Visa-Pak
WorldMail

Key Competitors
Airborne Freight
Consolidated Freightways
FedEx
Harper Group
Roadway
UPS
U.S. Postal Service
Yellow Freight

Industry
Package delivery

Overview
DHL Worldwide Express was the first company to provide air express service in overseas markets and is the world leader in international air express delivery. Its expertise in dealing with governments and customs has given it an edge over its competition. The company operates as 2 separate entities, with DHL Airways serving the US and DHL International serving the rest of the world. DHL International has about 5 times more offices than DHL Airways. Japan Airlines, Lufthansa, and Nissho Iwai are part owners of both DHL segments.

DI GIORGIO CORP.

RANK: 396

2 Executive Dr., Ste. 400
Somerset, NJ 08873
Phone: 908-469-4444
Fax: 908-469-9151

1993 Sales: $782 million
FYE: December
Employees: 561

Key Personnel
Chm, Pres & CEO: Arthur M. Goldberg
EVP & CFO: Richard B. Neff
Corp Acctg: Lawrence Grossman

Operating Units
Dairy products
Delicatessen products
Drugs
Fruits & vegetables
Frozen foods
Meats
Sundries

Key Competitors
Condal
Farmer Bros.
Fleming
JP Foodservice
Nash Finch
Richfood
Super Food Services
SUPERVALU

Industry
Food - wholesale to grocers

Overview
Wholesale grocer Di Giorgio, founded in 1920, is part of DIG Holding Corp., created by New Jersey investor and Bally Entertainment CEO Arthur Goldberg, who won the $1 billion public conglomerate in a 1990 takeover bid. Goldberg sold 4 of Di Giorgio's 5 divisions to focus on its White Rose food distribution operation and moved the headquarters from San Francisco to New Jersey. Goldberg then agreed to buy Royal Foods from Fleming in early 1994. Combined revenues of the 2 companies' sales to supermarkets, small stores, and delicatessens in the New York City/New Jersey/Connecticut area are approximately $1.1 billion.

THE DICK GROUP OF COMPANIES

RANK: 484

PO Box 10896
Pittsburgh, PA 15236
Phone: 412-384-1000
Fax: 412-384-1150

1993 Est. Sales: $575 million
FYE: December
Employees: 3,000

Key Personnel
VC: Aloysius T. McLaughlin
CEO: David E. Dick
Pres: Douglas P. Dick
Treas: Lon Susack
EVP: Stephen Peary
Gen Counsel: Roger J. Peters

Selected Services
Construction management
Cost estimating
Design
Engineering
Project planning
Renovations

Key Competitors
Bechtel
CRSS
Fluor
Gilbane Building
Morrison Knudsen
M. A. Mortensen
Parsons
H. B. Zachry

Industry
Construction - heavy

Overview
Pittsburgh-based Dick Group is a nationwide general contracting and construction management firm founded in 1922 by Noble J. Dick. Closely held, the company's major projects include the Allegheny County Jail, Bellingham Cogeneration Facility, the GM Saturn Plant (Springhill, Tennessee), the Los Angeles County Jail, the Pennsylvania Convention Center, and the rehabilitation of Union Station in Washington, DC. Types of projects managed include airport terminals, power plants, bridges, correctional facilities, treatment plants, hospitals, and office buildings.

DILLINGHAM CONSTRUCTION HOLDINGS INC. — RANK: 418

5960 Inglewood Dr.
Pleasanton, CA 94588
Phone: 510-463-3300
Fax: 510-463-1571

1993 Sales: $713 million
FYE: October
Employees: 1,050

Key Personnel
Chm & CEO: Donald K. Stager
Pres & COO: James R. Perry
VP Fin & CFO: Larry L. Magelitz
Treas: P. C. Freeman
VP & Gen Counsel: D. P. Haist
VP Personnel: Julian R. Hansen

Construction Projects
Commercial buildings
Dams
Docks
Hotels & motels
Industrial buildings
Marine projects
Office buildings
Warehouses

Key Competitors
Bechtel
Clark Enterprises
Fluor
McDermott
Parsons
Perini
Peter Kiewit Sons'
Turner Industries

Industry
Construction - heavy

Overview
Dillingham Construction Holdings has as its chief subsidiary Dillingham Construction Corp. Dillingham traces its beginnings to the Sandwich Islands' Oahu Railway & Land Co. (pre–Republic of Hawaii; 1894) and Hawaiian Dredging & Construction Co. (1902). These 2 Dillingham family companies merged in 1961 as Dillingham Corp., which was public until 1983 when it went private in a $350 million LBO financed by investment bankers Kohlberg Kravis Roberts & Co. In the 1980s Dillingham shared the construction industry's hard times. The company took on Japanese Shimizu Construction Co. as a 45% partner in 1987.

DOMINICK'S FINER FOODS INC. — RANK: 106

505 Railroad Ave.
Northlake, IL 60164
Phone: 708-562-1000
Fax: 708-409-3955

1993 Sales: $2,150 million
FYE: October
Employees: 18,000

Key Personnel
Chm & CEO: James DiMatteo
COO & Pres: Daniel Josephs
SVP & CFO: Charles R. Weber
VP & Controller: Joseph Addante
VP Legal: Thomas Roti
Dir HR: Charles Brazik

Selected Services
Banking
Coffee bar
Computer grocery orders
Food court
Restaurant
Shoe repair

Key Competitors
Aldi
American Stores
Eagle Food
Southland
Treasure Island Foods
Wal-Mart

Industry
Retail - supermarkets

Overview
Founded in 1925, Dominick's is the 2nd largest Chicago-area grocer (after American Stores's Jewel Food Stores), controlling 19% of the market. With 86 Dominick stores and 16 Omni Superstores, the company is bagging $2 billion in annual sales. Dominick's is checking out an in-store restaurant and upscale food court as well as marketing its own brands of prepared foods to keep its edge. Founder Dominick DiMatteo, Jr., died in late 1993.

DOMINO'S PIZZA, INC. — RANK: 99

30 Frank Lloyd Wright Dr.
Ann Arbor, MI 48106
Phone: 313-930-3030
Fax: 313-668-4614

1993 Sales: $2,200 million
FYE: December
Employees: 20,000

Key Personnel
Pres: Thomas S. Monaghan
VP Franchise Ops: Stuart Mathis
VP & CFO: Harry Silverman
VP Corp Ops: Nickep Romyananda
VP Dist: Mike Soignet
Dir HR: Mitch Srail

◀ **See page 51 for full-page profile.**

Major Products
Chicken wings
Garlic breadsticks
Pan pizza
Pizza
Salad
Soda
Submarine sandwiches
Thin-crust pizza

Key Competitors
Grand Metropolitan
International Dairy Queen
Little Caesars
McDonald's
Papa John's
PepsiCo
Subway

Industry
Restaurants

Overview
Founded in 1960, Domino's Pizza once dominated the delivery industry by offering nothing but pizza, Coke, and a 30-minute guarantee. Meanwhile, PepsiCo's Pizza Hut and Little Caesar have come close to nudging the company out of its #1 spot, and founder Monaghan hopes that fresh ideas like chicken wings and thin-crust pizza will deliver Domino's from stagnation. Domino's operates 5,000 stores in 30 countries. The company has recently eliminated its 30-minute delivery guarantee because of a legal judgment awarding $79 million to a woman seriously injured when her car was struck by a delivery driver running a red light.

DOW CORNING CORPORATION — RANK: 112

2200 W. Salzburg Rd.
Midland, MI 48686
Phone: 517-496-4000
Fax: 517-496-4511

1993 Sales: $2,044 million
FYE: December
Employees: 8,000

Key Personnel
Chm: Keith R. McKennon
Pres & CEO: Richard A. Hazleton
VP Fin & CFO: John Churchfield
EVP: Gary E. Anderson
VP, Sec & Gen Counsel: James R. Jenkins
Dir HR: James Chittick

Major Products
Fire protection products
Molybdenum silicon
Orthopedic silicone implants
Polycrystalline silicon
Sealants
Silicone gel
Silicone lubricants
Specialty lubricants

Key Competitors
Baxter
Bristol-Myers Squibb
Exxon
General Chemical
Heyer-Schulte
Huntsman Chemical
Union Carbide
Uniroyal Chemical

Industry
Chemicals - specialty

Overview
Founded in 1943 as a joint venture between owners Dow Chemical Company and Corning Inc., Dow Corning manufactures specialty chemicals and was once the world's largest maker of silicone breast implants. Beset by some 6,800 lawsuits by women claiming the implants harmed them, the company stopped making the devices in 1992. In February 1994 Dow Corning agreed to pay $2 billion over 30 years under a proposed settlement of a class action lawsuit. The company also makes polycrystalline silicon, a material used to manufacture semiconductors.

DRESSER-RAND COMPANY

RANK: 246

One Baron Steuben Place
Corning, NY 14830
Phone: 607-937-6400
Fax: 607-937-6405

1993 Sales: $1,116 million
FYE: September
Employees: 7,500

Key Personnel
Pres & CEO: Ben R. Stuart
VP & CFO: John A. Heldman
VP & Gen Counsel: Eugene H. Moore
VP HR: Lynn Sanberg
Controller: George W. Fray

Major Products
Control systems
Generators
Hot gas expanders
Motors
Power turbines
Steam turbines
Turbocompressors

Key Competitors
ABB
Cooper Industries
GEC
General Electric
Holt Cos.
McDermott
Siemens
Westinghouse

Industry
Machinery - general industrial

Overview
A joint venture born in 1987 when Dresser Industries believed it was best to "join them if you couldn't beat them," this 50-50 partnership between Dresser and Ingersoll-Rand is the nation's leading supplier of turbocompressors. Dresser-Rand also provides module engineering and construction services to the petroleum, gas, petrochemical, and electric power industries. The firm and its affiliates have 31 service centers worldwide and 12 manufacturing facilities, including plants in Olean, New York; Lethbridge, Canada; Le Havre, France; and Kongsberg, Norway.

DRUMMOND CO., INC.

RANK: 422

330 Beacon Pkwy. West
Birmingham, AL 35209
Phone: 205-945-6500
Fax: 205-945-4254

1993 Sales: $707 million
FYE: December
Employees: 2,600

Key Personnel
Chm & CEO: Garry N. Drummond
VC & VP: Elbert A. Drummond
Pres & COO: H. D. Dahl
SVP & Sec: Segal E. Drummond
SVP: Donald D. Drummond
Treas & CFO: Walter F. Johnsey

Business Lines
Coke manufacture
Mining, surface coal
Mining, underground coal
Real estate development

Key Competitors
Ashland Coal
Broken Hill
Coastal
CONSOL Energy
Hanson
Pittston
Walter Industries
Zeigler Coal

Industry
Coal

Overview
Founded in 1935 by Heman E. Drummond with a single mine, this coal company based in Birmingham, Alabama, is among the top 10 surface miners of bituminous coal in the US. The family-run firm also conducts underground mining operations and makes beehive coke oven products. Drummond also mines coal in South America and is preparing to open its La Loma mine in Colombia, which the company hopes will produce up to 2.5 million metric tons of coal each year. The company's real estate operation is currently working on its Rancho La Quinta project in Southern California, a 426-house community that has enjoyed almost immediate sales sucess.

DUCHOSSOIS INDUSTRIES, INC.

RANK: 364

845 N. Larch Ave.
Elmhurst, IL 60126
Phone: 708-279-3600
Fax: 708-530-6091

1992 Est. Sales: $837 million
FYE: December
Employees: 6,500

Key Personnel
Chm: Richard L. Duchossois
Pres: Craig J. Duchossois
VP Fin: James S. Yerbic
VP, Sec & Gen Counsel: Richard H. Irving
Dir HR: Lyn Fleichhacker

Business Lines
Ammunition
Auto buffer/polishers
Garage door openers
Radio broadcasting
Railroad freight car manufacturing
Television broadcasting
Thoroughbred breeding
Thoroughbred horse racetrack

Key Competitors
Genie Co.
Hawthorne Race Course
Itel
Morrison Knudsen
Overhead Door
Stanley Works
Sumitomo
Trinity Industries

Industry
Diversified operations

Overview
Duchossois, founded in 1906, has rolling stock, racing stock, and other interests. Its Thrall Car Manufacturing Co. makes railroad cars, which are leased through its Transportation Corp. of America. The company owns Arlington International Racecourse in Illinois (horseracing). Its electronics division makes garage door openers and car cleaning tools at a maquiladora on the Arizona-Mexico border. Duchossois also has munitions and broadcasting interests. Amid rumors that Duchossois was planning a riverboat casino for its racecourse pond, Illinois's governor required that such casinos be located on navigable waters.

DUKE UNIVERSITY

RANK: 220

Durham, NC 27706
Phone: 919-684-8111
Fax: 919-684-8547

1993 Sales: $1,249 million
FYE: June
Employees: 22,000

Key Personnel
Pres: Nannerl O. Keohane
Provost: Thomas A. Langford
EVP Admin: Charles E. Putman
EVP Asset Mgr: Eugene J. McDonald
VP & Corp Controller: John F. Adcock
University Counsel: David B. Adcock

Schools and Colleges
Divinity School
Fuqua School of Business
School of Engineering
School of Law
School of Medicine
School of Nursing
School of the Environment
Trinity College of Arts & Sciences

Industry
Schools

Overview
Trinity College was founded in 1838 as a private, coeducational institution affiliated with the United Methodist Church. It changed its name to Duke University and expanded considerably when endowed by American Tobacco Co. magnate James Duke in 1924. Duke left the school one of the US's largest private foundations, The Duke Endowment, now valued at over $1.25 billion. The endowment is mostly in the form of Duke Power Company stock, making the university Duke Power's largest shareholder. The Duke University Medical Center includes a number of hospitals and clinics that contribute almost half of the university's annual revenues.

DUNAVANT ENTERPRISES INC.

RANK: 222

3797 New Getwell Rd.
Memphis, TN 38118
Phone: 901-369-1500
Fax: 901-369-1608

1993 Est. Sales: $1,225 million
FYE: June
Employees: 2,500

Key Personnel
Chm: William B. Dunavant, Jr.
VP & Asst Treas: H. J. Weathersby
Controller: Perry Winstead
Sec: William Stubblefield
HR Mgr: Cheryl Cooley

Business Lines
Cotton brokering
Ginning
Merchandising & buying
Real estate
Warehousing

Key Competitors
Calcot
Cargill
Continental Grain
Natural Cotton Colours
Plains Cotton Co-op
Southwestern Irrigated Cotton Growers
Staple Cotton Co-op

Industry
Textiles - mill products

Overview
Founded in 1957, Dunavant Enterprises, run by Memphis cotton king Billy Dunavant (who is actually allergic to cotton), is one of the world's 2 largest cotton brokerages (the other is a Cargill subsidiary). Dunavant rose to the top by aggressively selling cotton to China and the Soviet Union. An avid sports fan, Dunavant, who owns a controlling interest in the company, has expressed interest in building a $1.3 billion PGA Tour–worthy golf course and resort in Florida.

DYNCORP

RANK: 309

2000 Edmund Halley Dr.
Reston, VA 22091
Phone: 703-264-0330
Fax: 703-264-8600

1993 Sales: $953 million
FYE: December
Employees: 22,000

Key Personnel
Chm: Herbert S. Winokur
Pres & CEO: Daniel R. Bannister
EVP: James H. Duggan
EVP: Paul V. Lombardi
SVP & CFO: T. Eugene Blanchard
SVP & Gen Counsel: David L. Reichardt

Business Lines
Adv. Technical Svcs. (commercial)
DynAir (commercial aviation)
Federal (government business)
- Aerospace technology
- Environment, energy, nat'l security
- Enterprise management
- Information & engineering

Key Competitors
British Airways
Dalfort
E-Systems
BFGoodrich
Lockheed
Lucas Aviation
Ogden
Primark

Industry
Business services

Overview
Founded in 1946 and taken private in a 1988 LBO, DynCorp provides diversified professional and technical services mostly to the US government. DynCorp's contracts include sorting mail for the US Postal Service, conducting research for Health & Human Services, and maintaining aircraft for the Pentagon (its #1 customer). President and CEO Dan Bannister, who says his firm is in the business of supplying people, has overseen expansion to new markets, including maintenance of commercial aircraft.

THE DYSON-KISSNER-MORAN CORPORATION

RANK: 73

230 Park Ave., Ste. 659
New York, NY 10169
Phone: 212-661-4600
Fax: 212-599-5105

1993 Est. Sales: $2,723 million
FYE: January
Employees: 4,798

Key Personnel
Chm & CEO: Robert R. Dyson
Pres: Joseph L. Aurichio
SVP Dev: Paul Rosetti
SVP & CFO: M.J. Zilinskas
Sec & Gen Counsel: John H. Fitzsimons
Office Mgr: Louise Donohue

Selected Affiliates
Burner Systems (gas burners)
Core-Mark International (food)
DKM Properties (real estate)
Kearney-National (electronics)
Muncy Building (modular housing)
Plaid Enterprises (craft products)
J.A. Sexauer (plumbing, heating)
Thetford (toilets, sanitation)

Key Competitors
Helmsley
Lefrak Organization
Tishman Speyer
Trammell Crow

Industry
Diversified operations

Overview
Begun in 1954 to acquire and operate businesses, Dyson-Kissner-Moran is 91% owned by the family of cofounder Charles Dyson, a decorated WWII colonel. DKM owns everything from electronics to food distribution to dry cleaning equipment and has operations across the US. Subsidiary DKM Properties, an aggressive developer that headed several important building projects in the 1980s, has 7 million square feet of space, mostly in New Jersey. The recession of the early 1990s has forced new CEO Robert Dyson to sell off companies and securities to improve liquidity.

EARLE M. JORGENSEN HOLDING COMPANY, INC.

RANK: 361

3050 E. Birch St.
Brea, CA 92621
Phone: 714-579-8823
Fax: 714-524-1072

1993 Sales: $843 million
FYE: March
Employees: 2,600

Key Personnel
Chm: David Roderick
Pres & CEO: Neven C. Hulsey
VP & COO: Lonnie Terry
VP & CFO: Charles P. Gallopo
VP Admin & HR: Steven Wild

Major Markets
Aerospace & aircraft parts
Agricultural equipment
Car & truck manufacturing
Construction machinery
Earth moving machinery
Fluid power components
Oil refining & exploration
Shipbuilding & repair

Key Competitors
Cargill
A.M. Castle
Inland Steel
Kaiser Aluminum
Lawson Products
Marmon Group
O'Neal Steel
Reliance Steel & Aluminum

Industry
Metal products - distribution

Overview
Earle M. Jorgensen was forged out of a 1990 buyout of a profitable steel service center chain of the same name and the subsequent consolidation of Jorgensen Steel & Aluminum, Kilsby-Roberts, and Republic Supply Co. of California. The merger created one of the US's largest independent steel distribution chains. However, a declining market (accompanied by declining prices) for steel and a heavy debt burden (despite the 1992 sale of Republic Supply Co. of California) have been squeezing margins. The company is majority-owned by the Kelso & Co. investment banking firm.

EDWARD D. JONES & CO.

RANK: 455

12555 Manchester Rd.
St. Louis, MO 63131
Phone: 314-851-2000
Fax: 314-984-3269

1993 Sales: $640 million
FYE: December
Employees: 8,330

Key Personnel
CEO & Managing Principal: John W. Bachmann
CFO: Ed Soule
Gen Counsel: Larry Sobol
Dir HR: Bob Pearce

Major Products
Annuities
Blue-chip stocks
Certificates of deposit
Insured tax-free bonds
Mutual funds

Key Competitors
Alex. Brown
Charles Schwab
Dean Witter, Discover
FMR
Kemper
Merrill Lynch
T. Rowe Price
Travelers

Industry
Financial - securities brokerage

Overview
With its strategy of providing financial services to rural Americans through one-broker offices, Edward D. Jones has become a major player in the securities industry. Founded in 1871, the firm has experienced explosive growth of late. Since 1980 the company's network of offices has grown tenfold, to 3,000 in 49 states (all but Alaska). Edward D. Jones now has more offices than any other broker. The company's philosophy has been to focus on providing middle-class investors with financial advice the firm characterizes as "conservative." But as the small-town market has been nearly tapped out, the company intends to expand into major US cities and Canada.

EDWARD J. DEBARTOLO CORPORATION

RANK: 136

7620 Market St.
Youngstown, OH 44513
Phone: 216-758-7292
Fax: 216-758-3598

1993 Est. Sales: $1,800 million
FYE: June
Employees: 15,000

Key Personnel
Chm & CEO: Edward J. DeBartolo, Sr.
Pres: Edward J. DeBartolo, Jr.
EVP Personnel : Marie Denise DeBartolo York
SVP Corp Planning & Fin: Anthony W. Liberati
SVP Dev & Gen Counsel: Richard S. Sokolov
SVP Leasing & Ops: William D. Moses

Major Projects
Century III Mall, Pittsburgh
The Florida Mall, Orlando
New Orleans Centre, New Orleans
Randall Park Mall, Cleveland
West Town Mall, Knoxville

Key Competitors
Crown General
JMB
LaSalle Partners
Lincoln Property
Melvin Simon
Prudential
Rouse
Trammell Crow

Industry
Real estate development

Overview
Edward J. DeBartolo Corporation is a leading builder and operator of enclosed shopping malls in the US. Founded in 1944 by Edward J. DeBartolo, Sr., now 84, the company has been plagued by crumbling commercial real estate values. With more than $4 billion in debt, DeBartolo issued an IPO in 1994, which left 48% of the company's retail operations in public hands in a spinoff subsidiary called DeBartolo Realty. The company also owns the San Francisco 49ers.

◀ See page 52 for full-page profile.

THE ELDER-BEERMAN STORES CORP.

RANK: 424

3155 El-Bee Rd.
Dayton, OH 45439
Phone: 513-296-2700
Fax: 513-296-2948

1993 Sales: $705 million
FYE: January
Employees: 9,000

Key Personnel
Chm & CEO: Milton E. Hartley
Pres & COO: Bruce A. Macke
EVP Fin & CFO: Michael E. Miller
EVP Mktg & Promotions: Jack Mullen
SVP & Controller: David W. Lovejoy
SVP HR: Patricia Gifford

Operating Units
Dayton Paper
El-Bee Shoe Outlet Stores
Elder-Beerman Stores
Margo's La Mode

Key Competitors
Anersons
Dayton Hudson
Dillard
May
Mercantile Stores
Montgomery Ward
J. C. Penney
Sears

Industry
Retail - regional department stores

Overview
Elder-Beerman has been retailing since 1883, when it was Elder & Johnston Co. In 1962 Arthur Beerman merged his stores with Elder & Johnston to form Elder-Beerman, which includes a chain of more than 50 department stores in malls and strip centers in 7 midwestern states (mostly in smaller towns), the Bee-Gee Shoe Division of 131 El-Bee Shoe Outlet Stores in 10 states, and Margo's La Mode women's stores in the Southwest. In 1987 Beerman family members and company directors engineered a $33 million buyout so that Elder-Beerman could operate free from disclosure requirements.

EMORY UNIVERSITY INC.

RANK: 350

1380 Oxford Rd. NE
Atlanta, GA 30322
Phone: 404-727-6123
Fax: 404-727-3750

1993 Sales: $862 million
FYE: August
Employees: 15,000

Key Personnel
Pres: William M. Chace
EVP: John L. Temple
VP Fin & Treas: Frank H. Huff
Controller: Edie Murphree
Sec: Gary S. Hauk
Assoc VP HR: Alice Miller

Selected Schools
Candler School of Theology
Carter Center for Policy Studies
Emory College
Emory University Hospital
Gozieuta Business School
School of Law
School of Medicine
Woodruff Health Sciences Center

Key Competitors

Industry
Schools

Overview
Coca-Cola is the drink of choice at Emory University. Asa Candler, who owned Coke at the turn of the century, endowed Emory and its hospital with over $8 million. In 1979 the Woodruff Foundation (Ernest Woodruff had bought Coke from Candler) gave $105 million. Founded in 1836 in Oxford, Georgia, the United Methodist–affiliated school has been in Atlanta since 1915. Its 1992–93 enrollment was 9,958 in 4 undergraduate and 6 graduate schools. Former university president James T. Laney left in 1993 to serve as the US ambassador to South Korea.

ENCYCLOPAEDIA BRITANNICA INC.

RANK: 497

310 S. Michigan Ave.
Chicago, IL 60604
Phone: 312-347-7000
Fax: 312-347-7135

1993 Sales: $540 million
FYE: September
Employees: 2,000

Key Personnel
Pres & CEO: Peter B. Norton
EVP: Joseph J. Esposito
Sec & Gen Counsel: William J. Bowe
SVP & CFO: Randall D. Johnson
VP HR: Karl Steinberg

Major Products
Audio-visual learning aids
Dictionaries
Encyclopedias
Films
Reading instruction
Reference books

Key Competitors
Berkshire Hathaway
Houghton Mifflin
K-III
Matra Hachette
Microsoft
Oxford University Press
Time Warner
Tribune

Industry
Publishing - books

Overview
Founded in Scotland in 1768, Britannica has had many owners. Sears ran it for over 20 years until 1943 when ownership transferred to master salesman William Benton (and in 1980 to the William Benton Foundation, the beneficiary of which is the University of Chicago). Britannica sells encyclopedias directly to the public, primarily on credit. Subsidiaries include Merriam-Webster (dictionaries) and Evelyn Wood (speed reading). In 1993 Britannica sold its Compton's Multimedia CD-ROM publishing unit. The company is publishing on the Internet, which it believes will give it control over its electronic sales channel.

ENTERPRISE RENT-A-CAR

RANK: 152

8850 Ladue Rd.
St. Louis, MO 63124
Phone: 314-863-7000
Fax: 314-863-7621

1993 Sales: $1,659 million
FYE: July
Employees: 14,000

Key Personnel
Chm: Jack C. Taylor
Pres & CEO: Andrew C. Taylor
EVP: Douglas S. Brown
SVP: Marcus T. Cohn
VP & CFO: John T. O'Connell
VP HR: Jerry Spector

See page 53 for full-page profile.

Business Lines
Adjuster referral service
Car & light truck leasing
Car rental
Cellular telecommunications
Hotel beverage service
New & used car sales
Prison commissary supplies
Vehicle fleet management

Key Competitors
Agency Rent-A-Car
Alamo Rent A Car
ARA
Avis
Budget Rent A Car
Dollar Rent A Car
Ford
General Motors

Industry
Leasing - autos

Overview
Founded in 1957 by Cadillac salesman Jack Taylor, Enterprise Rent-A-Car is one of the 5 largest car rental companies in the US. Taylor and his family own 85% of the company; management owns the rest. Enterprise concentrates on the replacement end of the market, providing replacement cars for customers whose cars have been damaged or stolen. Since the oil price shocks of the early 1970s, Enterprise has diversified into a variety of other businesses.

ERNST & YOUNG LLP

RANK: 33

787 Park Ave.
New York, NY 10019
Phone: 212-773-3000
Fax: 212-773-1996

1993 Sales: $5,839 million
FYE: September
Employees: 58,377

Key Personnel
Chm: Philip A. Laskawy
Co-Chm: William L. Kinsey
CEO Intl: Michael A. Henning
VC Fin: Hilton Dean
VC HR: Bruce J. Mantia
Gen Counsel: Carl D. Liggio

See page 54 for full-page profile.

Selected Services
Auditing
Cash management
Management consulting
Outsourcing (corporate tax)
Regulatory (environmental, health)
Relocation services
Restructuring & reorganization
Tax services

Key Competitors
Arthur Andersen
Booz, Allen
Coopers & Lybrand
Deloitte & Touche
KPMG
Marsh & McLennan
McKinsey & Co.
Price Waterhouse

Industry
Business services - accounting & consulting

Overview
The 2nd largest accounting firm in the US (after Arthur Andersen), Ernst & Young handles every kind of financial service, from corporate finance to health care. The firm was spawned by the 1980s Big 8 merger between Ernst & Whinney, a trend-setting company that dated back to the 1800s, and Arthur Young, long known as "old reliable." Ernst & Young has shed riskier clients like real estate ventures and financial services companies, but it has also led the Big 6 the past 2 years in a dubious category, client defections.

ESPRIT DE CORP.

RANK: 471

900 Minnesota St.
San Francisco, CA 94107
Phone: 415-648-6900
Fax: 415-550-3960

1993 Sales: $606 million
FYE: June
Employees: 4,150

Key Personnel
Pres & CEO: David Folkman
CFO & COO: Peter Hanelt
Pres Esprit Apparel: Andrew Cohen
Pres Footwear & Accessories: Engle Saez
Pres Susie Tompkins & Retail: Lisa Engler
VP HR: Debra J. Sisson

Major Products
Accessories
Bath & bed products
Children's clothing
Eyewear
Men's clothing
Socks & tights
Women's clothing

Key Competitors
Benetton
Calvin Klein
Donna Karan
The Gap
Levi Strauss
Liz Claiborne
Polo/Ralph Lauren
V. F.

Industry
Apparel

Overview
Founded in 1968 as the Plain Jane Dress Company by Doug and Susie Tompkins and Jane Tise, this apparel company became Esprit de Corp. in 1970. It designs and makes men's, women's, and children's clothing worldwide. Esprit de Corp. is known for encouraging social responsibility in its employees. In the late 1980s conflict between Doug and Susie Tompkins led to a company decline. In 1989 the couple filed for divorce and in 1990 Susie and some investors amicably bought Doug's interest. Susie made a number of executive changes in the 1990s, eventually retiring from day-to-day management.

ESSEX GROUP INC. — RANK: 348

1601 Wall St.
Ft. Wayne, IN 46802
Phone: 219-461-4000
Fax: 219-461-4150

1993 Sales: $869 million
FYE: December
Employees: 4,000

Key Personnel
Pres & CEO: Stanley C. Craft
CFO: David A. Owen
EVP: Thomas A. Twehues
Pres Wire & Cable Div: Steven R. Abbott
Pres Magnet Wire & Insulation Div: Charles W. McGregor
Pres Engineered Products Div: Robert J. Faucher

Major Products
Automotive wiring
Building wire
Electrical insulation
Electrical wire coatings
Magnet wire
Motor lead wire
Telecommunication cable

Key Competitors
Barnes Group
Communication Cable
Cooper Industries
Encore Wire
General Cable
Insteel
National-Standard
Northwestern Steel & Wire

Industry
Wire & cable products

Overview
Founded in 1930, Essex Group provides electrical wire and cable and electrical insulation products for automotive and other industrial markets. One of the world's largest producers of electric wire and cable, Essex Group was purchased by an affiliate of Bessemer Securities in 1992 from a unit of Morgan Stanley Leveraged Equity Fund II LP. Essex Group's ownership history also includes a period from 1974 to 1988 as a unit of United Technologies and a stint from 1965 to 1974 as a public company. The company has been hurt in recent years by falling copper prices, which have forced it to lower the cost of its own products in return.

ESTÉE LAUDER INC. — RANK: 81

767 Fifth Ave.
New York, NY 10153
Phone: 212-572-4200
Fax: 212-572-3941

1993 Sales: $2,614 million
FYE: December
Employees: 12,000

Key Personnel
Chm: Estée Lauder
Pres & CEO: Leonard A. Lauder
SCVP: Evelyn H. Lauder
EVP & COO: Fred H. Langhammer
SVP & CFO: Robert J. Bigler
Pres & CEO, Estée Lauder U.S.A.: Robin Burns

Major Brands
Aramis
Calyx
Clinique
Estée Lauder
New West
Origins
Prescriptives
Tuscany

Key Competitors
Avon
L'Oréal
LVMH
MacAndrews & Forbes
Mary Kay
Procter & Gamble
Shiseido
Unilever

Industry
Cosmetics & toiletries

Overview
Estée Lauder includes Aramis Inc., Clinique Laboratories Inc., Estée Lauder Inc., Estée Lauder International, Inc., Origins Natural Resources Inc., and Prescriptives, Inc. Together the group is the largest privately held cosmetic and fragrance marketer in the world. Group companies are controlled by the Lauder family, including Estée (who founded the company with her husband, Joseph, in 1946) and her 2 sons, Leonard and Ronald.

◀ See page 55 for full-page profile.

FAMILY RESTAURANTS INC. — RANK: 239

18831 Von Karman Ave.
Irvine, CA 92715
Phone: 714-757-7900
Fax: 714-757-7984

1993 Sales: $1,167 million
FYE: December
Employees: 55,200

Key Personnel
Chm & CEO: Jack Goodall
EVP & CFO: Mike Casey
COO: Barry Krantz
Chief Admin Officer: Patti Johnson

Selected Restaurant Chains
Carrows
Casa Gallardo
Charley Brown's
Chi-Chi's
Coco's
El Torito & El Torito Grill
JoJos
Reuben's

Key Competitors
Brinker
Carlson
General Mills
Metromedia
Outback Steakhouse
PepsiCo
Taco Cabana
Uno Restaurant

Industry
Restaurants

Overview
Family Restaurants Inc. is the new name of California-based Restaurant Enterprises Group Inc. (REGI). It was formed by Foodmaker (operator of Jack in the Box) and 2 investment groups after REGI, saddled with debt incurred in a 1986 management-led LBO of the W.R. Grace Restaurant Group, declared bankruptcy in 1993. Foodmaker spun off Chi-Chi's and merged it with REGI's more than 15 restaurant chains to create the new company. With over 700 units and a presence in 24 states, Family Restaurants is one of the industry's largest restaurant operators and owns the first national sit-down Mexican food restaurant chain.

FARMERS UNION CENTRAL EXCHANGE, INCORPORATED — RANK: 111

5500 Cenex Dr.
Inver Heights, MN 55077
Phone: 612-451-5151
Fax: 612-451-5568

1993 Sales: $2,048 million
FYE: September
Employees: 2,800

Key Personnel
Chm: Elroy Webster
Pres & CEO: Noel K. Estenson
VP & CFO: Joel M. Koonce
VP & Controller: Jodi Heller
Legal Counsel: David Baker
VP HR: Dick Baldwin

Business Lines
Convenience stores
Farm consulting services
Fertilizers
Herbicides & pesticides
Lubricants
Petroleum refining/production
Propane
Tires, batteries & accessories

Key Competitors
CF Industries
ConAgra
Deere
Farmland Industries
GROWMARK
Koch
Wilbur-Ellis

Industry
Agricultural operations

Overview
Founded in 1931 as the Farmers Union Central Exchange to purchase farm supplies, Cenex, as it is commonly known, is now an agricultural co-op operating in 15 states from the Great Lakes to the Pacific Northwest. Cenex supplies 1,925 local co-ops with crop protection products, fuel, tires, lubricants, and farm consulting services, serving 320,000 farmers and ranchers. A 1987 joint venture with Land O'Lakes created the nation's largest network of plant food dealers. Also a vertically integrated oil company, Cenex operates a 675-mile oil pipeline.

FARMLAND INDUSTRIES, INC.

RANK: 39

3315 N. Oak Trafficway
Kansas City, MO 64116
Phone: 816-459-6000
Fax: 816-459-6979

1993 Sales: $4,723 million
FYE: August
Employees: 8,155

Key Personnel
Pres & CEO: H. D. Cleberg
EVP & CFO: John F. Berardi
EVP Ag Input Ops: Robert W. Honse
EVP & Dir Gen, Farmland Industrias S.A.: Stephen P. Dees
VP HR: Holly McCoy

◀ **See page 56 for full-page profile.**

Major Products
Agricultural chemicals
Animal feeds & supplements
Brand name processed meats
Gas stations & convenience stores
Petroleum products

Key Competitors
ADM
Cargill
Continental Grain
DuPont
General Mills
W. R. Grace
Hormel
IBP

Industry
Agricultural operations

Overview
Farmland, founded in 1929 as a petroleum supply co-op, is the largest agricultural cooperative in the US, providing its members with fuels, fertilizers, and other chemicals; informational services relating to production; and, most important, marketing assistance that allows them to compete with major corporations. These services include grain trading, pork and beef processing, and the wholesaling of value-added finished meat products like ham and sausage.

FEDERATED INSURANCE COMPANIES

RANK: 389

121 E. Park Sq.
Owatonna, MN 55060
Phone: 507-455-5200
Fax: 507-455-5651

1993 Sales: $796 million
FYE: December
Employees: 2,500

Key Personnel
Chm & CEO: Charles I. Buxton II
Pres & COO: Kirk N. Nelson
SVP, CFO & Treas: Jairus E. Meilahm
SVP & Dir HR: James L. Sheard
SVP & Dir Mktg: Al Annexstad
SVP & Dir Claims: Jon R. Berglund

Principal Subsidiaries
Federated Acceptance Corp.
Federated Inv. & Prop. Management
Federated Life Insurance Co.
Federated Mutual Agency
Federated Mutual Insurance Co.
Federated Service Insurance Co.

Key Competitors
Aetna
Allstate
Blue Cross
CIGNA
Kemper
Prudential
St. Paul Cos.
Travelers

Industry
Insurance - misc.

Overview
Founded in 1904 by farm equipment dealer C.I. Buxton, Federated Insurance offers group accident and health coverage, as well as automobile, property and casualty, and life insurance. Group accident and health policies account for 30% of net premiums written, while automobile policies make up 23%. Since its inception, Federated has served a niche market of franchise automobile dealers, farm and power equipment dealers, bulk oil jobbers, and specialty trade contractors. The company operates nationwide, with Minnesota providing nearly 13% of the company's revenues.

FERRELLGAS, INC.

RANK: 500

One Liberty Plaza
Liberty, MO 64068
Phone: 816-792-1600
Fax: 816-792-7985

1993 Sales: $525 million
FYE: July
Employees: 2,800

Key Personnel
Chm & CEO: James Ferrell
VP & COO: Brad Cochennet
CFO: Danley K. Sheldon
VP HR: Michelle Warner
Gen Counsel: Rhonda Smiley

Major Products
Aromatics
Butanes
Gas oils
Naphthas
Olefins
Propane
Raffinates
Reformates

Key Competitors
Coast Gas
Empire Gas
Gas Equipment
GenEx
Heritage Propane
Quantum Chemical
Star Gas
USX - Marathon

Industry
Oil & gas - marketing & trading

Overview
Established in 1939, Ferrellgas is among the 3 largest propane dealers in the US, serving about 600,000 residential and commercial customers in 44 states. The company's largest market concentrations are in the Midwest, the Great Lakes area, and the Southeast. With a delivery fleet of 2,500 vehicles — all of which are fueled by propane gas — Ferrellgas sells more than 521 million gallons of fuel annually to retail customers. Headquartered in Liberty, Missouri, Ferrellgas has 2 divisions: Ferrell North America, which supplies propane to the firm's retail system, and Ferrell International, which markets propane in Europe.

FIESTA MART INC.

RANK: 448

5235 Katy Fwy.
Houston, TX 77007
Phone: 713-869-5060
Fax: 713-869-8210

1993 Sales: $650 million
FYE: May
Employees: 6,000

Key Personnel
Chm & CEO: Donald L. Bonham
Pres: Louis Katopodis
VC & Sec: O. C. Mendenhall
EVP & CFO: Robert Z. Walker
Treas: Victor R. Rodriguez
Dir HR: Juanita Elizando

Business Lines
Bakery
Clothing
General merchandise
Groceries
Liquor
Prepared foods
Seafood

Key Competitors
Albertson's
H. E. Butt
Circle K
Food Lion
Kroger
Randalls
Southland
Whole Foods Market

Industry
Retail - supermarkets

Overview
Donald Bonham founded Fiesta in 1972 with the strategy of cracking a long-neglected market: selling ethnic foods in minority neighborhoods. The Texas chain (with stores in Austin, Beaumont, Dallas, and Houston) is likely to offer more barbacoa than BBQ, more bok choy than broccoli. The first Fiestas attracted Hispanics; later stores catered to African Americans and Asians. The stores provide the fiesta atmosphere of a Mexican market by leasing outdoor kiosks that offer stereos, sombreros, and other merchandise. Fiesta also operates convenience stores and liquor stores.

FLINT INK CORPORATION

RANK: 490

25111 Glendale Ave.
Detroit, MI 48239
Phone: 313-538-6800
Fax: 313-538-3538

1993 Sales: $550 million
FYE: December
Employees: 2,200

Key Personnel
Chm & CEO: H. Howard Flint II
Pres & COO: Leonard D. Frescoln
EVP: David B. Flint
VP Fin & Admin: Michael J. Gannon
Sec & Gen Counsel: Lawrence E. King
VP HR: Glenn T. Autry

Major Products
Commercial & packaging ink
Gravure printing ink
High speed web printing ink
Offset printing blankets
Pigments & dispersions
Screen inks

Key Competitors
BASF
Braden Setphin Ink
Custom Chemical
Dai Nippon Ink
INX International Ink
Lawter International
Superior Printing Ink
Wikoff Color

Industry
Chemicals - specialty

Overview
Flint Ink, founded in 1920, is the largest US-owned manufacturer of printing inks and also makes pigments and offset printing blankets. In 1987 Flint led a leveraged buyout of Sinclair & Valentine, an Allied Signal division; the move greatly expanded the company's product lines and assets. The family-owned company (current chairman, H. Howard Flint II, is a 3rd generation family member) has more than 60 facilities in the US, Canada, and Mexico. Flint excels in making products easy on the environment, such as inks made with water and soy oils and those needing less solvent, and has staff specializing in environmental research.

FLORIST'S TRANSWORLD DELIVERY ASSOCIATION INC.

RANK: 457

29200–22 Northwestern Hwy.
Southfield, MI 48034
Phone: 810-355-9300
Fax: 810-355-6350

1993 Est. Sales: $640 million
FYE: June
Employees: 600

Key Personnel
Chm: Kenneth Coley
Pres: T. Mark Knox
EVP & Sec: John A. Borden
VP: John Partridge
Treas: Frank Campisi
Dir Mktg Svcs: Cliff McComb

Selected Products
Big Hug Bouquet
Birthday Party Bouquet
Bundle of Joy arrangement
FTD/Renaissance Greeting Cards
Gourmet food baskets
Pick Me Up Bouquet
Remembrance Collection
"Taste of the Seasons"

Key Competitors
American Floral Services
American Greetings
CUC International
Flowers Direct
Hallmark
Roll International
Teleway

Industry
Retail - direct

Overview
Michigan-based Florists' Transworld Delivery Association (FTD) began in 1910 when 15 retail florists agreed to exchange out-of-town deliveries using the telegraph. A nonprofit cooperative, FTD is owned by more than 24,000 independent retail florists in the US and is linked to florists in 142 countries. FTD revolutionized the floral industry with innovations such as flowers-by-wire, standardized special bouquets, and a catalog of its floral arrangements. But new competition and its delayed entry into the 1-800 arena ate into FTD's sales in the early 1990s, leading it to announce a merger with merchant banker Perry Capital in July 1994 and a change to for-profit status.

FLYING J INC.

RANK: 333

50 W. 990 South
Brigham City, UT 84302
Phone: 801-734-6400
Fax: 801-734-6556

1994 Sales: $900 million
FYE: January
Employees: 6,300

Key Personnel
Chm: O. Jay Call
Pres: J. Phillip Adams
CFO: Paul F. Brown
VP: Thad Call
VP: Richard E. Gerner
Dir Personnel: Robert O. Langford

Selected Services
Convenience stores
Fuel service
Lodging
Restaurants
Truck parking areas

Key Competitors
Ashland Oil
British Petroleum
Exxon
Petro
Rip Griffin Truck/Travel Centers
Texaco
Travel Ports of America
USX - Marathon

Industry
Truck stops

Overview
Founded in 1968 by O. Jay Call, Flying J operates a chain of truck stops (Flying J Travel Plazas) and a petroleum refinery. The company owns or franchises over 70 truck stops in 25 states, mostly in the South and the West, and is expanding into the eastern US. Flying J typically constructs its travel plazas and then sells them on a lease-buyback agreement to Scottsdale, Arizona–based Franchise Finance Corporation of America, a privately owned real estate and investment management firm. The truck stops include fuel stations, convenience stores, and lodging.

FMR CORPORATION

RANK: 83

82 Devonshire St.
Boston, MA 02109
Phone: 617-570-7000
Fax: 617-720-3836

1993 Sales: $2,570 million
FYE: December
Employees: 12,900

Key Personnel
Chm, Pres & CEO: Edward C. Johnson III
EVP: Mark A. Peterson
Pres Fidelity Brokerage: Roger T. Servison
SVP & CFO: Denis M. McCarthy
SVP Admin (HR): Jerry Lieberman
VP & Corp Counsel: David C. Weinstein

◀ **See page 57 for full-page profile.**

Principal Subsidiaries
Boston Coach Corp.
Community Newspaper Co.
Fidelity Brokerage Services, Inc.
Fidelity Investments (mutual funds)
Fidelity Investments Life Insurance Co.
Wentworth Gallery Ltd., Inc.
Worth (investment magazine)

Key Competitors
Aetna
Charles Schwab
John Hancock
Merrill Lynch
Oppenheimer
Prudential
T. Rowe Price
Vanguard Real Estate

Industry
Financial - mutual funds

Overview
Founded in 1930, FMR is the holding company for Fidelity Investments, the largest family of mutual funds in the world, with $258 billion in assets, and Fidelity Brokerage Services, the #2 discount brokerage operation in the US (after Charles Schwab). FMR also has operations in insurance, credit cards, real estate, transportation, and publishing, among other things, and owns an art gallery. CEO Edward (Ned) Johnson and his family own 47% of the company; management owns the rest.

FOLLETT CORPORATION

RANK: 470

2233 West St.
River Grove, IL 60171
Phone: 708-583-2000
Fax: 708-452-9347

1993 Sales: $612 million
FYE: March
Employees: 6,500

Key Personnel
Chm: Richard M. Traut
Pres & CEO: P.R. Litzsinger
VP Fin: Kenneth Hull
Treas: William Cook
Sec: Laverne Hosek
HR: Carl Dickes

Operating Units
Follett Campus Resources
Follett College Stores
Follett Collegiate Graphics
Follett Educational Services
Follett Library Book Company
Follett Software Company

Key Competitors
Ameritech
Baker & Taylor
Barnes & Noble
Blackwell
Ingram
Kinko's
Kmart

Industry
Wholesale distribution - books & software

Overview
Follett Corporation, founded in 1873, is one of the largest and oldest businesses dedicated exclusively to the education industry. Owned and operated by the Follett family since its inception, the company distributes textbooks, designs library computer products, runs on-campus Copy Stop shops, and leads the college bookstore market, with over 400 locations in 46 states and Canada. Chairman Richard Traut, son-in-law of former chairman Robert Follett, is the first company head not to carry the family name.

FORD FOUNDATION

RANK: 388

320 E. 43rd St.
New York, NY 10017
Phone: 212-573-5000
Fax: 212-599-4584

1993 Sales: $797 million
FYE: September
Employees: 590

Key Personnel
Chm: Henry B. Schacht
Pres: Franklin A. Thomas
VP Program Div: Susan V. Berresford
VP, Sec & Gen Counsel: Barron M. Tenny
Treas & Dir Fin Svcs: Nicholas M. Gabriel
Dir, Office of HR: Bruce D. Stuckey

◀ **See page 58 for full-page profile.**

Funding Categories
Education & Culture
Governance & Public Policy
International Affairs
Reproductive Health & Population
Rights & Social Justice
Rural Poverty & Resources
Urban Poverty

Industry
Foundation

Overview
The Ford Foundation is the largest philanthropic foundation in the US, giving millions of dollars annually in grants to organizations and institutions worldwide. In 1993 the foundation awarded $288 million in grants and for projects. Established in 1936 by Henry Ford and his son Edsel, the Ford Foundation no longer has stock in Ford Motor Co. or ties to the Ford family. The foundation's stock and bond portfolio supplies all funds; at year-end 1993 the portfolio's market value was more than $6.8 billion.

FORT HOWARD CORPORATION

RANK: 236

1919 S. Broadway
Green Bay, WI 54304
Phone: 414-435-8821
Fax: 414-435-3703

1993 Sales: $1,187 million
FYE: December
Employees: 6,600

Key Personnel
Chm & CEO: Donald H. DeMeuse
Pres & COO: Michael T. Riordan
VC & CFO: Kathleen J. Hempel
EVP: John F. Rowley
EVP: Andrew W. Donnelly
VP HR: David K. Wong

Major Products
Bathroom tissue
Facial tissue
Green Forest products (recycled)
Paper napkins
Paper towels
Wipers

Key Competitors
Georgia-Pacific
James River
Kimberly-Clark
Menasha
Potlatch
Procter & Gamble
Scott
Sweetheart Holdings

Industry
Paper & paper products

Overview
Started in 1919, Fort Howard is one of the largest makers of low-cost paper products, primarily serving commercial and institutional customers. Unable to afford a paper mill, founder Austin E. Cofrin used recycled materials to make paper. The company went public in 1971 and soon became a billion-dollar enterprise. In 1988 a management-led LBO, financed by Morgan Stanley, took the company private again but saddled it with staggering debt. Fort Howard has created a niche for itself with recycled products but is still highly leveraged. CFO Kathleen Hempel, who started at Fort Howard as a secretary, may be called upon to produce a miracle with the company's finances.

FOSTER POULTRY FARMS INC.

RANK: 381

1000 Davis St.
Livingston, CA 95334
Phone: 209-394-7901
Fax: 209-394-6342

1993 Sales: $800 million
FYE: December
Employees: 7,000

Key Personnel
Pres & CEO: Robert A. Fox
CFO: Jay Hicks
VP: George Foster
VP: Norma Foster
Gen Counsel: Thomas A. Lee, Jr.
Dir Personnel: Tim Walsh

Business Lines
Almond farming
Animal feeds
Dairy operations
Local trucking
Poultry hatching
Poultry processing
Poultry slaughtering
Prepared poultry

Key Competitors
ConAgra
Gold Kist
Hormel
Hudson Foods
Perdue
Pilgrim's Pride
Tyson Foods
Wayne Poultry

Industry
Food - meat products

Overview
Sick chicks in 1990 and 1991 threatened Foster's place in the pecking order. When Foster, California's #1 and the US's #8 poultry processor, had an outbreak of avian disease, national competitors got a leg up. The family-owned Foster Farms (founded 1939) responded with a restructuring — a new CEO, layoffs, moving some breeding operations to Arkansas and Colorado, and reduced production. The health of the poultry — corn-fed and hormone-free — improved also. Foster shifted some emphasis to bulk sales to restaurants instead of individual consumer sales.

FRANCISCAN HEALTH SYSTEM

RANK: 320

One MacIntyre Dr.
Aston, PA 19014
Phone: 215-358-3950
Fax: 215-358-4207

1993 Sales: $928 million
FYE: June
Employees: 14,000

Key Personnel
Pres & CEO: Ronald R. Aldrich
EVP: Mary E. O'Brien
SVP Sys Strategy: Ellen Barron
Controller: Sharon Laydon
VP HR: Edward T. Kane
Gen Counsel: Ellen Barton

Selected Services
Acute care hospital services
Eldercare services
Long-term care
Management services & programs
Mental health & substance abuse services
Mission & ministry programs
Outpatient diagnosis & treatment services
Rehabilitation services

Key Competitors
American Healthcare
Bon Secours Health System
Brim
Health & Hospital Services
Kaiser Foundation Health Plan
Legacy Health System
Main Line Health
Universal Health Services

Industry
Hospitals

Overview
Sponsored by the Sisters of St. Francis of Philadelphia, the Franciscan Health System is a national holding company of Catholic hospitals and related organizations. While its original hospital was founded in 1860, the system was formally organized in 1981. Franciscan Health consists of 12 member and 2 affiliate hospitals and 11 long-term care facilities located in the mid-Atlantic states and the Pacific Northwest. The system cares for about 115,000 hospital inpatients and long-term care residents annually.

FRANK CONSOLIDATED ENTERPRISES

RANK: 153

666 Garland Place
Des Plaines, IL 60016
Phone: 708-699-7000
Fax: 708-699-0681

1993 Sales: $1,658 million
FYE: August
Employees: 2,020

Key Personnel
Chm: Elaine Frank
Pres & CEO: James S. Frank
VP: Charles Frank
CFO: Ford Pearson
Dir Mktg: Dennis LaLiberty
Dir Personnel: Ruth Kurtz

Business Lines
Corporate travel services
Fleet administration
Fleet financing
Fleet management
New auto sales
Used auto sales

Key Competitors
AAA
American Express
Carlson
Celozzi-Edelson
Donlen
Holman Enterprises
Maritz
Thomas Cook Travel

Industry
Retail - new & used cars

Overview
Founded in 1939 by Zollie Frank, Frank Consolidated Enterprises operates a fleet leasing and management company (Wheels Inc.), a business travel service (IVI Travel), and several Chicago-area auto dealerships (Z Frank). Zollie died in 1990, and his wife, Elaine, now owns more than 60% of the company, which she helped start by selling used cars. Wheels, an industry pioneer, is the 3rd largest fleet management company in the US. IVI Travel, bought by Frank Consolidated Enterprises in 1986, is the 5th largest US travel agency.

FURR'S SUPERMARKETS, INC.

RANK: 311

1730 Montano Rd. NW
Albuquerque, NM 87107
Phone: 505-344-6525
Fax: 505-761-0866

1993 Sales: $950 million
FYE: December
Employees: 6,500

Key Personnel
CEO: Jan Friederich
Pres & COO: Walter "Buz" Doyle
CFO: Patrick Totman
VP, Treas & Controller: Mike Daly
Chief Admin Officer: Gene Denison
VP HR: Delwyn James

Operating Units
Furr's Supermarkets
SoLo

Key Competitors
Albertson's
Bashas'
H. E. Butt
Kroger
Megafoods
Safeway
Smith's Food & Drug
United Supermarkets

Industry
Retail - supermarkets

Overview
Founded in 1904, Albuquerque-based Furr's (not related to Furr's Cafeterias) operates 76 stores under the names Furr's and SoLo in West Texas and New Mexico. Owned by Ibero American Bank (Hamburg, Germany; 54%), Fleming Cos. of Oklahoma City (40%), and management (6%) since 1991, the chain recently rebuffed a merger bid by Arizona-based Megafoods. Furr's is adding bakeries, expanding produce and deli departments, and adding pharmacies and video rentals to upgrade its stores.

GAF CORP

RANK: 322

1361 Alps Rd.
Wayne, NJ 07470
Phone: 201-628-3000
Fax: 201-628-3311

1993 Sales: $926 million
FYE: December
Employees: 4,277

Key Personnel
Chm & CEO: Samuel J. Heyman
EVP: Carl R. Eckardt
EVP: John M. Sergey
SVP & CFO: James P. Rogers
VP & Asst Treas: Mark Presto
Asst Treas: Kathleen M. Guinnessey

Major Products
Acetylene chemicals
Fiberglass roofing
Fixative polymers
Gantrez resin
Simulated woodshake roofing

Key Competitors
Bayer
Dow Chemical
DuPont
Exxon
W. R. Grace
St.-Gobain
Union Carbide
Vulcan Materials

Industry
Chemicals - specialty

Overview
First a foreign company, then US government–owned, and later publicly traded, GAF began its 4th life in 1989 when Samuel J. Heyman led the company's management in an LBO. Founded in 1929 as American I.G. Chemical (later General Aniline and Film), a US division of the German chemical trust I.G. Farben-industrie, the company was seized by the US government during WWII and remained under federal control until its 1965 IPO. It became GAF in 1968. GAF currently manufactures chemicals and construction materials and owns a radio station. GAF's chief subsidiary is International Specialty Products.

GALILEO INTERNATIONAL — RANK: 480

9700 W. Higgins Rd., Ste. 400
Rosemont, IL 60018
Phone: 708-518-4000
Fax: 708-518-4085

1993 Sales: $584 million
FYE: December
Employees: 2,000

Key Personnel
Pres, CEO & Gen Counsel: Gregory L. Conley
SVP: Michael Foliot
SVP: Craig Thompson
CFO: Paul Bristow
VP Ops: Tom O'Key
HR: Kath Murphy

Major Owners
Alitalia (9%)
British Airways (15%)
KLM (12%)
Swissair (13%)
UAL (38%)
USAir (11%)

Key Competitors
ABACUS
AMR
Worldspan

Industry
Travel reservation services

Overview
Galileo International Partnership is the result of the 1993 merger of the Covia Partnership airline reservation system and the UK-based Galileo reservation system. Owners include UAL, USAir, Air Canada, and 9 European airlines. Galileo International is the world's 2nd largest reservation system (after AMR's Sabre Group), serving 25,000 travel agencies in 57 countries. Controversy erupted in 1994 when Galileo International dropped Southwest Airlines and a number of small airlines from its system, making it impossible for travel agents with the Galileo system to print tickets for those airlines.

E. & J. GALLO WINERY — RANK: 252

600 Yosemite Blvd.
Modesto, CA 95353
Phone: 209-579-3111
Fax: 209-579-3249

1993 Est. Sales: $1,100 million
FYE: December
Employees: 4,000

Key Personnel
Chm: Ernest Gallo
EVP: Albion Fenderson
VP Fin: Louis Freedman
VP: Joseph E. Gallo
VP: Robert J. Gallo
VP HR: Robert Deitrich

◀ See page 59 for full-page profile.

Major Brands
Andre
Ballatore
Bartles & Jaymes
Boone's Farm
Carlo Rossi
Ernest & Julio Gallo
Thunderbird
Wm. Wycliffe

Key Competitors
Adolph Coors
Allied-Lyons
Bacardi
Canandaguia
Kendall-Jackson Winery
Robert Mondavi
Seagram
Sebastiani Vineyards

Industry
Beverages - alcoholic

Overview
E. & J. Gallo sells more than one out of every 3 bottles of wine bought in the US. The winery, which opened at the end of Prohibition in 1933 with a $200 grape crusher and a rented warehouse, was operated by the Gallo brothers until the death of Julio in 1993. Today, with surviving brother Ernest still at the helm, Gallo boasts more than 1/4 of the domestic wine market, selling more than 50 types of wine, including varietals, "jug" wines, fortified wines, and wine coolers. Gallo entered the premium wine market in 1993 with a $30 chardonnay.

GATES CORPORATION — RANK: 197

900 S. Broadway
Denver, CO 80217
Phone: 303-744-1911
Fax: 303-744-4000

1993 Sales: $1,340 million
FYE: December
Employees: 12,730

Key Personnel
Chm & CEO: Charles C. Gates, Jr.
VC: Donald E. Miller
Pres & COO: John M. Riess
Pres No Am Ops, Gates Rubber: A. L. Stecklein
EVP, Sec & CFO: Thomas J. Gibson
Admin Svcs: D. R. Ahlman

Major Products
Car engine components
Molded fiber parts for cars
Oil & gas exploration
Rubber belts & hoses

Key Competitors
Carlisle Motors
Goodyear
HBD Industries
Kleer-Vu Industries
Plastic Specialties
Plymouth Rubber
Uniroyal Chemical

Industry
Rubber & plastic products

Overview
One of the world's leading manufacturers of rubber products, Gates was founded by Charles Gates, Sr., in 1917 to market the automotive V-belt his brother invented. Though for many years Gates primarily made specialty items for loyal clients in the US automotive and aerospace industries, the company now derives half its revenues from global operations. *Forbes* estimates that Chairman Charles Gates, Jr., is worth $680 million. The company formed a new subsidiary to buy, operate, and market US oil- and gas-producing leases.

GENERAL AMERICAN LIFE INSURANCE COMPANY — RANK: 79

700 Market St.
St. Louis, MO 63101
Phone: 314-231-1700
Fax: 314-525-5760

1993 Sales: $2,636 million
FYE: December
Employees: 2,700

Key Personnel
Chm: H. Edwin Trusheim
Pres & CEO: Richard A. Liddy
EVP Investment & Treas: Leonard M. Rubenstein
VP & Controller: John Barber
VP, Gen Counsel & Sec: Robert J. Banstetter
VP HR: Marsha McMillen

Selected Services
Brokerage services
Computer software & systems
Group life & health insurance
Group pensions
Individual health insurance
Investment management services
Life insurance & reinsurance
Managed health care

Key Competitors
Aetna
CIGNA
Equitable
John Hancock
MetLife
New York Life
Northwestern Mutual
Prudential

Industry
Insurance - life

Overview
Policyholder-owned General American Life Insurance, founded in 1933, provides life and health insurance and annuities to groups and individuals. Operating from 380 offices in 49 states, Puerto Rico, 8 Canadian provinces, and the District of Columbia, the St. Louis–based firm has 11 subsidiaries that offer services ranging from developing software to providing reinsurance to other insurance companies. Recently, General American began offering a variable annuity with 9 investment funds.

GENERAL CHEMICAL CORP. RANK: 436

Liberty Ln.
Hampton, NH 03842
Phone: 603-926-5911
Fax: 603-929-2404

1993 Sales: $690 million
FYE: December
Employees: 3,570

Key Personnel
Chm & CEO: Michael Dingman
Pres: Paul Montrone
CFO: Richard Russell
VP & Treas: Edward F. Kavanaugh
Controller: Larry Brock

Major Products
Aluminum sulfate
Calcium chloride
Methanol
Soda ash
Specialty chemicals
Sulfuric acid

Key Competitors
Elf Aquataine
Essex Group
FMC
Penrice
Rhône-Poulenc
Solvay
Tenneco
Union Carbide

Industry
Chemicals - specialty

Overview
Although it has been owned, sold, merged, and spun off by a number of companies, including AlliedSignal and Henley Manufacturing, General Chemical can trace its roots back to a chemical company founded in 1899. Now owned by its 2 top executives, Michael Dingman and Paul Montrone, the company has seen its fortunes improve in recent years. General has weathered several lawsuits and harsh cost-cutting to emerge as the leader in such niche markets as aluminum sulfate and regenerated sulfuric acid. In February 1994 it agreed to pay $1.18 million in fines and compensation after a sulfuric acid cloud escaped from its Richmond, California, facility.

GENERAL MEDICAL CORPORATION RANK: 300

8741 Landmark Rd.
Richmond, VA 23228
Phone: 804-264-7500
Fax: 804-264-7679

1993 Est. Sales: $1,000 million
FYE: December
Employees: 1,800

Key Personnel
Chm, Pres & CEO: Steven B. Nielsen
EVP & COO: James C. Robison
SVP, CFO & Treas: Donald B. Garber
SVP Corp Planning: Brian J. Fatzinger
VP & Gen Counsel: G. Keith Nedrow

Markets
Clinics
Hospitals
Nursing homes
Physicians

Key Competitors
Ballard Medical
C. R. Bard
Baxter
Medtronic
Mitek Surgical
Owens & Minor
U.S. Surgical
Vital Signs

Industry
Medical products - wholesale

Overview
Richmond, Virginia–based General Medical Corp. is the US's 3rd largest distributor of medical and surgical supplies and equipment. The company operates 45 distribution centers across the US, most of them in the East. It is also one of the largest distributors in the alternative care market. Formerly RABCO Health Services, the company was acquired in 1993 by 19 of its top managers from principal owner Richard Bernstein (owner of Western Publishing Group), with financial backing from Kelso & Co. Managers will retain about 15% ownership. General Medical's 1994 acquisition of California-based F.D. Titus & Son will add 10 distribution centers and a retail store.

GEORGE E. WARREN CORPORATION RANK: 176

605 17th St.
Vero Beach, FL 32960
Phone: 407-778-7100
Fax: 407-778-7171

1993 Est. Sales: $1,500 million
FYE: December
Employees: 30

Key Personnel
Pres: Thomas L. Corr
Treas & CFO: Jonathan W. Taylor
Controller: Michael E. George
Mgr Admin: Richard R. Cobb
Mgr Ops: Timothy J. Smith
Dir HR: Martin Paris

Major Products
Ethylene
Gasoline
Heating Oil
Propane
Propylene

Key Competitors
Coastal
Columbia Gas
Enron
Entergy
Koch
Occidental
Panhandle Eastern
Southern Co.

Industry
Oil & gas - distribution

Overview
George Warren Corp. is a refiner and major wholesale distributor of petroleum products in the southeastern US. The company has 8 refining facilities located in Florida (Port Everglades and Tampa), Mississippi (Greenville and Hattiesburg), Louisiana (Venice), Texas (Galena and Bellville), and New Mexico (Monument). The company distributes its products by tank trucks and pipeline.

THE GEORGE WASHINGTON UNIVERSITY RANK: 440

2121 I St. NW, 8th Fl.
Washington, DC 20037
Phone: 202-994-1000
Fax: 202-994-0654

1993 Sales: $677 million
FYE: June
Employees: 10,000

Key Personnel
Pres: Stephen J. Trachtenberg
Assoc VP & Comptroller: Ralph Olmo
Asst Controller: Colin Clasper
Dir Admissions: George W. G. Stoner
Registrar: Matthew Gaglione
Dir HR: Jim Clifford

Selected Programs of Study
Business & public management
Communication & the arts
Education & human development
Engineering & applied science
Health professions
Internal affairs
Law
Social Sciences

Industry
Schools

Overview
George Washington University, founded in 1821, offers degree programs in 6 undergraduate and 7 graduate schools. Business, engineering, and international studies are its strongest majors academically. Enrollment is about 15,200: 5,500 full-time and 700 part-time undergraduate and 9,000 graduate students. Of the school's nearly 1,400 full-time faculty members, about 90% hold doctorate degrees. More than half the faculty, about 2,700, are part-time. The school's 3 libraries contain 1.6 million volumes in addition to 6,800 audiovisual forms and 17,000 periodicals.

GEORGETOWN UNIVERSITY INC. RANK: 405

37th & O St. NW
Washington, DC 20057
Phone: 202-687-5055
Fax: 202-687-3608

1993 Sales: $749 million
FYE: June
Employees: 12,000

Key Personnel
Pres: Leo J. O' Donovan
EVP Health Sciences: John F. Griffith
EVP Campus Affairs: Patrick A. Heelan
VP: Michael J. Kelly
VP & Treas: Nicole F. Mandeville
Counsel: Lawrence White

Selected Programs of Study
Undergraduate
- Economics
- International business management
- Nursing
- Philosophy
- Physics
- Prelaw

Graduate
- Foreign service
- German
- Pathology
- Public policy
- Radiation science
- Spanish

Industry
Schools

Overview
Founded in 1789, Georgetown is the oldest Roman Catholic university in the US and is managed by the Jesuits. With over 1,700 faculty members, the university teaches approximately 11,500 grad and undergrad students. Situated on a 100-acre campus on the Potomac, the university has strong departments in international studies and foreign relations and boasts US president Bill Clinton as an alumnus. The university is known internationally for its medical school, which is almost 150 years old. In order to hold down tuition costs in a time of rising expenses, Georgetown is attempting to build its endowment, described by President Leo O'Donovan as "woefully inadequate."

GEORGIA LOTTERY CORPORATION RANK: 244

INFORUM, Ste. 3000
Atlanta, GA 30303
Phone: 404-215-5000
Fax: 404-215-8871

1994 Sales: $1,128 million
FYE: June
Employees: 266

Key Personnel
Pres & CEO: Rebecca Paul
CFO: M. W. Jordan
SVP: Candice Bluechel
SVP: Arville Brocksmith
SVP: Tom Shaheen
SVP: Jody Spicola

Major Products
Ca$h 3
Cool Cash
Georgia Millionaire
Instant Cash
Lotto Georgia
Lucky 7's
Magnolia Millions
Touchdown

Industry
Leisure & recreational services - lottery

Overview
Created as a public corporation by the Georgia General Assembly in 1992, the Georgia Lottery operates lottery games in that state. First-year sales set a record for per capita sales of start-up lotteries. The lottery's 16 instant games represent 50% of total sales, with Ca$h 3, a daily drawing, bringing in over 30% of revenues. A 7-member board, appointed by the governor, oversees lottery operations. At least 30% of all lottery sales must be spent on education. To maintain interest the lottery plans to continue adding new games, including a $2 instant game offering higher prizes.

GIANT EAGLE INC. RANK: 108

101 Kappa Dr.
Pittsburgh, PA 15238
Phone: 412-963-6200
Fax: 412-963-0374

1994 Sales: $2,100 million
FYE: June
Employees: 11,800

Key Personnel
Chm & CEO: David S. Shapira
Pres & COO: Raymond J. Burgo
SVP & CFO: Mark Minnaugh
SVP Merchandising: Joseph Faccenda
SVP Store Ops: Sam Amodeo
VP Personnel: Raymond A. Huber

Selected Services
Audio book rentals
Bottled water dispensing
In-store bank
Maestro (MasterCard debit card)
Video rentals

Key Competitors
American Stores
Great A&P
Kroger
Super Rite
SUPERVALU
Tamarkin
Wegmans Food Markets
Weis Markets

Industry
Retail - supermarkets

Overview
Founded in 1931, Giant Eagle is a chain of about 150 grocery stores with locations throughout western Pennsylvania, Ohio, and West Virginia. The company franchises almost half of its outlets. Giant Eagle, whose principal owner is CEO David Shapira's family, is the only remaining Pittsburgh, Pennsylvania–based supermarket chain. The company owns 39% of Phar-Mor, the superdiscount drugstore that declared bankruptcy in 1992 amid allegations of fraud by top executives.

GILBANE BUILDING COMPANY RANK: 316

7 Jackson Walkway
Providence, RI 02940
Phone: 401-456-5800
Fax: 401-456-5936

1993 Sales: $936 million
FYE: December
Employees: 828

Key Personnel
Chm: William J. Gilbane
Pres: Paul J. Choquette, Jr.
CFO: Charlie Salvator
VP Mktg: Alfred K. Potter
VP HR: Dan Kelly
Gen Counsel: John W. DiNicola

Selected Services
Commercial construction
Construction management
Industrial building construction
Office building construction
Repairs & renovations
Warehouse construction

Key Competitors
Bechtel
Fluor
Huber, Hunt & Nichols
Morrison Knudsen
Parsons
Peter Kiewit
Stone & Webster
Turner Industries

Industry
Construction - heavy

Overview
Gilbane Building is one of the top 20 construction firms in the US. Its projects include prisons, libraries, airport terminals, and medical research facilities. Its Gilbane Properties unit develops residential and commercial real estate. Gilbane was founded in 1873 by the chairman's grandfather, William Gilbane, and great uncle Thomas. President Paul Choquette, of the 4th generation, is the chairman's nephew.

GLAVAL CORPORATION

RANK: 337

29340 Lexington Park
Elkhart, IN 46514
Phone: 219-295-7178
Fax: 219-293-1294

1993 Est. Sales: $900 million

Employees: 1,400

Key Personnel
Pres: Richard Strefling
VP Mfg: Rita Gearhart
VP : Karl Strefling
VP Finance: Michael Givler
Treas and Sec: Nancy Ritchie
VP HR: Thomas Stutsman

Major Custom Van Products
Full-size Chevy vans
Full-size Dodge vans
Full-size Ford vans
Full-size GMC vans
Minivans - Chevy
Minivans - Dodge
Minivans - Ford

Key Competitors
Coachman
Cobra Industries
Fleetwood
Kentron
Mark III
Starcraft Automotive
Tiara Motor Coach
Winnebago

Industry
Automotive - van conversions

Overview
Located in the van-conversion center of America, Elkhart, Indiana (major van converters Kentron and Tiara Motor Coach are also there), Glaval is a close #2 in the van-conversion industry, after leader Mark III. Glaval was started in 1977 by Richard Strefling and Steve Kash as a hobby. Strefling now owns all of the concern. The company concentrates on generating high volume and serves the low- and mid-level van conversion market. Glaval is one of only 2 converters (the other is Mark III) that crash test their products.

GLOBAL PETROLEUM CORP.

RANK: 80

800 South St.
Waltham, MA 02154
Phone: 617-894-8800
Fax: 617-398-4160

1992 Est. Sales: $2,622 million
FYE: December
Employees: 150

Key Personnel
Pres & CEO: Alfred A. Slifka
SVP Fin: Thomas McManmon
VP Mktg: Joseph DeStefano
Gen Counsel: Edward Faneuil
Dir HR: Barbara Rosenblum

Selected Services
Diesel fuel distribution
Gasoline distribution
Heating oil distribution
Refined petroleum importing
Residual fuel distribution
Terminal operation

Key Competitors
Agway
Burmah
Chevron
Coastal
Exxon
Getty Petroleum
Transco Energy
Warren Equities

Industry
Oil refining & marketing

Overview
Global Petroleum, founded in 1950, is the leading independent supplier and marketer of gasoline, diesel fuel, heating oil, and heavy fuel in New England and a major supplier in the mid-Atlantic and midwestern states. Once just a regional company, it is now the largest US importer of refined petroleum products. Global also owns and operates storage terminals. With 2 other partners, Global is rehabilitating an old refinery in Nova Scotia at the deepest ice-free harbor on the North American East Coast.

GOLD KIST INC.

RANK: 184

244 Perimeter Center Pkwy.
Atlanta, GA 30346
Phone: 404-393-5000
Fax: 404-393-5061

1993 Sales: $1,401 million
FYE: June
Employees: 14,000

Key Personnel
Chm & CEO: Harold O. Chitwood
Pres & COO: Gaylord O. Coan
VP Fin: Peter J. Gibbons
VP, Sec & Gen Counsel: Jack L. Lawing
VP Info Svcs: Michael F. Thrailkill
VP HR: W. Andy Epperson

Business Lines
Farm equipment & supplies
Fertilizers
Peanut processing
Pork slaughtering & processing
Poultry farms
Poultry hatcheries
Poultry processing
Retail nurseries & garden stores

Key Competitors
ConAgra
Foster Poultry
Hudson Foods
Perdue
Pilgrim's Pride
Seaboard
Showell Farms
Tyson Foods

Industry
Food - meat products

Overview
Gold Kist, an Atlanta-based agricultural cooperative, is the US's 2nd largest poultry producer and processor, after Tyson Foods. It also produces game birds, processed pork, feeds, farm supplies, grains, and peanuts (with Archer-Daniels-Midland) and runs nurseries and garden stores. Gold Kist was founded in 1933 as the Georgia Cotton Producers Cooperative Association, but in response to changing economic conditions, it repositioned itself in poultry.

GOLDEN STATE FOODS CORPORATION

RANK: 240

18301 Von Karman Ave., Ste. 1100
Irvine, CA 92715
Phone: 714-252-2000
Fax: 714-252-2080

1993 Sales: $1,160 million
FYE: July
Employees: 1,700

Key Personnel
CEO: James E. Williams
Pres: Richard W. Gochnauer
SVP Fin & Sec: Gene L. Olson
VP Distribution: Joe Di Prima
VP Business Dev: Walter E. Kersten
Dir HR: Ron Childers

Major Products
Buns
Dairy items
Frozen fish & seafood
Paper products
Prepared meats
Produce
Syrups
Toppings

Key Competitors
AmeriServ Food
Earp Meat Co.
Martin-Brower
MBM
Perlman-Rocque
ProSource Distribution Services
JR Simplot

Industry
Food - wholesale to restaurants

Overview
Founded in 1969, Golden State is the nation's 7th largest food service distributor and has only one customer, McDonald's. Taken private by company executives in 1980, Golden State has supplied only McDonald's since 1972, but the relationship began in the late 1950s when both companies were only small fries. Golden State distributes self-manufactured products and other items to 2,000 "Golden Arches" in 25 states in the US and several countries overseas. Golden State is the 2nd largest McDonald's supplier, after Martin-Brower.

THE GOLDMAN SACHS GROUP, LP — RANK: 12

85 Broad St.
New York, NY 10004
Phone: 212-902-1000
Fax: 212-902-3925

1993 Sales: $13,200 million
FYE: November
Employees: 7,000

Key Personnel
Sr Partner & Chm of Mgmt Comm: Stephen Friedman
Partner & Intl Comptroller: David W. Blood
Partner & Co-Gen Counsel: Gregory K. Palm
Partner & Co-Gen Counsel: Robert J. Katz
Partner, Personnel: Jonathan L. Cohen

◀ See page 60 for full-page profile.

Selected Services
Commodity trading
Debt financing
Equity financing
Foreign exchange
Investment banking
Investment research
Mergers & acquisitions
Real estate

Key Competitors
General Electric
Bear Stearns
Lehman Brothers
Merrill Lynch
Morgan Stanley
Paine Webber
Prudential
Salomon

Industry
Financial - investment bankers

Overview
Founded in 1885 by Marcus Goldman and his son-in-law Samuel Sachs, Goldman Sachs is Wall Street's last major private partnership. Goldman Sachs has concentrated on traditional clientele (governments, wealthy individuals, and corporations) instead of becoming a financial supermarket. After losing some of its long-term underwriting clientele (Ford and GTE), the firm increased its presence overseas and is now making an increasingly large percentage of its income by trading on its own account. Recently, the company managed Daimler-Benz's first US issue of shares.

THE GOLODETZ GROUP — RANK: 195

142 W. 57th St., 8th Fl.
New York, NY 10019
Phone: 212-887-1601
Fax: 212-887-1650

1993 Est. Sales: $1,350 million
FYE: June
Employees: 850

Key Personnel
Pres: Gavin Parfit
Treas: David Ginzberg
VP Fin: Sharon Roth

Business Lines
Bulk liquid storage
Cattle feeding
Equipment leasing & financing
Farm management
Geothermal projects
Real estate investment
Sugar cane & sugar beets

Key Competitors
American Crystal Sugar
ConAgra
Connell
OESI Power
J.R. Simplot
Trammell Crow

Industry
Diversified operations

Overview
Founded in 1915, Golodetz Trading is a holding company controlling diverse service and manufacturing interests as well as stock and real estate investments. The company is owned by the various heirs of the original founders. Golodetz Trading is reportedly undergoing financial difficulties stemming from real estate investments, having been forced to sell off its steel operations.

THE GOLUB CORPORATION — RANK: 245

501 Duanesburg Rd.
Schenectady, NY 12306
Phone: 518-355-5000
Fax: 518-355-0843

1993 Sales: $1,120 million
FYE: April
Employees: 12,000

Key Personnel
Chm & CEO: Lewis Golub
Pres & COO: Neil Golub
CFO & Treas: Lawrence G. Olsen
VP, Sec & Gen Counsel: William Kenneally
SVP Store Ops: Frederick H. Bacheldor

Operating Units
Mini Chopper convenience stores
Price Chopper Market Center
Price Chopper supermarkets

Key Competitors
C&S Wholesaler Grocers
Cumberland Farms
Grand Union
Hannaford Bros.
Penn Traffic
Wawa
Wegmans Food Markets

Industry
Retail - supermarkets

Overview
Founded in 1931, Golub operates a chain of 81 Price Chopper supermarkets and 14 Mini Chopper convenience stores. Although Golub has a presence in 10 states, the stores are concentrated in New York, Massachusetts, and Pennsylvania. The company is owned by the Golub family and employees, who hold more than 1/3 of company stock. Formerly a low-price leader, Golub has been forced by competition to focus on quality service. The firm has introduced an expanded supermarket with a broader line of perishables and a food court. In an innovative move, Golub is having its advertising department work for outside clients.

GOODWILL INDUSTRIES INTERNATIONAL, INC. — RANK: 357

9200 Wisconsin Ave.
Bethesda, MD 20814
Phone: 301-530-6500
Fax: 301-530-1516

1993 Sales: $849 million
FYE: December
Employees: 94,621

Key Personnel
Pres & CEO: David M. Cooney
CFO: Michael Stephens
Dir Mktg: David Barringer
Dir Info Sys: Steven Snyderman
Dir HR: Doug Werber

Selected Services
Housing for the aged & disabled
Job training & placement
Medical treatment
Nursing care
Physical therapy
Psychological counseling
Secondhand retailing
Summer camps

Industry
Charitable organization

Overview
Goodwill Industries was founded as The National Cooperative Industrial Relief Association in Boston in 1910 by Dr. Edgar Helms, a Methodist minister whose goal was to offer people "not charity, but a chance." The organization collected used items, which were repaired by clients in trade and skills educational programs and sold through a network of retail stores. Although retailing is still important to Goodwill (renamed in 1946), the company now offers a wide variety of support programs for people, many of whom have disabilities, through 183 autonomous affiliates in the US and 50 organizations in 35 other countries.

GORDON FOOD SERVICE INC. RANK: 327

333 50th St. SW
Grand Rapids, MI 49548
Phone: 616-530-7000
Fax: 616-249-4165

1993 Sales: $910 million
FYE: October
Employees: 2,300

Key Personnel
Chm: Paul B. Gordon
Pres: Daniel Gordon
CFO: James Seiber
Dir Sys: Michael Clark
Dir Mktg: Ronald Miller
Dir HR: David Vickery

Major Products
Canned goods
Dairy products
Desserts
Disposable silverware
Meats
Paper napkins
Seafoods
Vegetables

Key Competitors
Ameriserv
JP Foodservice
SYSCO
US Foodservice

Industry
Food - wholesale to restaurants

Overview
Gordon Food Service (GFS), founded in 1942, is the largest family-owned food distributor in the US and is among the top 10 overall. In addition to food, GFS distributes beverages and paper products to hospitals, restaurants, hotels, and other institutions throughout Michigan, Ohio, Indiana, and Illinois. Known as an innovator within the industry, the company also operates 29 wholesale outlets that sell bulk food-service products to some of its smaller customers, as well as caterers and people planning large parties. Recently GFS announced plans to expand into Canada via acquisition.

THE GRAND UNION HOLDINGS CORPORATION RANK: 90

201 Willowbrook Blvd.
Wayne, NJ 07470
Phone: 201-890-6000
Fax: 201-890-6671

1994 Sales: $2,477 million
FYE: April
Employees: 18,500

Key Personnel
Chm: Gary D. Hirsch
Pres & CEO: Joseph J. McCaig
EVP & COO: William A. Louttit
SVP, CFO & Sec: Robert T. Galvin
SVP, NY Region: Darrell W. Stine
SVP Personnel: Charles Barrett

Selected Services
Bakery
Butcher shop
Floral department
Pharmacies
Produce department
Salad bar
Seafood department
Video rentals

Key Competitors
Big V Supermarkets
Golub
Great A&P
Key Food Stores
King Kullen Grocery
Pathmark
Victory Markets
Wakefern Food

Industry
Retail - supermarkets

Overview
Founded in 1872, privately held Grand Union was once one of the US's most prosperous food chains. Saddled with debt from a 1989 LBO, the chain is a subsidiary of Grand Union Holdings Corp., whose chairman, Gary Hirsch, owns 40% through various financial partnerships. Management owns 12%; outside investors, the remaining 48%. Revenues have been down since the sale of Grand Union's 48-store Big Star operation in the South in 1993, but the chain is acquiring more stores and renovating others. The company's 254 Grand Union stores now are concentrated in New York, New Jersey, Vermont, and 4 other northeastern states.

GRAYBAR ELECTRIC COMPANY, INC. RANK: 114

34 N. Meramec Ave.
St. Louis, MO 63105
Phone: 314-727-3900
Fax: 314-727-8218

1993 Sales: $2,033 million
FYE: December
Employees: 5,100

Key Personnel
Pres, CEO & CFO: Edward A. McGrath
SVP Sales & Mktg: Aubrey A. Thompson
SVP Distribution: James R. Hade
VP & Treas: John W. Wolf
VP, Sec & Gen Counsel: George S. Tulloch
VP HR: Jack F. Van Pelt

◀ **See page 61 for full-page profile.**

Major Products
Fiber optic equipment
Lighting fixtures
Motors
Power transmission equipment
Telephone station equipment
Transformers
Voice data equipment
Wiring devices

Key Competitors
Arrow Electronics
Avnet
General Electric
W. W. Grainger
Itel
Reliance Electric
Siemens
Westinghouse

Industry
Electrical products - wholesale

Overview
Founded in 1869, Graybar Electric is the largest independent electrical products distributor in the US. Graybar sells more than 100,000 electrical and telecommunications products from over 1,000 manufacturers, including AT&T, General Electric, IBM, Motorola, and 3M. The company's customers include electrical contractors, industrial plants, telephone companies, and utility companies. Graybar is owned by its current and retired employees. A 5-member board controls its voting shares.

GROCERS SUPPLY CO. INC. RANK: 187

3131 E. Holcombe Blvd.
Houston, TX 77021
Phone: 713-747-5000
Fax: 713-749-9320

1993 Est. Sales: $1,400 million
FYE: May
Employees: 1,275

Key Personnel
CEO: Milton Levit
Pres: Max Levit
VP, Sec & Treas: Gerald A. Levit
HR: Greg Belsheim

Major Products
Wholesale confectioneries
Wholesale frozen foods
Wholesale groceries

Key Competitors
Affiliated Foods
AmeriServ Food
Brenham Wholesale
Fleming
GSC Enterprises
Nash Finch
SUPERVALU
US Foodservice

Industry
Food - wholesale to grocers

Overview
Grocers Supply, originally incorporated in 1938, is directed by members of the Levit family — Milton, Max, and Gerald. Grocers is among the top 10 private employers in the greater Houston area. In addition to its wholesale grocery business, the company is an investor in Houston's own frankfurter company, the James Original Coney Island hot dog chain. The Texas Workers' Compensation Commission has cited Grocers as an "extra hazardous company," meaning the work-related injury and illness rates for its employees substantially exceed those of similar companies.

GROUP HEALTH COOPERATIVE OF PUGET SOUND — RANK: 318

521 Wall St.
Seattle, WA 98121
Phone: 206-448-6460
Fax: 206-448-2361

1993 Sales: $934 million
FYE: December
Employees: 9,000

Key Personnel
Pres & CEO: Phillip M. Nudelman
EVP & COO: Cheryl M. Scott
SVP & CFO: Grant E. McLaughlin
VP Legal & Gen Counsel: Gary Ikeda
Medical Dir: Al Truscott
VP HR: Brenda Tolbert

Selected Services
Family health centers
Health care financing
Hospitals
Medical research
Preventive-care services
Specialty medical centers

Key Competitors
Aetna
Blue Cross
First Choice Health Network
Health Systems
Kaiser Foundation Health Plan
PacifiCare
Prudential

Industry
Health maintenance organization

Overview
Group Health Cooperative of Puget Sound was formed in 1945 by Seattle-area citizens and claims to be the nation's largest consumer-governed health care organization. The co-op serves nearly 500,000 residents in Washington and Idaho by delivering integrated health care and providing health care financing. CEO Phil Nudelman has tried to get the cooperative's physicians involved in the administrative decision-making process. In 1993 *Money* magazine named the co-op one of the 10 best HMOs in the US, and Nudelman served on Hillary Clinton's White House Health-Care Reform Committee.

GROWMARK INC. — RANK: 370

1701 Towanda Ave.
Bloomington, IL 61701
Phone: 309-557-6000
Fax: 309-829-8532

1993 Sales: $827 million
FYE: August
Employees: 900

Key Personnel
Chm & Pres: O. Glenn Webb
CEO: Norman T. Jones
SVP Gen Counsel: R. Stephen Carr
VP Fin: Vern McGinnis
VP Grain Mktg: John McClenathan
VP Corp Svcs: Stan Nielsen

Major Products
Farm & garden machinery
Feed
Fertilizers
Garden seeds
Pesticides
Petroleum bulk stations

Key Competitors
Bartlett
Cargill
Countrymark Co-op
Effingham Equity
Farm Service Co-op
Southern States Co-op
Transammonia

Industry
Agricultural operations

Overview
Founded in 1927, GROWMARK is a farm supply cooperative serving agricultural interests primarily in Illinois, Iowa, and Wisconsin. GROWMARK ranks 15th among US agricultural cooperatives. Sales of fertilizers and pesticides account for the bulk of the cooperative's revenues. Responding to growing financial pressures in the farming industry, GROWMARK formed a joint venture with Archer-Daniels-Midland in 1985 to buy and market grain, the first such venture between a major regional cooperative and a public company. GROWMARK is also one of 12 cooperatives that own CF Industries, a manufacturer and distributor of fertilizers.

GSC ENTERPRISES, INC. — RANK: 404

130 Hillcrest Dr.
Sulphur Springs, TX 75483
Phone: 903-885-7621
Fax: 903-885-6928

1993 Sales: $757 million
FYE: December
Employees: 1,400

Key Personnel
Chm & CEO: Michael K. McKenzie
Pres & COO: Travis L. Owens
VP Fin & CFO: Ronald L. Folwell, Sr.
Dir MIS: Richard H. Chewning
Attorney: W. T. Allison
Dir HR: Theresa Patterson

Business Lines
Money orders
Wholesale confectioneries
Wholesale groceries
Wholesale tobacco products

Key Competitors
Affiliated Foods
AmeriServ Food
Brenham Wholesale
Fleming
Grocers Supply
Nash Finch
SUPERVALU
US Foodservice

Industry
Food - wholesale to grocers

Overview
GSC (Grocery Supply Company) Enterprises, founded in 1947, is a holding company for a number of wholesale grocers. It owns suppliers of wholesale and retail grocers and convenience stores throughout Texas and in parts of Arkansas, Kansas, and Oklahoma. The company has over 18,000 product lines, including general groceries and tobacco products, and is the 6th largest tobacco/candy/convenience products distributor in the US. GSC also owns Fidelity Express Money Order Company, which has agents in 13 states, primarily in the Southeast. In early 1994 GSC established a division in San Antonio to take advantage of new markets arising from NAFTA.

GUARDIAN INDUSTRIES CORP. — RANK: 231

43043 W. Nine Mile Rd.
Northville, MI 48167
Phone: 810-347-0100
Fax: 810-349-5995

1992 Est. Sales: $1,200 million
FYE: December
Employees: 1,000

Key Personnel
Pres & CEO: William Davidson
EVP Fin: Jeffrey A. Knight
EVP: Ralph J. Gerson
Pres, Auto Products Group: Jack W. Sights
Gen Counsel: Robert Gorlin
Dir Personnel: Kenneth Battjes

Major Products
Automobile windshields
Commercial window glass
Fiberglass insulation
Float glass

Key Competitors
AFG Industries
American Premier Underwriters
Apogee Enterprises
Asahi Glass
Corning
Pilkington
PPG
St.-Gobain

Industry
Glass products

Overview
Guardian Industries Corp. was founded in 1932 by the uncle of current president and CEO William Davidson, who in turn took the company private in 1985. Guardian Industries is one of the world's largest glassmakers. Davidson, who also owns the Detroit Pistons basketball team, has a reputation for playing rough, hiring top people from rivals. Davidson has also heavily lobbied Washington to push for more open markets in Asia. Guardian produces only big volume items, which allows it to keep its prices at the industry's bottom end.

THE GUARDIAN LIFE INSURANCE COMPANY OF AMERICA — RANK: 22

201 Park Ave. South
New York, NY 10003
Phone: 212-598-8000
Fax: 212-598-8813

1993 Sales: $7,069 million
FYE: December
Employees: 7,502

Key Personnel
Chm & CEO: Arthur V. Ferrara
Pres: Joseph D. Sargent
EVP & CFO: Peter L. Hutchings
SVP & Chief Investment Officer: Frank J. Jones
SVP & Gen Counsel: Edward K. Kane
VP HR: Douglas C. Kramer

Selected Services
Asset management
Group & individual disability
Group & individual life insurance
Group & individual medical
Variable annuities

Key Competitors
Aetna
CIGNA
Equitable
John Hancock
MassMutual
MetLife
New York Life
Prudential

Industry
Insurance - life

Overview
Guardian offers group and individual life, health, and disability insurance, as well as a variety of asset management funds. Founded in 1860 as Germania Life Insurance to tap the market for insurance among German-Americans, the company changed its name to Guardian during WWI in response to anti-German sentiment. Though it began as a mixed stock/mutual company, it went wholly mutual in 1944. Guardian pursues a conservative investment policy that has enabled it to pay a dividend every year since 1868.

◀ See page 62 for full-page profile.

GULF STATES TOYOTA, INC. — RANK: 169

7701 Wilshire Place Dr.
Houston, TX 77240
Phone: 713-744-3300
Fax: 713-744-3332

1993 Est. Sales: $1,534 million
FYE: July
Employees: 1,500

Key Personnel
Chm: Thomas H. Friedkin
Pres & CEO: Jerry Pyle
CFO: F. R. Mason
Controller: David Yellin
VP Mktg & Sales: John Bishop
VP Admin & HR: J. Brooks O'Hara

Selected Services
Automobile distribution
Automobile parts distribution
Buyer options installation
Computer marketing
Quality checks
Technician training

Key Competitors
Bill Heard
Frank Consolidated Enterprises
Holman Enterprises
JM Family Enterprises
Jordan Motors
Morse Operations
Prospect Motors
Santa Monica Ford

Industry
Wholesale distribution - automobiles

Overview
Founded in 1969, Gulf States Toyota (GST) performs quality checks on new Toyotas and installs buyer options, processing autos for distribution to 138 dealers in Texas, Oklahoma, Louisiana, Arkansas, and Mississippi. Owned by Thomas Friedkin, GST is one of only 2 of Toyota's 12 distributors serving the US that the Japanese automaker does not own. GST's new facility in Houston is expected to become the 3rd largest Toyota processing center in the US, increasing GST's yearly capacity from 86,000 vehicles to about 150,000.

GULFSTREAM AEROSPACE CORPORATION — RANK: 393

500 Gulfstream Rd.
Savannah, GA 31402
Phone: 912-965-3000
Fax: 912-965-3752

1992 Est. Sales: $790 million
FYE: December
Employees: 3,800

Key Personnel
Pres, CEO & COO: Fred Breidenback
CFO: Ms. Chris A. Davis
Principal: Steven B. Klinsky
SVP: W. W. Boisture , Jr.
VP & Gen Counsel: Donald L. Mayer
VP HR: Don Laidlaw

Airplane Models
Gulfstream I (1959)
Gulfstream II (1966)
Gulfstream III (1978)
Gulfstream IV (1987)
Gulfstream V (1992)

Key Competitors
Bombardier
Dassault-Breguet
Piper Aircraft
Raytheon
Textron

Industry
Aerospace - aircraft equipment

Overview
Gulfstream Aerospace, the world's leading manufacturer of long-distance business aircraft, was created in 1978 when aviation pioneer Allen Paulson purchased Grumman's corporate jet business for $52 million. Allen transformed this operation from mostly an aircraft assembly plant to a major high-tech jet aircraft manufacturer. When the aviation industry stagnated in the mid-1980s, Paulson sold Gulfstream to Chrysler. He repurchased it in 1990 with financing from Forstmann Little & Co., but later sold his interest. In a down market for corporate jets, Gulfstream is looking to foreign markets for a lift.

HALLMARK CARDS, INC. — RANK: 57

2501 McGee St.
Kansas City, MO 64108
Phone: 816-274-5111
Fax: 816-274-8513

1993 Sales: $3,400 million
FYE: December
Employees: 12,600

Key Personnel
Chm: Donald J. Hall
Pres & CEO: Irvine O. Hockaday, Jr.
EVP Corp Dev & Strategy & CFO: Henry F. Frigon
Pres, Hallmark Brand: Bob Firnhaber
Pres, Ambassador Cards: Lanny Julian
VP HR: Lowell J. Mayone

Major Brands
Ambassador (cards)
Crayola (crayons)
Hallmark (cards, gift wrap, mugs)
Liquitex (art supplies)
Magic Marker (markers)
Shoebox Greetings
Springbok (jigsaw puzzles)
Touch-Screen Greetings

Key Competitors
American Greetings
Artistic Greetings
Artistic Impressions
Deluxe
Gibson Greetings
Pearson
United Nations
Walt Disney

Industry
Greeting cards & related materials

Overview
The world's largest greeting card company, Hallmark started in 1910 with founder Joyce C. Hall's bedroom shoebox full of postcards. The company now offers 20,700 cards and commands a 42% US market share. It prints cards under several labels and also produces "Hallmark Hall of Fame." Hall's family owns 67% of the stock and Hallmark's employees own the rest. In 1994 Hallmark took a step toward the expansion of its in-house production department when it said it would buy RHI Entertainment, a TV movie and miniseries maker, for $365 million.

◀ See page 63 for full-page profile.

HARBOUR GROUP LTD. RANK: 478

7701 Forsyth Blvd.
St. Louis, MO 63105
Phone: 314-727-5550
Fax: 314-727-0941

1992 Sales: $590 million
FYE: December
Employees: 5,000

Key Personnel
Chm: Sam Fox
VC: William A. Schmalz
VC: Donald E. Nickelson
EVP Acquisitions: Samuel A. Hamacher
Pres & COO: James C. Janning
SVP Corp Dev: Peter S. Finley

Major Products
Air filtration systems
Compressed air dryers & filters
Cutting tools
Durable medical products
Machine tools & dies
Sealing components
Stamping equipment

Key Competitors
Abrasive Industries
Acme-Cleveland
Brown & Sharpe
Cincinnati Milacron
Detroit Center Tool
Giddings & Lewis
L. S. Starret

Industry
Diversified operations

Overview
Harbour Group is a congolmerate that acquires manufacturing companies through LBOs. Since its founding in 1976, Harbour Group has acquired more than 39 companies in 11 lines of business. Principal shareholder Sam Fox oversees the group's strategy of acquiring small manufacturers in slow-growth industries and boosting sales and profitability. Taking a hands-on approach, Harbour Group assists its portfolio companies in several areas, including corporate strategy and finances.

HARDWARE WHOLESALERS, INC. RANK: 160

6502 Nelson Rd.
Fort Wayne, IN 46803
Phone: 219-748-5300
Fax: 219-493-1245

1993 Est. Sales: $1,600 million
FYE: June
Employees: 100

Key Personnel
Pres & CEO: Michael J. McClelland
VP Fin: John C. Snider
VP Mktg Dev: David W. Dietz
VP Distribution: George Mattes
VP Ops: Douglas Dayton
HR Mgr: Dan Federspiel

Selected Services
Dataphone (warehouse info)
Do-it Center (retail display concept)
Do-it Center 2000
Do-it Express
New Resident Mailing Program
Power Program (design concept)
Private label products
VITAL video training program

Key Competitors
84 Lumber
Ace Hardware
Cotter & Co.
D.I.Y. Home Warehouse
Home Depot
Kmart
Lowe's
SERVISTAR

Industry
Building products - retail & wholesale

Overview
Hardware Wholesalers, Inc. (HWI) is a cooperative of hardware and building materials retailers. Founded in 1944, HWI operates 7 warehouses from which members buy a percentage of their retail products (a minimum of 80% of hardware and 65% of commodities) and offers store concepts to unify presentation among stores. The newest concept, Do-it Express, positions smaller stores to compete with chains and with larger Do-it Centers. HWI pays member rebates, never borrows or merges to expand, and channels ad dollars to retailers instead of advertising nationally.

HARTZ GROUP INC. RANK: 326

667 Madison Ave.
New York, NY 10021
Phone: 212-308-3336
Fax: 212-644-5987

1992 Est. Sales: $911 million
FYE: December
Employees: 4,000

Key Personnel
Chm & Pres: Leonard N. Stern
VP, Sec & Treas: Joseph A. Bardwil
VP & Gen Counsel: Arthur Andersen
VP: Richard Stern
VP & CFO: Curtis B. Schwartz
Dir HR: Charlotte Camino

Principal Subsidiaries
Cooper Square Advertising
Hartz Mountain (pet food, supplies)
Hartz Mountain Development Corp.
Village Voice (weekly newspaper)

Key Competitors
Grand Metropolitan
Heinz
Helmsley
Lefrak Organization
Mars
Quaker Oats
Ralston Purina Group
Trump

Industry
Diversified operations

Overview
Billionaire Leonard Stern's Hartz Group has interests in 3 areas: real estate (more than 200 buildings in New Jersey and New York), pet products (Hartz Mountain pet food and pet products), and publishing (New York's *Village Voice*). Stern's father, Max, started Hartz Mountain in 1926, selling birds, cages, and feed shortly after immigrating to the US from Germany with 2,100 canaries. Leonard Stern branched into real estate in 1962 and in 1985 bought the *Voice*. In 1994 Hartz sold its Harmon Publishing Co. (local real estate and automotive advertising periodicals) to British publisher United Newspapers PLC for $100 million.

HARVARD COMMUNITY HEALTH PLAN, INC. RANK: 285

10 Brookline Place West
Brookline, MA 02146
Phone: 617-731-8210
Fax: 617-730-4695

1993 Sales: $1,023 million
FYE: September
Employees: 6,489

Key Personnel
Chm: Alan R. Morse, Jr.
Pres & CEO: Manuel M. Ferris
SVP, Gen Counsel & Clerk: William F. Frado, Jr.
VP, CFO & Treas: Harold E. Putnam, Jr.
VP Mktg: William A. Schlag
VP HR: Larry Gibson

Selected Health Centers
Boston, MA
Cambridge, MA
Medford, MA
Peabody, MA
Providence, RI
Quincy, MA
Somerville, MA
Warwick, RI

Key Competitors
Blue Cross
Constitution Healthcare Inc.
Flagship Health Systems
New England Inc.
Prudential
Tufts Associated Health
U.S. Healthcare

Industry
Health maintenance organization

Overview
Founded in 1969 by the dean of Harvard Medical School and a group of colleagues, Harvard Community Health Plan (HCHP) is a nonprofit HMO. HCHP is the biggest HMO in New England and the 7th largest in the US, serving 565,000 members. HCHP operates more than 60 health care facilities in Massachusetts, Rhode Island, and New Hampshire. The company focuses on primary and specialty care; hospital care is offered through affiliated hospitals and in-house surgical specialty programs. Following the trend toward consolidation in the health care industry, HCHP began merger talks in 1994 with Pilgrim Health Care.

HARVARD UNIVERSITY

RANK: 203

1350 Massachusetts Ave.
Cambridge, MA 02138
Phone: 617-495-1000
Fax: 617-495-0754

1993 Sales: $1,306 million
FYE: June
Employees: 2,065

Key Personnel
Pres: Neil L. Rudenstine
VP Alumni Affairs & Dev: Fred L. Glimp
VP Fin: Robert H. Scott
VP & Gen Counsel: Margaret Marshall
Treas: D. Ronald Daniel
Dir HR: Diane Bemus Patrick

◀ See page 64 for full-page profile.

Schools & Colleges
Divinity School
Graduate School of Arts & Sciences
Graduate School of Business Administration
Harvard College
John F. Kennedy School of Government
Law School
Medical School
Radcliffe College

Industry
Schools

Overview
The oldest institution of higher education in the US, Harvard comprises a coeducational undergraduate school and 10 graduate schools. Founded in 1636, the university has grown to become one of the world's most competitive, boasting as graduates 6 US presidents and a host of Nobel laureates and Pulitzer Prize winners. Even though Harvard's $5.3 billion endowment is the US's largest, the university recently announced a 5-year fund-raising drive to raise $2.1 billion for the endowment.

HARVEST STATES COOPERATIVES

RANK: 56

1667 N. Snelling Ave.
St. Paul, MN 55164
Phone: 612-646-9433
Fax: 612-641-6579

1993 Sales: $3,482 million
FYE: May
Employees: 2,500

Key Personnel
Chm: Steven Burnet
Pres & CEO: Allen D. Hanson
Group VP Fin: T. F. Baker
SVP & Exec Counsel: Harvey S. Kaner
SVP Corp Planning: Patrick Kluempke
SVP Corp Admin: Allen J. Anderson

Business Lines
Agri Service Centers (storage)
Amber Milling (durum milling)
Country Hedging, Inc. (marketing)
Fin-Ag (credit)
Harvest Data (accounting)
Terminal Agency (insurance)

Key Competitors
Associated Milk Producers
Campbell Soup
Cargill
ConAgra
Continental Grain
General Mills
W. R. Grace
Koch

Industry
Agricultural operations

Overview
Harvest States is a regional grain marketing, farm supply, and food processing co-op that represents 150,000 farmers in the upper Midwest and the Pacific Northwest. Created from the merger of Grain Terminal Association and North Pacific Grain Growers in 1983, it is one of the US's largest farmer-owned grain co-ops and one with access to the Pacific, Great Lakes, and Gulf of Mexico. The co-op is expanding its food processing operations, which include Holsum Foods, Gregg's, Albert's Foods, Private Brands, Honeymead, and Great American Foods.

HAWORTH, INC.

RANK: 382

One Haworth Ctr.
Holland, MI 49423
Phone: 616-393-3000
Fax: 616-393-1570

1993 Est. Sales: $800 million
FYE: December
Employees: 7,000

Key Personnel
Founding Chm: Gerrard W. Haworth
Chm & CEO: Richard G. Haworth
COO & Pres: Gerald B. Johanneson
VP Fin & Admin: James J. Lehmann
VP Mktg: John C. Berrett
VP HR: Randy Evans

Principal Subsidiaries
Castelli (Italy)
Comforto (Germany)
Cortal-Seldex (Portugal)
Globe Business Furniture (US)
Haworth U.K.
Kinetics (Canada)
Mobilier International (France)
Ordo (France)

Key Competitors
American Seating
Ameriwood
Herman Miller
Hon Industries
Irwin Seating
Masco
Steelcase
Westinghouse

Industry
Furniture - office

Overview
In 1948 teacher Gerrard Haworth started in his garage what would become one of the world's largest office furniture companies. His ambitious son Richard patented in 1975 a movable office panel that was prewired with electrical cable, allowing companies to easily assemble work cubicles. Sales soared, leading Haworth down a path of growth that has included numerous acquisitions of both US and foreign furniture makers. These acquisitions allowed the company to enter the small office and home office markets in the early 1990s as commercial office construction slowed and a glut of used furniture came on the market.

HEALTH INSURANCE PLAN OF GREATER NY

RANK: 162

7 W. 34th St.
New York, NY 10001
Phone: 212-630-5000
Fax: 212-630-8747

1993 Sales: $1,583 million
FYE: December
Employees: 1,500

Key Personnel
Chm: Randi Weingarten
Pres & CEO: Anthony L. Watson
COO: Victor L. Ronding
EVP & CFO: Bernard J. Neeck
SVP, Gen Counsel & Sec: Maxine Fass
VP HR: Fred Blickman

Selected Services
HMO planning
Laboratory services
Medical care
Pharmacies

Key Competitors
Aetna
Blue Cross
Equitable
Healthsource
MetLife
New York Life
Prudential
Value Health

Industry
Health maintenance organization

Overview
Health Insurance Plan of Greater NY (HIP) is a not-for-profit HMO founded in 1944 to provide health care services for city workers. Today, HIP and its New Jersey-based affiliate HIP/Rutgers Health Plan serve almost 1.3 million members in the New York City metropolitan area through 70 medical facilities. Another affiliate, HIP Health Plan of Florida, founded in 1986, has an additional 35,000 members. City, state, and federal workers make up 37% of HIP's enrollment, with commercial sector employees accounting for an additional 42%. To cope with changes to the health care industry, HIP is investing in new technology, slashing costs, and aggressively expanding its service area.

THE HEARST CORPORATION

RANK: 96

959 Eighth Ave.
New York, NY 10019
Phone: 212-649-2000
Fax: 212-765-3528

1993 Sales: $2,300 million
FYE: December
Employees: 15,000

Key Personnel
Chm: Randolph A. Hearst
Pres & CEO: Frank A. Bennack, Jr.
VP & Gen Counsel: Jonathan E. Thackeray
EVP & COO: Gilbert C. Maurer
SVP, CFO & Chief Legal Officer: Victor F. Ganzi
Dir HR: Kenneth A. Feldman

◀ **See page 65 for full-page profile.**

Selected Services
Arts & Entertainment Network
Avon Books
Cable, TV
ESPN
Magazines
Newspapers
Radio stations
Ranching

Key Competitors
Advance Publications
CBS
Cox
Gannett
Heritage Media
New York Times
Time Warner
Washington Post

Industry
Publishing - magazines, newspapers, cable TV

Overview
Started in 1887, Hearst is 100% owned by the William Randolph Hearst Trust, named after the company's famous founder. It owns 17 newspapers, major US and UK magazines (such as Redbook and Good Housekeeping) published in 61 editions worldwide, and news distributors. Hearst's entertainment and syndication properties range from joint ventures in cable TV to a newspaper syndicate (King Features, the world's largest). The founder's son, a Pulitzer Prize winner and the company chairman, died in 1993.

HEICO ACQUISITIONS INC.

RANK: N/R

70 W. Madison St., Ste. 5600
Chicago, IL 60602
Phone: 312-419-8220
Fax: 312-419-9417

1993 Sales: $0 million
Employees: 5

Key Personnel
Chm: Michael E. Heisley

Selected Investments
Aelco Foundries
Davies Molding
Davis Wire
Newbury Industries
Nutri/System
Pettibone
Robertson Ceco
Tom's Foods

Industry
Financial - investors

Overview
Founded in 1979, Heico Acquisitions is an investment group controlled by Michael Heisley. Heico specializes in acquiring distressed low-tech manufacturing companies and turning them around by downsizing and selling off unprofitable subsidiaries. To direct the restructuring, Heisley usually takes a prominent role on the acquired company's board of directors or in management. The group controls 27 service and manufacturing companies, producing everything from snack foods to plastic injection molding machines to weight loss plans. Heico also holds a minority interest in Robertson Ceco, one of the largest metal building companies in the US.

G. HEILEMAN BREWING COMPANY, INC.

RANK: 385

9399 W. Higgins Rd., Ste. 700
Rosemont, IL 60018
Phone: 708-292-2100
Fax: 708-292-6870

1993 Sales: $800 million
FYE: December
Employees: 2,150

Key Personnel
Chm: William Turner
Pres & CEO: Richard F. Gaccione
EVP Fin: Daniel J. Schmid, Jr.
SVP Fin Sales: Thomas Koehler
VP & Corp Counsel: Randy Smith

Major Brands
Black Label
Colt-45
Henry Weinhard
Lone Star
Mickey's Malt
Old Style
Ranier
Special Export

Key Competitors
Adolph Coors
Anheuser-Busch
Genesee
Guinness
Heineken
Philip Morris
S&P Co.
Stroh

Industry
Beverages - alcoholic

Overview
Founded in 1853 as City Brewery, G. Heileman is the country's largest regional brewer as well as the 5th largest brewer in the US, holding a 5% market share. The company, which grew by acquiring other breweries, has over 30 different brand names. Once the US's fastest-growing brewer of premium beer, near beer, malt liquor, and low-calorie beer, it declared bankruptcy in 1991, burdened with debt from Australia-based Bond Corp.'s LBO in 1987. In 1993 niche-marketing specialists Hicks, Muse, Tate & Furst bought the company; they intend to revive sales by expanding into new markets and buying competitors while maintaining a regional focus.

HELMSLEY ENTERPRISES, INC.

RANK: 227

60 E. 42nd St.
New York, NY 10165
Phone: 212-687-6400
Fax: 212-687-6437

1992 Est. Sales: $1,200 million
FYE: December
Employees: 13,000

Key Personnel
Chm, Pres & CEO: Harry B. Helmsley
SVP: Joseph Licari
SVP: William La Blina
Treas, Sec & CFO: Martin S. Stone
Controller: Josephine Keenan
Mgr HR: Jennie Voscina

◀ **See page 66 for full-page profile.**

Principal Subsidiaries
Brown, Harris, Stevens, Inc.
Helmsley Hotels Inc.
Helmsley-Noyes Co., Inc.
Helmsley-Spear Conversion Sales
Helmsley-Spear Inc.
John J. Reynolds, Inc.
National Realty Corp.
Owners Maintenance Corp.

Key Competitors
Accor
Edward J. DeBartolo
Hilton
Hyatt
Lefrak Organization
Loews
Trammell Crow
Trump

Industry
Real estate operations

Overview
Helmsley Enterprises is a holding company owned by Harry and Leona Helmsley. The company manages the Helmsleys' real estate empire, which had its beginnings in the properties Harry began buying in 1929. Although the company has struggled since the Helmsleys' well-publicized brushes with the law, it still controls over 100 million square feet of commercial space, more than 100,000 apartments, and 13,000 hotel rooms. Its subsidiaries manage a number of properties, including the Empire State Building.

HENDRICK AUTOMOTIVE GROUP

RANK: 159

6000 Monroe Rd., Ste. 100
Charlotte, NC 28218
Phone: 704-568-5550
Fax: 704-535-5592

1993 Est. Sales: $1,600 million
FYE: December
Employees: 3,500

Key Personnel
Pres & CEO: J. R. Hendrick III
EVP & CFO: James F. Huzl
EVP: William Musgrave
Dir HR: Suzanne Wrenn

Business Lines
Auto dealerships
Auto leasing
Motorsports teams
Real estate
Sportswear
Truck dealerships

Key Competitors
Bill Heard
Frank Consolidated Enterprises
Holman Enterprises
Island Lincoln-Mercury
JM Family Enterprises
Morse Operations
Rosenthal Automotive
Royal Automotive Group

Industry
Retail - new & used cars

Overview
Joseph R. Hendrick, sole owner of Hendrick Automotive Group, rarely slows down. The 44-year-old North Carolina businessman runs one of the nation's largest auto dealer chains, which has almost 50 car and truck dealerships in 11 states, ranging from the Carolinas to northern California. Hendrick also owns a sportswear company and fields a NASCAR circuit team. In 1994 some of Hendrick's auto dealerships were caught up in a Justice Department investigation into bribes and kickbacks involving the American Honda Motor Company.

HENSEL PHELPS CONSTRUCTION CO.

RANK: 450

420 Sixth Ave.
Greeley, CO 80631
Phone: 303-352-6565
Fax: 303-352-9311

1993 Sales: $646 million
FYE: May
Employees: 1,688

Key Personnel
Pres & CEO: Jerry L. Morgensen
VP Fin: Stephen J. Carrico
VP: Victor McNallie
VP: Wayne S. Lindholm
VP: Ron Norby
VP & Gen Counsel: Eric L. Wilson

Major Projects
Colorado Convention Center
Embassy Suites Hotel (GA)
K Street Tower (CA)
Kodak Manufacturing Facility (CO)
Poudre Valley Hospital (CO)
Sea World (TX)
Space Shuttle Launch Site (CA)
Vista Dentention Facility (CA)

Key Competitors
Bechtel
Black & Veatch
CRSS
Fluor
McDermott
M. A. Mortensen
Parsons
H. B. Zachry

Industry
Construction - heavy

Overview
In 1989 Joseph Phelps gave away the company his father had founded in 1937. After watching employee stock options erode his holdings from 90% to 15%, Phelps turned over the general contracting interests to his employees, forming a new corporation from the remaining subsidiaries. One of the nation's largest and most diverse general contractors, Hensel Phelps has built everything from treatment plants and top-secret government facilities to resort hotels and health care facilities. Rather than rely exclusively on subcontractors, the company hires its own craftspeople.

HICKS, MUSE, TATE & FURST INC.

RANK: N/R

200 Crescent Ct., Ste. 1600
Dallas, TX 75201
Phone: 214-740-7300
Fax: 214-740-7313

FYE: December
Employees: 23

Key Personnel
Chm: Thomas O. Hicks
Managing Dir/Principal: Jack Furst
Managing Dir: John Muse
Managing Dir: Charles W. Tate
VP: Paul Stone

Selected Investments
Berg Electronics (connectors)
Dr. Pepper/Seven-Up Cos., Inc.
Hat Brands Inc. (headwear)
Healthco (dental products)
G. Heileman Brewing Co.
Home Interiors & Gifts (direct sales)
Life Partners Group, Inc. (insurance)
The Morningstar Group, Inc.
Spectradyne, Inc. (cable TV)
Trident NGL Inc. (natural gas)

Industry
Financial - investors

Overview
An investment banking and holding company that has made over 20 leveraged buyouts worth more than $3 billion, the company was founded as Hicks, Muse & Co. in 1989 (it took its present name in 1994) by Thomas Hicks and John Muse. Hicks was no stranger to LBOs: since 1977 he and then-partner Bobby Haas had turned heads with deals for companies like Dr Pepper and Seven-Up. At his new firm Hicks expanded operations but kept the same strategy of pursuing companies with strong niche markets, stable cash flow, and a willingness to be acquired. In 1994 the company acquired G. Heileman Brewing Co. and announced a $1 billion deal for Dallas-based Home Interiors & Gifts.

HOLIDAY COS.

RANK: 295

4567 W. 80th St.
Bloomington, MN 55437
Phone: 612-830-8700
Fax: 612-830-8864

1993 Est. Sales: $1,000 million
FYE: December
Employees: 5,000

Key Personnel
Chm: Ronald Erickson
Pres: Donovan Erickson
VP: Gerald Erickson
VP Fin: Arnold D. Mickelson
VP Retail Stores: Lyle Larson
Dir HR: Bob Nye

Operating Units
Convenience stores
- Holiday Express

Food distribution
- Fairway Foods

Grocery stores
- Food-4-Less
- Holiday Foods
- Holiday Plus

Key Competitors
American Stores
Circle K
Kroger
QuikTrip
Southland
Wal-Mart

Industry
Retail - convenience stores

Overview
Founded in 1928 as a general store in Centuria, Wisconsin, by 7 Erickson brothers, this secretive, family-held company (now owned and operated by the brothers' heirs) operates grocery and convenience stores primarily in Minnesota, Iowa, Wisconsin, and North and South Dakota. Holiday generates the lion's share of its sales from about 250 Holiday Express convenience stores. It also operates about 50 Holiday Foods, Holiday Plus, and Food-4-Less (of which it is a franchisee) supermarkets. In addition, the company runs its own wholesaling arm to supply its stores.

HOLMAN ENTERPRISES INC.

RANK: 282

7411 Maple Ave.
Pennsauken, NJ 08109
Phone: 609-663-5200
Fax: 609-665-1419

1992 Sales: $1,028 million
FYE: December
Employees: 2,300

Key Personnel
Chm: Joseph S. Holman
Treas: Ken T. Coppola
VP: Mindy Holman
VP: H. H. Herrington
VP: Larry E. Parent
Mgr HR: Frank J. Lepore

Business Lines
Automobile sales
Automotive parts remanufacturing
Fleet leasing
Passenger car rental
Truck rental

Key Competitors
Hendrick Automotive
JM Family Enterprises
Mid-Atlantic Cars
Morse Operations
Penske
Potamkin Manhattan
Ryder
U-Haul

Industry
Retail - new & used cars

Overview
Founded in 1924, Holman Enterprises is one of the largest auto dealers in the US, with Ford dealerships in New Jersey and Florida. The company, which is owned by the Holman family and headed by Joseph P. Holman, wholly owns each of its dealerships. A key focus of the auto dealer division is providing customers with increased service hours and maintaining a strong management training program. The company entered fleet leasing by supplying trucks for RCA TV repair technicians and expanded into passenger car and truck rentals. Its ARI subsidiary is one of the largest independently owned vehicle lease management groups in the world.

HOLY CROSS HEALTH SYSTEM

RANK: 234

3606 E. Jefferson Blvd.
South Bend, IN 46615
Phone: 219-233-8558
Fax: 219-233-8891

1993 Sales: $1,192 million
FYE: December
Employees: 18,360

Key Personnel
Chm: Edward Osborn
Pres: Sister P. Vandenberg
EVP Ops: Coyla Anderson
SVP Fin & CFO: Stephen A. Felsted
VP & Gen Counsel: Carolyn Pfotenhauer
VP HR: Dave Dickerson

Business Lines
Acute-care hospitals
Ambulatory & surgery centers
Clinics
Extended care facilities
Preferred provider organizations
Residential centers

Key Competitors
American Medical Holdings
Beverly Enterprises
Columbia/HCA
Hillhaven
Manor Care
Mercy Health Services
UniHealth America
Wheaton Franciscan Services

Industry
Hospitals

Overview
Holy Cross Health System (HCHS), with over 3,300 beds, is the nation's 21st largest health care system and 9th largest Catholic health care system. A nonprofit organization, it operates acute-care hospitals, extended care facilities, and several other health care operations in several states, from Maryland to California. HCHS is supervised by The Sisters of the Holy Cross, a congregation of Roman Catholic nuns, whose sisters first arrived in the US in 1843 from Le Mans, France. The sisters' mission is to meet the educational, health care, and social needs of people in their communities, especially the needs of children.

HOME INTERIORS & GIFTS, INC.

RANK: 355

4550 Spring Valley Dr.
Dallas, TX 75244-3705
Phone: 214-386-1000
Fax: 214-233-8825

1993 Sales: $850 million
FYE: December
Employees: 580

Key Personnel
CEO: Donald J. Carter
Fin Mgr: Leonard Shipley
SVP Sales: Barbara Hammond
VP Ops : Ronald Carter
VP Mktg: Joey Carter
HR Mgr: Bob McComas

Major Products
Artificial flowers
Baskets
Ceramics
Light fixtures
Mirrors
Picture frames
Wood home accessories

Key Competitors
50-Off Stores
Amway
Bombay Company
Hallmark
Montgomery Ward
J. C. Penney
Sears
Tuesday Morning

Industry
Retail - direct

Overview
Home Interiors and Gifts markets home decorative accessories through 42,000 independent contractors who stage home parties to sell the items throughout the US. The company was founded by Mary Crowley (Mary Kay Ash's sister-in-law) in 1957. Donald Carter, Crowley's son and owner of the Dallas Mavericks, recently sold a 51% stake in the company to buyout specialists Hicks, Muse, Tate & Furst. As part of the agreement, Carter's 3 children will remain in executive positions and the Carter family will retain a 49% ownership. To repay the debt, company officials plan to expand to foreign markets and take the company public in 2 to 3 years.

HOMELAND HOLDING CORPORATION

RANK: 374

400 NE 36th St.
Oklahoma City, OK 73105
Phone: 405-557-5500
Fax: 405-557-5600

1993 Sales: $811 million
FYE: December
Employees: 6,000

Key Personnel
Pres & CEO: Max E. Raydon
SVP: Jack Lotker
CFO, Sec & Treas: Mark Sellers
VP Mktg: Steve Slade
Dir Grocery Mktg: Kent Carlston
Dir HR: Prentess Alletag

Selected Departments
Bakery
Delicatessen & foods-to-go
Floral shop
Pharmacy
Post office
Salad bar
Seafood & meats
Video

Key Competitors
Albertson's
Food Lion
Furr's Supermarkets
Minyard Food Stores
QuikTrip
Wal-Mart
Winn-Dixie

Industry
Retail - supermarkets

Overview
Under the umbrella of Homeland Holding, Homeland Stores grew out of Safeway's Oklahoma division, which was acquired in 1987 in a $165 million management-led LBO and financed by New York investment firm Clayton & Dubilier. The new owners revamped the stores, and employees helped select the new name. With 115 stores operating in Oklahoma, southern Kansas, and the Texas Panhandle, the chain was initially successful. But higher costs, a lingering recession, and increased competition from nonunion, low-price chains may cause the Oklahoma-based grocery to take a business partner.

HOWARD HUGHES MEDICAL INSTITUTE

RANK: 247

4000 Jones Bridge Rd.
Chevy Chase, MD 20815
Phone: 301-215-8500
Fax: 301-215-8937

1993 Sales: $1,106 million
FYE: August
Employees: 2,145

Key Personnel
Chm: Irving S. Shapiro
Pres: Purnell W. Choppin
Chief Scientific Officer: W. Maxwell Cowan
CFO: Robert C. White
VP Admin & Gen Counsel: Joan S. Leonard
Dir HR: Donald C. Powell

Primary Research
Cell biology
Genetics
Immunology
Neuroscience
Structural biology

Industry
Foundation

Overview
The Howard Hughes Medical Institute is the largest private medical research sponsor in the US. Unlike most such agencies, including the National Institutes of Health, Hughes Medical directly employs the researchers it funds, along with assistants, and provides needed equipment or facilities. The institute also supports science education through a $50 million grant program. Founded in 1953 by Howard Hughes, Jr., as a tax shelter, the institute was tied up in estate litigation for 8 years following his death in 1976. It was the major beneficiary of the sale of Hughes Aircraft to GM.

THE HUB GROUP, INC.

RANK: 458

377 E. Butterfield, Ste. 700
Lombard, IL 60148
Phone: 708-964-5800
Fax: 708-964-6475

1993 Sales: $640 million
FYE: December
Employees: 600

Key Personnel
Chm : Phillip C. Yeager
Pres: Thomas L. Hardin
EVP Nat'l Sales: John Donnell
EVP Int'l Sales: Jerry Cople
CFO: William Crowder
Controller & Dir HR: James Blank

Selected Services
Distribution terminals
Highway trucking
Intermodal transportation
Railway transport
Sea freight services

Key Competitors
Alliance Shippers
American President
Consolidated Freightways
J. B. Hunt
Manufacturers Consolidation
Mark Industries
Rail-Van, Inc.
C. H. Robinson

Industry
Transportation - services

Overview
Started in 1971 with the intent of creating a small family business, Phillip Yeager's Hub Group is moving right along. This 3rd-party intermodal freight transporation company has seen sales recently expand from $350 million in 1990 to $640 million in 1993, making it the #1 intermodal marketing company. To keep this locomotive rolling, the company launched Hub Group International, looking to apply its domestic intermodal skills to sea freight. Hub operates a network of 29 terminals.

HUBER, HUNT & NICHOLS INC.

RANK: 452

2450 S.Tibbs Ave.
Indianapolis, IN 46241
Phone: 317-241-6301
Fax: 317-243-3461

1993 Sales: $645 million
FYE: December
Employees: 600

Key Personnel
Chm: Robert G. Hunt
CEO: Robert C. Hunt
CFO: Mack V. Furlow, Jr.
EVP: Jerry Kerr
EVP: Mike Kerr
EVP: Bill Mullin

Major Products
Convention centers
Corporate buildings
Educational facilities
Management services
Public buildings
Roads
Sports arenas

Key Competitors
Barton-Malow Enterprises
Bechtel
Centex
Fluor
HCB Contractors
M. A. Mortenson
Turner Industries
H. B. Zachry

Industry
Construction - heavy

Overview
Huber, Hunt & Nichols (HHN) is the world's leading builder of sports arenas and among the top 10 contractors in domestic general building contracts. Projects include the Alamo Dome in San Antonio, the Super Dome in New Orleans, Riverfront Stadium in Cincinnati, and the new central library in San Francisco. Huber Hunt was founded in 1944 by the grandfather of Robert G. Hunt, whose Hunt Corporation now owns HHN. Under his leadership the company has expanded nationally.

J. M. HUBER CORPORATION

RANK: 254

333 Thornall St.
Edison, NJ 08818
Phone: 908-549-8600
Fax: 908-549-2239

1992 Sales: $1,100 million
FYE: December
Employees: 3,000

Key Personnel
Chm, Pres & CEO: Peter T. Francis
CFO: W. J. Ryan
Treas: Fred S. Gersten
Sec & Gen Counsel: John G. Webb
VP HR: Joseph P. Matturro

Major Products
Calcium carbonate
Chemicals
Clay
Engineered carbons
Flow control equipment
Oil & gas
Polymer services
Solem

Key Competitors
ASARCO
Baker Hughes
Cabot Corp.
Dow Chemical
Monsanto
Nord Resources
St-Gobain
Vulcan Materials

Industry
Diversified operations

Overview
Founded in 1883, family-owned J. M. Huber produces a wide range of products used primarily by other manufacturers. The company's operations include kaolin (china) clay and limestone mining, carbon black production, and equipment manufacturing for the petroleum and pipeline industries. Huber's customers include oil refineries and pipeline companies, printers, and producers of paint, plastics, ceramics, animal feed, and insecticides.

HUGHES MARKETS, INC.

RANK: 258

14005 Live Oak Ave.
Irwindale, CA 91706
Phone: 818-856-6580
Fax: 818-856-6020

1993 Sales: $1,087 million
FYE: March
Employees: 5,100

Key Personnel
Chm: Roger K. Hughes
Pres & CEO: Fred B. McLaren
VP Fin: Allan P. Brennan
SVP Sales & Mktg: Harland Polk
SVP Ops: Michael L. Solem
Dir HR: David McMahon

Selected Departments
Bakery
Delicatessen
Fresh seafood
General merchandise
Liquor
Meat
Produce
Video

Key Competitors
Albertson's
American Stores
Certified Grocers
Edward J. DeBartolo
Smith's Food & Drug
Stater Bros.
Vons
Yucaipa

Industry
Retail - supermarkets

Overview
Founded in 1952, Hughes operates 52 grocery stores in the Los Angeles area. Now in its 2nd generation of family leadership, the company considers its stores family markets and has maintained a conventional approach to grocery retailing by managing relatively small stores (compared with superstores and warehouse clubs) that focus on quality, value, and service. Hughes, which has expanded through acquisition and new store development, finances growth with internally generated funds.

HUNT CONSOLIDATED INC.

RANK: 299

1445 Ross at Field
Dallas, TX 75202
Phone: 214-978-8000
Fax: 214-978-8888

1993 Est. Sales: $1,000 million
FYE: December
Employees: 2,600

Key Personnel
Chm & CEO: Ray L. Hunt
Pres: Gary T. Hurford
SVP Fin: Don F. Robillard
VP & Sec: John R. Scott
Gen Counsel: George Cunyus
Dir HR: Chuck Mills

Principal Subsidiaries
Bon Terre Partnership
Champion Property Co.
Hunt Financial Corp.
Hunt Oil Co.
Hunt Realty Services
Wilcox Realty Group
Woodbine Development Corp.
Yemen Hunt Oil Co.

Key Competitors
Amoco
Anschutz
Atlantic Richfield
Exxon
Koch
Petrofina
Phillips Petroleum
USX - Marathon

Industry
Oil & gas - US exploration & production

Overview
Hunt Consolidated is a holding company for the oil and real estate businesses of Ray Hunt, son of legendary Texas wildcatter H. L. Hunt. Hunt Oil, founded in 1934 (reportedly with H. L.'s poker winnings), is an independent oil and gas production and exploration company with interests throughout the South and the Rocky Mountain states as well as offshore operations in the Gulf of Mexico, the Mideast, and South America. Its high-risk, high-reward exploration strategy led to the discovery of a massive oil field in Yemen. Hunt's real estate operations are concentrated in Dallas and include commercial and residential development and 3rd-party property management.

HUNTSMAN CHEMICAL CORPORATION

RANK: 131

2000 Eagle Gate Tower
Salt Lake City, UT 84111
Phone: 801-532-5200
Fax: 801-536-1581

1993 Sales: $1,850 million
FYE: December
Employees: 5,000

Key Personnel
Chm & CEO: Jon Meade Huntsman
VC & CFO: Terry R. Parker
Pres & COO: Ronald A. Rasband
SVP: Randy Plant
VP & Treas: Lee S. Skidmore
VP HR: Winston H. Conners

◀ See page 67 for full-page profile.

Major Products
Expandable resins
Plastic compounds
Polyethylene & polypropylene films
Polypropylene
Polystyrene
Styrene monomer

Key Competitors
Akzo Nobel
American Cyanamid
Dow Chemical
DuPont
Formosa Plastics
Imperial Chemical
Rhône-Poulenc
Union Carbide

Industry
Chemicals - plastics

Overview
Hunstman Chemical is the largest US maker of polystyrene, a plastic used to make items ranging from coffee cups to appliances. The company is owned by Jon Huntsman, who has aggressively built a chemical empire by acquiring manufacturing facilities that other companies (e.g., Texaco and Monsanto) did not want. The company, which has operations in 15 countries, also manufactures styrene monomer (raw material used to make other plastics), expandable resins (for packaging and insulation), and polypropylene (for durable plastics).

HYATT CORPORATION

RANK: 85

200 W. Madison St.
Chicago, IL 60606
Phone: 312-750-1234
Fax: 312-750-8550

1993 Est. Sales: $2,500 million
FYE: January
Employees: 52,275

Key Personnel
Chm & CEO: Jay A. Pritzker
Pres: Thomas V. Pritzker
SVP & CFO: Ken Posner
SVP Sales & Mktg: Jim Evans
Gen Counsel: Michael Evanoff
SVP Planning & HR: Timothy Wolf

◀ See page 68 for full-page profile.

Operating Units
Classic Residence by Hyatt (retirement)
Grand Hyatt
Hyatt
Hyatt Hotels International
Hyatt Regency
Park Hyatt
Spectacor (arena management)

Key Competitors
Four Seasons
Helmsley
Hilton
ITT
Loews
Marriott International
Ritz-Carlton
Trump

Industry
Hotels & motels

Overview
Founded in 1957, Hyatt hotels are the best-known operations of Chicago's publicity-shy Pritzker clan, who own H Group Holding, the holding company of Hyatt Corporation. Known for superlative service, Hyatt introduced many amenities (free shampoo, restricted-access floors) that other chains have copied. Hyatt's sales have been falling for several years but should benefit from rising hotel occupancy rates. The company does not expand aggressively, opening only a few new hotels each year. In 1994 Hyatt began offering business travelers rooms equipped with fax machines and computer hookups.

HY-VEE FOOD STORES, INC.

RANK: 86

1801 Osceola Ave.
Chariton, IA 50049
Phone: 515-774-2121
Fax: 515-774-7211

1993 Sales: $2,500 million
FYE: September
Employees: 30,000

Key Personnel
Chm & CEO: Ronald D. Pearson
VP, CFO & Treas: Michael D. Wheeler
VP, Eastern Region: Charles R. Robertson
VP, Western Region: Charles M. Bell
Dir Communications: Ruth C. Mitchell
Mgr HR: Jerry Willis

Selected Departments
Apparel
Delicatessen
Food court
Greeting cards
Home-office supplies
Karaoke rental
Pharmacy
Video

Key Competitors
Affiliated Foods
Aldi
American Stores
Eagle Food
Fleming
Fred Meyer
Kroger
SUPERVALU

Industry
Retail - supermarkets

Overview
Hy-Vee Food Stores, founded in 1938, operates 220 Hy-Vee supermarkets and Save-U-More warehouse operations, 38 convenience stores (Handy Shops), and 20 drugstores (Drugtown) in Iowa, Illinois, Kansas, Michigan, Minnesota, Nebraska, and South Dakota. It is one of the first supermarket chains in the US to offer a store-affiliated national credit card (MasterCard). Hy-Vee, whose service area was overwhelmed by the 1993 midwestern floods, donated bottled water and acted as a middleman for distributing donated goods and merchandise to flood victims. Hy-Vee has recently expanded the line of merchandise it offers, adding home-supplies and apparel departments.

INDIANA UNIVERSITY

RANK: 179

212 Bryan Hall
Bloomington, IN 47405
Phone: 812-855-4004
Fax: 812-855-5678

1993 Sales: $1,460 million
FYE: June
Employees: 16,875

Key Personnel
Pres: Myles Brand
VP Planning & Fin: Judith G. Palmer
VP & Chancellor, IU Bloomington: K. R. Louis
Chancellor, IU Kokomo: Emita B. Hill
Chancellor, IU South Bend: H. Daniel Cohen
Chancellor, IU East: Charles Nelms

Schools & Colleges
Indiana University at Bloomington
Indiana University East (Richmond)
Indiana University at Kokomo
Indiana University Northwest (Gary)
Indiana University-Purdue at Fort Wayne
Indiana University-Purdue at Indianapolis
Indiana University at South Bend
Indiana University Southeast (New Albany)

Industry
Schools

Overview
Established in 1820, the Indiana University system has 8 public campuses. Its campuses at Fort Wayne and Indianapolis are operated jointly with Purdue University. Indiana University employs almost 5,000 faculty members and enrolls about 84,000 undergraduate students. The system's universities offer 313 baccalaureate, 207 master's, and 108 doctoral programs. Tuition in 1993 ranged from $2,068 per semester at the South Bend campus to $2,533 at Indiana University at Bloomington. The various campuses admit between 77% and 100% of student applicants.

INGRAM INDUSTRIES INC.

RANK: 26

One Belle Meade Place, 4400 Harding Rd.
Nashville, TN 37205
Phone: 615-298-8200
Fax: 615-298-8242

1993 Est. Sales: $6,163 million
FYE: December
Employees: 9,658

Key Personnel
Chm & CEO: E. Bronson Ingram
Pres: Linwood A. Lacy, Jr.
EVP & Chm Distribution Group: Philip M. Pfeffer
SVP: Roy E. Claverie
VP & Treas: Thomas H. Lunn
VP HR: W. Michael Head

◀ See page 69 for full-page profile.

Operating Units
Energy Group
Ingram Distribution Group
  Book Group
  Entertainment Group
  Microcomputer Group
Inland Marine Group
Insurance Group

Key Competitors
Advanced Marketing
Baker & Taylor
CSX
Handelman
Merisel
Pacific Pipeline
Software Spectrum
Wal-Mart

Industry
Wholesale - books and computer products

Overview
Ingram Industries was founded in 1946 and is owned by brothers Bronson and Fritz Ingram. Ingram Distribution Group is the world's #1 seller of general interest books (with nearly 200,000 titles), microcomputer products (hardware, software, and accessories), and videos (with 10% of the US market). Ingram Industries also operates the nation's #3 inland barge company (Ingram Barge), produces and installs petroleum drilling equipment (Ingram Cactus Co.), and sells auto insurance in Tennessee (Permanent General Companies).

INTERMOUNTAIN HEALTH CARE, INC.

RANK: 292

36 S. State St.
Salt Lake City, UT 84111
Phone: 801-442-3587
Fax: 801-442-3728

1993 Sales: $1,000 million
FYE: December
Employees: 18,000

Key Personnel
Pres & CEO: Scott S. Parker
SVP & CFO: William H. Nelson
SVP: Cecil O. Samuelson
SVP: Steven D. Kohlert
VP HR: Gary Hart
Gen Counsel: Douglass Hammer

Business Lines
Blood donor centers
Health insurance
Home health agencies
Hospitals
Pharmacies
Primary care & specialty clinics
Psychiatric hospitals
Women's centers

Key Competitors
Adventist Health
American Medical Holdings
Blue Cross
Columbia/HCA
Kaiser Foundation Health Plan
Prudential
Sierra Health Services
UniHealth America

Industry
Hospitals

Overview
Anchored by its 520-bed LDS (Latter-Day Saints) Hospital in Salt Lake City, Intermountain Health Care offers both urban and rural health care, operating 24 hospitals in Utah, Idaho, and Wyoming; 33 clinics; and other health care facilities. Intermountain also deals in health insurance for those who use IHC. The company was formed in 1975 as a nonprofit corporation to administer 15 hospitals sold by Mormon church leaders. By 1993 IHC hospitals ranked #35 nationally in number of beds (2,119).

INTERNATIONAL BROTHERHOOD OF TEAMSTERS

RANK: N/R

25 Louisiana Ave. NW
Washington, DC 20001
Phone: 202-624-6800
Fax: 202-624-6918

1993 Sales: $74 million
FYE: December
Employees: —

Key Personnel
Gen Pres: Ronald Carey
Gen Sec & Treas: Tom Sever
Gen Counsel: Richard Gilberg

◀ **See page 127 for full-page profile.**

Selected Trade Divisions
Airline
Building material & construction
Freight
Industrial
Laundry
Newspaper drivers
Public employees
Warehouse

Industry
Labor union

Overview
A merger in 1903 between 2 rival unions created the International Brotherhood of Teamsters, the US's largest and most diverse labor union. With about 1.4 million members, the Teamsters includes truckers, United Parcel Service workers, warehouse employees, cab drivers, airline employees, and factory workers. President Ronald Carey has sought to reform the union, historically plagued by corruption, by cutting expenses and perks. But Carey's reign has been tumultuous: members rejected a dues hike, and rivals allege he once had ties to "the mob."

INTERNATIONAL CONTROLS CORP.

RANK: 329

2016 N. Pitcher St.
Kalamazoo, MI 49007
Phone: 616-343-6121
Fax: 616-343-2244

1993 Sales: $909 million
FYE: December
Employees: 5,055

Key Personnel
Chm: Allan R. Tessler
VC: Wilmer J. Thomas , Jr.
VC & Sec: Martin L. Solomon
Pres & CEO: David R. Markin
EVP & COO: Jay H. Harris
Treas: Marlan R. Smith

Major Products & Services
Automotive stamping & assemblies
Property & casualty insurance
Taxicab service
Truck trailers
Workers' compensation insurance

Key Competitors
Dana
Distribution International Corp.
Dorsey Trailers
Magna International
A. O. Smith
Terex
Utility Trailer Manufacturing
Wabash National

Industry
Diversified operations

Overview
Founded in 1959, International Controls is a holding company for 2 key subsidiaries, Great Dane Trailers and Checker Motors. The company is owned by a partnership of top management headed by VC Martin Solomon. The expansion of intermodal shipping is fueling the growth of Great Dane, a leading US producer of over-the-road truck trailers and intermodal containers/chassis systems. Checker Motors makes automotive stampings and assemblies; General Motors accounts for 97% of sales. The last US producer of taxicabs, Checker controls 40% of the taxi medallions in Chicago and offers liability insurance for taxicabs.

INTERNATIONAL DATA GROUP

RANK: 306

One Exeter Plaza, 15th Fl.
Boston, MA 02116
Phone: 617-534-1200
Fax: 617-262-2300

1993 Sales: $980 million
FYE: October
Employees: 5,600

Key Personnel
Chm & CEO: Patrick J. McGovern
Pres: W. W. Boyd
EVP Fin: William P. Murphy
Dir Corp Communications: Mary Dolaher
Dir Info Sys: William Berghauer
Dir HR: Martha Stephens

Selected Publications
CD Review
Computer World
DOS for Dummies
Game Hits
InfoWorld
Macworld
PC World
Video Event

Key Competitors
CMP Publications
McGraw-Hill
Meckler
Reed Elsevier
Time Warner
Wired Ventures
Ziff Communications

Industry
Publishing - computer magazines & books

Overview
Founded in 1964, IDG is one of the world's largest publishers of information technology trade journals. Founder and majority owner Patrick McGovern oversees a publishing empire with more than 190 magazines and newspapers that reach over 40 million readers in 65 countries. Over 30% employee-owned, IDG consists of some 80 operating units designed to be autonomous and flexible. IDG is working on an on-line shopping network targeted at technology users.

IRVIN FELD & KENNETH FELD PRODUCTIONS, INC.

RANK: N/R

8607 Westwood Center Dr.
Vienna, VA 22182
Phone: 703-448-4000
Fax: 703-448-4100

1993 Est. Sales: $494 million
FYE: January
Employees: 2,500

Key Personnel
Pres: Kenneth Feld
SVP; VP & Treas, Ringling Bros: C. E. Smith
VP Mktg & Sales: Allen J. Bloom
Acct Fin Mgr: Joe Kobylski
Dir HR, Ringling Bros: Connie Kepple

See page 70 for full-page profile.

Principal Subsidiaries
Feld Brothers Management
Hagenbeck-Wallace (circus equip.)
Klowns Publishing Co. (programs)
Ringling Brothers Circus
Sells-Floto (concessions)

Key Competitors
Anheuser-Busch
Cirque du Soleil
Clyde Beatty-Cole Brothers Circus
Great American Circus
Hanneford Family Circus
Pickle Family Circus
Time Warner
Viacom

Industry
Leisure & recreational services - circus

Overview
Irvin Feld & Kenneth Feld Productions, the largest live entertainment company in the world, traces its roots back to the 1940s, when Irvin Feld opened a record store, then started his own record company and began to promote musical acts. Feld's son Kenneth took over in 1984 when Irvin died. The company produces the Ringling Brothers Circus, Walt Disney's World on Ice, the Siegfried & Roy magic show, and other acts. Kenneth owns 82% of the company, and 3 executives own the rest.

THE IRVINE COMPANY

RANK: 386

550 Newport Center Dr.
Newport Beach, CA 92660
Phone: 714-720-2000
Fax: 714-720-9453

1993 Est. Sales: $800 million
FYE: June
Employees: 200

Key Personnel
Chm: Donald L. Bren
VC & CFO: Norman J. Metcalfe
VC: Raymond L. Watson
EVP: William H. McFarland
EVP: Richard G. Sim
Dir HR: Bruce Endsley

Business Lines
Hotel development & mgmt.
Industrial development & mgmt.
Land development
Office development & mgmt.
Residential development
Retail development & mgmt.

Key Competitors
Britcher Real Estate
Centex
Chevron
Edward J. DeBartolo
Koll Co.
Presley
Walt Disney

Industry
Real estate development

Overview
The Irvine Co. is a developer and manager of residential and commercial real estate in Southern California. The company creates planned urban environments on the 62,000 acres it controls in Orange County (1/16th of the total land area in that county). The company's holdings are part of the original 120,000-acre Irvine Ranch formed from Spanish and Mexican land grants by James Irvine in 1876. Billionaire Donald Bren, who purchased the Irvine Ranch in 1977 with several other partners, whom he bought out in 1983, owns 93% of the company. The company leases 6,000 acres of its undeveloped land to tenant farmers.

ISLAND LINCOLN-MERCURY INC.

RANK: 378

1850 E. Merritt Island Causeway
Merritt Island, FL 32952
Phone: 407-452-9220
Fax: 407-453-3498

1993 Sales: $804 million
FYE: December
Employees: 101

Key Personnel
Pres: R. Bruce Deardoff
VP: Michael G. Deardoff
VP: Marie Fisher
Sec & Treas: Phyllis G. Walker
Comptroller: Rene Cheney
HR: Fran Parnell

Car Lines
Ford
Lincoln
Mercury

Key Competitors
Carlisle Motors
Coggin-O'Steen Investment
Ed Morse Chevrolet
Ferman Motor Car
King Motor Center
JM Family Enterprises
Mid-Atlantic Cars

Industry
Retail - new & used cars

Overview
R. Bruce Deardoff's Island Lincoln-Mercury has emerged as one of the largest private automotive dealers in the US, only 9 years after the company's 1984 founding. With the 1993 acquisition of Central Florida Lincoln-Mercury (Orlando), Deardoff has 2 Lincoln-Mercury dealerships and Griffin Ford (Frostproof), all in Florida. Island ranked #4 nationally and #2 in Florida (behind Ed Morse Chevrolet in Lauderhill) in new units sold, according to *Automotive News* in 1993.

J. CREW GROUP INC.

RANK: 460

625 Sixth Ave.
New York, NY 10011
Phone: 212-886-2500
Fax: 212-886-2666

1994 Sales: $636 million
FYE: January
Employees: 6,400

Key Personnel
Chm & CEO: Arthur Cinader
VC & Head Designer: Emily C. Woods
Pres & COO: Robert Bernard
VP Ops: Robert Paris
VP Fin & CFO: Michael P. McHugh
VP HR: Carol Dudgeon

◀ **See page 71 for full-page profile.**

Major Products
Furniture
Kitchen supplies
Men's sportswear
Women's career clothing
Women's sportswear

Key Competitors
L.L. Bean
Benetton
Blair
The Gap
Lands' End
May
Spiegel
Talbots

Industry
Retail - mail order

Overview
J. Crew Group Inc. is the parent company of 3 subsidiaries that sell casually elegant clothing and other items, mostly through mail order catalogs (J. Crew, Clifford & Wills, and Popular Club Plan). Started in 1947, the family-owned company is headed by the founder's son Arthur Cinader. Arthur's daughter Emily Woods designs the clothing and helped launch the company's foray into retailing. Facing more competition, J. Crew is marketing its apparel in Japan and starting an aggressive international expansion program that may include home furnishings and children's clothing.

JITNEY-JUNGLE STORES OF AMERICA, INC.

RANK: 241

453 N. Mill St.
Jackson, MS 39202
Phone: 601-948-0361
Fax: 601-352-0483

1993 Sales: $1,152 million
FYE: April
Employees: 10,000

Key Personnel
Chm, Pres & CEO: W. H. Holman, Jr.
VC, CFO & Sec: Roger P. Friou
EVP Retail Ops: David Essary
EVP Wholesale Ops: Claude W. Duvall
SVP Sales & Mktg: W. H. Holman III
VP HR: Jerry Jones

Selected Services
Deli & bakery departments
Floral departments
Grocery/dairy/frozen foods
Meats & seafood
Nonfood departments
Pharmacies (8 run by Jitney)
Produce departments
Video departments

Key Competitors
Bruno's
Delchamps
Fleming
Great A&P
Kroger
SUPERVALU
Winn-Dixie

Industry
Retail - supermarkets

Overview
Three cousins founded the Jitney-Jungle supermarket chain in 1919, pledging to help customers "save a nickel on a quarter." The chain takes its name from "jitney," a slang term for a nickel. With 109 sites in the Southeast, including units in Arkansas, Tennessee, and Florida, this family-owned, Mississippi-based chain has a wholesale division (McCarty Holman) and is run by William H. Holman, son of one of the founders. Jitney-Jungle claims a 50% market share in Jackson, Mississippi, where it recently opened Jitney Premier, an upscale gourmet specialty store.

JM FAMILY ENTERPRISES INC.

RANK: 82

100 NW 12th Ave.
Deerfield Beach, FL 33442
Phone: 305-429-2000
Fax: 305-429-2300

1993 Sales: $2,600 million
FYE: December
Employees: 2,300

Key Personnel
Chm: James M. Moran
Pres: Patricia Moran
EVP: L. Wayne McClain
SVP & CFO: Casey L. Gunnell
VP & Gen Counsel: Colin W. Brown
VP HR: Rhonda B. Gallaspy

◀ **See page 72 for full-page profile.**

Operating Units
JM Lexus
JM Pontiac
JM&A Group
Joyserv Co. Ltd.
Petro Chemical Products Inc.
Southeast Toyota Distributors
World Cars
World Omni Financial Corp.

Key Competitors
Chrysler
Ford
Island Lincoln Mercury
Mid-Atlantic Cars
Morse Operations
Potamkin Manhattan

Industry
Retail - new & used cars

Overview
Jim Moran began selling Hudsons on TV in 1948. He switched to Fords in 1955 and within 30 days was the world's #1 Ford dealer. This family-owned company runs one of the world's largest auto distributorships, Southeast Toyota, and the nation's largest Pontiac dealership and reaps profits from more than 20 auto-related enterprises, including an accessorizing plant; a parts supplier; and insurance, financing, and leasing firms. The company is run by Patricia Moran, who took over from her father in 1992.

JOHN HANCOCK MUTUAL LIFE INSURANCE COMPANY

RANK: 14

PO Box 111
Boston, MA 02117
Phone: 617-572-6000
Fax: 617-572-6451

1993 Sales: $12,732 million
FYE: December
Employees: 16,500

Key Personnel
Chm & CEO: Stephen L. Brown
Pres & COO: William L. Boyan
VC & Chief Investment Officer: Foster L. Aborn
CFO: Thomas E. Moloney
Gen Counsel: Richard S. Scipione
VP Corp HR: A. Page Palmer

◀ **See page 73 for full-page profile.**

Selected Services
Banking services
Group life, accident & health insurance
Group retirement funds
Life insurance & annuities
Long-term care insurance
Mortgage loans
Mutual funds
Property & casualty insurance

Key Competitors
Aetna
CIGNA
MassMutual
MetLife
New York Life
Northwestern Mutual
Prudential
Travelers

Industry
Insurance - life

Overview
John Hancock, the US's 9th largest life insurer according to *FORTUNE*, was founded in 1862. The mutual company has diversified into brokerage, limited banking services (First Signature Bank), and venture capital and other investment funds, especially in nontraditional areas: real estate syndicates, timber management, and asset management. It also operates in Belgium, Canada, and the UK and in recent years has established a strong presence in Indonesia, Malaysia, and Thailand.

THE JOHNS HOPKINS UNIVERSITY INC.

RANK: 198

3400 N. Charles St.
Baltimore, MD 21218
Phone: 410-516-8000
Fax: 410-516-8900

1993 Sales: $1,329 million
FYE: June
Employees: 17,397

Key Personnel
Pres: William C. Richardson
SVP Admin: Eugene S. Sunshine
VP & Sec: Ross Jones
Provost & VP Academic Affairs: Joseph Cooper
VP & Gen Counsel: Estelle A. Fishbein
VP HR: James R. Jones III

Schools & Colleges
School of Arts & Sciences
School of Hygiene & Public Health
School of Medicine
School of Nursing
G.W.C. Whiting School of Engineering

Industry
Schools

Overview
Founded in 1876 as the first graduate school in the US and known for its superior medical school, The Johns Hopkins University is among the most prestigious schools in the US. In 1993 U.S. News and World Report ranked this private school the #15 research-oriented university and rated it in the top 10 in geology, biology, history, and English programs. The school currently enrolls over 5,000 students. Faced with rising expenses Johns Hopkins has taken strong measures to cut costs: it has frozen salaries and laid off workers at its physics laboratory.

JOHNSON & HIGGINS

RANK: 307

125 Broad St.
New York, NY 10004
Phone: 212-574-7000
Fax: 212-574-7190

1992 Est. Sales: $970 million
FYE: December
Employees: 8,700

Key Personnel
Chm, Pres & CEO: David A. Olsen
Pres & COO: Richard A. Nielsen
CFO: Joseph D. Roxe
Chief Info Officer: Alan Page
Mgr HR: James R. Reardon

Selected Services
Benefit consulting
Compensation consulting
Insurance brokerage
Insurance services
Loss control
Reinsurance services
Risk management

Key Competitors
Acordia
Alexander & Alexander
Arthur J. Gallagher
Crawford & Co.
Hewitt Associates
Marsh & McLennan
Prometheus Funding
Willis Corroon

Industry
Business services - insurance brokerage

Overview
Johnson & Higgins, founded in New York in 1845, is the world's largest privately owned insurance brokerage and employee benefit consulting firm. UNISON, the firm's global network, includes 120 J&H offices around the world and exclusive partnerships with firms in over 135 cities. It recently opened a major office in the heart of London's financial district. J&H provides services to 70 of the top 100 US multinational companies. However, with limited growth potential among large corporations, J&H is going after "middle-market" companies previously left to smaller, regional brokers.

JOHNSON PUBLISHING COMPANY, INC.

RANK: N/R

820 S. Michigan Ave.
Chicago, IL 60605
Phone: 312-322-9200
Fax: 312-322-0918

1993 Sales: $294 million
FYE: December
Employees: 2,600

Key Personnel
Chm & CEO: John H. Johnson
Pres & COO: Linda Johnson Rice
Sec & Treas: Eunice W. Johnson
Controller: Gregory Robertson
Personnel Dir: La Doris Foster

Business Lines
Beauty aids
Books
Fashion
Magazines
Radio stations
Television production

Key Competitors
Advance Publications
Amway
Essence Communications
IVAX
L'Oréal
Luster Products
Pavion
Soft Sheen Products

Industry
Publishing - magazines

Overview
Founded by John Johnson in 1942, with $500 his mother raised by mortgaging family furniture, Johnson Publishing is the 2nd largest black-owned business in the US (after TLC Beatrice). The company's magazines include Ebony, Jet, and EM. It also publishes books by black authors, owns 2 radio stations, produces a fashion roadshow, and sells cosmetics (Fashion Fair, Ebone) and hair care products (Duke, Raveen). The company is owned by John Johnson; his wife, Eunice; and their daughter Linda Johnson Rice.

◀ See page 74 for full-page profile.

S.C. JOHNSON & SON, INC.

RANK: 53

1525 Howe St.
Racine, WI 53403
Phone: 414-631-2000
Fax: 414-631-2133

1993 Est. Sales: $3,550 million
FYE: July
Employees: 13,100

Key Personnel
Chm: Samuel C. Johnson
Pres & CEO: William D. George, Jr.
SVP & CFO: Neal R. Nottleson
SVP, Sec & Gen Counsel: Robert C. Hart
SVP HR & Corp Comm: M. Garvin Shankster

Major Brands
Drano (drain cleaner)
Edge (shaving products)
Future (floor care)
OFF! (insect repellent)
Pledge (furniture polish)
Raid (insecticide)
Shout (soil & stain remover)
Windex (glass cleaner)

Key Competitors
Amway
Bristol-Myers Squibb
Clorox
Dow Chemical
Johnson & Johnson
Pfizer
Procter & Gamble
Unilever

Industry
Soap & cleaning preparations

Overview
Founded in 1886, S.C. Johnson & Son is one of the world's largest makers of consumer chemical specialty products. It is a leader in insect control, cleaning products, and personal care products and has interests in real estate, recreational products, sanitation services, over-the-counter drugs, commercial pest control, and venture capital financing. About 60% of its sales are made outside of the US. Samuel C. Johnson, great-grandson and namesake of the founder, controls 60% of the company.

◀ See page 75 for full-page profile.

JORDAN CO.

RANK: N/R

9 W. 57th, 40th Fl.
New York, NY 10019
Phone: 212-755-9710
Fax: 212-477-2461

FYE: December
Employees: 16

Key Personnel
Partner: John W. Jordan II
Partner: David Zalaznick
Controller: Paul Rodzevik
Mgr HR: Margaret W. Nee

Selected Investments
American Safety Razor Co.
Great American Cookie Corp.
Jordan Industries Inc.
LePage's
Mezzanine Capital & Income Trust
Newflo Corp.
Penn Square Management Corp.

Industry
Financial - investors

Overview
Founded in 1982, Jordan Co. is a private investment firm specializing in leveraged buyout deals. Controlled by principal partners John W. Jordan and David Zalaznick, the firm purchases private manufacturing companies, especially those owned by aging single owners. Jordan Co. is also involved in money management, operating the London-based Mezzanine Capital and Income Trust. In 1988 Jordan spun off six manufacturing firms from its portfolio to form Jordan Industries, in which it retains an interest.

JORDAN MOTORS INC.

RANK: 170

609 E. Jefferson Blvd.
Mishawaka, IN 46545
Phone: 219-259-1981
Fax: 219-255-0984

1993 Sales: $1,532 million
FYE: December
Employees: 185

Key Personnel
Chm: Jordan H. Kapson
Pres: Craig Kapson
VP: James A. Hoffer
CFO: George Merryman
Dir HR: Sandra Eggers

Operating Units
Jordan Ford
Jordan Lincoln-Mercury
Jordan Mitsubishi
Jordan Toyota
Jordan Volvo

Key Competitors
DiFeo Automotive Network
Gulf States Toyota
Holman Enterprises
Island Lincoln-Mercury
Mid-Atlantic Cars
Morse Operations
Prospect Motors
Santa Monica Ford

Industry
Retail - new & used cars

Overview
Jordan Motors's owner, Jordan Kapson, who founded the automobile dealership in 1949, is bullish on the Ford Taurus. The nation's largest auto dealer in dollar sales, new unit sales, and fleet sales in 1993, Jordan Motors primarily sells Fords. Although the company has other retail franchises, fleet sales of Ford cars and trucks fuel the vast majority of its business. Kapson's son Craig, who has been with the company since 1972 and is now president, helped develop fleet sales of specialty vehicles to buyers such as utilities and railroads.

JP FOODSERVICE, INC.

RANK: 283

9830 Patuxent Woods Dr.
Columbia, MD 21046
Phone: 410-712-7111
Fax: 410-312-7591

1993 Sales: $1,026 million
FYE: June
Employees: 2,300

Key Personnel
Chm, Pres & CEO: James L. Miller
EVP: Pat Tolbert
CFO: Lew Hay
Dir HR: Dan Berliant

Major Clients
Food suppliers
Health care facilities
Hotels
Prisons
Restaurants
Schools

Key Competitors
Ameriserv
Gordon Food Service
SYSCO
US Foodservice

Industry
Food - wholesale to restaurants

Overview
Founded in 1989 by a group of PYA/Monarch executives as a spinoff of that company, JP Foodservice rapidly became the 6th largest broadline food-service distributor in the US. Its 10 distribution centers in the Midwest and Northeast distribute between 10,000 and 12,000 items in all major product categories. This closely held, secretive firm is owned by its management, other investors, and the Sara Lee Corporation.

JPS TEXTILE GROUP INC.

RANK: 339

555 N. Pleasantburg Dr., Ste. 202
Greenville, SC 29607
Phone: 803-239-3900
Fax: 803-271-9939

1993 Sales: $885 million
FYE: October
Employees: 8,000

Key Personnel
Chm & CEO: Steven M. Friedman
Pres: Jerry E. Hunter
EVP Fin & Sec: David H. Taylor
VP HR: Monnie L. Broome
Controller: Allen Hodges

Principal Subsidiaries
JPS Carpet Corp.
JPS Converter & Industrial Corp.
JPS Elastomerics Corp.

Key Competitors
Burlington Industries
Cone Mills
Galey & Lord
Greenwood Mills
Milliken
R. B. Pamplin
Springs Industries
Walton Monroe Mills

Industry
Textiles - mill products

Overview
JPS Textile Group, a holding company formed in 1988 to buy 5 J. P. Stevens & Co. units, manufactures textile and textile-related products, including apparel, industrial fabrics, carpet, and elastics. After the 1988 LBO by Odyssey Partners and a group headed by investor Grant Wilson, JPS's heavy debt burden and weak product markets led to a 1991 restructuring whereby the existing stockholders kept 51% of the stock and the bondholders got the rest. Reorganizing again, JPS has sold off its automotive products and synthetic industrial fabrics businesses.

K-III COMMUNICATIONS CORPORATION

RANK: 359

745 Fifth Ave.
New York, NY 10151
Phone: 212-745-0100
Fax: 212-745-0169

1993 Sales: $845 million
FYE: December
Employees: 3,600

Key Personnel
Chm & CEO: William F. Reilly
Pres: Charles G. McCurdy
VC, Gen Counsel & Sec: Beverly C. Chell
VP & Pres, K-III Magazine: Harry McQuillen
VP, Controller & CFO: Curtis A. Thompson
VP HR: Michaelanne C. Discepolo

◀ See page 76 for full-page profile.

Major Products
Daily Racing Form
Funk & Wagnalls encyclopedias
Premiere
Scientific & professional books
Seventeen
Soap Opera Digest
Trade magazines (Intertec)
Weekly Reader

Key Competitors
Advance Publications
Houghton Mifflin
MatraHachette
Pearson
Reed Elsevier
Thomson Corp.
Time Warner
Universal Press Syndicate

Industry
Publishing - periodicals; information services

Overview
Founded in 1989, K-III is a rapidly expanding publishing empire. Since it was formed by investment firm Kohlberg Kravis Roberts and its senior management, K-III has acquired a variety of publishing and information businesses, including Weekly Reader (the #1 publisher of student newspapers in the US), Funk & Wagnalls, and Daily Racing Form. In 1993 K-III acquired the World Almanac Education division of United Media Publishing.

KAISER FOUNDATION HEALTH PLAN, INC.

RANK: 15

One Kaiser Plaza
Oakland, CA 94612
Phone: 510-271-5910
Fax: 510-271-5917

1993 Sales: $11,930 million
FYE: December
Employees: 84,885

Key Personnel
Chm & CEO: David M. Lawrence
Pres & COO: Wayne R. Moon
SVP Legal, Gen Counsel & Sec: Jerry J. Phelan
SVP Fin: Susan E. Porth
VP HR Programs: Alfred Bolden

◀ See page 77 for full-page profile.

Selected Services
Home health
Hospitals
Insurance
Support function

Key Competitors
Aetna
Blue Cross
Foundation Health
Group Health Co-op of Puget Sound
PacifiCare
Prudential
Sierra Health Services
Travelers

Industry
Health maintenance organization

Overview
The Kaiser Foundation Health Plan is the umbrella for the Kaiser Foundation Hospitals and the Permanente Medical Groups, which together form the largest HMO in the US. Founded in 1946 by construction and shipbuilding magnate Henry Kaiser and building upon wartime production clinics, the Health Plan was, for a long time, limited to the West by physician resistance to HMOs. But as medical costs have risen, HMOs have become increasingly cost-effective, and Kaiser has become a national model.

KASH N' KARRY FOOD STORES INC.

RANK: 259

6422 Harney Rd.
Tampa, FL 33610
Phone: 813-621-0200
Fax: 813-621-0293

1993 Sales: $1,086 million
FYE: July
Employees: 9,900

Key Personnel
Chm, Pres & CEO: Ronald J. Floto
EVP Admin & CFO: Raymond P. Springer
EVP Ops: Dennis V. Carter
SVP Mktg: Joseph P. Bullara
VP HR: Andrea Guillo

Business Lines
Conventional supermarkets
Liquor stores
Multidepartment supermarkets
Super warehouse stores

Key Competitors
Albertson's
American Stores
Bruno's
Food Lion
Melville
Publix
Winn-Dixie

Industry
Retail - supermarkets

Overview
Kash n' Karry is a 115-unit chain of retail supermarkets in western and central Florida. In the Tampa Bay area it is the #2 chain (with about 25% of the market), after #1 Publix (with about 30%). After separating from Lucky Stores via a 1988 LBO, Kash n' Karry has been majority-owned by an investment fund controlled by Los Angeles–based Leonard Green & Partners. Debt left over from the LBO has contributed to a string of unprofitable years for the company. Kash n' Karry joined the super warehouse fray by acquiring 3 Save 'n Pack stores in 1993.

THE KEMPER NATIONAL INSURANCE COMPANIES

RANK: 61

One Kemper Dr.
Long Grove, IL 60049
Phone: 708-320-2000
Fax: 708-320-2494

1993 Sales: $3,166 million
FYE: December
Employees: 9,000

Key Personnel
Chm & CEO: Gerald L. Maatman
Pres & COO: Alfred K. Kenyon
EVP & CFO: Walter L. White
EVP: James S. Kemper III
EVP: Peter T. Standbridge
Gen Counsel: John K. Conway

Business Lines
Automotive insurance
Commercial multiperil
Homeowners insurance
Products liability
Surety
Workers' compensation

Key Competitors
AFLAC
Allstate
CIGNA
GEICO
Liberty Mutual
Nationwide
State Farm
Travelers

Industry
Insurance - property & casualty

Overview
Kemper National, a mutual company and one of the nation's leading property casualty insurance organizations, is led by its work horse Lumbermens Mutual Casualty and related affiliates American Motorists, American Protection, and Associated Mutual American Manufacturers. Kemper National, once closely tied to security broker Kemper Corp., has gradually been reducing ownership in that company and holds only 4%, down from 49% in 1988. Kemper National is primarily a commercial insurer, with such policies accounting for over 77% of total sales.

KEY FOOD STORES COOPERATIVE, INC.

RANK: 474

8925 Avenue D
Brooklyn, NY 11236
Phone: 718-451-1000
Fax: 718-451-1202

1993 Est. Sales: $600 million
FYE: April

Key Personnel
Chm: Sheldon Geller
CEO: Allen Newman
Pres: Lawrence Mandel
Treas: Sam Kristal
Controller: Ron Phillips
HR: Frank De Franco

Selected Products
Candy
Dairy products
Deli products
Frozen meat
Nursery items
Poultry
Produce
Specialty/gourmet items

Key Competitors
Di Giorgio
Fleming
SUPERVALU
Wakefern Food

Industry
Food - wholesale to grocers

Overview
Founded in 1937, the member-owned Key Food Stores Cooperative offers its 140 member stores in the New York City metropolitan area a full line of products, ranging from dairy products to fresh produce. Member stores also may use the co-op's banner name, Food Store. The co-op has experienced a stormy past with the mysterious disappearance at sea of its president in 1986 and allegations of links of key executives to the Mafia.

KEYSTONE FOODS CORPORATION

RANK: 173

401 City Ave., Ste. 800
Bala Cynwyd, PA 19004
Phone: 610-667-6700
Fax: 610-677-1460

1993 Est. Sales: $1,500 million
FYE: December
Employees: 1,875

Key Personnel
Chm & Pres: Herbert Lotman
SEVP: Jeff Lotman
EVP: Jerry Dean
SVP & Controller: Jack Conway, Sr.
VP & Treas: John J. Coggins
VP HR: Robert S. Weinberg

Business Lines
Frozen beef patties
Frozen chicken
Poultry slaughtering & processing
Processed meats & sausages
Reduced-fat meat mixtures
Refrigerated entrees
Restaurant supplies

Key Competitors
ConAgra
Farmland Industries
Perdue
Philip Morris
Pilgrim's Pride
Sara Lee
Smithfield Foods
Tyson Foods

Industry
Food - meat products

Overview
Keystone Foods is one of the nation's largest makers of sausage and other prepared and processed meats and one of the largest processors of poultry. The company is a major supplier to McDonald's; in the early 1970s Keystone developed a new method of freezing meat patties and persuaded McDonald's to switch to frozen beef to reduce the health risks associated with fresh beef. The company was also instrumental in developing Chicken McNuggets. In association with Wawa Food Markets, Keystone also produces refrigerated (not frozen) prepared entrees, under the name Fresh Buffet, which have a shelf life of up to 2 weeks.

KING KULLEN GROCERY COMPANY INC. — RANK: 414

1194 Prospect Ave.
Westbury, NY 11590
Phone: 516-333-7100
Fax: 516-333-7929

1993 Sales: $720 million
FYE: September
Employees: 4,500

Key Personnel
Chm & CEO: John B. Cullen
Pres & COO: Bernard D. Kennedy
EVP Fin & Admin: J. D. Kennedy
EVP Ops: Brian C. Cullen
VP Sales & Merchandising: Rudolph A. Becht
Dir Labor & Personnel: Thomas Nagle

Business Lines
Communications
Data processing
Grocery stores
Leasing & financial services
Real estate development
Specialty products & food services
Transportation

Key Competitors
Golub
Grand Union
Great A&P
Pathmark
Penn Traffic
Red Apple Group
Wakefern Food
Wegmans Food Markets

Industry
Retail - supermarkets

Overview
Long Island–based food retailer King Kullen (described by the company as the world's first supermarket chain) was founded in 1930 by Michael Cullen in a Queens, New York, warehouse. Today, the company is owned and operated by Cullen's descendants. King Kullen runs more than 50 supermarkets in New York and New Jersey. Although long known as a conservative company, in recent years King Kullen has branched into new nonfood areas, including real estate and data processing, in order to drive growth.

KOCH INDUSTRIES, INC. — RANK: 7

4111 E. 37th St. North
Wichita, KS 67220
Phone: 316-832-5500
Fax: 316-832-5739

1993 Est. Sales: $20,000 million
FYE: December
Employees: 12,000

Key Personnel
Chm & CEO: Charles G. Koch
Pres & COO: W.W. Hanna
EVP Fin & Admin: F. Lynn Markel
EVP & Chief Legal Officer: Donald L. Cordes
Sec & Gen Counsel: H. Allan Caldwell
Dir HR: R. A. Pohlman

◀ **See page 78 for full-page profile.**

Operating Units
Agriculture Group
Chemical Technology Group
Financial Services Group
Hydrocarbon Group
Materials Group
Minerals Group
Refining & Chemical Group
Supply, Trading & Transportation

Key Competitors
Amoco
Atlantic Richfield
Cargill
Continental Grain
Exxon
Mobil
Phillips Petroleum
Texaco

Industry
Oil & gas - US integrated

Overview
An integrated petroleum giant, Koch Industries is the 2nd largest family-held and family-run private company in the US. Koch also has operations in chemical technology, agriculture, and minerals. The company traces its roots to 1928, when Fred Koch developed a process to refine more gasoline from crude oil. Koch is controlled by brothers Charles and David Koch, survivors of a feud with their brother William; they own 80% of the company's stock.

KOHLBERG KRAVIS ROBERTS & CO. — RANK: N/R

9 W. 57th St., Ste. 4200
New York, NY 10019
Phone: 212-750-8300
Fax: 212-593-2430

Key Personnel
Founding Partner: Henry R. Kravis
Founding Partner: George R. Roberts
General Partner: James H. Greene, Jr.
General Partner: Robert I. MacDonnell
General Partner: Michael W. Michelson
General Partner: Paul E. Raether

◀ **See page 79 for full-page profile.**

Selected Investments
Duracell
Fred Meyer
K-III
Owens-Illinois
RJR Nabisco
Safeway
Stop & Shop
Walter Industries

Industry
Financial - investors

Overview
The LBO king of the 1980s, Kohlberg Kravis Roberts has spent the 1990s keeping its acquisitions afloat, especially the biggest, the $29.6 billion RJR Nabisco LBO. In addition to the value of stock ownership in companies it acquires, KKR receives various fees for managing the transactions. The fact that it takes its fees off the top, regardless of the profitability of the transaction, has irked some of its largest investors, state pension funds. KKR was founded in 1976 by cousins Henry Kravis and George Roberts and mentor Jerome Kohlberg, who left in 1987 in a dispute over KKR's direction.

KOHLER CO. — RANK: 178

444 Highland Dr.
Kohler, WI 53044
Phone: 414-457-4441
Fax: 414-459-1656

1992 Sales: $1,472 million
FYE: December
Employees: 14,000

Key Personnel
Chm & Pres: Herbert V. Kohler, Jr.
VC: Sam H. Davis
CFO: Richard A. Wells
Pres Plumbing & Spec Prods: J. W. Harbrecht
Gen Counsel: Natalie A. Black
VP HR: Kenneth W. Conger

Business Lines
Engines & generators
Furniture & interior design
Plumbing fixtures
Real estate development

Key Competitors
American Standard
Black & Decker
Bradley Corp.
Eljer Industries
Elkay Manufacturing
Jones Plumbing
Masco
NIBCO

Industry
Building products - plumbing fixtures

Overview
Founded in 1873, Kohler is a leading US producer of plumbing fixtures. Company paternalism and quality craftsmanship are Kohler tenets. The owners even built the company town of Kohler, Wisconsin, to produce "greater industry and happier workers." But "happy" the workers sometimes were not: bloodshed and 2 major strikes have marred Kohler's history. Owned by its founding family and led by ex-hippie Herbert Kohler, in 1993 Kohler won an undisclosed settlement from Eljer Industries, which had copied Kohler's designs.

KPMG PEAT MARWICK — RANK: 29

767 Fifth Ave.
New York, NY 10153
Phone: 212-909-5000
Fax: 212-909-5299

1993 Sales: $6,000 million
FYE: September
Employees: 76,200

Key Personnel
Chm: Hans Havermann
US Chm & CEO: Jon C. Madonna
Admin & Fin Partner: Joseph E. Heintz
Gen Counsel: Ed Scott
HR Partner: Mary L. Dupont

◀ See page 80 for full-page profile.

Selected Services
Auditing
Financial services
Management consulting
Tax

Key Competitors
Arthur Andersen
Coopers & Lybrand
Deloitte & Touche
Ernst & Young
Electronic Data Systems
Marsh & McLennan
McKinsey & Co.
Price Waterhouse

Industry
Business services - accounting & consulting

Overview
Klynveld Peat Marwick Goerdeler (KPMG) is the 2nd largest accounting firm in the world (after Arthur Andersen). The firm traces its roots to 1911, when William Peat and James Marwick met on an Atlantic crossing. Its US practice, KPMG Peat Marwick, is the nation's 4th largest accounting firm. The firm is expanding some of its services, forming an alliance with Toshiba to provide hardware and software for sales force automation applications.

K-VA-T FOOD STORES, INC. — RANK: 485

329 N. Main St.
Grundy, VA 24614
Phone: 703-935-4587
Fax: 703-628-6493

1993 Sales: $562 million
FYE: December
Employees: 5,000

Key Personnel
Chm & CEO: Jack C. Smith
VC, SVP Fin, Sec & Treas: Robert L. Neely
Pres & COO: Steven C. Smith
EVP Ops: Thomas R. Hembree
EVP Ops: Claude S. Trout
VP HR & Security: William L. Neely

Operating Units
Retail Supermarkets
- Food City
- Super Dollar

Wholesale grocery distribution
- Jif-E Mart
- Ole Town Market
- Piggly Wiggly

Key Competitors
Alex Lee
Fleming
Food Lion
Giant Food
Great A&P
Kroger
Safeway
Winn-Dixie

Industry
Food - wholesale to grocers

Overview
Founded in 1955, K-Va-T is a southern grocery distributor and wholesaler. Owned by Jack Smith, the company operates more than 60 Food City supermarkets in Kentucky, Virginia, and Tennessee. Some Food City supermarkets offer video rental, seafood service, and a restaurant. Half have in-store bakeries and most offer deli service and hot food bars. The company is majority owner of a wholesale cooperative, Mid-Mountain Foods, based in Abingdon, Virginia. Mid-Mountain also offers canned goods, bakery goods, dairy products, and frozen foods under the private labels of Food City and Real Value.

LAND O' LAKES, INC. — RANK: 72

4001 Lexington Ave. North
Arden Hills, MN 55126
Phone: 612-481-2222
Fax: 612-481-2022

1993 Sales: $2,733 million
FYE: December
Employees: 5,700

Key Personnel
Chm: Stan Zylstra
Pres & CEO: Jack Gherty
EVP & COO: Duane Halverson
Group VP & CFO : Ron Ostby
VP & Gen Counsel: John Rebane
VP HR: Jack Martin

◀ See page 81 for full-page profile.

Operating Units
Cenex/Land O' Lakes (mktg JV)
Food Ingredients (dried whey)
Lake to Lake Dairy
Land O' Lakes Inc., Agricultural
Land O' Lakes International Div.
Land O' Lakes Seed Division
Wilson Seeds Inc.

Key Competitors
Associated Milk Producers
ConAgra
Dairy Gold Foods
Darigold
Grassland Dairy Products
Mid-America Dairymen
Philip Morris
Steuben Foods

Industry
Food - dairy products

Overview
Formed in 1921 by more than 300 Minnesota dairy farmers seeking an outlet for their products, Land O' Lakes has grown into a major farm cooperative owned by more than 8,000 farmers and more than 1,000 member co-ops in 15 states from the Great Lakes to Idaho. The largest producer of butter in the US (with the first and only national brand of butter), it is also the leading maker of deli cheese and a major manufacturer of seeds, feeds, fertilizers, and chemicals.

LANOGA CORPORATION — RANK: 446

17946 NE 65th St.
Redmond, WA 98052
Phone: 206-883-4125
Fax: 206-882-2959

1993 Sales: $657 million
FYE: December
Employees: 2,900

Key Personnel
Chm: William Lucas
Pres & CEO: Daryl Nagel
Pres, United Building Centers: Robert D. Drumm
VP, CFO, Sec & Treas: William P. Brakken
VP: Dale Kukowski
VP: Douglas D. Johnson

Operating Units
Fish Building Supplies
Lumbermen's Building Centers
Spenard Building Supply
United Building Centers

Key Competitors
84 Lumber
Ace Hardware
Cotter & Co.
Hechinger
Home Depot
Kmart
Lowe's
McCoy

Industry
Building products - retail

Overview
Lanoga Corp. is a huge lumber and building supplies retailer that has 144 stores in 12 states. Lanoga caters to "do-it-yourself" customers and contractors and places its stores in rural areas, rather than city centers, to avoid competition. Started in 1955 by the Norton Clapp family, who were prominent in timber and real estate, the company began with Minnesota-based United Building Centers and later grew by acquiring other companies in the Northwest. The company officially became Lanoga when it merged with Spenard Builders of Alaska. Lanoga's majority stockholder is Seattle-based Laird Norton Co., an investment management firm.

LEFRAK ORGANIZATION INC. RANK: 60

97-77 Queens Blvd.
Rego Park, NY 11374
Phone: 718-459-9021
Fax: 718-897-0688

1992 Est. Sales: $3,200 million
FYE: November
Employees: 18,000

Key Personnel
Chm: Samuel J. LeFrak
Pres: Richard S. LeFrak
VP Fin: Arthur J. Phelan
VP & Gen Counsel: Howard Boris
VP Construction-Engineering: Anthony Scavo
HR: Cheryl Jensen

◀ See page 82 for full-page profile.

Business Lines
Commercial real estate constr.
Commercial real estate mgmt.
Entertainment (shows & records)
Oil & gas exploration
Residential real estate constr.
Residential real estate mgmt.

Key Competitors
Edward J. DeBartolo
Helmsley
Lincoln Property
Nederlander Organization
Port Authority
Shubert Organization
Tishman Speyer
Trump

Industry
Real estate development

Overview
The Lefrak Organization may be the US's largest private landlord, with more than 90,000 affordable apartments and extensive holdings in commercial and retail space. The company, owned by Samuel LeFrak and managed by his son, Richard, also has interests in oil and gas exploration and pumping and entertainment. The organization was founded by Samuel's father and grandfather in 1905 and grew by pursuing a strategy of providing low-cost housing in New York. The company's current project is Newport City, a planned community on the Hudson River.

LENNOX INTERNATIONAL INC. RANK: 273

2100 Lake Park Blvd.
Richardson, TX 75080
Phone: 214-497-5017
Fax: 214-497-5299

1993 Sales: $1,050 million
FYE: December
Employees: 7,500

Key Personnel
Chm & CEO: John W. Norris, Jr.
Pres & COO, Lennox Ind.: Thomas J. Keefe
Pres & COO, Armstrong A/C: Robert E. Schjerven
Pres & COO, Heatcraft: Robert Jenkins
EVP & Treas: Clyde Wyant
EVP HR: Harry Ashenhurst

Principal Subsidiaries
Armstrong Air Conditioning Inc.
Heatcraft Inc.
Lennox Industries Inc.

Key Competitors
American Standard
Electrolux
Fedders
Goodman Manufacturing
Scotsman Industries
Tecumseh Products
United Technologies
York International

Industry
Building products - a/c & heating

Overview
Through its 3 manufacturing subsidiaries, Lennox International provides a wide range of air conditioning, heating, and refrigeration equipment for commercial and residential uses. Flagship subsidiary Lennox Industries's products are marketed to 6,000 independent dealers in 70 countries. Named after inventor Dave Lennox, the company was acquired and incorporated (Iowa, 1904) by D. W. Norris, a newspaper publisher. The Norris family still controls the company.

LEO BURNETT COMPANY, INC. RANK: 468

35 W. Wacker Dr., Ste. 2200
Chicago, IL 60601
Phone: 312-220-5959
Fax: 312-220-6533

1993 Sales: $622 million
FYE: December
Employees: 6,581

Key Personnel
Chm & Chief Creative Officer: Richard B. Fizdale
Pres & CEO: William T. Lynch
Group Pres: Michael B. Conrad
Group Pres & CFO: Roger A. Haupt
EVP HR: Jerry L. Strimbu
Sec & Gen Counsel: Michael E. Breslin

Major Clients
Allstate Insurance Companies
Fiat
Goodyear
Kellogg
Kraft General Foods
Philip Morris
Procter & Gamble
United Distillers

Key Competitors
D'Arcy Masius
Foote, Cone & Belding
Grey Advertising
Interpublic Group
Omnicom Group
Saatchi & Saatchi
WPP Group
Young & Rubicam

Industry
Advertising

Overview
Founded in 1935, privately held advertising agency Leo Burnett is known for its timeless campaigns: Tony the Tiger, Charlie the Tuna, Marlboro Country, the Jolly Green Giant, and the Pillsbury Dough Boy, to name only a few. A worldwide operation, Burnett has 55 offices in 49 countries. Billings were down slightly in 1993 for the first time in 10 years, but that year the agency landed Reebok's worldwide account, American Tourister's national account, and Cadbury Schweppes's campaign in China. Founder Leo Burnett, who died in 1971, chose to sell the agency to employees instead of going public.

LEVI STRAUSS ASSOCIATES INC. RANK: 31

1155 Battery St.
San Francisco, CA 94111
Phone: 415-544-6000
Fax: 415-544-3939

1993 Sales: $5,892 million
FYE: November
Employees: 36,400

Key Personnel
Chm of the Exec Committee: Peter E. Haas, Sr.
Chm & CEO: Robert D. Haas
Pres & COO: Thomas W. Tusher
SVP, Gen Counsel & Sec: Thomas J. Bauch
SVP & CFO: George B. James
SVP HR: Donna J. Goya

◀ See page 83 for full-page profile.

Major Brands
501 jeans
Brittania
Brittgear
Dockers
Levi's Action
Little Levi's
Orange Tab
Red Tab

Key Competitors
Farah
The Gap
Guess?
Haggar
Jordache Enterprises
Liz Claiborne
Polo/Ralph Lauren
V. F.

Industry
Apparel

Overview
Since Levi Strauss made his first pair of sturdy pants in the mid-1800s, his company has become the world's #1 producer of brand-name clothing. Levi Strauss ranks 2nd in the domestic jean market, after V. F. (Wrangler and Lee), with about 18% of the domestic market (to V. F.'s 30%). Owned by the Haas family, descendants of the founder, the company is led by Strauss's great-great-grandnephew Robert Haas. The company's sewing plants recently adopted Japanese-style production techniques, which encourage more worker responsibility.

LEXMARK INTERNATIONAL INC. — RANK: 100

55 Railroad Ave.
Greenwich, CT 06836
Phone: 203-629-6700
Fax: 203-629-6725

1993 Est. Sales: $2,200 million
FYE: December
Employees: 4,000

Key Personnel
Chm, Pres & CEO: Marvin L. Mann
VP & CFO: Achim Knust
VP & Gen Mgr: Paul Curlander
VP Sales & Support: Douglas R. LeGrande
VP HR & Info Prgms: A. Richard Murphy

Major Products
Dot matrix printers
Ink-jet printers
Keyboards
Laser printers
Network systems
Laser printer cartridges
Ribbons
Typewriters

Key Competitors
Apple
Canon
Compaq
Hewlett-Packard
NEC
Oki
Olivetti
Smith Corona

Industry
Computers - peripheral equipment

Overview
A former division of IBM, Lexmark was sold to the investment firm of Clayton, Dubilier & Rice in an LBO in 1991. Lexmark makes and markets computer keyboards and printers, notebook computers, and typewriters under both its own name and the IBM logo, which it is licensed to use through 1996. IBM remains Lexmark's biggest customer and still owns 10% of the company. Lexmark's employees own 15%.

◀ See page 84 for full-page profile.

LIBERTY MUTUAL INSURANCE GROUP — RANK: 32

175 Berkeley St.
Boston, MA 02117
Phone: 617-357-9500
Fax: 617-350-7648

1993 Sales: $5,859 million
FYE: December
Employees: 22,000

Key Personnel
Chm & CEO: Gary L. Countryman
Pres & COO: Edmund F. Kelly
SVP, CFO & Treas: Robert H. Gruhl
SVP & Gen Counsel: Christopher C. Mansfield
Dir HR: Julie Baumgartner

Principal Subsidiaries
Liberty Financial Companies
Liberty Insurance Corporation
Liberty Life Assurance Company
Liberty Mutual (Bermuda) Ltd.
Liberty Mutual Fire Insurance Co.
Liberty Mutual Insurance Co. (UK)
Stein Roe & Farnham

Key Competitors
Aetna
Allstate
AIG
GEICO
Kemper
MassMutual
Prudential
State Farm

Industry
Insurance - multiline

Overview
Liberty Mutual, with 450 locations in the US and offices in Canada, Mexico, and the UK, is the leading insurer specializing in workers' compensation insurance and the related fields of loss prevention and physical rehabilitation. Founded in 1912 to specialize in the new field of workers' compensation, the company has diversified into other fields and has recently begun to pare back its workers' compensation business in some states. It now offers an HMO; individual and group life, health, and disability insurance; property/casualty insurance; and financial services.

◀ See page 85 for full-page profile.

LIFE CARE CENTERS OF AMERICA — RANK: 148

3570 Keith St. NW
Cleveland, TN 37320
Phone: 615-472-9585
Fax: 615-339-8337

1993 Est. Sales: $1,700 million
FYE: December
Employees: 18,000

Key Personnel
Chm & Pres: Forrest L. Preston
EVP: John O'Brien, Jr.
SVP & CFO: Jack Quigley
SVP Mktg: Greg Vital
SVP Ops: Tim Beaulieu
VP Professional Dev & HR: Mark Gibson

Selected Services
Cosmetology services
Diet planning
Family support activities
Housekeeping & laundry
Nursing care
Resident outings
Social activities

Key Competitors
Beverly Enterprises
Continental Medical
Hillhaven
Horizon Healthcare
Manor Care
Mid-America Health Centers
Regency Health Services
Sun City Industries

Industry
Nursing homes

Overview
Life Care Centers of America began in 1970 with the opening of a long-term nursing facility in Cleveland, Tennessee. Today the company is one of the largest nursing home systems in the US, operating more than 150 nursing centers and 14 retirement communities in 27 states. Its stated mission is to be the "premier provider of long-term health care in America." The company has division offices in Cleveland, Tennessee; Aurora, Colorado; Indianapolis, Indiana; and Scottsdale, Arizona.

LINCOLN PROPERTY COMPANY — RANK: 296

500 N. Akard, Ste. 3300
Dallas, TX 75201
Phone: 214-740-3300
Fax: 214-740-3313

1993 Sales: $1,000 million
FYE: June
Employees: 4,400

Key Personnel
Chm & CEO: Mack Pogue
Pres Commercial: William Duvall
Pres Residential: Tim Byrne
EVP & CFO : Mark Wallis
EVP Fin: Ken Mooter
VP & Sr Controller: T. W. Toomey

Selected Projects
Anaheim Village Apts. (CA)
Crossing Apts. (Wayne, NJ)
GSA Warehouse (Chicago, IL)
Lincoln Plaza (Dallas, TX)
Lincoln Tower Apts. (Arlington, VA)
NCNB Tower (Charlotte, NC)
Orlando City Hall (FL)
Village Apts. (Dallas, TX)

Key Competitors
Edward J. DeBartolo
Hines Interests
JMB Realty
Melvin Simon
Mitchell Energy & Development
Rouse
Trammell Crow

Industry
Real estate development

Overview
Founded on Lincoln's birthday in 1965, Lincoln Property is the 2nd largest property manager and the 5th largest property developer in the US. The company was formed as a partnership between Mack Pogue and Trammell Crow to build apartments in Dallas. Pogue bought out Crow in 1977 and diversified into commercial real estate. As the real estate market softened, Lincoln shifted more toward property management. The company created a real estate investment trust to hold $200 million of its apartment property.

LITTLE CAESAR ENTERPRISES, INC. — RANK: 105

2211 Woodward Ave.
Detroit, MI 48201
Phone: 313-983-6000
Fax: 313-983-6494

1993 Sales: $2,150 million
FYE: December
Employees: 92,000

Key Personnel
Pres & CEO: Michael Ilitch
VC: Charles P. Jones
Treas, Sec & CFO: Marian Ilitch
SEVP: Denise Ilitch Lites
Senior Group VP: Kim Pollack
Dir HR: Darrell Snygg

◀ **See page 86 for full-page profile.**

Major Products
Baby Pan! Pan! (small pan pizzas)
Caesars Sandwiches
Crazy Bread (with garlic & cheese)
Crazy Crust (flavored pizza crust)
Crazy Sauce (tomato sauce)
Pan! Pan! (deep-dish pizza)
Pizza! Pizza! (various sizes)
Slice! Slice! (2 slices of pizza)

Key Competitors
Checkers Drive-In
Domino's Pizza
Flagstar
International Dairy Queen
McDonald's
PepsiCo
Philip Morris
Subway

Industry
Restaurants

Overview
"Pizza! Pizza!" is the war cry of Detroit-based Little Caesar Enterprises in the battle for pizza dominance. Husband-and-wife team Michael and Marian Ilitch owns and operates one of the largest pizza chains in the US. Little Caesar claims to be the world's leading carry-out pizza provider and is growing faster than its 2 chief rivals, PepsiCo's Pizza Hut and Domino's. Little Caesar also owns the Detroit Tigers Baseball Club, the Detroit Red Wings hockey team, Olympia Arenas (which manages 3 arenas), The Fox Theatre, and Blue Line Distributing (which distributes products to the pizza franchises).

LONG JOHN SILVER'S RESTAURANTS, INC. — RANK: 345

101 Jerrico Dr.
Lexington, KY 40579
Phone: 606-263-6000
Fax: 606-263-6680

1993 Sales: $870 million
FYE: June
Employees: 26,000

Key Personnel
Pres & CEO: Clyde E. Culp
EVP & CFO: Gerald W. Deitchle
EVP Dev: Howard Singer
EVP Ops: Paul F. McFarland
EVP Mktg: Ted R. Murphy
VP HR: Wayne Hougland

Major Products
Baked fish & chicken meals
Batter-dipped fish & chicken
Chicken planks
Fingerfoods
Popcorn chicken & shrimp
Salads

Key Competitors
Carlson
Flagstar
General Mills
Little Caesars
McDonald's
Metromedia
PepsiCo
Subway

Industry
Restaurants

Overview
Founded in 1969, Long John Silver's is the nation's largest quick-service seafood restaurant chain. The company, which was a pioneer in bringing seafood into the fast-food arena, operates over 1,400 restaurants worldwide and controls 65% of the domestic market for quick-service seafood. Long John Silver's has operations in Canada, Mexico, Saudi Arabia, and Singapore. Approximately 2/3 of its stores are company-owned; the rest are franchises. Since being bought in a 1989 management-led LBO from Jerrico, Inc., Long John Silver's has been owned by senior management and CS First Boston.

LOUISIANA STATE UNIVERSITY SYSTEM — RANK: 235

3810 W. Lakeshore Dr.
Baton Rouge, LA 70808
Phone: 504-388-6935
Fax: 504-388-5524

1993 Sales: $1,191 million
FYE: June
Employees: 21,458

Key Personnel
Chancellor: William E. Davis
Vice Chancellor: Jerry J. Baudin
Vice Chancellor: Patrick M. Gibbs
Pres: Allen A. Copping
VP Admin & Fin: William L. Silvia , Jr.
VP Academic Affairs: H. Douglas Braymer

Schools & Colleges
LSU & A&M College, Baton Rouge
LSU Agricultural Center
LSU at Alexandria
LSU at Eunice
LSU Medical Center (New Orleans)
  School of Dentistry
  School of Medicine
  School of Nursing & Allied Health Professions
LSU at Shreveport
Paul M. Herbert Law Center
University of New Orleans

Industry
Schools

Overview
Founded in 1860, the Louisiana State University System consists of 8 publicly supported universities in 5 Louisiana cities. The system enrolls about 55,000 students, over 90% of whom are from Louisiana. LSU's main campus at Baton Rouge accepts about 79% of applicants and enrolls about 26,000 students in 4 graduate and 10 undergraduate schools. Academically, the strongest programs are engineering and basic science. The decades-long battle over college desegregation continues in Louisiana, as university officials have been scrambling for a solution to avoid federal intervention.

LOYOLA UNIVERSITY OF CHICAGO — RANK: 409

820 N. Michigan Ave.
Chicago, IL 60611
Phone: 312-915-6000
Fax: 312-915-6449

1993 Sales: $740 million
FYE: June
Employees: 10,500

Key Personnel
Pres & CEO: John J. Piderit
EVP: Ronald E. Walker
EVP Medical Center: Anthony Barbato
SVP & Dean of Faculty: James L. Wiser
SVP Admin: Stephen Kasbeer
Treas: David J. Meagher

Selected Programs of Study
Biological sciences
Business
Communications & the arts
Computer sciences
Education
Health professions
Human resources & ind. relations
Law
Medicine
Physical sciences
Social sciences

Industry
Schools

Overview
Loyola University of Chicago, founded in 1870, is a private Jesuit university. With 6 undergraduate and 10 graduate schools, the university has a total enrollment of about 16,000 — about 60% of whom are undergraduates — scattered over 5 campuses, including the 32-acre Lake Shore campus and the 65-acre Medical Center campus. Loyola is recognized as having one of the most innovative investment programs among major universities as it struggles to maximize its investment returns to compensate for increased operating costs.

LUTHERAN BROTHERHOOD

RANK: 98

625 Fourth Ave. South
Minneapolis, MN 55415
Phone: 612-340-7000
Fax: 612-340-8389

1993 Sales: $2,243 million
FYE: December
Employees: 1,864

Key Personnel
Chm: Robert O. Blomquist
VC: Judith K. Larsen
Pres & CEO: Robert P. Gandrud
EVP & CFO: Bruce J. Nicholson
SVP, Sec & Gen Counsel: David J. Larson
SVP Personnel: Harland J. Hogsven

Major Products
Disability income
Life insurance
- Term
- Universal

Major medical
Medicare supplement
Mutual funds

Key Competitors
Aetna
Equitable
John Hancock
MetLife
New York Life
Northwestern Mutual
Prudential
Travelers

Industry
Insurance - life

Overview
Minneapolis-based Lutheran Brotherhood, incorporated in 1917, is a one million–member fraternal benefit society that is also one of the US's top 50 insurance companies. The group has been transformed since 1980: assets have grown from $1.8 billion to $12 billion. Premium income in 1993 on its life, health, and annuity products was $1.5 billion. The brotherhood donates to Lutheran schools, charities, and other causes in exchange for paying no corporate income taxes. In 1993 it paid out almost $50 million for a wide range of charitable efforts. Life insurance represents almost 75% of its business.

LYKES BROS. INC.

RANK: 323

111 E. Madison St.
Tampa, FL 33602
Phone: 813-223-3981
Fax: 813-273-5493

1993 Est. Sales: $915 million
FYE: September
Employees: 3,200

Key Personnel
Chm, Pres & CEO: Thompson L. Rankin
Treas: David Schindler
SVP: David Knapp
SVP: Bill T. Bailey
VP: James M. Lykes
Dir HR: Ron Cox

Business Lines
Agriculture sales
Citrus
Coffee processing
Forestry
Meats
Packaging
Shipping
Transportation & distribution

Key Competitors
Alico
ConAgra
Del Monte
Dole
IBP
King Ranch
Orange Co.
Sunkist

Industry
Diversified operations

Overview
Tampa, Florida–based Lykes Brothers, incorporated in 1949, is a family-owned agribusiness conglomerate with interests in citrus, ranching, cattle, meat packing, insurance, banking, natural gas (Peoples Gas System), and shipping (Lykes Bros. Steamship Co.). It is one of the last major privately owned citrus producers as well as the largest meat packing operation in Florida. Lykes Bros. is known for its unique management, where family members learn the business from the bottom up.

MACANDREWS & FORBES HOLDINGS INC.

RANK: 70

35 E. 62nd St.
New York, NY 10021
Phone: 212-688-9000
Fax: 212-572-8400

1993 Est. Sales: $2,748 million
FYE: December
Employees: 23,500

Key Personnel
Chm & CEO: Ronald O. Perelman
VC: Howard Gittis
VC: Donald G. Drapkin
Pres: Bruce Slovin
EVP & Gen Counsel: Barry F. Schwartz
CFO: Erwin Engelman

◀ **See page 87 for full-page profile.**

Principal Subsidiaries
Boston Whaler
Consolidated Cigar Corp.
Marvel Entertainment Group (81%)
New World Communications
- Genesis Entertainment
- New World Television

Revlon Group, Inc.

Key Competitors
Amway
Avon
Black & Decker
Estée Lauder
L'Oréal
Time Warner
Tribune
Turner Broadcasting

Industry
Diversified operations

Overview
Led by owner Ronald Perelman since its founding in 1978, MacAndrews & Forbes Holdings has stakes in companies ranging from a licorice maker to a boat manufacturer to a cosmetics company (Revlon) to the US's #1 comic book publisher. The company also has interests in banking. In recent years MacAndrews & Forbes has systematically acquired media and communications companies, and in 1994 it combined them into a public entity named New World Communications Group, Inc.

R. H. MACY & CO., INC.

RANK: 24

151 W. 34th St.
New York, NY 10001
Phone: 212-494-4249
Fax: 212-629-6814

1993 Sales: $6,300 million
FYE: July
Employees: 51,000

Key Personnel
Chm & CEO: Myron E. Ullman III
Chm Macy's East: Arthur E. Reiner
Chm Macy's West: Michael Steinberg
Chm, I. Magnin, Inc.: Joseph Cicio
SVP Finance: Diane Price Baker
SVP HR: A. David Brown

◀ **See page 88 for full-page profile.**

Operating Units
Aeropostale
Bullock's
Charter Club
Macy's
Macy's East
Macy's West
I. Magnin

Key Competitors
Dayton Hudson
Dillard
The Gap
Harcourt General
May
Nordstrom
J. C. Penney
Saks

Industry
Retail - major department stores

Overview
Since its founding in 1858, retailer R. H. Macy has been associated with some of New York's grander traditions, like the Macy's Thanksgiving Day Parade. Unfortunately, since its 1986 management-led LBO, the company has mostly been associated with financial woes, culminating with its 1992 bankruptcy. Despite these troubles, Macy is still one of the world's largest and best-known retailers, operating 122 department stores and 84 specialty stores. A 1994 agreement to merge with retailer Federated may be Macy's salvation. The deal would take it out of bankruptcy and form the US's biggest department store chain with 450 stores and $14 billion in sales.

MAJOR LEAGUE BASEBALL

RANK: 142

350 Park Ave.
New York, NY 10022
Phone: 212-339-7800
Fax: 212-355-0007

1993 Sales: $1,775 million
FYE: October
Employees: 150

Key Personnel
Chm Exec Council: Alan H. Selig
Pres American League: Bobby Brown
Pres National League: Len Coleman
Deputy Commissioner & COO: Steve Greenberg
Gen Counsel: Tom Ostertag
Dir HR: John Honor

◀ **See page 89 for full-page profile.**

1993 Sales Leaders
New York Yankees/$108 mil.
Toronto Blue Jays/$88 mil.
Chicago Cubs/$83 mil.
Baltimore Orioles/$81 mil.
New York Mets/$81 mil.
Los Angeles Dodgers/$80 mil.
Atlanta Braves/$79 mil.
Chicago White Sox/$79 mil.

Industry
Leisure & recreational services - sports

Overview
Created in 1903 when the National League (founded 1876) and the American League (founded 1892) merged, Major League Baseball is the membership organization for baseball's owners. Each of baseball's 28 teams is a semi-independent franchise; run as separate businesses, the teams share national broadcasting revenue, gate receipts, and licensing fees. In 1994, in an effort to help small-market franchises, the owners agreed on a plan of revenue sharing that included a cap for players' salaries, a contentious issue that, along with other matters, led the players to strike in August 1994.

MARITZ INC.

RANK: 180

1375 N. Highway Dr.
Fenton, MO 63099
Phone: 314-827-4000
Fax: 314-827-4436

1994 Sales: $1,442 million
FYE: March
Employees: 6,000

Key Personnel
Chm & CEO: William E. Maritz
Pres & COO: Norman L. Schwesig
SEVP & CFO: David L. Fleisher
EVP & Sec: Jeffery D. Reinberg
SVP & Counsel: Henry S. Stolar
SVP HR: Terry Goring

Business Lines
Business group travel
Communications & training
Corporate travel
Marketing research
Performance improvement

Key Competitors
American Express
Carlson
Dun & Bradstreet
Frank Consolidated Enterprises
PS Group
Rosenbluth International
Thomas Cook Travel
Thomson Corp.

Industry
Business services - marketing

Overview
Founded in 1894 by CEO Bill Maritz's grandfather, Maritz Inc. provides a variety of services to businesses, including performance improvement seminars, marketing programs, sales incentive programs, and travel services. Bill Maritz and his sister Jean Maritz Hobler each own 20% of the company; 320 management stockholders own the rest. Hobler and her brother feuded recently over a price for Hobler's holdings, which she planned to sell. Recently, Maritz acquired telemarketing company Telecenter and signed on Ford Motor Co. as a new client.

MARK III INDUSTRIES, INC.

RANK: 338

5401 NW 44th Ave.
Ocala, FL 34482
Phone: 904-732-5878
Fax: 904-351-1017

1993 Sales: $900 million
FYE: December
Employees: 1,160

Key Personnel
Pres & CEO: Clark J. Vitulli
CFO: Randy Ellspermann
VP Prod: Larry Lincoln
VP R&D: James Hosack

Major Custom Van Products
Full-size Chevy vans
Full-size Dodge vans
Full-size Ford vans
Minivans - Chevy
Minivans - Dodge
Minivans - Ford
Sport utility vehicles
Trucks

Key Competitors
Coachman
Cobra Industries
Fleetwood
Glaval
Kentron
Starcraft Automotive
Tiara Motor Coach
Winnebago

Industry
Automotive - van conversions

Overview
Founded by Thadgard Boyd in 1978, Mark III is the U.S.'s #1 custom van converter. Thad Boyd died suddenly in 1992 at age 45, leaving the business to his wife, Sally. Mark III has grown rapidly in recent years because of its low-price, high-volume approach to the market and lower gas prices, which led to the popularity of the vans, trucks, and sport utility vehicles for which the company creates custom interiors. Mark III converts nearly 60,0000 vehicles per year. After letting her son and then a family friend run the company with unhappy results, Sally turned management over to Clark Vitulli. He brought in professional managers and has Mark III humming again.

THE MARMON GROUP, INC.

RANK: 43

225 W. Washington St.
Chicago, IL 60606
Phone: 312-372-9500
Fax: 312-845-5305

1993 Sales: $4,319 million
FYE: December
Employees: 27,700

Key Personnel
Chm: Jay A. Pritzker
Pres & CEO: Robert A. Pritzker
EVP, Treas & CFO: Robert C. Gluth
EVP: Sidney H. Bonser
VP, Gen Counsel & Sec: Robert W. Webb
Personnel Dir: George Frese

◀ **See page 90 for full-page profile.**

Business Lines
Automotive products
Building products
Medical products
Metals trading
Mining equipment
Office equipment
Rail car leasing
Water treatment systems

Key Competitors
Eaton
Equifax
Ingersoll-Rand
Itel
Manville
Masco
Peerless Manufacturing
TRW

Industry
Diversified operations

Overview
Founded in 1953, The Marmon Group is the manufacturing and services arm of the Pritzkers' empire and consists of over 60 autonomous companies making everything from seat belts and poultry incubator systems to gloves and copper plumbing. The group also provides services such as rail car leasing and consumer credit reporting. The company is owned by the Pritzker family, whose net worth is estimated at $4.4 billion by *Forbes*.

MARS, INC.

RANK: 13

6885 Elm St.
McLean, VA 22101
Phone: 703-821-4900
Fax: 703-448-9678

1993 Est. Sales: $13,000 million
FYE: December
Employees: 27,000

Key Personnel
Chm, CEO & Co-Pres: Forrest E. Mars, Jr.
Co-Pres: John F. Mars
VP & CFO: Joseph Danvers
VP Mktg, M&M/Mars: Paul Michaels
Dir External Relations: Jim Conlan
Sec: E. J. Stegeman

Major Brands
3 Musketeers
Kal Kan (pet food)
M&Ms
Mars
Milky Way
Skittles
Snickers
Uncle Ben's rice

Key Competitors
Cadbury Schweppes
Campbell Soup
General Mills
Hershey
Nestlé
Philip Morris
Quaker Oats
RJR Nabisco

Industry
Food - confectionery

Overview
Founded in 1922 by Frank Mars, the company battles with Hershey for supremacy in the US candy market, where it now holds the #2 spot. Mars is so publicity-shy that it refused to let M&Ms appear in the hit movie E.T., forfeiting a bonanza of free advertising. Family-owned Mars also produces rice, pet food, and electronic products like coin changers and scanning devices. The company is doing brisk business in Russia and other ex-Soviet states where a gargantuan ad campaign has made Snickers a household word.

◀ **See page 91 for full-page profile.**

MARY KAY COSMETICS INC.

RANK: 410

8787 Stemmons Fwy.
Dallas, TX 75247
Phone: 214-630-8787
Fax: 214-905-5699

1993 Sales: $737 million
FYE: December
Employees: 2,400

Key Personnel
Chm Emeritus: Mary Kay Ash
Chm & CEO: Richard R. Rogers
Pres & COO: Richard C. Bartlett
CFO: John P. Rochon
SVP, Sec & Legal Counsel: Bradley R. Glendening
SVP HR: Amy Digeso

Major Products
Accessories
Bath and body products
Clothing
Cosmetics
Fragrances
Jewelry
Skin care products
Toiletries

Key Competitors
Amway
Avon
Colgate-Palmolive
Estée Lauder
Helene Curtis
Jean Philippe Fragrances
L'Oréal
Shiseido

Industry
Retail - direct

Overview
Mary Kay Cosmetics is the US's 2nd largest direct seller of cosmetics (after Avon). Matriarch Mary Kay Ash founded the company in 1963. Mary Kay's cosmetics are sold by about 325,000 direct-sales consultants, who earn such prizes as pink Cadillacs, furs, diamonds, and Buicks. Ash and her family own the company, which has more women making more than $50,000 per year than any other US company; women account for 70% of the company's work force. Mary Kay is considered a good employer; in the past it has temporarily outsourced its employees to other companies instead of laying them off.

◀ **See page 92 for full-page profile.**

MASHANTUCKET PEQUOT GAMING ENTERPRISE INC.

RANK: 294

R.R. 2
Ledyard, CT 06339
Phone: 203-885-3000
Fax: 203-536-3412

1993 Est. Sales: $1,000 million
Employees: 9,100

Key Personnel
Chm: Richard "Skip" Hayward
VC Tribal Council: Kenneth Reels
Pres & CEO: G. Michael Brown
VP Resort Ops: Bob Levitt
Tribal Mgr: Phyllis Monroe
Dir PR & Cultural Resources: Theresa Bell

Operating Units
Casino
Cinema
Hotels
Native American museum
Restaurant
Theater

Key Competitors
Bally Entertainment
Circus Circus
Hilton
Mohegan tribe
Promus
Resorts International
Trump
Wampanoag tribe

Industry
Leisure & recreational services - gambling

Overview
Mashantucket Pequot Gaming Enterprise, which operates the Foxwoods High Stakes Bingo and Casino in Ledyard, Connecticut, is owned by the Mashantucket Pequot Native American tribe. Opened in 1992, the casino — the most successful in the Western hemisphere — is already raking in more than $600 million in profits per year. This has made the tribe, with only 307 members, very rich, as well as one of the largest taxpayers in the state (it shelled out $113 million in 1993 for its state-granted slot machine monopoly). Plans for a new hotel (2 are already in operation), a new bingo hall, a concert arena, an amusement park, and golf courses are underway.

MASSACHUSETTS INSTITUTE OF TECHNOLOGY

RANK: 215

77 Massachusetts Ave.
Cambridge, MA 02139
Phone: 617-253-1000
Fax: 617-253-8000

1993 Sales: $1,251 million
Employees: 10,826

Key Personnel
Chm: Paul E. Gray
Pres & CEO: Charles M. Vest
Provost: Mark S. Wrighton
VP & Treas: Glenn P. Strehle
Sec: Kathryn A. Willmore
VP & Dir Personnel: Joan Rice

Schools & Colleges
School of Architecture & Planning
School of Engineering
School of Humanities & Social Science
School of Science
Whitaker College

Industry
Schools

Overview
In 1994 *U.S. News and World Report* rated MIT as the #4 national university (after Harvard, Princeton, and Yale); as having the #1 graduate program in chemistry; and as #1 (in a tie with other universities) in computer science, economics, and math. But things are tough even at the top of the education mountain: MIT raised tuition $1,000 for 1993–94 and announced 400 layoffs and a $25 million expenses cut over 4 years to deal with a 1993 deficit of more than $10 million. Founded in 1861, MIT currently has a faculty of 960 professors and a student body of 9,800. Approximately 4,000 research projects are conducted annually.

MASSACHUSETTS MUTUAL LIFE INSURANCE COMPANY

RANK: 21

1295 State St.
Springfield, MA 01111
Phone: 413-788-8411
Fax: 413-744-8889

1993 Sales: $7,109 million
FYE: December
Employees: 6,428

Key Personnel
Pres & CEO: Thomas B. Wheeler
EVP & Chief Invest Officer: Gary E. Wendlandt
EVP Insurance & Fin Mgmt: Lawrence L. Grypp
EVP Corporate Fin Ops: Daniel J. Fitzgerald
EVP & Gen Counsel: Lawrence V. Burkett , Jr.
EVP Ops & HR: John J. Pajak

◀ **See page 93 for full-page profile.**

Selected Services
Disability income protection
Financial management
Health insurance
Investment management
Life insurance
Pension management

Key Competitors
CIGNA
Equitable
FMR
John Hancock
MetLife
New York Life
Prudential
T. Rowe Price

Industry
Insurance - life

Overview
Founded in 1851, MassMutual is the US's 12th largest life insurer. MassMutual's 4 core businesses are insurance and financial management, life and health benefits management, pension management, and investment management. The policyholder-owned company has been hard hit by the economic slowdown in the US. Because of a recent New York law that requires insurers to accept all applicants at one premium rate, MassMutual announced that it would stop selling new individual and small group policies in that state.

MASTERCARD INTERNATIONAL INCORPORATED

RANK: 498

888 Seventh Ave.
New York, NY 10106
Phone: 212-649-4600
Fax: 212-649-5046

1993 Sales: $540 million
FYE: December
Employees: 1,300

Key Personnel
Pres & CEO: H. Eugene Lockhart
Pres Asia/Pacific Region: James A. Cassin
Pres US Region: Peter S. P. Dimsey
SVP & CFO: Edward H. Brode
SVP & Gen Counsel: Robert E. Norton
SVP HR: Philip M. Thawley

Selected Services
CIRRUS (ATM Network)
Maestro (debit card)
MasterCard (credit card)
MasterCard Travelers Cheques

Key Competitors
American Express
Citicorp
Dean Witter, Discover
Visa

Industry
Financial - business services

Overview
Begun in 1966 as the Interbank Card Association and owned by its member banks, MasterCard now has 210 million cards being used to charge nearly $321 billion at 12 million locations worldwide. The MasterCard card is the world's #2 credit card (after VISA) but doesn't plan to stay that way for long – its volume grew 28% in 1993 compared with VISA's 17%. In addition to its ubiquitous credit cards, MasterCard owns the CIRRUS ATM Network (162,600 worldwide locations) and has recently developed the Maestro debit system, which now has over 110 million cards. MasterCard is a leader in co-branding credit cards; it has programs with AT&T, GM, and Shell Oil.

MAYO FOUNDATION

RANK: 163

Mayo Clinic
Rochester, MN 55905
Phone: 507-284-2511
Fax: 507-284-8713

1993 Sales: $1,579 million
FYE: December
Employees: 21,770

Key Personnel
Pres & CEO: Robert R. Waller
VP & Dir Education: Richard M. Weinshilboum
VP & Chief Admin Officer: John H. Herrell
Sec; Chair, Plng & Pub Aff: Robert K. Smoldt
Treas; Chair, Fin: David R. Ebel
HR: Greg Warner

◀ **See page 94 for full-page profile.**

Selected Care Facilities
Luther Hospital
Mayo Clinic, Jacksonville
Mayo Clinic, Rochester
Mayo Clinic, Scottsdale
Midelfort Clinic
Rochester Methodist Hospital
St. Luke's Hospital
St. Marys Hospital

Key Competitors
Baylor College of Medicine
Columbia/HCA
Detroit Medical Center
Harvard Medical School
Johns Hopkins
Lutheran Health Care
Unilab

Industry
Hospitals

Overview
William W. Mayo and 2 sons began operating St. Marys Hospital in 1889, changing the name to Mayo Clinic in 1905. In 1915 the brothers established the Mayo Graduate School of Medicine in affiliation with the University of Minnesota. In 1919 Mayo's sons formed a nonprofit foundation to run the clinic and, later, its subsidiaries. The clinic established the first blood bank in 1933 and saw its millionth patient in 1938. In 1939 both of the brothers died. The clinic, now the world's largest private medical facility, is named in *The Best Hospitals of America.* Mayo is known for its philanthropy, providing health care regardless of a patient's ability to pay.

MCCARTHY BUILDING COMPANIES

RANK: 430

1341 N. Rock Hill Rd.
Ladue, MO 63124
Phone: 314-968-3300
Fax: 314-968-0032

1993 Sales: $700 million
FYE: March
Employees: 1,700

Key Personnel
Chm & CEO: Michael M. McCarthy
CFO, Sec & Treas: George Scherer
EVP: Richard A. Vandegrift
Controller: Doug Audiffred
VP HR: James Faust
Gen Counsel: James Staskiel

Major Projects
Bridges
Convention centers
Medical facilities
Prisons
Public buildings

Key Competitors
Barton-Malow Enterprises
Bechtel
Fluor
Gilbane Building
Halliburton
Hensel Phelps
Morrison Knudsen
Peter Kiewit Sons'

Industry
Construction - heavy

Overview
McCarthy Building is the holding company for McCarthy Brothers, one of the largest heavy construction companies in the US. Founded in 1864, the company has been owned and operated by members of the McCarthy family for 130 years, which gives this company unusual longevity for a family-run business. McCarthy operates 6 offices nationally and is one of the largest contractors of health and medical facilities in the US. It also built the California State Prison at El Centro and the Cervantes Convention Center in St. Louis.

MCCRORY CORPORATION

RANK: 284

667 Madison Ave.
New York, NY 10021
Phone: 212-735-9500
Fax: 212-735-9450

1994 Sales: $1,024 million
Employees: 14,400

Key Personnel
Chm and CEO: Meshulam Ricklis
VC: Karl L. Margolis
Pres McCrory Stores: Steve Jackel
EVP: Jeff Safchik
SVP and Treasurer: Paul Weiner
SVP and Counsel: Dean Haskell

Stores
H. L. Green
S.H. Kress
McCrory
McLellan
GC Murphy
J. J. Newberry
T. G. & Y.

Key Competitors
Ames
Dayton Hudson
Kmart
Venture Stores
Wal-Mart
Woolworth

Industry
Retail - discount & variety

Overview
Founded by John McCrorey in Scottdale, PA in 1882, McCrory's five & dime store chain (he dropped the "e" to save space on signs) rose to greatness in the 1920s, went bankrupt during the Depression, rose again, only to crash to earth again, declaring bankruptcy in 1992. Owner Meshulam Ricklis, who acquired his initial interest in the company in 1960, still runs McCrory but has reduced the number of stores from 819 in 1992 to 740 in 1994. McCrory serves 36 states and the District of Columbia and sells to a customer base that is primarily low-income and innercity. Ricklis operates through Ricklis Family Corporation and is known for his flashy and litigious lifestyle.

MCKEE FOODS CORPORATION

RANK: 456

10260 McKee Rd.
Collegedale, TN 37315
Phone: 615-238-7111
Fax: 615-238-7170

1993 Sales: $640 million
FYE: July
Employees: 4,500

Key Personnel
Chm: O. D. McKee
Pres & CEO: Ellsworth McKee
VP & Treas: Barry Patterson
EVP: Jack McKee
Sec: Joe Davis
VP HR: Blair Lake

Major Products
Caravellas
Devil Cremes
Figaroos
Golden Cremes
Natural Grains Cereal
Nutty Bars
Oatmeal Creme Pies
Swiss Rolls

Key Competitors
Flowers Industries
General Mills
Interstate Bakeries
Kellogg
Quaker Oats
Ralston Continental
RJR Nabisco
Tasty Baking

Industry
Food - baked goods

Overview
The largest independently owned snack-cake company in the US, McKee Foods started in 1931 with founder O.D. McKee selling cupcakes and apple turnovers from the trunk of his car. Now with 4 bakeries in 3 states, family-owned and -operated McKee Foods has more than half the US snack-cake market. The key to its success is its 38 varieties of Little Debbie snack cakes, named after one of McKee's grandchildren. McKee Foods also sells its products to supermarkets at a steep discount and keeps its overhead low; its natural preservatives give products a longer shelf life than competitors'. Along with its Sunbelt label, the company markets over 50 products in 48 states.

MCKINSEY & COMPANY, INC.

RANK: 208

55 E. 52nd St.
New York, NY 10022
Phone: 212-446-7000
Fax: 212-446-8575

1993 Est. Sales: $1,300 million
FYE: December
Employees: 5,560

Key Personnel
Managing Dir: Rajat Gupta
CFO: James Rogers
Gen Counsel: Jean Molino
Dir London: Michael Patsalos-Fox
Dir Tokyo: Kenichi Ohmae
Principal & Dir Personnel: Jerome Vascellaro

◀ **See page 95 for full-page profile.**

Selected Services
Cost reduction & profit improvement
Electronic data processing
Management controls
Manufacturing management
Marketing
Operations research
Organizational change
Strategic planning

Key Competitors
Arthur Andersen
Arthur D. Little
Bain & Co.
Booz, Allen & Hamilton
Boston Consulting Group
Electronic Data Systems
KPMG
Marsh & McLennan

Industry
Consulting

Overview
Founded in 1926, McKinsey & Co. practically invented the profession of management consulting and is one of the country's oldest and most prestigious consulting firms. It is noted for the intense loyalty of its consulting staff, despite a high rate of attrition and a low rate of promotion to partnership. McKinsey has worked for many of the US's largest companies at fees of up to $1 million or more. The firm is managed by a team elected by its partners and led by a managing director elected triennially. In 1994 it elected its first managing director of non-European descent, US-educated Rajat Gupta.

MEDIANEWS GROUP INC.

RANK: 483

4888 Loop Central Dr., Ste. 525
Houston, TX 77081
Phone: 713-295-3800
Fax: 713-295-3893

1993 Sales: $575 million
FYE: December
Employees: 7,943

Key Personnel
Chm: Richard B. Scudder
VC, Pres & CEO: William D. Singleton
EVP & CFO: Joseph J. Lodovic
SVP Admin: E. M. Fluker
Controller: James McDougald
Dir HR: Pat Angel

Selected Newspapers
Alameda Times-Star (CA)
Denver Post
Express-Times (Easton, PA)
Gloucester County Times (NJ)
Houston Post
Las Cruces Sun-News (NM)
Woodbridge Potomac News (VA)
Ypsilanti Press (MI)

Key Competitors
Advance Publications
Gannett
Hearst
Knight-Ridder
New York Times
E. W. Scripps
Times Mirror Co.
Tribune

Industry
Publishing - newspapers

Overview
Founded in 1983, MediaNews Group controls 17 daily and 57 nondaily newspapers throughout the US, with a combined circulation of about 2 million. MediaNews Group's most prominent properties include the *Houston Post* and the *Denver Post*. About half of its newspapers are in New Jersey. The Houston-based company is managed by William Dean Singleton, who shares 50-50 ownership with Richard Scudder, the group's chairman. The company recently purchased 5 New Jersey and Pennsylvania newspapers from Virginia-based Media General.

MEIJER, INC.

RANK: 44

2929 Walker Ave. NW
Grand Rapids, MI 49504
Phone: 616-453-6711
Fax: 616-791-2572

1993 Est. Sales: $4,250 million
FYE: December
Employees: 60,000

Key Personnel
Chm Exec Committee: Fred Meijer
Co-Chm: Doug Meijer
Co-Chm: Hank Meijer
SVP Fin & Admin: Fritz Kolk
SVP, Gen Counsel & Sec: Bob Riley
SVP Personnel: Windy Ray

See page 96 for full-page profile.

Selected Services
Bakery
Bulk foods
Delicatessen
Food court
Pharmacy
Photo lab
Service meat & seafood
Video shop

Key Competitors
American Stores
Great A&P
Hi-Vee Food Stores
Kroger
Roundy's
Spartan Stores
SUPERVALU
Wal-Mart

Industry
Retail - supermarkets

Overview
With 85 Meijer combination stores, 69 gas stations, and 60,000 employees, Meijer is one of the largest food retailers in the US. Its giant superstores often have as many as 24 departments. Founded in 1934, Meijer is chaired by the founder's son and owned by the Meijer family. It still operates under the founder's standards: high regard for employees and customers, competitive pricing, and a strong focus on future growth. Meijer, with a strong presence in Michigan and Ohio, recently entered the Indiana market by opening 8 stores.

MENARD, INC.

RANK: 150

4777 Menard Dr.
Eau Claire, WI 54703
Phone: 715-874-5911
Fax: 715-876-5901

1994 Sales: $1,700 million
FYE: January
Employees: 6,500

Key Personnel
Pres & CEO: John R. Menard
CFO & Treas: Earl R. Rasmussen
Ops Mgr: Larry Menard
Senior Merchandiser: Ed Archibald
General Counsel & Sec: Warren R. Johnson
Dir HR, Office Mgr: Terri Jain

Major Products
Building supplies
Doors
Floor coverings
Hardware
Lumber
Prefabricated wood buildings
Steel trim

Key Competitors
84 Lumber
Ace Hardware
Cotter & Co.
Hardware Wholesalers
Home Depot
Kmart
SERVISTAR
Spahn & Rose Lumber

Industry
Building products - retail

Overview
John Menard founded Menard Inc. in 1960 at age 19 as a barn construction enterprise to fund his college years. Today the company, still owned by Menard, is one of the largest home improvement chains, with 90 stores located primarily in the upper Midwest. The Wisconsin-based chain sells low-priced hardware imported from the Far East and reportedly has no bank debt. Menard has recently expanded operations in the Chicago area and in Michigan, South Dakota, Nebraska, Wisconsin, and Iowa.

MENASHA CORPORATION

RANK: 444

1645 Bergstrom Rd.
Neenah, WI 54956
Phone: 414-751-1000
Fax: 414-751-1236

1993 Sales: $674 million
FYE: December
Employees: 4,500

Key Personnel
Chm: Bernard J. McCarragher
Pres & CEO: Robert D. Bero
SVP Packaging: Bruce T. Buchanan
VP Fin: William C. Griffith
VP & Gen Counsel: James J. Sarosiek
VP HR: David H. Rust

Business Lines
Forest products
Information graphics
Material handling products
Packaging
Plastics
Promotional graphics

Key Competitors
Boise Cascade
Canadian Pacific
Federal Paper Board
Georgia-Pacific
International Paper
Mead
Stone Container
Weyerhaeuser

Industry
Paper & paper products

Overview
Elisha Smith's pail factory, purchased in 1852, has evolved from a woodenware producer to a diversified paper packaging and material handling products company, with 53 operations in 17 US states and 3 other countries. The company's shareholders are still primarily Smith's descendants. In the 1980s the company grew rapidly and diversified through acquisitions, but the largest share of its sales is still generated by packaging (36%), with plastics coming in next (23%). The company sells logs to domestic mills and exports to such Pacific Rim countries as Japan, Korea, and China from its 100,000 acres of timberland.

MERCY HEALTH SERVICES

RANK: 125

34605 W. 12 Mile Rd.
Farmington Hills, MI 48331
Phone: 810-489-6000
Fax: 810-489-6932

1993 Sales: $1,900 million
FYE: June
Employees: 24,362

Key Personnel
Pres & CEO: Judith C. Pelham
CFO: James H. Combs
EVP: Michael R. Schwartz
EVP: Nancy Hart
EVP: Robert Laverty
VP & Gen Counsel: Agnes Hagerty

Selected Care Facilities
Mercy Hospital (Charlotte, NC)
Mercy Hospital (Detroit, MI)
Mercy Hospital (Port Huron, MI)
St. Lawrence Hospital (Lansing, MI)
Saint Mary's (Grand Rapids, MI)

Key Competitors
Aurora Health Care
Bronson Healthcare
Columbia/HCA
The Detroit Medical Center
Mayo Foundation
Prudential
Sinai Health Care
Travelers

Industry
Hospitals

Overview
Organized in 1984 by the Sisters of Mercy Regional Community of Detroit, Mercy Health Services Inc. is one of the largest health care systems in the US, with units in Michigan, North Carolina, and Iowa. Offering its Care Choices HMO program in Iowa and Michigan, the company is also aggressively entering the managed care market by merging services with other local hospitals and physicians to control costs. It is also negotiating with insurers such as Blue Cross/Blue Shield of Michigan and Aetna Life & Casualty to be their preferred provider organization.

MERCY HEALTH SYSTEM

RANK: 263

2335 Grandview Ave.
Cincinnati, OH 45206
Phone: 513-221-2736
Fax: 513-559-3835

1993 Sales: $1,076 million
FYE: December
Employees: 15,739

Key Personnel
Interim Pres & CEO: Sister Marjorie Bosse
EVP: Gary Campbell
SVP: Sister Beverly McGuire
SVP: Jay S. Herron
SVP HR: Ronald J. Baril
VP Legal Svcs: Susan Smith Makos

Selected Care Facilities
Lourdes Hospital (KY)
Mercy Hospital, Scranton (PA)
Mercy Hospital, Toledo (OH)
Mercy Hospital, Wilkes-Barre (PA)
Mercy Medical Ctr., Springfield (OH)
St. Charles Hospital (OH)
St. Mary's Medical Center (TN)
St. Rita's Medical Center (OH)

Key Competitors
Alliant Health System
Columbia/HCA
HealthTrust
Quorum Health Group
Sisters of Charity Health Care
Universal Health Services

Industry
Hospitals

Overview
The 6th largest catholic health care system in the US, Mercy Health System was formed in 1986, although its roots go back to hospital systems run by the Sisters of Mercy in the early 1960s. The system is a nonprofit organization run by the Sisters of Mercy, Cincinnati, Ohio, and the Sisters of Mercy, Dallas, Pennsylvania. Mercy Health System has 19 acute-care facilites and 10 long-term care facilities in Indiana, Kentucky, Ohio, Pennsylvania, and Tennessee. Overall, the system includes more than 60 corporations involved in health care activities.

METALLURG, INC.

RANK: 491

25 E. 39th St.
New York, NY 10016
Phone: 212-686-4010
Fax: 212-697-2874

1993 Sales: $550 million
FYE: December
Employees: 2,000

Key Personnel
Chm, CEO & Pres: Michael A. Standen
VP Fin, Treas & CFO: Barry C. Nuss
VP: Bill Kienke
Sec: Michael Finn
Controller: Tony Cocca
HR: Michael Banks

Major Products
Aluminum master alloys
Chromium
Cobalt
Metal Carbides
Tin
Titanium
Vanadium

Key Competitors
American Alloys
American Mine Services
Christensen Boyles
Globe Metallurgical
Keokuk Ferro-Sil
Macalloy
Reactive Metal & Alloys
Reading Alloys

Industry
Metal processing & fabrication

Overview
Metallurg, incorporated in 1946, is a producer and trader of specialty metal alloys used in automobiles and appliances and in the aerospace industry. Subsidiary Shieldalloy Metallurgical Corp. manufactures abrasive additives and metal powders used by the optical industry. In filing for Chapter 11 bankruptcy protection, Metallurg's CEO blamed the company's need to reorganize on an influx of metal exports from Russia, which caused prices for metal alloys to plummet, and the huge cost of environmental compliance.

METROMEDIA COMPANY

RANK: 134

One Meadowlands Plaza
East Rutherford, NJ 07073
Phone: 201-804-6400
Fax: 201-804-6540

1992 Est. Sales: $1,804 million
FYE: December
Employees: 20,400

Key Personnel
Gen Partner, Chm, Pres & CEO: John W. Kluge
Gen Partner & EVP: Stuart Subotnick
SVP, Sec & Gen Counsel: Arnold L. Wadler
SVP Fin: Robert A. Maresca
Dir HR: Beverly Scoggins

◄ See page 97 for full-page profile.

Principal Subsidiaries
Bristol Valley Foods
LDDS Metromedia Communications
Metbenale
Metromedia Steakhouses
MUZE, Inc.
North Communications
Orion Pictures
Radisson Empire Hotel

Key Competitors
AT&T
Carlson
General Mills
Lone Star Steakhouse
McDonald's
MCI
Outback Steakhouse
Sprint

Industry
Diversified operations

Overview
Started by John Kluge from a single radio station he purchased in 1946, Metromedia is now a telecommunications giant, with interests in restaurants (Ponderosa, Bonanza, Steak and Ale, and Bennigan's), filmmaking (Orion), and other businesses. Today Kluge is considered to be the 3rd richest man in the US, with an estimated $5.9 billion fortune. Metromedia is in the process of merging its long-distance subsidiaries with 2 other carriers; it will then become the 4th largest long-distance provider in the US (after AT&T, MCI, and Sprint).

METROPOLITAN LIFE INSURANCE COMPANY

RANK: 5

One Madison Ave.
New York, NY 10010
Phone: 212-578-2211
Fax: 212-578-3320

1993 Sales: $28,683 million
FYE: December
Employees: 55,000

Key Personnel
Chm & CEO: Harry Kamen
Pres & COO: Ted Athanassiades
SEVP & CFO: Stewart G. Nagler
EVP & Chief Investment Officer: Gerald Clark
SVP & Gen Counsel: Richard M. Blackwell
SVP HR: Anne E. Hayden

◄ See page 98 for full-page profile.

Principal Subsidiaries
Century 21 Real Estate Corporation
MetLife HealthCare Management Corporation
MetLife Securities, Inc.
MetLife (UK) Limited
Metropolitan Property & Casualty Insurance
Metropolitan Tower Life Insurance Company
Metropolitan Trust Co. of Canada
Seguros Génesis, S.A. (Mexico)

Key Competitors
Aetna
Allstate
Equitable
John Hancock
New York Life
Northwestern Mutual
Prudential
RE/MAX

Industry
Insurance - multiline

Overview
Founded in 1868, Metropolitan Life is the largest North American life insurer, with $1.2 trillion of life insurance in force. Its Century 21 subsidiary is the largest real estate franchise sales organization in the world. The policyholder-owned company is also involved in real estate leasing, appraising, mortgage banking, financing, asset management, and investment services. The company has been rocked by charges of corrupt sales practices in 13 states that sparked investigations in 1993 and 1994.

MID-AMERICA DAIRYMEN, INC. — RANK: 133

3253 E. Chestnut Expwy.
Springfield, MO 65802
Phone: 417-865-7100
Fax: 417-865-1093

1993 Sales: $1,832 million
FYE: December
Employees: 3,500

Key Personnel
CEO: Gary E. Hanman
Pres: Carl Baumann
VP Fin: Gerald Bos
VP Mktg & Planning: Bill Blakeslee
VP HR: Ray Silvey
Gen Counsel: Wayne Hoecker

Major Products
Butter
Cheeses & cheese sauces
Coffee creamers
Nonfat dry milk
Infant formula
Milk
Whey products
Yogurt

Key Competitors
Associated Milk Producers
Borden
Dairymen
Dean Foods
Farmland Industries
General Mills
Land O' Lakes
Wisconsin Dairies Co-op

Industry
Food - dairy products

Overview
Founded in 1968, Mid-America Dairymen is owned by 13,000 members located in 7 membership divisions covering 15 US states. The largest milk cooperative in the northern Midwest, Mid-America provides members with a variety of services, including hauling, sampling, and testing; field services; farm supplies; loans; insurance; and government lobbying. Nearly 90% of the milk produced at member farms is sold as Grade A milk; the rest is used to produce dairy products at the cooperative's plants.

MID-ATLANTIC CARS INC. — RANK: 186

10287 Lee Hwy.
Fairfax, VA 22030
Phone: 703-352-5555
Fax: 703-352-5591

1992 Sales: $1,400 million
FYE: December
Employees: 3,300

Key Personnel
Pres: John E. Wright
VP: Frank Cuteri
Treas: Charles Stringfellow
Sec: Catherine Parsell

Major Brands
Buick
Dodge
Lincoln-Mercury
Mazda
Nissan
Pontiac
Toyota
Volvo

Key Competitors
Bethesda Investment
Casey Auto Group
Hendrick Automotive
Holman Enterprises
Lustine Automotive Services
Rosenthal Automotive

Industry
Retail - new & used cars

Overview
Mid-Atlantic Cars, founded in 1983, sells a wide variety of new and used automobiles and trucks at more than 30 company-owned dealerships in Maryland and Virginia. Mid-Atlantic also operates parts and service centers. Founder William Schuiling started Mid-Atlantic when he bought a Pontiac dealership in Arlington, Virginia, where he was working as a sales manager. Mid-Atlantic expanded from being a "single-point" dealer who sold only one brand of automobile to a multidealer, selling a variety of domestic and international automobiles at several locations, and in the process became one of the region's largest automobile dealers.

MILLIKEN & CO. — RANK: 78

920 Milliken Rd.
Spartanburg, SC 29303
Phone: 803-573-2020
Fax: 803-573-2100

1992 Est. Sales: $2,640 million
FYE: November
Employees: 14,000

Key Personnel
Chm & CEO: Roger Milliken
Pres & COO: Thomas J. Malone
VP & CFO: Minot K. Milliken
VP & Gen Counsel: Bill Petry
Dir Mktg: Kay Shannon
VP HR: Tommy Hodge

Major Products
Automotive upholstery
Carpet & carpet tiles
Elastic fabrics
Lining fabrics
Machinery filters
Specialty chemicals
Stretch fabrics (Lycra)
Textured yarns

Key Competitors
Armstrong World
Burlington Industries
DuPont
Fieldcrest Cannon
Galey & Lord
W. R. Grace
JPS Textile
R. B. Pamplin

Industry
Textiles - mill products

Overview
Founded in 1865, Milliken is the largest privately held textile company in the US, manufacturing fabrics for everything from Burger King uniforms to Michelin tires. The company also produces chemicals used in dyes, plastics, petroleum products, and textiles. The company has about 200 shareholders (primarily Milliken family members), but a majority of the company's stock is controlled by CEO Roger "Big Red" Milliken, his brother Gerrish, and his cousin Minot.

◀ **See page 99 for full-page profile.**

THE MINNESOTA MUTUAL LIFE INSURANCE COMPANY — RANK: 140

400 Robert St. North
St. Paul, MN 55101
Phone: 612-298-3500
Fax: 612-223-4488

1993 Sales: $1,783 million
FYE: December
Employees: 1,860

Key Personnel
Chm: Coleman Bloomfield
Pres & CEO: Robert Senkler
EVP: Robert E. Hunstad
VP Fin Mgmt & CFO: Gregory S. Strong
VP, Gen Counsel & Sec: Robert J. Hasling
VP HR & Corp Svcs: Keith M. Campbell

Selected Services
Annuities
Asset management
Disability insurance
Financial services
Group insurance plans
Life insurance
Pension products

Key Competitors
Aetna
John Hancock
Kemper
MassMutual
MetLife
New York Life
Northwestern Mutual
Travelers

Industry
Insurance - life

Overview
Founded in 1880, Minnesota Mutual Life is among the largest mutual life insurers in the US, with more than $113 billion of life insurance in force. The company, which is owned by its 9 million policyholders, provides individual and group insurance and financial services through 86 general agencies. Subsidiary MIMLIC Asset Management Company manages the company's assets and about $1.6 billion in assets of corporate clients and individuals. After retiring in 1993, long-time chairman Coleman Bloomfield was forced to return in 1994 after his replacement, John Clymer, left to pursue private interests.

MINYARD FOOD STORES INC.

RANK: 400

777 Freeport Pkwy.
Coppell, TX 75019
Phone: 214-393-8700
Fax: 214-462-9407

1993 Sales: $770 million
FYE: July
Employees: 6,200

Key Personnel
Co-Chm: Elizabeth Minyard
Co-Chm: Gretchen M. Williams
Pres & CEO: J. L. "Sonny" Williams
SVP Wholesale Dist: Prudencio Pineda
Dir Fin: Mario LaForte
Dir HR: Alan Vaughan

Operating Units
Carnival Food Stores
Minyard Food Stores
Sack 'n Save Warehouse Food Stores

Key Competitors
Albertson's
Brookshire Grocery
H. E. Butt
Food Lion
Kroger
Randalls
Wal-Mart
Winn-Dixie

Industry
Retail - supermarkets

Overview
The Minyard family, who founded Minyard Food Stores in 1932, transformed a neighborhood grocery in East Dallas into one of the largest grocery chains in the area. Now owned by 2 sisters and one of their cousins, Minyard is experimenting with new ideas to attract customers. Recently, it started a new chain of ethnic foods supermarkets, under the name Carnival. Its Sack 'n Save warehouse chain has added walk-in beer coolers and upgraded its offerings of perishables to better compete with supermarkets.

MONTEFIORE MEDICAL CENTER

RANK: 321

111 E. 210th St.
Bronx, NY 10467
Phone: 718-920-4321
Fax: 718-652-2161

1993 Sales: $927 million
FYE: December
Employees: 10,500

Key Personnel
Pres: Spencer Foreman
EVP Corporate: Donald L. Ashkenase
EVP Ops: Robert B. Conaty
SVP & Gen Counsel: Nadia C. Adler
SVP Fin: Joel A. Perlman
SVP HR: Donald G. Revelle

Selected Services
Adolescent AIDS services
Child protection services
Geriatric education
Home health services
Psychiatric services
Sleep-wake disorder treatment

Key Competitors
Columbia/HCA
Eger Lutheran Healthcare Ctr.
Johns Hopkins
Kennedy Memorial
NY City Health & Hospitals
United HealthCare
West Jersey Health

Industry
Hospitals

Overview
As the University Hospital for the Albert Einstein College of Medicine, Montefiore Medical Center is the largest teaching hospital in the US, training 15% of America's doctors. Founded in 1884 as the Montefiore Home for Chronic Invalids, today the hospital is the main health provider for 1.2 million people in the Bronx, one of the nation's poorest areas. Proposed federal Medicare cuts threaten Montefiore, which serves more Medicare patients than any other hospital in the US and relies on that funding for almost 40% of its budget.

MONTGOMERY WARD HOLDING CORP.

RANK: 28

One Montgomery Ward Plaza
Chicago, IL 60671
Phone: 312-467-2000
Fax: 312-467-3975

1993 Sales: $6,002 million
FYE: December
Employees: 51,350

Key Personnel
Chm & CEO: Bernard F. Brennan
VC Ops & Specialty Catalogs: Richard M. Bergel
Pres & COO: Bernard W. Andrews
EVP, Sec & Gen Counsel: Spencer H. Heine
EVP & CFO: John L. Workman
EVP HR, Montgomery Ward: Robert A. Kasenter

◀ **See page 100 for full-page profile.**

Business Lines
Apparel
Appliances
Auto parts, tires & batteries
Car rental
Electronics & repair services
Home furnishings
Optometric/optician services
Photographic portraits

Key Competitors
Circuit City
Dillard
Federated
May
Melville
J. C. Penney
Sears
Wal-Mart

Industry
Retail - major department stores

Overview
Founded in 1872, Montgomery Ward is one of America's largest department store operators as well as one of its top furniture sellers. In 1988 CEO Bernard Brennan and other senior managers bought the company from Mobil in one of the biggest management-led LBOs in US history. Net income has fallen over the last several years as the company has struggled with depressed markets and intense competition, but sales seem to be rebounding. In February 1994 Ward announced it was buying Lechmere, an appliance and consumer electronics retailer with 24 stores in the northeastern US and annual sales of $800 million.

MOORMAN MANUFACTURING COMPANY

RANK: 372

1000 N. 30th St.
Quincy, IL 62301
Phone: 217-222-7100
Fax: 217-222-4069

1993 Sales: $820 million
FYE: March
Employees: 3,000

Key Personnel
Chm, Pres & CEO : Tom M. McKenna
VP Fin & CFO: W. T. Hurley
Sec: Betty Schappaugh
VP HR: Terry Lunt

Major Products
Cattle feed
Grain
Hog feed
Industrial equipment
Livestock equipment
Soybean products
Vegetable oils

Key Competitors
ADM
Ag Processing
Cargill
ConAgra
Ferruzzi
Riceland Foods
Southern States Coop
Tenneco

Industry
Food - flour & grain

Overview
One of the nation's largest animal feed and equipment suppliers and one of the world's largest soybean processors, Moorman Manufacturing was founded in 1885 by T. R. Moorman. The company's feed operations make more than 500 feed formulations for pork, beef, and dairy producers. Its livestock equipment subsidiary, Quincy Design and Manufacturing, produces more than 200 types of equipment, including feeders and confinement systems. Another subsidiary, Quincy Soybean, processes more than 70 million bushels of soybeans a year.

MORSE OPERATIONS

RANK: 128

6363 NW 6 Way, Ste. 400
Ft. Lauderdale, FL 33309
Phone: 305-351-0055
Fax: 305-771-6493

1993 Sales: $1,886 million
FYE: December
Employees: 1,563

Key Personnel
Chm: Edward J. Morse
Pres: Edward J. Morse, Jr.
VP & CFO: Donald A. MacInnes
VP: Richard V. Beaver
Mktg Dir: Myron R. May
HR: Betty Anne Beaver

Major Brands
Buick
Cadillac
Chevrolet
Dodge
Honda
Mazda
Saturn
Toyota

Key Competitors
Bill Heard
Carlisle Motors
Friendly Ford
Island Lincoln-Mercury
JM Family Enterprises
Potamkin Manhattan
Royal Automotive Group
Scott-McRae Group

Industry
Retail - new & used cars

Overview
Ft. Lauderdale–based and family-owned Morse Operations, founded in 1946, is one of the largest "megadealers" of new and used cars in the country. With a huge fleet operation and 17 auto dealerships, Morse is one of only a handful of US car megadealerships that dominate regional markets. Morse's operations include one of the country's largest Cadillac dealerships and Ed Morse Chevrolet, which is the #2 US car dealership (after Jordan Motor's Jordan Ford) based on fleet sales and new unit sales.

M. A. MORTENSON COMPANIES, INC.

RANK: 387

700 Meadow Ln. North
Minneapolis, MN 55422
Phone: 612-522-2100
Fax: 612-520-3430

1993 Sales: $798 million
FYE: December
Employees: 1,700

Key Personnel
Chm, Pres & CEO: M. A. Mortenson, Jr.
VP & CFO: Peter A. Conzemius
VP: John Wood
Sec: Earl Hacking
Gen Counsel: Jeanne Forneris
Dir Quality & Training: Jerry Pitzrick

Selected Projects
Denver International Airport
Lincoln Centre (Minneapolis)
Minneapolis Convention Center
National Sports Center (Blaine, MN)
Normandale Lake Office Park (MN)
Norwest Center (Minneapolis)
Target Center (Minneapolis)
VA Med. Center (Ft. Snelling, MN)

Key Competitors
Bechtel
Centex
Gilbane Building
Parsons
Pepper
Peter Kiewit Sons'
Turner Industries
H. B. Zachry

Industry
Construction - heavy

Overview
M. A. Mortenson founded his construction company in 1954; it is now one of the US's largest domestic contractors. The company is involved primarily in general building, water and sewer, and transportation construction. Mortenson conducts most of its operations in the Midwest and is one of the only major US contractors that does no business overseas. The company is shifting away from corporate/campus projects to a variety of other endeavors, including sports complexes and municipal buildings. Mortenson built Iowa's tallest building, the 44-story 801 Grand in Des Moines.

MTS INC.

RANK: 384

2500 Del Monte St., Bldg. C
West Sacramento, CA 95691
Phone: 916-373-2500
Fax: 916-373-2535

1993 Sales: $800 million
FYE: July
Employees: 5,269

Key Personnel
Pres & CEO: Russell M. Solomon
EVP, Sec & Treas: Walter S. Martin
VP Fin & CFO: Dee Searson
VP: Michael T. Solomon
Controller: Bernadette Markwood
Personnel Mgr: Genny Danielson

Major Products
Books
Cassettes
Compact discs
Pulse magazine
Videos

Key Competitors
Barnes & Noble
Best Buy
Blockbuster
Camelot Music
Hastings Manufacturing
Musicland
Trans World Music
Wherehouse Entertainment

Industry
Retail - books, music & video

Overview
MTS's Tower Records is the 2nd largest record store chain in the US (after Musicland). Russell Solomon founded MTS in 1960 with a $5,000 loan from his father, 10 days after his previous venture into record wholesaling went broke. The company took off in 1968 when Solomon opened his first Tower Records megastore in San Francisco. Stocking thousands of titles, Tower rode a rising interest in popular music. The company also owns bookstores and video stores. All of Solomon's stores, over 120 in all, use the same concept, staying open late and offering as many titles as possible in as large a space as possible.

THE MUTUAL LIFE INSURANCE COMPANY OF NEW YORK

RANK: 54

1740 Broadway
New York, NY 10019
Phone: 212-708-2000
Fax: 212-708-2056

1993 Sales: $3,493 million
FYE: December
Employees: 3,400

Key Personnel
Chm & CEO: Michael I. Roth
Pres & COO: Samuel J. Foti
SVP & CFO: Richard Daddario
SVP & Gen Counsel: Richard E. Mulroy
Dir HR: Catherine Gushue

Principal Subsidiaries
ARES Inc.
Bell Investment Acquisition Corp.
Enterprise Capital Management
MONY Brokerage, Inc.
MONY Funding, Inc.
MONY Life Insurance Company
MONY Securities Corp.

Key Competitors
Aetna
CIGNA
John Hancock
MetLife
Nationwide
New York Life
Principal Financial
Prudential

Industry
Insurance - life

Overview
Mutual of New York (MONY) is the 9th largest life insurer in the US. The company specializes in disability income, retirement funding, and securities brokerage and dealership. As part of its ongoing restructuring, aimed at streamlining for efficiency, MONY agreed to sell its group pension business to AEGON USA in late 1993. The company boasts many "firsts" in its 150-year history. For example, it was the first to offer life insurance both to women and to those serving in the military.

MUTUAL OF OMAHA COMPANIES

RANK: 52

Mutual of Omaha Plaza
Omaha, NE 68175
Phone: 402-342-7600
Fax: 402-978-2775

1993 Sales: $3,577 million
FYE: December
Employees: 7,665

Key Personnel
Chm & CEO: Thomas J. Skutt
Pres & COO: John Weekly
CFO: John W. Sturgeon
SEVP & Sec: Mary J. Huerter
EVP & Dir HR: Robert Bogart
SVP & Chief Counsel: Tom McCusker

Business Lines
Accident & health insurance
Automobile insurance
Foreign currency exchange
Health maintenance services
Homeowners insurance
Preferred provider organizations
Travel & baggage insurance

Key Competitors
AFLAC
Allstate
CIGNA
GEICO
Liberty Mutual
Nationwide
State Farm
Travelers

Industry
Insurance - property & casualty

Overview
Known almost as well for its sponsorship of the popular television series "Wild Kingdom" as for the insurance it sells, Mutual of Omaha is the largest writer of individual health and accident insurance in the US. Incorporated in 1909, this mutual insurance company operates in all 50 states, the District of Columbia, Puerto Rico, the Virgin Islands, and Canada. About 4,800 representatives work out of 125 branch offices. New York provides Mutual of Omaha with the largest chunk of policyholders (9.6%), followed by Canada (9.3%), Texas (6.0%), Florida (4.9%), and California (4.7%).

NATIONAL BASKETBALL ASSOCIATION

RANK: 281

645 Fifth Ave., 15th Fl.
New York, NY 10022
Phone: 212-826-7000
Fax: 212-754-6414

1993 Sales: $1,030 million
FYE: August
Employees: 450

Key Personnel
Commissioner: David J. Stern
Dep Comm & COO: Russell T. Granik
VP Fin: Robert Criqui
VP Human & Info Res: Leroy D. Nunery
VP Ops: Rod Thorn
Gen Counsel: Joel Litvin

1993 Sales Leaders
Los Angeles Lakers/$68.7 mil.
New York Knicks/$61.6 mil.
Detroit Pistons/$60.6 mil.
Phoenix Suns/$55.6 mil.
Chicago Bulls/$50.3 mil.
Boston Celtics/$41.9 mil.
Cleveland Cavaliers/$40.6 mil.
Utah Jazz/$39.7 mil.

Industry
Leisure & recreational services - sports

Overview
Formed in 1946, the NBA is a nonprofit, 27-team, professional basketball league. Rebounding from a poor image and an even poorer bank account in the early 1980s, the league currently is enjoying unprecedented success. In the last 10 years, the NBA has experienced soaring growth in attendance, merchandise sales, TV proceeds, and player salaries. However, Commissioner David Stern, credited for most of the league's recent success, now faces a host of new challenges, including diminished star power with the loss of megastars Michael Jordan and Magic Johnson and discord among the ranks of owners.

NATIONAL DISTRIBUTING COMPANY, INC.

RANK: 368

One National Dr. SW
Atlanta, GA 30336
Phone: 404-696-9440
Fax: 404-691-0364

1993 Sales: $830 million
FYE: December
Employees: 2,300

Key Personnel
Chm & CEO: Michael C. Carlos
Pres & COO: Jay M. Davis
EVP & Treas: Andrew C. Carlos
SVP: Shai Froelich
Sec: H. S. Selwyn
Controller: Bob Schussel

Selected Services
Beer distribution
Distilled spirits distribution
Linen services
Spring water distribution
Wine distribution

Key Competitors
ARA
Ben Arnold Company
Beverage Distributors
Georgia Crown Distributing
Magnolia Marketing
Seagram
Southern Wine & Spirits
Sunbelt Beverage

Industry
Beverages - alcoholic

Overview
Founded in 1937 by Alfred A. Davis and Chris Carlos, National Distributing Company is one of the nation's largest wholesale distributors of wine, distilled spirits, and beer. The company, which distributes beverages in Georgia, Florida, and Colorado, also has linen service operations in Georgia, North Carolina, and Virginia. In 1991 National Distributing Company acquired distribution rights to the Glen Ellen line of wines, one of the country's most popular labels. Cofounder Chris Carlos's son, Michael, with the company since 1946, is now chairman and CEO.

NATIONAL FOOTBALL LEAGUE

RANK: 146

410 Park Ave.
New York, NY 10022
Phone: 212-758-1500
Fax: 212-758-1742

1993 Sales: $1,753 million
FYE: March
Employees: 150

Key Personnel
Commissioner: Paul Tagliabue
VP Broadcasting: Val Pinchbeck
Dir Corp & Govt Communications: Joe Browne
Lead Counsel: Jay Moyer
Dir Admin (HR): John Buzzeo

1993 Sales Leaders
Dallas Cowboys/$92.9 mil.
Miami Dolphins/$74.4 mil.
San Francisco 49ers/$70.4 mil.
Philadelphia Eagles/$68.9 mil.
Chicago Bears/$65.4 mil.
New York Giants/$65.3 mil.
Cleveland Browns/$65.1 mil.
Buffalo Bills/$64.9 mil.

Industry
Leisure & recreational services - sports

Overview
Organized in 1920, the NFL, originally the American Professional Football Association, is big business disguised as sports. The NFL acts as a trade association to promote football, license teams, collect dues, and develop new programs to cash in on the entertainment value of athletics through the sale of retail paraphernalia and broadcast rights. For example, after 38 years on CBS, the NFL will be taking $1.6 billion from the Fox network over the next 4 years in exchange for broadcast rights to National Football Conference games. Two new franchises were added in 1994: the Carolina Panthers and the Jacksonville Jaguars.

NATIONAL HOCKEY LEAGUE

RANK: 433

1251 Avenue of the Americas, 47th Fl.
New York, NY 10020
Phone: 212-789-2000
Fax: 212-789-2020

1993 Sales: $694 million
Employees: 110

Key Personnel
Commissioner: Gary Bettman
SVP & COO: Steve Solomon
SVP & COO, NHL Enterprises: Richard Dudley
SVP & Dir Hockey Ops: Brian Burke
CFO: John Houston
Gen Counsel: Jeffrey Pash

1993 Sales Leaders
Detroit Red Wings/$47.9 mil.
Toronto Maple Leafs/$45.5 mil.
Los Angeles Kings/$43.8 mil.
Chicago Black Hawks/$42.1 mil.
Boston Bruins/$39.4 mil.
New York Rangers/$37.7 mil.
Philadelphia Flyers/$35.1 mil.
Montreal Canadiens/$35 mil.

Industry
Leisure & recreational services - sports

Overview
In 1993 the National Hockey League, founded in 1917, hired Gary Bettman, former general counsel at the NBA, to modernize hockey. Bettman has changed the conference names (from such names as Clarence Campbell and Prince of Wales to Northeast and Pacific), realigned the teams in the conferences, and changed the Stanley Cup playoff format. The league expanded to 26 teams, adding the Florida Panthers, owned by Blockbuster's Wayne Huizenga, and Disney's Anaheim Mighty Ducks. Former league chairman and L.A. Kings owner Bruce McNall was sent to the penalty box after defaulting on $162 million in loans.

NATIONAL LIFE INSURANCE CO.

RANK: 317

One National Life Dr.
Montpelier, VT 05604
Phone: 802-229-3333
Fax: 802-229-9281

1993 Sales: $935 million
FYE: December
Employees: 944

Key Personnel
Chm & CEO: Frederic H. Bertrand
Pres & COO: John H. Harding
EVP Mktg & Svcs: William L. Cassidy
EVP & CFO: Thomas H. Macleay
VP, Sec & Gen Counsel: Margaret K. Arthur
VP HR: Susan S. Chiapetta

Principal Subsidiaries
Administrative Services
Champlain Life Insurance
Equity Services
National Life Investment Mgt.
National Property Advisors
Sentinel Advisors
Vermont Life Insurance

Key Competitors
Aetna
Connecticut Mutual
John Hancock
Liberty Mutual
MetLife
New York Life
Prudential
Travelers

Industry
Insurance - life

Overview
One of the 10 oldest life insurance companies in the US, National Life was incorporated in 1850 by a Vermont physician. Licensed in all 50 states, National Life is owned by its policyholders and offers a complete portfolio of individual life as well as individual and group annuities, health, accident, and disability income policies. National Life cut staff, perks, and costs to offset significant operating losses suffered during the mid-1980s; the losses stemmed from a high cost structure and poor individual disability line results.

NATIONAL RAILROAD PASSENGER CORPORATION

RANK: 183

60 Massachusetts Ave. NE
Washington, DC 20002
Phone: 202-906-3860
Fax: 202-906-3865

1993 Sales: $1,403 million
FYE: September
Employees: 24,000

Key Personnel
Chm, Pres & CEO: Thomas M. Downs
EVP & COO: Dennis F. Sullivan
VP Fin & Admin: Norris W. Overton
VP Trans: Robert C. VanderClute
VP Passenger Svcs: Arthur F. McMahon
Asst VP Personnel: Neil D. Mann

◀ **See page 101 for full-page profile.**

Business Lines
Contract commuter travel
Mail & express delivery
Other contract services
Passenger railroad travel
Real estate

Key Competitors
AMR
Continental Airlines
Delta
Greyhound
Peter Pan Bus Lines
USAir

Industry
Transportation - rail

Overview
John Henry couldn't turn this train around. A private, for-profit enterprise, National Railroad Passenger Corporation, or Amtrak, is almost fully owned by the DOT. Founded in 1970 by an act of Congress, the company transported more than 51 million passengers in 1993. Amtrak has never once turned a profit, and it still faces a barrel of problems, among them a quickly aging fleet, a recent history of wrecks (the worst accident in Amtrak's history occurred in 1993), airfare wars, and a poor public image.

NATIONWIDE INSURANCE ENTERPRISE

RANK: 11

One Nationwide Plaza
Columbus, OH 43215
Phone: 614-249-7111
Fax: 614-249-9771

1993 Sales: $14,835 million
FYE: December
Employees: 32,583

Key Personnel
Chm, Pres & CEO: D. Richard McFerson
EVP Investments: Peter F. Frenzer
SVP & CFO: Robert A. Oakley
SVP Business Ops: William P. DeMeno
VP HR: Susan A. Wolken

◀ **See page 102 for full-page profile.**

Principal Subsidiaries
Colonial
Employers Insurance of Wausau
Farmland Insurance Group
GatesMcDonald
Nationwide Life
Scottsdale
Wausau General Insurance
West Coast Life

Key Competitors
CIGNA
Guardian Life
John Hancock
MetLife
Principal Financial
State Farm
USAA
USF&G

Industry
Insurance - multiline

Overview
Nationwide Insurance Enterprise, a mutual company, is one of the country's largest multiline insurers, with more than 11 million active policies and combined assets of more than $42 billion. Through 130 companies Nationwide, founded in 1919, provides property/casualty insurance, life and health insurance, and financial services throughout the US and in more than 30 other countries. It also has interests in 12 radio and 3 television stations and real estate. After some up-and-down profitability in the early 1990s, Nationwide is back on sound footing, citing better claims management, among other factors.

NATURAL GAS CLEARINGHOUSE

RANK: 69

13430 Northwest Fwy., Ste. 1200
Houston, TX 77040
Phone: 713-744-1777
Fax: 713-744-6207

1993 Sales: $2,791 million
FYE: December
Employees: 393

Key Personnel
Pres & CEO: C. L. "Chuck" Watson
EVP Mktg: Stephen W. Bergstrom
SVP & CFO: H. K. Kaelber
EVP Fin & Admin: James Hackett
SVP & Gen Counsel: Kenneth E. Randolph
VP HR: Dan Conner

Natural Gas Services
Gathering
Marketing
Processing
Storage

Key Competitors
Associated Natural Gas
Coastal
Columbia Gas
Enron
Koch
Occidental
Panhandle Eastern
Tenneco

Industry
Natural gas marketing & distribution

Overview
Founded in 1983, Natural Gas Clearinghouse is the largest independent marketer of natural gas in the US. The company moves about 4 billion cubic feet of gas per day through its gas gathering and gas processing systems. In 1994 Nova Corp. of Alberta, Canada, paid Louisville, Kentucky–based LG&E Energy Corp. $170 million for its 36.5% stake in the company. British Gas PLC also owns 36.5%. The company's management owns the remaining 27%. The company is planning to expand both its North American and worldwide operations.

NAVY EXCHANGE SYSTEM

RANK: 121

3280 Virginia Beach Blvd.
Virginia Beach, VA. 23452
Phone: 804-631-3600
Fax: 804-631-3659

1993 Sales: $1,977 million
FYE: January
Employees: 22,387

Key Personnel
Commander: John T. Kavanaugh
Vice Commander: James E. Jaudon
Chief Merchandising Officer: Elliot P. Zucker
CFO: Jack T. Feitelberg
Dir HR: Michael Marchesani
Gen Counsel: Randall Kennington

Selected Services
Automotive repair
Barber shops
Food outlets
Gas stations
General merchandise
Guest lodges
Laundry services
Optical goods stores

Key Competitors
Ames
Army & Air Force Exchange
Dayton Hudson
Kmart
Montgomery Ward
Sears
Wal-Mart

Industry
Retail

Overview
Since 1946, the Navy Exchange System (NEX) has been catering to sailors, outfitting them with everything from sweats to designer jeans at below-market prices. A full-line retail and service firm, NEX operates 130 exchanges that serve 12 million authorized customers — active duty navy personnel, reservists, and retirees and their families — through a network of nearly 500 food outlets, more than 200 hair care shops, over 100 gas stations, and dozens of flower shops. NEX operates under the Department of Defense and is overseen by navy officers but receives tax funds only for its stores on naval ships.

THE NEW ENGLAND

RANK: 66

501 Boylston St.
Boston, MA 02116
Phone: 617-578-2000
Fax: 617-578-3776

1993 Sales: $2,827 million
FYE: December
Employees: 2,600

Key Personnel
Chm & CEO: Robert A. Shafto
EVP & CFO: Robert E. Schneider
EVP & Chief Inv Officer: F. K. Zimmermann
EVP & Gen Counsel: H. James Wilson
SVP Fin & Admin: Chester R. Frost
SVP HR: Gail E. Weber

Operating Units
New England Annuity
New England Emp Ben Group
New England Investment Assoc. LP
New England Life
New England Services
New England Variable Life
TNE Investment Services, LP

Key Competitors
Aetna
AFLAC
Equitable
Kemper
Northwestern Mutual
New York Life
Prudential
Travelers

Industry
Insurance - life

Overview
The New England is a 160-year-old life insurance company that has diversified into a wide range of financial products and services. Edward Phillips, who recently retired as chairman, built the company into one of the country's largest investment management operations and a top seller of life insurance to the wealthy. Operating in every state, the company offers a complete line of life, health, and disability insurance in addition to such services as investment counseling, management services, and securities distribution services.

NEW UNITED MOTOR MANUFACTURING, INC.

RANK: 88

45500 Fremont Blvd.
Fremont, CA 94538
Phone: 510-498-5500
Fax: 510-498-1037

1993 Est. Sales: $2,500 million
FYE: December
Employees: 4,300

Key Personnel
Pres & CEO: Iwao Itoh
SVP Mfg: Gary Convis
VP Corp Plan/Ext Aff & Sec: Dennis C. Cuneo
VP Prod Control/Quality Assur: Mitsutoshi Sato
Gen Counsel & Asst Corp Sec: Patricia Pineda
VP HR: D. William Childs

Major Products
2-wheel-drive compact pickup
4-wheel-drive compact pickup
Geo Prizm
Toyota Corolla
Toyota trucks
Xtracab pickup

Key Competitors
Chrysler
Ford
Honda
Hyundai
Mazda
Mitsubishi
Nissan
Volkswagen

Industry
Automotive manufacturing

Overview
New United Motor Manufacturing, Inc. (NUMMI), is a 50-50 joint venture between General Motors and Toyota. Founded in 1984, NUMMI is an experiment to see if Toyota's manufacturing practices can be transplanted to the US. Toyota has responsibility for day-to-day management and appoints NUMMI's top 2 executives. Of the vehicles manufactured, about 74% are Toyotas and about 26% are GM cars. In 1993 NUMMI launched the Toyota Xtracab, an extended version of Toyota's pickup.

◀ See page 103 for full-page profile.

NEW YORK LIFE INSURANCE COMPANY

RANK: 55

51 Madison Ave.
New York, NY 10010
Phone: 212-576-7000
Fax: 212-576-6794

1993 Sales: $15,564 million
FYE: December
Employees: 17,169

Key Personnel
Chm & CEO: Harry G. Hohn
Pres: George A.W. Bundschuh
EVP & Gen Counsel: Alice T. Kane
VP & Treas: Jay S. Calhoun III
VP & Gen Auditor: Thomas J. Warga
SVP HR: George J. Trapp

◀ **See page 104 for full-page profile.**

Selected Services
Deferred annuities
Group life & health insurance
MainStay (mutual funds)
NYLIFE Securities, Inc. (brokerage)
Retirement investing
Term life insurance
Variable annuities
Whole life insurance

Key Competitors
Aetna
CIGNA
Equitable
John Hancock
MassMutual
MetLife
Northwestern Mutual
Prudential

Industry
Insurance - life

Overview
Founded in 1841, policyholder-owned New York Life is the 5th largest US life insurance company. The company offers life, health, and disability insurance; annuities; mutual funds and other investments; and health care management services. In 1994 the company sold most of its Canadian operations (which had been in existence since 1858). It was also operating under a cloud of suspicion following investigations in Florida and Texas into sales practices by agents.

NEW YORK POWER AUTHORITY

RANK: 181

1633 Broadway
New York, NY 10019
Phone: 212-468-6000
Fax: 212-468-6040

1993 Sales: $1,430 million
FYE: December
Employees: 3,500

Key Personnel
Pres & CEO: S. David Freeman
EVP & COO: Robert Schoenberger
EVP Fin & Admin: Robert L. Tscherne
EVP Mkt Dev: Robert A. Hiney
SVP & Gen Counsel: Charles M. Pratt
Dir HR: Deborah Estrin

Operating Units
Ashokan Project
Blenheim-Gilboa Power Project
Charles Poletti Power Project
FitzPatrick Nuclear Power Plant
Gregory Jarvis Power Plant
Indian Point 3 Nuclear Power Plant
Niagara Power Project
St. Lawrence-FDR Project

Industry
Utility - electric power

Overview
The New York Power Authority is the US's largest nonfederal public power organization, supplying nearly 1/4 of New York State's electricity and transmitting power to neighboring states. The authority finances, builds, and operates electrical generation and transmission facilities and functions as a wholesale power supplier to other utilities. Established in 1931, this state agency functions as a nonprofit, public benefit corporation and operates 6 major generating facilities and 5 small hydroelectric plants. In 1993 its chairman, Richard Flynn, resigned amid criticism over his use of the agency jet for personal trips.

NEW YORK UNIVERSITY

RANK: 200

70 Washington Sq. South
New York, NY 10012
Phone: 212-998-1212
Fax: 212-995-4040

1993 Sales: $1,324 million
FYE: August
Employees: 15,000

Key Personnel
Pres: L. Jay Oliva
Provost, Med Ctr: Saul J. Faber
Dep Provost & EVP, Med Ctr: Theresa A. Bischoff
Vice Chancellor: C. Duncan Rice
SVP & Gen Counsel: S. A. Schaffer
VP Fin: Harold T. Read

Schools & Colleges
College of Arts & Science
College of Dentistry
Leonard N. Steans School of Business
Robert F. Wagner Graduate School of Public Service
School of Continuing Education
School of Education
School of Law
School of Medicine
School of Social Work
Tisch School of the Arts

Industry
Schools

Overview
Founded in 1831, New York University is the largest private university in the US, with about 15,400 students. Located in Manhattan's Greenwich Village, NYU has 7 graduate and 7 undergraduate schools. Desiring to become the first truly global university, NYU offers students study opportunities in some 20 countries and is considering a requirement that every undergraduate spend a semester abroad. NYU came closer to its goal in 1994, when it received what may be the largest gift ever given to a US university: 5 villas filled with exquisite art, located on 57 acres of olive groves and gardens overlooking Florence, Italy.

NORTH PACIFIC LUMBER CO.

RANK: 362

1505 SE Gideon
Portland, OR 97208
Phone: 503-231-1166
Fax: 503-238-2650

1993 Est. Sales: $840 million
FYE: December
Employees: 450

Key Personnel
Chm, Pres & CEO: Thomas J. Tomjack
EVP & CFO: George R. Thurston
SVP: Donald R. Lester
SVP: Bradley A. Mannelin
SVP: Kenneth N. McCoun
HR: Mits Tamura

Business Lines
Ag-chemical distribution
Lumber manufacture & distribution
Millwork distribution
Plywood distribution
Pole & piling distribution
Seafood distribution
Steel products distribution

Key Competitors
Boise Cascade
Georgia-Pacific
Perry H. Koplik
RLC Industries
Sierra Pacific Industries
Simpson Investment
Universal Forest Products

Industry
Building products - wholesale

Overview
North Pacific Lumber Co. is a wholesaler, trader, and distributor of lumber and lumber products; 80% of its business is in wood products. The company's headquarters is in Portland, Oregon, and it has offices in British Columbia, Missouri, and Mississippi. Founded in 1948, the company was acquired by its employees in 1986 following the retirement of its founder, Douglas David. Environmental concerns about timber harvesting in Oregon have led the company to affiliate with mills in other countries, such as Chile.

NORTHWESTERN MUTUAL LIFE INSURANCE COMPANY

RANK: 17

720 E. Wisconsin Ave.
Milwaukee, WI 53202
Phone: 414-271-1444
Fax: 414-299-7022

1993 Sales: $8,778 million
FYE: December
Employees: 3,500

Key Personnel
Pres & CEO: James D. Ericson
EVP: Robert E. Carlson
VP & Treas: Mark G. Doll
VP, Gen Counsel & Sec: John M. Bremer
VP New Business: Deborah A. Beck
SVP HR & Admin: James W. Ehrenstrom

Selected Services
Annuities
Disability insurance
Mortgage insurance
Securities brokerage
Term life insurance
Variable life insurance
Whole life insurance

Key Competitors
Aetna
CIGNA
Equitable
John Hancock
MassMutual
MetLife
New York Life
Prudential

Industry
Insurance - life

Overview
Northwestern Mutual, founded in 1857, is the 8th largest life insurer in the US. The policyholder-owned company is renowned for its agent retention rate and its training programs, which include college internships in which students represent the company on their campuses. Northwestern markets its services through a network of 7,300 exclusive agents across the 50 states and the District of Columbia. *FORTUNE* has ranked Northwestern as "the most admired" of the largest life insurance companies for 12 consecutive years.

◀ See page 105 for full-page profile.

OCEAN SPRAY CRANBERRIES, INC.

RANK: 238

One Ocean Spray Dr.
Lakeville-Middleboro, MA 02349
Phone: 508-946-1000
Fax: 508-946-7704

1993 Sales: $1,168 million
FYE: August
Employees: 2,300

Key Personnel
Pres & CEO: John S. Llewellyn, Jr.
SVP & CFO: Alexander W. Turnbull
SVP Retail Markets: Thomas E. Bullock
Group VP, Sales/Mktg: Patrick M. McCarthy
VP, Gen Counsel & Sec: Kenneth J. Beeby
VP HR: Curtis L. Cowilson

Major Products
Blended juices (Cranapple)
Cookies (Cranberry Newtons)
Cranberry juice
Cranberry sauce
Dried cranberries (Craisins)
Fresh cranberries
Grapefruit juice (Ruby Red)
Lemonade

Key Competitors
Cadbury Schweppes
Chiquita Brands
Coca-Cola
Dole
Lykes Bros.
Northland Cranberries
Seagram
Sunkist

Industry
Food - juice and citrus products

Overview
Founded in 1930, Ocean Spray is owned by about 750 cranberry growers and 150 citrus growers. It harvests, markets, and distributes over 3/4 of North America's cranberries and makes blended cranberry drinks (Cranberry Juice Cocktail), grapefruit drinks (Ruby Red Grapefruit Juice), sauces, jellies, and other juice blends. Several growers have left the co-op recently to sell through independent buyers who offer prices up to 15% above those of Ocean Spray.

◀ See page 106 for full-page profile.

ODYSSEY PARTNERS, LP

RANK: N/R

31 W. 52nd St.
New York, NY 10019
Phone: 212-708-0600
Fax: 212-708-0770

FYE: December
Employees: 35

Key Personnel
Gen Partner: Leon Levy
Gen Partner: Jack Nash
Gen Partner: Joshua Nash
Gen Partner: Stephen Berger
CFO: Lawrence Levitt

Selected Investments
Avatar Holdings (23%)
Caldor (24%)
Chicago Milwaukee (9.6%)
Eagle Food Centers (52%)
Forstmann & Co. (51%)
Gundle Environmental (20%)
JPS Textile
Thackeray (26%)

Industry
Financial - investors

Overview
Two former executives from Oppenheimer & Co., Jack Nash and Leon Levy, created Odyssey in 1982 as a boutique to specialize in leveraged buyouts and portfolio management. Odyssey's strength is as a global money manager, while its record as a buyout specialist is mixed: its 1989 buyout of Caldor (now public) was a big success, but several other deals have had to be restructured. Nonetheless, Odyssey is still focusing on the buyout game. In 1993 it bought Scotsman, a mobile and modular office manufacturer.

OGLETHORPE POWER CORPORATION

RANK: 249

2100 E. Exchange Pl.
Tucker, GA 30085
Phone: 404-270-7600
Fax: 404-270-7872

1993 Sales: $1,101 million
FYE: December
Employees: 560

Key Personnel
Chm: J. Calvin Earwood
VC: Benny W. Denham
Pres & CEO: Tom D. Kilgore
SVP & CFO: Eugen Heckl
SVP & Gen Counsel: Charles T. Autry
SVP & Group Exec: W. Clayton Robbins

Power Generation Facilities
Alvin W. Vogtle (Waynesboro, GA)
Edwin I. Hatch (Baxley, GA)
Hal B. Wansley (Carrollton, GA)
Robert W. Scherer (Forsyth, GA)
Rocky Mountain (Rome, GA)
Tallassee Project (Athens,GA)

Industry
Utility - electric power

Overview
Incorporated in 1972, Oglethorpe Power Corporation is an electricity generation and transmission cooperative. It supplies power from 5 owned and leased generating plants and is constructing #6 (Rocky Mountain). Oglethorpe also has long-term contracts to purchase power from other suppliers. The cooperative is owned by 39 retail distribution companies that provide power to some 2.3 million Georgians. It is the primary power supplier for rural Georgia and supplies power to 94% of the state's counties, an area of about 40,000 square miles. It is one of the 10 largest US electric utilities in terms of service area.

THE OHIO STATE UNIVERSITY

RANK: 182

190 N. Oval Mall
Columbus, OH 43210
Phone: 614-292-2424
Fax: 614-292-1231

1993 Sales: $1,409 million
FYE: June
Employees: 29,576

Key Personnel
Pres: Gordon Gee
Treas: James Nichols
VP Fin: William Shkurti
Controller: Don Seidelman
VP Legal Affairs: Robert Duncan
VP HR: Linda Tom

Schools & Colleges
Agricultural Technical Institute at Wooster
Ohio State University, Columbus
Ohio State University, Lima
Ohio State University, Mansfield
Ohio State University, Marion
Ohio State University, Newark

Industry
Schools

Overview
Founded in 1870, Ohio State University at Columbus is one of the nation's largest universities, enrolling more than 58,000 graduate and undergraduate students at its 6 campuses. The 3,297-acre campus in Columbus is a city in itself, with an airport, golf course, 90,000-seat stadium, and housing for 8,500 students. The university offers 220 bachelor's, 132 master's, and 100 doctorate programs. Students come from every state and 117 countries. OSU's athletic program, the largest in the Big 10, has produced 5 Heisman Trophy winners and captured 4 national football championships.

OXBOW CORPORATION

RANK: 255

1601 Forum Place
West Palm Beach, FL 33402
Phone: 407-697-4300
Fax: 407-640-8747

1993 Est. Sales: $1,100 million
FYE: December
Employees: 1,500

Key Personnel
Pres: William I. Koch
VP Fin: Zachary Shipley
Pres, Owbow Energy Inc.: Mike Mustafoglu
Pres, Oxbow Power Corp.: Bernard H. Cherry
Dir Personnel: Karen Brannon

Business Lines
Coal products
Geothermal & alternative energy
Petroleum products
Publishing
Real estate
Research

Key Competitors
AES
Atlantic Richfield
California Energy
CONSOL Energy
Destec Energy
Magma Power
Peter Kiewit Sons'
Westmoreland Coal

Industry
Diversified operations

Overview
Oxbow Corp. was started by America's Cup winner William Koch, whose father cofounded Koch Industries. Oxbow, known for its development of alternative energy sources, is a diversified energy and real estate conglomerate. The company has offices in Oklahoma and Nevada and supplies geothermal power to Southern California Edison and a cogeneration plant in New York State. Koch made an unsucessful bid to acquire MGM in 1993. He also controls Kendall Square Research.

PACIFIC MUTUAL LIFE INSURANCE COMPANY

RANK: 59

700 Newport Center Dr.
Newport Beach, CA 92660
Phone: 714-640-3011
Fax: 714-640-7614

1993 Sales: $2,400 million
FYE: December
Employees: 2,400

Key Personnel
Chm & CEO: Thomas C. Sutton
VC & Chief Inv Officer: William D. Cvengros
EVP & CFO: Glenn S. Schafer
SVP & Gen Counsel: David R. Carmichael
SVP Pension Investments: Daryle G. Johnson
SVP Investment Ops: Larry J. Card

◀ **See page 107 for full-page profile.**

Selected Services
Asset management
Employee benefits
Individual life insurance
Pension investments
Variable annuities

Key Competitors
Aetna
CIGNA
Connecticut Mutual
Equitable
John Hancock
Liberty Mutual
MetLife
Prudential

Industry
Insurance - life

Overview
Founded in 1868 by several prominent California business and political leaders, including Leland Stanford, Pacific Mutual is the US's 25th largest life insurer and the largest life and health insurer domiciled in California. In 1992 Pacific Mutual obtained approval to rehabilitate First Capital Life Insurance, an insurer taken over by the California State Insurance Commissioner in 1991. The transaction, to be completed in 1997, will boost Pacific Mutual's assets by about 30% and double its individual insurance base.

PACKARD BELL ELECTRONICS INC.

RANK: 218

31717 La Tienda Dr.
Westlake Village, CA 91362
Phone: 818-865-1555
Fax: 818-865-0379

1993 Est. Sales: $1,250 million
FYE: December
Employees: 2,000

Key Personnel
Chm, CEO & Pres: Beny Alagem
COO: Brent Cohen
VC, Fin: Jeffrey Scheinrock
VP: Michael Burney
VP Mktg: Mal D. Ransom
Dir HR: Larry Levinsohn

Major Brands
Axcel
Executive
Force
Legend
Packard Bell
Packmate

Key Competitors
Apple
AST
AT&T
Compaq
Dell
Everex Systems
Gateway 2000
IBM

Industry
Computers - PCs

Overview
Named for a popular brand of console radio, Packard Bell, founded in 1986 and owned by 3 Israeli immigrants, is leading the booming home-computer market. The company mass-merchandises its low-cost IBM clones through 7,000 retailers, among them Wal-Mart, Circuit City, and Sears. After tabling an IPO in 1992, Packard Bell sold a 20% stake to France's Groupe Bull, gaining deeper pockets to compete in a crowded market, expand internationally, and, through an alliance with Groupe Bull's Zenith Data Systems, diversify into notebook computers.

R. B. PAMPLIN CORPORATION

RANK: 432

900 SW 5th Ave., Ste. 1800
Portland, OR 97204
Phone: 503-248-1133
Fax: 503-248-1175

1994 Sales: $695 million
FYE: May
Employees: 5,728

Key Personnel
Chm & CEO: Robert B. Pamplin, Sr.
Pres, COO & Sec: Robert B. Pamplin, Jr.
Treas: David Meek
VP: Katherine Pamplin
VP: Marilyn Pamplin

Major Products
Apparel & work clothes
Blankets
Fabric & printed cloth
Gauze & yarn
Home furnishings
Infantwear
Mattress pads
Towels & table napkins

Key Competitors
Burlington Industries
Cone Mills
Galey & Lord
Greenwood Mills
JPS Textile
Milliken
Springs Industries
Walton Monroe Mills

Industry
Textiles - mill products

Overview
Founded in 1957 by former Georgia-Pacific executive Robert B. Pamplin, Sr., family-owned and -managed R. B. Pamplin Corporation is a holding company for an unlikely mix of textiles, sand and gravel, and concrete and asphalt companies. With 19 mills in Alabama, Georgia, South Carolina, and Texas, the company is best known for its American-made textiles. The firm also operates the world's largest denim mill, which produces enough denim for 45 million pairs of jeans each year.

PAN-AMERICAN LIFE INSURANCE COMPANY

RANK: 445

601 Poydras St.
New Orleans, LA 70130
Phone: 504-566-1300
Fax: 504-566-3950

1993 Sales: $663 million
FYE: December
Employees: 763

Key Personnel
Chm: G. Frank Purvis, Jr.
Pres & CEO: John K. Roberts, Jr.
EVP: M. Stevens Bumpas
EVP: Warren S. Newton, Jr.
SVP Fin Planning: Sydney Le Blanc
VP HR: P. W. Polk

Principal Subsidiaries
Argus Life Insurance Company
Compania de Seguros PALIC
Comp. de Seguros Panamericana
International Reinsurance Co.
PANACON
Pan-American Assurance Co.
Pan-American de Colombia
Pan-American de Panama

Key Competitors
Aetna
AIG
CIGNA
General Re
John Hancock
MetLife
Northwestern Life
New York Life

Industry
Insurance - life

Overview
Pan-American was founded as a stock company in 1911 to write insurance in the Caribbean basin but converted to mutual status in 1952. The company sells life and health insurance and annuities in 36 US states, the District of Columbia, and 7 Central and South American countries. Traditional life insurance products are a declining portion of sales, but Pan-American's strength in the Hispanic market and a new emphasis on pension products provide a base for new growth.

PARSONS AND WHITTEMORE INC.

RANK: 437

4 International Dr.
Rye Brook, NY 10573
Phone: 914-937-9009
Fax: 914-937-2259

1992 Est. Sales: $685 million
FYE: December
Employees: 1,500

Key Personnel
Chm: George F. Landegger
VC & VP; Chm, Black-Clawson: C. C. Landegger
CEO & Pres: Arthur L. Schwartz
VP & CFO: Robert Masson
Mgr HR: Richard Martin

Principal Subsidiaries
Alabama Pine Pulp Co.
Alabama River Newsprint Co.
Alabama River Pulp Co.
Black-Clawson
St. Anne-Nackawic Pulp & Paper
St. Anne Pulp Sales Co.

Key Competitors
Boise Cascade
Champion International
ITT
Kimberly-Clark
Mead
Southeast Paper Mfg.
Weyerhaeuser

Industry
Paper & paper products

Overview
Parsons and Whittemore is one of the world's largest producers of wood pulp (it has more than 50% of the US market and is the largest supplier to Japan and Korea) and commercial papers. It is also a major pulp mill contractor, its Black-Clawson subsidiary is a major manufacturer of paper machinery, and it makes machinery for recycling paper. The company is owned by George and Carl Landegger, whose Austrian father, Karl, came to the US in 1940 and bought Parsons and Whittemore, then a small pulp trading firm.

THE PARSONS CORPORATION

RANK: 168

100 W. Walnut St.
Pasadena, CA 91124
Phone: 818-440-2000
Fax: 818-440-2630

1993 Sales: $1,547 million
FYE: December
Employees: 10,000

Key Personnel
Chm & CEO: Leonard J. Pieroni
Pres: Thomas L. Langford
SVP & CFO: Curtis A. Bower
VP, Gen Counsel & Sec: Gary L. Stone
Dir HR: Graydon Thayer

Business Lines
Aviation
Community & leisure
Environmental services
Government services
Ground transportation
Petroleum & chemical
Power generation & distribution
Pulp & paper & industrial

Key Competitors
Bechtel
Dresser
Fluor
McDermott
Morrison Knudsen
Peter Kiewit Sons'
Turner Corp.
WMX Technologies

Industry
Construction - heavy

Overview
One of the largest firms of its kind in the world, Parsons provides one-source design and engineering services to a wide array of customers. The company has transformed a small fishing village into an industrial city of 100,000 in Saudi Arabia, built the first permanent oil and gas production facility in Arctic waters, and built the first reef runway on a man-made island. Founded in 1944, Parsons is also one of the largest 100% employee-owned companies in the US.

◀ **See page 108 for full-page profile.**

PATHMARK STORES, INC.

RANK: 45

301 Blair Rd.
Woodbridge, NJ 07095
Phone: 908-499-3000
Fax: 908-499-3072

1994 Sales: $4,207 million
FYE: January
Employees: 28,000

Key Personnel
Chm & CEO: Jack Futterman
Pres & CFO: Anthony J. Cuti
SVP Retail Dev: Harvey M. Gutman
SVP Ops: Bernard Kenny
VP, Gen Counsel & Sec: Marc A. Strassler
VP HR: Maureen McGurl

◀ **See page 109 for full-page profile.**

Business Lines
Distribution facilities
Pathmark Drugstores
Pathmark Supermarkets
  Pathmark 2000
  Super Center Format
  Supermarkets

Key Competitors
American Stores
Grand Union
Great A&P
Key Food Stores
King Kullen Grocery
Penn Traffic
Red Apple Group
Walgreen

Industry
Retail - supermarkets

Overview
Formed in 1956, Pathmark Stores (formerly known as Supermarkets General) is one of the leading grocery retailers in the Northeast and the #1 filler of prescriptions in New York City. The company operates 143 Pathmark grocery stores and 33 free-standing drugstores. To dodge a hostile takeover effort, Merrill Lynch Capital Partners took the company private in 1987 and still retains control. The company has one of the strongest private-label food lines in the grocery business (accounting for 23% of revenues), with more than 3,300 products.

PATRICOF & CO. VENTURES, INC.

RANK: N/R

445 Park Ave.
New York, NY 10022
Phone: 212-753-6300
Fax: 212-319-6155

FYE: January
Employees: 75

Key Personnel
Chm: Alan J. Patricof
Pres: Patricia M. Cloherty
SVP: Wilmer R. Bottoms
VP Fin: Arthur Burach
VP: George M. Jenkins
Office Mgr: Susan Smith

Selected Investments
Creative BioMolecules
Dakin
FORE Systems
Modern Coupon Systems
Sunglass Hut
Xpedite Systems

Industry
Financial - investors

Overview
Founded in 1969 by Alan Patricof, this leading venture capital firm manages $1.5 billion in investments worldwide and has had a hand in the startup of such ventures as Apple Computer and New York Magazine. Recent investments include Dakin (stuffed dinosaurs) and Modern Coupon Systems (mail-order catalogs selling home health care products). In 1993 Patricia Cloherty was named Patricof's president, becoming the first woman to head a major venture capital firm.

THE PAUL ALLEN GROUP

RANK: N/R

110 110th Ave. NE, Ste. 530
Bellevue, WA 98004
Phone: 206-453-6101
Fax: 206-453-6106

Employees: 3

Key Personnel
Chm: Paul Allen
Pres & CEO: Vern Raburn
Sec: Pia Fessenden

Selected Investments
America Online
Asymetrix
Cardinal Technologies
Interval Research
Metricom Inc.
Portland Trail Blazers
StarWave Corp.
Telescan
Ticketmaster Corp.
Vulcan Ventures

Industry
Financial - investors

Overview
The Paul G. Allen "family of companies" is a loose federation of at least 15 high-tech, multimedia, and telecommunications companies acquired or invested in by the billionaire cofounder of Microsoft, Paul Allen. His group of companies is strategically located on the information superhighway and includes on-line services, software companies, and a ticketing concern, along with think tank Interval Research and investment organization Vulcan Ventures. Allen, who owns the Portland Trail Blazers basketball team, also is building his team a new sports and entertainment arena.

PENN MUTUAL LIFE INSURANCE CO.

RANK: 463

510 & 530 Walnut St.
Philadelphia, PA 19106
Phone: 215-956-8000
Fax: 215-956-8347

1993 Sales: $635 million
FYE: December
Employees: 900

Key Personnel
Chm & CEO: John E. Tait
Pres & COO: Robert E. Chappell
CFO: Nancy S. Brodie
EVP & Gen Counsel: Joseph J. Horvath
EVP & Chief Investment Officer: William V. Ferdinand
VP HR: Catherine B. Strauss

Business Lines
Annuities
Asset management
Individual disability insurance
Individual life insurance
Pensions
Universal life

Key Competitors
Aetna
CIGNA
Equitable
MetLife
New York Life
Provident Mutual
Prudential
Travelers

Industry
Insurance - life

Overview
Founded in 1847, Penn Mutual Life has carved itself a bigger niche of the insurance market lately by purchasing Monarch Life, a financially troubled Massachusetts insurer. Penn Mutual has prospered by focusing on the individual life and individual and group pension markets. The company reached an agreement with UNUM Life Insurance Co. in 1993 whereby Penn Mutual would sell disability insurance products developed by UNUM under the Penn Mutual name.

THE PENNSYLVANIA STATE UNIVERSITY

RANK: 172

408 Old Main
University Park, PA 16802
Phone: 814-865-4700
Fax: 814-865-7145

1994 Sales: $1,504 million
FYE: June
Employees: 15,838

Key Personnel
Pres: Joab L. Thomas
EVP & Provost: John A. Brighton
SVP & Dean, Coll of Med: C. McCollister Evarts
SVP Community Education: Robert E. Dunham
SVP Dev & Univ Relations: G. David Gearhart
VP Finance: Gary C. Schultz

Selected Programs of Study
Undergraduate
- Agronoma
- Astronomy
- Banking & finance
- Botany
- East Asian studies
- Film arts

Graduate
- Aerospace engineering
- Cell & molecular biology
- Health policy & administration
- Pharmacology
- Theater arts

Industry
Schools

Overview
Founded in 1855, Penn State University at University Park is the largest and oldest of the 22 campuses in the Penn State system. Of the 32,000 students at the University Park campus, 80% are enrolled in 10 undergraduate schools; there is one graduate school. The university is a major medical education center, operating a 4-year medical school and a hospital in Hershey. The medical center contributes 17% of university revenues, tuition provides 26%, and more than 31% comes from state and federal funds. Penn State recently announced that AT&T would provide $27 million toward making the university a leading center of telecommunications.

PENSION BENEFIT GUARANTY CORPORATION

RANK: 312

1200 K St. NW
Washington, DC 20005
Phone: 202-326-4000
Fax: 202-326-4042

1993 Sales: $950 million
FYE: September
Employees: 687

Key Personnel
Exec Dir: Martin Slate
Deputy Exec Dir & COO: William B. Posner
Deputy Exec Dir & CFO: N. Anthony Calhoun
Deputy Exec Dir & Chief Mgmt Officer: John Seal
Deputy Exec Dir & Chief of Staff: William DeHarde
Dir HR: R. Frank Tobin

Selected Services
Multiemployer programs
Private benefit pensions
Single-employer plans

Key Competitors
CIGNA
GEICO
MassMutual
New York Life
Northwestern Mutual
Prudential
State Farm
Travelers

Industry
Insurance - misc.

Overview
Pension Benefit Guaranty Corporation (PBGC) was established in 1974 as a federal corporation to insure private pension plans. By 1993 the agency was protecting almost 41 million people in about 66,000 plans. PBGC receives no tax funds; its income is generated by premiums, investments, and the pension plans that it oversees. The agency has a deficit approaching $3 billion (from covering underfunded plans) but has been whittling away at its yearly losses. PBGC is instituting reforms, such as higher premiums, to avoid a federal bailout.

PENSKE CORPORATION

RANK: 58

13400 Outer Dr. West
Detroit, MI 48239
Phone: 313-592-5000
Fax: 313-592-5256

1992 Est. Sales: $3,250 million
FYE: December
Employees: 11,000

Key Personnel
Chm, Pres & CEO: Roger S. Penske
CFO & Treas: Richard J. Peters
EVP Fin: Walter P. Czernecki
Controller: James H. Harris
VP Personnel: Robert Carter
VP Communications: Dan Luginbuhl

Business Lines
Auto racing team
Auto racing tracks
Car dealerships (Cadillac & Toyota)
Diesel engines (Detroit Deisel)
Internal combustion engines
Methanol engines
Truck rental (Hertz-Penske)

Key Competitors
Allison Engine
Caterpillar
Chrysler
Cummins Engine
Daimler-Benz
General Motors
Ryder
U-Haul

Industry
Diversified operations

Overview
The Penske Corporation was founded in 1969 by Roger Penske, a former race car driver who is now CEO and owns more than 50% of the company's stock. The Penske Corporation has a reputation for creating successful auto-related businesses and champion car racing teams. Its truck leasing division is the #9 lessor of trucks to fleets. Penske sold about 27% of its Detroit Diesel Corporation in 1993 through a public stock offering. The Penske auto racing team has won 10 Indianapolis 500 races, including the 1994 competition.

PERDUE FARMS INCORPORATED

RANK: 207

PO Box 1537
Salisbury, MD 21801
Phone: 410-543-3000
Fax: 410-543-3874

1993 Sales: $1,300 million
FYE: March
Employees: 13,300

Key Personnel
Chm & CEO: James A. Perdue
Chm Exec Committee: Franklin Parsons Perdue
Pres & COO: Robert A. Turley
CFO: George C. Reiswig
VP Sales: Roger Covey
VP HR: Tom Moyers

◀ **See page 110 for full-page profile.**

Major Products
Chicken parts
Fully cooked chicken products
Ground chicken & turkey
Skinless & boneless chicken
Turkey parts
Turkey sausages
Whole chickens
Young whole turkeys

Key Competitors
Cargill
ConAgra
Continental Grain
Farmland Industries
Foster Poultry
Gold Kist
Hormel
Tyson Foods

Industry
Food - meat products

Overview
Perdue Farms is the largest chicken producer in the northeastern US and the 4th largest in the country (after Tyson Foods, ConAgra, and Gold Kist). Family-owned and -managed, the company in 1983 was first in the industry to add nutritional labels to its products. Growing with the rising demand for healthy foods in the 1970s and 1980s, the company boosted sales with clever advertising and became famous through family spokesman Frank Perdue, who claimed, "It takes a tough man to make a tender chicken."

PETER KIEWIT SONS', INC.

RANK: 103

1000 Kiewit Plaza
Omaha, NE 68131
Phone: 402-342-2052
Fax: 402-271-2829

1993 Sales: $2,179 million
FYE: December
Employees: 10,620

Key Personnel
Chm & Pres: Walter Scott, Jr.
VC: Charles H. Campbell
VC: William L. Grewcock
EVP: Kenneth E. Stinson
EVP & CFO: Robert E. Julian
VP HR: Brad Chapman

◀ **See page 111 for full-page profile.**

Subsidiaries & Affiliates
Kiewit Coal Properties Inc.
Kiewit Construction Group Inc.
Kiewit Energy Company
Kiewit Mining Group Inc.
MFS Communications Co., Inc.
PKS Information Services, Inc.

Key Competitors
Bechtel
Cyprus Amax
Fluor
Halliburton
Ogden
Parsons
Turner Industries
U S West

Industry
Construction - heavy

Overview
Peter Kiewit Sons' is one of the US's largest construction and mining businesses and has been owned by its employees since the death of the founder's son in 1979. The company started in masonry but grew during the Depression through huge public works projects and later through wartime emergency projects. Construction now accounts for over 80% of sales, and the company mines coal in Wyoming, Texas, and Montana. Major customers include Commonwealth Edison and Detroit Edison. Other interests include geothermal energy and telecommunications.

PHAR-MOR INC.

RANK: 117

20 Federal Plaza West
Youngstown, OH 44501
Phone: 216-746-6641
Fax: 216-740-2915

1993 Est. Sales: $2,000 million
FYE: June
Employees: 6,500

Key Personnel
Chm: David S. Shapira
CEO: Antonio C. Alvarez
Pres & COO: David Schwartz
CFO: Daniel J. O'Leary
Treas: Peter Austin
VP HR: Robert C. Miller

Major Products
Cleaning supplies
Cosmetics
Film
Groceries
Packaged foods
Pharmaceuticals
Video sales & rentals

Key Competitors
Drug Emporium
Eckerd
Payless Cashways
Revco D.S.
Rite Aid
Walgreen
Wal-Mart

Industry
Retail - drugstores

Overview
Once celebrated as the country's largest and fastest-growing deep discount drugstore chain, Phar-Mor, founded in 1982 in Youngstown, Ohio, filed for bankruptcy in August 1992, reeling from allegations of fraud and embezzlement by top executives. Once boasting 300 stores in 32 states and sales of about $3 billion, the company has hired new management, closed about 150 stores, cut overhead, and focused on its core products and more profitable stores. The company's principal shareholders are supermarket chain Giant Eagle and its CEO David Shapira (who is also Phar-Mor's chairman).

PMC INC.

RANK: 416

12243 Branford St.
Sun Valley, CA 91352
Phone: 818-896-1101
Fax: 818-897-0180

1993 Sales: $715 million
FYE: December
Employees: 3,700

Key Personnel
Pres & CEO: Philip E. Kamins
CFO: Thian C. Cheong
VP & Treas: Lori M. Johnson
Sec: Dorothy A. Kamins
Asst Treas: Peter Gamboa
Dir HR: Karen Ferguson

Major Products
Chemicals
Dyes
Fiberglass
Military instruments
Neurosurgical devices
Paint
Plastic foam products
Varnish

Key Competitors
Amoco
Foamex
Formosa Plastics
James River
Sealed Air
Sherwin-Williams
Valspar
Wellman

Industry
Chemicals - plastics

Overview
PMC (an acronym for Plastic Management Corp) is the biggest manufacturer of plastic foam products in the US. Launched in 1964 and started as a plastics scrap yard, PMC grew into a diverse international company, with interests in paint, medical goods, plastics, chemicals, aspirin, textiles, food dyes, consulting services, and a machine shop. Founder-owner Philip Kamins's first overseas venture was a Belgian acetateflake shop, which he purchased in 1982. PMC sold its EPA-hounded specialty chemicals division, Hilton Davis Co., in 1993.

POLO/RALPH LAUREN CORPORATION

RANK: 137

650 Madison Ave.
New York, NY 10022
Phone: 212-318-7000
Fax: 212-318-5780

1993 Est. Sales: $1,800 million
FYE: April
Employees: 2,800

Key Personnel
Chm & CEO: Ralph Lauren
Pres: Cheryl Sterling
CFO: Michael J. Newman
VP Fin: Joanne Mandry
Dir Mktg & Sales: Tracie Nelson
Dir HR: Karen Rosenback

◀ **See page 112 for full-page profile.**

Business Lines
Polo by Ralph Lauren (menswear)
Polo for Boys
Polo/Ralph Lauren (accessories)
Ralph Lauren Fragrances
Ralph Lauren Home Collection
Womenswear collections

Key Competitors
AnnTaylor
Anne Klein
L. L. Bean
Calvin Klein
Donna Karan
Geoffrey Beene
Lands' End
Liz Claiborne

Industry
Apparel

Overview
Polo/Ralph Lauren is the licensing company for Ralph Lauren designs for men, women, and children. Its marketing image depends heavily on idealized images of upper-class life. The company began in 1968 as Polo, invoking that sport's aristocratic image and focusing on tailored menswear; it later branched out into accessories and womenswear, most of it licensed to various manufacturers and sellers. The company derives its sales primarily from licensing operations.

THE PORT AUTHORITY OF NEW YORK AND NEW JERSEY

RANK: 123

One World Trade Center
New York, NY 10048
Phone: 212-435-7000
Fax: 212-435-4660

1993 Sales: $1,921 million
FYE: December
Employees: 9,200

Key Personnel
Chm: Kathleen A. Donovan
Exec Dir: Stanley Brezenoff
CFO: Barry Weintrob
Gen Counsel: Jeffrey S. Green
Dir HR: Louis J. LaCapra
Treas: John E. Haupert

Selected Services
Airport operations
Bus terminal
Cargo handling
Hotel operation
Marine terminals
Rail passenger operations
Real estate ownership
Tunnel operations

Key Competitors
Helmsley
Lefrak Organization
Parkchester Management
Pembrook Management
J.I. Sopher and Company
Tishman Speyer
Trump
Zeckendorf

Industry
Diversified operations

Overview
Established in 1921 as the first interstate agency created with consent of the US Congress, the Port Authority operates and maintains 39 regional facilities, including airports, toll bridges, wharves, and tunnels. It also promotes commerce and trade for a 17-county region of New York and New Jersey. Governors of the 2 states appoint commissioners and have ultimate decision-making authority. One of the Port Authority's most visible and lucrative operations, the World Trade Center, was reopened for business less than 2 months after a terrorist bombing in 1993. The authority is nearing completion of a fully automated passenger monorail at Newark International Airport.

POTAMKIN MANHATTAN CORP.

RANK: 354

787 Eleventh Ave.
New York, NY 10019
Phone: 212-603-7200
Fax: 212-603-7035

1992 Sales: $850 million
FYE: December
Employees: 2,000

Key Personnel
Pres: Victor Potamkin
Co-CEO: Robert Potamkin
Co-CEO: Alan Potamkin
CFO: Peter Paris
Gen Partner: Ted Bessen
VP HR: Jack Calumusa

Operating Units
Potamkin Auto Center (New York)
Potamkin Chevrolet (Hialeah, FL)
Potamkin NYLP (New York)
Potamkin Leasing Corp. (New York)
Potamkin Paramus (Paramus, NJ)
Potamkin Toyota (Springfield, PA)
Potamkin Toyota Corp. (New York)
Potamkin Volkswagen (New York)

Key Competitors
Dorschel Group
Holman Enterprises
Island Lincoln-Mercury
JM Family Enterprises
McCafferty Sales
Morse Operations
Warnock Automotive
West-Herr Ford

Industry
Retail - new & used cars

Overview
Auto magnate Victor Potamkin specializes in the turning radius. He has a reputation for acquiring ailing car dealerships and turning them around until they are profitable enterprises with added franchises. He and his 2 sons (co-CEOs) own more than 50 auto franchises in 5 states. Potamkin started the company with a Ford-Lincoln-Mercury showroom in 1949 but closed that and tried again with 3 Chevrolet dealerships in the 1950s. In 1979 he added a Dodge agency and soon after took on import lines. Potamkin raised eyebrows at GM when he sold Cadillacs below cost, but the tactic drew customers.

PRAIRIE FARMS DAIRY INC.

RANK: 420

1100 N. Broadway St.
Carlinville, IL 62626
Phone: 217-854-2547
Fax: 217-854-6426

1993 Sales: $709 million
FYE: September
Employees: 1,843

Key Personnel
Pres: Melvin Schweizer
EVP & CEO: Leonard J. Southwell
VP Fin: Paul Benne
VP Eng: Ronald Dierolf
VP Mktg: Donald Kullmann
Dir Personnel: Tom Beichler

Principal Subsidiaries
ABC Dairies Inc.
East Side Jersey Dairy Inc.
Ice Cream Specialties Inc.
Pevely Dairy
PFD Supply Corp.

Key Competitors
Associated Milk Producers
Ben & Jerry's
Borden
Dairyland Farms
Farmland Dairies
General Mills
Philip Morris
Wisconsin Dairies Co-op

Industry
Food - dairy products

Overview
Prairie Farms, a dairy cooperative founded in 1938, is one of the largest dairies in the Midwest. With 850 producers and 27 plants in 7 states, the co-op also produces frozen desserts as well as juice drinks for schools through its subsidiaries. Prairie Farms owns and operates other dairies through joint ventures with Mid-America Dairymen, the US's 2nd largest dairy cooperative. Prairie Farms, like many dairy cooperatives, is struggling with the issue of whether to process or sell milk from cows treated with the growth hormone BST, which boosts milk production.

PRICE WATERHOUSE LLP

RANK: 46

1251 Avenue of the Americas
New York, NY 10020
Phone: 212-819-5000
Fax: 212-790-6620

1993 Sales: $3,890 million
FYE: June
Employees: 48,781

Key Personnel
World & US Chm: Shaun F. O'Malley
Chm Europe & Dep World Chm: Jermyn Brooks
CFO: Thomas H. Chamberlain
Gen Counsel: Eldon Olson
VC HR: Richard P. Kearns

Selected Services
Audit & business advisory services
Employee benefits services
International trade services
Inventory services
Investment management
Management consulting
Personal financial services
Tax services

Key Competitors
Arthur Andersen
Coopers & Lybrand
Deloitte & Touche
Electronic Data Systems
Ernst & Young
KPMG
Marsh & McLennan
McKinsey & Co.

Industry
Business services - accounting & consulting

Overview
A high-prestige accounting firm founded in 1850, London-based Price Waterhouse is a worldwide organization of management consultants, accountants, tax advisors, and auditors. The company is an international association of partnerships. The company's growth has been spurred by its management consulting business, including its growing information technology services business. Of late Price Waterhouse has been plagued by legal issues.

◀ See page 113 for full-page profile.

PRINCETON UNIVERSITY

RANK: 496

One Nassau Hall
Princeton, NJ 08544
Phone: 609-258-3000
Fax: 609-258-1294

1993 Sales: $541 million
FYE: June
Employees: 4,931

Key Personnel
Pres: Harold T. Shapiro
Provost: Stephen M. Goldfeld
VP Fin & Admin: Richard Spies
VP HR: Audrey S. Smith
Controller: Henry J. Murphy
Treas: Raymond J. Clark

Selected Programs of Study
Undergraduate
- Archeology
- Architectural engineering
- Astrophysics
- Classics
- Near Eastern studies

Graduate
- African studies
- Economics
- Molecular biology
- Public affairs
- Transportation

Industry
Schools

Overview
Princeton (founded in 1746) focuses on vigorous undergraduate liberal arts programs — there are no law, business, or medical schools. Three current faculty members are Nobel laureates. The university has the 2nd largest endowment in the country ($3.29 billion) and an enrollment of 4,500. In recent years the endowment's investments were diversified to include international stocks and foreign-based securities. Appointed president in 1987, Harold Shapiro has helped the university continue to prosper in the face of tightening budgets and increasing competition for federal research dollars.

PRINCIPAL FINANCIAL GROUP

RANK: 23

711 High St.
Des Moines, IA 50392
Phone: 515-247-5111
Fax: 515-247-5930

1993 Sales: $12,370 million
FYE: December
Employees: 13,583

Key Personnel
Chm & CEO: G. David Hurd
VC: Roy W. Ehrle
Pres: David J. Drury
EVP: Theodore M. Hutchinson
VP & Gen Counsel: Gregg R. Narber
VP HR: Donald Keown

◀ See page 114 for full-page profile.

Selected Services
Annuities & IRAs
Disability income insurance
Health insurance
Life insurance
Mutual funds
Pension plans
Rehabilitation services

Key Competitors
Aetna
Allstate
CIGNA
John Hancock
MassMutual
Northwestern Mutual
Prudential
Travelers

Industry
Insurance - life

Overview
Founded in 1879, Principal Financial Group is the holding company for Principal Mutual Life Insurance, the largest life insurer headquartered west of New York City and the 4th largest in the US in premium and annuity income. The Principal serves more than 8.4 million customers and operates in all 50 states; Washington, DC; Puerto Rico; and Canada. Its 3 core areas of business are group life and health insurance, pension plans, and a wide variety of insurance services offered directly to individuals.

PROSPECT MOTORS INC.

RANK: 276

645 Hwy. 49 & 88 North
Jackson, CA 95642
Phone: 209-223-1740
Fax: 209-223-0395

1994 Sales: $1,047 million
FYE: May
Employees: 100

Key Personnel
CEO & Pres: William Halvorson
VP: Frank E. Halvorson
VP: W. B. Smallfield
Sec & Treas: Lorraine Halvorson
Dir Business Dev & HR: Linda Hamilton

Major Brands
Buick
Cadillac
Chevrolet
Chrysler
Oldsmobile
Plymouth
Pontiac
Toyota

Key Competitors
Fornaca
Frank Consolidated Enterprises
Galpin Motors
Lloyd A. Wise Co.
Lucas Dealership Group
S and C Motors
Santa Monica Ford
Tasha

Industry
Retail - new & used cars

Overview
Prospect Motors is among the top 5 dealers of fleet vehicles in the US, whether ranked by dollar sales (well over $1 billion) or by units sold (about 35,000). The company is one of the top 10 dealers of GM's 5 main brands and the nation's #1 Buick franchise. Founded in 1970, the Halvorson family's Prospect Motors has made its name by selling and leasing in bulk — mostly fleet sales and leases to car rental agencies in California and other western states. Prospect Motors owns 2 other California dealerships: American Chevrolet-Geo (Modesto) and Amador Motors (Chrysler-Plymouth, Dodge, Jeep-Eagle; Sutter Creek).

PROVIDENT MUTUAL LIFE INSURANCE COMPANY OF PHILADELPHIA

RANK: 286

1600 Market St.
Philadelphia, PA 19101
Phone: 215-636-5000
Fax: 215-636-8166

1993 Sales: $1,023 million
FYE: December
Employees: 700

Key Personnel
Chm, Pres & CEO: L. J. "Bud" Rowell, Jr.
EVP & CFO: John R. McClelland
EVP & Chief Mktg Officer: Robert S. Johnson
EVP Corp: Gerald B. Beam
VP & Gen Counsel: George Lambert
VP HR: Charlene Parsons

Products and Services
Annuities
Group pension
Individual insurance
Investment management
Securities
Trust funds
Variable life

Key Competitors
Aetna
MetLife
Nationwide
New York Life
Penn Mutual
Principal Financial
State Farm
Travelers

Industry
Insurance - life

Overview
Founded in 1865, Provident Mutual Life is among the top 25 mutual life insurers in the US, with more than $4 billion in assets. The company offers a range of life insurance products, from traditional to variable life, as well as retirement fund products. Its Sigma American and PML Securities subsidiaries offer trust and investment management and securities services. The company emphasizes customer service to hold on to existing customers and gain new ones.

THE PRUDENTIAL INSURANCE COMPANY OF AMERICA

RANK: 4

751 Broad St.
Newark, NJ 07102
Phone: 201-802-6000
Fax: 201-802-6092

1993 Sales: $45,974 million
FYE: December
Employees: 105,534

Key Personnel
Chm, Pres & CEO: Robert C. Winters
VC: Garnett L. Keith Jr.
SVP, Comptroller & CFO: Eugene M. O'Hara
SVP & Gen Counsel: James R. Gillen
SVP HR: Donald C. Mann

Selected Services
Annuities
Asset management
Credit card services
Deposit accounts
Estate & financial planning
Life, health & property insurance
Reinsurance
Residential real estate services

Key Competitors
Aetna
CIGNA
Equitable
MetLife
New York Life
Northwestern Mutual
State Farm
Travelers

Industry
Insurance - multiline

Overview
Founded in 1873 as the Widows and Orphans Friendly Society, Prudential is the US's largest insurance company and one of the largest life insurers in the UK. Prudential's health plans, including PruCare HMO and PruCare Plus, enroll 3.8 million people. The company also offers financial services through Prudential Securities. Regulatory investigations relating to the sale of risky real estate partnerships and unscrupulous sales methods have plagued this policyholder-owned company since 1991.

◀ See page 115 for full-page profile.

CORPORATION FOR PUBLIC BROADCASTING

RANK: 190

901 E Street NW
Washington, DC 20004
Phone: 202-879-9600
Fax: 202-879-1039

1992 Sales: $1,390 million
FYE: September
Employees: 900

Key Personnel
Pres & CEO : Richard W. Carlson
EVP: Robert T. Coonrod
SVP: Frederick L. DeMarco
SVP: Eugene Katt
SVP: Carolyn Reid-Wallace
Treas: Renee Ingram

Operating Units
American Public Radio
National Public Radio
Public Broadcasting Service

Key Competitors
Capital Cities/ABC
CBS
Cox
General Electric
TCI
Time Warner
Turner Broadcasting
Viacom

Industry
Broadcasting - radio & TV

Overview
Created by the Public Broadcasting Act of 1967, the Corporation for Public Broadcasting (CPB) is a nonprofit organization charged with providing high-quality, educational, informational, and cultural programming to the American viewing public. CPB's operating units, The Public Broadcasting Service and National Public Radio, oversee, respectively, the 354 member television stations and 584 member radio stations. Much of public broadcasting's revenues come from funds raised by member stations, with most of the rest from government sources and grants. Each week 61% of US households with TVs watch public television.

PUBLIX SUPER MARKETS, INC.

RANK: 18

1936 George Jenkins Blvd.
Lakeland, FL 33801
Phone: 813-688-1188
Fax: 813-680-5257

1993 Sales: $7,554 million
FYE: December
Employees: 82,000

Key Personnel
Chm & CEO: Howard M. Jenkins
Chm Exec Committee: Charles H. Jenkins, Jr.
Pres & COO: Mark C. Hollis
EVP: Hoyt R. Barnett
EVP & Principal Fin Officer: William H. Vass
VP Personnel: Edward H. Ruth

Business Lines
Baking plants (Danish Bakery line)
Dairy processing plants
Delicatessen plants
Food/drug supermarkets
- Deli
- Groceries
- Pharmacy
- Produce

Key Competitors
Bruno's
Food Lion
Jitney-Jungle Stores
Kash n' Karry
Pueblo XTRA International
Wal-Mart
Winn-Dixie

Industry
Retail - supermarkets

Overview
George Jenkins founded the original Publix store in 1930 with money he had saved to buy a car. Publix is now the largest grocery chain in Florida, with almost 1/2 the market in the state's heavily populated southeastern region and about 1/4 of the Gulf Coast area; it also operates stores in Georgia and South Carolina. Publix operates 425 supermarkets as well as dairy, bakery, and deli processing plants, which supply the supermarkets with private label products. The company is one of the largest employee-owned firms in the US.

◀ See page 116 for full-page profile.

PUEBLO XTRA INTERNATIONAL, INC.

RANK: 233

1300 NW 22nd Ave.
Pompano Beach, FL 33069
Phone: 305-977-2500
Fax: 305-979-5770

1994 Sales: $1,199 million
FYE: January
Employees: 10,600

Key Personnel
Chm: Gustavo A. Cisneros
Pres & CEO: David W. Morrow
Pres, Puerto Rico Div: Hector Quinones
EVP, CFO, Sec & Treas: Jeffrey P. Freimark
SVP Florida & Virgin Islands Div: Gary J. Allen

Operating Units
Blockbuster video stores
Pueblo supermarkets
Xtra superstores

Key Competitors
Publix
Wal-Mart
Winn-Dixie

Industry
Retail - supermarkets

Overview
Pueblo Xtra operates 55 supermarkets in Puerto Rico, Florida, and the US Virgin Islands under the Xtra and Pueblo names. It also has 21 Blockbuster video stores in these same markets. Founded by Harold Toppel, who took the company private in 1988, Pueblo Xtra was acquired by the Venezuelan-based Cisneros Group (management still has an ownership position) in 1993. Pueblo Xtra is the #1 grocery chain in Puerto Rico and derives 72% of its sales from Puerto Rico. Intense competition in the Florida market has depressed earnings. In response the company has decided to concentrate its efforts on Florida's Hispanic consumers.

QUAD/GRAPHICS, INC. — RANK: 426

W224 N3322 Duplainville Rd.
Pewaukee, WI 53072
Phone: 414-246-9200
Fax: 414-246-4322

1993 Sales: $700 million
FYE: December
Employees: 6,800

Key Personnel
Chm: Harry R. Quadracci
Pres & CEO: Harry V. Quadracci
CFO: John C. Fowler
VP Mfg: Tom Quadracci
Gen Counsel: Debra Kraft
Dir Employee Svcs: Emmy Labode

Business Lines
Commericial art & graphic design
Gravure printing
Lithographic printing
Periodical publishing & printing

Key Competitors
Banta
R.R. Donnelley
Graphic Industries
John H. Harland
Quebecor
Treasure Chest
Western Publishing
World Color Press

Industry
Printing - commercial

Overview
Quad/Graphics was founded in 1971 by Harry V. Quadracci. The company is one of the largest privately owned commercial printers in the US; 80% is worker owned. Its presses work 24 hours a day, 7 days a week, printing primarily magazines such as *Newsweek* and *Playboy,* catalogs, free-standing inserts, and commercial products.The company runs only 2 shifts of 12 hours each; operators work 3 days one week and 4 days the next. The firm has never been unionized and the management-worker relationship is relaxed and unstructured. Quadracci has a unique style of participative management that has been celebrated by numerous management gurus.

QUALITY KING DISTRIBUTORS INC. — RANK: 399

2060 Ninth Ave.
Ronkonkoma, NY 11779
Phone: 516-737-5555
Fax: 516-737-5154

1992 Sales: $775 million
FYE: October
Employees: 650

Key Personnel
Chm, Pres & CEO: Bernard Nussdorf
CFO: Mike Katz
Sec & Treas: Lillian N. Broder
Dir HR: Glenn Satur

Distribution Lines
Cosmetics
Fragrances
Health aids
Nonperishable groceries
Pharmaceuticals

Key Competitors
Alco Health Services
Bergen Brunswig
Cardinal Health
McKesson
Moore Medical
National Intergroup
Pharmacy Network Direct
Whitmire Distribution

Industry
Drugs & sundries - wholesale

Overview
Bernard Nussdorf started Quality King in a Queens, New York, storefront in 1960. Today it is one of the US's 20 largest distributors of drugs, cosmetics, and sundries. Quality King buys large lots of goods from unspecified sources at bargain prices and resells them. The company, which operates 5 facilities on Long Island, has been known as a "gray marketeer" because it often sells exclusive brands to unauthorized outlets, such as discounters. Its subsidiary, Deborah International, makes cosmetics and toiletries, as well as low-priced knock-offs of designer fragrances.

QUIKTRIP CORPORATION — RANK: 304

901 N. Mingo Rd.
Tulsa, OK 74101
Phone: 918-836-8551
Fax: 918-834-4117

1994 Sales: $985 million
FYE: April
Employees: 2,500

Key Personnel
Chm & Pres: Chester Cadieux
EVP Store Dev: Alvin Howerton
SVP Fin: Terry Carter
SVP Ops: Mike Stanford
VP Info Svcs: Dave Reid
VP HR: Jim Denny

Selected Services
ATMs
Drinks
Food
Gasoline
Money orders

Key Competitors
Circle K
Diamond Shamrock
Exxon
Kroger
Mobil
Phillips Petroleum
Southland
Texaco

Industry
Retail - convenience stores

Overview
Founded in 1958 by young entrepreneur Chester Cadieux and partners, QuikTrip grew gradually at first. In the late 1960s, however, the upstart chain began to expand rapidly, growing into Kansas, Iowa, and Georgia, and now has over 300 stores. In the 1980s QuikTrip remodeled, entered the gasoline business, and embarked upon another ambitious expansion plan. To ensure food quality QuikTrip supplies its stores with its own food brand, Quick 'n Tasty. The company recently placed a stone gorilla in front of its Tulsa headquarters, symbolizing its ambitious expansion strategy: like the 900-pound gorilla, QuikTrip plans to go anywhere it wants.

RACETRAC PETROLEUM, INC. — RANK: 390

300 Technology Ct.
Smyrna, GA 30082
Phone: 404-431-7600
Fax: 404-431-7612

1993 Sales: $795 million
FYE: December
Employees: 2,100

Key Personnel
Chm & CEO: Carl E. Bolch, Jr.
Pres: Max Lenker
CFO & Personnel: Robert J. Dumbacher
VP HR: Bob Stier
Gen Counsel: Harriet Landau

Business Lines
Flixx Video
Powers Ferry Realty
Racetrac (gas/convenience stores)
Raceway (gas stations)

Key Competitors
Blockbuster
Circle K
National Convenience
Pilot
Southland
Star Enterprise
Sunshine-Jr. Stores
Turtles

Industry
Retail - convenience stores

Overview
The largest independent gasoline marketer in the Southeast, Racetrac Petroleum was founded in Missouri in 1934 as a gasoline wholesaler by Carl Bolch, Sr. His son, CEO Carl Bolch, Jr., moved the company to the Atlanta metropolitan area and into retailing, putting convenience stores and gas stations together. The company that claims the distinction of opening Georgia's first self-service gas station now operates over 450 stores in 14 states in the Southeast. Racetrac added video stores to its line but shed its ethanol supply and transport companies in 1992.

RALEY'S INC.

RANK: 130

500 W. Capitol Ave.
West Sacramento, CA 95605
Phone: 916-373-3333
Fax: 916-444-3733

1993 Sales: $1,850 million
FYE: June
Employees: 11,000

Key Personnel
Co-Chm: Joyce Raley Teel
Co-Chm: James E. Teel
Pres & CEO: Charles L. Collings
EVP: David Steitz
CFO: Keith F. Tronson
VP HR: Sam McPherson

Operating Units
Bel Air Markets
Raley's Food & Drug
Sunny Select
Super Store Industries
WestPac Pacific Foods

Key Competitors
Albertson's
American Stores
Certified Grocers
Edward J. DeBartolo
Safeway
Save Mart Supermarkets
Southland
Yucaipa

Industry
Retail - supermarkets

Overview
Raley's is a leading supermarket and drugstore chain in Northern California and Nevada, as well as Sacramento's #1 food store chain. The company, which was founded in 1935 and now consists of over 80 stores, is owned by Joyce Teel and her husband and company veteran, Jim. Joyce Teel, who inherited the company from her father, Thomas Raley, in 1994, was listed in *Working Woman* as the US's #2 woman business owner.

RANDALLS FOOD MARKETS

RANK: 93

3663 Briarpark Dr.
Houston, TX 77042
Phone: 713-268-3500
Fax: 713-268-3601

1993 Est. Sales: $2,400 million
FYE: June
Employees: 7,800

Key Personnel
Chm, Pres & CEO: Robert Randall Onstead, Jr.
EVP Fin & Admin: Bob L. Gowens
EVP: Ronnie W. Barclay
SVP Mktg: Joseph Livorsi
VP Mktg & Public Relations: Cindy Garbs
VP HR: Jan Gillespie

◀ See page 117 for full-page profile.

Selected Services
Bakery
Bank
Coffee shop
Deli
Pharmacy
Prepared food counter
Seafood market
Video rental shop

Key Competitors
Albertson's
H. E. Butt
Fiesta Mart
Food Lion
Kroger
Minyard Food Stores
Whole Foods Market
Winn-Dixie

Industry
Retail - supermarkets

Overview
Founded in 1966 with only 2 stores, Randalls Food Markets is now the operator of some 70 Texas supermarkets and the leading grocer in Houston. Chaired by R. Randall Onstead, Jr., Randalls made a name for itself by targeting upscale clientele and offering exemplary services. Onstead is now expanding his vision, moving into other areas of Texas, particularly Dallas and Austin. A recent push into the Austin market has vaulted Randalls into that city's #2 spot.

RED APPLE GROUP

RANK: 91

823 Eleventh Ave.
New York, NY 10019
Phone: 212-956-5803
Fax: 212-262-4979

1993 Sales: $2,425 million
FYE: May
Employees: 9,300

Key Personnel
Chm & CEO: John Andreas Catsimatidis
Pres: Charles Criscoula
CFO: Stuart Spivak
EVP: Robert Scwartz
SVP: Vito Aviola
Dir HR: Ben Focarinio

Business Lines
Convenience stores
Corporate jet leasing
Petroleum refineries
Real estate
Supermarkets
  Gristede's
  Red Apple
  Sloan's

Key Competitors
American Stores
Grand Union
Great A&P
King Kullen Grocery
Koch
Penn Traffic
Wegmans Food Markets

Industry
Diversified operations

Overview
Red Apple Group has interests in everything from supermarkets to gasoline refineries. With 93 Red Apple, Sloan's, and Gristede's food markets in the New York City area, Red Apple is the #1 grocer in the Big Apple. The company also owns Pantry Pride and Grand Union stores in Florida and the Carribean. Chairman John Catsimatidis, a Greek immigrant who founded the company in 1969 and still owns it, also controls 33% of a jet leasing firm, 100% of United Refining, and about $250 million worth of real estate. *Forbes* estimates Catsimatidis's worth to be about $375 million.

RENCO GROUP INC.

RANK: 194

45 Rockefeller Plaza
New York, NY 10111
Phone: 212-541-6000
Fax: 212-541-6197

1992 Est. Sales: $1,350 million
FYE: October
Employees: 6,000

Key Personnel
Pres & CEO: Ira L. Rennert
VP Fin: Roger L. Fay
EVP: Marvin Koenig
Sec & Gen Counsel: Justin W. D'Atri

Selected Operating Units
AM General
Ascan Ohio
Consolidated Sewing Machine
Magnesium Corp. of America
Republic Drainage Products
Sabel Industries
R.L. Sweet Lumber
Warren Consolidated Industries

Key Competitors
Armco
Bethlehem Steel
Dow Chemical
Inland Steel
LTV
Republic Engineered Steels
Tremont
Worthington Industries

Industry
Diversified operations

Overview
New York–based Renco Group is a diversified investment company with various wholesale and manufacturing operations ranging from fasteners to industrial sewing machines. It is a subsidiary of Renco Holdings Inc., founded in 1980 by former business consultant Ira Rennert. Renco moved into steel in 1988, buying 2 companies from LTV Steel, and magnesium, by purchasing Amax's operations on the Great Salt Lake, in 1989. Renco recently bought LTV's AM General Corp., which manufactures Hummer military vehicles for the US military.

REPUBLIC ENGINEERED STEELS, INC.

RANK: 454

410 Oberlin Rd. SW
Massillon, OH 44648
Phone: 216-837-6000
Fax: 216-837-6204

1993 Sales: $642 million
FYE: June
Employees: 4,900

Key Personnel
Chm, Pres & CEO: Russell Maier
EVP & CFO: James Riley
Treas: John B. George
Controller: John Sears
VP & Gen Counsel: Harold V. Kelly
VP HR: Rick Miller

Operating Units
Cold Finished Division
Rolling Division
Specialty Steel Group
Steel Division

Key Competitors
Armco
Bethlehem Steel
Bliss & Laughlin Industries
Inland Steel
Nucor
USX - U.S. Steel
Worthington Industries

Industry
Steel - production

Overview
Organized in 1989 through an employee stock ownership plan that bought the assets of LTV Steel's bar division, Republic is the largest US producer of hot-rolled and cold-finished steel bars and specialty steels. The company operates 6 facilities in Ohio, Illinois, Indiana, Pennsylvania, and Connecticut that produce carbon, alloy, stainless, and tool steels. Automotive manufacturers such as Chrysler, Ford, GM, and Honda account for more than half of Republic's revenues. Other customers include Rockwell, TRW, American Steel & Aluminum, Caterpillar, John Deere, and Mercury Marine.

RGIS INVENTORY SPECIALISTS

RANK: 477

805 Oakwood Dr.
Rochester, MI 48307
Phone: 810-651-2511
Fax: 810-651-6787

1993 Sales: $590 million
FYE: December
Employees: 20,000

Key Personnel
Partner/Owner: Raymond J. Nicholson
Treas: Mark Papak
Personnel: Susan Kingman

Selected Customers
Albertson's
Barnes & Noble
Great A&P
Kmart
Sears
TravelFest
Wal-Mart

Key Competitors
Arthur Andersen
Coopers & Lybrand
Deloitte & Touche
Ernst & Young
Huffy
KPMG
Price Waterhouse

Industry
Business services - inventory taking

Overview
RGIS Inventory Specialists is the largest 3rd-party inventory taker in America. Using largely part-time employees who frequently work at night, the company takes inventory for its customers, primarily large retailers. Inventory takers use scanners to send information to a sophisticated computer system at RGIS headquarters. RGIS can take an inventory in the evening and deliver a report to its customer the next morning. RGIS also does fixed-asset and warehouse inventory from its 280 offices in the US, Canada, and Mexico. The company is owned by Ray Nicholson in partnership with a trust that benefits his deceased brother's estate.

RICELAND FOODS, INC.

RANK: 435

2120 S. Park Ave.
Stuttgart, AR 72160
Phone: 501-673-5500
Fax: 501-673-3366

1993 Sales: $692 million
FYE: July
Employees: 1,848

Key Personnel
Chm: Tommy Hillman
Pres: Richard E. Bell
VP & CFO: Harry E. Loftis
SVP: Carl Brothers
Legal Counsel: Terry Richardson
Dir HR: George Vickers

Major Products
Corn oil
Cottonseed oil
Packaged & flavored rice
Rice bran
Rice flour
Shortening
Soybean oil
Vegetable oil

Key Competitors
ADM
American Rice Growers Co-op
Cargill
ConAgra
Continental Grain
ERLY Industries
Farmers Rice Co-op
Riviana Foods

Industry
Food - flour & grain

Overview
In 1921 in Stuttgart, Arkansas, a group of farmers formed a co-op to sell their rice. Today, Riceland Foods has grown into the US's largest rice marketer and is a *FORTUNE* 500 company, selling crops grown by its 11,000 owners. In addition to storing, transporting, and processing rice (it is the world's largest rice miller) and soybeans, Riceland markets wheat, corn, oats, and milo. A poor rice harvest and a food shortage have pried open Tokyo's long sealed rice market, and in 1994 Riceland made its first sales to Japan.

RICH PRODUCTS CORPORATION

RANK: 302

1150 Niagara St.
Buffalo, NY 14213
Phone: 716-878-8000
Fax: 716-878-8266

1993 Sales: $990 million
FYE: December
Employees: 7,000

Key Personnel
Chm: Robert E. Rich, Sr.
Pres: Robert E. Rich, Jr.
Asst Treas: James Haddad
Sec: David A. Rich
VP Gen Counsel: Maureen O. Hurley
VP HR: Brian Townson

Principal Subsidiaries
Byron's, Inc.
Casa Di Bertacchi Corporation
Nanticoke Seafood Corporation
Rich Baseball Operations
Rich Communications Corporation
Rich-SeaPak Corporation
Rich Transportation Services
Stadium Services Inc.

Key Competitors
Borden
ConAgra
Dean Foods
Land O' Lakes
Nestlé
PET
Philip Morris
RJR Nabisco

Industry
Food - dairy substitute products

Overview
Robert Rich, Sr., bought a milk company in 1935, learned about product substitution during WWII, and then pioneered the nondairy industry. In 1945, en route to a customer, he packed a soybean-based whipped topping in dry ice, inadvertently founding the frozen nondairy industry. Later he developed Coffee Rich, the first nondairy creamer. Now the world's largest family-owned frozen food manufacturer, the company has expanded into frozen doughs and pies and also owns 3 minor league baseball teams and a Florida golf course. With operations throughout North America, Europe, and the Far East, the firm is now planning to move into the Russian market.

THE RITZ-CARLTON HOTEL COMPANY, INC. — RANK: 397

3414 Peachtree Rd. NE, Ste. 300
Atlanta, GA 30326
Phone: 404-237-5500
Fax: 404-261-0119

1993 Sales: $781 million
FYE: December
Employees: 14,000

Key Personnel
Chm & CEO: William B. Johnson
Pres & COO: Horst H. Schulze
CFO: Richard Stephens
EVP: Larry P. Martindale
VP & Gen Counsel: Terry Stinson
VP HR: Leonardo Inghilleri

Selected Hotels
Ritz-Carlton - Cleveland
Ritz-Carlton - Laguna Beach
Ritz-Carlton - Naples, FL
Ritz-Carlton - New York
Ritz-Carlton - Philadelphia
Ritz-Carlton - San Francisco
Ritz-Carlton - Washington

Key Competitors
Fairmont Management
Four Seasons
Hilton
Hyatt
ITT
Loews
Marriott International
Trump

Industry
Hotels & motels

Overview
Established in 1983 when William B. Johnson acquired the rights to the name made famous by hotelier Cesar Ritz, Ritz-Carlton in 1992 was the first hotel company to win the Malcolm Baldrige quality award. Of 30 hotels worldwide, the company owns 3 and has equity in 10 more. The rest are owned by others, but Ritz-Carlton receives handsome management fees for running them. Since the fees are usually based on gross revenue (typically 5%), critics contend the company emphasizes great service over profitability. The management strategy stresses training and employee retention.

RLC INDUSTRIES CO. INC. — RANK: 493

One Mile South on Hwy 99
Dillard, OR 97432
Phone: 503-679-3311
Fax: 503-679-9683

1993 Est. Sales: $548 million
FYE: March
Employees: 3,360

Key Personnel
Chm & Pres: Kenneth W. Ford
CEO: William Whelan
Pres, Sales & Mktg: Lyle Thompson
EVP: Allyn C. Ford
VP Fin & CFO: Ronald Parker
Personnel Mgr: Bob Wilson

Selected Services
Logging services
Lumber manufacturing
Road building
Timberland management
Wood product manufacturing
Woodchip exporting

Key Competitors
Georgia-Pacific
International Paper
Manville
North Pacific Lumber
Potlatch
Sierra Pacific Industries
Simpson Investment
Weyerhaeuser

Industry
Building products - wood

Overview
Started in 1936 with one sawmill assembled from junk parts, Kenneth Ford's RLC had become by 1989 the #1 US family-owned forest products firm, with timber and logging interests (Roseburg Lumber) and mills for lumber, plywood, and particle board (Roseburg Forest Products, Diamond Lands). In 1990 Ford put Roseburg Forest Products up for sale (it didn't sell) in an industry atmosphere of increased regulation. Logging shortages caused by restrictive federal forest policies are putting pressure on the company to downsize.

C.H. ROBINSON COMPANY — RANK: 229

8100 Mitchell Rd., Ste. 200
Eden Prairie, MN 55344
Phone: 612-937-8500
Fax: 612-937-7809

1993 Est. Sales: $1,200 million
FYE: December
Employees: 1,400

Key Personnel
Pres: D. R. Verdoorn
CFO: Dale S. Hanson
VP Legal & Sec: Owen P. Gleason
VP: Looe Baker III
VP: Barry Butzow
Dir Branch Resources: Colleen Zwach

Principal Subsidiaries
Allstates Warehousing
Meyer Customs Brokers
C.H. Robinson Air Cargo
C.H. Robinson Intermodal/Rail
C.H. Robinson International, Inc.
C.H. Robinson LTL
C.H. Robinson Pallet
Robinson Special Services

Key Competitors
Consolidated Freightways
Hub Group
J.B. Hunt
Norfolk Southern
Roadway
Union Pacific
Werner
Yellow Corporation

Industry
Transportation - services

Overview
Incorporated in 1905 as a produce broker, C.H. Robinson expanded into transportation services in the 1930s. Robinson owns no equipment but contracts with 5,200 companies — including all the major railroads and airlines as well as trucking, shipping, and leasing companies — for intermodal services to serve its 14,000 customers. The 100%-employee-owned firm is one of the nation's largest produce distributors, serving both national and international wholesale, retail, and foodservice markets.

THE ROCKEFELLER FOUNDATION — RANK: N/R

420 Fifth Ave.
New York, NY 10018
Phone: 212-869-8500
Fax: 212-398-1858

1993 Sales: $208 million
FYE: December
Employees: 147

Key Personnel
Chm: John R. Evans
Pres: Peter C. Goldmark, Jr.
SVP: Kenneth Prewitt
Treas & Chief Investment Officer: David A. White
Comptroller: Charles J. Lang
Mgr HR: Charlotte Church

◀ **See page 118 for full-page profile.**

Selected Programs
Agricultural Sciences
Arts & Humanities
Equal Opportunity Program
Global Environmental Program
Health Sciences
International Security
Population Sciences
School Reform

Industry
Foundation

Overview
Founded by oil baron John D. Rockefeller in 1913, The Rockefeller Foundation is one of the largest and oldest private charitable organizations in the world. The foundation supports grants, fellowships, program-related investments, and conferences for activities in 3 areas: science-based development, the arts and humanities, and equal opportunity programs. The foundation maintains no ties to the Rockefeller family or its other philanthropic activities. A board of trustees sets program guidelines and approves expenditures.

ROLL INTERNATIONAL

RANK: 308

12233 W. Olympic Blvd., Ste. 380
Los Angeles, CA 90064
Phone: 310-442-5700
Fax: 310-207-1557

1992 Est. Sales: $962 million
FYE: December
Employees: 7,500

Key Personnel
Co-Chm & Pres: Stewart A. Resnick
Co-Chm: Lynda Rae Resnick
CFO: Neil R. Bersch
VP Fin & Acctg: Peter R. Gurney
VP & Gen Counsel: Richard S. Kolodny
Dir HR: Tim Zeleny

Principal Subsidiaries
Bundy Properties (commercial)
Franklin Mint Corp. (collectibles)
Jay Dee Transportation (buses)
Paramount Citrus Association Inc.
Paramount Farming Co. (nuts)
Paramount Farms (nut sales)
Teleflora (floral marketing services)

Key Competitors
Calyx & Corolla
Dole
FTD
Jostens
QVC
Royal Citrus
Stanhome
Sun-Diamond Growers

Industry
Retail - mail order & direct

Overview
Roll International (fruit, almond, and pistachio farming) was part of American Protection Industries, but owners Stewart and Lynda Resnick sold the protection firm (alarms) in 1989, keeping the API name until 1993 when they gave Roll's name to the holding company. Roll International's other holdings include commercial properties in Los Angeles (Bundy Properties); New York school buses (Jay Dee Transportation); florist service Teleflora (founded 1934); and the Franklin Mint, which withdrew an IPO in 1992. The Franklin Mint manufactures money for foreign governments but is best known for mail-order collectibles.

ROTARY INTERNATIONAL

RANK: N/R

One Rotary Center, 1560 Sherman Ave.
Evanston, IL 60201
Phone: 708-866-3243
Fax: 708-328-8554

1993 Sales: $52 million
FYE: June
Employees: 617

Key Personnel
Gen Sec: Herbert A. Pigman
Pres: Robert R. Barth
Pres-Elect: Bill Huntley
VP: Wilfrid J. Wilkinson
CFO: Mary Wolfenberger
Treas: Takuomi Matsumoto

◀ **See page 119 for full-page profile.**

Major Programs
Cultural exchange program
Educational activities
International humanitarian projects
Local community service

Industry
Membership organization

Overview
Rotary International, started in 1905 by Paul Percy Harris and 3 other small businessmen, is the world's oldest service and business organization. It promotes the goals of international fellowship and goodwill through a variety of programs. Its Rotary Foundation, founded 1917, administers service projects, which include the largest privately sponsored scholarship program in the world, childhood immunization and nutritional programs, and relief efforts to such troubled areas as Bosnia and Croatia.

ROUNDY'S INC.

RANK: 89

23000 Roundy Dr.
Pewaukee, WI 53072
Phone: 414-547-7999
Fax: 414-547-4540

1992 Sales: $2,490 million
FYE: January
Employees: 5,000

Key Personnel
Chm & CEO: John R. Dickson
Pres & COO: Gerald F. Lestina
CFO: Robert D. Ranus
VP Mktg: Marion H. Sullivan
Gen Counsel: Robert G. Turcott
VP Admin: David C. Busch

Business Lines
Wholesale grocery distribution
Retail grocery store chains:
Pick 'n Save Warehouse Foods
Shop-Rite Food Stores

Key Competitors
American Stores
Fleming
Holiday Cos.
Kohl's
Kroger
Schultz Sav-O-Stores
SUPERVALU
Wal-Mart

Industry
Food - wholesale to grocers

Overview
Founded in 1872, Roundy's, one of the largest wholesale grocers in the US, distributes to retailers throughout the Midwest. Organized as a cooperative, Roundy's is owned by the store operators it supplies. Roundy's retail supermarket group includes Pick 'n Save stores (Wisconsin's largest chain, with over 60 units, several owned by the company) and Shop-Rite stores (mostly in smaller communities). Facing fierce industry competition, Roundy's is adding larger stores that offer more varied products.

S&P CO.

RANK: 465

100 Shoreline Hwy., Bldg. B, Ste. 315
Mill Valley, CA 94941
Phone: 415-332-0550
Fax: 415-332-0567

1993 Sales: $628 million
Employees: 2,800

Key Personnel
Chm & Pres: Lutz Issleib
EVP & Sec: Bernard Orsi
EVP & Gen Counsel: William Bitting
VP Fin: John Schiess

Major Beverage Brands
Ballantine
Falstaff
Hamm's
Olde English 800
Olympia
Pabst Blue Ribbon
Pearl
Texas Pride

Key Competitors
Adolph Coors
Anheuser-Busch
Gambrinus
Genesee
Heileman Brewing
Philip Morris
Stroh
Tsing Tao

Industry
Beverages - alcoholic

Overview
Trouble is no longer brewing at S&P, the holding company for Pabst, Pearl, and Falstaff breweries, which is owned by a testamentary trust established by Paul Kalmanovitz and by his widow, Lydia Kalmanovitz. Sales of flagship brand Pabst plunged from 17 million barrels in 1976 to under 6 million barrels in 1988. But aggressive pricing strategies have added fizz to the sales, which are back up over 7 million barrels, making Pabst the 6th largest brewery in the US. S&P, which purchased Pabst in 1985, has spent $58 million on capital improvements and trimmed middle management. S&P recently established the first US-owned brewery in China.

SACRAMENTO MUNICIPAL UTILITY DISTRICT

RANK: 447

6201 S St.
Sacramento, CA 95817
Phone: 916-452-3211
Fax: 916-732-6027

1993 Sales: $656 million
FYE: December
Employees: 2,411

Key Personnel
Gen Mgr & CEO: Jan E. Schori
Asst Gen Mgr & COO: Leo A. Fassler
Asst Gen Mgr & CFO: Gail R. Hullibarger
Asst Gen Mgr & Chief Eng: Richard G. Ferreira
Gen Counsel & Sec: Dana S. Appling
Mgr Personnel Svcs: Shirley Lewis

Selected Services
Agricultural electricity services
Energy conservation services
Ethanol production
Industrial electricity services
Residential electricity services

Industry
Utility - electric power

Overview
The Sacramento Municipal Utility District (SMUD) is the US's 5th largest publicly owned electric utility, based on customers served. Founded in 1923, SMUD generates electricity using geothermal energy, natural gas, solar power, and water and is building a wind-generated plant. SMUD is also working on projects to share power generation with Campbell Soup and Procter & Gamble, among other organizations. The utility shut down its Rancho Seco nuclear facility in 1989 and is awaiting regulatory permission to decommission the plant. SMUD generates about 1/3 of the electricity it supplies and buys the remainder.

SAKS HOLDINGS, INC.

RANK: 185

12 E. 49th St.
New York, NY 10017
Phone: 212-940-4180
Fax: 212-940-4103

1993 Sales: $1,400 million
FYE: January
Employees: 8,000

Key Personnel
Chm & CEO: Philip B. Miller
VC: Gary Witkin
Pres: Rose Marie Bravo
EVP & CFO: Brian E. Kendrick
SVP HR: Owen Dorsey
Legal Counsel: Joan F. Krey

Major Products
Accessories
Career wear
Men's clothing
Shoes
Sportswear
Women's clothing

Key Competitors
AnnTaylor
Barneys
Federated
The Gap
The Limited
Harcourt General
May
J. C. Penney

Industry
Retail - major department stores

Overview
Saks, best known for its New York City flagship store Saks Fifth Avenue, is a chain of 49 full-line department stores, resort stores, and clearance centers. Founded in 1924 and acquired by Investcorp in 1990, Saks plans to open a new line of specialty stores and expand its full-line stores overseas. Former chairman and industry notable Melvin Jacobs, who died unexpectedly in 1993, led Saks into the home shopping arena in a venture with QVC Network.

SALT RIVER PROJECT AGRICULTURAL IMPROVEMENT & POWER DISTRICT

RANK: 192

1521 N. Project Dr.
Tempe, AZ 85281
Phone: 602-236-5900
Fax: 602-236-4350

1993 Sales: $1,360 million
FYE: April
Employees: 4,600

Key Personnel
Pres: William P. Schrader
Gen Mgr: Richard H. Silverman
CFO: Mark B. Bonsall
Treas: Dean K. Yee
Legal Counsel: Jane Alfano
Mgr HR: Kathy Haake

Selected Services
Drinking water supply
Electric power distribution
Electric power generation
Electric services
Irrigation systems
Irrigation water supply

Industry
Utility - electric power

Overview
Incorporated in 1903, Salt River is the nation's 3rd largest power utility and Arizona's largest water provider. The water branch is a private corporation owned by landowners; the power utility, formed in 1937, is a subdivision of the state government. They are led by 2 boards with a total of 24 members, all but 4 elected according to their land holdings. The power division generates the lion's share of revenue and subsidizes the water district, resulting in a classic Old West clash of interests: the townsfolk (power users) vs. the farmers (heavy water users).

THE SALVATION ARMY

RANK: 188

615 Slaters Ln.
Alexandria, VA 22313
Phone: 703-684-5500
Fax: 703-684-5538

1992 Sales: $1,398 million
FYE: September
Employees: 5,842

Key Personnel
National Advisory Board Chm: Arthur J. Decio
General: Bramwell H. Tillsley
National Commander: Kenneth L. Hodder
Eastern Territorial Commander: Ronald G. Irwin
Southern Territorial Commander: Kenneth Hood
Western Territorial Commander: Paul A. Rader

Selected Services
Adult rehabilitation
Christmas sharing
Correctional services
Day care centers
Disaster relief
Homeless shelters
Missing persons assistance
Summer camps

Industry
Religious & charitable organization

Overview
Founded in 1865 in the East End of London by ex–Methodist preacher William Booth, The Salvation Army quickly grew into a global grassroots movement, combining evangelical Christianity with innovative social programs. Established in the US by 8 young British Salvationists in 1880, the "army" steadily gained acceptance. Although the uniforms of its "soldiers" catch the eye primarily at Christmas and during disasters, the "army" operates community centers and social service programs year-round in almost 10,000 locations across the US.

◀ **See page 120 for full-page profile.**

SAMMONS ENTERPRISES, INC.

RANK: 202

300 Crescent Ct., Ste. 700
Dallas, TX 75201
Phone: 214-855-2800
Fax: 214-855-2899

1993 Sales: $1,308 million
FYE: December
Employees: 3,900

Key Personnel
Pres & CEO: Robert W. Korba
EVP & COO: James N. Whitson
CFO: Joseph A. Ethridge
Gen Counsel: John H. Washburn
Dir Communications: Joe Barta
Dir Real Estate: Bill Daves

Principal Subsidiaries
Adventure Tours USA
Briggs-Weaver
Jack Tar Village Beach Resorts
Midland National Life Insurance
Mountain Valley Spring Water
Sammons Communications Group
Texas Marine & Industrial Supply
Vinson Supply

Key Competitors
Carlson
Equitable
Danone
Marriott International
Nestlé
New York Life
Prudential
TCI

Industry
Diversified operations

Overview
Founded in 1962, Dallas-based Sammons Enterprises has become the holding company for the diversified businesses of billionaire Charles Sammons, an orphan who started a grain and hay business at age 19. The business was a success, but Sammons lost his money in 1928 when his bank went broke. Sammons moved into insurance and made his fortune with Reserve Life Insurance Co., which he founded in 1938. Sammons Enterprises is now a conglomerate of insurance, cable television, hotel, travel, industrial supply, and bottled water companies. A well-known philanthropist, Sammons died at age 90 in 1988.

SANTA MONICA FORD

RANK: 398

1230 Santa Monica Blvd.
Santa Monica, CA 90404
Phone: 310-451-1588
Fax: 310-394-8115

1992 Sales: $778 million
FYE: December
Employees: 110

Key Personnel
Chm: L. Wayne Harding
Pres: Robert Karlin
VP: Mark Harding
VP: William Topping
Sec & Treas: Edith Harding
Bus Mgr & Controller: Charlotte Richardson

Business Lines
Auto dealerships
Body shops
Fleet sales
Service departments

Key Competitors
Galpin Motors
Holman Enterprises
Kramer Motors
Martin Cadillac
Prospect Motors
Walker Motor Co.

Industry
Retail - new & used cars

Overview
Founded in 1947 by Roy Pierce and bought in 1963 by Wayne Harding and Robert Karlin, Santa Monica Ford is the nation's 4th largest auto dealership ranked by new unit sales. The dealership, which realizes most of its business from fleet sales, is also the country's 4th largest fleet dealer. Apparently unimpressed by star status alone, Santa Monica Ford made headlines by asking a former Miss America to have her father cosign her lease on a Ford Explorer.

SAVE MART SUPERMARKETS

RANK: 250

1800 Standiford Ave.
Modesto, CA 95350
Phone: 209-577-1600
Fax: 209-526-4396

1993 Sales: $1,100 million
FYE: December
Employees: 7,000

Key Personnel
Chm, Pres & CEO: Robert M. Piccinini
CFO: Ronald Riesenbeck
Dir Mktg: Cecil Russell
VP Ops: Art Patch
VP HR: John Bacon

Operating Units
Fry's Food Stores
Mid-Valley Dairy
Save Mart Supermarkets
Super Store Industries (JV)

Key Competitors
Albertson's
American Stores
Kroger
Raley's
Safeway
Wal-Mart
Whole Foods Market
Yucaipa

Industry
Retail - supermarkets

Overview
Founded in 1952, Save Mart operates more than 90 supermarkets in California, mostly in the San Joaquin Valley and the Bay Area. The company, owned by the Piccinini family, significantly expanded with the 1989 acquisition of 27 Fry's stores from Kroger. In an effort to reduce costs and compete with large, vertically integrated grocers, Save Mart and 2 other local grocery chains jointly operate 2 dairies and a grocery warehouse.

SCHNEIDER NATIONAL INC.

RANK: 216

3101 S. Packerland Dr.
Green Bay, WI 54306
Phone: 414-592-2000
Fax: 414-592-3565

1993 Sales: $1,250 million
FYE: December
Employees: 13,950

Key Personnel
Pres: Donald J. Schneider
Pres Trans Sector: James Olson
Pres Schneider Natl Logistics: Larry Sur
CFO: Tom Gannon
Chief Info Officer: Larry Tieman
Mgr HR: Mary Vogel

Operating Units
Bulk Group (tankers)
Dedicated Operations (pvt. fleets)
Schneider Communications
Specialized Carriers
Van Group

Key Competitors
American Freightways
Cannon Express
Consolidated Freightways
J.B. Hunt
Leaseway Transportation
Roadway
Transcon
Yellow Corporation

Industry
Transportation - truck

Overview
A. J. "Al" Schneider founded Schneider National in 1935 with one truck; today it is North America's largest truckload carrier, with 9,000 tractors and 22,000 trailers on the road. The company has grown quickly since industry deregulation and is noted for its participatory (generally non-Teamster) culture and its up-to-the-minute technology. All units are linked by satellite, which enhances scheduling and loading efficiency. Schneider, now piloted by Al's son Donald, is enlarging its intermodal capacity and foresees increased business with the passage of NAFTA. It also owns a communications firm.

SCHNUCK MARKETS INC.

RANK: 221

11420 Lackland Rd.
St. Louis, MO 63146
Phone: 314-994-9900
Fax: 314-994-4465

1993 Sales: $1,225 million
FYE: September
Employees: 14,000

Key Personnel
Chm & CEO: Craig D. Schnuck
Pres & COO: Scott C. Schnuck
CFO: Todd R. Schnuck
Counsel: Terry Schnuck
VP HR: William Jones

Selected Services
Bakery
Delicatessen
Florist
Fresh seafood shop
Pharmacy
Prepared foods
Video rental

Key Competitors
Aldi
Eagle Food
Fleming
George Weston
Hy-Vee Food Stores
Kroger
National Supermarkets
SUPERVALU

Industry
Retail - supermarkets

Overview
Founded in 1939 and in its 3rd generation of family leadership, Schnuck Markets is a chain of over 60 supermarkets located in the St. Louis area (49 stores), Kansas City (5), Columbia, Missouri (2), and Evansville, Indiana (4). Schnuck also owns a major egg business (Agri Foods Inc.) and a dairy (Mid States Dairy). In an effort to bag upscale shoppers, a new Schnuck store includes an espresso bar, an herb garden, and a stone hearth oven in the bakery.

SCHOTTENSTEIN STORES CORPORATION

RANK: 225

1800 Moler Rd.
Columbus, OH 43207
Phone: 614-221-9200
Fax: 614-443-5810

1993 Sales: $1,204 million
FYE: July
Employees: 15,000

Key Personnel
Chm & CEO: Jay Schottenstein
Pres: Saul Schottenstein
Pres, Value City: George Iacono, Sr.
VP Fin: Thomas Ketteler
VP Info Sys: Jerry Kerr
VP HR: Herbert E. Minkin

Operating Units
American Eagle Outfitters
Dollar Bargain stores
Englander Sleep products
Schottenstein's
Shiffren Willens Jewelry
Valley Fair Department Stores
Value City Department Stores
Value City Furniture stores

Key Competitors
Dayton Hudson
Heilig-Meyers
Levitz
May
Mercantile Stores
J. C. Penney
Sears
Tuesday Morning

Industry
Retail - regional department & specialty retail stores

Overview
Founded in 1917 and largely family owned, Schottenstein Stores (SSC) is now, after the 1992 death of retail liquidation industry pioneer Jerome Schottenstein, in its 3rd generation of family leadership. Jerome's son Jay heads this chain of retail department, furniture, and clothing stores in 11 midwestern and eastern states. The family also has substantial real estate holdings in central Ohio. The Value City Department Store Division (a discount chain with over 60 stores) was spun off in a 1991 public offering, but SSC still controls a majority of the stock and elects all of its directors.

SCHREIBER FOODS INC.

RANK: 217

425 Pine St.
Green Bay, WI 54301
Phone: 414-437-7601
Fax: 414-436-2205

1993 Est. Sales: $1,250 million
FYE: September
Employees: 2,800

Key Personnel
Chm: Robert G. Bush
Pres & CEO: John C. Meng
Treas: Bob Paruess
EVP Ops & Tech: Thomas F. Badciong
SVP Acquisitions: Thomas L. Krautkramer
VP HR: Sherry W. Featherstone

Major Products
Bacon
Cheese
Cheese processing equipment
Packaging machinery

Key Competitors
Darigold
Land O' Lakes
Lapreno Foods
Marathon Cheese
Prairie Farms Dairy
Philip Morris
Western Dairymen Co-op
Wisconsin Dairies Co-op

Industry
Food - dairy products

Overview
Founded in 1962, Schreiber Foods is a major cheese processor. The company operates a number of cheese processing plants, selling to institutional and retail buyers. Under the brand Premium Cooper, the company sells 22 cheese products. Its plant in Logan, Utah, supplies most of the major grocery chains and fast food chains in the western US. The company also makes prepared meats. CEO Jack Meng believes in participatory management, and the company is organized into work teams with rotating leaders.

SCHWAN'S SALES ENTERPRISES, INC.

RANK: 141

115 W. College Dr.
Marshall, MN 56258
Phone: 507-532-3274
Fax: 507-537-8145

1992 Est. Sales: $1,780 million
FYE: December
Employees: 6,500

Key Personnel
Pres & CEO: Alfred Schwan
VP: Adrian J. Anderson
Mgr Fin & Acctg: Dan Herrmann
Dir Info Svcs: Bob Hefti
Head of Personnel: Larry Gibbs
Controller: Don Miller

Major Products
Better Baked Pizza
Chicago Bros. Frozen Pizza
Panzerotti (stuffed pastries)
RAM Center (robotics)
Red Baron Pizza
Sabatasso Foods
Syncom Magnetic Media (disks)
Tony's Pizza

Key Competitors
ConAgra
Fleming
General Mills
Philip Morris
Quaker
RJR Nabisco
Sara Lee
SUPERVALU

Industry
Food - frozen & prepared

Overview
Founded in 1944, Schwan's is a leader in preparing and delivering foods to customers' homes as well as the leading supplier of frozen pizza to school lunch programs and grocery stores in the US. The company's 2,300-van home delivery service operates in rural areas of 49 states. Products delivered include dairy products, frozen meats, fish, bread, casseroles, and fruits, some of which Schwan's processes itself. The family-owned company was started by Paul Schwan, a milk delivery man, and developed by his son Marvin, who died in 1993.

SCIENCE APPLICATIONS INTERNATIONAL CORPORATION

RANK: 151

10260 Campus Point Dr.
San Diego, CA 92121
Phone: 619-546-6000
Fax: 619-546-6777

1993 Sales: $1,680 million
FYE: January
Employees: 16,200

Key Personnel
Chm & CEO: J. Robert Beyster
Pres & COO: Lorenz A. Kull
SVP & CFO: William A. Roper
SVP & Sec: J. Dennis Heipt
VP HR: Bernard Theule
Gen Counsel: Douglas Scott

Selected Services
Systems integration
R&D in the areas of:
- Energy
- Environment
- Health
- National security
- Sciences

Key Competitors
Arvin
Battelle
Bolt Beranek
EG&G
Electronic Data Systems
IBM
Mitre

Industry
Engineering - R&D services

Overview
Founded in 1969 by physicist J. Robert Beyster with a $20,000 contract, SAIC has grown into a large, diversified high-tech research and engineering firm. Historically highly secretive and dependent on defense industry contracts, including work for Star Wars, SAIC is now undertaking more nonmilitary projects such as hazardous waste cleanup, global warming research, and electric vehicle development. But SAIC continues to benefit from Defense Department contracts and is helping the military engineer its downsizing. SAIC employees and directors own 46% of the company's shares, and another 41% is reserved for ESOP and 401(k) plans.

THE SCOULAR COMPANY INC.

RANK: 270

2027 Dodge St.
Omaha, NE 68102
Phone: 402-342-3500
Fax: 402-342-5568

1993 Sales: $1,053 million
FYE: May
Employees: 250

Key Personnel
Chm: Marshall E. Faith
Pres: Duane A. Fischer
VP: John M. Heck
VP: John M. Zenner
VP: Randal L. Linville
VP, Controller: Timothy J. Regan

Major Products
Corn
Field beans
Grain
Soybeans
Wheat

Key Competitors
ADM
Ag Processing
Bartlett
Cargill
ConAgra
Continental Grain
Farmland Industries
Harvest States Co-ops

Industry
Food - brokerage

Overview
Providing storage and transportation for domestic and international sales of grains and other farm products, The Scoular Company began in the 1890s in Nebraska. Consolidating with 2 other companies in 1967, Scoular now operates 20 grain storage facilities and 13 grain elevators. The company also operates 4 grain terminals in Nebraska (in Lincoln, Omaha, Sidney, and Venango) as well as terminals in Salina, Kansas, and Butte, Montana. With the hope of becoming more competitive with Canadian grain dealers, Scoular recently made the first direct shipment of 3,080 metric tons of high-protein Nebraska wheat to Mexico.

SEALY CORPORATION

RANK: 438

1228 Euclid Ave.
Cleveland, OH 44115
Phone: 216-522-1310
Fax: 216-522-1366

1993 Sales: $683 million
FYE: November
Employees: 4,844

Key Personnel
Chm & Pres: Lyman M. Beggs
CFO: Douglas R. Schrank
VP HR: Jeffrey C. Claypool
Treas: John G. Bartik
Sec & Gen Counsel: John D. Moran
Controller: Frank Abbatomarco

Major Products
Bedside stands
Box springs
Couches
Davenports
Dressers
Mattresses
Sofa beds
Waterbed frames

Key Competitors
Jamison Bedding
Leggett & Platt
National Bedding and Furniture
Olympic Spring
Ortho Mattress
Serta Inc.
Simmons Co.
Spring Air Co.

Industry
Furniture

Overview
The world's largest manufacturer of mattresses dates back to 1881, when a Sealy, Texas, cotton gin builder devised a tuftless mattress. Takeover maven Sam Zell acquired 94% of Sealy from First Boston in 1993. The remaining 6% is owned by management and another investment group. Sealy, which has over 20% of the market for bedding, promotes its products' construction and Posturepedic brand name as major selling points.

SENTRY INSURANCE, A MUTUAL COMPANY

RANK: 165

1800 Northpoint Dr.
Stevens Point, WI 54481
Phone: 715-346-6000
Fax: 715-346-7516

1993 Sales: $1,568 million
FYE: December
Employees: 4,500

Key Personnel
Chm & Pres: Larry C. Ballard
SVP & CFO: Wayne Ashenberg
SVP Mktg: Dale R. Schuh
VP HR: Alfred C. Noel
VP Investments: Steven R. Boehlke
Sec & Gen Counsel: William M. O'Reilly

Principal Subsidiaries
Dairyland County Mutal Ins. Co.
Dairyland Insurance Co.
Middlesex Insurance Co.
Patriot General Insurance Co.
Sentry Investors Life Insurance Co.
Sentry Life Insurance Co.
Sentry Life Insurance Co. of NY
Sentry Lloyds of Texas

Key Competitors
Aetna
AIG
Chubb
CIGNA
GEICO
SAFECO
State Farm
USF&G

Industry
Insurance - multiline

Overview
Sentry Insurance, of Stevens Point, Wisconsin, is a mutual company which offers, through its nationally operating subsidiaries, a variety of insurance, including fire and marine, auto and other property/casualty, life, and health and disability insurance. The company was formed as Wisconsin Hardware Limited Mutual Liability Insurance Co. in 1913 to provide insurance to hardware dealers. In 1971 it merged with the Hardware Dealers Mutual Fire Insurance Co. and changed its name to Sentry Insurance.

SERVICES GROUP OF AMERICA INC. RANK: 210

4025 Delridge Way SW
Seattle, WA 98106
Phone: 206-933-5000
Fax: 206-933-5279

1993 Est. Sales: $1,275 million
FYE: January
Employees: 3,000

Key Personnel
Chm: Thomas J. Stewart
Pres: Dennis J. Specht
Treas: Greg Stevenson
Dir HR: Jacqueline Steven

Business Lines
Fire & casualty insurance
Fruits & vegetables
Real estate
Wholesale groceries
Workers' compensation insurance

Key Competitors
Allstate
AmeriServ Food
Associated Grocers
Fred Meyer
Mutual of Omaha
Philip Morris
Rykoff-Sexton
SYSCO

Industry
Food - wholesale to grocers

Overview
Services Group of America, through its largest subsidiary, Food Services of America (FSA), is the 8th largest broadline distributor in the US, supplying groceries, produce, and cleaning products to supermarkets, hospitals, schools, and restaurants in 17 western states, including Alaska. Fresh produce purchased through a subsidiary, Amerifresh, Inc., accounts for about 25% of FSA's sales. Services Group of America, organized in 1954, also owns Eagle Pacific Insurance, which sells insurance to West Coast longshoremen, and Development Services of America, a real estate developer.

SERVISTAR CORP. RANK: 157

PO Box 1510
East Butler, PA 16029
Phone: 412-283-4567
Fax: 412-284-6320

1993 Sales: $1,619 million
FYE: June
Employees: 2,007

Key Personnel
Pres & CEO: Paul E. Pentz
SVP Fin & CFO: Albert Mielcuszny
SVP Mktg: Don E. Belt
SVP Mdse: Gene O'Donnell
SVP Sales: Donald J. Hoye
SVP HR: Russell A. Thomas

Business Lines
Equipment rental
Hardware wholesaling
Home & garden supplies
Marketing assistance to members

Key Competitors
84 Lumber
Ace Hardware
Cotter & Co.
Hardware Wholesalers
Home Depot
Kmart
Menard

Industry
Building products - retail & wholesale

Overview
SERVISTAR, one of the largest hardware wholesalers in the US, is a co-op controlled by more than 4,000 hardware store–owning members in the US and Canada. In addition to providing members with merchandise, it sponsors a variety of marketing, pricing, and educational programs to help its members compete with hardware industry giants like Home Depot and Kmart's Builder's Square. SERVISTAR (formerly American Hardware Supply) also has the largest general consumer rental operation in the US, renting everything from party supplies to construction machinery. SERVISTAR plans to expand into industrial distribution.

SHURFINE INTERNATIONAL, INC. RANK: 256

2100 N. Mannheim Rd.
Northlake, IL 60164
Phone: 708-681-2000
Fax: 708-681-5862

1994 Sales: $1,100 million
FYE: May
Employees: 130

Key Personnel
Chm: Virgil Froehlich
Pres & CEO: Paul T. Jasper
VP & CFO: Eric Stuhlmann
VP Mktg Stores: David LaPlante
VP Mktg Service: Bill Maier
Personnel Mgr: Carol Lemmer

Major Brands
Award Winner
Price-Saver
Quality Choice
Shurfine
Shurfresh
Shur-Valu
Ultimate Choice

Key Competitors
American Stores
Daymon Associates
Fleming
George Weston
Kroger
Jitney-Jungle Stores
Topco Associates

Industry
Food - wholesale to grocers

Overview
Shurfine-Central is a food buying co-op that markets private label products to 33 warehouses serving 12,000 retailers in 48 states. It controls about 8% of the booming private label market, and plans to boost its market share by increasing sales to retailers, expanding its product line into perishables, personal and general products, and beer, and expanding overseas, especially in Eastern Europe, Latin America, and Asia. The company also makes grocery bags.

SIERRA PACIFIC INDUSTRIES RANK: 472

3735 El Cajon Ave.
Shasta Lake, CA 96019
Phone: 916-275-8812
Fax: 916-365-9475

1992 Sales: $604 million
FYE: December
Employees: 2,800

Key Personnel
Pres & CEO: A. A. "Red" Emmerson
VP Fin: Mark Emmerson
VP Mfg: George Emmerson
VP Resources: Dan Thomascheski
Controller: Ray Lowry
Dir HR: Ed Bond

Business Lines
Lumber
Millwork products
Planing mills
Sawmills
Wood windows

Key Competitors
Canfor
Georgia-Pacific
International Paper
Louisiana-Pacific
North Pacific Lumber
RLC Industries
Simpson Investment
Weyerhaeuser

Industry
Building products - wood

Overview
Founded in 1969, Sierra Pacific Industries is the largest private timberland owner in California, with 1.1 million acres. Owned by the Emmerson family, it operates 9 mills. Decreasing access to national forests, strong environmental interests, and catastrophic fires have besieged the industry in recent years. In 1994 Sierra Pacific convinced the federal government that the company's purchase of Michigan-California Lumber Co. did not constitute a regional monopoly; the deal went through, saving 280 jobs.

SILGAN HOLDINGS INC.

RANK: 451

4 Landmark Sq.
Stamford, CT 06901
Phone: 203-975-7110
Fax: 203-975-7902

1993 Sales: $646 million
FYE: December
Employees: 3,980

Key Personnel
Chm & Co-CEO: R. Philip Silver
Pres & Co-CEO: D. Greg Horrigan
CFO & EVP: Harley Rankin , Jr.
Pres, Silgan Containers: James D. Beam
Pres, Silgan Plastics: Russell F. Gervais
HR: Sharon Budds

Subsidiaries
California-Washington Can
Express Plastic Containers
Silgan Containers
Silgan Plastics

Key Competitors
American National Can
Ball
Continental Can
Crown Cork & Seal
Graham Packaging
Johnson Controls
Owens-Illinois

Industry
Containers - metal and plastic

Overview
Former Continental Can executives Philip Silver and Greg Horrigan formed Silgan in 1987 by purchasing the containers divisions of such companies as Nestlé, Dial, and Monsanto. The company, which has manufacturing facilities across the US and in Ontario, is split into 2 principal subsidiaries: Silgan Containers (steel and aluminum containers for the food and pet food markets) and Silgan Plastics (plastic containers for the personal care, food, pharmaceutical, and household markets). Each is an industry leader. Silgan Containers recently acquired Del Monte's container business, giving them a market share of over 20%.

J.R. SIMPLOT COMPANY

RANK: 149

999 Main St., Ste. 1300
Boise, ID 83702
Phone: 208-336-2110
Fax: 208-389-7515

1993 Sales: $1,700 million
FYE: August
Employees: 9,000

Key Personnel
Pres & CEO: Stephen A. Beebe
CFO: Lawrence E. Costello
VP Govt & Pub Rel: Fred Zerza
VP Info Sys: Ray Sasso
VP HR: Ted Roper
Counsel: Ronald N. Graves

Major Products
Cheese
Fertilizers
Frozen foods
Livestock
Potatoes
Prepared meats

Key Competitors
Cargill
ConAgra
Koch
Sara Lee
Schwan's Sales Enterprises
Universal Foods
Vigoro

Industry
Food - potatoes

Overview
Tater titan J. R. Simplot, who founded his company in 1941, practically guaranteed his success in the potato processing industry over 30 years ago when he convinced McDonald's pioneer Ray Kroc to go with his frozen french fries. Today, industry leader J.R. Simplot Co. produces 1.5 billion pounds of fries annually, including half of McDonald's. Making good use of leftover potato peels, Simplot also produces prepared feeds and operates beef cattle feedlots. J.R. Simplot retired from day-to-day operations in 1994, turning over his role to a 4-person Office of the Chairman made up of 3 of his children and one grandchild.

SIMPSON INVESTMENT CO.

RANK: 351

1201 Third Ave., Ste. 4900
Seattle, WA 98101
Phone: 206-224-5000
Fax: 206-224-5060

1992 Sales: $860 million
FYE: December
Employees: 7,600

Key Personnel
Chm: William G. Reed, Jr.
Pres: Furman C. Moseley
CFO: J. Thurston Roach
Dir Sys: A. J. Berger
VP & Gen Counsel: Joseph R. Breed
VP HR: Cynthia Sonstelie

Operating Units
PW Pipe Co.
Simpson Paper Co.
Simpson Timber Co.

Key Competitors
Boise Cascade
Champion International
Georgia-Pacific
International Paper
James River
North Pacific Lumber
Sierra Pacific Industries
Weyerhaeuser

Industry
Paper & paper products

Overview
Simpson Investment Co. is the holding company for Simpson Timber, founded by Sol Simpson in 1890. The company diversified into paper making in the 1950s and today is one of the largest makers of fine papers in the US. Simpson Timber pursues a strategy of acquiring cheap tracts of land, replanting them, and operating them for the long term. In recent years the company has struggled with declining pulp prices, which forced it to consolidate facilities. The Reed family, descendants of founder Sol Simpson, own all of the company's stock.

SINCLAIR OIL CORPORATION

RANK: 191

550 E. South Temple St.
Salt Lake City, UT 84102
Phone: 801-363-5100
Fax: 801-524-2773

1993 Sales: $1,385 million
FYE: June
Employees: 3,000

Key Personnel
Pres: Robert E. Holding
VP: Carol Holding
VP & Treas: Charles Barlow
Sec: Lynn S. Richards
Dir HR: Wendel White
Gen Counsel: Peter M. Johnson

Business Lines
Gas stations
Hotels
Oil distribution
Oil exploration
Oil pipelines
Oil refining
Ranching
Ski resorts (Sun Valley)

Key Competitors
Accor
Amoco
Ashland Oil
Chevron
Exxon
Mobil
Wainoco Oil

Industry
Oil & gas - US integrated

Overview
Sinclair Oil is the jewel in the crown of Robert Earl Holding's business empire, which, apart from oil, includes hotels, ski resorts, and one of the largest ranching operations in the Rockies. Founded in 1916 by oilman Harry Sinclair, the company was owned by Atlantic Richfield in 1976 when Holding bought the name and some facilities. Sinclair produces gas locally and sells in the Rocky Mountain states where transport costs from outside are high. The company can thus supply its 225 gas stations more cheaply with a higher margin than most other companies can.

SISTERS OF CHARITY HEALTH CARE SYSTEMS, INC.　RANK: 124

345 Neeb Rd.
Cincinnati, OH 45233
Phone: 513-347-1000
Fax: 513-922-0762

1993 Sales: $1,911 million
FYE: June
Employees: 17,300

Key Personnel
Pres: Sister Celestia Koebel
CEO, St. Mary-Corwin: Sister Sally Duffy
CEO Samaritan Health: K. Douglas Deck
CEO, Provenant Health: Thomas H. Rockers
CEO, Penrose-St. Francis: Leonard A. Farr
Dir Sys Fin Svcs : Karen A. Dugan

Selected Operating Units
Good Samaritan Health Systems
Penrose-St. Francis Healthcare
Provenant Health Partners
Saint Elizabeth Health Systems
Saint Francis Health Systems
St. Joseph Healthcare System
St. Mary-Corwin Medical Center
Samaritan Health Resources

Key Competitors
Columbia/HCA
HealthTrust
Mercy Health Systems
Quorum Health Group
SSM Health Care
US Health Services

Industry
Hospitals

Overview
Incorporated in 1979 as a nonprofit organization, Sisters of Charity Health Care Systems (SCHCS) is a multi-institutional health care system cosponsored by the Sisters of Charity of Cincinnati, Ohio, and the Sisters of St. Francis of Perpetual Adoration of Colorado Springs, Colorado. Serving 5 states (Colorado, Kentucky, Nebraska, New Mexico, and Ohio), SCHCS has 20 hospitals with nearly 5,000 beds, 4 long-term care facilities, and 5 retirement communities. The sisters also run community programs, including wellness summer camps for asthmatic children and parenting education for teens.

SLIM-FAST NUTRITIONAL FOODS INTERNATIONAL, INC.　RANK: 442

919 Third Ave., 26th Fl.
New York, NY 10022
Phone: 212-415-7100
Fax: 212-415-7171

1993 Est. Sales: $675 million
FYE: November
Employees: 5,000

Key Personnel
Co-Chm: Daniel Abraham
Co-Chm: Edward Steinberg
Pres: John Costa
CFO: Carl Tfang
HR Dir: Jack Portlock
Gen Counsel: Barbara Waitman

Major Products
Cookies
Meal replacement drink powders
Nutritional bars
Premixed shakes
Snacks

Key Competitors
Grand Metropolitan
Heico
Heinz
Jenny Craig
RJR Nabisco
Nestlé
Quaker Oats

Industry
Food - diet

Overview
Wholly owned by fitness fanatic Daniel Abraham, who created an empire from Dexatrim (1976) and Slim-Fast (1977) diet aids, New York–based Slim-Fast Foods was spun off from Thompson Medical Co. in 1991 to capitalize on the needs of weight-conscious consumers. Because sales of prepared entrees have been anemic, the company is expanding its line of popular meal-replacement drinks and snacks. Aggressively marketed, the diet shakes are best known for celebrity endorsements by L.A. Dodger manager Tommy LaSorda and entertainer Kathie Lee Gifford.

SMITHSONIAN INSTITUTION　RANK: 413

1000 Jefferson Dr. SW
Washington, DC 20560
Phone: 202-357-2700
Fax: 202-786-2515

1993 Sales: $729 million
FYE: September
Employees: 6,800

Key Personnel
Sec: I. Michael Heyman
Under Sec: Constance B. Newman
Treas: Sudeep Anand
Gen Counsel: Peter G. Powers
Asst Sec Fin & Adm & CFO: Nancy D. Suttenfield
Personnel Dir: Marilyn Marton

◀ **See page 121 for full-page profile.**

Selected Museums
Air & Space Museum
Anacostia Museum
Freer Gallery of Art
Museum of African Art
Museum of American Art
Museum of American History
Museum of the American Indian
Portrait Gallery

Industry
Leisure & recreational services - museum

Overview
With money bequeathed to the US by English chemist James Smithson, the Smithsonian Institution was created by an act of Congress in 1846. The world's largest museum complex, the Smithsonian houses over 130 million items in 16 facilities and also runs the National Zoo, conducts research in its own laboratories at field locations around the world, and publishes Smithsonian magazine. The institution is operated as a private organization, but it is largely funded by government appropriations.

SOUTHERN STATES COOPERATIVE, INCORPORATED　RANK: 315

6606 W. Broad St.
Richmond, VA 23230
Phone: 804-281-1000
Fax: 804-281-1383

1993 Sales: $937 million
FYE: June
Employees: 3,539

Key Personnel
Pres & CEO: Gene A. James
EVP & COO: M. T. Ragsdale
SVP & CFO: Jonathan A. Hawkins
Group VP Agriculture: George W. Winstead
VP & Gen Counsel: N. Hopper Ancarrow, Jr.
VP HR: Richard G. Sherman

Selected Services
Farm supply sales
Feed sales
Fertilizer sales
Financial services
Fuel sales
Grain marketing
Seed sales
Vegetable seed packaging

Key Competitors
Bayer
Cargill
ConAgra
Continental Grain
GROWMARK
Louis Dreyfus Natural Gas
Transammonia
Wilbur-Ellis

Industry
Agricultural operations

Overview
Founded in 1923, Southern States Cooperative (SSC) is a diversified agricultural cooperative that serves farmers and nonfarmers in Delaware, Kentucky, Maryland, North Carolina, Virginia, and West Virginia. Individuals and local farm cooperatives own SSC, which distributes to over 168,000 clients through 550 local dealers and markets grains, corn, and soybeans for farmers in selected areas. Statesman Financial Corp., an affiliate of SSC, has initiated a private-label credit card program to provide a convenient source of credit to members of the cooperative.

SOUTHERN WINE & SPIRITS OF AMERICA — RANK: 156

1600 NW 163rd St.
Miami, FL 33169
Phone: 305-625-4171
Fax: 305-625-4720

1993 Sales: $1,620 million
Employees: 3,000

Key Personnel
Chm: Isidore Becker
Pres: Harvey Chaplin
VP: Wayne Chaplin
VP: Elliot Dinnerstein
Sec & Treas: Herbert Joseph
Controller: Lee Hager

Major Products
Ale
Beer
Distilled spirits
Wine

Key Competitors
Chairmen Industries
Glazer's Wholesale Drug
National Distributing
Sunbelt Beverage
Young's Market

Industry
Beverages - alcoholic

Overview
Southern Wine & Spirits is the nation's largest wine distributor and wine and spirits importer. In the face of criticism in California that the company neglects wine in favor of beer and hard liquor, Southern created American Wine and Spirits to emphasize fine wines in 1993. The company recently bought a South Carolina distributor, which provided wholesale distribution centers in Arizona, California, Florida, Nevada, and South Carolina.

SOUTHWIRE COMPANY, INC. — RANK: 209

One Southwire Dr.
Carrollton, GA 30119
Phone: 404-832-4242
Fax: 404-832-4929

1993 Est. Sales: $1,300 million
FYE: December
Employees: 5,000

Key Personnel
Chm & CEO: Roy Richards, Jr.
Pres: James C. Richards
VP & Treas: Anna Berry
VP Mktg: Bob Sullivan
VP Manufacturing: Jim Blevins
VP HR & Gen Counsel: William Hearnburg

Business Lines
Aluminum smelting
Cable-in-conduit products
Copper processing
Nonferrous rod manufacture
Nonferrous wire manufacture
Scrap metal recycling
Wood pallets & skids

Key Competitors
Belden
Communication Cable
Cooper Industries
Essex Group
General Cable
Insteel
Pirelli
Raychem

Industry
Wire & cable products

Overview
Southwire is the US's largest maker and seller of nonferrous rods, wire, and cables for use in the construction and power industries. It also smelts copper and aluminum. Growth slowed during the 1990s recession, but Southwire has rebounded with a program of acquisitions (Georgia Wire Products, Integral Corp.). The family-owned company was founded in 1950 by Roy Richards, Sr., to supply wire for the Rural Electrification Administration wire-stringing contracts.

SPARTAN STORES INC. — RANK: 102

850 76th St. SW
Grand Rapids, MI 49518
Phone: 616-878-2000
Fax: 616-878-2775

1993 Sales: $2,189 million
FYE: March
Employees: 2,300

Key Personnel
Pres & CEO: Patrick M. Quinn
SVP & CFO: James B. Meyer
SVP Bus Dev: Charles B. Fosnaugh
SVP Mgmt Info Svcs: William E. May
VP Customer Support: Dennis Otto
VP HR: Robert C. Morse

Major Products
Bakery products
Dairy products
Fresh fruits
Fresh meats & meat products
Fresh vegetables
Groceries
Packaged frozen foods

Key Competitors
Capistar
Fleming
Foodland Distributors
Nash Finch
SUPERVALU
Wal-Mart

Industry
Food - wholesale to grocers

Overview
Spartan Stores was founded in 1917 in Grand Rapids when a group of local retailers gathered to discuss the threat of growing national chains. Now one of the nation's top food wholesalers, Spartan serves grocers in Indiana, Ohio, and Michigan. The company distributes both food and nonfood items and provides its clients with a variety of services, such as advertising and accounting assistance. A cooperative, Spartan is owned by its employees and the more than 500 supermarkets and supermarket chains that it serves and their employees.

SPECIALTY FOODS CORP. — RANK: 120

520 Lake Cook Rd., Ste. 520
Deerfield, IL 60015
Phone: 708-267-3000
Fax: 708-267-0015

1993 Sales: $1,998 million
FYE: December
Employees: 13,100

Key Personnel
Chm: Robert B. Haas
Pres & CEO: Thomas Herskovits
VP, Sec & Gen Counsel: John E. Kelly
VP Mktg & Strategy: Robert E. Baker
VP & CFO: Paul J. Liska
VP HR: John D. Reisenberg

Major Brands
B&G Pickles
Burns & Ricker Bagel Chips
Colombo Bread
Mother's Cookies
Old Home Bread
San Francisco French Bread
Stella Cheese

Key Competitors
Alpine Lace
CPC
GF Industries
Heinz
Interstate Bakeries
J & J Snack Foods
Sara Lee
Schreiber Foods

Industry
Food - baked goods

Overview
Specialty Foods was organized in 1993 when 8 food businesses were purchased by an investor group consisting of Haas, Wheat & Partners; Keystone, Inc. (formerly the Robert M. Bass Group); Acadia Partners; UBS Capital Corp.; and Donaldson, Lufkin & Jenrette. To improve efficiency the company has since reorganized into 5 geographic divisions: Stella Foods (cheese) in Wisconsin, Metz Baking Co. in the Midwest, Western Bakery Group on the West Coast, H&M Food System (prepared meats) in Texas, and B&G/DSDB&R (pickles and chips) on the East Coast.

SSM HEALTH CARE SYSTEM INC.

RANK: 293

477 N. Lindbergh Blvd.
St. Louis, MO 63141
Phone: 314-994-7800
Fax: 314-994-7900

1993 Est. Sales: $1,000 million
FYE: December
Employees: 16,051

Key Personnel
CEO: Sister Mary Jean Ryan
EVP & CFO: William C. Schoenhard
SVP & Treas: Suzanne M. Petru
SVP HR: Steven Barney
VP Strategic Dev: William Thompson
SVP & Asst Sec: Vito F. Tamboli

Business Lines
Clinics
Home health care
Hospice
Hospitals

Key Competitors
Carondelet Health
Columbia/HCA
Deaconess Health
Sisters of Charity of Leavenworth
Sisters of the Sorrowful Mother
St. Louis University Health Sciences

Industry
Hospitals

Overview
Founded in 1874 by the Sisters of St. Mary, the SSM Health Care System operates 14 hospitals, 4 nursing homes, and a hospice and provides related health care services in Georgia, Illinois, Missouri, Oklahoma, South Carolina, and Wisconsin. To cut costs, SSM recently joined forces with 3 otherSt. Louis–based health care organizations to form an integrated health delivery network to negotiate managed-care contracts and develop a unified patient information and access system. Facilities operated by SSM include St. Mary's Health Center and the Cardinal Glennon Children's Hospital.

STANDARD INSURANCE CO.

RANK: 267

1100 SW 6th Ave.
Portland, OR 97204
Phone: 503-248-2700
Fax: 503-796-7935

1993 Sales: $1,063 million
FYE: December
Employees: 1,500

Key Personnel
Chm & CEO: Benjamin R. Whiteley
Pres & COO: Ronald E. Timpe
SVP: Edward T. Reynolds
SVP: Gerald B. Halverson
VP & CFO: James R. Bloyer
Corp Sec & Personnel - Benefits: Ivy Lenz

Products & Services
Accidental death coverage
Brokerage services
Dental insurance
Disability income coverage
Disability reinsurance
Group insurance
Life insurance
Retirement plan products

Key Competitors
Aetna
John Hancock
MetLife
New York Life
Northwestern Mutual
Pacific Mutual
Prudential
Travelers

Industry
Insurance - multiline

Overview
Founded in 1906 as Oregon Life Insurance Company, Standard Insurance adopted its current name in 1946. The company is licensed in all 50 states, although in New York State it may provide only reinsurance services. This mutual company offers a wide range of insurance products through about 300 agents and managers in the western states and some 70 agents in 4 regional offices around the US. A majority of the company's premiums are written in Oregon and California. A subsidiary, StanWest Equities, provides brokerage services.

STANFORD UNIVERSITY

RANK: 211

857 Serra St.
Stanford, CA 94305
Phone: 415-725-8396
Fax: 415-725-3326

1993 Sales: $1,268 million
FYE: August
Employees: 14,000

Key Personnel
Pres: Gerhard Casper
Provost: Condoleezza Rice
CFO: Peter Van Etten
VP Faculty-Staff Svcs: Barbara Butterfield
Gen Counsel: Michael Roster
Controller: Joanne M. Coville

Schools & Colleges
Graduate School of Business
Graduate School of Education
School of Earth Sciences
School of Engineering
School of Humanitites & Sciences
School of Law
School of Medicine

Industry
Schools

Overview
Widely regarded as one of the US's finest schools, Stanford is a private, coed institution founded in 1891 and located about 30 miles south of San Francisco. Admission is highly competitive: only about 20% of applicants are accepted. Notable alumni include Herbert Hoover, William Rehnquist, Sandra Day O'Connor, John Elway, Ted Koppel, and former Harvard president Derek Bok. The university is still working to repair the damage done by the Loma Pieta earthquake of 1989.

STAR ENTERPRISE

RANK: 25

12700 Northborough Dr.
Houston, TX 77067
Phone: 713-874-7000
Fax: 713-874-7760

1993 Sales: $6,252 million
FYE: December
Employees: 5,000

Key Personnel
Pres & CEO: Lester A. Wilkes
VP Fin & CFO: William J. Mathe
VP Mktg: Joseph W. Bernitt
VP Refining: Reidar O. Fauli
Gen Counsel & Sec: Clydia J. Cuykendall
Dir HR: Floyd Chaney

Major Products
Asphalt
Aviation fuel
Diesel fuel
Gasoline
Home heating oil
Natural gas liquids
Petrochemical feedstocks
Propane

Key Competitors
Amoco
Ashland Oil
Coastal
Diamond Shamrock
Exxon
Mobil
Phillips Petroleum
Royal Dutch/Shell

Industry
Oil refining & marketing

Overview
Star Enterprise is a joint venture between Texaco and Saudi Arabia Oil Company (Saudi Aramco). Formed in 1989, Star is the 4th largest branded gasoline retailer in the US. Star supplies gasoline to 9,500 Texaco-branded outlets in 26 states in the eastern and southern US and in the District of Columbia. Saudi Aramco provides crude oil for Star's 3 refineries, located in Delaware, Louisiana, and Texas. The company is upgrading its refining facilities to comply with new, stricter emission standards.

◀ **See page 122 for full-page profile.**

STATE FARM MUTUAL AUTOMOBILE INSURANCE COMPANY

RANK: 6

One State Farm Plaza
Bloomington, IL 61710
Phone: 309-766-2311
Fax: 309-766-6169

1993 Sales: $24,463 million
FYE: December
Employees: 64,520

Key Personnel
Chm, Pres & CEO: Edward B. Rust, Jr.
EVP & COO: Vincent J. Trosino
SVP & Treas: Roger S. Joslin
Senior Agency VP: Chuck Wright
VP & Gen Counsel: Cranford A. Ingham
VP Personnel: John Coffey

◀ See page 123 for full-page profile.

Business Lines
Automobile insurance
Fire insurance
Health insurance
Homeowners insurance
Inland marine insurance
Life insurance

Key Competitors
Aetna
AFLAC
Allstate
GEICO
Liberty Mutual
Nationwide
Travelers
USAA

Industry
Insurance - property & casualty

Overview
State Farm has been the nation's largest auto insurance company for more than 50 years. Owned by policyholders, the company has been run since its beginning by 2 families (the Mercheles [1922-54] and the Rusts [1954-present]). Its Fire and Casualty Company affiliate is also the largest US homeowners' insurer. Other affiliate companies offer life and health insurance. In 1993, after paying claims from Hurricane Andrew, State Farm reported its first annual loss since 1969.

STATE UNIVERSITY OF NEW YORK

RANK: 50

State University Plaza
Albany, NY 12246
Phone: 518-443-5313
Fax: 518-443-5322

1993 Sales: $3,700 million
FYE: June
Employees: 47,964

Key Personnel
Chancellor: Joseph C. Burke
Sr Vice Chancellor Fin & Mgt: William H. Anslow
Vice Chan & Provost: Richard S. Jarvis
Vice Chan Legal Aff & Counsel: Sanford H. Levine
EVP Research Foundation: Peter Tenbeau
Assoc Vice Chan HR: Thomas Mannix

Schools & Colleges
SUNY-Binghamton
SUNY-Buffalo
SUNY-College at Buffalo
SUNY-College at Fredonia
SUNY-College at Geneseo
SUNY-College at New Paltz
SUNY-College at Old Westbury
SUNY-College at Oswego
SUNY-College at Purchase
SUNY-Empire State College
SUNY-Health & Science Ctr.
SUNY-Stony Brook

Industry
Schools

Overview
SUNY is tied with the University of California as the 2nd largest university system in the US, with over 162,000 full-time students at 34 campuses. SUNY's campuses include 4 university centers, 4 health science centers, and colleges for forestry, agriculture, optometry, human ecology, and ceramics, among others. New York was the last state to establish a statewide higher education system, waiting until 1948 because it did not wish to create competition for private schools. SUNY gets 56% of funds from the state and federal governments.

STATER BROS. HOLDINGS INC.

RANK: 167

21700 Barton Rd.
Colton, CA 92324
Phone: 909-783-5000
Fax: 909-783-5035

1993 Sales: $1,550 million
FYE: October
Employees: 8,200

Key Personnel
Chm, Pres & CEO: Jack H. Brown
VP & CFO: Dennis N. Beal
Group SVP Retail Ops: H. Harrison Lightfoot
Group SVP Mktg: Richard C. Moseley
Group SVP HR: Donald Baker
Sec & Gen Counsel: Bruce D. Varner

Business Lines
Dairy food processing
Shopping center construction
Shopping center management
Supermarkets

Key Competitors
Albertson's
American Stores
Edward J. DeBartolo
Hughes Markets
Smart and Final
Smith's Food & Drug
Vons
Yucaipa

Industry
Retail - supermarkets

Overview
The 108-store Stater Brothers Markets is the dominant supermarket chain in the Inland Empire area of Southern California, which includes San Bernardino and Riverside counties. It also has a presence in Los Angeles, Kern, and Orange counties. In 1987 the then-50-year-old company was taken private by a management group with the aid of Craig Corp., which bought about 50% of Stater's stock. In 1993 the company agreed to buy out Craig's interest.

STEELCASE INC.

RANK: 87

901 44th St. SE
Grand Rapids, MI 49508
Phone: 616-247-2710
Fax: 616-246-9015

1994 Sales: $2,500 million
FYE: February
Employees: 17,800

Key Personnel
Chm: Robert Pew
Interim Pres: Frank H. Merlotti
EVP Ops: William S. Elston
EVP & CFO: William Williams
EVP Sales & Mktg: Roger L. Choquette
VP, Sec & Gen Counsel: David S. Fry

◀ See page 124 for full-page profile.

Major Products
Bookcases
Desks
Lateral & vertical files
Modular storage cabinets
Seating
Systems furniture
Tables

Key Competitors
American Brands
Hanson
Haworth International
Herman Miller
Hon Industries
Krueger International
Masco
Westinghouse

Industry
Furniture - office

Overview
Founded in 1912, Steelcase is the world's largest office furniture manufacturer, providing a wide variety of products — from swivel tilt chairs to entire office furniture systems. Credited with creating "the look of the modern office," the company has long been an innovator in office furniture, introducing the first metal wastepaper basket and patenting the suspension filing cabinet. Listed in *The 100 Best Companies to Work For in America,* Steelcase has developed strong employee loyalty and provides workers with a profit-sharing plan. Steelcase recently experienced its first annual loss ($70 million) ever.

THE STROH COMPANIES INC.

RANK: 289

100 River Place
Detroit, MI 48207
Phone: 313-446-2000
Fax: 313-446-2206

1993 Est. Sales: $1,010 million
FYE: March
Employees: 3,200

Key Personnel
Chm & CEO: Peter W. Stroh
Pres & COO: William L. Henry
SVP Ops: James R. Avery
SVP & CFO: Christopher T. Sortwell
SVP, Gen Counsel & Sec: George E. Kuehn
SVP Cust Mktg & Admin: Joseph J. Franzem

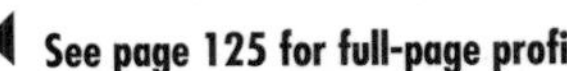
See page 125 for full-page profile.

Major Brands
Augsburger
Chaos (iced teas)
Old Milwaukee
Piels
Schaefer
Schlitz
Stroh's
White Mountain Cooler

Key Competitors
Adolph Coors
Anheuser-Busch
Boston Beer
Genesee
Heileman Brewing
John Labatt
Philip Morris
S&P Co.

Industry
Beverages - alcoholic

Overview
The 4th largest brewer in the US, Stroh was founded in 1850 by Bernhard Stroh, whose descendants still own the company. Stroh's main business is brewing, but it is also involved in real estate, malt cooler production, and iced tea production. The company rose to prominence during the 1980s with the acquisitions of F&M Schaefer and Schlitz, but it has lost money for several years, which could mean a return to regional, rather than nationwide, marketing. Stroh's brands have fared better overseas, posting double-digit growth rates.

SUBWAY SANDWICHES

RANK: 119

325 Bic Dr.
Milford, CT 06460
Phone: 203-877-4281
Fax: 203-876-6688

1993 Est. Sales: $2,000 million
FYE: December
Employees: 400

Key Personnel
Pres & CEO: Peter Buck
VP & COO: Frederick A. DeLuca
Treas: Haydee Buck
Sec: Carmela DeLuca
Controller & Data Processing: Ralph Slivka

Major Products
Cold sandwiches
Hot sandwiches
Kids' Pack
Made-to-order salads
Platters
Round sandwiches

Key Competitors
Blimpie
Domino's Pizza
Flagstar
Grand Metropolitan
Little Caesars
McDonald's
PepsiCo
Wendy's

Industry
Restaurants

Overview
Fred DeLuca launched Subway Sandwich Shops in 1965 at age 17 with $1,000 in starting capital, which he got from partner Peter Buck. Still owned by the founding partners, Subway Sandwiches is the most rapidly growing fast food chain in the world: it has opened about 1,100 new franchises each year since 1988. The chain had 8,640 outlets in early 1994, when *Entrepreneur Magazine* named it Franchise of the Year for the 5th time in 6 years. Some franchisees have claimed that Subway overstated potential sales and earnings, sparking a 9-month FTC probe that was dropped in 1993.

SUNBELT BEVERAGE CORPORATION

RANK: 481

2330 W. Joppa Rd., Ste. 330
Lutherville, MD 21093
Phone: 410-832-7740
Fax: 410-832-7730

1993 Sales: $580 million
Employees: 1,200

Key Personnel
Chm: Raymond R. Herrmann
Pres & CEO: Charles E. Andrews
EVP & CFO: Gene Luciana
Dir HR: Ronald Meliker

Operating Units
Arizona Beverage
Ben Arnold-Heritage Beverage
Churchill Distributors
Premier Beverage

Key Competitors
Charmer Industries
Glazer's Wholesale Drug
National Distributing
National Wine & Spirits
Southern Wine & Spirits
Young's Market

Industry
Alcoholic beverages - distribution

Overview
Sunbelt began life as the alcoholic beverage distribution division of McKesson. In 1988 McKesson decided to get out of the business. Division head Raymond Herrmann, with the help of investment firm Weiss, Peck & Greer, bought the division and renamed it Sunbelt Beverage. Sunbelt, now led by Charles Andrews, has grown from $400 million in revenues at the time of the buyout to $580 million today and is among the top 30 beverage companies in the nation according to *Beverage World*.

SUN-DIAMOND GROWERS OF CALIFORNIA

RANK: 449

5568 Gibraltar Dr.
Pleasanton, CA 94588
Phone: 510-463-8200
Fax: 510-463-7492

1993 Sales: $649 million
FYE: July
Employees: 1,860

Key Personnel
Pres: Larry D. Busboom
VP Fin: William P. Beaton
VP, Gen Counsel & Sec: George O. Petty
VP Consumer Sales: Ben H. Body
VP Intl Sales: Robert A. Beckwith
Dir HR: Sally Klein

Members
Diamond Walnut Growers
Hazelnut Growers of Oregon
Sun Land Products
Sun Maid
Sunsweet Growers
Valley Fig Growers

Key Competitors
Azar Nut
Basic American
Dole
Georgia Nut
John B. Sanfilippo
Nonpareil Corp.
Philip Morris

Industry
Agricultural operations

Overview
Sun-Diamond is the marketing and distribution co-op for 5 of the largest agricultural specialty co-ops in the US, including Sun Maid (raisins), Sunsweet (prunes), and Diamond Walnut. It was formed in 1974 when Sunsweet and Diamond Walnut decided to pool their marketing resources in order to achieve greater efficiency and economies of scale. They were joined by the other members in the 1980s. Sun-Diamond sells and ships its members' products worldwide. Its business has been particularly strong in Europe and Japan.

SUNKIST GROWERS, INC. RANK: 269

14130 Riverside Dr.
Sherman Oaks, CA 91423
Phone: 818-986-4800
Fax: 818-379-7511

1993 Sales: $1,054 million
FYE: October
Employees: 1,200

Key Personnel
Pres & CEO: Russell L. Hanlin
SVP & Gen Counsel: Dale V. Cunningham
VP Research & Tech Svcs: Owen W. Belletto
VP Fin & Admin: H. B. Flach
Sec: Eileen H. Fowler
Treas & Controller: Richard G. French

Business Lines
Brandname licensing
Canned fruit
Electronic fruit grading systems
Electronic fruit packers
Fresh fruit
Fruit juices
Real estate

Key Competitors
Calavo Growers
ConAgra
Dole
Lykes Bros.
Ocean Spray
Orange Co.
Snokist Growers
United Foods

Industry
Agricultural operations

Overview
Sunkist Growers, an agricultural co-op and distributor that represents about 6,500 orange, lemon, and grapefruit growers, evolved from a group of small California citrus growers who pooled their resources in the early 1890s. The name Sunkist, devised by an advertising copywriter in 1908, was adopted in 1952. It is now one of the most widely recognized brand names in the world, used on more than 400 products and found in 30 countries. Sunkist's market share has fallen because of international competition, corporate infighting, and loss of federal price supports.

THE SVERDRUP CORP. RANK: 462

13723 Riverport Dr.
Maryland Heights, MO 63043
Phone: 314-436-7600
Fax: 314-770-5105

1993 Sales: $635 million
FYE: December
Employees: 4,500

Key Personnel
Chm: B. R. Smith , Jr.
Pres & CEO: Richard E. Beumer
SVP & CFO: Robert J. Messey
Treas: T. E. Wehrle
Gen Counsel: A. S. Morrison
Dir HR: Marge Anderson

Projects
Busch Stadium
Camden Yards
Fort McHenry Tunnel
New Orleans Superdome
Space shuttle launch complex

Key Competitors
Bechtel
Black & Veatch
Halliburton
Day and Zimmermann
Fluor
Morrison Knudsen
Parsons
Peter Kiewit Sons'

Industry
Construction - heavy

Overview
A leading engineering and architectural firm founded in 1928, St. Louis–based Sverdrup has played a role in designing projects ranging from the new baseball stadium in Baltimore to an underground military-command network in Saudi Arabia. In addition to providing architectural and engineering services worldwide, the company builds and operates capital facilities, including airports and public-transit systems. Sverdrup is also a real estate developer, counting among its projects the 500-acre Riverport Development in its hometown of Maryland Heights, which it owns along with McDonnell Douglas.

SWEETHEART HOLDINGS, INC. RANK: 367

7575 S. Kostner Ave.
Chicago, IL 60652
Phone: 312-767-3300
Fax: 312-767-9454

1993 Sales: $830 million
FYE: September
Employees: 8,500

Key Personnel
Chm: Burnell Roberts
Pres & CEO: William F. McLaughlin
VP Fin & Treas: Roger Cregg
Dir Mktg: Marguerite Davis
VP & Gen Counsel: Daniel Carson
VP HR: James Mullen

Business Lines
Converted paper products
Food containers
Food packaging machinery
Ice cream cones
Paper & plastic cups
Paper & plastic plates
Plastic utensils

Key Competitors
Champion International
Dart Container
Envirodyne
International Paper
James River
Kimberly-Clark
Mead
Scott

Industry
Paper & paper products

Overview
Sweetheart Holdings is the parent of Sweetheart Cup Co., North America's #1 maker of disposable paper and plastic food-service items and plastic eating utensils. The company also makes food-service packaging and ice cream cones. Sweetheart traces its roots to the Maryland Cup Co., founded in Boston in 1911. Paper goods maker Fort Howard Co. purchased the company in 1983 and merged it with its Lily-Tulip division to form Sweetheart Cup (named after Maryland Cup's most famous product). Today, Sweetheart is owned by investment group American Industrial Partners (66.3%) and GM's employee benefit plans (33.7%).

TANG INDUSTRIES, INC. RANK: 341

1699 Wall St., Ste. 720
Mt. Prospect, IL 60056
Phone: 708-228-1860
Fax: 708-228-0456

1993 Sales: $878 million
FYE: December
Employees: 3,500

Key Personnel
Pres & CEO: Cyrus Tang
Controller: Kurt Swanson

Business Lines
Electric generation & distribution
Metal distribution
Metal fabrication
Natural gas distribution
Office furniture manufacturing
Pharmaceuticals
Real estate development
Scrap metal brokerage

Key Competitors
Cargill
Haworth International
Illinois Tool Works
Inland Steel
Olympic Steel
Peltz
Steelcase
Transco Energy

Industry
Metal products - fabrication

Overview
Tang Industries had its beginnings in 1964 when Chinese immigrant Cyrus Tang purchased a metal stamping shop in Illinois. Since then, Tang Industries, which was incorporated in 1970, has specialized in buying and reviving distressed businesses. The largest holding in Tang's international empire is National Material, a metal fabricating and distributing company. Tang also owns National Gas Resources, which buys gas for Tang-owned facilities, including steel-processing and aluminum plants and office furniture manufacturers. Tang recently has ventured into homebuilding, hoping to profit from 150 acres of Chicago-area real estate.

TAUBER OIL COMPANY

RANK: 407

55 Waugh Dr., Ste. 700
Houston, TX 77007
Phone: 713-869-8700
Fax: 713-869-8069

1993 Sales: $747 million
FYE: September
Employees: 52

Key Personnel
Pres: O. J. Tauber, Jr.
CFO: Steve Hamlin
EVP Residual Fuels: David W. Tauber
EVP, Refined Products: Richard E. Tauber
VP Administration: Gerrilyn Fortino
HR: Nancy Dillard

Major Products
Chemicals
Gasoline
Liquified Petroleum Gas
Oil
Petrochemicals
Residual fuels

Key Competitors
Tesoro Petroleum
Vanguard Energy
Xeron

Industry
Oil refining & marketing

Overview
Houston-based Tauber Oil, founded in 1953, markets and wholesales petroleum products, chemicals, and petrochemicals. The company began natural gas operations in 1993.

TEACHERS INSURANCE AND ANNUITY ASSOCIATION - COLLEGE RETIREMENT EQUITIES FUND

RANK: 16

730 Third Ave.
New York, NY 10017
Phone: 212-490-9000
Fax: 212-916-6231

1992 Sales: $11,900 million
FYE: December
Employees: 4,000

Key Personnel
Chm & CEO: John H. Biggs
Pres & COO: Thomas W. Jones
EVP Fin & Planning: Richard L. Gibbs
EVP Law & Gen Counsel: Charles H. Stamm
EVP TIAA Investments: J. Daniel Lee, Jr.
EVP HR: Matina S. Horner

◀ **See page 126 for full-page profile.**

Business Lines
Bond Market Account (CREF)
Group life insurance (TIAA)
Group total disability ins. (TIAA)
Individual life insurance (TIAA)
Long-term care insurance (TIAA)
Money Market Account (CREF)
Retirement annuities (TIAA)
Stock Account (CREF)

Key Competitors
American Express
Charles Schwab
CIGNA
Equitable
FMR
Merrill Lynch
MetLife
T. Rowe Price

Industry
Financial - retirement funds

Overview
Teachers Insurance and Annuity Association–College Retirement Equities Fund (TIAA–CREF) was founded in 1905. The nonprofit organization is one of the US's largest insurers and one of the world's largest private pension systems, providing pensions and life, disability, and long-term care insurance to 1.7 million educators and researchers. TIAA provides annuities and insurance while CREF offers investment funds. In 1993 Chairman and CEO Clifton Wharton resigned his post after being named US deputy secretary of state.

TENNESSEE RESTAURANT CO.

RANK: 369

One Pierce Place, Ste. 100E
Itasca, IL 60143
Phone: 708-250-0471
Fax: 708-250-0382

1993 Sales: $829 million
FYE: December
Employees: 35,000

Key Personnel
Chm & CEO: Donald N. Smith
VP & Controller: Michael Donahoe
VP, Sec & Gen Counsel: Larry W. Browne
VP Corp Fin: Joe Colonneta

Operating Units
Friendly Ice Cream Corp.
Perkins Family Restaurants (51%)
Perkins Management Co.

Key Competitors
Buffets
Cracker Barrel Old Country Store
Flagstar
Furr's/Bishop's Cafeterias
Homestyle Buffet
IHOP
Luby's Cafeterias
Restaurant Enterprises

Industry
Restaurants

Overview
Tennessee Restaurant, paradoxically headquartered near Chicago, is one of the top 20 restaurant chains in the US. It was formed in 1985 to acquire the 330-store Perkins restaurant chain, which is based in Tennessee. TRC is owned by Holiday Corp., the Bass Investment Limited Partnership, and Chairman Donald Smith, a restaurant industry veteran. In 1989 it acquired the Friendly Ice Cream Corp., a chain of family-style restaurants, from Hershey for $375 million.

TENNESSEE VALLEY AUTHORITY

RANK: 35

400 W. Summit Hill Dr.
Knoxville, TN 37902
Phone: 615-632-2101
Fax: 615-632-6783

1993 Sales: $5,276 million
FYE: September
Employees: 18,974

Key Personnel
Chm: Craven Crowell
Pres, Generating Group: Oliver D. Kingsley, Jr.
Pres, Customer Group: Mary Sharpe Hayes
EVP & CFO: William F. Malec
SVP & Gen Counsel: Edward S. Christenbury
Employment Svcs Mgr: Kathleen Branson

See page 128 for full-page profile.

Selected Services
Agricultural development
Coal gasification
Electric power
Environmental research
Flood control
Recreation projects
Rural development
Water quality projects

Industry
Utility - electric power

Overview
Created in 1933 by an act of Congress, the TVA provides power and nonpower programs. Nonpower programs, including flood control and river management, are funded by congressional appropriations ($135 million in 1993); power programs are required to be self-supporting. The TVA supplies electricity to 7 million people in the 7 states of the Tennessee Valley. The agency is run by a 3-member board appointed by the president and approved by the Senate.

THE TEXAS A&M UNIVERSITY SYSTEM — RANK: 224

State Headquarters Building
College Station, TX 77843
Phone: 409-845-4331
Fax: 409-862-2679

1993 Sales: $1,212 million
FYE: August
Employees: 19,000

Key Personnel
Chancellor: Barry P. Thompson
Vice Chancellor & Gen Counsel: Mary Beth Kurtz
Vice Chancellor Fin & Ops (HR): Richard Lindsay
Vice Chancellor Academic Aff: David A. Sanchez
Vice Chancellor State & Public Affairs: James B. Bond
Vice Chancellor Strategic Prog: William J. Merrell

Schools & Colleges
Prairie View A&M University
Tarleton State University
Texas A&M Intl. U. (Laredo)
Texas A&M Univ. (College Station)
Texas A&M Univ. (Corpus Christi)
Texas A&M Univ. (Kingsville)
West Texas A&M Univ.

Industry
Schools

Overview
The Texas A&M University System is one of the 10 largest university systems in the US, with an annual budget of more than $1 billion. The school was founded at College Station in 1876 under the federal land-grant system. In addition to administering 7 universities, the system oversees research facilities and public services in agriculture and engineering (including agricultural extension services), state forest services, a transportation institute, and a veterinary diagnostic laboratory. In 1993 and 1994 the system was rocked by financial scandals and the resignation of its chancellor, William H. Mobley, after only a year in office.

THOMAS H. LEE COMPANY — RANK: N/R

75 State St.
Boston, MA 02109
Phone: 617-227-1050
Fax: 617-227-3514

Employees: 40

Key Personnel
Pres: Thomas H. Lee
CFO: Wendy L. Masler
Dir Mktg: Kristina A. Weinberg

Selected Investments
Amerace
ATP Holdings
Ghirardelli Chocolate
GNC
Petco
Playtex Family Products
Snapple
Stanley Interiors

Industry
Financial - investors

Overview
Thomas H. Lee has been doing LBOs for 20 years. In 1974 he began investing his own money in small companies that he thought could do better. Lee differs from many other LBO artists in that his takeovers are not hostile and do not result in mass sell-offs of assets. In addition, unlike some LBO companies, Lee has always deducted the costs of bad deals from his company's management fees. Although some deals fell victim to the recession of the early 1990s, Lee has taken many of its acquisitions public.

THRIFTY OIL CO. — RANK: 488

10000 Lakewood Blvd.
Downey, CA 90240
Phone: 310-923-9876
Fax: 310-869-9739

1993 Est. Sales: $560 million
FYE: September
Employees: 800

Key Personnel
Pres: Ted Orden
EVP: Barry Berkett
CFO: Jack Elgin
Controller: Mike Hewell
Sec & Treas: Hedy Orden
Dir HR: Beverly Brooks

Principal Subsidiaries
Benzin Supply Co.
Cluj Distributing Co.
Golden West Distributing Co.
Golden West Refining Co.

Key Competitors
Atlantic Richfield
Chevron
Exxon
Koch
Mobil
Royal Dutch/Shell
Texaco
Unocal

Industry
Oil refining & marketing

Overview
Founded in 1961, Thrifty Oil Co. is a diversified Southern California company engaged in oil refining, gasoline retailing, convenience store operations (Sunshine Food Stores), and development and leasing of commercial properties. Once the state's largest independent gasoline retailer, with over 300 outlets, Thrifty and its 4 subsidiaries filed for bankruptcy in 1992 after poor profit margins at its Golden West refinery (purchased to supply the retail outlets) forced its closure. The company also cited a glutted oil market and the high expenditures needed to meet California's environmental laws.

THRIFTY PAYLESS INC. — RANK: 42

9275 SW Peyton Ln.
Wilsonville, OR 97070
Phone: 503-682-4100
Fax: 503-685-6140

1993 Sales: $4,454 million
FYE: September
Employees: —

Key Personnel
Pres & CEO: Tim R. McAlear
SEVP: Gordon Barker
EVP Store Ops: Ken Flynn
EVP & CFO: Dave Jessick
EVP Merch & Mktg: Gary Rocheleau
SVP HR: Jeannette Stone

Products and Services
Beverages
Cosmetics
Health & beauty aids
Household products
Over-the-counter drugs
Photofinishing
Prescription drugs

Key Competitors
Albertson's
American Stores
Longs
Melville
Price/Costco
Vons
Walgreen
Wal-Mart

Industry
Retail - drugstores

Overview
The 2nd largest drugstore chain in the US and the largest on the West Coast, Thrifty PayLess was formed in 1994 when Thrifty Drugs and PayLess Drug Stores Northwest merged. Thrifty Drugs was originally founded in 1919, and PayLess in 1939. Kmart, which owned PayLess prior to the merger, owns approximately 46% of the new company's stock. Leonard Green & Partners, which owned Thrifty, owns the remainder. The company operates PayLess Drug Stores, Thrifty Drugs, and Bi-Mart discount membership clubs.

◀ See page 129 for full-page profile.

TLC BEATRICE INTERNATIONAL HOLDINGS, INC.

RANK: 154

9 W. 57th St.
New York, NY 10019
Phone: 212-756-8900
Fax: 212-888-3093

1993 Sales: $1,656 million
FYE: December
Employees: 4,700

Key Personnel
Chm: Loida N. Lewis
EVP Fin & CEO: John R. Ranelli
EVP Legal Affairs: Albert M. Fenster
EVP Ops: Dennis P. Jones
SVP Strat Planning & Proj Fin: David A. Guarino
SVP, Gen Counsel & Sec: W. Kevin Wright

◀ **See page 130 for full-page profile.**

Business Lines
Artic & Artigel (ice cream, Europe)
Boissons du Monde (beer, France)
Établissements Baud (France)
Gelati Sanson (ice cream, Italy)
Interglas (ice cream, Canary Is.)
La Menorquina (ice cream, Spain)
Minimarché Group (France)
Tayto (potato chips, Ireland)

Key Competitors
Allied-Lyons
Borden
Cadbury Schweppes
Coca-Cola
Danone
Nestlé
PepsiCo
Philip Morris

Industry
Food - wholesale to grocers

Overview
TLC Beatrice, an international food distributor and grocery manufacturer, operates primarily in Western Europe. Founder Reginald F. Lewis, who died of brain cancer in 1993, formed TLC Group in 1983 as a holding company. The company acquired Beatrice International in 1987 and changed its name to TLC Beatrice. TLC Beatrice has 19 operating companies, with sales in over 20 countries and manufacturing facilities in 8. After only a year on the job, Lewis's handpicked successor and half-brother Jean S. Fugett, Jr., was replaced as chairman by Lewis's widow, Loida Lewis, who owns 55% of the company's stock.

TOPCO ASSOCIATES, INC.

RANK: 64

7711 Gross Point Rd.
Skokie, IL 60077
Phone: 708-676-3030
Fax: 708-676-4949

1993 Sales: $2,927 million
FYE: March
Employees: 395

Key Personnel
Pres & CEO: W. Steven Rubow
SVP Planning Dev: Frank G. Mayes
SVP Fin & CFO: Steven Lauer
SVP Grocery & Corp. Brands: Dan Mazur
SVP HR: Ron Ficks

Major Brands
Food Club
GreenMark (paper products)
Top Care (cosmetics)
World Classics (gourmet foods)

Key Competitors
Associated Grocers
Fleming
Grocers Supply
GSC Enterprises
Shurfine
Spartan Stores
SUPERVALU

Industry
Food - wholesale to grocers

Overview
Member-owned Topco distributes a wide variety of processed, preserved, and perishable foods, as well as paper products and cosmetics, for 44 retail supermarket chains throughout the US. Members include Dominick's Finer Foods, in the Chicago area, and Randalls, in Texas. Founded in Wisconsin in the mid-1940s, Topco moved to Skokie, Illinois, in 1961. After years of sticking to its main private label line, Food Club, Topco expanded its lines, beginning with World Classics in 1989.

TOWERS PERRIN

RANK: 419

245 Park Ave.
New York, NY 10167
Phone: 212-309-3400
Fax: 212-309-3760

1993 Sales: $709 million
FYE: December
Employees: 4,730

Key Personnel
Chm, Pres & CEO: John T. Lynch
CFO: Patrick Gonnelli
VP & Treas: Paul Clark
VP Technical: Harry Allan
Dir Mktg: Dallas Kersey
Mgr HR: Ken Ranftle

Operating Units
Cresap (management consulting)
Tillinghast (insurance consulting)
TPF&C Reinsurance

Key Competitors
Booz, Allen
Coopers & Lybrand
Deloitte & Touche
Ernst & Young
Hewitt Associates
McKinsey & Co.
Price Waterhouse
Wyatt Co.

Industry
Consulting

Overview
In the management consulting business since 1934, Towers Perrin (formerly Towers, Perrin, Forster & Crosby) traces the roots of its family tree to a company founded in 1871. With offices around the globe, the firm serves more than 8,000 clients worldwide, including 3/4 of the top 1,000 US industrial and service companies. Towers Perrin consults in the areas of human resources and benefits, general management, insurance and risk management, and reinsurance. In the early 1990s Towers Perrin downsized in 2 ways: it laid off 10% of its benefits staff, and 6'7" Chairman James Kielley retired.

TRAMMELL CROW RESIDENTIAL

RANK: 291

2859 Paces Ferry Rd.
Atlanta, GA 31400
Phone: 404-801-1600
Fax: 404-801-5395

1993 Sales: $1,007 million
FYE: December
Employees: 18

Key Personnel
Natl Managing Partner: J. Ronald Terwilliger
Group Managing Partner: Leonard W. Wood
Partner: William W. Thompson
Partner: Bruce C. Ward
Partner: Chris D. Wheeler
CFO & Dir HR: Randy J. Pace

Selected Services
Property management
Real estate development
Renovations
Residential construction

Key Competitors
Centex
JMB Realty
Kaufman and Broad
NVR
Paragon Group
Pulte
Ryland
U.S. Home

Industry
Real estate operations

Overview
Founded in 1945, Trammell Crow Residential, a spinoff of Trammell Crow Company, primarily builds and manages apartment complexes in 70 cities throughout the US. Owned by 80 partners, the company pulled out of the single-family home market in 1990. Trammell Crow Residential is one of the nation's top builders of low-rise rental units and is also among the largest homebuilders in terms of revenue. The Atlanta, Dallas, and Houston divisions of Trammell Crow Residential recently formed a real estate investment trust, Gables Residential, which includes 30 complexes in Georgia, Tennessee, and Texas.

TRANSAMMONIA, INC.

RANK: 196

350 Park Ave.
New York, NY 10022
Phone: 212-223-3200
Fax: 212-759-1410

1993 Est. Sales: $1,350 million
FYE: April
Employees: 190

Key Personnel
Chm & CEO: Ronald P. Stanton
VC: Elias R. Gonzalez
SVP & Gen Counsel: Fred M. Lowenfels
VP & CFO: Edward G. Weiner
VP & Treas: James H. Benfield
VP & Controller: H. Lawrence Berman

Business Lines
Fertilizer products
Methanol
Petroleum products

Key Competitors
Chevron
Coastal
Enron
GROWMARK
Hoechst
Southern States Co-op
Terra Industries
Wilbur-Ellis

Industry
Fertilizers

Overview
Founded in 1971, Transammonia distributes fertilizer and petroleum products in the US, Central America, Europe, and South America. The New York–based company's most widely publicized activity in recent years has been its role as a producer and distributor of the alternative fuel methanol, a liquid form of natural gas that burns cleaner than gasoline and improves engine performance.

TREASURE CHEST ADVERTISING COMPANY, INC.

RANK: 376

511 W. Citrus Edge
Glendora, CA 91740
Phone: 818-914-3981
Fax: 818-852-3056

1994 Sales: $807 million
FYE: June
Employees: 4,000

Key Personnel
Chm: R. Theodore Ammon
Pres & CEO: Sanford G. Scheller
EVP: Donald E. Roland
SVP Fin & CFO: Kenneth B. Erickson
SVP Mktg & Sales: Herbert W. Moloney
VP HR: Robert J. Turner

Operating Units
BFP Holdings Corp.
Big Flower Press
KTB Associates
Retail Graphics
Treasure Chest Advertising

Key Competitors
Century Graphics
R.R. Donnelley
Printco
Quad/Graphics
Quebecor
Sullivan Graphics
World Color Press

Industry
Printing - commercial

Overview
Treasure Chest Advertising is the centerpiece of Ted Ammon's burgeoning printing empire. Ammon, only the 2nd partner ever to leave the KKR fold, departed in 1992 in search of a business he could develop; about a year later he engineered the LBO of Treasure Chest, the 4th largest printer in the US and a leader in the printing of advertising circulars and newspaper roto sections. The holding company created to acquire Treasure Chest is owned by a group including Ammon's company, TCA, Bankers Trust, Apollo Advisors, and members of management. Treasure Chest had been founded in 1967 to produce a retail ad circular entitled Treasure Chest of Values.

TRI VALLEY GROWERS

RANK: 371

101 California St.
San Francisco, CA 94120
Phone: 415-837-4000
Fax: 415-837-3900

1993 Sales: $821 million
FYE: January
Employees: 3,000

Key Personnel
Chm : James Cooley
CEO: David Hash
EVP Sales: Paul McGinty
Treas: James R. Salisbury
Dir HR: Edward Miller
Counsel: Linda McSweyn

Major Products
Apricots
Cherries
Fruit cocktail
Grapes
Olive oil
Peaches
Roasted coffee
Tomatoes

Key Competitors
Campbell Soup
Del Monte
Dole
Grand Metropolitan
Heinz
Pacific Coast Producers
RJR Nabisco
TLC Beatrice

Industry
Food - canned

Overview
The fruit of a 1963 merger, Tri Valley Growers is among the nation's largest grower-owned agricultural co-ops and canned food companies. The company processes its member's fruits and vegetables in its 10 plants and markets the products under the brand names S&W Fine Foods, Oberti Olives, and Libby Lite Fruit. Facing layoffs, withering income, and changing consumer preferences for fresh fruit and vegetables, Tri Valley has turned to foreign fields. It heads a federally funded consortium to provide money, equipment, and know-how to fix Russia's decrepit food system while cultivating potentially huge new markets for its products.

TRUMP ORGANIZATION

RANK: 113

725 Fifth Ave.
New York, NY 10022
Phone: 212-832-2000
Fax: 212-935-0141

1992 Est. Sales: $2,037 million
FYE: December
Employees: 15,000

Key Personnel
Chm: Donald J. Trump
Pres: Nicholas Ribis
VP Fin: John Burke

Major Properties
Plaza Hotel
Trump Castle casino
Trump Plaza casino
Trump Taj Mahal casino
Trump Tower

Key Competitors
Bally Entertainment
Carlson
Circus Circus
Helmsley
Hilton
Lefrak Organization
Marriott International
Mashantucket Pequot Gaming

Industry
Leisure & recreational services - gambling

Overview
The Trump Organization is one of the best-known real estate development companies in the US, thanks to its flamboyant founder, Donald Trump. After scoring on several big deals in the 1980s (The Grand Hyatt Hotel, Trump Tower), the organization began foundering in the late 1980s when operating revenues no longer covered debt service. The firm is now largely occupied with managing its debt, preserving Trump's ownership of properties, and running 3 casinos in Atlantic City.

◀ **See page 131 for full-page profile.**

TWIN COUNTY GROCERS INC. — RANK: 232

145 Talmadge Rd.
Edison, NJ 08817
Phone: 908-287-4600
Fax: 908-287-6027

1993 Est. Sales: $1,200 million
FYE: August
Employees: 925

Key Personnel
Chm: Martin Vitale
Pres: James A. Burke
VC & VP: Hyman Shulman
VP Fin: Victor L. Bonini
VP HR: Joseph Casemento

Selected Products
Dairy products
Drugs, proprietaries & sundries
Fruits & vegetables
Groceries
Meats & meat products
Packaged frozen goods
Pet food

Key Competitors
Associated Food
Di Giorgio
Grand Union
Great A&P
King Kullen Grocery
Pathmark
SUPERVALU
Wakefern Food

Industry
Food - wholesale to grocers

Overview
Founded in 1944 and based in Edison, New Jersey, Twin County Grocers is the 7th largest retailer-owned buying cooperative in the US and is among the top 100 grocery companies. It serves 121 Foodtown supermarkets and 38 independent stores in New Jersey and New York. Its largest owner participant is Mayfair Super Markets, which runs the Foodtown grocery chain. Other participants include D'Agostino, Manyfoods, Food Circus, and Melmarkets. Twin County's chairman, Martin Vitale, owns at least 12 Foodtown grocery stores in New York and New Jersey.

U-HAUL INTERNATIONAL, INC. — RANK: 278

2727 N. Central Ave.
Phoenix, AZ 95004
Phone: 602-263-6011
Fax: 602-277-4329

1993 Sales: $1,041 million
FYE: March
Employees: 10,900

Key Personnel
Chm, Pres & CEO: Edward J. Shoen
EVP: Harry B. DeShong, Jr.
VP: James P. Shoen
VP HR: Dick B. Renckly
Sec & Gen Counsel: Gary V. Kleinefelter
Treas: Gary Horton

◀ **See page 132 for full-page profile.**

Operating Units
AMERCO (holding company)
Amerco Real Estate
Ponderosa Holdings, Inc.
  Oxford Life Insurance Co.
  Republic Western Insurance Co.
U-Haul International, Inc.

Key Competitors
Budget Rent A Car
Mayflower Group
Penske
Public Storage Properties
Rollins Leasing
Ryder
Shurgard
Unigroup

Industry
Leasing - trucks

Overview
U-Haul is the US's 2nd largest truck and trailer rental company, after Ryder, with over 1,000 outlets and 10,400 franchisees. It is also the nation's 3rd largest self-storage operator. Its parent company, AMERCO, oversees U-Haul's real estate holdings and attends to its insurance needs. U-Haul was founded in 1945 by L. S. Shoen to fill a niche for do-it-yourself movers. In recent years it has suffered from discord among Shoen's children, who own more than 95% of its stock.

UIS, INC. — RANK: 415

600 5th Ave., 27th Fl.
New York, NY 10020
Phone: 212-581-7660
Fax: 212-581-7517

1992 Sales: $716 million
FYE: December
Employees: 7,100

Key Personnel
Chm, Pres & CEO: Andrew E. Pietrini
EVP: Richard Pasculano
EVP & Treas: Joseph Arrigo
VP: Thomas W. Mellars
Asst VP: Brian McDonnell

Principal Subsidiaries
Champion Laboratories
Mid-South Manufacturing
Neapco
New England Confectionery
UIS Export
Union Forging
Wells Manufacturing
Wells Manufacturing Canada

Key Competitors
AlliedSignal
Borg-Warner Automotive
Dana
Eaton
General Motors
Hershey
Standard Motor Products
TRW

Industry
Auto parts - retail

Overview
UIS is one of the top US car parts makers; it also makes iron and steel forgings, electrical components for cars, and candy (Necco Wafers); and it does wood millwork. Founder Harry Lebensfeld started the company in 1945 with the purchase of an Indiana desk maker. He has pursued a strategy of buying small firms that have a potential for growth, often hanging on to existing management. In 1959 he started a charitable foundation. UIS is owned by a trust for Lebensfeld's only child (who is married to EVP Richard Pasculano) and her children.

UNIHEALTH AMERICA — RANK: 204

4100 W. Alameda Ave.
Burbank, CA 91505
Phone: 818-566-6300
Fax: 818-566-7070

1993 Sales: $1,303 million
FYE: September
Employees: 11,367

Key Personnel
Chm: David R. Carpenter
Pres & CEO: Terry Hartshorn
EVP & COO: Gary L. Leary
SVP & CFO: Eric S. Benveniste
SVP Corp Dev: Dennis W. Strum
SVP HR: Stanley M. Croonquist, Jr.

◀ **See page 133 for full-page profile.**

Principal Subsidiaries
CareAmerica Health Plans
CaseCARE
CliniShare
ElderMed America
Pacific Health Resources
Pacific Health Systems
UniMed America
VertiHealth

Key Competitors
Aetna
Blue Cross
CIGNA
Columbia/HCA Health Systems
Kaiser Foundation Health Plan
MassMutual
Sierra Health Services

Industry
Health maintenance organization

Overview
UniHealth was created in 1988 by the merger of the 2 largest secular, nonprofit health systems in Los Angeles: LHS Corp. and HealthWest Foundation. The company is the 5th largest nonprofit health care organization in the US. It operates 11 hospitals, a home health care service, a senior medical service, and a physician network. It also owns CareAmerica, an HMO serving more than 3,000 employer groups in Southern California, and 49% of publicly traded PacificCare Health Systems, which has 925,000 members in 5 states.

THE UNION CENTRAL LIFE INSURANCE COMPANY

RANK: 375

1876 Waycross Rd.
Cincinnati, OH 45240
Phone: 513-595-2200
Fax: 513-595-2206

1993 Sales: $810 million
FYE: December
Employees: 994

Key Personnel
Chm, Pres & CEO: Larry R. Pike
EVP: Lother A. Vasholz
SVP & CFO: Stephen R. Hatcher
VP & Treas: Marilyn R. Mitchell
VP, Sec & Gen Counsel: David F. Westerbeck
VP HR: Donna L. Sanders

Principal Subsidiaries
Carillon Advisers Inc.
Carillon Investments Inc.
Carillon Marketing Agency Inc.
Manhattan Life Insurance Co.

Key Competitors
Aetna
Allstate
CIGNA
Equitable
John Hancock
MetLife
Northwestern Mutual
Prudential

Industry
Insurance - life

Overview
Incorporated in 1867, Cincinnati-based The Union Central Life Insurance Company is one of the US's top 30 mutual life insurance companies. It operates in all 50 states and the District of Columbia. The company offers a range of ordinary and group life policies, group annuities, and individual disability insurance. While it dropped its group health insurance in 1988, Union Central has diversified its portfolio by offering a mutual fund and other annuities through its subsidiary Carillon Advisers.

UNIROYAL CHEMICAL COMPANY, INC.

RANK: 330

World Headquarters
Middlebury, CT 06749
Phone: 203-573-2000
Fax: 203-573-2265

1993 Sales: $908 million
FYE: September
Employees: 2,700

Key Personnel
Chm, Pres & CEO: Robert J. Mazaika
VP Ops: Eric W. Johnson
VP & Gen Counsel: Ira J. Krakower
VP & Gen Mgr Intl Ops: Michael M. Powers
VP Corp Business Dev: Edward L. Hagen
VP HR: Neil A. Melore

Business Lines
Agricultural seed treatments
Antioxidants
Antiozonants
Castable urethanes
Plastics additives
Specialty rubbers & polymers

Key Competitors
Bridgestone
DuPont
Exxon
Gates
Goodyear
Rhône-Poulenc
Union Carbide
Univar

Industry
Chemicals - diversified

Overview
Uniroyal Chemical is the #1 maker of synthetic rubbers and chemicals in the US. The company uses these synthetics to make a variety of rubber, plastic, electronic, petrochemical, and paint items. The company also makes agricultural treatment additives. Uniroyal Chemical was part of Uniroyal Inc. until 1986, when it was sold to Avery Inc. Three years later, the company went private in a management-led LBO. Despite a heavy debt load and a failed IPO in 1992, Uniroyal Chemical has increased its overseas presence in Asia and Europe.

UNITED ARTISTS THEATRE CIRCUIT, INC.

RANK: 453

9110 E. Nichols Ave., Ste. 200
Englewood, CO 80112
Phone: 303-792-3600
Fax: 303-790-8907

1993 Sales: $643 million
FYE: December
Employees: 12,000

Key Personnel
Chm & CEO: Stewart Blair
President: Peter Warzel
EVP & CFO: Kurt Hall
EVP: Thomas Elliot
Dir HR: Elizabeth Moravak
Gen Counsel: Gene Hardy

Theatres/Screens by State
California: 68/315
New York: 43/193
Pennsylvania: 36/150
Texas: 35/199
Florida: 31/243

Key Competitors
AMC
Carmike
Cinemark USA
Cineplex Odeon
GC Companies
National Amusements
Regal Cinemas
Sony

Industry
Motion pictures - theaters

Overview
United Artists Theatre Circuit is the #1 US movie theater chain, operating 429 locations with 2,231 screens. The company derives its name from the United Artists studio, founded by D.W. Griffith, Charlie Chaplin, and actors Douglas Fairbanks and Mary Pickford in 1926. United Artists's complex history includes a stint as a Transamerica subsidiary and a period when investor Kirk Kerkorian ran it as part of MGM/UA. The theater operator and other portions of the company finally came under the control of cable-operator TCI in 1986. In 1992 TCI sold the theater chain to management, led by CEO Stewart Blair and backed by Merrill Lynch.

UNITED GROCERS INC.

RANK: 342

PO Box 22187
Portland, OR 97222
Phone: 503-833-1001
Fax: 503-833-1491

1993 Sales: $877 million
FYE: September
Employees: 1,250

Key Personnel
Chm: Marlin Smythe
VC: Craig Danielson
Pres, CEO, Sec & Treas: Alan C. Jones
VP & CFO: John White
Controller: Lyman Brown
Dir HR: Susan Weber

Major Products
Coffee
Dairy
Delicatessen products
Disposables
Groceries
Light equipment
Perishables
Smallwares

Key Competitors
Albertson's
Associated Grocers
Fleming
Fred Meyer
Safeway
Services Group of America
SUPERVALU
US Food service

Industry
Food - wholesale to grocers

Overview
Headquartered in Milwaukie, Oregon, and founded in 1915, United Grocers is a wholesale grocery cooperative that serves more than 350 supermarkets in Oregon, Washington, and Northern California. Its food service division, made up of 26 cash-and-carry stores, sells only to traditional food service operations, daycare, and foster care facilities. The company handles more than 10,000 products, and it services such chains as Sentry Supermarkets, Select Markets, and Price Chopper as well as individual stores.

UNITED PARCEL SERVICE OF AMERICA, INC. — RANK: 8

55 Glenlake Pkwy.
Atlanta, GA 30328
Phone: 404-828-6000
Fax: 404-828-6593

1993 Sales: $17,782 million
FYE: December
Employees: 286,000

Key Personnel
Chm & CEO: Kent C. Nelson
EVP & COO: James P. Kelly
SVP, Treas & CFO: Robert Clanin
SVP, Legal & Regulatory: Joseph R. Moderow
SVP: Charles L. Schaffer
SVP HR: John J. Kelley

◀ See page 134 for full-page profile.

Selected Services
2nd Day Air
3 Day Select
Customs & brokerage
GroundSaver (package delivery)
GroundTrac (electronic tracking)
Hundredweight Service
Next Day Air
On Call Air Pickup

Key Competitors
Airborne Freight
Consolidated Freightways
DHL Worldwide Express
FedEx
Harper Group
Roadway
Pittston
U.S. Postal Service

Industry
Package delivery

Overview
UPS traces its roots to 1907, when 2 Seattle teenagers began delivering telephone messages. Since then UPS has grown into the world's largest package delivery service. While most people associate the company with ground delivery services, UPS is now #2 in air express and is giving #1 Federal Express a run for its money. Employees, their families, and their heirs own this package delivery giant. UPS now transmits delivery information from its 50,000 package trucks to UPS computers via a cellular phone system.

UNITED STATES ENRICHMENT CORPORATION — RANK: 174

2 Democracy Ctr., 6903 Rockledge Dr.
Bethesda, MD 20817
Phone: 301-564-3200
Fax: 301-564-3201

1993 Est. Sales: $1,500 million
FYE: September
Employees: 110

Key Personnel
Pres & CEO: William H. Timbers , Jr.
EVP Ops: George Rifakes
VP & CFO: Henry Z Shelton, Jr.
VP Mktg & Sales: Richard Kingdon
Gen Counsel: Robert Moore
VP HR: Yvonne Herndon

Selected Services
Research
Uranium enrichment

Industry
Metal ores - uranium

Overview
Customer complaints about inflexible pricing and an operating loss of $178 million in 1991 led the government to begin privatizing its uranium business. On July 1, 1993, the DOE's Uranium Enrichment Enterprise, organized in 1964, was transformed into United States Enrichment Corporation, a government-owned corporation. One of its first actions, however, had a governmental feel: citing national security, it bought 15,260 tons of Russian uranium for more than the market price. USEC's 2 gaseous diffusion plants in Ohio and Kentucky process the uranium for 60 nuclear power plants. USEC must come up with a privatization plan by 1995.

UNITED STATES POSTAL SERVICE — RANK: 2

475 L'Enfant Plaza SW
Washington, DC 20260
Phone: 202-268-2000
Fax: 202-268-2175

1993 Sales: $47,418 million
FYE: September
Employees: 691,723

Key Personnel
Chm: Bert H. Mackie
Postmaster General & CEO: Marvin Runyon
EVP & COO: Joseph R. Caraveo
SVP Fin & CFO: Michael J. Riley
SVP & Gen Counsel: Mary S. Elcano
VP Employee Relations: Suzanne J. Henry

◀ See page 135 for full-page profile.

Selected Services
Box rentals
Certified mail
Collection-on-Delivery
Express Mail
First-Class Mail (letters)
Mailgram
Money orders
Priority mail

Key Competitors
Airborne Freight
Consolidated Freightways
DHL Worldwide Express
FedEx
Harper Group
Pittston
Roadway
UPS

Industry
Mail & package delivery

Overview
Created by the Continental Congress in 1775 (with Benjamin Franklin as its first postmaster general), the United States Postal Service delivers more than 550 million pieces of mail every day. The service is the largest independent agency of the executive branch of the US government and boasts the nation's largest civilian work force. An 11-member board of governors sets policy, and a 5-member Postal Rate Commission recommends postage rates. Facing increased competition, the postal service lost more than $4.6 billion between 1990 and 1993.

UNITED VAN LINES, INC. — RANK: 325

One United Dr.
Fenton, MO 63026
Phone: 314-326-3100
Fax: 314-326-1106

1993 Sales: $912 million
FYE: December
Employees: 950

Key Personnel
Chm & CEO: Maurice Greenblatt
Pres: Robert J. Baer
CFO: Douglas H. Wilton
EVP Mktg: James L. Wilson
VP Intl: Richard Sullivan
Mgr HR: Sherry Fagan

Operating Units
United Capital Services, Inc.
United Leasing, Inc.
United Van Lines, Inc. (moving)
Vanliner Group, Inc. (insurance)

Key Competitors
Atlas Van Lines Internationa
Bekins
Mayflower Group
Norfolk Southern
Roadway
Ryder
U-Haul
Yellow Corporation

Industry
Transportation - truck

Overview
With 1,065 agents in 130 countries, United Van Lines is one of the largest moving companies in the world and is in a dead heat with American Van Lines to claim the title of largest moving company in the US (each has about a 20% market share). Other subsidiaries of its holding company, UniGroup, lease and finance trucks and sell insurance to truckers. Formed in 1928 as Return Loads Services, United Van Lines was bought by an alliance of independent movers and reorganized in 1947. It is owned by 120 of its agents, who have bought shares in UniGroup. Although agents are theoretically able to sell their shares, UniGroup usually exercises its right of first refusal.

UNITED WAY OF AMERICA

RANK: N/R

701 N. Fairfax St.
Alexandria, VA 22314
Phone: 703-836-7100
Fax: 703-836-7840

1993 Sales: $27 million
FYE: December
Employees: —

Key Personnel
Chm: Thomas F. Frist, Jr.
VC: Edward A. Brennan
VC: Paul J. Tagliabue
Pres: Elaine L. Chao
Treas: Ragan A. Henry
Sec: Cathleen P. Black

 See page 136 for full-page profile.

Selected Recipients
American Heart Association
American Red Cross
Big Brothers/Big Sisters
Boy Scouts/Girl Scouts
Goodwill Industries
Jewish Federations
Planned Parenthood
YMCA/YWCA

Industry
Charitable organization

Overview
Incorporated in 1932, United Way of America (UWA) is a national nonprofit service agency that helps some 1,400 local chapters with fund-raising, volunteer training, management, communications, and long-range planning. Through "one-stop" donations from corporations and their employees, UWA raised over $3 billion in 1991 before a scandal forced its president to resign a year later. UWA responded by shaving staff, expanding its board, and instituting more accountability. But other charitable organizations took advantage of UWA's troubles and cut into its fund-raising efforts.

THE UNIVERSITY OF ALABAMA

RANK: 332

701 20th St. South, Ste. 1070
Birmingham, AL 35294
Phone: 205-934-4636
Fax: 205-975-8505

1993 Sales: $904 million
Employees: 15,000

Key Personnel
Chancellor: Philip E. Austin
Pres: J. Claude Bennett
EVP: Kenneth J. Roozen
VP Fin Affairs: Linda Flaherty-Goldsmith
VP Planning & Info Mgmt: John M. Lyons
VP Admin & HR: John H. Walker

Schools & Colleges
School of Arts & Humanities
School of Business
School of Dentistry
School of Education
School of Engineering
School of Medicine
School of Natural Sciences & Mathematics
School of Optometry
School of Public Health
School of Social & Behavioral Sciences

Industry
Schools

Overview
The University of Alabama has 43,000 students and campuses in Huntsville, Tuscaloosa, and Birmingham. The Birmingham campus began in 1944 as a separate entity to provide the state with its first medical school. Birmingham was chosen as the site for the new center, rather than the campus at Tuscaloosa or Huntsville, because of the city's large number of poor people who could become patients for the teaching hospital. Other disciplines were added in 1954 when the university's 2-year Birmingham Extension (opened in 1936) moved to the campus.

UNIVERSITY OF CALIFORNIA

RANK: 319

300 Lakeside Dr., 22nd Fl.
Oakland, CA 94612
Phone: 510-987-0700
Fax: 510-987-0894

1993 Sales: $7,548 million
FYE: December
Employees: 131,661

Key Personnel
Pres: Jack W. Peltason
Chancellor: Chang-Lin Tien
SVP Academic Affairs & Provost: Walter E. Massey
SVP Business & Fin: Wayne Kennedy
SVP: William R. Frazer
Dir Personnel: Alice Gregory

 See page 137 for full-page profile.

Schools & Colleges
UC/Berkeley
UC/Davis
UC/Irvine
UC/Los Angeles
UC/Riverside
UC/San Diego
UC/San Francisco
UC/Santa Barbara
UC/Santa Cruz

Industry
Schools

Overview
The largest public university in the country, the University of California has 9 main campuses and enrolls more than 162,000 students. The system offers a place to every California high school student in the top 1/8 of his or her class. Its campus in Los Angeles (UCLA) is one of the largest university campuses in the US. The system's Berkeley campus is famous for its political protests of the 1960s and 1970s. UC is a leader in the fields of engineering and physical sciences. It had a hand in the development of the atomic bomb and today runs 3 laboratories for the DOE. Medical research is also a strong suit; UC owns and operates a number of hospitals.

THE UNIVERSITY OF CHICAGO

RANK: 242

5801 S. Ellis Ave.
Chicago, IL 60637
Phone: 312-702-1234
Fax: 312-702-8324

1993 Sales: $1,150 million
FYE: June
Employees: 11,800

Key Personnel
Chm: Howard G. Kane
Pres: Hugo F. Sonnenschein
Provost: Edward O. Laumann
VP & CFO: Lawrence J. Furnstahl
Gen Counsel & VP Admin: Arthur M. Sussman
Assoc VP HR: Henry Webber

Schools & Colleges
Graduate School of Business
Graduate School of Public Policy Studies
Irving B. Harris
School of Divinity
School of Law
School of Medicine
School of Social Sciences
School of Social Service Administration

Industry
Schools

Overview
The University of Chicago (enrollment: 11,000), founded in 1891 with Rockefeller gifts, is renowned for its commitment to the Great Books as well as for its voluminous production of Nobel laureates (64 at last count). Hanna Gray retired in 1993 after 15 years as the university's president. Though Gray produced operating surpluses of as much as $24 million, she did so, in part, by deferring building maintenance. New president Hugo Sonnenschein initiated a plan to modernize buildings and cut costs, primarily through administrative layoffs. Despite financial strains, the school maintains a $1.2 billion endowment.

UNIVERSITY OF FLORIDA

RANK: 373

226 Tigert Hall
Gainesville, FL 32611
Phone: 904-392-3261
Fax: 904-392-6278

1993 Sales: $816 million
FYE: June
Employees: 21,404

Key Personnel
Chancellor: Charles B. Reed
Pres: John V. Lombardi
Provost & VP: Andrew A. Sorenson
VP Admin Affairs: Gerald Schaffer
Controller: John P. Kruczek
Dir HR: Jack Hidler

Schools & Colleges
College of Architecture
College of Building Construction
College of Dentistry
College of Division of Continuing Education
College of Engineering
College of Fine Arts
College of Forest Resources & Conservation
College of Health & Human Performance
College of Health Related Professions
College of Journalism & Communicaion
College of Law
College of Liberal Arts & Sciences
College of Medicine
College of Veterinary Medicine

Industry
Schools

Overview
Founded in 1853, the University of Florida is a public, coeducational, liberal arts institution. The university, located on a 2,000-acre campus 115 miles north of Orlando, is Florida's oldest and largest university. With an enrollment of almost 36,000 students, the school is the nation's 11th largest university by enrollment. The University of Florida offers 114 majors in 52 undergraduate degree programs, 123 master's and 76 doctoral programs in 87 academic departments, and professional post-baccalaureate degrees in law, dentistry, medicine, and veterinary medicine.

UNIVERSITY OF ILLINOIS

RANK: 109

346 Henry Admin. Bldg.
Urbana, IL 61801
Phone: 217-333-2464
Fax: 217-244-5821

1993 Sales: $2,069 million
FYE: June
Employees: 20,000

Key Personnel
Pres: Stanley O. Ikenberry
Chancellor, Urbana-Champaign: Michael Aiken
Chancellor, Chicago: James J. Stukel
Vice Chancellor HR & Admin: Charles Colbert
VP Business & Fin & Comptroller: Craig S. Bazzani
Counsel: Byron H. Higgins

Selected Programs of Study
Undergraduate
- Chemical engineering
- Graphic design
- Horticulture
- Physics
- Speech pathology
- Social work

Graduate
- Biophysics
- Comparative literature
- Computer science
- Kinesiology
- Slavic languages & literature
- Textiles & clothing

Industry
Schools

Overview
Founded in 1867, the University of Illinois is a public, coeducational school. Its oldest and largest campus, Urbana-Champaign, is located in a suburban area 130 miles south of Chicago (the other campus is in Chicago). The school's 35,000 students, 94% of whom are from Illinois, can choose from 150 majors and 4,000 courses. The curriculum includes a heavy orientation toward science and industry and a highly regarded accounting program. The school also boasts the 3rd largest academic library, after Harvard and Yale. With 53 national fraternities and 27 sororities, the University of Illinois has the world's largest Greek system.

THE UNIVERSITY OF IOWA

RANK: 305

105 Jessup Hall
Iowa City, IA 52242
Phone: 319-335-0062
Fax: 319-335-2951

1993 Sales: $984 million
FYE: June
Employees: 22,410

Key Personnel
Pres: Hunter R. Rawlings III
Provost: Peter E. Nathan
VP Fin & Treas: Doug True
VP Research: David J. Skorton
Controller & Sec: Doug Young
Dir Personnel: Marvin Lynch

Selected Programs of Study
Undergraduate
- Astronomy
- Banking & finances
- Biochemistry
- Dental hygiene
- Health education
- Mechanical engineering

Graduate
- Afro-American studies
- Biomedical engineering
- Linguistics
- Mass communications
- Orthodontics
- Urban & regional planning

Industry
Schools

Overview
Founded in 1847, The University of Iowa is a comprehensive public university with an enrollment of 26,000. The university's health care units include a general and a pyschiatric hospital, as well as a hospital school, and contribute 35% of total revenues. With more than 50 separate research centers and programs, the university receives numerous grants and appropriations to conduct research in areas ranging from physics to cardiovascular science. The National Insititute of Health is the largest source of federal research support to the university, providing 45% of such funds.

THE UNIVERSITY OF KENTUCKY

RANK: 360

111 Administration Bldg.
Lexington, KY 40506
Phone: 606-257-9000
Fax: 606-257-4000 (mail room)

1993 Sales: $844 million
FYE: June
Employees: 12,021

Key Personnel
Pres: Charles T. Wethington, Jr.
Asst to Pres, Admin: Robert G. Lawson
VP Mgmt & Budget: Edward A. Carter
Gen Counsel: Richard E. Plymale
Controller & Treas: Henry C. Owen
Dir HR: James Webb

Schools & Colleges
College of Agriculture
College of Business Economics
College of Communications
College of Dentistry
College of Education
College of Human Environmental Sciences
College of Library & Information Sciences
College of Medicine
College of Pharmacy
School of Music

Industry
Schools

Overview
The University of Kentucky traces its roots to 1865, when the Agriculture and Mechanical College was founded as a public land-grant institution. The university took its current name in 1916. Serving some 24,000 students, the main campus at Lexington offers 13 undergraduate schools and one graduate school. The university also has a system of 14 community colleges, which enroll more than 48,000 students. In 1993 *Money Magazine* ranked the University of Kentucky 15th among US colleges in terms of value.

THE UNIVERSITY OF MARYLAND SYSTEM

RANK: 177

3300 Metzerott Rd.
Adelphi, MD 20783
Phone: 301-445-1905
Fax: 301-445-2761

1993 Sales: $1,481 million
FYE: June
Employees: 20,000

Key Personnel
Chancellor: Donald N. Langenberg
Vice Chancellor Fin: Brenda Albright
Vice Chancellor Advancement: John K. Martin
Vice Chancellor Acad Affairs: George Marks
Controller: James Sansbury
Dir HR: Karen Farber

Schools & Colleges
Bowie State University
Center for Environmental & Estuarine Studies
Coppin State College
Frostburg State University
Maryland Biotechnology Institute
Maryland Institute for Agriculture & Natural Resources
Salisbury State University
Towson State University
Univ. of Baltimore
Univ. of Maryland at Baltimore
Univ. of Maryland at College Park
Univ. of Maryland at Eastern Shore
Univ. of Maryland at University College

Industry
Schools

Overview
The University of Maryland System was founded in 1856 as a public land-grant system. Its 11 public campuses enroll about 100,000 students, who may choose between 115 doctoral, 212 master's, and 347 baccalaureate programs of study. An adult continuing education school, the University of Maryland/University College offers evening and weekend classes at 30 locations in Maryland and Washington, DC. Financial problems have plagued the system in recent years, and efforts to merge various campuses as a cost-saving measure have failed to win approval in the state's legislature.

THE UNIVERSITY OF MASSACHUSETTS

RANK: 275

18 Tremont St.
Boston, MA 02108
Phone: 617-287-7000
Fax: 617-287-7044

1993 Sales: $1,049 million
FYE: June
Employees: 12,935

Key Personnel
Chm, Board of Trustees: Daniel A. Taylor
Pres: Michael K. Hooker
EVP: Allen L. Sessoms
VP & Gen Counsel: Joyce A. Kirby
VP Mgmt & Fiscal Affairs: Stephen W. Lenhardt, Sr.
Dir Labor Affairs: Roy Milbury

Selected Programs of Study
Undergraduate
- Botany
- Chemical engineering
- Computer science
- Design
- Forestry
- Secondary education

Graduate
- Animal science
- Communication disorders
- Engineering management
- Entomology
- Hispanic literature & linguistics
- Wildlife & fisheries biology

Industry
Schools

Overview
The University of Massachusetts operates 4 graduate and undergraduate campuses and a medical center (Worcester), with a total enrollment approaching 60,000. The school at Amherst is the oldest and the largest, founded in 1863. Michael Hooker, president of UMASS since 1992, is fighting legislators' image of UMASS's administration, reported in the *Boston Herald* as "avaricious, mendacious, and not trustworthy." With financial needs exceeding the funds commonwealth leadership is willing to grant, Hooker has considered layoffs and higher student fees.

THE UNIVERSITY OF MICHIGAN

RANK: 104

503 Thompson St.
Ann Arbor, MI 48109
Phone: 313-764-1817
Fax: 313-747-3529

1993 Sales: $2,162 million
FYE: June
Employees: 37,013

Key Personnel
Pres: James J. Duderstadt
VP & CFO: Farris W. Womack
Provost & VP: Gilbert R. Whitaker, Jr.
VP Dev: Jon Cosovich
VP Research: Homer A. Neal
Exec Dir HR: Jackie McClain

Schools & Colleges
College of Engineering
College of Pharmacy
Horace H. Rackham School of Graduate Studies
School of Business Administration
School of Dentistry
School of Law
School of Medicine
School of Public Health
School of Social Work

Industry
Schools

Overview
Founded in 1817, the University of Michigan is a public, coeducational institution with campuses in Dearborn, Flint, and Ann Arbor (its main campus, 50 miles west of Detroit). With a total enrollment of over 51,000 (over 36,500 are undergraduates), the school ranks as one of the nation's largest universities. It also ranks highly in terms of academic reputation, especially among public schools, garnering top 10 rankings at the graduate and undergraduate levels.

UNIVERSITY OF MINNESOTA

RANK: 164

202 Morrill Hall, 100 Church St. SE
Minneapolis, MN 55445
Phone: 612-625-5000
Fax: 612-626-1332

1993 Sales: $1,572 million
FYE: June
Employees: 18,212

Key Personnel
Chm: Jean B. Keffeler
Pres & Chancellor: Nils Hasselmo
Exec Dir & Corp Sec: Barbara Muesing
Treas: Roger Paschke
SVP Fin & Ops: Robert O. Erickson
Assoc VP HR: Carol Carrier

Selected Programs of Study
Agriculture
Biological sciences
Business
Communication & the arts
Computer sciences
Education
Engineering
Health Professions
Physical sciences
Social sciences

Industry
Schools

Overview
Founded as a preparatory school in 1851 (7 years before the territory of Minnesota became a state), the University of Minnesota is a public, land-grant institution with 4 campuses and over 67,000 students. The main campus, Twin Cities, has 20 colleges and offers nearly 200 undergraduate majors and degrees in roughly 175 graduate and professional fields of study. In the late 1980s, the university and the state legislature sought to improve academic quality by cutting enrollment by 20% while keeping state appropriations constant. But even though the university closed its Waseca campus in 1992, state financial crises have forced it to expand enrollment once again.

THE UNIVERSITY OF MISSOURI SYSTEM — RANK: 303

321 University Hall
Columbia, MO 65211
Phone: 314-882-6211
Fax: 314-882-2721

1993 Sales: $990 million
FYE: June
Employees: 17,060

Key Personnel
Pres: George A. Russell
VP Academic Affairs: Richard L. Wallace
Gen Counsel: Robert L. Ross
VP Admin Affairs (Fin): James T. McGill
Asst Vice-Chancellor HR: Karen Touzeau
Controller: James U. Weaver

Schools & Colleges
Univ. of Missouri at Columbia
Univ. of Missouri at Kansas City
Univ. of Missouri at Rolla
Univ. of Missouri at St. Louis

Industry
Schools

Overview
With more than 54,000 students, the University of Missouri is among the 20 largest university systems in the US. Forty percent of the system's revenues come from federal and state government appropriations, while less than 20% come from tuition and fee payments by students. Teaching accounts for only 38% of total expenditures. The largest campus, Columbia, was founded in 1839, with others following in 1871 (Rolla), 1933 (Kansas City), and 1963 (St. Louis).

THE UNIVERSITY OF NEBRASKA — RANK: 363

3835 Holdrege St.
Lincoln, NE 68583
Phone: 402-472-2111
Fax: 402-472-2410

1993 Sales: $839 million
FYE: June
Employees: 1,237

Key Personnel
Pres: L. Dennis Smith
VP Fin: James C. Van Horn
Chancellor, U. of N. at Kearney: Gladys Johnston
Chancellor, U. of N. at Lincoln: Graham B. Spanier
Chancellor, U. of N. at Omaha: Del D. Weber
Chancellor, U. of N. Med Ctr: C. A. Aschenbrener

Selected Programs of Study
Undergraduate
- Advertising
- Aeronautical engineering
- Business economics
- Dramatic arts
- Information sciences & systems
- Political science

Graduate
- Biometry
- Community & regional planning
- Educational technology
- Exercise science
- Mathematics
- Social sciences

Industry
Schools

Overview
Established in 1869 as a land-grant, 4-year, coeducational institution, the University of Nebraska is a public system with 4 campuses, 51,000 students, and more than 3,200 faculty members. The university, which offers 263 baccalaureate, 137 master's, and 40 doctoral programs, lists its primary goals as teaching, research, and service. Minority students account for less than 10% of the student population. New president L. Dennis Smith began his 3-year term in March 1994 in the midst of debate over a controversial plan to open an engineering school at the university's Omaha campus.

UNIVERSITY OF PENNSYLVANIA — RANK: 161

3451 Walnut St.
Philadelphia, PA 19104
Phone: 215-898-5000
Fax: 215-898-9659

1993 Sales: $1,594 million
FYE: June
Employees: 20,000

Key Personnel
Pres: Judith Rodin
EVP: Jack Freeman
VP & Sec: Barbara R. Stevens
Treas: Scott C. Lederman
Gen Counsel: Shelley Z. Green

Schools & Colleges
Annenberg School of Communication
Graduate School of Education
Graduate School of Fine Arts
School of Arts & Sciences
School of Dental Medicine
School of Engineering & Applied Sciences
School of Law
School of Medicine
School of Nursing
School of Social Work
Wharton School of Finance & Commerce

Industry
Schools

Overview
The University of Pennsylvania, founded in 1740 as the College, Academy, and Charitable Schools of the Province of Pennsylvania, is one of the nation's oldest private universities. Of its 22,000 students, 49% are enrolled in the 12 graduate schools (there are only 4 undergraduate schools). The university is a major medical education center, and its clinics and hospitals contribute 46% of university revenues. Tuition provides 21%; only 14% comes from government funds.

UNIVERSITY OF PITTSBURGH — RANK: 379

4200 Fifth Ave.
Pittsburgh, PA 15260
Phone: 412-624-4141
Fax: 412-624-1150

1993 Sales: $801 million
FYE: June
Employees: 9,299

Key Personnel
Chm: Farrell Rubenstein
Chancellor: J. Dennis O'Connor
SV Chancellor & Treas: Ben J. Tuchi
Controller & Asst Treas: William G. Laird
Asst Controller: Vince Kreuer
Sec: Robert E. Dunkelman

Schools & Colleges
Faculty of Arts & Sciences
Graduate School of Public Health
Graduate School of Public & International Affairs
Joseph M. Katz Graduate School of Business
School of Dental Medicine
School of Engineering
School of Health & Rehabilitation Sciences
School of Law
School of Library & Information Science
School of Medicine

Industry
Schools

Overview
The University of Pittsburgh of The Commonwealth System of Higher Education is the official name for this university. Founded in 1787, the university includes 9 undergraduate and 11 graduate schools. The focal point of the urban Pittsburgh campus is the 42-story Cathedral of Learning. Also part of the system is the University of Pittsburgh Medical Center, nationally acclaimed for its quality. The university has campuses in Bradford, Greensburg, Johnstown, and Titusville, which offer bachelor and associate degrees.

UNIVERSITY OF ROCHESTER

RANK: 402

Administration Bldg.
Rochester, NY 14627
Phone: 716-275-2121
Fax: 716-275-2190

1993 Sales: $764 million
FYE: June
Employees: 11,249

Key Personnel
Pres & CEO: Thomas Jackson
VP & Treas: Richard W. Green
VP Budgets-Financial: Ronald J. Paprocki
VP External Affairs: Richard P. Miller
VP Dean of Students: Paul J. Burgett
Dir of Personnel: B. E. Donbaugh

Schools & Colleges
College of Arts & Science
College of Engineering & Applied Sciences
Eastman School of Music
Margaret Warner Graduate School of Education & Human Development
School of Medicine & Dentistry
School of Nursing
William E. Simon Graduate School of Business Administration

Industry
Schools

Overview
Founded in 1850, the University of Rochester is a private institution with 4 undergraduate and 7 graduate schools, including the famous Eastman School of Music. With a student body of about 8,500 (around 5,000 are undergraduates), the university has a highly competitive admissions policy, granting entrance to 70% of the applicants; 53% of undergraduates are from New York.

UNIVERSITY OF SOUTHERN CALIFORNIA

RANK: 271

3620 S. Vermont Ave.
Los Angeles, CA 90089
Phone: 213-743-2111
Fax: 213-740-7750

1993 Sales: $1,052 million
FYE: June
Employees: 17,000

Key Personnel
Chm, Board of Trustees: Forrest N. Shumway
Pres: Steven B. Sample
Provost: Lloyd Armstrong, Jr.
SVP Academic Affairs: Lloyd Armstrong
SVP Admin: Dennis F. Dougherty
Exec Dir Personnel Svcs: Janis Romero

Schools & Colleges
School of Architecture
School of Business Administration
School of Dentistry
School of Education
School of Engineering
Schoool of Fine Arts
School of Law
School of Medicine
School of Music
School of Public Administration
School of Social Work

Industry
Schools

Overview
The University of Southern California — the largest private university in California — has 41 schools and almost 28,000 students at its campus near South Central Los Angeles. Founded in 1880, USC is dedicated to higher education from the first-year level through the postdoctoral level. The school views itself as a global university despite the regional limitations of its name and emphasizes its accomplishments in research along with its strong tradition of excellence in intercollegiate athletics.

THE UNIVERSITY OF TENNESSEE

RANK: 266

305 Student Services Bldg.
Knoxville, TN 37996
Phone: 615-974-2105
Fax: 615-974-6341

1993 Sales: $1,071 million
FYE: June
Employees: 14,967

Key Personnel
Pres: Joseph E. Johnson
EVP & VP Bus & Fin: Emerson H. Fly
SVP: Homer S. Fisher
Treas: Charles M. Peccolo , Jr.
Gen Counsel & Sec: Beauchamp E. Brogan
Dir HR: Lola Dodge

Selected Programs of Study
College of Agricultural Sciences & Natural Resources
College of Allied Health Sciences
College of Dentistry
College of Pharmacy
College of Social Work
College of Veterinary Medicine
School of Business Administration
School of Medicine

Industry
Schools

Overview
The University of Tennessee, founded in 1794 as Blount College, is one of the oldest universities in the country. Established when George Washington was president of the United States, the school predates Tennessee statehood by 2 years. For a short period in the early 1800s, the university admitted women, becoming the first coeducational college in the nation. Today, the university system comprises several campuses and institutions across the state and boasts an enrollment of 42,000 students. The governor of Tennessee, Ned McWherter, serves as chairman of the Board of Trustees.

THE UNIVERSITY OF TEXAS SYSTEM

RANK: 48

O. Henry Hall
Austin, TX 78701
Phone: 512-499-4201
Fax: 512-499-4215

1993 Sales: $3,744 million
FYE: August
Employees: 71,109

Key Personnel
Chm, Board of Regents: Bernard Rapoport
Chancellor: William H. Cunningham
Exec Vice Chan Academic Aff: James P. Duncan
Exec Vice Chan Health Aff: Charles B. Mullins
Exec Vice Chan Business Aff: R. Dan Burck
Dir, System Personnel Office: Trennis Jones

Schools & Colleges
UT at Arlington
UT at Austin
UT at Brownsville
UT at Dallas
UT at El Paso
UT Health Science Center at Houston
UT M.D. Anderson Cancer Center
UT-Pan American
UT at San Antonio

Industry
Schools

Overview
Be careful when you equate Texas with the Longhorns — The University of Texas System operates 15 institutions in the state. Much of the system's support comes from more than $4 billion in oil money, which is split between the UT and Texas A&M systems. Fall 1993 enrollment for all UT schools was 151,835. With the 2nd largest student body in the nation (behind Ohio State), UT-Austin, where they "hook 'em horns," had 48,555 students. In 1994 *U.S. News* rated UT-Austin as the most efficient national university (in spending per student on education). The first classes met in Austin in 1883; the system was established in 1950.

UNIVERSITY OF WASHINGTON

RANK: 212

Administrative Offices, AH-30
Seattle, WA 98195
Phone: 206-543-8812
Fax: 206-543-3951

1993 Sales: $1,260 million
FYE: June
Employees: 21,536

Key Personnel
Pres: William P. Gerberding
Provost & VP Academic Affairs: G. W. Clough
EVP: Tallman Trask III
VP Minority Affairs: Myron Apilado
VP University Relations: James R. Collier
Treas: V'Ella Warren

Schools & Colleges
College of Arts & Sciences
College of Education
College of Engineering
College of Forest Resources
College of Nursing
Graduate School of Public Affairs
School of Public Health & Community Medicine

Industry
Schools

Overview
The University of Washington, a state-controlled institution founded in 1861, is located 10 miles from downtown Seattle on a 690-acre campus. Enrollment at the main campus (Seattle) and 2 branch campuses (Tacoma and Bothell) is almost 35,000. Minorities, mostly Asian-American, account for 23% of undergraduates, and Washington residents make up 85% of the student population. The university has 16 schools and colleges that offer programs of study in over 100 academic disciplines. Over 34% of the university's revenues come from gifts, grants, and contracts; tuition and fees contribute just 11%.

THE UNIVERSITY OF WISCONSIN SYSTEM

RANK: 92

1220 Linden Dr.
Madison, WI 53706
Phone: 608-262-2321
Fax: 608-265-3175

1993 Sales: $2,424 million
FYE: June
Employees: 28,606

Key Personnel
Pres: Katharine C. Lyall
SVP Academic Affairs: Stephen R. Portch
SVP Admin: Ronald Bornstein
VP Business & Fin: Raymond Marnocha
VP Physical Planning & Dev: Paul Brown
Assoc VP HR: Charles Wright

Schools & Colleges
UW/Eau Claire
UW/Green Bay
UW/La Crosse
UW/Madison
UW/Milwaukee
UW/Oshkosh
UW/Parkside
UW/Platteville
UW/River Falls
UW/Stevens Point
UW/Stout
UW/Superior
UW/Whitewater

Industry
Schools

Overview
The University of Wisconsin System has 26 campuses, over 162,000 students, and 7,200 faculty members. The system offers 400 baccalaureate, 300 master's, and 137 doctoral programs. Founded in 1849, the university is a public, land-grant institution, whose 900-acre main campus at Madison includes 8 undergraduate and 4 graduate schools. The university attracts 70% of its undergraduates from in state. A new study by the Wisconsin Policy Research Institute recommends that the university system shift its focus to include the education of returning adult students.

THE UNO-VEN COMPANY

RANK: 230

3850 N. Wilke Rd.
Arlington Heights, IL 60004
Phone: 708-818-1800
Fax: 708-818-7155

1993 Est. Sales: $1,200 million
FYE: December
Employees: 1,150

Key Personnel
Pres & CEO: Edward T. DiCorcia
VP, Sec & Chief Legal Officer: Brian A. Loftus
VP & CFO: Richard J. Estlin
VP & COO: Leonardo E. Wilthew
VP & Chief Commercial Officer: J. Michael Gibbs
Gen Mgr, Sales: Samuel H. Bailey

Major Products
Aviation turbine fuel
Diesel fuels
Fuel oils
Gasoline
Kerosene
Lubricants
Solvents
Sponge

Key Competitors
Amoco
Atlantic Richfield
Chevron
DuPont
Exxon
Mobile Gas Service
Phillips Petroleum
Texaco

Industry
Oil refining & marketing

Overview
Petroleum refiner and marketer UNO-VEN is a 50-50 joint venture between Unocal Corp. and Petróleos de Venezuela, S.A., a government-owned entity. Started in 1989, the company serves 2,700 retail outlets and 200 midwestern petroleum wholesalers and sells Unocal's "76" brand of products in 15 states. The company operates a refinery near Chicago, a lubricants blending plant in Cincinnati, and 72 terminals in 12 midwestern states. Its crude oil supply is purchased under a long-term contract from an affiliate of Petróleos de Venezuela, shipped to Louisiana, and delivered via pipeline to the UNO-VEN refinery in Illinois.

UOP

RANK: 334

25 E. Algonquin Rd.
Des Plaines, IL 60017
Phone: 708-391-2000
Fax: 708-391-2253

1992 Est. Sales: $900 million
FYE: December
Employees: 4,000

Key Personnel
Chm: Joseph C. Soviero
Pres & CEO: Michael D. Winfield
VP Fin & CFO: Herbert G. Lawrence
VP Process Licensing: Robert A. Lengemann
VP HR: Aaron R. Phillips
Gen Counsel: Harold W. Bergendorf

Business Lines
Contractual R&D
Petrochemical services
Petrochemical technologies
Refining services
Refining technologies

Key Competitors
ARCO
Chevron
Dow Chemical
DuPont
Engelhard
Great Lakes Chemical
Institut Français du Pétrole
Lyondell Petrochemical

Industry
Chemicals - specialty

Overview
Jointly owned by Allied-Signal and Union Carbide since 1988, UOP, which provides chemical catalysts and technologies for the petroleum industry, was founded in 1914 as National Hydrocarbon and later renamed Universal Oil Products. After several changes in ownership, UOP became wholly owned by Allied Signal in 1985 and then jointly owned when merged with Union Carbide's catalysts, adsorbents, and process systems division. About 70% of UOP's revenues flow from the refining sector, and the balance from petrochemicals. Almost 2/3 of UOP's business is overseas. UOP spends more than 10% of its revenues on R&D and holds thousands of patents.

US FOODSERVICE INC. — RANK: 171

1065 Hwy 315, Ste. 203
Wilkes-Barre, PA 18702
Phone: 717-822-0902
Fax: 717-822-0909

1993 Sales: $1,530 million
FYE: December
Employees: 3,725

Key Personnel
Chm & CEO: Frank H. Bevevino Bevevino
Pres & COO: Ronald E. Elmquist
VP & CFO: David F. McAnally
Sec: Ann B. Cianflone
EVP: Thomas G. McMullen
VP Admin: William Griffin

Principal Subsidiaries
Bevaco Food Service
Biggers Brothers, Inc.
Kings Foodservice, Inc.
Roanoke Restaurant Service
White Swan

Key Competitors
Consolidated Foodservice
Fleming
JP Food Service
Philip Morris
Sara Lee
SYSCO
Wal-Mart

Industry
Food - wholesale to restaurants

Overview
US Foodservice is the 3rd largest food and merchandise wholesale distributor in the US. It distributes food and other products to restaurants, schools, hospitals, and other institutions. The company was formed when Merrill Lynch Capital acquired Dallas-based wholesaler White Swan and merged it into its US Foodservice unit (formed from Pennsylvania-based distributor Unifax). Merrill Lynch Capital continues to hold a controlling interest in the company. US Foodservice maintains 15 distribution centers in 8 states. It operates under the name White Swan in the western US and as US Foodservice in the eastern portion of the country.

USAA — RANK: 30

9800 Fredericksburg Rd., USAA Building
San Antonio, TX 78288
Phone: 210-498-2211
Fax: 210-498-9940

1993 Sales: $5,990 million
FYE: December
Employees: 15,905

Key Personnel
Chm & CEO: Robert T. Herres
VC: H.T. Johnson
EVP & Chief Admin Officer: Herbert L. Emanuel
SVP, CFO & Controller: Josue Robles
SVP, Gen Counsel & Sec: William McCrae
SVP HR: William B. Tracy

◀ See page 138 for full-page profile.

Selected Services
Auto insurance
Banking
Health insurance
Homeowners'/property insurance
Investment services
Life insurance
Retirement facilities
USAA/Sprint Long-Distance Program

Key Competitors
Aetna
Allstate
CIGNA
GEICO
Kemper
Liberty Mutual
Prudential
State Farm

Industry
Insurance - multiline

Overview
Founded in 1922 by US Army officers gathered in a hotel room, USAA is the nation's 4th largest home insurer and its 5th largest automobile insurer. It has more than 2.5 million members, including 95% of active-duty US military officers. Policyholder-owned USAA limits its membership to retired and active military officers, Secret Service and FBI agents and other government officials, and their families. USAA's CEO and chairman, Robert McDermott, resigned in 1993 after 25 years in company leadership.

VANDERBILT UNIVERSITY — RANK: 358

110 21st Ave. South
Nashville, TN 37203
Phone: 615-322-7311
Fax: 615-343-7286

1993 Sales: $848 million
FYE: June
Employees: 11,781

Key Personnel
Chancellor: Joe B. Wyatt
Pres, Board of Trustees: E. Bronson Ingram
Provost: Thomas G. Burish
Treas: William T. Spitz
Controller: J. Walton Lipscomb
Assoc. Vice Chancellor, HR: H. Clint Davidson

Selected Programs of Study
Business
Engineering
Health science
Law
Liberal & fine arts
Military science
Music
Religion

Industry
Schools

Overview
Vanderbilt, a private coeducational university, was founded in 1873 with a $1 million grant from wealthy industrialist Cornelius Vanderbilt. Located on 330 acres near downtown Nashville, the Vanderbilt campus is a leafy haven where over 9,700 students are enrolled in 4 undergraduate and 6 graduate schools. Of the 84% of undergraduates from out of state, most are from the South. Fraternities and sororities draw about half the student population and influence much of the campus social activity. Since 1985, the market value of the university's endowment has more than doubled, keeping Vanderbilt on firm financial footing.

VANSTAR, INC. — RANK: 101

5964 W. Las Positas Blvd.
Pleasanton, CA 94588
Phone: 510-734-4000
Fax: 510-734-4802

1993 Est. Sales: $2,200 million
FYE: September
Employees: 3,295

Key Personnel
Chm, Pres & CEO: William Y. Tauscher
SVP Ops: Robert C. Kuntzendorf
SVP Fin & Controller: Michael Fung
SVP & Gen Counsel: Richard F. Vitkus
SVP & Chief Info Officer: Michael J. Moore
Dir HR: Judith Marshall

◀ See page 139 for full-page profile.

Business Lines
Computer accessories
Computers
LAN & WAN coordination
Peripherals
Software
Systems consulting
Training & educational services

Key Competitors
Best Buy
Circuit City
Compaq
DEC
Dell
Gateway 2000
Tandy
Technology Solutions

Industry
Computers - wholesale

Overview
Once the cutting edge computer retailer to individuals, Vanstar (formerly Computerland) has repositioned itself as a reseller to businesses. It sold its US franchise operations in 1994 and converted company-owned stores to sales offices, enhancing its service and support functions by strategic purchases from NYNEX and TRW. Started in 1973 to sell mail order computer kits, the company soon became the premier seller of Apple and IBM computers. In 1987 founder William Millard sold his majority interest to a group led by E.M. Warburg.

VISA INTERNATIONAL — RANK: 401

900 Metro Center Blvd.
Foster City, CA 94404
Phone: 415-570-3200
Fax: 415-378-4129

1993 Est. Sales: $770 million
FYE: September
Employees: 2,000

Key Personnel
Chm, Visa International: Peter Ellwood
Pres & CEO, Visa International: Edmund P. Jensen
Pres & CEO, Visa USA: Carl F. Pascarella
Pres, Visa Asia-Pacific: Lindsay C. Pyne
EVP & CFO, Visa USA: Victor Dahir
EVP HR, Visa International: John Van Aken

Selected Services
Electron (deposit access card)
Interlink (debit product)
Travelers checks
Visa CardShield (card security)
Visa credit cards
Visa Debit (account debit card)
VisaNet 2000 (authorizations)
Visa/PLUS (ATM network)

Key Competitors
American Express
Citicorp
Dean Witter, Discover
MasterCard

Industry
Financial - business services

Overview
Visa International, a consortium of 19,000 member financial institutions, is the largest bill payment system in the world, with 333 million cards in circulation in 69 countries (less than half of the cards are in the US). In 1970, under the leadership of Dee Ward Hock, the company was incorporated as BankAmericard and became Visa in 1977. In 1983 Hock (who retired in 1984) pioneered the extensive use of the now common automated teller machine (ATM), revolutionizing the credit card industry. Visa's goal to become the universal payment system is summed up in its motto "One World, One Currency, Visa."

VOUGHT AIRCRAFT COMPANY — RANK: 383

PO Box 655907
Dallas, TX 75265
Phone: 214-266-2446
Fax: 214-266-4140

1993 Est. Sales: $800 million
FYE: December
Employees: 5,800

Key Personnel
Chm: Frank Carlucci
Pres: Gordon L. Williams
SVP & CFO: W. J. McMillan
SVP Admin & Support (HR): Jerry P. Carr
VP, Sec & Gen Counsel: W. B. White
VP Gen Mgr, Military Programs: Henry Spence

◀ **See page 140 for full-page profile.**

Major Products
Bulkheads
Engine housings
Propulsion systems
Skin panels
Structures
Tail sections

Key Competitors
AlliedSignal
EG&G
Fairchild Corp.
Lockheed
Lucas Industries
Martin Marietta
Moog
Textron

Industry
Aerospace - aircraft equipment

Overview
Vought Aircraft is one of the oldest aircraft manufacturers in the US. The company derives most of its revenues from contract work, such as the manufacture of airplane parts for industry giants like Boeing and McDonnell Douglas. Founded in 1917, the company is now 51%-owned by the Carlyle Group, a Washington investment bank. The remainder is owned by Northrop Grumman, which in 1994 announced its intention to exercise its option to purchase Carlyle's 51%. For the military, the company does work on the B-2 Stealth Bomber and the C-17 Globemaster transport plane.

VT INC. — RANK: 257

8500 Shawnee Mission Pkwy., Ste. 200
Merriam, KS 66202
Phone: 913-432-6400
Fax: 913-789-1039

1992 Sales: $1,088 million
Employees: 2,500

Key Personnel
Co-CEO: Cecil Van Tuyl
Co-CEO: Larry Van Tuyl
Sec & Treas: Robert J. Holcomb
VP Personnel: John A. Morford

Business Lines
Body shop
F&I sales
Fleet sales
New car sales
Parts & service
Used car sales

Key Competitors
Don Massey Cadillac
Frank Consolidated Enterprises
Hendrick Management
Holman Enterprises
Morse Operations
Penske
Potamkin Manhattan

Industry
Retail - new & used cars

Overview
Founded in 1955 by Cecil Van Tuyl, VT is one of the nation's largest car dealers, with over 20 dealerships in the Midwest and Arizona. Once the dominant car dealer in the Kansas City area, VT sold most of its operations there as part of a long-planned downsizing program. Larry Van Tuyl, Cecil's son and company co-owner, oversees operations in Phoenix, which include several dealerships and a management training center. VT receives about 20% of its revenues from "backshop" operations such as parts and service and body shop sales. Cecil Van Tuyl has also poured his energy and capital into such areas as airplane dealerships, banking, insurance, and real estate.

W. L. GORE & ASSOCIATES INC. — RANK: 377

555 Papermill Rd.
Newark, DE 19711
Phone: 302-738-4880
Fax: 302-738-7710

1993 Sales: $804 million
FYE: March
Employees: 5,170

Key Personnel
Pres & CEO: Robert W. Gore
CFO: Shanti Mehta
Sec & Treas: Genevieve W. Gore
Mgr Personnel: Barbara Debnam

Major Products
Electronic connectors
Gore-Tex fabrics
Industrial filters
Medical patches & implants

Key Competitors
DuPont
Essex Group
General Cable
General Instrument
Hercules
Raychem
Southwire
Union Carbide

Industry
Diversified operations

Overview
Delaware-based W. L. Gore was founded in 1958 in the basement of a former DuPont employee who wanted to market Teflon as an insulator for electrical wires. While insulated wire and cable spurred early growth, the high-tech company, which eschews typical corporate hierarchies, trappings, and titles, manufactures fabric, electronic, medical, fiber, and filtration products at 44 plants worldwide. "Miracle fabric" Gore-Tex, which allows perspiration to pass through it but blocks out rain, is used in sports equipment, NASA spacesuits, sutures, and artificial ligaments and arteries.

WAKEFERN FOOD CORPORATION

RANK: 51

600 York St.
Elizabeth, NJ 07207
Phone: 908-527-3300
Fax: 908-906-5038

1993 Sales: $3,600 million
FYE: September
Employees: 4,760

Key Personnel
Chm and CEO: Thomas P. Infusino
Pres: Jerome D. Yaguda
EVP: Dean Janeway
Treas: Dominick V. Romano
VP HR: Marty Glass

Major Products
Cigarettes
General groceries
Private label goods
Elizabeth York
Farm Flavor
ShopRite
Specialty foods
Store supplies

Key Competitors
Associated Food
Fleming
Grand Union
King Kullen Grocery
Pathmark
Spartan Stores
SUPERVALU
Twin County Grocers

Industry
Food - wholesale to grocers

Overview
Founded in the late 1940s, Wakefern Food is a cooperative owned by the 30 operators of the 180 ShopRite grocery stores located in Connecticut, Delaware, New Jersey, New York, and Pennsylvania. Wakefern supplies ShopRite stores with food (including an extensive selection of private labels), cigarettes, and store supplies. The company is a leader in cost cutting and claims to be the largest grocery cooperative in the nation and the market share leader in the region that it serves.

WALTER INDUSTRIES INC.

RANK: 199

1500 N. Dale Mabry Hwy.
Tampa, FL 33607
Phone: 813-871-4811
Fax: 813-871-4430

1994 Sales: $1,329 million
FYE: May
Employees: 7,500

Key Personnel
Chm: James W. Walter
Pres & CEO: G. Robert Durham
EVP & CFO: Kenneth J. Matlock
VP Legal & Sec: John F. Turbiville
VP HR & Public Relations: David L. Townsend

Business Lines
Coal mining
Coke production
Home building
Insurance
Mineral wool manufacture
Mortgage financing
Petroleum products
Pipe & fittings manufacture

Key Competitors
American Standard
Centex
Cyprus Amax
Manville
Masco
PHC
USG
Ziegler Coal

Industry
Diversified operations

Overview
Walter Industries is a diversified corporation resulting from the 1987 LBO of the Jim Walter Corp. engineered by Kohlberg Kravis Roberts. The Jim Walter company was split into Hillsborough Holdings (renamed Walter Industries), which kept, among others, the building, insurance, and mortgage units, and the new Jim Walter Corp., which owns Celotex, an asbestos case defendant. Walter Industries is in Chapter 11, but a 1994 ruling that it bears no asbestos liability may expedite its emergence from bankruptcy.

WARREN EQUITIES INC.

RANK: 431

One Warren Way
Providence, RI 02905
Phone: 401-781-9900
Fax: 401-941-2570

1993 Sales: $700 million
FYE: May
Employees: 1,600

Key Personnel
Chm & CEO: Warren Alpert
VC & VP: Edward Cosgrove
Pres: Herbert Kaplan
Treas & CFO: John Dziedzic
Sec: Benjamin Alpert
Dir HR: Thomas Palumbo

Principal Subsidiaries
Auburn Merchandise Distributors
Drake Petroleum Company
Kenyon Oil Company, Inc.
Cazeault Oil Corporation
Mid-Valley Petroleum Corporation
Puritan Oil Company, Inc.
Warren Oil Company

Key Competitors
Agway
Amoco
Circle K
Cumberland Farms
Fleming
Global Petroleum
Southland
Wawa

Industry
Oil refining & marketing; convenience stores

Overview
Warren Equities operates several petroleum and food product companies owned by Harvard Business School graduate Warren Alpert. It includes Extra•Mont gas and convenience stores, which are located in the Northeast, as well as a New England grocery, tobacco, candy, and paper goods distributor (Auburn Merchandise Distributors). Other companies transport and market gasoline, fuel oil, lubricants, and diesel fuel. Alpert started with a single distributorship, which was given to him by Standard Oil in the early 1950s. Now Warren operates in 11 states. Bachelor Alpert recently gave Harvard Medical School its largest gift ever: $20 million.

WASHINGTON CORPORATIONS

RANK: 464

101 International Dr.
Missoula, MT 59807
Phone: 406-523-1300
Fax: 406-523-1399

1993 Sales: $629 million
FYE: December
Employees: 3,450

Key Personnel
Pres: Dorn Parkinson
EVP: Leroy E. Wilkes
VP Acctg: Mike Haight
VP Mgmt Info Sys: Mike Ragbourn
Sec & Treas: Helen B. Miller
Personnel Mgr: Jim Brouelette

Business Lines
Copper mining
Heavy construction
Mining equipment leasing
Rail services
Underground coal mining

Key Competitors
CSX
Cyprus Amax
Industrial Constructors
Peter Kiewit Sons'
Rogers Group
Union Pacific
Walsh Group
Zeigler Coal

Industry
Construction - heavy

Overview
Washington Corporations is a Montana-based mining, construction, machinery, and railroad operation. Owner Dennis R. Washington, who founded the company in 1964 with a $30,000 loan, built the highway construction company into Montana's largest contractor. In 1985 Washington bought the Anaconda copper mine from Atlantic Richfield for $20 million and, 4 years later, sold half for $125 million. In 1987 the company purchased a rail line from Burlington Northern that is now generating profits. In 1993 Washington merged its construction and mining unit with Kasler Corp., a Southern California contractor.

WASHINGTON UNIVERSITY

RANK: 277

1 Brookings Dr.
St. Louis, MO 63130
Phone: 314-935-5000
Fax: 314-935-5146

1993 Sales: $1,046 million
FYE: June
Employees: 7,162

Key Personnel
Chancellor: William H. Danforth
Vice Chan & Gen Counsel: Michael R. Cannon
Vice Chan Admin: Richard E. Anderson
Gen Counsel: Peter H. Ruger
Treas: Jerry Woodham
Sec: Harriet K. Switzer

Selected Programs of Study
Undergraduate
- Architecture
- Asian/Oriental studies
- Comparative literature
- Early childhood education
- Earth sciences
- Occupational therapy

Graduate
- Communication sciences
- European studies
- Human resources management
- Latin American studies
- Physics
- Technology & human affairs

Industry
Schools

Overview
Founded in 1853, Washington University grew from a regional school into a major research university under the leadership of Chancellor William Danforth, who plans to retire in June 1995 after 24 years of service. During Danforth's tenure, people connected with the university won 10 Nobel prizes and the endowment grew to $1.7 billion. The university's medical school is considered one of the top 5 in the country. Proposed US health care reform is of primary concern because 30% of the school's revenue comes from health care services.

WATCHTOWER BIBLE & TRACT SOCIETY OF NEW YORK INC.

RANK: 219

25 Columbia Hts.
Brooklyn, NY 11201
Phone: 718-625-3600
Fax: 718-625-3066

1992 Est. Sales: $1,250 million
FYE: August
Employees: 1,100

Key Personnel
Pres: Milton G. Henschel
Treas & Sec: Lyman A. Swingle
Treas & Asst Sec: John C. Booth
VP: George M. Couch
VP HR: Max H. Larson

Major Publications
Awake! magazine
Devotional literature
Yearbook of Jehovah's Witnesses
The Watchtower magazine

Industry
Religious organization

Overview
The Watchtower Bible & Tract Society is the governing and publishing arm of the Jehovah's Witnesses religion, which claims about 4.4 million members worldwide. Some 914,000 adherents live in the US. With about 2,900 missionaries evangelizing in 229 countries, the organization is growing most rapidly outside the US. Members believe that soon the world will end with a great battle and that Christ and 144,000 righteous followers will then rule the earth. The sect is known for being nonpolitical, abhorring blood transfusions, and hawking its publications and beliefs door-to-door.

WAWA INC.

RANK: 417

260 Baltimore Pike
Wawa, PA 19063
Phone: 610-358-8000
Fax: 610-358-8878

1992 Sales: $715 million
FYE: December
Employees: 1,900

Key Personnel
Pres & CEO: Richard D. Wood
EVP Fin & Admin: Edward Chambers
SVP Store Ops & Purchasing: Donald Price
SVP Store Ops: Henry McHugh
SVP Mktg: Howard Stoeckel
SVP HR: Vincent P. Anderson

Major Products
Custom-made sandwiches
Dairy products
Fountain soft drinks
Groceries
Health & beauty products
Juices
Prepackaged salads
Yogurt

Key Competitors
American Stores
Circle K
Cumberland Farms
Grand Union
Kroger
Pathmark
Southland
Twin County Grocers

Industry
Retail - convenience stores

Overview
Wawa is one of the largest privately held convenience store chains in the US, with over 500 mostly suburban outlets in the mid-Atlantic and New England regions. The company built its operations around selling high-quality perishables (delicatessen and salad bar items). Wawa promotes itself by emphasizing its prepared foods line (especially hoagies, a Philadelphia specialty) and low-price cigarettes. In addition to its convenience stores, Wawa also runs a dairy and a wholesale cigarette operation.

WEGMANS FOOD MARKETS INC.

RANK: 135

1500 Brooks Ave.
Rochester, NY 14624
Phone: 716-328-2550
Fax: 716-464-4626

1993 Sales: $1,800 million
FYE: December
Employees: 21,100

Key Personnel
Chm & CEO: Robert B. Wegman
Pres: Daniel Wegman
CFO & Dir of Fin: Mark Kindig
Controller: Jim Leo
Sec & Gen Counsel: Paul S. Speranza
Dir HR: Gerald Pierce

Selected Services
Bakery
Chase-Pitkin Home & Garden
Delicatessen
Health food line
Market Cafe
Old World Cheese Shops
Wegmans Transaction Services
Xerox Document Centers

Key Competitors
American Stores
Fleming
Golub
Great A&P
Penn Traffic
SUPERVALU
Tamarkin
Tops Markets

Industry
Retail - supermarkets

Overview
Family-owned Wegmans was founded by brothers Jack and Walter Wegman in 1916 as the Rochester Fruit and Vegetable Company and became one of the first self-service grocers in the U.S. in the 1930s. It is now one of America's top 50 supermarket chains. Its nearly 50 stores are clustered in the Rochester, Syracuse, and Buffalo areas. Wegmans is also expanding into Pennsylvania. Known for creative merchandising, the chain is a leader in adopting such concepts as private labeling, restaurant-quality in-store cafes, store-affiliated national credit cards, and (as partners with Xerox) a home office department. CEO Robert Wegman is a nephew of the founders.

WEST PUBLISHING CO. RANK: 495

610 Opperman Dr.
Eagan, MN 55123
Phone: 612-687-7000
Fax: 612-687-5388

1993 Est. Sales: $541 million
FYE: July
Employees: 5,300

Key Personnel
Chm & CEO: Dwight D. Opperman
Pres: Vance K. Opperman
VP, CFO & Sec: Grant E. Nelson
VP, Asst to the Pres: Jerrol M. Tostrud
VP Mktg & Sales: Gerard L. Cafesjian
HR: Barbara Christenson

Major Products
Federal Securities
Federal Taxation Library
Military Justice Reporter
Social Security Library
US Supreme Court Reporter
WESTLAW (on-line service)
West's Bankruptcy Digest
West's Legal Directory

Key Competitors
Commerce Clearing House
John Wiley & Sons
Mead
Reed Elsevier
Thomson Corp.
Time Warner
Times Mirror
Ziff Communications

Industry
Publishing - books

Overview
Founded in 1872, West Publishing is the preeminent publisher of legal books. Consisting of 3 divisions (Law Books, Law School, and College and School), West publishes more than 55 million volumes and pamphlets a year. Critical to the company's success was its development more than a century ago of the Key Number System, a way of organizing and summarizing the thousands of legal decisions handed down every year. In the early 1970s, West countered Mead Corp.'s introduction of LEXIS/NEXIS, an on-line legal information service, with WESTLAW, which has been successful.

WESTFIELD COMPANIES RANK: 459

One Park Circle
Westfield Center, OH 44251
Phone: 218-887-0101
Fax: 216-887-0840

1993 Sales: $638 million
FYE: December
Employees: 1,840

Key Personnel
Pres & CEO: R. C. Blair
SVP & CFO: Otto Bosshard
SVP: T. H. Pickering
SVP: R. H. Thompson
VP HR: R. D. Sondles
Gen Counsel: Ed Lytle

Major Products
Annuities
Automobile insurance
Fire, marine & casualty insurance
Life insurance
Property & casualty insurance

Key Competitors
Allstate
CIGNA
GEICO
Liberty Mutual
MetLife
New York Life
Prudential
State Farm

Industry
Insurance - property & casualty

Overview
An operating arm for its parent company — Ohio Farmers Insurance, founded in 1848 — Westfield operates 6 insurance companies. They sell commercial and personal insurance policies through 1,300 independent agents in Florida, Illinois, Indiana, Kentucky, Michigan, Minnesota, Ohio, and West Virginia; 47% of the company's business is in Ohio. The company writes coverage in states known for favorable operating and regulatory environments. Company profits are divided among employees and agents. Westfield's purchase of Beacon Insurance is expected to strengthen its position in such niche markets as religious and trade groups.

WICKLAND CORPORATION RANK: 412

3640 American River Dr.
Sacramento, CA 95864
Phone: 916-978-2500
Fax: 916-978-2408

1993 Sales: $732 million
FYE: December
Employees: 140

Key Personnel
Chm: John A. Wickland, Jr.
Pres: John A. Wickland III
CFO: John W. Reho
EVP: Roy L. Wickland
Gen Counsel: Jay Fortun

Business Lines
Bunker oil
Chemical bulk stations
Gasoline distribution
Natural gas
Oil marketing
Oil trading
Petroleum terminals
Real estate

Key Competitors
Chevron
Coastal
Enron
Getty Petroleum
Tesoro Petroleum
Unocal
Valero Energy
Western Gas

Industry
Oil & gas - marketing & trading

Overview
Wickland operates domestic and international petroleum terminals, distributes fuel oils and natural gas, and invests in real estate. Owned and operated by CEO John Wickland and his family, the company, which has divested its retail and wholesale gasoline businesses in recent years, expanded into the natural gas business in 1993 when it bought Mock Resources, which is also the largest nonretail marketer of gasoline and diesel fuels in California. Wickland has bulk terminals in San Francisco, Los Angeles, Singapore, and Aruba.

WILBUR-ELLIS COMPANY RANK: 336

320 California St., Ste. 200
San Francisco, CA 94104
Phone: 415-772-4000
Fax: 415-772-4011

1993 Sales: $900 million
FYE: December
Employees: 2,000

Key Personnel
Pres & CEO: Brayton Wilbur, Jr.
VP & Treas : Herbert B. Tully
Sec: Ingrid Kroneberg
Controller: Robert T. Pantzer
Gen Counsel: Ellen Maldonado
Dir Personnel: Ofelia Uriarte

Business Lines
Agricultural chemicals
Animal feed
Fertilizer
Gear boxes & switches
Industrial chemicals
Insecticides
Machinery
Seed

Key Competitors
Agway
Ashland Oil
Cargill
W. R. Grace
GROWMARK
Terra Industries
Transammonia
Western Farmco

Industry
Chemicals - specialty

Overview
Founded in 1921 by Brayton Wilbur, Sr., and his partner Floyd Ellis as a fish oil supplier, San Francisco–based Wilbur-Ellis is now the #10 distributor of fertilizers and agricultural chemicals in the US, according to *Farm Chemicals*. Managed by the son of a founder, the company markets and distributes products through nearly 200 warehouses, plants, offices, and retail centers in North America, Asia, and Africa. Wilbur-Ellis has grown its business by acquiring other companies, which the company believes is more efficient than setting up its own new operations. The company also has an equity interest in about 1/3 of the companies whose products it sells.

WISCONSIN DAIRIES COOPERATIVE — RANK: 492

PO Box 111
Baraboo, WI 53913-0111
Phone: 608-356-8316
Fax: 608-356-9005

1994 Sales: $548 million
FYE: March
Employees: 946

Key Personnel
Chm: Edward Brooks
Pres: Donald C. Storhoff
VP Fin: Duaine T. Kamenick
VP Mktg: Curtis Kurth
VP Mfg: Dave Fuhrmann
VP HR: John Murphy

Major Products
American cheese
Butter
Condensed milk products
Italian cheese
Liquid milk
Milk powder products
Specialty cheeses
Whey products

Key Competitors
Associated Milk Producers
Dairyman's Co-op Creamery
Dairymen
Darigold
Mid-America Dairymen

Industry
Food - dairy products

Overview
Founded in 1963 when 2 dairies in south-central Wisconsin merged to become a farm cooperative, Wisconsin Dairies now has 3,810 member farms in Wisconsin, Minnesota, and Iowa that produce 2.7 billion pounds of milk annually. Over 70% of the co-op's revenue is derived from turning that milk into cheese, which the co-op sells to the food industry, including Kraft and Dean Foods. Wisconsin Dairies produces a wide variety of cheeses ranging from the traditional cheddar to a new Hispanic style. The co-op also is a major player in whey (through its Foremost unit) and butter, which it sells exclusively to Land O' Lakes (in which it has an equity interest).

WOODWARD & LOTHROP, INCORPORATED — RANK: 356

1025 F St. NW
Washington, DC 20002
Phone: 202-879-8000
Fax: 202-879-8397

1994 Sales: $849 million
FYE: January
Employees: 12,702

Key Personnel
Chm & CEO: Robert B. Mang
Pres & COO: Robert J. Mulligan
SVP Fin: Joseph F. Gallucci
Sec & Gen Counsel: Judith Pickering
SVP Personnel: Joseph Culver

Operating Units
Bethesda Furniture & Design Ctr.
The Home Store (2 stores)
John Wanamaker (16 stores)
Woodward & Lothrop (19 stores)

Key Competitors
Federated
Harcourt General
Jos. A. Bank
May
Nordstrom
J. C. Penney
Saks
Strawbridge & Clothier

Industry
Retail - regional department stores

Overview
One of the last over-leveraged, upscale retailers, 114-year-old Woodies succumbed to the high debt left over from its 1984 LBO, declaring bankruptcy in 1994. Owned by financier Alfred Taubman (84%) and its management (16%) before the bankruptcy, Woodies was once the premier retailer in the Washington, DC, area. Too much debt, new competition from high-end out-of-town retailers like Nordstrom, and its small scale compared to other department store chains brought the venerable retailer down. The company also owns Philadelphia retailer John Wanamaker (acquired in 1986) and several specialty furniture stores in the DC area.

WORLD COLOR PRESS, INC. — RANK: 353

101 Park Ave.
New York, NY 10178
Phone: 212-986-2440
Fax: 212-455-9266

1993 Sales: $850 million
FYE: December
Employees: 6,219

Key Personnel
Chm, Pres & CEO: Robert G. Burton
VC: Jerome B. Spier
VP Fin & CFO: Marc Reisch
VP & Gen Counsel: Jennifer L. Adams

Selected Printing Services
Catalogs
Directories
Magazines
Newspaper inserts

Key Competitors
Banta
R.R. Donnelley
Graphic Industries
Quad/Graphics
Quebecor
Stevens Graphics
Sullivan Graphics
Treasure Chest

Industry
Printing - commercial

Overview
Founded in St. Louis in 1903 as the World's Fair Color Printing Company, this firm originally produced weekly newspapers, circulars, and Sunday comics. Now World Color Press is the #3 printer of directories in the US and also prints catalogs, consumer magazines (e.g., *McCall's*, *TV Guide*), and other materials. It is owned by a limited partnership led by Kohlberg Kravis Roberts (KKR). In 1993 the company agreed to purchase specialty catalog printer Alden Press for about $110 million.

YALE UNIVERSITY — RANK: 352

451 College St.
New Haven, CT 06520
Phone: 203-432-2321
Fax: 203-432-7891

1993 Sales: $852 million
FYE: June
Employees: 8,500

Key Personnel
Pres: Richard C. Levin
Acting VP Fin: Joseph Mullinix
VP Dev & Alumni Affairs: Terry Holcombe
Sec: Linda K. Lorrimer
Gen Counsel: Dorothy Robinson
VP HR: Peter Vallone

Selected Programs of Study
Undergraduate
- Afro-American studies
- Chemical engineering
- Comparative literature
- Computer science
- Molecular biophysics
- Russian

Graduate
- American studies
- Economics
- Engineering & applied science
- Neurobiology
- Pharmacology
- Political science

Industry
Schools

Overview
Founded in 1701, Yale University, a private liberal arts institution, is one of the nation's oldest and most prestigious universities. Yale, which has about 11,000 students enrolled in one undergraduate and 11 graduate schools, is located 75 miles northeast of New York City in an urban area of Connecticut. Only about 15% of undergraduates are from in-state; the rest are from the other 49 states and 52 foreign countries. Although academically rigorous, Yale makes student comparisons difficult because the university has no GPAs and no class rankings. Social life is centered on the residential college system in which all Yale freshmen are placed.

YOUNG MEN'S CHRISTIAN ASSOCIATION — RANK: 144

101 N. Wacker Dr., Ste. 1400
Chicago, IL 60606
Phone: 312-977-0031
Fax: 312-977-9063

1993 Sales: $1,762 million
FYE: December
Employees: 10,299

Key Personnel
Chm: E. H. Clark
VC: George Rehnquist
VC: Daniel E. Emerson
CEO: David Mercer
CFO: Michael Renehan
HR: Wyley Moore

Selected Services
Athletic facilities
Child care
Civic training
Cultural programs
Recreational facilities
Social events
Vocational instruction

Key Competitors
24 Hour Nautilus
Bally Entertainment
Gold's Gym
Kinder-Care Learning Centers
La Petite Academy
Northwest Raquet Swim and Health
Weider Franchising
YWCA

Industry
Leisure & recreational services - athletic facilities

Overview
The YMCA is a national leader in health club facilities. Founded in England in 1844 and started in the US in 1851, the YMCA is a worldwide network of nonsectarian facilities providing athletic, recreation, and learning activities for members. Low dues maximize access; half of its members are children. The 2,200 community Y's in the US have an estimated 19,000 rooms for rent, and many have cafeterias. Each Y is a nonprofit corporation. With large national revenues, the YMCA's nonprofit status has been challenged by for-profit health clubs and other competitors.

YOUNG & RUBICAM INC. — RANK: 290

285 Madison Ave.
New York, NY 10017-6486
Phone: 212-210-3000
Fax: 212-210-9073

1993 Sales: $1,009 million
FYE: December
Employees: 9,846

Key Personnel
Chm: Alexander S. Kroll
VC & Worldwide Creative Dir: Ted Bell
Pres & CEO: Peter A. Georgescu
EVP & CFO: Dave Greene
EVP & Gen Counsel: R. John Cooper
Dir HR: Raquel Suarez

◀ See page 141 for full-page profile.

Representative Clients
American Express
Clorox
Dr. Pepper/7 Up
Ford
MetLife
PepsiCo
Sears
Time Warner

Key Competitors
N W Ayer
Bozell
D'Arcy Masius
Grey Advertising
Interpublic Group
Leo Burnett
Saatchi & Saatchi
WPP Group

Industry
Advertising

Overview
Raymond Rubicam and John Orr Young founded Young & Rubicam in 1923. Today Y&R is the US's 2nd largest consolidated advertising agency, with 304 offices in 64 countries. Its 5 main divisions provide services in advertising, public relations, sales promotion/direct marketing, corporate and product identity consulting, and health care communications. The employee-owned agency recently announced its 4th major restructuring in the last 8 years. The agency is concentrating on making its operations more client-driven.

YOUNG'S MARKET CO. — RANK: 328

2164 N. Batavia St.
Orange, CA 92665
Phone: 714-283-4933
Fax: 714-283-6176

1993 Sales: $910 million
FYE: February
Employees: 1,500

Key Personnel
Pres & CEO: Vernon O. Underwood, Jr.
SVP & CFO: Dennis J. Hamann
VP Mktg: Mark Sneed
Dir Info Sys: Steve Schaad
VP HR: Naomi Buenaslor

Business Lines
Food processing
Specialty foods
Wholesale food
Wholesale liquor
Wines & distilled beverages

Key Competitors
Magnolia Marketing
Martine's Wines
Mountaintop
National Distributing
Seagram
Southern Wine & Spirits
Sunbelt Beverage

Industry
Food - wholesale to grocers

Overview
One of the top 20 beverage companies in the US, Los Angeles–based Young's Market was founded in 1888 by John Young, who started with a concession stand and incorporated in 1906 with his brothers. After the repeal of Prohibition, the brothers focused on the liquor market but some 20 years later moved into wholesale foods. In 1985 the family- owned company expanded into Northern California, acquiring other wine and spirits wholesale operations (Rathjen, Berberian Bros.). The company's CEO is a grandson of one of the founding Young brothers.

YUCAIPA COMPANIES — RANK: 71

777 S. Harbor Blvd.
La Habra, CA 90631
Phone: 714-738-2000
Fax: 714-738-2522

1993 Sales: $2,742 million
FYE: June
Employees: 13,596

Key Personnel
Chm: Ronald W. Burkle
EVP & CFO: Greg Mays
EVP: Joe S. Burkle
VP HR: Don Ropele
Gen Counsel: Robert Birmingham
Sec: George G. Golleher

Selected Chains
ABC
Alpha Beta
Boys Market
Falley's
Food 4 Less
Marina
Viva

Key Competitors
Albertson's
American Stores
Certified Grocers
Edward J. Debartolo
Hughes Markets
Smith's Food & Drug
Vons

Industry
Retail - supermarkets

Overview
Yucaipa Companies is an investment group formed in 1986 that controls various supermarket franchise chains, including its flagship company Food 4 Less Supermarkets. Yucaipa, owned by Ronald Burkle, Mark Resnik, and 5 others, uses LBOs to acquire older, underperforming grocery chains. With a chain of 251 groceries, Food 4 Less Supermarkets is Southern California's 2nd largest supermarket operator. Under the banners of ABC, Boys, and Viva, Food 4 Less has created a niche in the inner-city communities of Watts and East Los Angeles. Acquired in a 1989 LBO, Food 4 Less is heavily leveraged, with a long-term debt of $500 million.

H. B. ZACHRY COMPANY

RANK: 392

527 W. Harding Blvd.
San Antonio, TX 78221
Phone: 210-922-1213
Fax: 210-927-8060

1993 Sales: $792 million
FYE: December
Employees: 8,000

Key Personnel
Chm & CEO: Henry B. Zachry, Jr.
Pres: Peter Van Nort
CFO: J. J. Lozano
VP Ops: John B. Zachry
VP & Sec: Murray L. Johnson
VP HR: Steve Hoech

Business Lines
Bridge & highway construction
Cement
Construction sand
Gravel mining
Heavy construction
Hotels
Insurance
Water, sewer & utility lines

Key Competitors
Bechtel
Black & Veatch
Clark Enterprises
CRSS
Fluor
Foster Wheeler
Hensel Phelps
Parsons

Industry
Construction - housing

Overview
H. B. Zachry began business in 1924 as a bridge builder and expanded into construction of power plants, highways, missile sites, hotels, dams, and airfields in the US and the South Pacific. Among the projects managed by Zachry are the runways at DFW Airport, the Alaska Pipeline Project, the Navajo Generating Station in Arizona, 2 coal units for Old Dominion Electric Cooperative in Virginia, and the J. C. Penney headquarters in Plano, Texas. A pioneer in the development of modular construction, Zachry also owns Tower Life Insurance, hotels, ranches, oil & gas interests, and an interest in the San Antonio Spurs. CEO Henry Zachry is the son of the founder.

ZEIGLER COAL HOLDING COMPANY

RANK: 343

50 Jerome Ln.
Fairview Heights, IL 62208
Phone: 618-394-2400
Fax: 618-394-2473

1993 Sales: $873 million
FYE: December
Employees: 4,000

Key Personnel
Chm & CEO: Michael K. Reilly
Pres & COO: Chand B. Vyas
VP Govt Rel & Comm: Francis L. Barkofske
VP & CFO: George J. Holway
VP HR: William Kuzma, Jr.
VP & Gen Counsel: Brent L. Motchan

Operating Units
Americoal Services Company
Encoal Corporation
Franklin Coal Sales Company
Marrowbone Development
Old Ben Coal Company
Phoenix Land Company
SMC Mining Company
Wolf Creek Collieries Company

Key Competitors
CONSOL Energy
Cyprus Amax
Drummond
Exxon
Kerr-McGee
Occidental
Pittston
Walter Industries

Industry
Coal

Overview
Zeigler Coal began in 1904 as the dream of Joseph Leiter, who hoped to supply Illinois and the nation with coal from Illinois's own mine reserves. In 4 years Leiter's first mine became the 3rd largest coal producer in the nation. Today the Zeigler family of companies has an annual production of approximately 40 million tons. Zeigler Coal nearly tripled its revenues shortly after acquiring Shell Mining Company.

ZELL/CHILMARK FUND LP

RANK: N/R

2 N. Riverside Plaza
Chicago, IL 60606
Phone: 312-984-9711
Fax: 312-984-0317

Employees: 12

Key Personnel
Partner: Samuel Zell
Partner: Joel S. Freidland

Selected Investments
American Classic Voyages (46%)
Broadway Stores (54%)
Jacor Communications (66%)
Midway Airlines (90%)
Revco D.S. Inc. (20%)
Schwinn Bicycle Co. (56%)
Sealy Corporation (94%)

Industry
Financial - investors

Overview
Self-proclaimed grave dancer Samuel Zell, who began his business career as a teen selling *Playboy* magazines to friends for a profit, has made millions in the distressed real estate market. His Zell/Chilmark Fund partnership (founded in 1984) specializes in reviving companies considered to be dead and buried. Zell became department store giant Carter Hawley Hale's (now Broadway Stores) white knight when he rescued it from a 1991 bankruptcy by buying 80% of its $600 million in unsecured debt. With a range of investments from bedding to bicycles, Zell/Chilmark got into the Cincinnati broadcasting market in 1994 with the purchase of Jacor Communications.

ZIFF COMMUNICATIONS COMPANY

RANK: 297

One Park Ave.
New York, NY 10016
Phone: 212-503-3500
Fax: 212-503-4599

1993 Est. Sales: $925 million
FYE: December
Employees: 4,300

Key Personnel
Chm & CEO: Eric Hippeau
VP & Publisher, PC Magazine: Jim Stafford
VP: Jeff Ballowe
VP & CFO: Bruce Barnes
VP Ziff-Davis: Sam Huey
VP HR: Fred Staudmyer

Operating Units
Information Access Co.
Interchange Network Co.
Ziff-Davis Publishing Company
- Business Media Group
- Consumer Media Group
- International Media Group

Key Competitors
America Online
CMP Publications
H&R Block
International Data Group
McGraw-Hill
Meckler
Reed Elsevier
Wired Ventures

Industry
Publishing - periodicals

Overview
Founded in 1927, Ziff Communications Company is now the #1 computer magazine publisher in the US. The company's roster includes *PC Magazine*, *PC Computing*, and *MacUser*. Ziff also has operations in electronic information (including 2 on-line services), trade shows, and newsletters. Son of a cofounder, Bill Ziff, Jr., retired as chairman and CEO in 1993, having run, and built up, the company since 1953. Ownership now rests in the hands of Ziff's heirs (3 sons and 3 nephews), who have announced their intention to sell the company.

◀ **See page 142 for full-page profile.**

THE
Indexes

Index of Companies by Industry

Index of Companies by Headquarters Location

Index of Brands, Companies, and People Named in the Profiles

MANUFACTURING

Building Materials and Components, Furniture, Glass and Containers

Chemicals

Computers and Peripherals

Defense and Aerospace

Drugs and Medical Equipment

Electronics and Electrical Equipment

Food, Beverages, and Tobacco

Forest and Paper Products

Household and Personal Products

Mining and Metals

Motor Vehicles, Parts, and Tires

Office and Photographic Equipment

Textiles, Apparel, and Shoes

Tools and Industrial Equipment

SERVICES

Business Services

Note: Page numbers in **boldface** indicate the company's profile. Lightface numbers indicate references in other profiles.

Numbers

A

B

C

E

F

G

H

I

J

K

L

M

N

S

T

U

X

Y

Z

MORE BUSINESS RESOURCES FROM

THE REFERENCE PRESS — PUBLISHER OF  OOVER'S 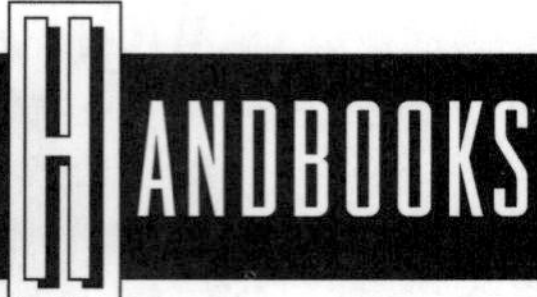 ANDBOOKS

STOCK GUIDES

NASDAQ Fact Book & Company Directory 1994	$19.95
New York Stock Exchange Fact Book 1994	$9.95
American Stock Exchange Fact Book 1994	$14.95
The 100 Best Stocks to Own in America	$22.95
Standard & Poor's 500 Guide 1994	$19.95
Standard & Poor's Midcap 400 Guide 1994	$19.95
Standard & Poor's Stock and Bond Guide 1994	$19.95
The Dow Jones Guide to the World Stock Market	$39.95
The World's Emerging Stock Markets	$64.95
Asia Pacific Securities Handbook 1994–95	$99.95

LOGO BOOKS

Logos of America's Largest Corporations	$39.95
Logos of America's Fastest Growing Corporations	$39.95
Logos of Major World Corporations	$39.95
Living Logos: How U.S. Corporations Revitalize Their Trademarks	$22.95

FOREIGN TRADE INFORMATION

Cracking Latin America	$44.95
Mexico Business	$24.95
Trade Directory of Mexico 1994	$89.95
The U.S.–Mexico Trade Pages 1994	$59.95
Cracking the Pacific Rim	$44.95
China Business	$24.95
Singapore Business	$24.95
Taiwan Business	$24.95
Japan Business	$24.95
Korea Business	$24.95
Hong Kong Business	$24.95
Asian and Australasian Companies: A Guide to Sources of Information	$94.95
Cracking Eastern Europe	$44.95
European Companies: A Guide to Sources of Information	$89.95
The African Business Handbook 1993–1994	$34.95
American Companies: A Guide to Sources of Information	$94.95
Dictionary of International Trade	$16.45

FOREIGN COMPANY HANDBOOKS

Mexico Company Handbook 1994–95	$34.95
Brazil Company Handbook 1994–95	$34.95
Venezuela Company Handbook 1992–93	$29.95
Company Handbook—Hong Kong 1994	$44.95
Thailand 1994	$46.95
Access Nippon 1994	$34.95
Canada Company Handbook 1994	$39.95
French Company Handbook 1994	$59.95
Germany's Top 500: 1994/95	$49.95
The Guardian Guide to the UK's Top Companies 1995	$49.95
The Times 1000 1995	$49.95
Company Handbook Spain 1994	$84.95
Directory of East European Businesses	$74.95
Russia 1994	$64.95

OTHER BUSINESS REFERENCES

The American Forecaster Almanac 1994	$14.95
The Computer Industry Almanac 1994–1995	$59.95
Association Directories (2-volume set) 1994	$134.95
The Competitive Intelligence Handbook	$24.95
The 1994 National Directory of Addresses and Telephone Numbers	$84.95
1994 Information Please Business Almanac & Desk Reference	$29.95
The Fortune Encyclopedia of Economics	$49.95
The Ernst & Young Almanac and Guide to U.S. Business Cities	$16.95
The 100 Best Companies to Work for in America	$27.95
The National Book of Lists	$19.95
National Directory of Corporate Public Affairs	$89.95
Net Guide	$18.95
Net Games	$18.95
Net Chat	$18.95
Weissmann Travel Planner for Western and Eastern Europe 1994–1995	$49.95

TO ORDER CALL 1-800-486-8666

 The Reference Press, Inc., 6448 Highway 290 E., Suite E–104, Austin, Texas 78723
512-454-7778 • Fax 512-454-9401

ELECTRONIC MEDIA FROM THE REFERENCE PRESS

The Reference Press offers business information in more electronic formats than any other publisher. You can choose from CD-ROMs, floppy disks, electronic books, personal digital assistants, or on-line services.

HOOVER'S ELECTRONIC MASTERLIST OF MAJOR U.S. COMPANIES — $199.95

Hoover's MasterList of Major U.S. Companies 1994–1995 is now available in an easy-to-use software program for Macintosh and PC Windows users. Developed in Claris's Filemaker Pro, the program combines a simple intuitive interface (no user manual required) with a powerful yet flexible search engine. This versatile tool contains information on approximately 7,200 companies and over 14,000 CEOs and CFOs. In addition to search, sort, and retrieval features, the software includes a built-in mailing label capability. The license permits use of the data for creating letters and labels for personal use only (not for resale). A version of the product that includes quarterly updates (the original plus 3 updates) is available for only $100 more — just $299.95. A data-only version is available for DOS users in an ASCII-delimited format. This version requires users to import the data into their own database, contact management, or spreadsheet program.

HOOVER'S COMPANY AND INDUSTRY DATABASE ON CD-ROM — $249.95

Get over 1,100 in-depth company profiles and nearly 200 detailed industry profiles with the Hoover's CD. This intuitive, no-nonsense CD-ROM is loaded with valuable business information that will make your business research tasks quick and easy. Each database is fully searchable, and the profiles are displayed in an easy-to-read format. Hoover's CD includes all company profiles in *Hoover's Handbook of American Business, Hoover's Handbook of Emerging Companies, Hoover's Handbook of World Business*, and *Hoover's Guide to Private Companies*, plus many company profiles not available in print format. In addition, it includes over 200 industry profiles from the *U.S. Industrial Outlook 1994*. Available with quarterly updates for $399.95. **Available January 1995.**

TEXAS AND BAY AREA REGIONAL BUSINESS LISTS ON DISK — $49.95 EACH

Both the top 500 companies in Texas and the top 500 companies in the San Francisco Bay Area are available in easy-to-use Macintosh or Windows software programs. In addition to search, sort, and retrieval features, the software includes a built-in mailing label capability. A separate file is included on each disk with the names and addresses of the area's largest public-sector employers, key employers headquartered outside the areas, top media companies, and the most influential accounting firms, banks, and law firms with offices in the areas. Ideal for sales and marketing professionals, job seekers, career placement offices, and researchers. A data-only version is available for DOS users in an ASCII-delimited format. This version requires users to import the data into their own database, contact management, or spreadsheet program.

HOOVER'S MULTIMEDIA BUSINESS 500 — $49.95

This CD-ROM contains the entire contents of *Hoover's Handbook of American Business 1995*. Search by company, key word, region, or industry. Access competitive information by using the hot spot to jump to numerous competitors. See and hear 30 minutes of multimedia video clips from over 50 top corporations. Cut and paste information into your own word processing documents and generate mailing lists. CD-ROM drive and DOS Windows required for use.

HOOVER'S CATALOG ON THE INTERNET

The Reference Press catalog of all print and electronic products is available on the Internet on both World Wide Web (http://kaleidoscope.bga.com/RP/top_page.html) and Gopher (gopher.bga.com) servers. Look for our most current product offerings at these sites.

HOOVER'S ON-LINE

Company profiles from all *Hoover's Handbooks*, plus many profiles not in print format and additional business information from The Reference Press are available on the following on-line services:

- America Online (1-800-827-6364) — in the "News and Finance" section under Company Profiles
- Apple's eWorld (1-800-521-1515) — in the Business and Finance Plaza under Resources and Reference
- CompuServe (1-800-848-8199) — Go Hoover
- Mead's LEXIS/NEXIS (1-800-227-4908) — under "Hoover" in the "COMPNY" file
- Bloomberg Financial Network (1-800-448-5678) — type HHB
- The Library Corporation's NlightN (1-800-654-4486)

INTERNET ACCESS — QUOTECOM

Hoover's Company Profiles and the U.S. Industrial Outlook Industry Profiles can also be found on the Internet through QuoteCom (http://www.quote.com/ or telnet quote.com). QuoteCom is a commercial Internet service that supplies financial market data to the Internet community. In addition to Hoover's Company Profiles, the service provides stock quotes, historical data, end-of-day updates, intraday alarm triggers, research reports, investment newsletters, and much more. QuoteCom offers services both free and for pay. For more information, send a blank e-mail message to info@quote.com or call (702) 324-7129.

FARCAST™

Hoover's Company Profiles, *Hoover's Masterlist of Major U.S. Companies*, and the *U.S. Industrial Outlook* are also available through Farcast. Farcast is an agent-based news and information service that lets you tap its collection of news, industry-wide press releases, reference material, and stock quotes 24 hours a day. Set it up to automatically send you news articles that match your interests or create information robots to retrieve news of interest to you. And since Farcast works through your e-mail account, you're probably ready to start using it today. You get all this for one flat-rate price, less than $1 a day! For information, send an e-mail message to info@farcast.com or call (415) 321-3720.

VENCAP DATA QUEST™ — $89.95 EACH

LOOKING FOR MONEY? VenCap is a great place to start. VenCap Data Quest™ is a comprehensive database of U.S. venture capital firms containing detailed information on venture capital sources, including names of principals and investment preferences by industry and region and more. VenCap is the quickest and easiest way to find venture capital sources and is ideal for entrepreneurs, venture capitalists, consultants, and financial investors. VenCap Data Quest™ comes in two versions: a western version covering the western and southwestern states, and an eastern version covering the eastern and southeastern states. Each version contains those venture capital firms in the U.S. which prefer to invest in that specific geographical area. Each database contains over 375 venture capital firms and costs $89.95. Together they cover over 750 venture capitalists. (Save $30 and get both versions for $149.95).

To place an order or for more information about our electronic products, contact Tom Linehan at 800-486-8666, by fax at (512) 454-9401, or send e-mail to refpress6@aol.com

UPDATE YOUR BUSINESS REFERENCE COLLECTION WITH NEW EDITIONS AND ALL-NEW TITLES FROM THE REFERENCE PRESS

HOOVER'S GUIDE TO PRIVATE COMPANIES 1994–1995
$79.95 hardcover, ISBN 1-878753-55-X

Profiles the 500 largest private companies in the U.S., ranked by sales. Includes in-depth profiles of 125 of the largest and most interesting companies and quarter-page capsule profiles of all 500 companies. Fully indexed.

HOOVER'S HANDBOOK OF AMERICAN BUSINESS 1995
$39.95 hardcover, ISBN 1-878753-65-7
$49.95 CD-ROM (requires Windows)

Profiles over 500 of the largest and most influential enterprises in America, including company histories and strategies, up to 10 years of key financial and employment data, products, competitors, key officers, addresses, and phone and fax numbers. Fully indexed.

HOOVER'S HANDBOOK OF EMERGING COMPANIES 1995
$37.95 hardcover, ISBN 1-878753-51-7

The only reasonably priced guide to 250 of America's most exciting growth enterprises. Company profiles include overviews and strategies, up to 6 years of key financial and stock data, lists of products and key competitors, names of key officers, addresses, and phone and fax numbers. **Available December 1994.**

HOOVER'S HANDBOOK OF WORLD BUSINESS 1995–1996
$37.95 hardcover, ISBN 1-878753-44-4

Profiles 200 non-U.S.–based companies that employ thousands of Americans in the U.S. and abroad. Includes a discussion of the world economy and business/economic profiles of 66 countries and 5 regions. **Available March 1995.**

HOOVER'S MASTERLIST OF MAJOR U.S. COMPANIES 1994–1995
$49.95 hardcover, ISBN 1-878753-56-8
$199.95 Computer Disk

Names, addresses, phone and fax numbers, key officers, industry descriptions, sales and employment data, stock symbols, and stock exchanges for over 7,300 of the largest public and private companies in the U.S. Also available on computer disk.

HOOVER'S MASTERLIST OF MAJOR EUROPEAN COMPANIES 1995
$79.95 hardcover, ISBN 1-878753-70-3
$249.95 Computer Disk

Organized in the same format as *Hoover's MasterList of Major U.S. Companies*, this book covers the top 2,500 public and private companies in Western Europe, Greece, and Turkey and includes all companies on the major European stock indexes. Also available on computer disk. **Available January 1995.**

HOOVER'S MASTERLIST OF MAJOR LATIN AMERICAN COMPANIES 1995
$79.95 hardcover, ISBN 1-878753-69-X
$249.95 Computer Disk

Organized in the same format as *Hoover's MasterList of Major U.S. Companies*, this book covers the top 2,500 public and private companies in Latin America, from Argentina to Venezuela. Also available on computer disk. **Available February 1995.**

THE TEXAS 500: HOOVER'S GUIDE TO THE TOP TEXAS COMPANIES 1994–1995
$24.95 hardcover, ISBN 1-878753-46-0

THE BAY AREA 500: HOOVER'S GUIDE TO THE TOP SAN FRANCISCO AREA COMPANIES 1994–1995
$24.95 trade paper, ISBN 1-878753-52-5

Each regional guide covers the top 500 public and private companies from the region and features in-depth profiles of 50 or more of the largest and fastest-growing companies. Each book also includes an overview of the area's economy, information on major employers, and much more. Mailing lists available on disk for $49.95 each.

U.S. INDUSTRIAL OUTLOOK 1994
$27.95 hardcover, ISBN 1-878753-54-1

The U.S. Commerce Department's forecast for hundreds of industries includes 280 easy-to-read charts and tables. Available from The Reference Press in hardcover at 25% off the government's paperback edition price.

STATISTICAL ABSTRACT OF THE UNITED STATES 1994
$24.95 hardcover, ISBN 1-878753-67-3

The Bureau of the Census's annual compendium of who we are, where we live, what we do, and how we spend our national resources. Available from The Reference Press at 35% off the government price.

DIRECTORY OF BUSINESS PERIODICAL SPECIAL ISSUES
by Trip Wyckoff, $49.95 hardcover, ISBN 1-878753-60-6

The definitive guide to special issues and annual index issues of business, science, and technology periodicals. Includes virtually all general business-oriented indexes. **Available December 1994.**

Company profiles also available in electronic format — See reverse for details.

TO ORDER CALL 1-800-486-8666

The Reference Press, Inc., 6448 Highway 290 E., Suite E–104, Austin, Texas 78723
512-454-7778 • Fax 512-454-9401